P9-DHN-504

Maps

CloseUps

ABOUT THIS BOOK

There's no doubt that the best source for travel advice is a like-minded friend who's just been where you're headed. But with or without that friend, you'll have a better trip with a Fodor's guide in hand. Once you've learned to find your way around its pages, you'll be in great shape to find your way around your destination.

SELECTION

Our goal is to cover the best properties, sights, and activities in their category, as well as the most interesting communities to visit. We make a point of including local food-lovers' hot spots as well as neighborhood options, and we avoid all that's touristy unless it's really worth your time. You can go on the assumption that everything you read about in this book is recommended wholeheartedly by our writers and editors. It goes without saying that no property mentioned in the book has paid to be included.

RATINGS

Orange stars ★ denote sights and properties that our editors and writers consider the very best in the area covered by the entire book. These, the best of the best, are listed in the Fodor's Choice section in the front of the book. Black stars ★ highlight the sights and properties we deem Highly Recommended, the don't-miss sights within any region. Fodor's Choice and Highly Recommended options in each region are usually listed on the title page of the chapter covering that region. Use the index to find complete descriptions. In cities, sights pinpointed with numbered map bullets ❶ in the margins tend to be more important than those without bullets.

SPECIAL SPOTS

Pleasures & Pastimes focuses on types of experiences that reveal the spirit of the destination. Watch for Off the Beaten Path sights. Some are out of the way, some are quirky, and all are worth your while. If the munchies hit while you're exploring, look for Need a Break? suggestions.

TIME IT RIGHT

Wondering when to go? Check On the Calendar up front and chapters' Timing sections for weather and crowd overviews and best days and times to visit.

SEE IT ALL

Use Fodor's exclusive Great Itineraries as a model for your trip. (For a good overview of the entire destination, follow those that begin the book, or mix regional itineraries from several chapters.) In cities, Good Walks guide you to important sights in each neighborhood; ► indicates the starting points of walks and itineraries in the text and on the map.

BUDGET WELL

Hotel and restaurant price categories from ¢ to $$$$ are defined in the opening pages of each chapter—expect to find a balanced selection for every budget, from amazing bargains to luxurious blowouts. For attractions, we always give standard adult admission fees; reductions are usually available for children, students, and senior citizens.

BASIC INFO

Smart Travel Tips lists travel essentials for the entire area covered by the book; city- and region-specific basics end each chapter in the A to Z sections. To find the best way to get around, see the transportation section; see individual modes of travel ("By Car," "By Train") for details. We assume you'll check Web sites or call for particulars.

ON THE MAPS	Maps throughout the book show you what's where and help you find your way around. Black and orange numbered bullets ➊ ➊ in the text correlate to bullets on maps.
BACKGROUND	In general, we give background information within the chapters in the course of explaining sights as well as in CloseUp boxes and in Understanding Naples, Capri & the Amalfi Coast at the end of the book. To get in the mood, review the suggestions in Books & Videos. The Italian vocabulary can be invaluable.
FIND IT FAST	The Naples chapter explores the main sightseeing neighborhoods of the city, then goes on to detail its dining, lodging, arts, nightlife, shopping, and sports scenes. The other chapters are divided into small regions, within which towns are covered in logical geographical order; attractive routes and interesting places between towns are flagged as En Route. Heads at the top of each page help you find what you need within a chapter.
DON'T FORGET	Restaurants are open for lunch and dinner daily unless we state otherwise; we mention dress only when there's a specific requirement and reservations only when they're essential or not accepted. Unless we note otherwise, most hotels have private baths, phone, TVs, and air-conditioning and operate on the European Plan (without meals). Meal Plans are listed for all hotels (but added costs for these plans are not). We list facilities but not if you'll be charged extra to use them (some hotels in Naples even charge an additional fee for air-conditioning), so when pricing accommodations, find out what's included.
SYMBOLS	

Many Listings

★ Fodor's Choice
★ Highly recommended
⊠ Physical address
✢ Directions
🕮 Mailing address
🕾 Telephone
🖷 Fax
⊕ On the Web
🖎 E-mail
🕗 Open/closed times
▶ Start of walk/itinerary
Ⓜ Metro stations
▭ Credit cards

Hotels & Restaurants

🏨 Hotel
🛏 Number of rooms
♨ Facilities
🍽 Meal plans
✕ Restaurant
🍴 Reservations
👗 Dress code
🚭 Smoking
🍺 BYOB
✕🏨 Hotel with restaurant that warrants a visit

Other

☷ Family-friendly
🛈 Contact information
⇨ See also
⊠ Branch address
☞ Take note

ON THE ROAD WITH FODOR'S

Although there's no substitute for travel advice from a good friend who knows your style, our contributors are the next best thing—the kind of people you would poll for travel advice if you knew them.

Many months with his nose buried in art history books helped Gregory W. Bailey cast his Texas days aside and blossom as a full-fledged Italian after relocating to Rome in 1996. On a side trip, he discovered and fell in love with Naples, quickly learning to remain *sempre tranquilla* (always calm) when riding in a taxi that never bothered to stop for red lights or speeding buses. Even so, Gregory has decided to remain in much more tranquilla Rome, where he has contributed to publications such as *Saveur* and the *International Herald Tribune*.

A native Neapolitan, Francesca Marretta has left a trail of ink on 1,000 kilometers of Italy's southern coastlines, having worked on several guide books. An English-language intepreter and teacher, she has traveled to Russia, the Czech Republic, and the United Kingdom, but is always exhilarated (and exasperated) upon her return to the high-heeled boot.

A love for Renaissance history first brought Londoner Victoria Primhak to Italy to research her Ph.D in the mid-1980s, where she fell in love with the charm and chaos that is Naples. She now splits her daytime job between university teaching and working as a consultant on international relations for the region. As for her home base, it is divided between the bustle of the *centro storico*—her apartment shares a wall with the city's famed cathedral—and the calm of the bay island of Procida. The best of both worlds, as she point out.

Lea Lane Stern covers the world in varied guises: She was a columnist at Gannett newspapers, managing editor of the newsletter "Travel Smart," author of a cruise book, and a talking head on Travel Channel. Having been to more than 100 countries, she has a special place in her heart for Italy—after all, she spent two honeymoons there.

Chris Rose arrived in Naples from Manchester, England, planning to stay for three months. After twelve years in Campania, he fully understands southern Italy is its own country. Currently, he writes travel guides, teaches English, and organizes events with artists and writers visiting from Britain. He's finishing his first novel but, in the meantime, you can read his short story, "The Shoemaker General of Naples," in *New Writing 10,* published by Picador.

Language editor, travel consultant, and naturalist, British-born Mark Walters has been able to practice French, German, *napolitano,* and on occasion even Italian for many years now from his base in Naples. His Classics degree from Cambridge, a first career in English language teaching, and a recent qualification in environmental management help him to juggle a wide variety of activities from his home in San Martino high above the city. He spends several months every year leading tours in the Mediterranean for California-based Betchart Expeditions, with a current program that includes prehistoric France, the Etruscans, Sicily, and northern Greece.

All that studying of art and architecture paid off for editor Robert I. C. Fisher on his frequent trips to Naples, especially when he accurately guessed the date of the Palazzo Donn'Anna based solely on its architectural ornament, which he viewed as he fell from the palazzo's terrace into the Bay of Naples (it's much saltier than he had imagined). Part of Fodor's full-color Escape series, his *Escape to the Amalfi Coast* (2nd edition, 2001) captures in text and color photographs 20 of the dreamiest destinations in Campania, from Greta Garbo's Villa Cimbrone to the sky-kissing Hotel Cappuccini Convento, and can serve as a handy travel aperitif to the region.

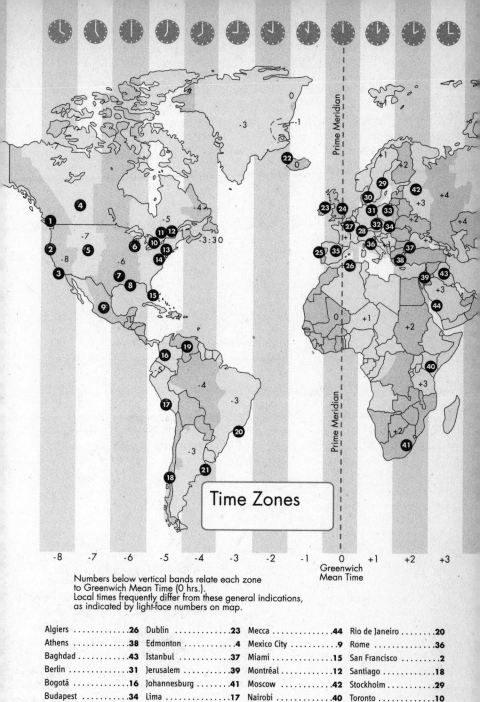

Time Zones

Numbers below vertical bands relate each zone
to Greenwich Mean Time (0 hrs.).
Local times frequently differ from these general indications,
as indicated by light-face numbers on map.

Band	GMT offset
-8	-7	-6	-5	-4	-3	-2	-1	0 Greenwich Mean Time	+1	+2	+3

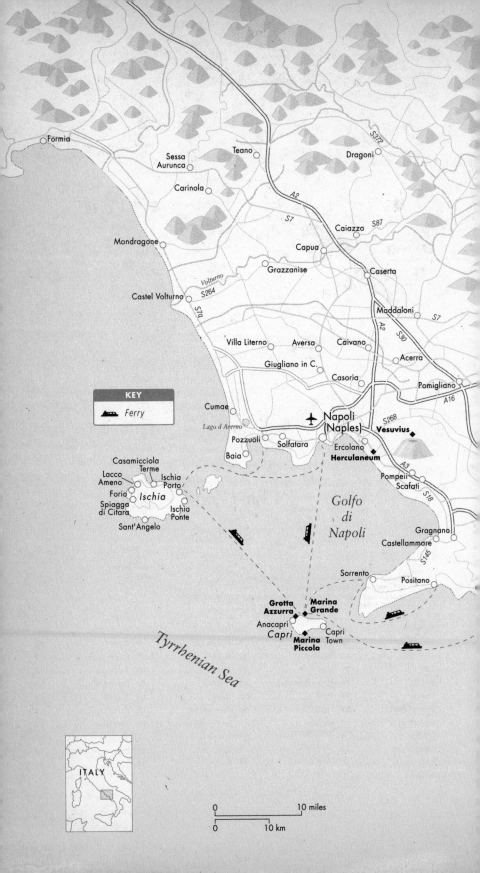

Campania is a region of names—Capri, Sorrento, Pompeii, Paestum, Positano, Amalfi, Ravello—that evoke visions of cliff-shaded coves, sun-dappled waters, and mighty ruins. And Naples, a tumultuous, animated city, the very heart of Campania, stands guard over these treasures. Campania stretches south in flat coastal plains and low mountains from Baia Domizia, Capua, and Caserta to Naples and Pompeii on the magnificent bay; past the isles of Capri and Ischia; along the rocky coast to Sorrento, Amalfi, and Salerno; and farther still past the Cilento promontory to Sapri and the Calabria border. Inland lie the bleak fringes of the Apennines and the rolling countryside around Benevento.

Many of Campania's attractions are on the Golfo di Napoli (Bay of Naples)—including the city itself and its satellite islands, Capri and Ischia, and the archaeological sites of Pompeii, Herculaneum, and the Campi Flegrei (Phlegrean Fields), at the northern end of the bay. At the southern end, Sorrento also lies within this charmed circle, within easy distance of Positano, Amalfi, and the pleasures of the Amalfi Coast. Farther afield, Paestum offers more classical sights, and inland, Caserta and Benevento have a Bourbon palace and more majestic Roman remains.

① Naples

The most operatic of Italy's cities, Naples is extraordinary, and it's the Neapolitans who make it so. Their capacity for warmth, friendliness, and *amore* is amazing. They love you, they love their city, and they want you to love it back. But to win her loving heart, you must woo her, just as Clark Gable did Sophia Loren in the 1956 film *It Happened in Naples*. That heart is the Spaccanapoli, the kaleidoscopic 5-km-long (3-mi-long) pedestrian ribbon that cuts the inner city in two. This is the historic center of Naples, and any city tour should include this open-air museum of a neighborhood, studded with some of the city's most famous churches and palaces, including the Gesù Nuovo, the Cappella Sansevero, and the city duomo. In the streets, the atmosphere is almost carnival-like, as crowds at the many sidewalk cafés overflow into the narrow, canyonlike roadways.

Spaccanapoli is an oasis sheltered from the grandeur of classical Naples, which is centered around the Piazza del Plebiscito, a vast square laid out in the Napoleonic era and today the eye of the urban storm swirling around it. Around this square and the nearby Piazza Municipio are the great urban monuments—whose style is best described as overblown imperial—erected by many of Naples's invaders and conquerors: the brooding medieval keep of the Castel Nuovo; the Palazzo Reale, where the Bourbon kings lived in awe-inspiring splendor; the glittering 19th-century Teatro San Carlo opera house; and the elegant Church of San Francesco di Paola. Just to the north is Via Toledo (often called Via Roma)—the "Broadway" of Naples, which bisects the city north to south and stretches from the harbor to the hill of Capodimonte. This grand thoroughfare runs by the world-famous Museo Archeologico Nazionale, packed with archaeological relics of the Classical era, and a must-see before venturing out of town to see Pompeii and Herculaneum. Their most important finds are on display here—everything from sculpture to carbonized fruit—and seeing them will add to the pleasure of your trip to the two excavated towns. Near the museum is the neighborhood of I Vergini, where some famous Baroque palaces designed by Ferdinando Sanfelice can be seen. From here, footsore and weary, you deserve a taxi or bus to reach the Capodimonte hill, high over Naples, where the Museo di Capodimonte, the greatest of the Bourbon palaces, has artistic masterpieces and royal apartments to ogle as well as incomparable views over the entire city from its Bosco di Capodimonte (park).

Just to the south of the Piazza del Plebiscito is Naples's famous harbor and the elegant stretch of waterfront that runs from the Lungomare over to the Riviera di Chiaia. Here is Castel dell'Ovo, a 12th-century fortress built over the ruins of an ancient Roman villa, whose site commands a view of the whole harbor—proof, if you need it, that the Romans knew a premium location when they saw it. Under the walls of the castle is the Borgo Marinaro, a toylike fishing village built at the end of the 19th century for the fishermen of the Santa Lucia district. Nearby is the diamond-shape Piazza dei Martiri, center of chic Naples and surrounded by streets lined with elegant boutiques and antiques shops. Other must-dos include the world-famous Aquarium; the sumptuous Villa Pignatelli; the historic Pizzofalcone quarter; and the grand 19th-century bayside promenades of Via Partenope and Via Caracciolo, lined with luxury hotels and Belle Epoque mansions and backdropped by a vista of Vesuvius.

Funiculars link this part of town with Naples's steep Vomero Hill, today a gentrified residential quarter and home to three important museums: Villa La Floridiana, the Castel Sant'Elmo, and the Certosa di San Martino. They have treasures galore, but you might be content just to take in the heart-stopping views from the slopes of the Vomero neighborhood. If you can adapt to its ways, Naples may become your favorite city in Italy. After all, who really needs stoplights?

(2) **Around the Bay: From Pompeii to the Phlegrean Fields**
The area surrounding Naples has a Greco-Roman history that makes the city look like the new kid on the block. The Greeks set out to Hellenize Italy's boot in the 6th and 7th centuries BC by settling here at Cumae. Later, the Romans used the area as one giant playground, paving the roads from their colonies to numerous pleasure villas along the sea. Both groups left ruins for modern-day explorers to peruse. West of Naples is the Campi Flegrei—the fields of fire—alternatively condemned by the ancient Greeks as the entrance to Hades and immortalized as the Elysian Fields, a paradise for the righteous dead. This whole area floats freely on a mass of molten lava very close to the surface (Italy's two major seismic faults intersect here). Such sights as the Solfitara, or "little Vesuvius," inspired Dante when he wrote his *Inferno*. Here's where Nero and Hadrian had summer villas, Virgil composed his poetry, and the Apostle Paul landed to spread the Gospel. Also here are ancient sites, such as the Greeks' first mainland city, Cumae—home of the fabled Antro della Sibilla (Cave of the Cumaean Sibyl); Nero's Baths of Baia; the ancient Roman amphitheater of Pozzuoli, the third-largest arena in Italy; and the Lago d'Averno (Lake Avernus), which the ancients thought to be the very gates of hell. Today water-skiers glide over its surface without getting sucked in.

To the east of Naples around the bay lie Pompeii and Herculaneum (Ercolano), the most completely preserved cities of classical antiquity, along with their nemesis, the dream volcano, Vesuvius. Volcanic ash and mud from Il Vesuvio preserved these towns almost exactly as they were on the day it erupted in AD 79, leaving them not just archaeological ruins but testimonies of daily life in the ancient world. All three sites can be visited from either Naples or Sorrento using the Circumvesuviana railway, the suburban line, which provides fast, frequent, and economical service. Pompeii, noted for its romantic legend (thanks to Sir Edward

Bulwer-Lytton's Victorian potboiler *The Last Days of Pompeii*) as well as its actual artifacts, is the most famous system of Roman excavations anywhere, but perhaps Herculaneum—Pompeii's smaller but wealthier and more cultured neighbor—is the more interesting. Above all looms the profile of Vesuvius, the cause of all this ruin and, as a concomitant, of all this preservation. Its ominous, towering profile is so inseparable from the Bay of Naples area and the ferocious power it can unleash so vivid as you tour the sights of the cities that it destroyed, you may be overwhelmed by the urge to explore the crater itself.

③ The Islands: Capri, Ischia & Procida

History's hedonists have long luxuriated on Campania's famous islands. The Roman emperor Tiberius built a dozen villas on Capri to indulge his sexual whims. Later residents have included dancer Rudolf Nureyev and droves of artists and writers. These days day-trippers make up the bulk of the visitors, and they can easily turn Capri from a pint-size paradise into pure purgatory on summer weekends, when the fabled isle is packed with far too many people. Yet even the crowds are not enough to destroy Capri's very special charm. The town is a Moorish opera set of shiny white houses, tiny squares, and narrow medieval alleyways hung with bougainvillea. Although there are famous man-made sights—the Villa of Tiberius, the Certosa di San Giacomo, and the Villa San Michele, among them—it's the island's natural wonders that are the main lure. The famed Blue Grotto is but one of many such caverns, and some connoisseurs think it's not even the most beautiful of the grottoes, instead giving the laurel variously to its Green, Yellow, Pink, or White counterpart. Elsewhere are the geologic marvels of the Arco Naturale, the Pizzolungo stone pinnacle, and the famed I Faraglioni rocks, which anchor the island's southern coast. At night everyone congregates on the Piazzetta to search for heavenly bodies—of the Hollywood, not the astral, variety.

Twice the size of Capri, the neighboring island of Ischia promises more peace and quiet, although the hordes of Germans who take over in summer can make this island as congested as Capri. Ischia's volcano, Monte Epomeo, shoots up to a height of 2,585 ft, but don't be alarmed—it hasn't erupted for nearly seven centuries. Around the rim of the island are Campania's most beautiful white-sand beaches and a number of towns, including Casamicciola and Lacco Ameno, which trade on the island's greatest drawing cards: spas, thermal baths, and mineral springs. For a break from a mud bath, explore the Castello at Ischia Porto or La Mortella, the gardens designed by Sir William Walton, which are at Forio. Nearby Procida is a wild and rugged island of great charm. Its small population of fishermen, vineyard workers, domed houses, and sweeping views were immortalized in the Academy Award–winning film *Il Postino*.

④ Sorrento & the Amalfi Coast

Emperors and kings, popes, the greatest musicians, writers, and artists have made Sorrento their preferred abode for more than 2,500 years—and it just takes one look at the view over the Bay of Naples to tell you why. Directly across the water from Naples, Sorrento was until the mid-20th century a small, genteel resort favored by central European princes, English aristocrats, and American literati. Now the town has grown and spread out along the crest of its famous cliffs, and apartments stand where citrus groves once bloomed. Still, the old historic town is a Belle Epoque treasure, with picturesque alleyways, palm tree–shaded caffès, and some of Italy's most gorgeous hotels. Like most resorts, Sorrento is best off-season, either in spring and early autumn or in winter, when Campania's mild climate can make a stay pleasant anywhere along the coast.

Sorrento is the leading jewel of the Sorrentine peninsula, but there are other destinations to explore along the promontory: the gracious villa-hotels of Sant'Agnello; the idyllic fishing port of Massa Lubrense; the mountaintop aerie of Sant'Agata sui Due Golfi (which offers a Cineramaic vista over both the bays of Naples and Salerno); the beach at Marina del Cantone; and the ancient Roman villas of Castellamare di Stabia.

Heading south from Sorrento the south side of the peninsula leads to the dramatically scenic, spectacularly beautiful Amalfi Coast, linked together by a road that must have a thousand turns, each with a different view, on a dizzying 69-km (43-mi) journey from Sorrento to Salerno. Crystal lagoons where the water is emerald-green, small boats lying in sandy coves like brightly colored fish, vertiginous cliffs hollowed out with fairy grottoes where the air is turquoise and the water an icy blue, and white, sunbaked villages dripping with flowers all join together in a single scenic masterpiece. Whatever town you pick as your favorite, you'll have a battle on your hands if you insist that it deserves the title of Most Beautiful. Some prefer Positano, the world's most photographed fishing village and once called "the poor man's Capri" until the jet set discovered it. Others choose Amalfi, a city adorned with medieval monasteries, Arab-Sicilian cloisters, souk-like passageways, and the coast's grandest cathedral. Creative souls, from Boccaccio to Greta Garbo, have always preferred Ravello, perched 1,500 ft over the famously blue Bay of Salerno, a town blessed with some of Italy's most beautiful gardens and villas. To the south, beyond modern Salerno, lies ancient Paestum, where three of the best-preserved ancient Greek temples anywhere, including Greece itself, stand sharp against the cobalt sky.

If art and antiquity are high on your list, consider spending a few days in Naples before retreating to the beauty of Capri, Ischia, or the Amalfi Coast. Now that the city has made great strides in combating urban decay, practically everyone who takes the time and trouble to discover its artistic riches and appreciate its vivacious nature considers it well worth the effort. Naples is close to Italy's most fabled classical ruins, and you should dedicate at least a morning or afternoon to Pompeii or Herculaneum.

If You Have 3 Days

In **Naples,** a visit to the **Museo Archeologico Nazionale** is an essential preparation (or follow-up) for an expedition to **Herculaneum** (Ercolano) and **Pompeii,** indispensable sights for anyone visiting Campania. The islands of **Ischia** and **Capri** can also be reached from Naples and make an ideal antidote to the city's noise. It's worth spending at least one night outside Naples, and a good alternative to the islands would be **Sorrento,** an easy hydrofoil ride away and a good base from which to tour the nearby Amalfi Coast, where you could visit small towns—**Positano, Amalfi, Ravello,** and/or **Vietri sul Mare,** for instance—on a third day's excursion.

If You Have 5 Days

In **Naples,** more time will enable you to take in one of the region's greatest palace-museums, the **Museo Capodimonte,** housed in one of the Bourbon royal palaces. Outside town you could also see more than just one of the classical sights, including a visit to the Greek temples of **Paestum,** highly recommended for a glimpse at some of Magna Graecia's most stunning relics. You might also venture north to **Caserta** to wander around the royal palace. Back in the Bay of Naples, spend your fourth and fifth days exploring **Ischia** and **Sorrento,** both undemanding holiday resorts with plenty of natural beauty.

If You Have 7 Days

A week in Campania will allow you to discover some of the more esoteric pleasures that Naples has to offer. Apart from the sheer vibrancy of its shopping streets and alleys and the glorious views over the waterfront, **Naples** has plenty of diversions within its tight mesh of streets, and you should make time for visiting some of the many famous churches of the historic Spaccanapoli district, including the **Duomo,** of course, but also **Santa Chiara** and the **Cappella Sansevero,** with its 18th-century sculptures. Outside town head west to the volcanic region of the **Phlegrean Fields,** where Roman remains lie within a smoking, smoldering area rich with classical history. Spend three nights on the Amalfi Coast, making sure to visit inland **Ravello,** and pass some time in pretty **Positano,** which requires at least a day and a half. **Capri,** too, deserves a couple of nights to appreciate fully its beauty—of secluded coves and beaches, not to mention the famous Blue Grotto—easily eclipsing the island's more lurid tourist trappings. You might pass a last day, perhaps en route out of Campania, in **Benevento,** which holds a well-preserved Roman theater and the renowned Arco di Traiano.

By Public Transportation Given low average traffic speeds in and around Naples, always opt for rails rather than wheels. Take one of the metropolitana lines where possible within Naples or the Cumana railway to gain access to the Campi Flegrei. The Circumvesuviana train gets you to sites around Vesuvius. Only buses run to the Amalfi coast (best from Sorrento or Salerno), except in summer when it is served by ferries and hydrofoils. Thanks to a novel integrated-transport system called *Campania Unica,* you can travel all over Campania combining several transportation modes on just one ticket, the Biglietto Unico, which will vary in price and time validity depending on how many zones you have to cross. A cheap and scenic way of traveling across the Bay of Naples and further afield is the Metro del Mare (sea metro), which uses routes and ports often overlooked by the major maritime carriers.

Campania is not always at its best in high summer: Naples can become a sweltering inferno, the archaeological sites swarm, and the islands and Amalfi Coast resorts are similarly overrun with tour buses and bad tempers. Any other time of year would be preferable, including even winter, when the temperature rarely falls below the comfort threshold and rain is relatively rare. Optimum times are May–June and September–October. Due to the temperate climate, bougainvillea and other floral displays can bloom through Christmas, while swimming is possible year-round, though you will only see the hardiest bathers out between October and May.

Summer is also the worst time for ascents to Vesuvius; the best visibility occurs around spring and fall. Watch the clock, however, as the days get shorter; excursions to Vesuvius, Pompeii, Herculaneum, and the islands all require some traveling, and it's easy to get caught with little daylight left. At most archaeological sites, you are rounded up two hours before sunset, but by that time most crowds have departed so late afternoon is an optimum time to enjoy Pompeii and Herculaneum in peace and quiet. Remember that a good number of hotels, restaurants, and other tourist facilities in Sorrento, the Amalfi Coast, and the islands close down from November until around Easter.

If you can avoid it, don't travel at all in Italy in August, when much of the population is on the move, especially around Ferragosto, the national holiday period that begins August 15 and generally extends to the beginning of September; at this time, Naples is fairly deserted and many of its restaurants and shops are closed. Of course, with residents away on vacation, this makes crowds less of a bother for tourists.

Climate

Weatherwise, the best months for sightseeing are April, May, June, September, and October—generally pleasant and not too hot. The hottest months are July and August, when humidity can make things pretty unpleasant. However, most of the places covered in this book lie along the seashore, if not actually in the sea (Capri, Ischia, Procida), which takes some of the curse off the heat. Winters are relatively mild but cold fronts can arrive and stay for days.

🔲 Forecasts **Weather Channel Connection** ☎ 900/932-8437, 95¢ per minute from a Touch-Tone phone ⊕ www.weather.com.

NAPLES

Jan.	53F	12C	May	72F	22C	Sept.	79F	26C
	40	4		54	12		61	16
Feb.	55F	13C	June	79F	26C	Oct.	71F	22C
	41	5		61	16		54	12
Mar.	59F	15C	July	84F	29C	Nov.	63F	17C
	44	6		65	18		48	9
Apr.	65F	18C	Aug.	84F	29C	Dec.	56F	14C
	48	9		65	18		44	6

ON THE CALENDAR

Campania's top seasonal events are listed below, and any one of them could provide the stuff of lasting memories. It's revealing that the Italian *festa* can be translated either as "festival or holiday" or "party"—with food being a key feature of most Italian celebrations. For further information contact the Italian Government Tourist Board (*see* Visitor Information *in* Smart Travel Tips A to Z) and the regional visitor centers, listed in the A to Z section at the end of each chapter in this book.

WINTER

Dec.	**Christmas in Naples** (Natale a Napoli) is celebrated through December until January 6 (Epiphany). The season officially opens December 8th on the day of the Immacolata (Immaculate Conception), when the mayor lays wreaths on the Guglia dell'Immacolata and when the *Presepe* (crèche) shops of Via Gregorio Armeno are thronged by Neapolitans. Historic crèches are on view in many churches, including Santa Chiara, San Domenico Maggiore, and the Gesù Nuovo.
Dec.–June	The **Opera Season** is in full swing at Teatro San Carlo in Naples. ✉ *Via San Carlo 101–3* ☎ *081/7972412 ticket office* 🖷 *081/400902* ⊕ *www.teatrosancarlo.it.*
Dec. 31	Naples stages a rousing **New Year's Eve** celebration, with the focal point being the concert in Piazza Plebiscito, concluding with a public fireworks display over the bay and an open-air disco till dawn at the Stazione Marittima. At about 2 AM many Neapolitans pile into their cars and regroup for a *Veglione* (New Year's Eve party). The night winds up with a dawn espresso at the châlets in Mergellina or at other panoramic spots along the bay, as well as gridlock traffic along the waterfront and in San Martino. As a general rule, avoid walking the streets of residential areas from 11 PM to 1 AM: some Neapolitans still take their celebrations far too seriously and—despite police warnings and civic initiatives—continue to indulge in a variety of banned pyrotechnics from their windows and balconies, though the days of flying refrigerators are thankfully over. Fashionable merrymakers zero in on Capri, where islanders stir from their wintry pace to welcome hordes for days-long celebrations.
Jan. 5–6	**Epiphany Celebrations** (Epifania). Roman Catholic Epiphany decorations are evident throughout Campania. Notable is the celebration in Naples when the Befana witch arrives on the Piazza Plebiscito; she generally performs a similar function to that of the more northern European Santa Claus, with "good" children being rewarded with sweets and "naughty" children being given lumps of coal. This is still a major occasion—perhaps even more important than Christmas—for the *popolino* (common people) in Naples and the surrounding area: streets close to Piazza Garibaldi, like Via Foria and Via Carbonara, are lined for the January 5th and 6th events with a welter of market stalls selling toys and other goodies, and locals are busy making last-minute purchases until the early hours of the morning.

SPRING	
Early Apr.	**Easter in Naples** (Pasqua a Napoli) is celebrated around Easter Monday (Pasquetta). Throughout the Settimana Santa (Holy Week), choral concerts are offered in churches. Sorrento hosts two torch-lit Good Friday processions, one at 4 AM and the other on the evening of the same day, involving the local **Incappucciati** (Brotherhoods). Easter Monday sees a mass exodus from Naples for a *scampagnata* (day trip into the surrounding countryside) or a boat ride across to the islands in the Bay of Naples.
End Apr.–Early May	**Maggio dei Monumenti** (Monuments of May) opens Neapolitan palazzi, churches, and landmarks usually closed to the public. This time also sees the **Notti d'Arte**, a series of concerts and performances in historic settings, such as the Cappella Palatina of the Castel Nuovo, the Salone da Ballo of the Museo di Capodimonte, and the Salone d'Ercole of the Palazzo Reale.
Early May	In Naples the first of the two annual celebrations of the **Feast of San Gennaro** is marked on the first Sunday in May at the Duomo of Naples (the ceremony of the Liquefaction of the Blood begins at 9 AM, but arrive by 7 or you'll wind up far from the altar and the action). Unlike the similar festa held in September, this one includes a *Processione di San Gennaro*—a procession of the saint's relics—through the streets of Spaccanapoli to the Church of Santa Chiara.
SUMMER	
Early June	The **Regatta of the Great Maritime Republics** (Regatta Storica dell'Antiche Repubbliche Marinare) sees keen competition among the four former maritime republics—Amalfi, Genoa, Pisa, and Venice. The regatta is held every four years in Amalfi, with the next scheduled for the first Sunday in June 2005.
Late June	On the fourth Sunday of every June, the **Festa dei Gigli** (Feast of the Lilies) is held in Nola, just to the north of Naples. Spectacular wooden floats, often bearing orchestras, celebrate the homecoming of Bishop Paolino from Africa in 394.
Late June–Late Sept.	**Estate a Napoli** (Summer in Naples) is a summer-long schedule of concerts and performances. In general, entertainment in the summer months in Naples moves outdoors. Cinemas often close for their *riposo estivo* (summer break), while cultural associations stage shows and festivals in historical venues throughout Campania. In recent years, special events have included *concerti a mezzanotte* (midnight concerts, which actually start at 11 PM) in parks; Baroque, Neapolitan, and jazz concerts at the Borgo Marinaro; and a comedy festival at the Castel Nuovo. During the last week of June the **Napoli Cinefest Film Festival** is held in the city, featuring some outdoor movies. The main Piazza D'Armi at the top of Castel Sant'Elmo in the Vomero, towering over the rest of the city, hosts open-air movies in the Rassegna Cinematografica festival and avant-garde theater. The suburb of Fuorigrotta is another fulcrum for entertainment, with the Neapolis festival taking place in the San Paolo soccer stadium and the nearby Arena Flegrea a good open-air concert venue throughout the summer.

July 16	The Feast of the Feast of the Madonna del Carmine is held on Naples's Piazza Mercato and is celebrated by the "burning" of the campanile of Santa Maria del Carmine with fireworks.
July–Aug.	Estate Musicale Sorrentina is the summer music festival in Sorrento. Concerts are held in historic cloisters and churches.
July–Aug.	The Fèstival Musicale di Ravello actually schedules concerts throughout most of the year (except January–March) at Ravello's spectacular Villa Rufolo, but the annual highlights are the operatic concerts scheduled during July to commemorate the 1880 visit of Richard Wagner to the villa's famous gardens. ⊠ *Piazza Vescovado, Ravello* ☎ *089/858149* ⊕ *www.ravelloarts.org.*
Aug. 15	The traditional beginning of the Ferragosto, the traditional vacation period in Italy, is marked by an exodus from Naples and many regional celebrations, including the Assunta, or Feast of the Assumption of the Virgin Mary, in Positano, which commemorates the defeat of the Saracens with a procession and mass held on the main beach.
Early Sept.	The first week in September usually sees the Vittorio de Sica Film Festival in Positano. The Premio Leonide Massine dance awards are also held in Positano during September.
FALL	
Mid-Sept.	You can't see *Il Vesuvio* erupt on command, but many regional organizations sponsor dinner sunset cruises on the Bay of Naples, with a fireworks display to re-create the eruption of Vesuvius. One celebrates the Festa di S. M. del Lauro a Meta di Sorrento in mid-September, leaving from the Molo Beverello of Naples. For information contact: ⊠ *Ascultur Campania* ☎ *081/665532* ⊠ *Associazione Aliseo* ☎ *081/5265780.*
Sept. 19	The main celebration of the Feast of San Gennaro is held at Naples's duomo on this day. *Il Miracolo* begins (hopefully) shortly after 9 AM, but the best seats are grabbed hours earlier. Once the blood of St. Gennaro liquefies, a ceremonial cortege is paraded from Piazza del Duomo to Piazza del Carmine. For details contact: ⊠ *Comitato Diocesano S. Gennaro* ☎ *081/446103.*

The Art of Enjoying Art

You could select almost any three paintings in Naples's museums or churches and spend not only weeks or months but a lifetime in their company. But when you get all that beauty wholesale—a slew of Titians, great Baroque altarpieces, acres of painted Annunciations—your eyes can glaze over from the heavy downpour of images, dates, and names, and you begin to lean, Pisa-like, on your companion for support. The secret, of course, is to act like a turtle—not a hare—and take your sweet time. Instead of trotting after briskly efficient tour guides, allow the splendors of Italy's artistic heritage to unfold—slowly. Get out and explore the actual settings—medieval chapels, Rococo palaces, and Romanesque cloisters—for which these marvelous examples of Italy's art and sculpture were conceived centuries ago and where many of them may still be seen in situ.

Museums are only the most obvious places to view art; there are always the trompe l'oeil renderings of Assumptions that float across Baroque church ceilings and piazza scenes that might be Renaissance paintings brought to life. Instead of studying an 18th-century altarpiece in the Museo di Capodimonte, spend an hour in the Rococo cloisters of the Church of Santa Chiara. An hour walking through the open-air museum of Naples's Spaccanapoli district will reveal more about the artistic energy of Naples than a day spent in its art collections. Of course, chances are you'll also see a Caravaggio altarpiece so perfect, so beautiful, that your knees will buckle.

Buon Appetito!: The Pleasures of Dining

It's no wonder Neapolitan food has won the hearts (and stomachs) of millions: The rich volcanic soil and fertile waters surrounding the city provide abundant and varied seafood, Vesuvian wines, vine-ripe tomatoes, and luscious fruits. Simple, earthy, at once wholesome and sensual, as sophisticated in its purity as the most complex cuisine, as inspired in its aesthetics as the art and architecture of its culture, the cooking of Campania strikes a chord that resonates today as it did when it was served up centuries ago. Its enduring appeal can be traced to an ancient principle: respect for the essence of the thing itself. Naples—the homeland of pizza—is most famous for pizza *alla Margherita* (with tomato, mozzarella, and basil) and marinara (with tomato, garlic, and oregano). Nothing could be simpler, yet nothing is more delicious. That is the wonder of the cuisine of Campania. Like Michelangelo freeing the prisoners that dwelt within the stone—innate, organic—a chef in Campania seems intuitively to seek out the crux of the thing he is about to cook and flatter it, subtly and with the purest of ingredients.

Today the newest trend in southern Italian cooking is to serve up the old—the simple, rustic, time-honored forms of *cucina simpatica, rustica*, and *trattoria*—with a nouvelle flair. Just venture to Campania's greatest restaurant, Don Alfonso 1890, in Sant'Agata sui Due Golfi, and discover how famed chef Alfonso Iaccarino's gastronomic brilliance has made *la nouvella cucina* newer still. Yet Signore Iaccarino also stays true to Campania's roots, using spices brought to the region by Arab traders and luxuries *à la française* that would have delighted the Bourbons who ruled Naples in the 18th century (try his cannelloni stuffed with asparagus, truffles, *and* foie gras). Above all, this chef insists that Campanian cooking remains *puro* and *sincero*—true to the region's culinary traditions.

Whether a slice of pizza from a street vendor in Naples or a culinary extravaganza at Don Alfonso 1890, dining is a marvelous part of the total southern Italian experience, a chance to enjoy authentic specialties and ingredients. Visitors have a choice of eating places, ranging from a *ristorante* (restaurant) to a trattoria, *tavola calda*, or *rosticceria*. The line separating ristoranti from trattorie have blurred of late, but a trattoria is usually a family-run place, simpler in decor, menu, and service than a ristorante and slightly less expensive. Some rustic-looking spots call themselves *osterie* but are really restaurants (a true osteria is a basic, down-to-earth tavern). At a tavola calda or rosticceria, prepared food is sold to be consumed on the spot or taken out; you choose what you want at the counter and pay at the cashier. An *enoteca* is a wine bar where you can order wine by the glass or bottle; most have tables, and many serve savory light meals and snacks.

None of the above eateries serves breakfast; in the morning you go to a *caffè* (coffee bar), where you can also find sandwiches, pastries, and other snacks that are perfect for later in the day. Tell the cashier what you want, pay for it, and then take the stub to the counter, where you restate your order and then drink and eat standing at the counter. Remember that table service costs extra, almost double; don't sit at a table unless you want to be served. On the other hand, if you do sit down, you'll be allowed to linger as long as you like.

In eating places of all kinds the menu is posted in the window or just inside the door so you can see what you're getting into (in a snack bar or tavola calda the price list is usually displayed near the cashier). In all but the simplest places there's a *coperto* (cover charge) and usually also a *servizio* (service charge) of 10%–15%, only part of which goes to the waiter. A *menù turistico* (tourist menu)—which usually means you've stepped into tourist territory, beware—includes taxes and service, but beverages are usually extra.

Generally, a typical meal in a restaurant or trattoria consists of at least two courses: a first course of pasta, risotto, or soup and a second course of meat or fish. Side dishes such as vegetables and salads cost extra, as do desserts. There's no such thing as a side dish of pasta; pasta is a course in itself, and Italians would never think of serving a salad with it; the salad comes later. Years ago pasta dishes were inexpensive because restaurateurs made their profit on the total of the first and second courses. Now tourists and even some diet-conscious Italians tend to order only one course—usually a pasta, perhaps followed by a salad or vegetables—so hosts have jacked up the price of first courses. Now, about antipasti: many a misunderstanding arises over a lavish offering of antipasti, which literally means "before the pasta." No matter how generous and varied the antipasti, the host expects you to order at least one other course. Pizza is in a category by itself and is a one-dish meal, even for the Italians. But some replace the starter course of pasta with a small pizza.

Tap water is safe almost everywhere unless labeled "*non potabile.*" Most people order bottled *acqua minerale* (mineral water), either *gassata* (carbonated), or *naturale,* or *nongassata* (without bubbles). In a restaurant you order it by the *litro* (liter) or *mezzo litro* (half-liter); often the waiter will bring it without being asked, so if you don't like it or want to keep your check down, make a point of ordering *acqua semplice* (tap water). You can also order *un bicchiere di acqua minerale* (a glass of mineral water) at any bar. Italians mostly go heavy on the salt: If you're on a low-sodium diet, ask for everything (within reason) *senza sale* (without salt).

Lunch is served in Campania from 1:30 to 3:30, dinner from 8:30 to 10:30, or later in some restaurants. Almost all eating places close one day a week and for vacations in summer, especially during the last two weeks in August.

Il Dolce Far Niente

The idea of vacation was probably invented when some hardworking Roman emperor escaped Rome for a villa on the Bay of Naples, and ever since the denizens of Campania have been fine-tuning what they call il dolce far niente—the sweet art of idleness. In today's hectic age, even relaxing can feel like a chore, but thanks to Campania's opulent villas, picture-perfect coastal resorts, and dreamy hill towns, you can idle here more successfully than anywhere else. But it takes more than trading in a silk tie for a T-shirt; you have to adjust to the deeper, subtler rhythms of leisure Italian style. Hours spent over a Campari in a sun-splashed caffè; days spent soaking up the sun on the beach at Positano; an afternoon spent painting a watercolor at the gardens of Ravello's Villa Cimbrone: you may be pleasantly surprised to find that such pursuits prove more beneficial than forced marches through the obligatory sights of Naples, Pompeii, or Amalfi. The luxury is often in the lingering.

FODOR'S CHOICE

The sights, restaurants, hotels, and other travel experiences listed below are our editors' top picks—the *crème de la crème* chosen from the lists of Fodor's Choices found on the opening pages of regional chapters in this book. They're the best of their type in the area covered by the book. In addition, the list incorporates many of the highly recommended restaurants and hotels our reviewers have come to treasure. In the destination chapters that follow, you will find all the details for these memories-in-the-making.

LODGING

$$$$ **Bellevue-Syrene,** Sorrento. Long the darling of crowned heads (and heads that were once crowned), this legendary hotel is a fantasia of ducal salons, violet posies, Venetian chandeliers, and muted champagne corks. Today old-world guests still arrive—invariably greeting each other with "Haven't I seen you . . ."—to savor its unique ambience and to marvel at its grand vista of the Bay of Naples.

$$$$ **Excelsior-Vittoria,** Sorrento. Magnificently set overlooking the Bay of Naples, this is a Belle Epoque dream come true, with gilded salons elegant enough to make a Proust heroine swoon, stunning gardens, and a romantic terrace where musicians lull guests with equal doses of Cole Porter and Puccini.

$$$$ **Le Sirenuse,** Positano. As legendary as its namesake sirens, this hotcool, exquisite 18th-century palazzo shimmers with stylish glamour: Venetian and Neapolitan museum-quality antiques, vine-entwined terraces with breathtaking views, a private yacht, Italy's most beautiful pool terrace, and the priciest—probably the best—restaurant on the Amalfi Coast are just some of the pleasures here.

$$$$ **Punta Tragara,** Capri. Pity the billionaire who thinks his ship has sailed in but has never enjoyed a blissful stay here. Built by Le Corbusier, set at the very end of Via Tragara (Capri's, perhaps the world's, prettiest street), and perched over the rocks of I Faraglioni, this hotel has baronial guest rooms and a poolside restaurant whose beauty stops conversation.

$$$$ **San Pietro,** Positano. Set like a gull's nest high over the Bay of Positano, this is the favorite Amalfi Coast "forgetaway" of Julia Roberts, Princess Caroline of Monaco, and a gaggle of Agnellis. Part De Mille, part de Milo—the giddily pretty rooms here are accented with antique statues—the San Pietro remains the hotel wonder of the Amalfi Coast.

$$$–$$$$ **Caruso Belvedere,** Ravello. With regal Empire-era salons and terraced gardens offering spellbinding views of the blue Bay of Salerno, this aristocratic hotel fairly purrs with gentility and style. No wonder authors like Virginia Woolf, Graham Greene, and Tennessee Williams often booked this place. Let's hope everything is intact when this hotel opens in 2004 after a long renovation.

$$$	**Cappuccini Convento**, Amalfi. Like Richard Wagner, you may be tempted to abandon your room and camp out under the stars on this hotel's legendary verandah, set high on a cliff over the sea. Originally a medieval convent, then a fabled inn in the Grand Tour era, this is still southern Italy's most sublime hotel. Touched by peace and quietude, guests enjoy more than a hint of the blessed isolation in which the monks once lived. However, the hotel is now shut for a major refurbishment.
$$–$$$	**La Fenice**, Positano. All the scenic magic of the Amalfi Coast is distilled into one tiny package at this hotel, whose castaway cottages cascade down a hill in an ambuscade of bougainvillea.

BUDGET LODGING

$	**Lorelei et Londres**, Sorrento. *O Sole Mio!* The 19th-century music-box tinkle of Sorrento can still be clearly heard at this pensione, once favored by *Room with a View* ladies from England. With a terracotta facade sunburned by a century of sun and a caffè that seems to levitate over the Bay of Naples, this albergo (small hotel) should be declared a national monument by the Italian government.
$	**Soggiorno Sansevero**, Naples. Set in the former palazzo of the Princes Sansevero, just a block away from the floridly magnificent Capella Sansevero and right on the most charming square of Spaccanapoli, this tiny pensione can't be beat for the location—or price.

RESTAURANTS

$$$$	**Don Alfonso 1890**, Sant'Agata. Haute-hungry pilgrims know the road up to mountaintop Sant'Agata is the *strada* to culinary glory: a table at Don Alfonso, southern Italy's finest restaurant. We recommend *gamberi crude al caviale blue con sucito di limone,* or red shrimp with blue caviar—it's also Prince Rainier's favorite.
$$$$	**Eolo**, Amalfi. The room is small, elegant, with a Gothic window framing a view of the harbor; the kitchen is superlative, with an eye for the spectacular (just order the scampi risotto, adorned with a jewel-like crustacean). Opened in 1998, this restaurant is run by the Gargano family, whose famous Hotel Santa Caterina is just across the bay.
$$$–$$$$	**La Terrazza**, Naples. The new roof-top aerie of the famous Hotel Excelsior, this glam spot comes replete with eye-knocking views of the gulf, city, and Vesuvius, a super-ambitious menu, and a dressy clientele.
$$$$	**Villa Pompeiana**, Sorrento. Here, on the site of the seaside villa where Emperor Augustus once dined on moray eels fattened on human flesh, William Waldorf Astor built a re-creation of the glory that was Rome—a tiny villa set with Pompeiian murals, mosaic floors, and a stone terrace worthy of a Caesar. Now it's the restaurant of the Hotel Bellevue Syrene, and you can dine here on fine regional delicacies like Li Galli lobster with melon pearls. No moray eels, however.

$$–$$$	**Ristorante il Ritrovo,** Montepertuso. Set in Montepertuso, 1,500 ft up the mountainside from Positano, the beloved Ritrovo has a dizzying view over the coast, famous *frutti di mare,* and infamously delicious hazelnut *semifreddi* mousses.
$$	**O' Capurale,** Positano. Positano is all about easy elegance, and this dining spot sums it all up. Graced with a coved ceiling awash with colorful Fauvist-style frescoes, the dining room hums with happy, stylish diners unwinding before your eyes. All it takes is one blissful lunch here to forget all about those newspaper headlines.
$–$$	**Lo Scoglio,** Marina di Cantone. Dramatically set on a pier by the beach, you can hear, smell—even *taste*—the waves from here on a rough day. The cuisine, not unexpectedly, is freshly caught seafood, but even if you only stop by for a gelato at this informal *ristorante,* you'll enjoy yourself immensely (especially if you're a water baby, or are accompanied by one).
$–$$	**Lombardi à Santa Chiara,** Naples. Naples is the home of pizza and this place offers some of the best, served up in the adorable neighborhood of Spaccanapoli, opposite the Palazzo Croce.

BUDGET RESTAURANTS

$	**Timpani e Tempura,** Naples. A sublime bite of Napoli is this tiny shrine's *mangiamaccheroni,* or spaghetti in broth with caciocavallo cheese.
¢	**Friggitoria Vomero,** Naples. For some oil-based bliss, try the deep fried eggplant, dough balls, or potato croquettes here—they are the memory-triggering, Neapolitan equivalents of Proust's madeleines.

QUINTESSENTIAL CAMPANIA

Dawn Concert at the Villa Rufolo, Ravello. The soul of serenity, this hilltop village, suspended between sea and sky, is home to the Fèstival Musicale di Ravello. Experience its extraordinary midnight concerts and the even more extraordinary *concerto all'alba*—a dawn concert that serenades the rising sun beginning at 4 AM, usually held in the first week of August—to enjoy a fitting encore to Ravello's stirring scenery.

Festa di San Gennaro, Naples. Everything in Naples is brought to a boil twice a year—on the first Saturday in May and on September 19—when the Liquefaction of the Blood of San Gennaro is celebrated at the city duomo. If you want to "assist" at *Il Miracolo,* arrive as early as 7 AM.

Ancient Temples, Paestum. Paestum is blessed by its remoteness from the main tourist routes. The best times to absorb the grandeur and desolation of these noble ruins are daybreak and dusk.

Spaccanapoli, Naples. For perfect people-watching, promenade through Spaccanapoli, the historic district of Naples, whose packed streets, pungent aromas, and operatic hawking offer an unforgettable Punch-and-Judy show. Towering tenements (the tallest of 19th-century Europe) jostle with grand palazzi, while the district's swirling Baroque architecture melts even the stoniest hearts.

Twilight, Positano. The utter tranquillity of Positano at sunset is a balm to the soul. Whitewashed houses tumble down to the azure sea, shimmering under a blood-orange sky. Reserve an alfresco table at a caffè and let it all soak in. *This* is why you came to Italy.

Villa Cimbone, Ravello. No one should miss the breathtaking gardens of this villa—whose roses once warmed Greta Garbo's chilly heart—and its sky-touching Belvedere of Infinity.

Villa of the Mysteries, Pompeii. Enter this private house—adorned with the most famous frescoes surviving from antiquity—and the days of the Caesars won't seem so remote.

Villa San Michele, Capri. Emperor Tiberius himself would have loved this 19th-century, antique-inspired villa. Make a wish standing on the Sphinx Parapet—here, high atop Anacapri, your spirit will shed its earthly bonds, and, hey, you never know. When you return by bus, be sure to be nice to the driver—you're 1,800 ft above the Bay of Naples on this road.

SMART TRAVEL TIPS

Half the fun of traveling is looking forward to your trip, but when you look forward, don't just daydream. There are plans to be made, things to learn about, serious work to be done. Finding out about your destination before you leave home means you won't squander time organizing everyday minutiae once you've arrived. You'll be more streetwise when you hit the ground as well, better prepared to explore the aspects of Naples and the Amalfi Coast that drew you here in the first place. The organizations in this section can provide information to supplement this guide; contact them for up-to-the-minute details. Note that some of the information in this section is Italy-wide; for all the specific details about the various topics covered below within Campania itself, consult the A to Z sections at the end of each regional chapter in this book. Happy landings!

ADDRESSES

Addresses in Italy are fairly straightforward: the street is followed by the street number. However, you might see an address with a number plus "bis" or "A"; for instance, "Via Verdi 3/bis" or "Via Mazzini 8/A." This indicates that 3/bis and 8/A are the next door down from Via Verdi 3 and Via Mazzini 8, respectively. In rural areas, some addresses give only the route name or the distance in kilometers along a major road (e.g., Via Fabbri, km 4.3), or sometimes only the name of the small village in which the site is located.

AIR TRAVEL TO & FROM NAPLES

BOOKING

When you book, look for nonstop flights and remember that "direct" flights stop at least once. Try to avoid connecting flights, which require a change of plane. Two airlines may operate a connecting flight jointly, so ask whether your airline operates every segment of the trip; you may find that the carrier you prefer flies you only part of the way. To find more booking tips and to check prices and make on-line flight reservations, log on to www.fodors.com.

CARRIERS

When flying internationally, you must usually choose between a domestic carrier, the national flag carrier of the country, and a foreign carrier from a third country. You may, for example, choose to fly Alitalia to Italy—as the national flag carrier it has the greatest number of nonstops. Domestic carriers, such as Air One, AlpiEagles, AirEurope, and Meridiana, may have better connections to smaller destinations as well as a slight price advantage.

No international carrier makes a transatlantic flight to Naples, but Alitalia offers an extensive and varied schedule of flights connecting Naples with Rome and Milan and numerous other Italian and European cities. It continues to offer more nonstop flights to Italy from the United States than any other airline, including a nonstop flight from San Francisco to Milan's Malpensa Airport. Among the cities that Alitalia connects with Naples (often with daily flights) are Milan (both Linate and Malpensa), Paris, Rome, Turin, and Venice, while connections to lesser airports in Italy—Bologna, Catania, Genoa and Trieste—are run by Alitalia partner, Minerva Airlines. Alitalia's North American gateways are Boston, Chicago, Los Angeles, Miami, San Francisco, New York City, Montreal, and Toronto. The main sales offices for the airline in the United States is in New York City, with other offices in Washington, D.C. and San Francisco; the main reservations number and sales office numbers are listed below. For further information about schedules, special fare promotions, and Italiatour—Alitalia's tour-group agency—visit www.alitalia.com or www.alitaliausa.com.

Several other carriers link major European cities with Naples—for instance, British Airways offers a direct route between London-Gatwick and Naples, Air France offers a direct route between Paris and Naples, Lufthansa serves Naples–Munich passengers, and AlpiEagles flies to Barcelona. Most Mediterranean country-hoppers are now re-routed via Milan Malpensa or Rome, though Air Littoral still conveniently flies between Naples and Nice. Internet bargain-hunters are appreciating the cut-price fares from London-Stansted to Naples with the carrier EasyJet, while Ryan Air continues to deliver unbelievable fares to Pescara, 4½ hours away by bus. Milan and Rome are also served by Continental Airlines and Delta Air Lines. American Airlines, United

Airlines, and Northwest Airlines fly into Milan. US Airways serves Rome. Lower-price charter flights to a range of Italian destinations are available throughout the year.

To & From Italy Air France ☎ 800/237-2747; 848/884466 within Italy ⊕ www.airfrance.com. **Air Littoral** ☎ 06/841-8120; within Italy, 848/878510. **Alitalia** ☎ 800/223-5730 or 020/760-27111; 0990/448259 in Britain; 848/865641 within Italy ⊕ www.alitalia.it ✉ Individual sales offices in U.S. ☎ 212/903-3300 New York; 310/568-5941 Los Angeles; 312/644-0404 Chicago; 617/267-2882 Boston. **American Airlines** ☎ 800/433-7300 ⊕ www.im.aa.com. **British Airways** ☎ 848/812266 ⊕ www.britishairways.com. **Continental Airlines** ☎ 800/231-0856 ⊕ www.continental.com. **Delta Air Lines** ☎ 800/241-4141 ⊕ www.delta.com. **EasyJet** ☎ 848/887766 ⊕ www.easyjet.com. **Lufthansa** ☎ 800/247-9297; 06/6568-4004 in Rome ⊕ www.lufthansa.it. **Meridiana** ☎ 0171/839-2222; 800/555092 in Italy ⊕ www.meridiana.it. **Northwest Airlines** ☎ 800/225-2525 ⊕ www.nwa.com. **Ryan Air** ☎ 899/889-973 ⊕ www.ryanair.com. **United Airlines** ☎ 800/538-2929 ⊕ www.united.com. **US Airways** ☎ 800/428-4322 ⊕ www.usairways.com.

Within Italy AirEurope ☎ 848/824425 within Italy. **Air One** ☎ 06/488800; 848/48880 within Italy. **Alitalia** ☎ 06/65621; 06/65643 in Rome; 02/24991 in Milan; 848/865641 within Italy. **Alpieagles** ☎ 081/5992351 in Naples. **Meridiana** ☎ 06/478041; 800/555092 within Italy. **Minerva Airlines** ☎ 848/865641 within Italy ⊕ www.minerva-airlines.it/.

CHECK-IN & BOARDING

Always **find out your carrier's check-in policy.** Plan to arrive at the airport about two hours before your scheduled departure time for domestic flights and 2½ to 3 hours before international flights. You may need to arrive earlier if you're flying from one of the busier airports or during peak air-traffic times. To avoid delays at airport-security checkpoints, try not to wear any metal. Jewelry, belt and other buckles, steel-toe shoes, barrettes, and underwire bras are among the items that can set off detectors.

Assuming that not everyone with a ticket will show up, airlines routinely overbook planes. When everyone does, airlines ask for volunteers to give up their seats. In return, these volunteers usually get a several-hundred-dollar flight voucher, which can be used toward the purchase of another ticket, and are rebooked on the next flight out. If there are not enough volunteers, the airline must choose who will be denied boarding. The first to get bumped are passengers who checked in late and those flying on discounted tickets, so get to the gate and check in as early as possible, especially during peak periods.

Always **bring a government-issue photo I.D.** to the airport; even when it's not required, a passport is best.

CUTTING COSTS

The least expensive airfares to Italy are priced for round-trip travel and must usually be purchased in advance. Airlines generally allow you to change your return date for a fee; most low-fare tickets, however, are nonrefundable. It's smart to call a number of airlines and check the Internet; when you are quoted a good price, **book it on the spot**—the same fare may not be available the next day, or even the next hour. Always check different routings and look into using alternate airports. Also, price off-peak flights, which may be significantly less expensive than others. Travel agents, especially low-fare specialists (*see*:Discounts and Deals *below*), are helpful.

Consolidators are another good source. They buy tickets for scheduled flights at reduced rates from the airlines, then sell them at prices that beat the best fare available directly from the airlines. Sometimes you can even get your money back if you need to return the ticket. Carefully read the fine print detailing penalties for changes and cancellations, purchase the ticket with a credit card, and **confirm your consolidator reservation with the airline.**

🔢 Consolidators **AirlineConsolidator.com** ☎ 888/468-5385 ⊕ www.airlineconsolidator.com for international tickets. **Best Fares** ☎ 800/576-8255 or 800/576-1600 🖥 www.bestfares.com; $59.90 annual membership. **Cheap Tickets** ☎ 800/377-1000 or 888/922-8849 ⊕ www.cheaptickets.com. **Expedia** ☎ 800/397-3342 or 404/728-8787 ⊕ www.expedia.com. **Hotwire** ☎ 866/468-9473 or 920/330-9418 ⊕ www.hotwire.com. **Now Voyager Travel** ☎ 212/459-1616 🖥 212/243-2711 ⊕ www.nowvoyagertravel.com. **Orbitz** ☎ 888/656-4546 ⊕ www.orbitz.com. **Priceline.com** ⊕ www.priceline.com. **Travelocity** ☎ 888/709-5983; 877/282-2925 in Canada; 0870/111-7060 in the U.K. ⊕ www.travelocity.com. 🔢 Courier Resources **Air Courier Association/Cheaptrips.com** ☎ 800/282-1202 ⊕ www.aircourier.org or www.cheaptrips.com; $29 annual membership. **International Association of Air Travel Couriers** ☎ 308/632-3273 ⊕ www.courier.org; $45 annual membership.

ENJOYING THE FLIGHT

State your seat preference when purchasing your ticket, and then repeat it when you confirm and when you check in. For more legroom, you can request one of the few emergency-aisle seats at check-in, if you are capable of lifting at least 50 pounds—a Federal Aviation Administration requirement of passengers in these seats. Seats behind a bulkhead also offer more legroom, but they don't have under-seat storage. Don't sit in the row in front of the emergency aisle or in front of a bulkhead, where seats may not recline.

Ask the airline whether a snack or meal is served on the flight. If you have dietary concerns, **request special meals when booking.** These can be vegetarian, low-cholesterol, or kosher, for example. It's a good idea to pack some healthful snacks and a small (plastic) bottle of water in your carry-on bag. On long flights, try to maintain a normal routine, to help fight jet lag. At night, get some sleep. By day, eat light meals, drink water (not alcohol), and **move around the cabin** to stretch your legs. For additional jet-lag tips consult *Fodor's FYI: Travel Fit & Healthy* (available at bookstores everywhere).

All flights within Italy are smoke-free. Smoking is allowed on an ever-dwindling number of international flights; **contact your carrier about its smoking policy.**

FLYING TIMES

Flying time to Rome is 8½ hours from New York, 10–11 hours from Chicago, 11½ hours from Dallas (via New York), 11½ hours from Los Angeles, 2½ hours from London (to Naples), and 12½ hours from Sydney.

HOW TO COMPLAIN

If your baggage goes astray or your flight goes awry, complain right away. Most carriers require that you **file a claim immediately.** The Aviation Consumer Protection Division of the Department of Transportation publishes *Fly-Rights,* which discusses airlines and consumer issues and is available on-line. You can also find articles and information at mytravelrights.com, the Web site of the nonprofit Consumer Travel Rights Center.

🔢 Airline Complaints **Aviation Consumer Protection Division** ✉ U.S. Department of Transportation, C-75, Room 4107, 400 7th St. SW, Washington, DC

20590 ☎ 202/366-2220 ⊕ airconsumer.ost.dot.gov.
**Federal Aviation Administration Consumer Hot-
line** ✉ For inquiries: FAA, 800 Independence Ave.
SW, Washington, DC 20591 ☎ 800/322-7873
⊕ www.faa.gov.

RECONFIRMING

Check the status of your flight before you
leave for the airport. You can do this on
your carrier's Web site, by linking to a
flight-status checker (many Web booking
services offer these), or by calling your carrier or travel agent. Always confirm international flights at least 72 hours ahead of
the scheduled departure time.

AIRPORTS & TRANSFERS

Located just outside Naples, **Aeroporto
Capodichino** serves the Campania region.
It handles domestic and international
flights, including several flights daily between Naples and Rome (flight time 45
minutes). The airport is currently run by
the local handler GESAC with some logistical assistance from BAA (British Airports
Authority), the majority stakeholder. From
May to September there's a direct **helicopter service** (☎ 081/5844355 ⊕ www.
cabair.it) between Aeroporto Capodichino
and Capri, Ischia, and Praiano (near Positano). The major gateways to Italy include
Rome's **Aeroporto Leonardo da Vinci,** better known as **Fiumicino,** and Milan's **Aeroporto Malpensa** (MXP). Smaller, minor
gateways are served by domestic and some
international flights.

🔁 Airport Information **Aeroporto Capodichino**
✉ Via Umberto Maddalena, 5 km [3 mi] north of
Naples ☎ 081/7896111 ⊕ www.gesac.it. **Aeroporto
Leonardo da Vinci** (Fiumicino) ✉ 35 km [20 mi]
southwest of Rome ☎ 06/65953640 ⊕ www.adr.it.
Aeroporto Malpensa ✉ 45 km [28 mi] north of
Milan ☎ 02/74852200 ⊕ www.sea-
aeroportimilano.it/malpensa.

Bologna: **Aeroporto Guglielmo Marconi** ✉ Borgo
Panigale, 7 km [4½ mi] from Bologna ☎ 051/
6479615 ⊕ www.bologna-airport.it. Genoa: **Aeroporto Cristoforo Colombo** ✉ 6 km [4 mi] west of
Genoa ☎ 010/6512577 ⊕ www.airport.genova.it.
Milan: **Aeroporto Linate** ✉ 10 km [6 mi] east of
Milan ☎ 02/74852200. Pescara: **Aeroporto
d'Abruzzo** ✉ 5 km [3 mi] southwest of Pescara
☎ 085/4324200 ⊕ www.abruzzo-airport.it. Turin:
Aeroporto Caselle ✉ 15 km [9 mi] north of Turin
☎ 011/5676361 ⊕ www.turin-airport.com. Venice:
Aeroporto Marco Polo ✉ Tessera, about 10 km [6
mi] north of Venice ☎ 041/2609260.

AIRPORT TRANSFERS

Bus 3S runs from Piazza Garibaldi to
Naples' airport (every 30 minutes, the
journey lasts around 30 minutes) between
5:30 AM and midnight, and costs €.77.
The quicker shuttle bus, Alibus, also runs
from 6:30 AM to midnight between the airport, Piazza Garibaldi (where the main
railroad terminal is), the port, and the very
center of town, the Piazza Municipio
(every 30 minutes, the journey lasts approximately 20 minutes, €3). If you take a
taxi from Piazza Garibaldi, expect to pay
€13–€17 for the 15-minute trip.
🔁 Taxis & Shuttles **Shuttle bus** ☎ 081/5311706.

BOAT & FERRY TRAVEL

As one of the great harbors of the world,
Naples offers a wide array of boat, ferry
(*traghetti*), and hydrofoil (*aliscafo*) services
between the city, the islands of the bay, the
Sorrentine peninsula, and other Mediterranean destinations. The main station is at
the Molo Beverello—the port of Naples opposite the Castel Nuovo (and near the
Montesanto and future Piazza Municipio
metro stops)—along the waterfront of Piazza Municipio. Here, hydrofoils and ferries run by Caremar, Linee Lauro, SNAV,
and Alilauro connect Naples with Sorrento,
Capri, Ischia, and Procida. More hydrofoils
depart for Capri, Ischia, and Procida, as
well as the further-flung islands of Ponza
and Ventotene to the northwest and the Aeolian islands off Sicily's northern coast,
from the Mergellina harbor (a short walk
from the Mergellina train station) at the far
western end of the Riviera di Chiaia; the
trip to Ischia and Procida is shorter and
cheaper if you use the ferry that departs
from Pozzuoli harbor (the nearest metro
station is on the Cumana line at Pozzuoli).
Next to the Molo Beverello is the Stazione
Marittima (Molo Angioino), where larger
ferries make trips to Ponza, the Aeolian islands, Sicily, and Sardinia.

In 2002, Campania unveiled its exciting
and extensive new Metro del Mare public
transport system. This ambitious new network is headquarted at the Molo Beverello
port in downtown Naples. From this
major harbor hub, and sailing north as far
as the Phelegrean Fields and as south as
Salerno, a web of ferries and fastjet boats
connect the top ports of call, including Bacoli, Pozzuoli, Naples (Molo Beverello),
Torre Annunziata, Sorrento, Positano, and

Amalfi. There are six lines of the Metro del Mare, with some running only on weekends (e.g. MM4, which runs from Naples to Sapri in the Cilento south of Maiori) and others running on a daily basis (e.g. MM1, which goes four times daily from Sorrento to Monte di Procida, stopping at Castellammare, Torre del Greco, Portici, Napoli Mergellina, Pozzuoli, and Bacoli). If you want to go directly from Naples to Positano, you will have to pay more a ticket on one of the three daily express boats. **Note that the Metro del Mare service runs from Easter time through October only.** Check the local papers (*Il Mattino* or *La Repubblica*) for timetables or go to www.metrodelmare. com. Prices are highly competitive and make this the cheapest way to get around by sea. One-way fares vary from as little as €2 (Naples to Pozzuoli) to €12 (Naples to Salerno). Better, if you purchase a three-day Campania *Artecard* (*see* the introduction to Exploring Naples *in* Chapter 1), you also get a three-day travelcard and two free Metro del Mare tickets.

Hydrofoil service is generally twice as fast as ferries and almost double the price. The service is considerably more frequent in summer. For specific information about boat, ferry, and hydrofoil travel between Naples and other destinations on the Bay of Naples and the Amalfi Coast, *see* the A to Z sections at the end of each regional chapter. Car ferries operate to the islands of the Bay of Naples, but advance reservations are best.

FARES & SCHEDULES

The most comprehensive coverage of ferry, hydrofoil, and boat services and schedules is found in the local paper *Il Mattino,* which features a *Per chi Parte* ("For Those Departing") section every day. *Qui Napoli,* the helpful monthly English-language periodical for visitors to Naples, as well as the handy events booklet, *Le Pagine dell' Ozio,* also lists ferry and hydrofoil schedules. As there are substantial seasonal variations, double-check departure times and days, especially when traveling further afield on low-frequency services. Alternatively, consult the excellent Web site, ⊕ www.campaniatrasporti. it for a helpful overview of most public transport lines in Campania.
🚢 Boat & Ferry Information **Alilauro** ☎ 081/ 7614909 ⊕ www.alilauro.it. **Caremar** ☎ 081/5513882

⊕ www.caremar.it. **Linee Lauro** ☎ 081/5522838 ⊕ www.lineelauro.it. **Metro del Mare** ☎ 199/ 446644 ⊕ www.metrodelmare.com. **Navigazione Libera del Golfo** ☎ 081/5527209 ⊕ www.navlib.it. **SNAV** ☎ 081/7612348 ⊕ www.snavali.com. **Siremar** ☎ 081/5800340 ⊕ www.siremar.it. **Tirrenia** ☎ 8408/99000 or 081/7201111 ⊕ www.tirrenia.it.

BUSINESS HOURS

BANKS & POST OFFICES

Banks are open weekdays 8:30 to 1:15 and 2:45 to 3:45.

Post offices are open Monday through Saturday 9 to 1; central and main district post offices stay open until 6 PM weekdays, 9 to 2 on Saturday.

GAS STATIONS

Gas stations open about 7 AM and close at about 8 PM. In sleepy country areas away from major roads they will close for lunch between 1 PM and 4 PM, so make sure you fill up beforehand. Services open around the clock can be found on autostrade and the tangenziale around Naples, and there are about 20 *benzinai notturni* (night-shift gas-stations) operating in various parts of Naples. Details can be found in local newspapers. See also the Car Travel section in Naples A to Z in the Naples chapter.

MUSEUMS & SIGHTS

The major museums in Naples, such as Museo Archeologico Nazionale, Museo di Capodimonte, Palazzo Reale, and San Martino are open through to the evening, although you may find some rooms closed in the afternoons due to lack of staff. Many smaller private museums are only open from 9 AM to 1 or 2 PM. The opening times of archaeological sites are subject to seasonal variations, with most sites closing an hour before sunset, and preventing access as much as two hours before. When this book refers to summer hours, it means approximately Easter to October; winter hours run from November to Easter. Most museums are closed one day a week, often Monday. Always check locally.

Most churches are open from early morning until noon or 12:30, when they close for three hours or more; they open again in the afternoon, closing about 7 PM or later.

PHARMACIES

Pharmacies are generally open Monday–Friday from 8:30 to 1 and from 4 to 8, and Saturday mornings 9 to 1. Local pharmacies cover the off-hours in shifts: on the door of every pharmacy is a list of pharmacies that will be open in the vicinity on Saturday afternoon, Sunday, or 24 hours.

SHOPS

As in most European countries, shop opening times vary according to the retail sector. Clothing shops open from 10 to 1:30 and from 4:30 to 8, Tuesday through Saturday. They are generally closed on Monday mornings, but open regular afternoon hours, except from July to mid-September when they close Saturday afternoons and open on Monday mornings. *Alimentari* (grocers) and *panifici* (bakeries) open as early as 8 AM every day except Sunday, but are closed on Thursday afternoons and Sundays. Barbers and hairdressers, with some exceptions, are closed Sunday and Monday. On Sundays the *pasticcerie* (cake shops) do a roaring trade, as most southern Italians like to round off their luncheon ritual with a calorie-rich *pasticcino* (little cake). The smaller shops in town will usually close for a week either side of Ferragosto (August 15th), when most larger urban areas are transformed into ghost towns and city-dwellers flock to seaside or mountain resorts.

BUS TRAVEL AROUND CAMPANIA

Campania's bus network is extensive and in some areas buses can be more direct (and therefore, faster) than local trains, so it's a good idea to **compare bus and train schedules.** Bus services outside cities are organized on a regional level, and often by private companies. Campania has three main bus companies, listed below. ANM handles buses within Naples, CTP usually handles medium- and long-distance routes out of Naples, while SITA services the Amalfi Coast. Taking buses from Naples requires both research and patience, since there is no central bus station as such: Different bus lines leave from different city squares, with the situation being compounded by recent traffic reorganization in Piazza Garibaldi. For more specific information, *see* the A to Z sections at the end of each regional chapter or ask at a tourist information office.

PAYING

Tickets are not sold on board buses so you must purchase your tickets in advance by machine, at newsstands, or at tobacconists. Remember to time-stamp your ticket after you board as conductors often make spot-checks. Keep in mind that many ticket sellers close for several hours at midday, so it's always wise to stock up on bus tickets when you have the chance. **⚡ Bus Information ANM** ✉ Piazza Garibaldi, main Servizio CTP bus stop, Napoli ☎ 081/7632177 ⊕ www.anm.it. **CTP** ✉ Via Sannio 19, Napoli ☎ 081/7005091. **SITA** ✉ Via Pisanelli 3, south of Piazza Municipio, Napoli ☎ 081/5522176 or 081/5934644 ⊕ www.sita-on-line.it.

CAMERAS & PHOTOGRAPHY

The *Kodak Guide to Shooting Great Travel Pictures* (available at bookstores everywhere) is loaded with tips. **⚡ Photo Help Kodak Information Center** ☎ 800/242-2424 ⊕ www.kodak.com.

EQUIPMENT PRECAUTIONS

Don't pack film or equipment in checked luggage, where it is much more susceptible to damage. X-ray machines used to view checked luggage are extremely powerful and therefore are likely to ruin your film. Try to ask for hand inspection of film, which becomes clouded after repeated exposure to airport X-ray machines, and keep videotapes and computer disks away from metal detectors. Always keep film, tape, and computer disks out of the sun. Carry an extra supply of batteries, and be prepared to turn on your camera, camcorder, or laptop to prove to airport security personnel that the device is real.

FILM & DEVELOPING

Better to get your film developed back home. Other than serious camera shops, most "quickie" film developers are substandard and your pictures can turn out to be grainier than usual. Kodak film is widely distributed and can be purchased at tobacconists (average price €3–€3.50), while other brands (Fuji, Agfa) can be found at specialist dealers at similar prices.

VIDEOS

The local standard for videotape is PAL (not the American-used NTSC). A blank videotape (E120) will typically cost between €1.50–€2.20.

CAR RENTAL

Renting a car in Italy is helpful when exploring the off-the-beaten-track countryside, but not necessary, as the bus system throughout Campania is excellent and far-flung. Signage on country roads is usually pretty good, but be prepared for fast and impatient fellow drivers. Major car-rental companies have boxy "utility" cars and Fiats in various sizes that are always in good condition.

🚗 Major Agencies **Alamo** ☎ 800/522-9696 ⊕ www.alamo.com. **Avis** ☎ 800/331-1084; 800/879-2847 in Canada; 0870/606-0100 in the U.K.; 02/9353-9000 in Australia; 09/526-2847 in New Zealand ⊕ www.avis.com. **Budget** ☎ 800/527-0700; 0870/156-5656 in the U.K. ⊕ www.budget.com. **Dollar** ☎ 800/800-6000; 0124/622-0111 in the U.K., where it's affiliated with Sixt; 02/9223-1444 in Australia ⊕ www.dollar.com. **Hertz** ☎ 800/654-3001; 800/263-0600 in Canada; 0870/844-8844 in the U.K.; 02/9669-2444 in Australia; 09/256-8690 in New Zealand ⊕ www.hertz.com. **National Car Rental** ☎ 800/227-7368; 0870/600-6666 in the U.K. ⊕ www.nationalcar.com.

CUTTING COSTS

Most major American rental-car companies have offices or affiliates in Italy, but the rates are generally better if you make a reservation from abroad rather than from within Italy.

For a good deal, **book through a travel agent who will shop around.** Also, price local car-rental companies—whose prices may be lower still, although their service and maintenance may not be as good as those of major rental agencies—and research rates on the Internet. Remember to ask about required deposits, cancellation penalties, and drop-off charges if you're planning to pick up the car in one city and leave it in another. If you're traveling during a holiday period, also make sure that a confirmed reservation guarantees you a car.

Do look into wholesalers, companies that do not own fleets but rent in bulk from those that do and often offer better rates than traditional car-rental operations.

Prices are best during off-peak periods. Rentals booked through wholesalers often must be paid for before you leave home.

🚗 Wholesalers **Auto Europe** ☎ 207/842-2000 or 800/223-5555 🖷 207/842-2222 ⊕ www.autoeurope.com. **Europe by Car** ☎ 212/581-3040 or 800/223-1516 🖷 212/246-1458 ⊕ www.europebycar.com. **Destination Europe Resources** (DER) ☎ 800/782-2424 ⊕ www.der.com. **Kemwel** ☎ 800/678-0678 🖷 207/842-2124 ⊕ www.kemwel.com.

INSURANCE

When driving a rented car you are generally responsible for any damage to or loss of the vehicle. Collision policies that car-rental companies sell for European rentals typically don't cover stolen vehicles. Indeed, all car-rental agencies operating in Italy require that you buy a theft-protection policy. Before you rent—and purchase collision coverage—see what coverage you already have under the terms of your personal auto-insurance policy and credit cards.

REQUIREMENTS & RESTRICTIONS

In Italy you must be 21 years of age to rent an economy or subcompact car and at least 25 years of age to rent a bigger car.

SURCHARGES

Before you pick up a car in one city and leave it in another, **ask about drop-off charges or one-way service fees, which can be substantial.** Note, too, that some rental agencies charge extra if you return the car before the time specified in your contract. To avoid a hefty refueling fee, fill the tank just before you turn in the car, but be aware that gas stations near the rental outlet may overcharge. It's almost never a deal to buy the tank of gas that's in the car when you rent it; the understanding is that you'll return it empty, but some fuel usually remains.

CAR TRAVEL

There's an extensive network of *autostrade* (toll highways), complemented by equally well-maintained but free *superstrade* (expressways). The ticket you are issued upon entering an autostrada must be returned when you exit and pay the toll; on some shorter highways, like the *Tangenziale* around Naples, the flat rate toll €.65 is paid upon exiting; the Naples–Salerno toll €1.30 is paid on entry. Viacard cards, on sale at many autostrada locations, make paying tolls easier and faster, although if you are just using the car on local autostrade within Campania you may find yourself with substantial surplus credit on your card at the end of your trip. A *raccordo* or *tangenziale* is a ring road surrounding a city. *Strade statali* (state highways, denoted by S or SS numbers) may be single-lane roads, as are all secondary roads; directions and turnoffs are not always clearly marked.

Your driver's license may not be recognized outside your home country. An International Driver's Permit is a good idea; it's available from the American or Canadian automobile association, and, in the United Kingdom, from the Automobile Association or Royal Automobile Club. These international permits are universally recognized, and having one in your wallet may save you a problem with the local authorities.

AUTO CLUBS

There are two major automobile clubs operative in Italy: ACI (Automobil Club D'Italia), which is in fact less of a club and more of a vehicle ownership registration service, which also provides breakdown assistance coverage; subscription to the TCI (Touring Club Italiano) provides motorists with maps and logistical assistance when planning journeys and holidays, besides taking an active interest in Italian heritage preservation. For a small annual surcharge, the TCI will also provide breakdown assistance.

In Australia Australian Automobile Association ☎ 02/6247-7311 ⊕ www.aaa.asn.au.

In Canada Canadian Automobile Association (CAA) ☎ 613/247-0117 ⊕ www.caa.ca.

In Italy Automobil Club D'Italia ☎ 081/5931301 ⊕ www.aci.it. Touring Club Italiano ☎ 02/5359971 ⊕ www.touringclub.it.

In New Zealand New Zealand Automobile Association ☎ 09/377-4660 ⊕ www.aa.co.nz.

In the U.K. Automobile Association (AA) ☎ 0870/600-0371 ⊕ www.theaa.com. Royal Automobile Club (RAC) ☎ 0990/722-722 membership; 0345/121-345 insurance ⊕ www.rac.co.uk.

In the U.S. American Automobile Association ☎ 800/564-6222 ⊕ www.aaa.com.

EMERGENCY SERVICES

ACI Emergency Service offers 24-hour road service. Dial 116 from any phone to reach the ACI dispatch operator.

GASOLINE

Gas stations are generally open Monday through Saturday from 7 AM to 7 PM with a break at lunchtime. Many stations also have self-service pumps, which usually accept bills of €5, €10, or €20. Gas stations on autostrade are open 24 hours. Gas costs about €1.20 per liter. Almost all rental cars take so-called *benzina verde* (unleaded fuel known as green gasoline).

PARKING

Parking space is at a premium in Naples and most towns, but especially in the *centri storici* (historic centers), which are filled with narrow streets and restricted circulation zones. It's often a good idea (if not the only option) to park your car in a designated (preferably attended) lot. Parking in an area signposted ZONA DISCO (disk zone) is allowed for limited periods (from 30 minutes to 2 hours or more—the limit is posted); if you don't have the cardboard disk (inquire at the local tourist office) to show what time you parked, you can use a piece of paper. The *parcometro*, the Italian version of metered parking in which you purchase prepaid tickets (from a newsstand or tobacconist's) that you scratch to indicate time and date of arrival and leave on the dashboard, has been introduced both in Naples and in many of the towns around. Within Naples, it's advisable to **leave your car only in designated parking areas,** usually marked out by blue lines. A red sign with a horizontal white stripe through it means do not enter; a blue circular sign with a red slash or an X means no parking, as do the signs VIETATO SOSTARE, DIVIETO DI SOSTA, and NON PARCHEGGIARE. If you have baggage in the car, always park your car in an attended car park or garage.

ROAD CONDITIONS

Autostrade are well maintained, as are most interregional highways. The condition of provincial (county) roads varies, but road maintenance at this level is generally good in Italy. Street and road signs are often challenging—a good map and patience are essential. Italians drive fast and are impatient with those who don't. Tailgating is the norm here—the only way to avoid it is to get out of the way.

RULES OF THE ROAD

Driving is on the right. Regulations are similar to those in Britain and the United States. It's obligatory to drive with headlights on, even during the day, on trunk roads and highways. In most Italian towns the use of the horn is forbidden in certain, if not all, areas; a large sign, ZONA DI SILENZIO, indicates where. Elsewhere, according to the Italian Highway Code, horns can only be used in situations where there is "immediate and real danger." Some drivers interpret this as covering every sharp bend on the Amalfi Coast, although an alternative noise-free technique is to slow down and keep a foot hovering over the brake pedal. Speed limits are 130 kph (80 mph) on autostrade and 90 kph (55 mph) on state and provincial roads, unless otherwise marked. Fines for driving after drinking are heavy, including the suspension of license and the additional possibility of six months' imprisonment.

COMPUTERS ON THE ROAD

Getting on-line in Italian cities isn't difficult: public Internet stations and Internet cafés, some open 24 hours a day, are becoming more and more common. Prices differ from place to place, so spend some time to find the best deal. This isn't always readily apparent: a place might have higher rates, but because it belongs to a chain you won't be charged an initial flat fee again when you move to a different city that has the same chain. Some hotels have in-room modem lines, but, as with phones, using the hotel's line is relatively expensive. Always check modem rates before plugging in. You may need an adapter for your computer for the European-style plugs. As always, if you're traveling with a laptop, carry a spare battery and an adapter. Never connect your computer to any socket before asking about surge protection. IBM sells a pea-size modem tester that plugs into a telephone jack to check whether the line is safe to use.

CONSULATES & EMBASSIES

🇦🇺 Australia **Australian Consulate** ✉ Via Alessandria 215 00198 Rome ☎ 06/852721 ⊕ www.australian-embassy.it.
🇨🇦 Canada **Canadian Embassy** ✉ Via Zara 30, Rome ☎ 06/445981 ⊕ www.canada.it.
🇳🇿 New Zealand **New Zealand Embassy** ✉ Via Zara 28, Rome ☎ 06/4417171 ⊕ www.nzembassy.com.

🇬🇧 United Kingdom **British Consulate** ✉ Via Dei Mille 40, Napoli ☎ 081/4238911 ⊕ www.ukinitalia.it.
🇺🇸 United States **U.S. Consulate** ✉ Piazza della Repubblica 2, at west end of Villa Comunale, Napoli ☎ 081/5838111 ⊕ www.usembassy.it.

CONSUMER PROTECTION

Whether you're shopping for gifts or purchasing travel services, **pay with a major credit card** whenever possible, so you can cancel payment or get reimbursed if there's a problem (and you can provide documentation). If you're doing business with a company for the first time, contact your local Better Business Bureau and the attorney general's offices in your state and (for U.S. businesses) the company's home state as well. Have any complaints been filed? Finally, if you're buying a package or tour, always consider travel insurance that includes default coverage (⇨ Insurance).
🇺🇸 BBBs **Council of Better Business Bureaus** ✉ 4200 Wilson Blvd., Suite 800, Arlington, VA 22203 ☎ 703/276-0100 🖷 703/525-8277 ⊕ www.bbb.org.

CUSTOMS & DUTIES

When shopping abroad, keep receipts for all purchases. Upon reentering the country, **be ready to show customs officials what you've bought.** Pack purchases together in an easily accessible place. If you think a duty is incorrect, appeal the assessment. If you object to the way your clearance was handled, note the inspector's badge number. In either case, first ask to see a supervisor. If the problem isn't resolved, write to the appropriate authorities, beginning with the port director at your point of entry.

IN AUSTRALIA

Australian residents who are 18 or older may bring home A\$400 worth of souvenirs and gifts (including jewelry), 250 cigarettes or 250 grams of cigars or other tobacco products, and 1,125 ml of alcohol (including wine, beer, and spirits). Residents under 18 may bring back A\$200 worth of goods. Members of the same family traveling together may pool their allowances. Prohibited items include meat products. Seeds, plants, and fruits need to be declared upon arrival.
🇦🇺 **Australian Customs Service** ⌂ Regional Director, Box 8, Sydney, NSW 2001 ☎ 02/9213-2000 or

1300/363263; 02/9364-7222 or 1800/803-006 quar-
antine-inquiry line 🖴 02/9213-4043 ⊕ www.
customs.gov.au.

IN CANADA

Canadian residents who have been out of
Canada for at least seven days may bring
in C$750 worth of goods duty-free. If
you've been away fewer than seven days
but more than 48 hours, the duty-free allowance drops to C$200. If your trip lasts
24 to 48 hours, the allowance is C$50.
You may not pool allowances with family
members. Goods claimed under the C$750
exemption may follow you by mail; those
claimed under the lesser exemptions must
accompany you. Alcohol and tobacco
products may be included in the seven-day
and 48-hour exemptions but not in the 24-
hour exemption. If you meet the age re-
quirements of the province or territory
through which you reenter Canada, you
may bring in, duty-free, 1.5 liters of wine
or 1.14 liters (40 imperial ounces) of
liquor *or* 24 12-ounce cans or bottles of
beer or ale. Also, if you meet the local age
requirement for tobacco products, you
may bring in, duty-free, 200 cigarettes and
50 cigars. Check ahead of time with the
Canada Customs and Revenue Agency or
the Department of Agriculture for policies
regarding meat products, seeds, plants,
and fruits.

You may send an unlimited number of
gifts (only one gift per recipient, however)
worth up to C$60 each duty-free to
Canada. Label the package UNSOLICITED
GIFT—VALUE UNDER $60. Alcohol and to-
bacco are excluded.
🚩 **Canada Customs and Revenue Agency** ⊠ 2265
St. Laurent Blvd., Ottawa, Ontario K1G 4K3 ☎ 800/
461-9999, 204/983-3500, 506/636-5064 ⊕ www.
ccra.gc.ca.

IN ITALY

Of goods obtained anywhere outside the
EU or goods purchased in a duty-free shop
within an EU country, the allowances are:
(1) 200 cigarettes or 100 cigarillos or 50
cigars or 250 grams of tobacco; (2) 2 liters
of still table wine or 1 liter of spirits over
22% volume or 2 liters of spirits under
22% volume or 2 liters of fortified and
sparkling wines; and (3) 50 ml of perfume
and 250 ml of toilet water.

Of goods obtained (duty and tax paid)
within another EU country, the guidance

levels are: (1) 800 cigarettes or 400 cigarillos or 400 cigars or 1 kilogram of tobacco; (2) 90 liters of still table wine plus
(3) 10 liters of spirits over 22% volume
plus 20 liters of spirits under 22% volume
plus 60 liters of sparkling wines plus 110
liters of beer.
🚩 **Italian Customs** (Dipartimento delle Dogane e
Imposte Indirette) ⊠ Via A. de Gasperi 20, Naples
☎ 081/7803036 🖴 081/5528234 ⊕ www.
agenziadogane.it.

IN NEW ZEALAND

All homeward-bound residents may bring
back NZ$700 worth of souvenirs and
gifts; passengers may not pool their allowances, and children can claim only the
concession on goods intended for their
own use. For those 17 or older, the duty-
free allowance also includes 4.5 liters of
wine or beer; one 1,125-ml bottle of spirits; and either 200 cigarettes, 250 grams of
tobacco, 50 cigars, *or* a combination of
the three up to 250 grams. Meat products,
seeds, plants, and fruits must be declared
upon arrival to the Agricultural Services
Department.
🚩 **New Zealand Customs** ⊠ Head office: The Cus-
tomhouse, 17–21 Whitmore St., Box 2218, Wellington
☎ 09/300-5399 or 0800/428-786 ⊕ www.customs.
govt.nz.

IN THE U.K.

If you are a U.K. resident and your journey was wholly within the European
Union, you probably won't have to pass
through customs when you return to the
United Kingdom. If you plan to bring back
large quantities of alcohol or tobacco,
check EU limits beforehand. In most cases,
if you bring back more than 200 cigars,
3,200 cigarettes, 10 liters of spirits, 110
liters of beer, and/or 90 liters of wine, you
have to declare the goods upon return.
🚩 **HM Customs and Excise** ⊠ Portcullis House, 21
Cowbridge Rd. E, Cardiff CF11 9SS ☎ 0845/010-
9000 or 0208/929-0152; 0208/929-6731 or 0208/
910-3602 complaints ⊕ www.hmce.gov.uk.

IN THE U.S.

U.S. residents who have been out of the
country for at least 48 hours may bring
home, for personal use, $800 worth of for-
eign goods duty-free, as long as they
haven't used the $800 allowance or any
part of it in the past 30 days. This exemption may include 1 liter of alcohol (for
travelers 21 and older), 200 cigarettes, and

Eating & Drinking > **F 39**

100 non-Cuban cigars. Family members from the same household who are traveling together may pool their $800 personal exemptions. For fewer than 48 hours, the duty-free allowance drops to $200, which may include 50 cigarettes, 10 non-Cuban cigars, and 150 ml of alcohol (or 150 ml of perfume containing alcohol). The $200 allowance cannot be combined with other individuals' exemptions, and if you exceed it, the full value of all the goods will be taxed. Antiques, which the U.S. Bureau of Customs and Border Protection defines as objects more than 100 years old, enter duty-free, as do original works of art done entirely by hand, including paintings, drawings, and sculptures. This doesn't apply to folk art or handicrafts, which are in general dutiable.

You may also send packages home duty-free, with a limit of one parcel per addressee per day (except alcohol or tobacco products or perfume worth more than $5). You can mail up to $200 worth of goods for personal use; label the package PERSONAL USE and attach a list of its contents and their retail value. If the package contains your used personal belongings, mark it AMERICAN GOODS RETURNED to avoid paying duties. You may send up to $100 worth of goods as a gift; mark the package UNSOLICITED GIFT. Mailed items do not affect your duty-free allowance on your return.

To avoid paying duty on foreign-made high-ticket items you already own and will take on your trip, register them with Customs before you leave the country. Consider filing a Certificate of Registration for laptops, cameras, watches, and other digital devices identified with serial numbers or other permanent markings; you can keep the certificate for other trips. Otherwise, bring a sales receipt or insurance form to show that you owned the item before you left the United States.

▐ **U.S. Bureau of Customs and Border Protection** ✉ for inquiries and equipment registration, 1300 Pennsylvania Ave. NW, Washington, DC 20229 ⊕ www.customs.gov ☎ 877/287-8667 or 202/354-1000 ✉ For complaints, Customer Satisfaction Unit, 1300 Pennsylvania Ave. NW, Room 5.5D, Washington, DC 20229.

DISCOUNTS & DEALS

Be a smart shopper and compare all your options before making decisions. A plane ticket bought with a promotional coupon from travel clubs, coupon books, and direct-mail offers or purchased on the Internet may not be cheaper than the least expensive fare from a discount ticket agency. And always keep in mind that what you get is just as important as what you save.

DISCOUNT RESERVATIONS

To save money, look into discount reservations services with Web sites and toll-free numbers, which use their buying power to get a better price on hotels, airline tickets (⇨ Air Travel), even car rentals. When booking a room, always **call the hotel's local toll-free number** (if one is available) rather than the central reservations number—you'll often get a better price. Always ask about special packages or corporate rates.

When shopping for the best deal on hotels and car rentals, look for guaranteed exchange rates, which protect you against a falling dollar. With your rate locked in, you won't pay more, even if the price goes up in the local currency.

▐ Airline Tickets **Air 4 Less** ☎ 800/AIR4LESS, low-fare specialist.

▐ Hotel Rooms **Accommodations Express** ☎ 800/444-7666 or 800/277-1064 ⊕ www.accommodationsexpress.com. **Hotels.com** ☎ 800/246-8357 ⊕ www.hotels.com. **Steigenberger Reservation Service** ☎ 800/223-5652 ⊕ www.srs-worldhotels.com. **Turbotrip.com** ☎ 800/473-7829 ⊕ www.turbotrip.com.

PACKAGE DEALS

Don't confuse packages and guided tours. When you buy a package, you travel on your own, just as though you had planned the trip yourself. Fly–drive packages, which combine airfare and car rental, are often a good deal. In cities, ask the local visitor bureau about hotel packages that include tickets to major museum exhibits or other special events. If you **buy a rail–drive pass,** you may save on train tickets and car rentals. All Eurailpass holders get a discount on Eurostar fares through the Channel Tunnel and often receive reduced rates for buses, hotels, ferries, and car rentals.

EATING & DRINKING

The restaurants we list are the cream of the crop in each price category. Properties indicated by a ✕▥ are lodging establishments whose restaurant warrants a special trip. For price categories, *see* the price charts found under "About the Restaurants & Hotels" in each regional chapter.

MEALTIMES

Breakfast (*la colazione*) is usually served from 7 to 10:30, lunch (*il pranzo*) from 12:30 to 2:30, dinner (*la cena*) from 8 PM until midnight. While it's not usually necessary to reserve a table, remember that you'll find restaurants deserted before 8 in the evening and packed by 11, while lunch can extend until as late as 5 PM. Menus often seem to be an optional extra in many restaurants, and even if one exists it often bears little relation to what is actually on offer that day. Tune in carefully as the waiter reels off a list of what's good today—following their advice often pays off. A full-scale meal consists of a selection of antipasti followed by a *primo* (pasta or rice), then a *secondo* (meat or fish), rounded off with *frutta o dolci* (fruit or dessert). And unless you want to shock the locals, never, ever order a cappuccino after dinner (all that hot milk on a heavy stomach!)—but a regular espresso is a perfectly acceptable way to finish a meal.

Enoteche (wine bars) are open also in the morning and late afternoon for a snack at the counter. Most pizzerias open at 8 PM and close around midnight–1 AM, or later in summer and on weekends. Most bars and caffès are open nonstop from 7 AM until 8–9 PM; a few stay open until midnight or so. Unless otherwise noted, the restaurants listed in this guide are open daily for lunch and dinner.

PAYING

As indicated on *il conto*—the restaurant check—prices for goods and services in Italy include tax. Restaurant menu prices usually include service (*servizio*), unless indicated on the menu (in which case it's added to the prices listed on the menu). In addition, it's customary to leave a small tip (several euro) in appreciation of good service. Remember that there's no line to write a tip on the credit card receipt; you will be presented with a slip that includes only the cost of the meal. Tips are made in cash. Most restaurants charge a separate cover charge per person, usually listed on the menu as *"pane e coperto."* It should be a modest charge (€1.50 to €3 per person), except at the most expensive restaurants.

Some restaurants instead charge for bread, which should be brought to you (and paid for) only if you order it. The price of fish dishes is often given by weight (before cooking), so the price you see on the menu is for 100 grams of fish, not for the whole dish. An average fish portion is about 350 grams. When it comes to smaller *caffès* (cafés) and pizzerias, you sometimes place your order and then show your *scontrino* (receipt) when you move to the counter.

RESERVATIONS & DRESS

Reservations are always a good idea: we mention them only when they're essential or are not accepted. Book as far ahead as you can, and reconfirm as soon as you arrive. (Large parties should always call ahead to check the reservations policy.) Remember that when dining out in a nice restaurant (that is, not a caffè or casual trattoria) for dinner, most Italians will make an effort to smarten up: even when you're in a low-key seaside location, blue-jean shorts and sandals can attract "can-only-be-a-tourist" stares.

ELECTRICITY

To use your U.S.-purchased electric-powered equipment **bring a converter and adapter.** The electrical current in Italy is 220 volts, 50 cycles alternating current (AC); wall outlets take Continental-type plugs, with two round prongs.

If your appliances are dual-voltage you'll need only an adapter. Don't use 110-volt outlets, marked FOR SHAVERS ONLY, for high-wattage appliances such as blow-dryers. Most laptops operate equally well on 110 and 220 volts and so require only an adapter.

EMERGENCIES

Also see Emergencies *in* the A to Z section in regional chapters.

No matter where you are in Italy, **dial 113 for all emergencies,** or find somebody (your concierge, a passerby) who will call for you, as not all 113 operators speak English; the Italian word to use to draw people's attention in an emergency is *"Aiuto!"* (Help!, pronounced "ah-YOU-toh"). *"Pronto soccorso"* means "first aid" and when said to an operator will get you an *ambulanza* (ambulance). If you just need a doctor, you should ask for *un medico*;

most hotels will be able to refer you to a local doctor. Don't forget to ask the doctor for *una ricevuta* (an invoice) to show to your insurance company in order to get a reimbursement. Other useful Italian words to use in an emergency are *"Al fuoco!"* (Fire!, pronounced "ahl fuh-WOE-co"), and *"Al ladro!"* (Follow the thief!, pronounced "ahl LAH-droh").

Italy has a national police force *(carabinieri)* as well as local police *(polizia)*. Both are armed and have the power to arrest and investigate crimes. Always report the loss of your passport to either the carabinieri or the police, as well as to your embassy. Local traffic officers are known as *vigili* (though their official name is *polizia municipale*)—they are responsible for, among other things, giving out parking tickets and clamping cars, so before you even consider parking the Italian way, make sure you are at least able to spot their white (in summer) or black uniforms (many are women). Should you find yourself involved in a minor car accident in town, you should contact the vigili.

🚩 General emergencies: ☎ 113

🚩 Emergency Services **Police:** ☎ 112 Naples's **main police station** ✉ Via Medina 75 ☎ 081/7941111 ✉ Foreigners' office: Via Ferraris 131 ☎ 081/6064111 has an *ufficio stranieri* (foreigners' office) that usually has an English speaker on staff and can help with passport problems.

Ambulance: ☎ 081/7520696 **Medical emergency:** ☎ 081/7613466 after 8 PM (ask for an English-speaking nurse). **Car breakdowns & emergencies:** ☎ 116.

🚩 Hospitals ☎ 081/7471111.

🚩 24-Hour Pharmacies If the *farmacia* (pharmacy) in Naples' Stazione Centrale is closed, it will post the address of one that's open; the newspaper *Il Mattino* also prints a list of pharmacies that are open nights and weekends.

ENGLISH-LANGUAGE & ITALIAN MEDIA

The Azienda Autonoma di Soggiorno, Cura e Turismo publishes *Qui Napoli,* an English-language monthly periodical for visitors to Naples listing all the special events held in the city, along with complete listings of train, bus, subway, ferry, and hydrofoil routes and schedules. In addition, there are exhaustive listings of the city's libraries, theaters, cinemas, and sports facilities. A gratis publication, it's available at all visitor information centers in Naples and at many hotels. *Le Pagine*

dell'Ozio (€1.50 at newsstands) is a useful monthly guide to local events which might otherwise go unadvertised.

BOOKS

For a fair range of books in English, late opening hours, a busy basement caffè and a generally browse-friendly environment, head to the Piazza dei Martiri branch of **Feltrinelli Libri e Musica** (✉ Via S. Caterina 23 ☎ 081/2402511 🖱 www.lafeltrinelli.it).

NEWSPAPERS & MAGAZINES

Il Mattino (🌐 www.ilmattino.it) is the leading newspaper of Naples, while the national dailies, *Corriere della Sera* (🌐 www.corriere.it), *La Repubblica* (🌐 www.repubblica.it), and *La Stampa* (🌐 www.lastampa.it) also offer multipage Naples sections in their local editions.

RADIO & TELEVISION

One of the main regional papers, *Il Mattino,* lists the various local TV stations in its entertainment pages. Viewers are fed a fairly indigestible diet of television auctions, dubbed B movies from the United States, soccer highlights, soft porn (after midnight), and the odd tidbit of news. If you have a smattering of Italian, watch the better-quality state-funded RAI TRE station with local news and weather coverage at 2, 7, and 10:40 PM (approximately) every day (🌐 www.rai.it). The main private radio station is the curiously named Kiss Kiss (103.0 MHz), which broadcasts late-night music directly from its own disco up on the Vomero hill, but also does a fair amount of handy traffic news for those on the move (🌐 www.kisskissnapoli.it). For a good blend of traffic news (a permanent topic of conversation), interviews, news, and music, the state-run ISO Radio broadcasts on 103.3 MHz and is designed for those using the Italian motorway network.

GAY & LESBIAN TRAVEL

In keeping with its reputation as a city of stark contrasts, Naples combines a macho heterosexual image with a strong gay undercurrent. Several gay clubs—for both men and women—have sprung up in the past few years in various parts of town.

🚩 Local Resources **Arci-GAY/Lesbica** ✉ Vico S. Geronimo 17/20, Napoli ☎ 081/5528815 or 081/5518293 🌐 www.gay.it; this is the main clearinghouse for information in Naples and the region.

Bar B-Discobar ⊠ Via Giovanna Manna 14, Napoli ☎ 081/287681 opens all evenings (8:30 PM–3 AM to a very varied clientele. It has the added attraction of a sauna and disco and is close to the university. A minimum of €13 has to be spent on drinks. **Freezer** ⊠ Via Lauria 6, Napoli ☎ 081/7502457 is set in the thick of the post-modern jungle of the *Centro Direzionale* (Naples Business Center); this disco-bar is popular with visitors from other European countries. A minimum of about €8 has to be spent on drinks.

🏳 Gay- & Lesbian-Friendly Travel Agencies **Different Roads Travel** ⊠ 8383 Wilshire Blvd., Suite 520, Beverly Hills, CA 90211 ☎ 323/651–5557 or 800/429–8747 (Ext. 14 for both) 🖷 323/651–3678 ✆ lgernert@tzell.com. **Kennedy Travel** ⊠ 130 W. 42nd St., Suite 401, New York, NY 10036 ☎ 212/840–8659 or 800/237–7433 🖷 212/730–2269 ⊕ www.kennedytravel.com. **Now, Voyager** ⊠ 4406 18th St., San Francisco, CA 94114 ☎ 415/626–1169 or 800/255–6951 🖷 415/626–8626 ⊕ www.nowvoyager.com. **Skylink Travel and Tour** ⊠ 1455 N. Dutton Ave., Suite A, Santa Rosa, CA 95401 ☎ 707/546–9888 or 800/225–5759 🖷 707/636–0951, serving lesbian travelers.

GUIDEBOOKS

Plan well and you won't be sorry. Guidebooks are excellent tools—and you can take them with you. You may want to check out the color-photo-laden *Fodor's Escape to the Amalfi Coast,* which highlights 20 unique experiences and is available at on-line retailers and bookstores everywhere.

HEALTH

The Centers for Disease Control and Prevention (CDC) in Atlanta caution that most of Southern Europe is in the "intermediate" range for risk of contacting traveler's diarrhea. Part of this risk may be attributed to an increased consumption of olive oil and wine, which can have a laxative effect on stomachs used to a different diet. The CDC also advises all international travelers to swim only in chlorinated swimming pools, unless they are absolutely certain the local beaches and freshwater lakes are not contaminated.

In 2003, just under one-fourth of the coastline in the region of Campania was considered by local health authorities unfit for bathing. The main areas off-limits stretch from the Naples waterfront to the Vesuvian towns as far as Castellammare di Stabia—places where you wouldn't choose to swim anyway. Fortunately, this leaves a lot of coastal mileage for potential bathers, and many beaches in the area received a clean bill of health.

FOOD & DRINK

Contaminated seafood *is* a risk in Naples as elsewhere, and if you are going to indulge in oysters or other raw seafood, choose your restaurant wisely. Resist the temptation of prying open and eating mussels, clams, or other delicacies on your platter. If the shell doesn't open on cooking, then it's best left alone.

In bars and caffès, especially around areas with heavy human traffic like the Stazione Centrale in Naples or in the depressed areas around Vesuvius, you can ask for your espresso or cappuccino in a *bicchiere monouso* (nonreusable plastic cup), rather than opting to drink out of the local crockery. However, most mainstream bars and restaurants take hygiene ultra-seriously.

OVER-THE-COUNTER REMEDIES

Aspirin (*l'aspirina*) can be purchased at any pharmacy, but Tylenol and Advil are unavailable.

PESTS & OTHER HAZARDS

Thanks to the prevailing westerly winds, Naples does not suffer such acute air pollution as its Greek neighbor, Athens. However, when the winds drop, WHO safety thresholds are sometimes exceeded, especially for nitrogen oxides, while the excessive number of polluting two-stroke motorcycles can make the air thick with partially combusted hydrocarbons. As a general rule, for those who are highly sensitive to air quality, try not to linger in traffic-ridden areas like Piazza Garibaldi in Naples, and take a bus or metro to avoid direct exposure to pollutants.

Out in the country, health risks are minimal. There's no poison ivy or poison oak in the countryside around Naples, although if you stray off beaten paths you might become entangled in the smilax plant or in blackberry bushes, both of which have persistent thorns. The vast majority of the snakes you might meet will be harmless, and are likely to be far more frightened of you—and more innocuous— than vice versa.

HOLIDAYS

National holidays include January 1 (New Year's Day); January 6 (Epiphany); Easter Sunday and Monday; April 25 (Liberation Day); May 1 (Labor Day or May Day); June 2 (Founding of the Italian Republic); August 15 (Assumption of Mary, also known as Ferragosto); November 1 (All Saints' Day); December 8 (Immaculate Conception); and December 25 and 26 (Christmas Day and St. Stephen's Day). During these holidays many shops and restaurants are closed, while decisions about whether to open major museums and archaeological sites like Pompeii and Herculaneum are usually made at the eleventh hour.

The feast days of patron saints are observed locally in various towns and villages; some of the more famous festas are: San Costanzo, Capri, May 14; San Antonio, Anacapri, June 13; Sant'Andrea, Amalfi, June 25–30; San Pietro, Positano, June 29; Sant'Anna, Ischia, July 26; and San Pantaleone, Ravello, July 27. In Naples, two annual celebrations are held at the Duomo on the first Sunday in May and on September 19 to celebrate the Festa di San Gennaro, or the Liquefaction of the Blood of San Gennaro. For information on these and other holidays, see also "On the Calendar in the Destination chapter.

LANGUAGE

In Naples and the leading resorts, language is not a big problem. You can always find someone who speaks at least a little English; remember that the Italian language is pronounced exactly as it is written (many Italians try to speak English by enunciating every letter, with disconcerting results). You may run into a language barrier in the countryside, but a phrase book and close attention to the Italians' use of expressive gestures will go a long way. Try to **master a few phrases for daily use** (⇨ Italian Vocabulary at the back of this book) and familiarize yourself with the terms you'll need to decipher signs and museum labels.

LANGUAGES FOR TRAVELERS

A phrase book and language-tape set can help get you started. Fodor's Italian for Travelers (available at bookstores everywhere) is excellent.

LODGING

The lodgings we review in this book are the cream of the crop in each price category. We always list the facilities that are available—but we don't specify whether they cost extra: when pricing accommodations, always ask what's included and what costs extra. Extra fees can be charged for everything from breakfast to use of parking facilities to air-conditioning. For price categories, consult the price charts found under "About the Restaurants & Hotels" in Chapters 1, 2, 3, and 4.

Note that this region of Italy has many resort hotels and in peak-season months (usually June to September), some of them require either half- or full-board arrangements, whereby your (increased) room tab includes lunch or lunch and dinner provided by the hotel restaurant. Hotels operate on the European Plan (EP, with no meal provided) unless we note that they offer the Breakfast Plan (BP), Modified American Plan (MAP, with breakfast and dinner daily, known as mezza pensione), or Full American Plan (FAP, or pensione completa, with three meals a day); board plans, which are usually an option offered in addition to the basic room plan, are generally only available with a minimum two- or three-night stay and are, of course, more expensive than the basic room rate, running anywhere from €15 to €50 per meal. Note that the hotel price charts in this book reflect basic room rates only. Inquire about board plans when making your reservations; details and prices are often stated on hotel Web sites.

Properties indicated by a ✕⌂ are lodging establishments whose restaurants warrant a special trip.

APARTMENT RENTALS

If you want a home base that's roomy enough for a family and comes with cooking facilities, consider a furnished rental. These can save you money, especially if you're traveling with a group. Home-exchange directories sometimes list rentals as well as exchanges.

🄵 International Agents **Drawbridge to Europe** ⊠ 98 Granite St., Ashland, OR 97520 ☏ 541/482-7778 or 888/268-1148 🖷 541/482-7779 ⊕ www.drawbridgetoeurope.com. **Hideaways International** ⊠ 767 Islington St., Portsmouth, NH 03801 ☏ 603/430-4433 or 800/843-4433 🖷 603/430-4444

⊕ www.hideaways.com, membership $145. **Home-tours International** ✉ 1108 Scottie La., Knoxville, TN 37919 ☎ 865/690-8484 or 866/367-4668 ⊕ http://thor.he.net/~hometour/. **Interhome** ✉ 1990 N.E. 163rd St., Suite 110, North Miami Beach, FL 33162 ☎ 305/940-2299 or 800/882-6864 🖷 305/940-2911 ⊕ www.interhome.us. **Solemar** ✉ 1990 N.E. 163rd St., Suite 110, North Miami Beach, FL 33162 ☎ 305/940-2299 or 800/882-6864 🖷 305/940-2911 ⊕ www.visit-toscana.com. **Villanet** ✉ 1251 N.W. 116th St., Seattle, WA 98177 ☎ 206/417-3444 or 800/964-1891 🖷 206/417-1832 ⊕ www.rentavilla.com. **Villas International** ✉ 4340 Redwood Hwy., Suite D309, San Rafael, CA 94903 ☎ 415/499-9490 or 800/221-2260 🖷 415/499-9491 ⊕ www.villasintl.com.

🗹 Local Agents **Cuendet USA** ✉ 165 Chestnut St., Allendale, NJ 07041 ☎ 201/327-2333 ✉ Suzanne T. Pidduck, c/o Rentals in Italy, 1742 Calle Corva, Camarillo, CA 93010 ☎ 800/726-6702 ⊕ www.rentvillas.com. **Vacanze in Italia** ✉ 22 Railroad St., Great Barrington, MA 01230 ☎ 413/528-6610 or 800/533-5405 ⊕ www.homeabroad.com.

🗹 In the U.K. **CV Travel** ✉ 43 Cadogan St., London SW3 2PR, England ☎ 020/7581-0851 ⊕ www.cvtravel.net. **Magic of Italy** ✉ 227 Shepherds Bush Rd., London W6 7AS, England ☎ 020/8748-7575.

BED & BREAKFASTS

Increasing numbers of southern Italians, especially Neapolitans, are following the long-tried British formula of bed and breakfast. Besides the substantial cost savings, this may be your only chance to peek into an Italian home and experience *vita* (life) as lived by the locals. When booking, try to find out exactly what's on offer: it could be a cramped room in a faceless suburb with overly inquisitive hosts, or you could strike it lucky with a room with an 18th-century frescoed ceiling in a quiet city-center location. For further information, contact the local tourist information office or one of the agencies below.

🗹 Reservation Services **Associazione Bed & Breakfast** ✉ Cupa Camaldoli 18, Napoli ⊕ www.tightrope.it/bbnaples/index.htm. **Rent a Bed** ✉ Vico San Carlo alle Mortelle 14, Napoli ☎ 081/417721 ⊕ www.rentabed.com.

FARM HOLIDAYS & AGRITOURISM

Rural accommodations in the *agriturismo* (agritourism) category are increasingly popular with both Italians and visitors to Italy. A little surfing on the Internet can pay dividends: just call up a search engine and key in the words, say, "agriturismo" and "Campania," and see what gives. Al-though technologically literate, few farms in the Naples area accept credit cards, so remember to load up with cash before your stay.

🗹 Agencies **Italy Farm Holidays** ✉ 547 Martling Ave., Tarrytown, NY 10591 ☎ 914/631-7880 🖷 914/631-8831. **Agriturist** ✉ Corso Vittorio 101, 00186 Rome ☎ 06/6852342 ⊕ www.agriturist.it. **Turismo Verde** ✉ Via Flaminia 56, 00196 Rome ☎ 06/3611051 ⊕ www.turismoverde.it.

HOSTELS

No matter what your age, you can save on lodging costs by staying at hostels. In some 4,500 locations in more than 70 countries around the world, Hostelling International (HI), the umbrella group for a number of national youth-hostel associations, offers single-sex, dorm-style beds and, at many hostels, rooms for couples and family accommodations. Membership in any HI national hostel association, open to travelers of all ages, allows you to stay in HI-affiliated hostels at member rates; one-year membership is $28 for adults (C$35 in Canada, £13.50 in the U.K., $52 in Australia, and $40 in New Zealand); hostels run about $12–$25 per night. Members have priority if the hostel is full; they're also eligible for discounts around the world, even on rail and bus travel in some countries. The Naples area has several new hostels, including ones in the towns of Pompeii and Positano. In Naples itself, the youth hostel has a neat location in Mergellina and maintains high standards of food and accommodation. Italy's main hostelling association (AIG) has an exhaustive Web site giving all the hostels in the various regions, complete with facilities and prices.

🗹 Organizations **AIG Italy** ✉ Via Cavour 44, 00184, Rome ☎ 06/4871152 🖷 06/4880492 ⊕ www.hostels-aig.org. **Hostelling International–USA** ✉ 8401 Colesville Rd., Suite 600, Silver Spring, MD 20910 ☎ 301/495-1240 🖷 301/495-6697 ⊕ www.hiayh.org. **Hostelling International–Canada** ✉ 205 Catherine St., Suite 400, Ottawa, Ontario K2P 1C3 ☎ 613/237-7884 or 800/663-5777 🖷 613/237-7868 ⊕ www.hihostels.ca. **YHA England and Wales** ✉ Trevelyan House, Dimple Rd., Matlock, Derbyshire DE4 3YH, U.K. ☎ 0870/870-8808, 0870/770-8868, or 0162/959-2700 🖷 0870/770-6127 ⊕ www.yha.org.uk. **YHA Australia** ✉ 422 Kent St., Sydney, NSW 2001 ☎ 02/9261-1111 🖷 02/9261-1969 ⊕ www.yha.com.au. **YHA New Zealand** ✉ Level 4, Torrens House, 195 Hereford St., Box 436,

Christchurch ☎ 03/379-9970 or 0800/278-299 🖷 03/365-4476 🌐 www.yha.org.nz.

HOTELS

Italian hotels are awarded stars (one to five) by the national government based on their facilities and services. Those with three or more stars have bathrooms in all rooms. Keep in mind, however, that these are general indications, and that a charming three-star might make for a better stay than a more expensive four-star. In Naples, room rates can be on a par with other European metropolises: Deluxe and four-star rates can be downright extravagant. In those categories, **ask for one of the better rooms,** since less desirable rooms—and there usually are some—don't give you what you're paying for. Except in deluxe and some four-star hotels, bathrooms usually have showers rather than bathtubs.

In all hotels there's a rate card inside the door of your room, or inside the closet door; it tells you exactly what you will pay for that particular room (rates in the same hotel may vary according to the location and type of room). On this card, breakfast and any other options must be listed separately. Any discrepancy between the basic room rate and that charged on your bill is cause for complaint to the manager and to the police.

Although, by law, breakfast is supposed to be optional, most hotels quote room rates including breakfast. When you book a room, specifically **ask whether the rate includes breakfast** (*prima colazione*). You are under no obligation to take breakfast at your hotel, but in practice most hotels expect you to do so. It's encouraging to note that many of the hotels we recommend are offering generous buffet breakfasts instead of simple, even skimpy "Continental breakfasts."

Hotels that we list as ($$), ($), and (cen)—moderate to inexpensively priced accommodations—may charge extra for optional air-conditioning; somewhat surprisingly, this is usually the case for luxury hotels in southern Italy. In older hotels the quality of the rooms may be uneven; if you don't like the room you're given, request another. This applies to noise, too. Front rooms may be larger or have a view, but they also may have a lot of street noise—happily, many of Naples's finer hotels offer windows with double-pane glass to effectively silence the noise. If you're a light sleeper, **request a quiet room when making reservations.** Rooms in lodgings listed in this guide have a shower and/or bath, unless noted otherwise. Remember **to specify whether you care to have a bath or shower** because not all rooms, especially lodgings outside major cities, have both.

RESERVING A ROOM

Useful terms to know when booking a room are *aria condizionata* (air-conditioning), *bagno in stanza* (private bath), *letto matrimoniale* (double bed), *letti singoli* (twin beds), *letti singoli uniti* (twin beds pushed together). Italy does not really have queen- or king-size beds, although some beds, particularly in four- and five-star accommodations, can be larger than standard. Phrases that could come in handy include: *Vi prego di fornire informazioni riguardo il vostro albergo/pensione. Vorrei una camera doppia/camera matrimoniale con bagno in camera.* (Please supply me with information regarding your hotel/pensione. I would like a room with two single beds/a double bed with private bath); *Una camera su un piano alto e con vista.* (A room on a high floor with a view.); *Una camera a un piano basso.* (A room on a low floor.); *Una camera silenziosa.* (A quiet room).

It's always a good idea to have your reservation, dates, and rate confirmed by fax or e-mail. If you need to cancel your reservation, be sure to do so by fax or e-mail and keep a record of the transmission.

MAIL & SHIPPING

The Italian mail system has made great progress in speed and reliability, although it can still be slow, so allow up to 10 days for mail to and from the United States and Canada, about a week to and from the United Kingdom.

POSTAL RATES

Airmail letters and postcards (lightweight stationery) to the United States and Canada cost €0.52 for the first 20 grams and €1.03 up to 100 grams. Always stick the blue airmail tag on your mail, or write "airmail" in big, clear characters to the side of the address. Postcards and letters (for the first 20 grams) to the United Kingdom, as well as to any other EU country, including Italy, cost €0.41. The priority mail system (*Posta Prioritaria*) is about 50% more expensive but almost guarantees delivery in Italy within 2–3 days (€0.77 for the first 20 grams and €1.55 up to 100 grams for the USA and Canada). As regular stamps are not valid for this service, make sure you buy the gold Posta Prioritaria stamps. You can buy stamps for standard and priority mail at post offices and tobacconists. To send urgent letters and papers to the United States and elsewhere, consider the *Posta Celere* (swift mail) system, which tends to be cheaper than having them couriered. This service is offered at several major post offices in Naples and in town post offices throughout the area.

RECEIVING MAIL

Correspondence can be addressed to you care of the Italian post office. Letters should be addressed to your name, "c/o Ufficio Postale Centrale," followed by "Fermo Posta" on the next line, and the name of the city (preceded by its postal code) on the next. You can **collect it at the central post office** by showing your passport or photo-bearing I.D. and paying a small fee. American Express also has a general-delivery service. There's no charge for cardholders, holders of American Express traveler's checks, or anyone who booked a vacation with American Express.

MONEY MATTERS

The days when Italy's high-quality attractions came with a comparatively low Mediterranean price tag are long gone. Italy's prices are in line with those in the rest of Europe, with costs in its main cities comparable to those in other major capitals, such as Paris and Madrid. As in most countries, prices vary from region to region and are a bit lower in the countryside than in the cities. Good value for money can still be had in many places in Campania, especially in Naples and on the Amalfi Coast.

Here are some sample prices: Admission to the Museo Archeologico Nazionale is €8; the cheapest seat at Naples's Teatro San Carlo runs €18; a movie ticket is about €8. Going to a Naples nightclub might set you back about €15. A daily English-language newspaper is about €2.50. A Naples taxi ride (1⅗ km, or 1 mi) costs

about €8. An inexpensive hotel room for two, including breakfast, in Naples is about €80–€120; an inexpensive Naples dinner is €15–€25, and a ½ liter carafe of house wine, €4. A simple pasta item on the menu runs €5–€7, a cup of coffee €0.70, and a rosticceria lunch about €8. A Coca-Cola (standing) at a caffè is €1.50 and a pint of beer is €3.50.

Prices throughout this guide are given for adults. Substantially reduced fees are almost always available for children, students, and senior citizens. For information on taxes, *see* Taxes.

ATMS

Fairly common in cities and towns as well as in airports and train stations, ATMs are the easiest way to get euros in Italy. Don't, however, count on finding ATMs in tinier towns and rural areas. Italian ATMs are reliable, and are commonly attached to a bank—you won't find one, for example, in a supermarket. Do check with your bank to confirm you have an international PIN number, to find out your maximum daily withdrawal allowance, and to learn what the bank fee is for withdrawing money. The word for ATM in Italian is *bancomat*, for PIN, *codice segreto*.

CREDIT CARDS

Throughout this guide, the following abbreviations are used: **AE**, American Express; **DC**, Diners Club; **MC**, MasterCard; and **V**, Visa.

Reporting Lost Cards **American Express** ☎ 336/668-5110 international collect. **Diners Club** ☎ 702/797-5532 collect. **MasterCard** ☎ 800/870866. **Visa** ☎ 800/819014.

CURRENCY

The unit of currency in Italy is the euro, currently adopted in 12 countries of the European Union (the only EU Member States not to adopt the euro were Britain, Denmark, and Sweden). Italian banks no longer accept the lira—the currency used prior to 2002—but if you have some left over from a previous visit it can be changed at the **Banca D'Italia** (✉ Via Cervantes 71 ☎ 081/7975111), in the center of Naples, until the year 2012. The euro is printed in bills of 500 (practically impossible to change outside of banks), 200, 100, 50, 20, 10, and 5. Coins are €2, €1, 50 cents, 20 cents, 10 cents, 5 cents, 2 cents, and 1 cent. All coins have one side that has the value of the euro on it and the other side with each countries' unique symbol. Notes have principal architectural styles from antiquity onward on one side and the map and the flag of Europe on the other and are the same for all countries. **When changing money, make sure you ask for small denomination notes, preferably of 50 euros and below, as retailers in Naples and the surrounding area are notoriously bereft of small change.**

The euro continues to fluctuate considerably against other currencies. At the time of writing the exchange rate was about €.86 to the U.S. dollar; €.63 to the Canadian dollar; €1.40 to the pound sterling; €.56 to the Australian dollar; and €.50 to the New Zealand dollar.

CURRENCY EXCHANGE

The U.S. dollar (and all other currencies that are not part of the EU community) and the euro are in direct competition—in fact, this is the reason why the euro was created in the first place, so it could box with the big boys. Therefore, you still need to pay attention to where you exchange your dollars—**shop around for the best exchange rates (and also check the rates before leaving home) when it comes to non-EU currencies, such as the U.S. dollar, the Japanese yen, and the British pound.**

For the most favorable rates, **change money through banks.** Although ATM transaction fees may be higher abroad than at home, ATM rates are excellent because they're based on wholesale rates offered only by major banks. You won't do as well at exchange booths in airports or rail and bus stations, in hotels, in restaurants, or in stores. To avoid lines at airport exchange booths, get a bit of local currency before you leave home.

🖪 Exchange Services **International Currency Express** ✉ 427 N. Camden Dr., Suite F, Beverly Hills, CA 90210 ☎ 888/278-6628 orders 🖷 310/278-6410 ⊕ www.foreignmoney.com. **Thomas Cook International Money Services** ☎ 800/287-7362 orders and retail locations ⊕ www.us.thomascook.com.

TRAVELER'S CHECKS

Do you need traveler's checks? It depends on where you're headed. If you're going to rural areas and small towns, go with cash; traveler's checks are best used in cities. Lost or stolen checks can usually be re-placed within 24 hours. To ensure a speedy refund, buy your own traveler's checks—don't let someone else pay for them: irregularities like this can cause delays. The person who bought the checks should make the call to request a refund.

PACKING

The weather is considerably milder in Italy than in the north and central United States or Great Britain. In summer, stick with clothing that is as light as possible, although a sweater may be necessary for cool evenings, especially in the Lattari mountains along the Amalfi Coast (even during the hot months). Sunglasses, a hat, and sunblock are essential. Contrary to myth, the sun does not shine all day, every day on Campania: brief summer thunderstorms are common in Naples, while typhoonlike storms occasionally arrive along the Amalfi Coast, so an umbrella will definitely come in handy. In winter bring a medium-weight coat and a raincoat; winters in Naples can be both humid *and* cold. Even in Naples, central heating may not be up to your standards, and interiors can be chilly and damp; take wools or flannel rather than sheer fabrics. Bring sturdy shoes for winter, and comfortable walking shoes in any season.

In Campania, laid-back style is the way to go. However, even on sweltering days residents do not usually wear shorts unless they're somewhere close to a beach resort. Men aren't required to wear ties or jackets anywhere, except in some of the grander hotel dining rooms and top-level restaurants, but are expected to look reasonably sharp—and they do. Formal wear is the exception rather than the rule at the opera nowadays, although people in expensive seats usually do get dressed up, especially for "First Nights." A certain modesty of dress (no bare shoulders or knees) is expected in churches.

For sightseeing, **pack a pair of binoculars;** they will help you get a good look at Naples's wondrous painted ceilings and domes. If you stay in budget hotels, **take your own soap;** many such hotels do not provide it, or allot only one tiny bar per room.

In your carry-on luggage, pack an extra pair of eyeglasses or contact lenses and enough of any medication you take to last a few days longer than the entire trip. You may also ask your doctor to write a spare prescription using the drug's generic name, as brand names may vary from country to country. In luggage to be checked, **never pack prescription drugs, valuables, or undeveloped film.** And don't forget to carry with you the addresses of offices that handle refunds of lost traveler's checks. Check *Fodor's How to Pack* (available at on-line retailers and bookstores everywhere) for more tips.

To avoid customs and security delays, carry medications in their original packaging. Don't pack any sharp objects in your carry-on luggage, including knives of any size or material, scissors, and corkscrews, or anything else that might arouse suspicion.

To avoid having your checked luggage chosen for hand inspection, don't cram bags full. The U.S. Transportation Security Administration suggests packing shoes on top and placing personal items you don't want touched in clear plastic bags.

CHECKING LUGGAGE

You're allowed to carry aboard one bag and one personal article, such as a purse or a laptop computer. Make sure what you carry on fits under your seat or in the overhead bin. Get to the gate early, so you can board as soon as possible, before the overhead bins fill up.

Baggage allowances vary by carrier, destination, and ticket class. On international flights, you're usually allowed to check two bags weighing up to 70 pounds (32 kilograms) each, although a few airlines allow checked bags of up to 88 pounds (40 kilograms) in first class. Some international carriers don't allow more than 66 pounds (30 kilograms) per bag in business class and 44 pounds (20 kilograms) in economy. On domestic flights, the limit is usually 50 to 70 pounds (23 to 32 kilograms) per bag. In general, carry-on bags shouldn't exceed 40 pounds (18 kilograms). Most airlines won't accept bags that weigh more than 100 pounds (45 kilograms) on domestic or international flights. Check baggage restrictions with your carrier before you pack.

Airline liability for baggage is limited to $2,500 per person on flights within the United States. On international flights it amounts to $9.07 per pound or $20 per kilogram for checked baggage (roughly $640 per 70-pound bag), with a maximum of $634.90 per piece, and $400 per passenger for unchecked baggage. You can buy additional coverage at check-in for about $10 per $1,000 of coverage, but it often excludes a rather extensive list of items, shown on your airline ticket.

Before departure, itemize your bags' contents and their worth, and label the bags with your name, address, and phone number. (If you use your home address, cover it so potential thieves can't see it readily.) Include a label inside each bag and **pack a copy of your itinerary.** At check-in, make sure each bag is correctly tagged with the destination airport's three-letter code. Because some checked bags will be opened for hand inspection, the U.S. Transportation Security Administration recommends that you leave luggage unlocked or use the plastic locks offered at check-in. TSA screeners place an inspection notice inside searched bags, which are re-sealed with a special lock.

If your bag has been searched and contents are missing or damaged, file a claim with the TSA Consumer Response Center as soon as possible. If your bags arrive damaged or fail to arrive at all, file a written report with the airline before leaving the airport.

▪ Complaints U.S. Transportation Security Administration Consumer Response Center ☎ 866/289-9673 ⊕ www.tsa.gov.

PASSPORTS & VISAS

When traveling internationally, carry your passport even if you don't need one (it's always the best form of I.D.) and **make two photocopies of the data page** (one for someone at home and another for you, carried separately from your passport). If you lose your passport, promptly call the nearest embassy or consulate and the local police.

U.S. passport applications for children under age 14 require consent from both parents or legal guardians; both parents must appear together to sign the application. If only one parent appears, he or she must submit a written statement from the other parent authorizing passport issuance for the child. A parent with sole authority must present evidence of it when applying; acceptable documentation includes the child's certified birth certificate listing only the applying parent, a court order specifically permitting this parent's travel with the child, or a death certificate for the non-applying parent. Application forms and instructions are available on the Web site of the U.S. State Department's Bureau of Consular Affairs (⊕ www.travel.state.gov).

ENTERING ITALY

Travelers need only a valid passport to enter Italy for stays of up to 90 days.

PASSPORT OFFICES

The best time to apply for a passport or to renew is in fall and winter. Before any trip, check your passport's expiration date, and, if necessary, renew it as soon as possible.

🔝 Australian Citizens **Passports Australia** ☎ 131-232 ⊕ www.passports.gov.au.

🔝 Canadian Citizens **Passport Office** ✉ To mail in applications: 200 Promenade du Portage, Hull, Québec J8X 4B7 ☎ 819/994-3500 or 800/567-6868 ⊕ www.ppt.gc.ca.

🔝 New Zealand Citizens **New Zealand Passports Office** ☎ 0800/22-5050 or 04/474-8100 ⊕ www.passports.govt.nz.

🔝 U.K. Citizens **U.K. Passport Service** ☎ 0870/521-0410 ⊕ www.passport.gov.uk.

🔝 U.S. Citizens **National Passport Information Center** ☎ 900/225-5674 or 900/225-7778 TTY, calls are 55¢ per minute for automated service or $1.50 per minute for operator service; 888/362-8668 or 888/498-3648 TTY, calls are $5.50 each ⊕ www.travel.state.gov.

REST ROOMS

Public rest rooms are rather rare in Italy; the locals seem to make do with well-timed pit stops and rely on the local bar. Although private businesses can refuse to make their toilets available to the passing public, some bars will allow you to use the rest room if you ask politely. Alternatively, it is not uncommon to pay for a little something—a few cents for a mineral water or coffee—to get access to the facilities. Standards of cleanliness and comfort vary greatly. In cities, restaurants, hotel lobbies, department stores such as La Rinascente and Coin, and McDonald's restaurants tend to have the cleanest rest rooms. Pubs and bars rank among the worst and, for these, it may help to have your own small supply of tissues. There are bathrooms in all airports and train stations (in major train stations you'll also

find well-kept pay toilets for €.25–.50) and in most museums. There are also bathrooms at highway rest stops and gas stations: a small tip to the cleaning person is always appreciated. There are no bathrooms in churches, post offices, public beaches, or subway stations.

SAFETY

Don't wear a visible money belt or a waist pack, both of which peg you as a tourist. Distribute your cash and any valuables (including your credit cards and passport) between a deep front pocket, an inside jacket or vest pocket, and a hidden money pouch. Do not reach for the money pouch once you're in public.

Most of the destinations in this guide book are among the safest spots in Italy. Naples, like any modern metropolis, has had certain problems with crime. Although great inroads have been made in the past decade and the city today is as safe as many other big urban centers in Europe, you should continue to be vigilant, especially around the main rail station of Piazza Garibaldi. For special provisos, *see* Being Streetwise in Naples *in* Naples A to Z *in* Chapter 1.

WOMEN IN NAPLES

The difficulties encountered by women traveling alone in Italy are often overstated. Younger women have to put up with much male attention, but it's rarely dangerous. Ignoring whistling and questions is the best way to get rid of unwanted attention.

SENIOR-CITIZEN TRAVEL

To qualify for age-related discounts, mention your senior-citizen status up front when booking hotel reservations (not when checking out) and before you're seated at restaurants (not when paying the bill). Be sure to have identification on hand. When renting a car, ask about promotional car-rental discounts, which can be cheaper than senior-citizen rates. To qualify for senior-citizen discounts in museums and at archaeological sites, you should be from a European Union Member State. This will entitle you on most occasions to free or reduced admission.

🔝 Educational Programs **Elderhostel** ✉ 11 Ave. de Lafayette, Boston, MA 02111-1746 ☎ 877/426-8056; 978/323-4141 international callers; 877/426-2167 TTY 🖶 877/426-2166 ⊕ www.elderhostel.org.

SHOPPING

The notice PREZZI FISSI (fixed prices) means just that; in shops displaying this sign it's a waste of time to bargain unless you're buying a sizable quantity of goods or a particularly costly object. Always try to bargain, however, at outdoor markets (except food markets) and when buying from street vendors.

For any purchase you make, you should receive a regular receipt, which will list the amount spent, the name and—importantly—the *Partita IVA* (tax code) of the business concerned. You should have the receipt on you when you leave the shop; if you are stopped by the *Guardia di Finanza* (Revenue Police) and cannot produce a receipt, then both you and the retailer will be subject to a hefty fine. In Naples, which has a widespread "black" economy, the Guardia di Finanza has been known to swoop down on unsuspecting clients as late as 1 AM, so it is definitely worth asking for *la ricevuta* (the receipt). For information on VAT refunds, *see* Taxes.

SIGHTSEEING TOURS

See Tours *in* Chapter 1 (Naples) and Chapter 4 (Sorrento and the Amalfi Coast).

STUDENTS IN NAPLES

Italy is a popular student destination, and in Naples there are facilities (information, lodging) geared to students' needs, though they are not always easy to locate. Students with identification cards may obtain discounts at museums, galleries, exhibitions, entertainment venues, and on some transportation. The main faculties of the Università degli Studi di Napoli can be found in buildings extending the length of Via Mezzocannone, off Corso Umberto I, near the district of Spaccanapoli, and on Via Porta di Massa. Another university, the Orientale, is located on and around the nearby Piazza Bovio. Both universities sport areas with noticeboards with advertisements for lodgings, forthcoming events, private tutoring, etc., although facilities like university common rooms, student bars, and premises for university clubs and societies remain the stuff of pipedreams. For more structured information about university life, **buy a copy of the periodical Ateneapoli** (⌖ www.ateneapoli.it), available at newsstands.

LOCAL RESOURCES

If in Naples for a prolonged stay, you might want to join **CUS Napoli** (✉ Cupa Poligono 5 ☎ 081/5512623), the university sports club, which has extensive facilities in the west of town in Fuorigrotta. Apart from mainstream sports like soccer, tennis, and basketball, it also has a swimming pool, fitness center, and athletics track. The **Centro Turistico Studentesco** (CTS; ⇨ Travel Agencies) is a student and youth travel agency with an office in Naples; CTS helps its clients find low-cost accommodations and bargain fares for travel in Italy and elsewhere, but to avail yourself of CTS's student discount you need to purchase a membership card (€28). CTS is also the Rome representative for EuroTrain International. The **Associazione Italiana Alberghi per la Gioventù** operates hostels for student members, including the famous Ostello Mergellina in Naples.

🄸 I.D.s & Services **Associazione Italiana Alberghi per la Gioventù** ✉ Salita della Grotta 23, Napoli ☎ 081/7612346. **Associazione Italo-Americana (American Studies Center)** ✉ Via D'Isernia 36, Napoli ☎ 081/660562 ⊕ www.usembassy.it/usa/amstudies/italy.htm. **British Council** ✉ Via Crispi 92, Napoli ☎ 081/667410 ⊕ www.britishcouncil.it. **Centro Turistico Studentesco (CTS)** ✉ Via Mezzocannone 25, Napoli ☎ 081/5527960 ⊕ www.cts.it. **STA Travel** ✉ 10 Downing St., New York, NY 10014 ☎ 212/627-3111; 800/777-0112 24-hr service center ⊟ 212/627-3387 ⊕ www.sta.com. **Travel Cuts** ✉ 187 College St., Toronto, Ontario M5T 1P7, Canada ☎ 800/592-2887 in U.S.; 416/979-2406 or 866/246-9762 in Canada ⊟ 416/979-8167 ⊕ www.travelcuts.com.

Università degli Studi di Napoli ✉ Via Mezzocannone, Napoli ☎ 800/322020 ⊕ www.unina. it.

TAXES

HOTELS

The service charge and the 10% IVA, or value-added tax, are included in the rate except in five-star deluxe hotels, where the IVA (10%) may be a separate item added to the bill at departure.

RESTAURANTS

A service charge of approximately 15% is added to all restaurant bills; in some cases the menu may state that the service charge is already included in the menu prices.

VALUE-ADDED TAX

Value-added tax (IVA or V.A.T.) is 20% on clothing and luxury goods. On most consumer goods, it's already included in the amount shown on the price tag, whereas on services it may not be.

To **get an IVA refund,** take the goods and the invoice when you are leaving Italy to the customs office at the airport or other point of departure and have the invoice stamped. (If you return to the United States or Canada directly from Italy, go through the procedure at Italian customs; if your return is, say, via Britain, take the Italian goods and invoice to British customs.) Under Italy's IVA-refund system, a non-EU resident can obtain a refund of tax paid after spending a minimum of about €155 in one store (before tax—and note that price tags and prices quoted, unless otherwise stated, include IVA). Shop with your passport and ask the store for an invoice itemizing the article(s), price(s), and the amount of tax. In most cases, you will be given a form called a Global Refund Cheque to take to the customs desk on departure from Italy, where the procedure for the tax rebate will begin. Although even small stores in resort areas and larger department stores in Naples will be familiar with this and similar procedures, you may find some retailers in Naples are wholly unversed in tax-free shopping.

Fortunately, a growing number of stores in Italy (and Europe) are members of the Tax-Free Shopping System, which expedites things by providing an invoice that is actually a Tax-Free Cheque in the amount of the refund. Once stamped, it can be cashed at the Tax-Free Cash refund window at major airports and border crossings; you can also opt to have the refund credited to your credit card or bank account, or sent directly home. To save a step at the airport or border, you can send the Cheque to a Tax-Free Shopping address.

There are also many business services that facilitate quicker refunds—for an extra fee; one of the largest network services is called Europe Tax-Free Shopping.

When making a purchase, **ask for a V.A.T. refund form** and find out whether the merchant gives refunds—not all stores do, nor are they required to. Have the form stamped like any customs form by customs officials when you leave the country or, if you're visiting several European Union countries, when you leave the EU. Be ready to show customs officials what you've bought (pack purchases together, in your carry-on luggage); budget extra time for this. After you're through passport control, take the form to a refund-service counter for an on-the-spot refund, or mail it back to the store or a refund service after you arrive home. Note that many readers have reported that in spite of following all the regulations and forms, they never received a refund at all.

A refund service can save you some hassle—for a fee. Global Refund is a Europe-wide service with 190,000 affiliated stores and more than 700 refund counters—located at every major airport and border crossing. Its refund form is called a Tax Free Check. The service issues refunds in the form of cash, check, or credit-card adjustment, minus a processing fee. If you don't have time to wait at the refund counter, you can mail in the form instead.

🚩 V.A.T. Refunds **Global Refund** ✉ 99 Main St., Suite 307, Nyack, NY 10960 ☎ 800/566-9828 🖷 845/348-1549 🌐 www.globalrefund.com.

TELEPHONES

AREA & COUNTRY CODES

The country code for Italy is 39. The area code for Naples is 081. Essentially, the region from Naples to the islands (Capri, Ischia, Procida) and around the Bay of Naples to Sorrento uses the area code 081; the region along the Amalfi Coast from Positano to Salerno uses the area code 089. For example, a call from New York City to Naples would be dialed as 011 + 39 + 081 + phone number. From the U.K., dial 00 + 39 + 081 + phone number. When dialing an Italian number from abroad, you do not drop the initial 0 from the local area code. The same goes for when you are in Italy. When dialing numbers within Italy, you must always use the area code (e.g., 081 for Naples) even if the number you're calling is just down the road. When dialing from Italy overseas, the country code is 001 for the U.S. and Canada, 0061 for Australia, 0064 for New Zealand, and 0044 for the U.K.

Mobile phone numbers can be easily recognized; they begin with the digit 3, and run up to about 10 numbers. The first three numbers indicate the service provider (for example, 347 is an OMNITEL prefix, 330 is TIM) and are followed by another six or seven digits. Both OMNITEL and TIM have good network coverage throughout the Naples area.

DIRECTORY & OPERATOR ASSISTANCE

For general information in English, dial 176. To place international telephone calls via operator-assisted service, dial 170 or long-distance access numbers (⇨ International Calls).

INTERNATIONAL CALLS

Since hotels tend to charge handsomely for long-distance and international calls, it's best to make calls from public phones using telephone cards. These can be purchased from newsstands and tobacconists (⇨ Public Phones). You can **make collect calls from any phone by dialing 172–1011,** which will get you an English-speaking operator. Rates to the United States are lowest around the clock on Sunday and 10 PM–8 AM (Italian time) on weekdays.

LOCAL & LONG-DISTANCE CALLS

For all calls within Italy—local and long distance—you must dial the area code (*prefisso*), which begins with a 0, as 081 for Naples, 089 for Amalfi, etc. If you are calling from a public phone you must deposit a coin or use a calling card to get a dial tone.

Here are area codes for major cities in Italy: Bologna, 051; Brindisi, 0831; Florence, 055; Genoa, 010; Milan, 02; Palermo, 091; Perugia, 075; Pisa, 050; Rome, 06; Siena, 0577; Turin, 011; Venice, 041; and Verona, 045.

LONG-DISTANCE SERVICES

AT&T, MCI, and Sprint access codes make calling long-distance relatively convenient, but you may find the local access number blocked in many hotel rooms. First ask the hotel operator to connect you. If the hotel operator balks, ask for an international operator, or dial the international operator yourself. One way to improve your odds of getting connected to your long-distance carrier is to travel with more than one company's calling card (a

hotel may block Sprint, for example, but not MCI). If all else fails, call from a pay phone.

🚩 **Access Codes** **AT&T USADirect** ☎ 172–1011. **MCI Call USA** ☎ 172–1022. **Sprint Express** ☎ 172–1877.

PHONE CARDS

With a prepaid Eurocity card (€5 or €10), available at larger newsstands, you can make telephone calls for a fraction of standard charges. Phone the local (Naples) number listed on the card, key in the PIN, and you will be able to speak for more than 200 minutes to any destination in Western Europe, the U.S., and Canada on the lowest denomination card (€5), excluding the cost of the local call. For Australia and New Zealand, ask for a Gold Card. All cards have a one-month validity after the first day of use.

PUBLIC PHONES

Pay phones that accept coins are gradually being phased out. Therefore, for calls within Italy, **buy a *carta telefonica* (prepaid calling card).** Card phones are becoming common everywhere. You buy the card (values vary) at Telecom centers, post offices, and tobacconists. Tear off the corner of the card, and insert it in the slot on the phone. When you dial, the card's value appears in the window. After you hang up, the card is returned so you can use it until its value runs out.

TIME

Italy is six hours ahead of New York (so when it's 1 PM in New York it's 7 PM in Naples). Like the rest of Europe, Italy uses the 24-hour (or "military") clock, which means that after noon you continue counting forward: 13:00 is 1 PM, 23:30 is 11:30 PM. Daylight-saving time begins on the last Sunday in March, when clocks are set forward one hour; on the last Sunday in October, clocks are set back one hour. When it's 3 PM in Naples, it's 2 PM in London, and 6 AM in Los Angeles.

TIPPING

The following guidelines apply in Naples and most areas in southern Italy, where tipping effectively subsidizes fairly low wages and may ensure good service on return visits. In restaurants a service charge of about 15% sometimes appears as a separate item on your check. A few restaurants state on the menu that cover and service charge are included. Either way, it's customary to leave an additional 5%–10% tip for the waiter, depending on the service. Tip checkroom attendants €.25 per person, rest room attendants €.10 lire (more in expensive hotels and restaurants). Tip €.05–€.10 for whatever you drink standing up at a coffee bar, €.25 or more for table service in caffès. At a hotel bar tip €.50 and up for a round or two of cocktails.

If your car is being looked after by that southern Italian institution, the *posteggiatore* (parking attendant) found outside many city restaurants, then a tip of €1–€1.5 will usually be sufficient. Before you leave your car, make sure it's properly parked, as you will be liable for any fines incurred.

Tip taxi drivers 5%–10% of the meter amount. Railway and airport porters charge a fixed rate per bag. Tip an additional €.25 per person, more if the porter is very helpful. Theater ushers expect €.50 per person, and more for very expensive seats. Give a barber €1–€1.50 and a hairdresser's assistant €1.50–€4 for a shampoo or cut, depending on the type of establishment.

On sightseeing tours, tip guides about €1.50 per person for a half-day group tour, more if they are very good. In museums and other places of interest where admission is free, and a museum official has opened up a display specially for you, a tip of €2 or more would be appreciated, although this must be done with discretion. Service station attendants are tipped only for special services; for example, €.50 for checking your tires.

In hotels, some clients round up the bill when checking out or leave cash for *il personale* (the staff), say €10 depending on the establishment and the length of stay. For two people in a double room, leave the chambermaid about €.50–€1 per day, or about €3–€5 a week, in a moderately priced hotel; tip a minimum of €.50 for valet or room service. Double these amounts in a very expensive hotel. In very expensive hotels, tip doormen €1 for carrying bags to the check-in desk, bellhops €1.50–€2.50 for carrying your bags to the room, and the same for room service.

TOURS & PACKAGES

Because everything is prearranged on a prepackaged tour or independent vacation, you spend less time planning—and often get it all at a good price.

BOOKING WITH AN AGENT

Travel agents are excellent resources. But it's a good idea to collect brochures from several agencies, as some agents' suggestions may be influenced by relationships with tour and package firms that reward them for volume sales. If you have a special interest, find an agent with expertise in that area; the American Society of Travel Agents (ASTA; ⇨ Travel Agencies) has a database of specialists worldwide. You can log on to the group's Web site to find an ASTA travel agent in your neighborhood.

Make sure your travel agent knows the accommodations and other services of the place being recommended. Ask about the hotel's location, room size, beds, and whether it has a pool, room service, or programs for children, if you care about these. Has your agent been there in person or sent others whom you can contact?

Do some homework on your own, too: local tourism boards can provide information about lesser-known and small-niche operators, some of whom may sell only direct.

BUYER BEWARE

Each year consumers are stranded or lose their money when tour operators—even large ones with excellent reputations—go out of business. So check out the operator. Ask several travel agents about its reputation, and try to **book with a company that has a consumer-protection program.** (Look for information in the company's brochure.) In the United States, members of the National Tour Association and the United States Tour Operators Association are required to set aside funds to cover payments and travel arrangements in the event that the company defaults. It's also a good idea to choose a company that participates in the American Society of Travel Agents' Tour Operator Program; ASTA will act as mediator in any disputes between you and your tour operator.

Remember that the more your package or tour includes, the better you can predict the ultimate cost of your vacation. Make sure you know exactly what is covered, and beware of hidden costs. Are taxes, tips, and transfers included? Entertainment and excursions? These can add up.

🚈 Tour-Operator Recommendations American Society of Travel Agents (⇨ Travel Agencies). **National Tour Association (NTA)** ⊠ 546 E. Main St., Lexington, KY 40508 ☎ 859/226-4444 or 800/682-8886 🖷 859/226-4404 ⊕ www.ntaonline.com. **United States Tour Operators Association (USTOA)** ⊠ 275 Madison Ave., Suite 2014, New York, NY 10016 ☎ 212/599-6599 🖷 212/599-6744 ⊕ www.ustoa.com.

TRAIN TRAVEL

The fastest trains in Italy are the Eurostar trains, operating virtually the length and breadth of Italy, including Naples–Milan via Rome, Florence, and Bologna; seat reservations and supplement are included in the fare. Some of these (the ETR 460 trains) have little aisle and luggage space (although there's a space near the door where you can put large bags). To avoid having to squeeze through narrow aisles, board at your car (look for the number on the reservation ticket). Car numbers are displayed on their exterior. Next-fastest trains are the Intercity (IC) trains, for which you pay a supplement and for which seat reservations may be required and are always advisable. *Interregionale* trains usually make more stops and are a little slower. *Regionale* and *locale* trains are the slowest; many serve commuters.

Note that in some Italian cities (including Milan, Turin, Genoa, Naples, and Rome) there are two or more main-line stations, although one is usually the principal terminal or through-station. Be sure of the name of the station at which your train will arrive, or from which it will depart. Naples has at least four main-line stations: If your train leaves from Piazza Garibaldi, it means you must take the escalator down to the level below Napoli Centrale (follow signs to the *Metropolitana*). Some trains to Rome leave from the classy station of Mergellina, four stops away from Piazza Garibaldi on the Metropolitana. Potential confusion can also arise in Pompeii, as the main-line station is a good 20-minute walk from the archaeological site. For this site, you need to take the Circumvesuviana network from Naples to Sorrento and get off at Pompei Scavi.

There is refreshment service on all long-distance trains, with mobile carts and a cafeteria or dining car. Tap water on trains is not drinkable.

🚈 From the U.K. Rail Europe ⊠ 178 Piccadilly, London W1 ☎ 08705/848-848 ⊕ www.raileurope.co.uk.

CLASSES

All Italian trains have first and second classes. On local trains the higher first-class fare gets you little more than a clean doily on the headrest of your seat, but on long-distance trains you get wider seats, more legroom, and better ventilation and lighting. At peak travel times, first-class train travel is worth the difference. Remember **always try to make seat reservations in advance,** for either class, as you can easily run into long ticket lines at the station just when you are hoping to board a train. One advantage of traveling first class is that the cars are almost always not crowded—or, at the very least, less crowded than the second-class compartments. A first-class ticket, in Italian, is *prima classe*; second is *seconda classe*.

CUTTING COSTS

To save money, **look into rail passes.** But be aware that if you don't plan to cover many miles, you may come out ahead by buying individual tickets. If Italy is your only destination in Europe, **consider purchasing an Italian Railpass,** which allows unlimited travel on the entire Italian Rail network. The Italy Flexi Rail Card allows a limited number of travel days within one month: $239 for four days of travel in first class ($191 second class); 8 days of travel ($335 first class, $267 in second class); and 10 days of travel ($383 first class, $305 second class).

Once in Italy, **inquire about the Carta Verde (Green Card) if you're under 26** (€26 for one year), which entitles the holder to a 20% discount on all first and second-class tickets. Those under 26 should also inquire about discount travel fares under the Billet International Jeune (BIJ) and Euro Domino Junior schemes. Also in Italy, you can **purchase the Carta d'Argento (Silver Card) if you're over 60** (€26 for one year), which also allows a 20% discount on all first and second-class rail travel. For further information, check out the Ferrovie dello Stato (FS) Web site (⊕ www.fs-on-line.com).

Italy is one of 17 countries in which you can use **Eurailpasses,** which provide unlimited first-class travel in all of the participating countries. If you plan to rack up the miles, get a standard pass. Train travel is available for 15 days ($588), 21 days ($762), one month ($946), two months ($1,338), and three months ($1,654). You can also receive free or discounted fares on some ferry lines.

If your plans call for only limited train travel, **look into the Eurail Selectpass,** which costs less money than a Eurailpass and allows train travel in several (three, four, or 5) adjoining Eurail countries. For the minimum of three adjoining countries (say Italy, France, and Spain) rail travel within a two-month period will cost $356 for 5 days of travel, $394 for 6 days, $470 for 8 days, and $542 for 10 days). Extra countries cost about $40 each. You can receive discounts for two or more people. Please note that these fares are subject to change in 2004 and/or 2005.

In addition to standard Eurailpasses, **ask about special rail-pass plans.** Among these are the Eurail Youthpass (for those under age 26), Eurail Saverpass and Eurail Saver Flexipass (which give a discount for two or more people traveling together), Eurail Flexipass (which allows a certain number of travel days within a set period), and the EurailDrive Pass, which combines travel by train and rental car.

Whichever pass you choose, remember that you must **purchase your Eurailpass or Eurail Selectpass before you leave** for Europe. You can get further information and order tickets at the Rail Europe Web site (⊕ www.raileurope.com).

Many travelers assume that rail passes guarantee them seats on the trains they wish to ride. Not so. You need to book seats ahead even if you are using a rail pass. Seat reservations are required on some European trains, particularly high-speed trains, and are a good idea on trains that may be crowded—particularly in summer on popular routes. You will also need a reservation if you purchase sleeping accommodations. Trains going from the north of Italy via Naples through to Reggio Calabria in the toe of Italy will be particularly tightly packed, especially around weekends and public holidays. If traveling on a Saturday evening or Sunday, it may

be worth finding out about important soccer matches and steering well clear of local fans by upgrading to first class or changing your schedule.

If you're on a tight schedule or just want to avoid unpleasant surprises, double-check beforehand whether there is a strike (*sciopero*) planned for the day you're traveling. On average, industrial action is usually planned for 24-hour periods at weekends, and only a limited service may be provided while the strike lasts.

FARES & SCHEDULES

Trains can be very crowded; it's always a good idea to make a reservation. To avoid long lines at station windows, **buy tickets and make seat reservations up to two months in advance** at travel agencies displaying the FS emblem. Tickets can be purchased at the last minute, but seat reservations can be made at agencies (or the train station) up until about three hours before the train departs from its city of origin. For trains that require a reservation (all Eurostar and some Intercity), you may be able to get a seat assignment just before boarding the train; look for the conductor on the platform. On Eurostar trains you will have to pay a surcharge of €8 if you board without a reservation.

All **tickets must be date-stamped in the small yellow or red machines near the tracks before you board.** Once stamped, your ticket is valid for six hours if your destination is within 200 km (124 mi), for 24 hours for destinations beyond that. You can get on and off at will at stops in between for the duration of the ticket's validity. If you forget to stamp your ticket in the machine, or you didn't buy a ticket, you must actively seek out a conductor and pay a €6 fine. Don't wait for the conductor to find out that you are without a valid ticket (unless the train is overcrowded and walking becomes impossible), as he might charge you a much heavier fine. You can buy train tickets for nearby destinations (within a 200-km [120-mi] range) at tobacconists and at ticket machines in stations.

🚹 Information and Passes Eurailpasses are available through travel agents and **Rail Europe** ✉ 226–230 Westchester Ave., White Plains, NY 10604 ☎ 914/682–5172 or 800/438–7245 ✉ 2087 Dundas E., Suite 105, Mississauga, Ontario L4X 1M2 ☎ 416/602–4195. **DER Travel Services** 🚲 Box

1606, Des Plaines, IL 60017 ☎ 800/782-2424 ☎ 800/282-7474 ⊕ www.der.com. **CIT Tours Corp.** ✉ 342 Madison Ave., Suite 207, New York, NY 10173 ☎ 212/697-2100 or 800/248-8687; 800/2487245 in western U.S. ⊕ www.cit-tours.com. Italian rail passes can be purchased through DER Tours or CIT Tours as well.

❼ Train Information The main train station in Campania is Naples's **Stazione Centrale** ✉ Piazza Garibaldi ☎ 848/888088 ⊕ www.fs-on-line.it. The Ferrovia Circumvesuviana leaves for points east from the **Stazione Circumvesuviana** ✉ Corso Garibaldi ☎ 081/7722244 ⊕ www.vesuviana.it; all trains also stop on the lower level of Stazione Centrale. Destinations include Ercolano (Herculaneum), Pompei Scavi-Villa dei Misteri (Pompeii), and Sorrento. Note that there are two Circumvesuviana stations in the town of Pompeii, served by different lines. For the archaeological site, take the Sorrento line. SEPSA manages two railway lines that leave from the **Stazione Cumana** ✉ near Montesanto Metro station ☎ 081/7354111 ⊕ www.sepsa.it. Both end at Torregaveta, at the west end of the Bay of Naples; the Cumana line goes along the coast and stops at Pozzuoli and Lucrino (near Baia), among other places. **Salerno's train station** ✉ Piazza V. Veneto ☎ 848/888088 ⊕ www.fs-on-line.it is a stop on the Milan–Reggio Calabria line.

❼ Unique Guidebook *Italy by Train* by Tim Jepson (Fodor's Travel Publications, ☎ 800/533-6478 or from bookstores; $16).

TRANSPORTATION AROUND NAPLES & CAMPANIA

Public transportation is the fastest mode of travel among Italy's cities. It's also relatively inexpensive in comparison to the costs of renting a car and paying for gas and tolls. The big news is that the regional authorities in Campania have accomplished their ambitious integration of all its transport firms by tying together the metro and bus lines into one ticketing scheme called *Campania Unico*. Under this system, Campania has been divided into 11 travel zones, radiating out of Naples and all called *fascia* ("travel zone"). This means that you don't need to buy separate tickets for all the various stretches of the journey, even if you're traveling with different carriers. A single ticket, called the biglietto unico, allows you to travel across the zones. A Fascia 1 ticket (€1.40 for 100 minutes) covers trips between Naples and a radius of about 10 km (6 mi), which includes Pozzuoli and Portici; Fascia 2 (€1.70 for 120 minutes) takes in Ercolano (Herculaneum), Baia, and Cuma; Fascia 3

(€2.20 for 140 minutes) includes Pompeii, Boscoreale, and Castellammare; Fascia 4 (€2.70 for 160 minutes) will take you as far as Vico Equense; and Fascia 5 (€3.10 for 180 minutes) covers trips to Sorrento and beyond.

For one example, if you want to go from your hotel in Naples to Pompeii (zone 3, €2.20) just get a single Fascia 3 ticket and time-stamp it on the first leg of your journey (e.g. the city's metropolitana subway system). Then you'll find you don't need to buy another ticket for the other leg(s) of your journey (e.g. Circumvesuviana train from Napoli Centrale to Pompei-Villa dei Misteri). The same principles apply to trips between zones not passing through Naples (e.g. from Sorrento to Pompeii). If you are, say, based in Ravello and want to get to Positano (same travel zone, No. 5) you can buy a *biglietto orario*, (one-way ticket, €1.80) or a *biglietto giornaliero* (day pass, €3.60). The zone system only applies to land-based travel.

Italy's cities are served by an extensive state railway system (FS; ⇨ Train Travel), with fast service on main lines (Milan–Venice–Florence–Rome–Naples) that in some cases beats plane travel in time as well as cost. A complete schedule of all trains in the country and fares can be bought from most newsstands for about €4, or can be accessed via the Ferrovie Dello Stato Web site at ⊕ www.fs-on-line. it. Buses (⇨ Bus Travel), somewhat less comfortable than trains and slightly less expensive, offer more frequent service to certain smaller cities and towns that are served only by secondary train lines or are inaccessible by train. Ferries and hydrofoils (⇨ Boat & Ferry Travel) ply among the islands; some islands, such as Capri and Ischia, have helicopter service, a more expensive alternative.

TRAVEL AGENCIES

A good travel agent puts your needs first. Look for an agency that has been in business at least five years, emphasizes customer service, and has someone on staff who specializes in your destination. In addition, **make sure the agency belongs to a professional trade organization.** The American Society of Travel Agents (ASTA)—the largest and most influential in the field with more than 20,000 members in some 140 countries—maintains and enforces a strict code of ethics and will step in to help mediate any agent-client disputes involving ASTA members if necessary. ASTA (whose motto is "Without a travel agent, you're on your own") also maintains a Web site that includes a directory of agents.

🛈 Local Agent Referrals **American Society of Travel Agents (ASTA)** ✉ 1101 King St., Suite 200, Alexandria, VA 22314 ☎ 703/739-2782 or 800/965-2782 24-hr hot line 🖷 703/739-3268 ⊕ www. astanet.com. **Association of British Travel Agents** ✉ 68-71 Newman St., London W1T 3AH ☎ 020/7637-2444 🖷 020/7637-0713 ⊕ www.abta.com. **Association of Canadian Travel Agencies** ✉ 130 Albert St., Suite 1705, Ottawa, Ontario K1P 5G4 ☎ 613/237-3657 🖷 613/237-7052 ⊕ www.acta.ca. **Australian Federation of Travel Agents** ✉ Level 3, 309 Pitt St., Sydney, NSW 2000 ☎ 02/9264-3299 🖷 02/9264-1085 ⊕ www.afta.com.au. **Travel Agents' Association of New Zealand** ✉ Level 5, Tourism and Travel House, 79 Boulcott St., Box 1888, Wellington 6001 ☎ 04/499-0104 🖷 04/499-0786 ⊕ www. taanz.org.nz.

VISITOR INFORMATION

Learn more about foreign destinations by checking government-issue travel advisories and country information. For a broader picture, consider information from more than one country.

🛈 At Home **Italian Government Tourist Board (ENIT)** ✉ 630 5th Ave., New York, NY 10111 ☎ 212/245-4822 🖷 212/586-9249 ⊕ www.italiantourism.com ✉ 500 N. Michigan Ave., Chicago, IL 60611 ☎ 312/644-0996 🖷 312/644-3019 ✉ 12400 Wilshire Blvd., Suite 550, Los Angeles, CA 90025 ☎ 310/820-1898 🖷 310/820-6357 ✉ 175 Bloor Street East, Suite 907, Toronto, Ontario M4W 3R8 ☎ 416/925-4882 🖷 416/925-4799 ✉ 1 Princes St., London W1R 8AY ☎ 020/7408-1254 🖷 020/7399-3567 ⊕ www.enit.it.

🛈 Tourist Offices in Italy **Rome** ✉ Via Parigi 5, 00185 ☎ 06/48899255. **Naples** ✉ Piazzadei Martiri 58, 80121 ☎ 081/405311 ⊕ www.ept.napoli.it; for further listings of tourist offices in Naples and the Amalfi Coast, *see* the A to Z section at the end of each regional chapter in this book. Official sites of the Italian National Tourist Board (⊕ www.enit.it), the local region (⊕ www.regione.campania.it), and the provincial tourist boards (⊕ www.ept.it.) also provide fair coverage.

🛈 Government Advisories **U.S. Department of State** ✉ Overseas Citizens Services Office, Room 4811, 2201 C St. NW, Washington, DC 20520 ☎ 202/647-5225 interactive hot line ⊕ www.travel.state.gov; enclose a cover letter with your request and a business-size SASE. **Consular Affairs Bureau of Canada** ☎ 800/267-6788 or 613/944-6788 ⊕ www.voyage.gc.ca. **U.K. Foreign and Commonwealth Office** ✉ Travel Advice Unit, Consular Division, Old Admiralty Building, London SW1A 2PA ☎ 020/7008-0232 or 020/7008-0233 ⊕ www.fco.gov.uk/travel. **Australian Department of Foreign Affairs and Trade** ☎ 02/6261-1299 Consular Travel Advice Faxback Service ⊕ www.dfat.gov.au. **New Zealand Ministry of Foreign Affairs and Trade** ☎ 04/439-8000 ⊕ www.mft.govt.nz.

WEB SITES

Do check out the World Wide Web when planning your trip. You'll find everything from weather forecasts to virtual tours of famous cities. Be sure to visit Fodors.com (⊕ www.fodors.com), a complete travel-planning site. You can research prices and book plane tickets, hotel rooms, rental cars, vacation packages, and more. In addition, you can post your pressing questions in the Travel Talk section. Other planning tools include a currency converter and weather reports, and there are loads of links to travel resources.

🛈 Suggested Web Sites For more information specifically on Italy, visit ⊕ www.initaly.com, a constantly updated Web site with good-quality cultural information. The site for Ferrovie dello Stato, ⊕ www.fs-on-line.com is a good source for train information and journey planning, although at a local level ⊕ www.campaniatrasporti.it provides an easily downloadable overview of local transport networks. Two handy sites for Capri are ⊕ www.caprinet.it and ⊕ www.caprionline.com. The island of Ischia is now on the cyberspace map at ⊕ www.ischia.com and, for last minute travel bargains, ⊕ www.lastminuteischia.com. Many hotels now have on-line reservation facilities and several restaurants have thoughtfully posted menus to whet the appetites of Internet surfers. Where known, sites have been included at the end of individual listings.

NAPLES

FODOR'S CHOICE

Borgo Marinaro, *the fishermen still sing "Santa Lucia" here*

Castel dell'Ovo, *standing guard over the bay*

Cappella Sansevero, *the most macabre chapel in Naples*

Monte di Pietà, *if you want to "go for Baroque"*

Museo Archeological Nazionale, *for ancient treasures*

Palazzo Reale, Napoli *splendorissimo*

Pio Monte, *home to Caravaggio's bravura altarpiece*

Santa Chiara's Clarisse Cloister, *a masterpiece in majolica*

Spaccanapoli, *the Punch and Judy street of Naples*

Teatro San Carlo, *even Caruso was hissed here*

San Gregorio Armeno, *where every morning is Christmas*

HIGHLY RECOMMENDED

RESTAURANTS   Da Cicciotto, *Posillipo*

Lombardi à Santa Chiara, *Spaccanapoli*

La Terrazza in the Hotel Excelsior, *Santa Lucia*

Mimì alla Ferrovia, *Piazza Garibaldi*

HOTELS   Il Convento, *Piazza Municipio*

Parker's, *the Vomero hill*

Pinto Storey, *Chiaia*

San Francesco al Monte, *the Vomero hill*

Santa Lucia, *on the Lungomare*

Soggiorno Sansevero, *Spaccanapoli*

Many other great sights, restaurants, and hotels enliven this area. For other favorites, look for the black stars as you read this chapter.

By Gregory
W. Bailey

Updated by
Francesca
Marretta,
Victoria
Primhak, and
Chris Rose

BUILT LIKE A GREAT AMPHITHEATER around her beautiful bay, Naples is an eternally unfolding play acted by a million of the best actors in the world," Herbert Kubly observed in his *American in Italy.* "The comedy is broad, the tragedy violent. The curtain never rings down." Is it a sense of doom from living in the shadow of Vesuvius that makes some Neapolitans so volatile, so blind to everything but the pain or pleasure of the moment? More likely, a huge zest for living and overcrowding are the more probable causes. But whatever the reason, Naples remains the most vibrant city in Italy—a steaming, bubbling, reverberating minestrone in which each block is a small village, every street the setting for a Punch-and-Judy show, and everything seems to be a backdrop for an opera not yet composed. It is said that northern Italians vacation here to remind themselves of the time when Italy was *molto Italiano—really* Italian. In this respect, Naples—Napoli in Italian—doesn't disappoint: Neapolitan rainbows of laundry wave in the wind over alleyways open-windowed with friendliness, mothers caress children, men break out into impromptu arias at sidewalk cafés, street scenes offer Fellini-esque slices of life, and everywhere contrasting elements of faded gilt and romance, rust and calamity, grandeur and squalor form an intoxicating pageant of pure *Italianità*—Italy at its most Italian.

From the moment you arrive at swirling Piazza Garibaldi, the city envelops you with its mix of beauty, chaos, and a glorious past. The piazza, which is home to the Stazione Centrale, the main railroad terminal, seems at first glance a battered place—crowded, messy, and inhospitable, the local bus station perched in the middle of seemingly never-ending roadworks (even the locals find the one-way system confounding, so visiting drivers beware). Long-time home to the standard complement of street sharks and souvenir-hawkers, the piazza is now a meeting point for immense numbers of eastern Europeans; thanks to its age-old traditions of tolerance and hospitality, Naples is a welcome destination for increasing hoards of guest workers. But once you get away from Piazza Garibaldi and its rail lines (which run adjacent to the modern and ugly Centro Direzionali business sector, located far away from the historic city), first impressions begin to mellow: the pace changes, and your point of view along with it. Delightfully and unforgettably, Naples now unfolds as a cornucopia of elegant boulevards, treasure-stocked palaces, the world's greatest museum of classical antiquities, the stage-set neighborhood of Spaccanapoli, and hundreds of historic churches. For the serious-minded, walking, cathedral-visiting tourist, Naples becomes *Napoli la bella,* a city that centuries of romantics have deemed one of the most beautiful in the world, a designation that owes much to its location on the sweeping expanse of the Bay of Naples, plus an immense past attested to by its grand monuments and a mode of life that never fails to fascinate.

Despite these attributes, in the 1970s a different, rather seedy image was beginning to emerge: *Napoli la terribile.* Horror stories abounded about the *scippatori,* Vespa-riding muggers who yanked purses from unsuspecting sightseers; hospitals so terrible that patients were said to dial 113, the emergency number, from their beds because they despaired of ever seeing the ward nurse; and the juvenile *scugnizzi,* the street children who would pry off your license plate at one traffic light and sell it back to you at the next. Unemployment reached 30%, the infrastructure was rotting (government subsidies were simply being *mett'in tasca*—"put into pocket," as the local phrase had it, by the Camorra, the Neapolitan version of the Mafia)—and the threat of earthquakes and ever-present gridlock turned sectors of the city into an Italian Los Angeles.

A kinetic gust of 3-D garlic-and-basil aromatherapy for the soul, Naples is a destination no one ever forgets. The most operatic of cities, it blasts you with a heady mix of beauty, chaos, and a glorious past. If your eye is greedy for splendor, many treasures beckon—the world's finest museum of classical antiquities, opulent palaces, and bravura Caravaggio altarpieces—but the greatest treasure of all is the Neapolitan people themselves.

Numbers in the text correspond to numbers in the margin and on the Naples and From La Sanità to Capodimonte maps.

If you have 1 day

Begin with the Naples you have always imagined: Spaccanapoli—the historic quarter where palaces and slums, neon-lighted pizzerias and gilded cathedrals, organ-grinders and Mercedes create an open-air museum. Ground zero here is Piazza Gesù Nuovo, site of the churches of the Gesù Nuovo and Santa Chiara and entryway to the spectacular 5-km-long (3-mi-long) pedestrian ribbon called the Spaccanapoli. Explore the memorable sights of this quarter—the Cappella Sansevero, the crèche shops of Via Gregorio Armeno, the Caravaggio altarpiece at the Pio Monte, and the Chapel of San Gennaro at the Duomo—by first walking east along the Spacca, then returning west one block north along Via Tribunali. After lunch at a Spacca pizzeria or caffè, head over to Via Toledo, Naples's main thoroughfare, and walk back to the ceremonial center of the city: Piazza del Plebiscito, bookended on one side by the Church of San Francesco di Paola, and on the other by the Bourbons' palace, the Palazzo Reale. Combine sightseeing with shopping by touring the Galleria Umberto I and the shops of nearby Via Chiaia, which leads to the *"salone"* of Naples, chic Piazza dei Martiri. Continue south to the bayside Lungomare and walk over to the Castel dell'Ovo for a sunset dinner—with Vesuvius front and center—at one of the restaurants at the harbor port, the Borgo Marinaro.

If you have 3 days

Having survived your first whirlwind day in Naples, begin your second day at the world-famous Museo Archeologico Nazionale (be there when the doors open in the morning to get a jump on the crowds). Packed with archaeological relics of the Classical era, it's a must before venturing out of town to see Pompeii and Herculaneum. After viewing the *Hercules Farnese* and other ancient masterworks, you deserve a taxi or bus to reach Museo di Capodimonte, high above the city center and the greatest of the Bourbon palaces. Amble through its grand ballrooms and take in the great art collection (with its modern art collection housed on the top floor), then promenade in its park to admire the views over the bay and city. Return to the city center and bustling Piazza Municipio to view the collections on view at the brooding Castel Nuovo. For your third day take the Funicolare Centrale opposite Galleria Umberto I up the Vomero Hill to explore the Certosa di San Martino, a Baroque extravaganza of a monastery, and the mighty Castel Sant'Elmo. Then walk through the pretty residential quarter to the Villa Floridiana's decorative-arts museum and sylvan park, which has wonderful views high over the city. Take the Funicolare di Chiaia back down to the Lungomare to visit the aristocratic Villa Pignatelli and the celebrated aquarium. Head over to the west end of the Riviera di Chiaia by foot or bus to Mergellina for dinner and an evening boat tour of the waterfront, or opt for an opera performance at the Teatro San Carlo.

On your fourth day, take a vacation from your Neapolitan vacation by heading out of town to the nearby 18th-century Palace of Caserta, planned by the Bourbon king Charles III. Tour the gilded salons, majestic park, and English Garden designed by the Habsburg queen Maria Carolina along guidelines suggested by Sir William Hamilton and his wife, the celebrated Emma. Or, instead, venture out past Posillipo to the Phlegrean Fields and pay a call on the Cave of the Cumaean Sibyl. On your fifth day, don't miss the grandiose interior of the Palazzo Reale, and devote more time to the museums and galleries mentioned above—along with the many others covered in the pages below—that interest you most. Return to further explore a kindred neighborhood—the elegant Chiaia and Vomero or the picturesque Spaccanapoli—allowing plenty of time for poking into odd corners and courtyards and churches, and for caffè-sitting to watch the passing Neapolitan parade. Wherever you head, why not enjoy a truly Neapolitan grande finale and return to the Borgo Marinaro for your last view over the gulf? Don't forget to give thanks that Vesuvius—the spectacular backdrop for this vista—continues to be well-behaved.

By the early 1980s Neapolitans said *Basta*—"Enough!" Baroness Mirella Barracca mobilized the city's rich and powerful into Committee Naples Ninety-Nine, an organization whose mission was to uplift both the city's historic structures and its public image. The turnaround was confirmed with Antonio Bassolino's election as mayor: in the 1990s, he jumpstarted the city's economic development, threw the cars out of the piazzas, cleaned up the streets, and crowded more policemen than travelers into the main railway terminal. Palaces were restored, churches reopened, city museums refurbished, conferences encouraged; the Camorra was out and art was in. Today, more than a decade later, it is Naples that has erupted in an unending flow of cultural excitement while Il Vesuvio (Vesuvius) slumbers: The city's new state-of-the-art metro system is now a showcase graced with artworks by contemporary greats and young local sculptors; a renaissance of southern Italian cooking is making headlines around the world; and more and more travelers with a been-there, done-that take on Rome, Florence, and other capitals of northern Italy are setting a southward course. Only a few years ago, Naples was a "don't," and almost all of the thousands who entered the city's Stazione Centrale only did so because it was the gateway to Pompeii, Sorrento, Capri, and the Amalfi Coast. Since then, tourists alighting here are pleasantly discovering that Naples is much more than a railway station—it is a civilization.

Ultimately, the origin of Naples, once called Parthenope and later Neapolis, can be traced to the nearby ruins of Cumae, the earliest Greek colony in Italy, founded around 750 BC. Greek civilization flourished for hundreds of years along this coastline, but there was nothing in the way of centralized government until the Roman Empire, uniting all of Italy for the first time, surged southward and, with little opposition, absorbed the Greek colonies in the 4th century BC. The Romans were quick to appreciate the sybaritic potential of the region, and wealthy members of the empire flocked here to build palatial country residences. Generally, the peace of Campania was undisturbed during the centuries of Roman rule.

Naples and Campania, with the rest of Italy, decayed with the Roman Empire and collapsed into the abyss of the Middle Ages. In 1130 the Norman king, Roger II, King of the Two Sicilies, made Naples the capital of his empire, until Henry VI of Hohenstaufen captured it in 1194; his enlightened son, Frederick II, endowed the city with a university that attracted many scholars and poets. By now the popes had an eye on Naples, and together with the French king Louis IX and Charles of Anjou, the papal troops and the French Angevin government conquered the Hohenstaufen forces in 1268. Charles of Anjou and Robert the Wise sponsored the construction of several important buildings, including the Church of Santa Chiara, which introduced the style of Provençal Gothic to the city. Aragonese rule arrived in 1442 with the siege of Alfonso I of Aragon, but his line was driven from the city in turn by the alliance between King Louis XII of France and Ferdinand of Spain. The nobles who served under the Spanish viceroys in the 16th and 17th centuries, when their harsh rule made all Italy quake, enjoyed their libertine pleasures, resulting in the flourishing of taverns and gaming houses, even as Spain milked the citizenry with burdensome taxes. During this time Naples became second only to Paris as Europe's largest city (and also its most densely populated—to accommodate the crowds, tenements rose as high as seven stories).

After a short-lived Austrian occupation, Naples became the capital of the Kingdom of the Two Sicilies, established by the Bourbon kings in 1738. This somewhat garbled kingdom was made up of Naples (which included most of the southern Italian mainland) and the island of Sicily, which had been conjoined in the Middle Ages, then separated and unofficially reunited under Spanish domination during the 16th and 17th centuries. With the rule of the Bourbon kings, the Neapolitan "golden age" began in earnest, as their rule was generally benevolent, as far as Campania was concerned, and their support of the papal authority in Rome was an important factor in the development of the rest of Italy. The rule of Charles III of Bourbon, along with that of his son Ferdinand IV, was influential artistically: Both kings not only built many of the architectural showpieces of the city—the Palace of Capodimonte, Teatro San Carlo, and the Palaces of Caserta and Portici, to name a few—they also sponsored noted musicians, artists, and writers, who were only too willing to submit to court life in such magnificent natural surroundings. But the modern world came knocking in the person of Napoléon, whose forces dethroned the Bourbons in 1799. The glamour of the Empire style came to the city when Napoléon appointed his brother-in-law, Joachim Murat, as king of Naples. In 1815 the Bourbons returned to power, Murat was shot, and Ferdinand IV exclaimed that poor general Murat had been a better upholsterer than administrator. In 1816, with Napoléon out of the way on St. Helena, Ferdinand once again merged the two kingdoms, proclaiming himself Ferdinand I of the Kingdom of Two Sicilies. His reactionary and repressive rule earned him other, more colorful titles among his rebellious subjects. Finally, Giuseppe Garibaldi launched his expedition, and in 1860 Naples was united with the rest of Italy.

Clearly, as the historic capital of Campania, Naples has been perpetually and tumultuously in a state of flux. Neapolitans are instinctively the most hospitable of people, and they've often paid a price for being so, having unwittingly extended a warm welcome to wave after wave of invaders. Lombards, Goths, Normans, Swabians, Spanish viceroys and kings, and Napoleonic generals arrived in turn; most of them proved to be greedy and self-serving. Still, if these foreign rulers bled the populace dry with taxes, they left the impoverished city with a rich architectural inheritance.

Much of that inheritance is on display in Spaccanapoli, the historic center, where the Piazza Gesù Nuovo and the surrounding blocks are a showplace for the city's most beloved churches and a showcase for the city's greatest attraction, the Neapolitan people. On the piazza, watch and rub elbows with them. Let their charm, gaiety, effervescence, and undiluted spontaneity pull you into their unique but glorious concept of life and living. You'll soon begin to sense that Neapolitans are possibly the happiest people in the world. In an hour or two you'll feel like part of the *famiglia* yourself. Compared to most other great metropolises of the world, Naples has little tourist infrastructure, forcing you to become a native very quickly, as you'll find out if you spend some time wandering through the gridlike narrow streets of the old center. Lost? You'll be taken in hand (probably by way of mamma's house). Hungry? Hey, *paisan,* bring over a slice! Can't think of the right word? A translation is shouted out over the din, and a single word is never sufficient when 10 will do—as you could have seen one September afternoon when an English couple asked for directions to the Church of Pio Monte della Misericordia. One passerby started explaining, but another man suddenly thought of a still shorter way and butted in. In no time eight or ten people were volubly offering their own directions. The arguing that ensued was not unfriendly; a torn racing form was the only casualty. The inquiring couple never learned the shortest—or, for that matter, any other—way to Pio Monte. But the sun was warm, the sky was blue, and there are plenty of other beautiful churches in Naples.

— Robert I. C. Fisher

EXPLORING NAPLES

Updated by
Victoria
Primhak

Naples, a bustling city of some 1.2 million people, presents a particular challenge for visitors because of its hilly terrain and its twisty, often congested streets. Though spread out, Naples invites walking; the bus system, funiculars, and subways are also options for dealing with weary legs. Sightseeing days should begin no later than 9, as most churches are usually open only from 7:30 until noon or 12:30, reopening only after the afternoon siesta, which could run from 4 or 4:30 until about 7. In winter, schedule church visits for mornings only, as the grayish afternoon light can make even the most spectacular church seem dull and gloomy. Some museums now have extended hours, with a few even open in evenings; however, this usually means that rooms may be open on a rotating basis, and if you are making a special journey to see a particular exhibit, it's worth phoning to check if it's viewable. If you come to Naples by car, park it in a garage as fast as you can, agree on the cost in advance, and then forget it for the duration of your stay (otherwise, city driving is not for the faint-hearted, theft is a constant risk, and parking a nightmare).

The city of Naples stretches along the Bay of Naples from Piazza Garibaldi in the east to Mergellina in the west, with its back to the Vomero Hill. From Stazione Centrale, on Piazza Garibaldi, Corso Umberto I (known as the "Rettifilo") heads southwest to the monumental city center—commonly known as "Toledo"—around the piazzas Bovio, Municipio, and Trieste e Trento; here is the major urban set piece composed of the Palazzo Reale, Teatro San Carlo, and Galleria Umberto Primo. To the north are the historic districts of old Naples, most notably, Spaccanapoli, I Vergini, and La Sanità; to the south, the port. Farther west along the bay are the more fashionable neighborhoods of Santa Lucia and Chiaia, and finally the waterfront district of Mergellina. The residential area of Vomero sits on the steep hills rising above Chiaia and

La Cucina Napoletana

If you love food you'll love Naples, the birthplace of several of the world's most popular dishes and culinary delights: pizza, spaghetti *al pomodoro* (with tomatoes), mozzarella cheese, as well as most of the pasta shapes everyone knows, like ziti, vermicelli—what most Italians call spaghetti—fusilli, *bucatini,* and linguine, as well as some of the most *delizioso* coffee and desserts served up anywhere. For the most part, these dishes reflect the schizophrenic split of rich and poor that has always characterized the city. Since most Neapolitans as well have long been both very poor and very creative, *cucina povera*—subsistence nourishment alchemically raised to culinary gold—is at its best here. This species of "poor people's food" is best represented by pizza. By the 18th century, fishermen were eating like kings and kings like fishermen: Neapolitan royalty was known for its love of the sturdy and virtuous "common" food. Forks were supposedly invented so that Ferdinand II could indulge in spaghetti at state banquets in a dignified manner, and Ferdinand IV used the porcelain kilns at Capodimonte for cooking pizza so he wouldn't have to go out late at night to satisfy his cravings.

Beyond pizza and pasta, a number of other specialties take cheap, abundant ingredients and produce solid and dazzlingly delicious nourishment: the local version of Italian bean stew, *pasta e fagioli,* can suffice for a meal. The profusion of fried foods, and small take-out eateries—the *friggitorie*—serving only those items, grew out of the resilience of the many poor Neapolitans, who couldn't afford cooking facilities, if they had a home at all, and so took whatever items they had down to the local fryer and then either brought them home to eat or ate them standing up. There are more variations on fried dough than you may ever have time to try, but no one should miss the famous pea-studded rice croquettes bound with béchamel, best enjoyed at the pizzeria Da Matteo. *Arancini,* large rice croquettes with tomato and meat sauce and cheese, make a great snack, and fried zucchini flowers are a popular appetizer at pizzerias. Neapolitan *ragù,* slowly simmered, renders humble cuts of meat (roughly hewn) into ambrosia; and simple pasta with fresh tomato sauce is always a good bet, given the quality of the tomatoes. A number of dishes bear witness to the importance of communal eating (not to mention efficiently recycled leftovers), including *sartù,* an aristocratic and suitably elaborate rice casserole and, if you're around at Easter, *casatiello,* a golden ring of tender dough filled with everything on hand. Spaghetti *alla puttanesca,* tarted up with olives and capers, is a superquick pasta dish said to have been cooked up, as its name indicates, by ladies of the night who didn't have time to slave over the stove.

In part, Neapolitan cooking derives its quality from the availability of superb local ingredients: the rich volcanic soil surrounding the city, nurtured by abundant sun and benevolent breezes, has from ancient times been famous for the quality of its produce. *Friarielli* are a local type of broccoli, almost all stems and no flower, which are blanched like collard greens and tossed on pizza or sautéed with garlic and red pepper and served, delicious and remineralizing, with grilled sausage (*salsiccia e friarielli*). True mozzarella is the property of Campania; the best is made from 100% river-buffalo milk and has a unique tang and velvety consistency. Most *latte di bufala* is mixed (legally) with cow's milk, which tends to dilute its character, but still earns it the title of mozzarella. A slightly different fresh cheese product is *fior di latte*, made entirely from cow's milk (which lightly smoked is called *provola*). But be sure to try a good *mozzarella di vera bufala* (real buffalo milk mozzarella) while in Naples—it's a revelation: the cheese must be eaten very fresh and doesn't like to travel. An absolutely simple dish, though, such as the *insalata caprese* (tomato, mozzarella, and basil salad), becomes a voluptuous Titianesque masterpiece when all the ingredients are right—typical of the best dishes of *cucina napoletana*. To top it all off, critics consider southern Italian cooking among the healthiest in the world—unlike the cholesterol-laden butters used in northern Italian cuisine, most Campanian dishes use olive oils. And don't forget that Campania is really one great wine flask. Among the region's wines, Gragnano, Falerno, and Greco di Tufo are fine whites. Ischia and Ravello also produce good white wine. Campania's best-known reds are Aglianico, Taurasi, and the red version of Falerno. The most famous wines, of course, are the Lacrima Christi ("Christ's Tears") whites—named because Christ, looking down on the beautiful Bay of Naples, supposedly wept over the sins of the people.

Passion on the High C's

Opera is an art form peculiarly suited to the Neapolitan temperament, so do try to attend a performance of, let's say, *Lucia di Lammermoor,* at the Teatro San Carlo (where it received its premiere in 1835). Some may find stylized acting and great singing a bad mixture aesthetically, some will be embarrassed by the naked emotion on display and the clichéd sentimentality or incomprehensibility of the plot, and some may ridicule the convention that permits a dying Edgardo to rise and sing a powerful aria and perhaps an encore before lying down again to die. But whatever naysayers may think, opera is the lifeblood of Neapolitans, a reflection of the drama of their existence, a sublimation of their collective mythology; their melodrama, burlesque, pantomime, circus, and celebrity concert all rolled into one. Back when the Teatro San Carlo was built (1737), Naples was the musical capital of Italy, and here many of the greatest operas of the melodious trio of Rossini (1792–1868), Bellini (1801–35), and Donizetti (1797–1848) received their loudest ovations, since they often showcased bel canto singing to bravura effect. The bel canto style—in which libretto and dramatic tension are sacrificed to virtuoso singing—produced a typically Neapolitan being, the prima donna: haughty, tempestuous, temperamental, a despot in all her glory. The greatest singers flocked to the San Carlo since they knew Neapolitans were more prepared to stomach over-the-top emotional excess (on and off the stage) than anyone else in Italy. Today opera in Naples is a medium that grows neither old nor old-fashioned. The season lasts from early December to June, and the audience's dress and jewelry on premiere nights sometimes matches the extravagant red-and-gold decor of the auditorium. Under huge clusters of candelabra, the full house resembles an overflowing basket of flowers—a sight to remember, even before the curtain has gone up.

Beyond Baroque

Naples is commonly categorized as a Baroque city, and it's true that this 17th- and 18th-century style produced defining monuments for the city, but it's a mistake to define Naples simply as Baroque. The city is so much older than that—almost as old as Rome (the city that actually gave rise to the Baroque style). In any case, the "Baroque" exuberance of Naples goes back to ancient times; the style found fertile ground here underneath the volcano. But this chapter aims to introduce the reader to other facets of the city as well, by including unjustly neglected monuments, for Naples has ancient Greek and Roman ruins, vertical heaven-seeking Medieval churches, first-rate chapels of the Renaissance, elegant 19th-century Empire and Neo-classical palaces, and important Modernist buildings from the 20th century as well, much of which tends to be obscured by all the polychrome-marble flourishes of the Baroque style. In the end, the Naples of today is the sum of all these periods—and something timeless as well.

---

downtown. At the center of it all is Naples's picturesque quarter, Spaccanapoli—the heart of the *centro storico* (historic center), called the Decumanus Inferior in Roman times. The entire quarter takes its name from its main street, a pedestrianized promenade called Spaccanapoli. Rather confusingly, this street changes its name—Via Benedetto Croce and Via San Biagio dei Librai, among others—as it runs its way through the heart of old Naples. All of these neighborhoods are marked on the Exploring Naples map.

Tying much of this geographic layout together is the "spine" of the city, Via Toledo—Naples's major north–south axis, which begins at Piazza Trieste e Trento and heads up all the way up to Capodimonte. It's basically one straight road with four different names (five if you count the official name of Via Roma, which is how the locals refer to it). Via Toledo links Piazza Trieste e Trento with Piazza Dante. Going farther north you get into Via Pessina for about 100 yards, which takes you up to the mega-junction with the Museo Archeologico Nazionale. North of that, you head up to the peak of Capodimonte by traveling along Via Santa Teresa degli Scalzi and then Corso Amedeo di Savoia. To make things a bit more confusing, parts of Via Toledo are pedestrianized—that means no buses or scooters, thankfully—from just south of Piazza Carità (where Via Toledo/Roma intersects with Via Diaz) all the way to Piazza Trieste e Trento. Currently Via Diaz is closed to through traffic, which means that southbound buses from Piazza Dante have to turn left in Piazza Carità, pass in front of the main post office, and then join the maelstrom heading downtown toward Piazza Bovio and Corso Umberto. Bear in mind that mobility is further disrupted thanks to the various work sites on the new Metropolitana extension running through the heart of the city: Piazza Municipio is boarded off, as is Piazza Bovio and Piazza Amore, but to compensate you can now take a state-of-the art subway train from the Museo Archeologico up to Piazza Vanvitelli in Vomero without passing through some of the more congested parts of the city.

As for public transportation, there are several main ways to go. Use the funiculars to get up and down the towering hills. Use the Metropolitana—the city's main (if now, in parts, somewhat rundown) subway system—to link such destinations as Piazza Garibaldi, Chiaia, Mergellina, and Pozzuoli. The subway system is now undergoing a major expansion and many more city sites are reachable by train (in our sightseeing write-ups below, you will find the most convenient train station listed, with stations set to open in 2004 and 2005 listed as "in construction"). A new metro line now allows you to whiz up and down the Vomero—Naples's largest hill—to the area around the city's famed archaeological museum. A second state-of-the-art metro line (yet to be linked to the main metro network) runs between the historic center and Vomero and will run to the airport by 2006. For outlying Pozzuoli and the Phlegrean Fields, both west of Naples, take the Cumana line at the Montesanto Metropolitana station at Piazza Montesanto. East of Naples, the aptly named Circumvesuviana skirts the volcano to Pompeii, Herculaneum, and the towns of the Sorrento Coast. Finally, from Easter time through October, you can enjoy the Metro del Mare hydrofoil service, which whisks you right along the coastline from Baia in the north down to the far Cilento Coast (south of the Amalfi Coast)—and also to popular destinations, such as Positano, found in between—connecting with buses for the best sites, including Paestum. With enough riders complaining about the plethora of tickets needed to travel through the region if using metro, boats, and buses, a single ticketing system has now been introduced for all overland public transport in the region, whatever company, called *Campania Unico* (for more information on this, *see* Transportation Around Naples & Campania *in* the Smart Travel Tips chapter).

Long considered a threatened species, the Naples pedestrian is gradually being provided with a more friendly eco-niche, although it must be said that promenading in Naples sometimes takes a little practice. In a city where a red light is often looked at as merely a suggestion, walking across a busy avenue can be like a game of chess—if you hesitate, you capitulate. Most residents just forge out into the unceasing flow of traffic, knowing cars invariably slow down to let them cross (trick for the fainthearted: look for an elderly couple—when they cross, you *know* it will be safe). Essentially, you should cross big streets one or two lanes at a time, and don't ever hesitate in the middle of a lane—keep moving so motorcycles can avoid you. In any event, once you've dealt with the hurtling traffic at Piazza Municipio, you'll be prepared for almost anything in life.

ARTECARD   Introduced in 2002, the Campania Artecard is a big boon for museum-lovers. This pass offers free or discounted admission to 33 museums and monuments over a three- or seven-consective-day period for the city or the whole region. The main attraction is that you get free admission to the first two sites you visit, then half price for the others, plus free transport in the region. The cost for the basic three-day card for Naples and the Campi Flegrei is €13 for adults over 25. A card costing €8 is for visitors ranging in age from 18 to 25 and gives them free access to all sites. A more expensive three-day card for €25 includes free entrance to any two sites anywhere in the region (including Pompeii, Herculaneum, Caserta, and Paestum—not available on the cheaper card) and half-price for the other sites, plus free transport including the special Archeobuses; this card for ages 18 to 25 costs €18 and allows free entrance to all sites. Finally, there is a seven-day card with free entrance to all sites but no free transport; this costs €28 for adults and €21 for the younger set. The ticket includes discounts to the city's biggest museums as well as lesser known options, such as the Capella Sansevero, the Solfatara, and Underwater Baia. Special buses have been organised for cardholders to make access to the sites easier: the Archeobus Flegreo running Friday through Sunday links all the sites in the Campi Flegrei (which count as just one entrance); the Archeobus Vesuviano running Friday through Sunday links all the sites near Vesuvius; and special shuttle buses run every day from Salerno to Paestum, Velia, Padula, and Pertosa. As sites and discounts are frequently updated, check www.campaniartecard.it for the latest information. The card is available at all the participating museums, as well as at the airport and the station.

Napoli Nobilissima: The Monumental City Center

Naples's setting on what is possibly the most beautiful bay in the world has long been a boon for its inhabitants—the expansive harbor has always brought great mercantile wealth to the city—and, intermittently, a curse. Throughout history, a who's who of Greek, Roman, Norman, Spanish, and French despots has quarreled over this gateway to Campania. Each set of conquerors recognized that the area around the city harbor—today occupied by the Molo Beverello hydrofoil terminal and the 1928 Stazione Marittima—functioned as a veritable welcome mat to the metropolis and consequently should be a fitting showcase of regal and royal authority. This had become imperative because of explosive population growth, which, by the mid-16th century, had made Naples the second-largest city in Europe, after Paris. With the mass migration of the rural population to the city, Naples had grown into a capricious, unplanned, disorderly, and untrammeled capital. Thus, the central aim of the ruling dynasties became the creation of a *Napoli nobilissima*— a "most noble" Naples.

The monuments they created remain prominent features of the city center: one of the most magnificent opera houses in Europe, a palace that rivals Versailles, an impregnable *castello* (castle), a majestic church modeled on Rome's Pantheon, and a 19th-century shopping galleria are landmarks that characterized the shifts among the ruling powers, from the French Angevins to the Spanish Habsburgs and Bourbons and, later, the postunification rise of the bourgeoisie and the regime of Mussolini. This historic sector is the much-put-upon Cinderella—as Naples is seen by many of her fans—but dressed up in her *principessa* finery, all ready to wow the spectators at the royal ball. In contrast to the intense intimacy of the Spacca, the official center of Naples unrolls its majesty with great pomp along its spacious avenues and monumental piazzas.

Numbers in the text correspond to numbers in the margin and on the Naples and From La Sanità to Capodimonte maps.

a good walk

In a day filled with monarchist grandeur, it may be fitting to start out with breakfast at **Caffè Gambrinus,** on Piazza Trieste e Trento, the very center of Naples and set between Piazza del Plebiscito and Piazza Municipio. Gilded and mirrored, its Liberty-style, delicately painted tearooms newly renovated, this 19th-century caffè was once the rendezvous for Italian dukes, prime ministers, and writers like Oscar Wilde, Guy de Maupassant, and Gabriele d'Annunzio (although, truth to tell, you'll find more local professionals and politicians than authors here today). Treat yourself to a cappuccino and a pastry as rich and velvety as the surroundings, then head directly outside the door to the grand Piazza del Plebiscito. Neapolitans are too often caught up in the present to appreciate their past, and one sad example of this was the decades-long use of this urban showpiece as a parking lot. Now it makes an imposing setting for **San Francesco di Paola ❶ ▶**, the domed 19th-century church built by Ferdinand I, and its grand Doric hemicycle. Inside, the Roman-style "temple" is Naples at its most Neoclassic—imperial, aloof, funereal, and Olympian. From here head directly across the piazza to the main entrance of Naples's Royal Palace. Note the niches on its facade, filled in 1888 on order of King Umberto I of Italy with a series of rather ungainly statues of the kings of Naples, including, on the far right, his own static and unexpressive father, Victor Emanuel II, who had seized the palace (and the kingdom) from the Bourbons. Of all these figures, Joachim Murat comes out looking the most dignified, even if, as Vittorio Gleisejes writes, he appears "a bit too . . . virile in his revealing uniform."

At the **Palazzo Reale ❷** (use the entrance from Piazza Trieste e Trento), walk up the grand staircase of its Scalone d'Onore and tour the spectacular 18th- and 19th-century salons of the Museo dell'Appartmento Reale. You can't enter the hallway that was constructed by the Bour-

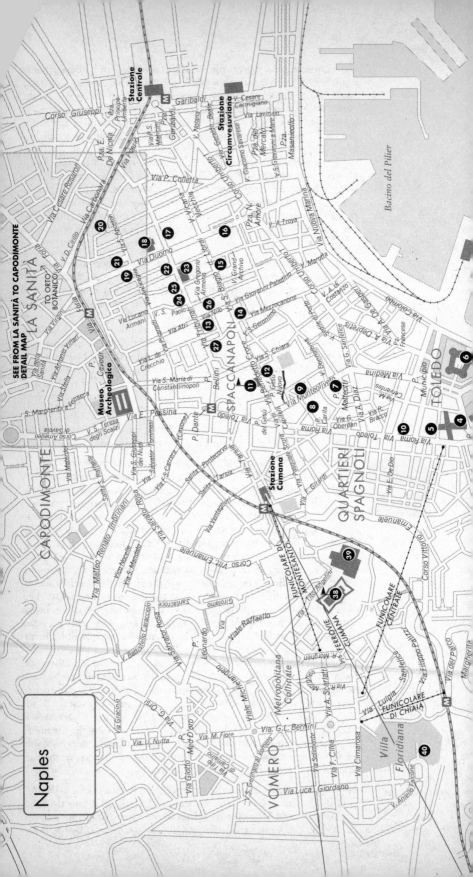

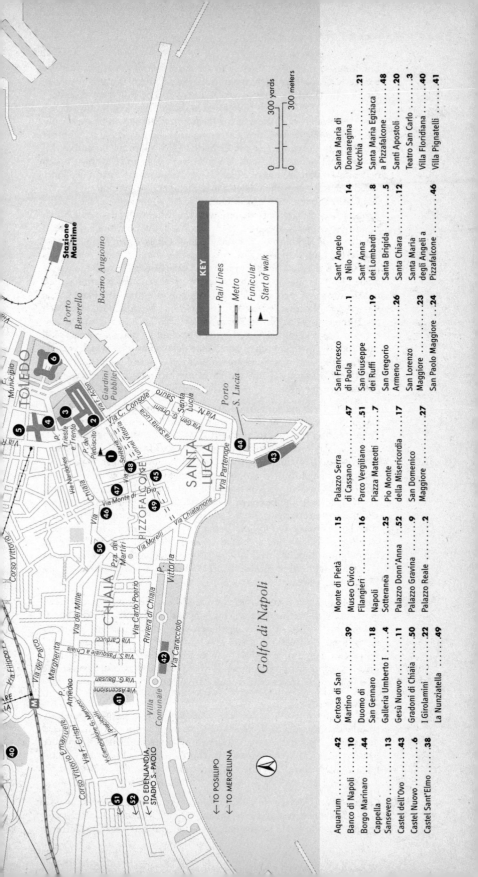

bon kings to take them directly to the royal box of the adjacent **Teatro San Carlo** ❸, so head back down to the piazza and make a right turn to the Piazza Trieste e Trento, where opera lovers will want to take a guided tour of the famous red-and-gold theater (weekends only; if a rehearsal is going on, porters at the theater may allow you to see the auditorium in return for a tip). Directly across the way is the fastidiously elegant vastness of the **Galleria Umberto I** ❹. Walk to the far end of this ancestor of the shopping mall to Via Santa Brigida and tour the Church of **Santa Brigida** ❺, burial place of renowned artist Luca Giordano. Head back through the Galleria and then gently downhill on the Via San Carlo and the Via Vittorio Emanuele III; you'll come to the usually light-drenched Piazza Municipio, with the delightfully discreet Church of San Giacomo ai Spagnoli. It is camouflaged within the bay side of the Banco di Napoli building and a pile of Greek ruins, forming an island in the middle of a daunting expanse of vehicular chaos. Above this piazza rises the civilized fortress of the **Castel Nuovo** ❻, with the bay as a backdrop. From the outside, study its great sculpted triumphal arch of Alfonso of Aragon; inside, explore the museum and Hall of the Barons. Head across Piazza Municipio to Via Medina until you reach the 20th-century complex at **Piazza Matteotti** ❼. Then trip across the centuries by continuing up Via Monteoliveto and its piazza, where you'll find both the quiet church of **Sant' Anna dei Lombardi** ❽, which is a fascinating and very digestible museum of Renaissance sculpture (with a great frescoed sacristy), and the Tuscan-influenced rusticated facade of **Palazzo Gravina** ❾.

Make a left leaving Sant'Anna dei Lombardi and head over to Piazza Carità for ice cream at La Scimmia and the Broadway of Naples, Via Toledo (often referred to as Via Roma). On the opposite side of the wide thoroughfare are some of Naples's most fascinating (and sometimes dangerous) *quartieri,* including the famous Spanish Quarter, or Quartieri Spagnoli. If you don't opt to make this detour, walk the 15 or so blocks back down Via Toledo to the Piazza Trieste e Trento; along the way, take in the **Banco di Napoli** ❿, do some window-shopping, and pick up a hot, flaky *sfogliatella* pastry at Pinturchio, or some cool chocolates at Gay-Odin. Back around Piazza Trieste e Trento make a stop for a leisurely lunch: Ciro a Santa Brigida and Amici Miei are in the neighborhood, as well as a number of places on nearby Via Santa Lucia, while Pizzeria Brandi is just up Via Chiaia. From here on you can take things easy.

TIMING Not including time spent in the enormous Palazzo Reale and Castel Nuovo museums, walking this route will take approximately three leisurely hours. There's no chance of escaping the crowds—this is the very heart of metropolitan Naples, but it's always best to get up early and get a head start—especially as this allows you to see the spectacular Piazza del Plebiscito *senza gente* (without people). With no backpacks or Ray-Bans to be seen, the square looks little changed from the early 19th century.

Sights to See

❿ **Banco di Napoli** (Bank of Naples). The oldest credit institution in Italy (founded as the *Monte di Pietà* in 1539), this bank is currently housed in an imposing marble swath designed by Marcello Piancentini, leader of the Historical Monumentalism school of early 20th-century architecture and "official" architect of the Fascist regime. ⊠ *Via Toledo 178, Toledo* Ⓜ *Metro: Montesanto (in construction: Toledo).*

★ ❻ **Castel Nuovo** (New Castle). Brooding over the modern traffic that swirls around it, this castle is one of the most famous landmarks of the city and is often referred to by Neapolitans as the Maschio Angioino (Angevin

Keep, in reference to its Angevin builders). Today it's the seat of the city government, with its courtyard filling up in June with couples registering their wedding vows, and the moat outside is the site of a morning flower market. The castle's shadows, however, hide some legend-haunted events that played out within the dark, *piperno*-stone walls, along with—rumor once had it—King Ferrante's crocodile, which was said to dispatch prisoners. The founder of the Angevin dynasty, Charles I d'Anjou, built this fortress, known from its beginning, in 1279, as the "new castle" (to differentiate it from the Castel dell'Ovo and the Castel Capuano). Under his successor, Robert the Wise, it became a center of culture, with the castle library attracting such luminaries as Petrarch and Boccaccio. Alfonso d'Aragona took up residence here when he conquered Naples in 1443 and marked his rule with a fairly complete rebuilding, including the five defensive towers now visible and, especially, the impressive marble **Arco di Trionfo** at the entrance. This highly important work of the first Renaissance (1443–68) consciously takes its inspiration from ancient Roman triumphal arches, recombining the elements, however, in a completely innovative composition of two superimposed arches so as to fit the tall, narrow space. Many noted sculptors worked on the arch. The most celebrated was Francesco Laurana, who carved the bas-relief above the lower arch, which shows, appropriately, the triumphal entrance of Alfonso into Naples on February 26, 1443. This grand depiction effectively overrides any memory of Alfonso's earlier foray through the city's underground sewer system (in the middle of the night of June 12, 1442, he emerged from underground into the home of a Neapolitan matron by the name of La Ceccarella, who, betraying her rightful king, guided the regal-looking intruder and his dashing band of armed men to the gates of the city, which they threw open to allow their troops to advance).

To the left inside the Arco di Trionfo is the ticket office. Across the imposing courtyard is the Palatine Chapel, one of the few remaining structures of the Angevin Palace, its austere facade graced by a portal with delicate reliefs and a Madonna by Francesco Laurana (1474). Decorated inside by Giotto and friends in the 14th century, the frescoes are now reduced to a few fragments, none of which can be attributed to the master. The chapel now houses paintings from the 14th through the early 16th centuries and graceful sculptures by Laurana and Domenico Gagini. Next to the chapel in the left corner is the **Sala dell'Armeria,** the Armory, where part of the flooring has been glassed over to reveal the remains of a Roman villa and a medieval necropolis. Above the Armeria, with access up a long ramp of steps, is the current Naples city council chamber, the **Sala dei Baroni,** or Hall of the Barons, built for Alfonso by the Majorcan architect Guglielmo Sagrera in 1446–54. Its simple volume is topped with a late-Gothic Moorish-inspired octagonal star vault whose ribs, in gray *piperno,* provide a harmonious accent to the yellow-tufa walls. The hall gets its name from a famous party held here in 1486, when Ferdinand I of Aragon invited a number of troublesome, powerful lords to dinner and then had them arrested and executed. For souvenirs of the event, he had several of the victims embalmed; their bodies were brought out from time to time to entertain more fortunate guests, who still must have been a bit nervous. The dungeons where the unlucky lords were to await death are below the Palatine Chapel (you would think that their moans would have disturbed any mass being held) and can be viewed today.

The rest of the public space of the castle houses the **Museo Civico,** which holds an interesting, low-key collection of painting and sculpture, especially strong in 19th-century landscapes with views of a lost or transformed Naples, but also with some nice 17th-century paintings and the bronze doors that Ferrante commissioned from William the Monk in 1475 to record his victory over John d'Anjou. ⊠ *Piazza Municipio, Toledo* ☎ *081/7952003* ▣ *€5* ⊘ *Mon.–Sat. 9–7, Sun. 9–1 (courtyard only)* Ⓜ *Metro: Montesanto (in construction: Piazza Municipio).*

❹ **Galleria Umberto I.** In 1885, in reaction to the devastating cholera epidemic of the previous year, authorities hastily implemented a massive urban renewal plan whose "clean-up" of Naples entailed the destruction of slum areas between Spaccanapoli and the Palazzo Reale. With facades on Via Toledo—the most animated street in Naples at the time— and across from the Teatro San Carlo, this galleria, built in 1887–90 according to a design by Emanuele Rocca, had a prestigious and important location from the start. As with its larger predecessor, the Galleria Vittorio Emanuele II in Milan, the Galleria Umberto Primo exalts the taste of the postunification commercial elite in a virtuoso display of late-19th-century technology clothed in traditional style. Here are the iron-ribbed glass barrel vault and 188-ft-high dome by Paolo Boubée, which represented the latest advance in modern form yet is layered over with the reassuring architectural ornament of the 14th century (another era when the bourgeoisie triumphed in Italy). The ground floor was designed to offer weatherproof shopping for the new-rich of the day; professional studios, fashion ateliers, and newspaper offices occupied the three upper stories. A small underground theater, the *Salone Margherita,* was constructed near the Via Toledo entrance for chamber music concerts, but within a few months of opening it evolved into a legendary nightclub and a center of Naples's turn-of-the-20th-century nightlife.

As the favored hangout for American soldiers (and their Neapolitan fans), the gallery throbbed with life during the American liberation of Italy in 1943–44. The locals used to come here for a leisurely Campari; today they occasionally visit for a quick espresso, since despite pricey designer outlets the grand gallery has a somewhat forlorn air today and at night seems unprepossessing. Still, it makes a soothing passageway by virtue of its sumptuous marble inlay, while light streaming through one of the upper-level loggias into the magnificent vastness of the arcade makes for a great scene. At Christmastime a huge crèche is set up, and the space becomes quite festive. ⊠ *Entrances on Via San Carlo, Via Toledo, Via Santa Brigida, Via Verdi, Toledo* Ⓜ *Metro: Montesanto (in construction: Piazza Municipio).*

❾ **Palazzo Gravina.** A dignified Renaissance palace in the Tuscan style with a vigorous *bugnato* (diamond-point) facade, the palazzo was begun in 1513 for Ferdinando Orsini, duke of Gravina, by Gabriele d'Angelo, a student of Alberti and Brunelleschi. The monumental doorway was added by Mario Giuffredo in a restoration of 1762–72, and an extra story was added in 1839, which is clearly visible from the beautiful courtyard. Largely burned down in 1848 by Swiss Guards trying to flush out a group of armed patriots, it now houses the modern School of Architecture, so feel free to wander around to observe how, typically in Naples, the lack of space forced overlapping styles to coexist. ⊠ *Via Monteoliveto 3, Monteoliveto* Ⓜ *Metro: Montesanto (in construction: Toledo).*

❷ **Palazzo Reale.** One of the showplaces of Naples, the Palazzo Reale, or FodorśChoice Royal Palace, was meant to be the apotheosis of Bourbon power in the ★ city. Renovated and redecorated by successive rulers in a style that can only be called overblown imperial, once lorded over by a dim-witted king who liked to shoot his hunting guns at the birds in his tapestries, and filled with salons designed in the most deliciously lavish 18th-century Neapolitan taste, it remains a palatial pile. The Spanish viceroys commissioned it in 1600, ordering Swiss architect Domenico Fontana to build a suitable new residence for Philip III, should he chance to visit Naples (which he didn't); the immense complex was not completed until 1843 (by Gaetano Genovese). The palace saw its greatest moment of splendor in the 18th century, when Charles III of Bourbon became the first permanent resident; during that century Luigi Vanvitelli filled in half the arcades in the lower register of the facade to strengthen it, and Ferdinando Fuga created the State Wing after the accession of Ferdinand IV in 1759. Today this wing comprises the Museo dell'Appartamento Storico, or **Royal Apartments,** where visitors can get a taste of Bourbon glory.

To view these 30 rooms on the first floor, enter the courtyard and ascend the monumental Scalone d'Onore on the left (the vaulted chambers housing the ticket booth are near the Piazza Plebiscito entrance), keeping to the left side of the stairway. Montesquieu, the French 18th-century writer, considered this to be the finest staircase in Europe, and it does set a tone for the glitter and grandeur to come. The first doors on the right open into the **Court Theater,** built by Ferdinando Fuga for Charles III, who in 1763 had created an opera company for private performances of comic opera. The theater was inaugurated in 1768 in honor of the royal wedding between Ferdinand I and Maria Carolina of Habsburg with *Peleo e Teti,* by Giovanni Paisiello, but soon afterward fell into disuse. Damaged by World War II bombing, it was restored in 1950; note the resplendent royal box, which abandons the lure of monumentality for intimate luxury. Following are the suite of rooms around the courtyard that constitute the royal apartments. Through a series of antechambers, you eventually reach Room VI, the **Throne Room,** with wine-red striped-silk walls and gilded stuccos representing the 12 provinces of the Kingdom of the Two Sicilies; the ponderous Empire-style throne in fact dates from after 1850. Giuseppe Bonito painted the two portraits of the ambassadors from Turkey and Tripoli in 1741; the entourage from Tripoli (to the right of the throne) looks like they'd be much more fun, but of course they were still pirates.

The decoration picks up in the **Room of the Ambassadors** (Room VIII), where a pair of choice 18th-century Gobelin tapestries grace the light-green walls together with a lovely Annunciation by Artemisia Gentileschi. The ceiling painting honoring Spanish military victories is by local artist Belisario Corenzio and his school (1610–20). Room IX, with pale gold walls and a simple white vault, was the bedroom of Charles's queen, Maria Amalia of Saxony, and hides a small, brilliantly gold private oratory in the corner, with beautiful paintings by Francesco Liani of Parma (1760). Above the exit door is a Madonna and Child attributed to the charming Spanish mannerist Ruviales. This door takes you a bit toward the courtyard to rejoin the inner rooms along the third side.

The **Great Captain's Room** (Room XI), small and square, has wonderful ceiling frescoes by Battistello Caracciolo (1610–16)—all velvet, fire, and smoke, they reveal the influence of the visit by Caravaggio to Naples—a jolly series by Federico Zuccari depicting 12 proverbs on small wood panels, along with, last but not least, a Titian portrait (circa 1543) of Pier Luigi Farnese. Room XII, the Flemish Hall, has a rather brash 19th-century gilded ceiling with 12 paintings representing the coats-of-arms of the kingdom's provinces and a large neo-Gothic centerpiece depicting the 12th-century Tancred and Constance. At eye level is a curious 18th-century "musical" clock by Charles Clay and a spectacularly overdone enamel and gilt-bronze birdcage on a flower stand, given by Czar Nicholas I to Ferdinand when he visited in 1846; the table flaunts views of the czar's various palaces. As for paintings, there's a simpatico portrait of a flutist by Alexis Grimou and a wonderfully hard-edged and cynical depiction of two tax collectors by van Roymerswaele (1538).

Room XIII was **Joachim Murat's writing room** when he was king of Naples; he brought with him from France some regal furniture by the great French *ébeniste* (cabinetmaker) Weisweiller, originally commissioned by Marie Antoinette and completed through commissions of his own (including the desk and two dignified clocks) in 1812. The next few rooms combine ponderous 19th-century furnishings and rather better Baroque paintings: Room XVII, in particular, has a good selection of paintings by followers of Caravaggio; Room XVIII has an intensely colored Guercino depiction of the biblical Joseph dreaming; and Room XIX is full of still lifes from the important Neapolitan school. The huge Room XXII, painted in green and gold with kitschy faux tapestries, is known as the **Hercules Hall,** for in a moment of glory it once housed the *Hercules Farnese.* The authentic tapestries are from the Royal Factory of Naples (1783–89), but the things to look at here are the porcelain creations from Sèvres, including the Atlas with his starry globe and the huge green chrome vase (1812), painted by Louis Béranger.

The **Palatine Chapel,** redone by Gaetano Genovese in the 1830s, is, as chapels go, a disappointing affair, having been gussied up with an excess of gold, but it has a stunning Technicolor intarsia altar from the previous chapel (Dionisio Lazzari, 1678). Note the false-perspective panels, which almost propel the altar into the stratosphere of bad taste. Also here on a long-term loan is the famous *Presepio* (Nativity) scene of the Banco di Napoli—it may lack the spectacular setting of the *Presepio Cuciniello* in the Museo di San Martino but has even better sculpture, with pieces by important sculptors such as Giuseppe Sammartino (the shepherdess at the table in the tavern scene on the right), Francesco and Antonio Viva, Francesco Celebrano, and others. There are some pleasant 19th-century landscapes in the next few rooms, as well as Queen Maria Carolina's Ferris wheel–like reading lectern (which enabled her to do a 19th-century reader's version of channel surfing). Speaking of reading, another wing of the complex holds the **Biblioteca Nazionale Vittorio Emanuele III,** the largest library in southern Italy and one of the most important in the country. Begun, as with so many other Bourbon collections, with Farnese bits and pieces, it was enriched with the priceless papyri from Herculaneum found in 1752 and opened to the public in 1804. You can view these and a splendid selection of manuscripts and rare editions in the elegant rooms open to visitors. To use the library for scholarly research, one needs to apply for a card. The library also has a lovely garden, which looks out on the Castel Nuovo. ⊠ *Piazza del Plebiscito, Toledo* ☎ *081/5808111* ☞ *€4* ☉ *Sun.–Tues. and Thurs.–Sat. 9–8* Ⓜ *Metro: Montesanto (in construction: Piazza Municipio).*

> **need a break?** Rub shoulders with politicians at classy **Gambrinus** (⊠ Via Chiaia 1, Piazza Trieste e Trento ☎ 081/417582), as you sip tea in its neoclassically grand rooms or people-watch from the sidewalk tables. Alternatively, cool down with a gelato at **Gelateria della Scimmia** (⊠ Piazza Trieste e Trento 54, Piazza Trieste e Trento ☎ 081/410322)

❼ **Piazza Matteotti.** In 1925 Mussolini issued a famous (now notorious) call for "good Italian architecture," hoping to revive its glories and underline the power of the modern Italian state. He was fortunate in having a flood of talented architects answer the call, but the troublesome political context of the resulting constructions has tended to allow a number of these magnificent structures to fall into oblivion. The area between Piazza Carità and Piazza Municipio in Naples represents one of the most significant and successful urban transformations of this period, and the pride of this vast program is the Piazza Matteotti, object of a 1927 competition.

The piazza, which combines a number of important civic buildings in a modern forum, is dominated by the strong parabolic curve of the post office, or **Palazzo delle Poste e Telegrafi,** a surprisingly contemporary building by Bolognese architect Giuseppe Vaccaro. The post office combines elements of the Rationalist Functional style—in which the plan and decoration of the building clearly articulate its functions—with subtle historical references. The lower band of dark gray diorite not only alludes to the gray *piperno* of local Renaissance construction, it also delineates the large public spaces on the ground floor. Inside, the building refreshingly retains its original interior furnishings, and the streamlined decoration of the public rooms buffers the boredom of waiting in endless lines with *Metropolis*-style elegance.

The other jewel of the piazza is the **Palazzo della Provincia,** to the left of the post office, by the young Neapolitan engineer Marcello Canino. This is a good example (along with the Banco di Roma) of the other predominant architectural current in the fascist era: Historical Monumentalism, a style that sought to translate ancient forms (arches, colonnades, basilical structures, and so forth) into a modern idiom. The Rational Functionalist school was generally judged too international and rootless a style for an Italy intent on reviving its past glory. Although the **Questura** looks every bit the totalitarian police station that it once was, with a stubbornly horizontal and forbiddingly spartan mass of travertine seeming to announce "Abandon hope, all ye who enter here," it should be said in its defense that at least its form expresses function. ✉ *Intersection of Via Monteoliveto, Via A. Diaz, and Via Battisti., Toledo* Ⓜ *Metro: Montesanto (in construction: Toledo).*

★ ❶ **San Francesco di Paola.** Modeled after Rome's Pantheon, this circular basilica is the centerpiece of the Piazza del Plebiscito and remains one of the most frigidly voluptuous examples of the Stil Empire, or Neoclassic style, in Italy. Commissioned by Ferdinand I in 1817 to fulfill a vow he had made in order to enlist divine aid in being reinstated to the throne of the Kingdom of the Two Sicilies, it rose at one end of the vast parade ground built several years earlier by Joachim Murat. It managed to transform Murat's inconveniently grandiose colonnade—whose architect was clearly inspired by the colonnades of St. Peter's in Rome—into a setting for restored Bourbon glory. The church also usefully fulfilled a prophecy by the 15th-century saint Ferrante d'Aragona, for whom it is named, that one day a large church and square would occupy the crowded site. Pietro Bianchi from Lugano in Switzerland won a competition and built a slightly smaller version of the Pantheon, with a beautiful coffered dome and a splendid set of 34 Corinthian columns in gray Mondragon marble; but the overall lack of color (so different from the warm interior of the Pantheon) combined with the severe geometrical forms produces an almost defiantly cold space. To some, this only proves the ancients did sometimes know their own architecture better. Art historians find the spectacle of the church to be the ultimate in Neoclassic *grandezza*; others think this Roman temple is only fitting to honor Jove, not Christ. In any event, the main altar, done in gold, lapis lazuli, and other precious stones by Anselmo Caggiano (1641), was taken from the destroyed Church of the Santi Apostoli and provides some relief from the oppressive perfection of the setting. ✉ *Piazza del Plebiscito, Toledo* ☎ *081/7645133* ◷ *Mon.–Sat. 8–1 and 3:30–5:30, Sun. 8–noon* Ⓜ *Metro: Montesanto (in construction: Piazza Municipio).*

❺ Santa Brigida. The Lucchesi fathers built this church around 1640 in honor of the Swedish queen and saint who visited her fellow queen, Naples's unsaintly Giovanna I, in 1372 and became one of the first persons to go on record as denouncing the loose morals and irrepressible sensuality of the Neapolitans. The height of the church's dome was limited to prevent its interfering with cannon fire from nearby Castel Nuovo, but Luca Giordano, the pioneer painter of the trompe l'oeil Baroque dome, effectively opened it up with a spacious sky serving as the setting for an *Apotheosis of Saint Bridget* (1678), painted (and now in need of restoration) in exchange for his tomb space, marked by a pavement inscription in the left transept. ✉ *Via Santa Brigida 72, Toledo* ☎ *081/5523793* ☯ *Daily 7:30–12:30 and 5:30–7* Ⓜ *Metro: Montesanto (in constuction: Piazza Municipio).*

❽ Sant' Anna dei Lombardi. Long favored by the Aragonese kings, this church, simple and rather anonymous from the outside, houses some of the most important ensembles of Renaissance sculpture in southern Italy. Begun with the adjacent convent of the Olivetani and its four cloisters in 1411, it was given a Baroque makeover in the mid-17th century by Gennaro Sacco, although this is no longer so visible, as the bombs of 1943 rather radically altered the decoration and led to a modern restoration favoring the original *quattrocento* (15th-century) lines. The wonderful coffered wooden ceiling, currently under restoration, will add a bit of pomp. Inside the porch is the tomb of Domenico Fontana, one of the major architects of the late 16th century, who died in Naples after beginning the Palazzo Reale. Once inside the entrance door, you enter a simple single-nave church with side chapels. Turn around and you will see, on either side of the entrance wall, two fine Renaissance tombs. The one on the left as you face the door belongs to the Ligorio family (whose descendant Pirro designed the Villa d'Este in Tivoli) and is a work by Giovanni da Nola (1524); the tomb on the right is a masterpiece by Giuseppe Santacroce (1532) done for the del Pozzo family. To the left of the Ligorio Altar (the corner chapel on the immediate right as you face the altar) is the Mastrogiudice Chapel, whose altar contains precious reliefs of the *Annunciation* and *Scenes from the Life of Jesus* (1489) by Benedetto da Maiano, a great name in Tuscan sculpture. On the other side of the entrance is the Piccolomini Chapel, with a Crucifixion by Giulio Mazzoni (circa 1550), a refined marble altar (circa 1475), a funerary monument to Maria d'Aragona by another prominent Florentine sculptor, Antonello Rossellino (circa 1475), and on the right, a rather sweet fresco of the Annunciation by an anonymous follower of Piero della Francesca.

The true surprises of the church, however, are off to the right of the altar, in the presbytery and adjoining rooms. The chapel just to the right of the main altar, belonging to the Orefice family, is richly decorated in pre-Baroque (1596–98) polychrome marbles and frescoes by Luis Rodriguez; from here you continue on through the Oratory of the Holy Sepulchre, with the tomb of Antonio D'Alessandro and his wife, to reach the church's showpiece: a potently realistic life-size group of eight terra-cotta figures by Guido Mazzoni (1492), which make up a Pietà; the faces are said to be modeled from people at the Aragonese court. Toward the rear of the church is Cappella dell'Assunta, with a fun painting in its corner of a monk by Michelangelo's student Giorgio Vasari, and the lovely Sacrestia Vecchia (Old Sacristy), adorned with one of the most successful decorative ensembles Vasari ever painted (1544) and breathtaking wood-inlay stalls by Fra' Giovanni da Verona and assistants (1506–10) with views of famous buildings (ask the attendant for access to the Old Sacristy). ✉ *Piazza Monteoliveto 15, entrance through a black gate to the right*

of church, Toledo ⊙ *Tues.–Thurs. and Sat. 8:30–12*
tesanto (in constuction: Toledo).

❸ Teatro San Carlo. La Scala in Milan is the famous one, but .
Fodor'sChoice more beautiful, and Naples is, after all, the most operatic of citi.
★ in eight months and 10 days in 1737 by Angelo Carasale for Cha.
III of Bourbon—and opened on the king's saint's name day—it burned
down in 1816 and was rebuilt, with its facade of five rustic arches in
gray piperno surmounted by an elegant loggia, in a mere nine months.
This time the architect was Antonio Niccolini, working under the impetus of Domenico Barbaja, the Milanese director appointed by Joachim
Murat in 1810. Barbaja, San Carlo's most legendary director, started
out as a waiter in a tavern and enriched himself through a talent for
gambling. Obviously wanting to remain part of the new regime, he bet
the king that he could have the theater open within nine months. More
important, he also managed in the same year to convince Gioacchino
Rossini to come to Naples as conductor and house composer; Stendhal
hailed Ferdinand's wise retaining of Barbaja and his prompt sponsor-
ship of the theater as a "coup d'état" for the deep and immediate bond
it created between the ruler and his opera-loving populace. This was further cemented by the many operas composed for the house, including
Donizetti's *Lucia di Lammermoor* and Rossini's *La Donna del Lago*.

In the theater, nearly 200 boxes are arranged on six levels, and the huge
stage (12,000 square ft; 3,600 meters) permits productions with horses,
camels, and elephants and even boasts a removable backdrop that can
lift to reveal the Palazzo Reale Gardens. Above the rich red-and-gold
auditorium is a breathy ceiling fresco, by Giuseppe Camarano, suitably
representing Apollo presenting poets to Athena. At many performances,
however, all eyes strayed to the sumptuous royal box, which seats 15
and is topped by a gigantic gilded crown. Check the local press (*Il Mattino, La Repubblica, Corriere della Sera*) or the *Qui Napoli* for information on performances, or pick up a schedule at the ticket office and
get ready for a great evening of opera. Performance standards are among
the highest in Europe at the San Carlo—even the great Enrico Caruso
was hissed here—although some locals really come to study the fashion show in the auditorium, not the Verdi on stage. If you can't catch
a performance, try to take the 30-minute guided tour (€2.58) to see the
splendid theater—as Stendhal wrote: "The first impression one gets is
of being suddenly transported to the palace of an oriental emperor. There
is nothing in Europe to compare with it, or even give the faintest idea
of what it is like." ⊠ *Via San Carlo 101–103, Toledo* ☎ *081/7972331;
ticket office, 081/7972412* 🖷 *081/400902* ⊕ *www.teatrosancarlo.it*
⊙ *Guided tours weekends 2–3:30* Ⓜ *Metro: Montesanto (in construction: Piazza Municipio).*

Spaccanapoli: The Heart & Soul of Naples

If your plan for Naples is just to do the sights, you'll see the city, but you'll
Fodor'sChoice miss its essence. To do that, you need to discover Spaccanapoli, the un-
★ forgettable neighborhood that is the heart of old Naples. A buzzing hive
of daily chaos in a constantly re-created grid of ancient patterns, this densely
populated neighborhood presents the city's most familiar face. This is
the Naples of peeling facades spackled with enough waving laundry to
suggest a parade; of arguments in the streets (or are they gossiping? it's
sometimes hard to tell) swelling to operatic proportions, often with on-
lookers adding their comments to supplement the lyrical principals; of
small alleyways fragrant with freshly laid flowers at the many shrines to
the Blessed Virgin. Here, where the cheapest pizzerias in town feed the

locals like kings, the full raucous street carnival of Neapolitan popular culture is punctuated with improbable oases of spiritual calm. All the contradictions of Naples—splendor and squalor, palace and slum, triumph and tragedy—meet here and sing a full-throated chorale. The amazing thing is that it seems, somehow, more real in its conscious theatricality. And, paradoxically, it also seems impossible to remain stressed out in the midst of all this ricocheting vitality.

Spaccanapoli (literally, "Split-Naples") is actually the name of the ruler-straight street that divides the neighborhood in half—a fantastic 5-km-long (3-mi-long) pedestrian ribbon that was originally the ancient Roman Decumanus Maximus, or main thoroughfare. Today the street changes names six times along its route, with Via Benedetto Croce and Via S. Biagio dei Librai among the most prominently used. This breathtaking roadway-cum-piazza is bordered by a palisade of 19th-century tenements (once the highest in Europe, they soared up to eight floors because of the population density and their tufa-rock construction), faded palazzi, and Baroque churches. But the Spacca is not simply picturesque. It also contains some of Naples's most important sights, including a striking conglomeration of churches—Lombard, Gothic, Renaissance, Baroque, Rococo, and Neoclassical. Here are the majolica-adorned cloister of Santa Chiara; the sumptuous Church of the Gesù Nuovo; two opera-set piazzas; the city duomo (where the Festa di San Gennaro is celebrated every September); the Cappella Sansevero; the greatest painting in Naples—Caravaggio's *Seven Acts of Mercy* altarpiece—on view at the Church of Pio Monte; and Via Gregorio Armeno, where shops devoted to *Presepe* nativity scene (crèche) wares make every day a rehearsal for Christmas. And even though this was the medieval center of the city, night owls will find that many of Naples's most cutting-edge clubs and bars are hidden among its nooks and alleys. This area is best explored by starting out at its heart, the Piazza Gesù Nuovo (approachable from all directions but easily reachable by cutting over about eight blocks east from the main avenue of Via Toledo where intersected by Via di Capitelli), then heading east along the Spacca street to the Duomo, then back along Via dei Tribunali. The Via dei Tribunali is often referred to as part of the city's Decumano Maggiore, but as it is only one block over from the Spacca, the entire region is also commonly grouped under the name Spaccanapoli. Wherever you head, you'll find half of Naples's populace crowded at your elbow, all pursuing life *con gusto*. The beautiful thing is that despite the Punch-and-Judy overtones, almost everyone turns out to be a sweetheart. If the Spacca is the heart of Naples, it pumps for all.

a good walk

Begin at Piazza Gesù Nuovo with a visit to the Church of **Gesù Nuovo** ⑪ ► (1584) to give a shot of Jesuit pomp to your morning cappuccino. As you exit, admire the piazza's extravagant carved-stone spire honoring the Virgin Mary, the Guglia dell'Immacolata, whose saints and cherubs, sculpted by Francesco Pagano and Matteo Bottigliero after a design by Giuseppe Genuino (1743), are considered a high point of 18th-century Neapolitan sculpture. Across the square, immerse yourself in the 14th century at **Santa Chiara** ⑫, a broodingly severe Gothic monument built by Robert of Anjou. In noisy Spaccanapoli, peace breaks out in the cloisters of the district, none more beautiful than the Chiostro delle Clarisse, transformed in 1742 into a Rococo-era showpiece by a colorful majolica-tile overlay on its columns and benches. In the grounds of the convent, visit the Roman baths and gymnasium to really see how the city was built up, layers and civilizations crammed on top of each other. At this point the piazza debouches into the pedestrian roadway nicknamed the Spaccanapoli. Past a block full of moldering palazzi—

note Palazzo Filmarino at the corner of Via S. Sebastiano, the home of Benedetto Croce, the noted aesthete and philosopher, and now the site of his library—is the Piazza San Domenico Maggiore, where the Guglia di San Domenico (1737) and the apse of San Domenico Maggiore create one of Naples's most charming urban set pieces. Residents of the district move into this piazza during spring and summer months, making it a "living room"—their furniture the umbrella-topped tables of Scaturchio, Naples's celebrated *gelateria* (ice cream parlor). After enjoying a time-out here, head up the right-hand side of the piazza swinging first right to Via Francesco de Sanctis and the **Cappella Sansevero** ⑬ (1590), the tomb-chapel of the Sangro di San Severo family, which features three showstopping 18th-century sculptures, including Giuseppe Sammartino's *Veiled Christ*.

Backtrack to the Spaccanapoli roadway and take in the pretty 18th-century Church of **Sant' Angelo a Nilo** ⑭ and picturesque Largo Corpo di Napoli (at press time hidden by renovation work), where the statue of the Egyptian river god Nile reclines on a pedestal. Somewhat bizarrely, but all too representative of the soccer-loving Neapolitan people, a shrine has been put up opposite it dedicated to the fabled Argentinian striker, Maradona. A few steps beyond, the street name changes from Via Benedetto Croce to Via S. Biagio dei Librai and at No. 81 you'll find that prime Spacca photo-op, the charming Ospedale delle Bambole, a "hospital" for dolls. Farther down the Spaccanapoli more wares can be found at the tiny Church of San Nicola a Nilo, whose horseshoe-shape steps serve as an open-air antiques store most days. Just across the street is the **Monte di Pietà** ⑮, whose Cappella della Pietà and spectacularly opulent 17th-century salons can be found just beyond the courtyard (open weekends only). Continue down the Spacca to view the storefront Ospedale delle Bambole—a doll hospital—at No. 81, then make a right turn on Via Duomo to the atmospheric **Museo Civico Filangieri** ⑯. Head back up Via Duomo two blocks to Via Tribunali and make a right to the **Pio Monte della Misericordia** ⑰, whose church contains one of the greatest 17th-century altarpieces in Europe, Caravaggio's *Seven Acts of Mercy*. The Baroque-era, floridly ornamented Guglia di San Gennaro spire in the piazza opposite was dedicated to the saint whose intervention had legendarily saved the city from the eruption of Vesuvius in 1631.

Head back to the Via Duomo and turn right to the **Duomo di San Gennaro** ⑱, the majestic cathedral built for Charles I of Anjou in the 14th century and home to the Cappella del Tesoro di San Gennaro. If you have more adrenaline to burn for Baroque, turn right from the duomo up the avenue to Via Apostoli to see **San Giuseppe dei Ruffi** ⑲ and Santi Apostoli ⑳. Nearby is a monument of Neapolitan Gothic, **Santa Maria di Donnaregina Vecchia** ㉑.

Head back down Via Duomo one block to the Via dei Tribunali—this is the other great historic thoroughfare of the district. Turn right along the street and discover the first of the street's many imposing churches—the elegant **I Girolamini** ㉒ and the gigantic **San Lorenzo Maggiore** ㉓, whose 18th-century facade hides a Gothic-era nave and—surprise—one of the most interesting archaeological sites in the city, showing the streets of ancient Naples as they were 2,000 years ago. The church is at the corner of Via San Gregorio Armeno, probably the most charming street in Naples. Famed for its lavishly Rococo church of **San Gregorio Armeno** ㉖, whose towering campanile arches over the street, this thoroughfare is lined with nearly a dozen Presepe (crèche) stores. After exploring the shops along the street, head back up to Via dei Tribunali and the impressive 16th-century church of **San Paolo Maggiore** ㉔, diagonally across small Piazza San Gaetano (former site of the Greek and Roman Agora marketplace) from San Lorenzo; on San Paolo's left-hand flank, you'll find one of the entrances to **Napoli Sotterranea** ㉕, the fascinating route through underground Naples. Coming out of San Paolo Maggiore, turn right and head east for about 10 blocks—passing the mammoth **San Domenico Maggiore** ㉗ on your way—to find pretty Piazza Bellini, whose literary caffès are perfect for a time-out and restorative espresso. You'll learn that, for the price of an aperitif or an ice cream, the caffès of the Spaccanapoli bestow instantaneous club membership on a patron (you may even find yourself taking part in a poetry-reading). From the moment you settle into a seat, you belong.

TIMING Because many churches open at 7:30 and close for the afternoon around 1, it's imperative to get an early start to fit in as many sights as possible before the midday break. It's worth remembering that most churches also close for visits during mass (times clearly indicated on the door). The famous Cappella Sansevero is open through the day, while the Monte di Pietà is only open on weekends. During the midday break, wander around savoring *colore locale* and enjoy lunch at any of a number of good inexpensive restaurants in this neighborhood (it's best to plan on paying cash for this lunch)—as always, the best advice is to opt for whatever's chalked up on the sidewalk board. Scaturchio in Piazza San Domenico is the perfect place for a post-lunch espresso. Then fit in a bit of shopping by browsing around Piazza Dante, Port'Alba, and the Via Santa Maria di Costantinopoli for used books and antiques, or head over to the Via San Gregorio Armeno to pick out a manger figure to take back home—but remember that many shops close for three hours, from 1:30 to 4:30. By 4 many of the churches reopen. Plan on a good two hours to walk this route, plus a quarter to a half hour for each of the principal churches you decide to visit. However, Spaccanapoli is the most memorable part of Naples so take a full day, if you can, to explore its varied pleasures.

Sights to See

⓭ **Cappella Sansevero.** Rightly one of the emblematic monuments of Naples in the popular imagination, this dazzling masterpiece, the funerary chapel of the Sangro di Sansevero princes, combines noble swagger, overwhelming color, and a touch of the macabre—which is to say, it expresses Naples perfectly. The di Sangros were renowned military leaders as far back as the Dark Ages, and they boast no fewer than six saints in their family (who are portrayed in the chapel's painted roundels between the windows). The chapel was begun in 1590 by Giovan Francesco di Sangro, the result of a vow to be fulfilled if he were cured of a dire illness. He lived for another 14 years, which was good for the building campaign, but the present aspect of the chapel is due to his descendant Raimondo di Sangro, prince of Sansevero, who had it completely redone between 1749 and 1770.

FodorśChoice ★

Youthful portraits show this fascinating character with a pronounced pointy chin. Confident and sophisticated in his tastes, legendarily brilliant, and an important mover in Naples's Enlightenment, this princely intellectual, mad scientist, and inventor was accused of just about everything then considered base: atheism, alchemy, and Freemasonry. The last two are likely: he seems to have been a Grand Master of the Freemasons, and his claim to be able to reproduce the miracle of St. Gennaro's blood got him kicked out of the Fraternity of the Treasure of St. Gennaro. He left a personal touch in the basement, down the stairs to the right, where two glass cases house a pair of "anatomical machines," which are astonishing even if fake. Purporting to be an encyclopedic reconstruction of the blood vessels of an adult male and a pregnant female, they are supposedly based on two of the prince's servants, who fell victim to his curiosity when he injected them while still alive with what is conjectured to be a mercury solution that hardened their arteries.

Prince Raimondo is generally credited with the design of the splendid marble-inlay floor; he hired Francesco Maria Russo to paint the ceiling with a *Glory of Paradise* (1749) and also hired a team of up-and-coming sculptors, whose contributions remain the focal point for most visits here: the showpiece is smack in the middle of the chapel, Giuseppe Sammartino's *Veiled Christ* (1753). The artist was only 33 years old when he sculpted this famous work, which was originally meant to be placed in the crypt. It was too good to leave down below with *those things;* the audacious virtuosity of the clinging drapery showing the wounds underneath is one of the marvels of Neapolitan sculpture. A taste for the outré and extravagant had already been demonstrated by other statues in the chapel, especially Francesco Quierolo's *Disillusion,* to the right of the altar, with its chisel-defying net making a spectacular transition to empty space. This Genovese sculptor also did the female statue representing *Sincerity* on the right and the commemorative *Altar to St. Odorisio* between the two Allegories. Antonio Corradini, who came to Naples from the Veneto region via Rome, is responsible for the allegorical statue to the left of the altar, *Veiled Modesty* (1751), widely considered his masterpiece; he also sculpted the funerary monument and allegorical figure of *Decorum,* on the inside of the front wall to the right of the exit. The main altar and its reliefs are the work of Francesco Celebrano, and the angels on either side are by a sculptor from nearby Sorrento, Paolo Persico. Celebrano also contributed the stunning funerary monument above the front door, with Cecco di Sangro leaping out of his coffin in commemoration of one of his most famous exploits—when, having been left for dead, he suddenly reappeared, fully armed, in the thick of the battle. Celebrano also did the tomb on the left of this monument. This team of sculptors is essentially responsible for the remainder of the sculptural decor as well, with the notable exception of the three 17th-century tombs in the front bays of the side walls. ⊠ *Via Francesco di Sanctis 19, Spaccanapoli* ☎ *081/5518470* 🖾 *€5* 🕑 *Easter–Sept., Mon., Wed.–Sat. 10–4:40, Sun., 10–1; Oct.–Easter, Mon., Wed.–Sat. 10–6:40* Ⓜ *Metro: Piazza Cavour (in construction: Piazza Borsa-Università).*

★ ⑱ **Duomo di San Gennaro.** The shrine to the paterfamilias of Naples, San Gennaro, the city's cathedral is home to the saint's devotional chapel, among the most spectacular—in the show-biz sense of the word—in the city. With a colonnade leading to an apse bursting with light and Baroque splendor, the duomo's nave makes a fitting setting for the famous **Miracle of the Blood,** when the blood of the martyred St. Gennaro liquifies (hopefully) in its silver ampule every September 19 before an audience of thousands massed in front of the duomo's altar. *San Genna, fa'o miracolo! Fa ampresso! Nun ce fa suffrì!* yell the congregants during the ritual—"Saint Genna, do the miracle! Hurry up! You'll pay for it if you don't do it!" If St. Januarius (to use his ancient Latin name) doesn't cooperate, however, it's usually the city that winds up paying, or so the locals believe: eruptions of Vesuvius, cholera outbreaks, and defeats of the Naples soccer team have all been blamed on the saint when the *miracolo* has failed to occur.

The duomo was first established by Charles II of Anjou, using imported French architects, on the site of a previous structure, the Cattedrale Ste-

CloseUp

THE GLITTER & THE GOLD: NEAPOLITAN BAROQUE ART & ARCHITECTURE

Naples is a city of dramatic pairings: Baroque with medieval, plenty with want, grandeur with muddle. Of the numerous artistic styles that comprise this feast, however, none suited the Neapolitan temperament better than the Baroque—the style that came to the fore in the 17th century and continued in the 18th century under the Bourbon kings.

In a city of volcanic passions, the flagrantly emotional, floridly luxurious Baroque—a style that seems perpetually on the point of bursting its bonds—found immediate favor. The departure of the austere Spanish viceroys in the 17th century gave free rein to the city's natural inclination for this extroverted style, allowing artists like Caravaggio and the Spaniard Il Ribera, and architects like Ferdinando Sanfelice and Cosimo Fanzago, to strut their aesthetic stuff.

With untrammeled individualism given full play, the results, most still visible today, were theatrical, dramatic, dynamic, vivid, alive, and sometimes wonderfully showy. Venture into the Gesù Nuovo (mother church of the Padri Gesuiti, or Jesuit Fathers) and note the buoyant swirl of stucco, inlaid marble, and gilt work, a florid tangle that mirrors the chaos of the piazza outside its door. Like the city itself, the decorative scheme is diffuse and disjunctive, with little effort to organize everything into an easily understood scheme.

Throughout the city, artists loved using illusionistic trompe l'oeil tricks of ingenious device on church cupolas, as in the Cappella di San Gennaro at the Duomo. Here, as in other churches, you'll see reliquaries studded with semiprecious stones and covered with gold, gold, and more gold.

Elsewhere, statues were made hyper-real, either thanks to amazing technique, such as the marble figures in the Cappella Sansevero, where fishing nets and veils were carved from pure stone, or by being dressed in silk and velvet garments. Thanks to the Counter-Reformation, the Catholic Church was then busy making an overt appeal to the congregant, using emotion and motion to get the message across—no more so than in 17th- and 18th-century Naples, a city which, incidentally, had some 20,000 clerics, more than Rome itself.

The most representative practitioner of Neapolitan Baroque was Cosimo Fanzago (1591–1678). A Lombard by birth, he arrived in Naples to study sculpture, so even when he decorated a church, he usually covered it head to toe with colored and inlaid marbles, as in his work at the Church of San Martino in the Certosa (charter house) that sits atop the Vomero hill.

Two decades earlier, Caravaggio (1571–1610) had arrived in Naples from Rome and this great painter of chiaroscuro took the city by storm. He was on the point of bringing the Baroque style back to earth in Naples—thanks to the unflinching truthfulness and extroverted sensuality in his paintings—but other forces prevailed.

Neapolitan Baroque painters were generally a mediocre bunch. Many, in fact, banded together to form a "Facione de' Pittori" (Painters' Faction) headed by the favored painter of the Spanish viceroyalty, Il Ribera.

These Dependentii, or disciples, formed more than just a "union": they were a full-fledged gang and spearheaded the persecution that plagued most painters who came to Naples for work, such as Domenichino and Guido Reni, both of whom fled the city and the cabal to save their lives (or nearly so: it was widely believed that Domenichino was mysteriously poisoned shortly after leaving the city).

Thanks to the disciples of Spagnoletto (Il Ribera's nickname), pride, pomposity, glitter, and gold conquered all.

fania (AD 570), and next to an even earlier structure, the still-extant Basilica di Santa Restituta (4th century AD). Already restored in 1456 and 1484, it was largely redesigned in 1787 and 1837. The original facade collapsed in the earthquake of 1349, and the present pseudo-Gothic concoction is a modern (1877–1905) fake by Enrico Alvino and Giuseppe Pisanti, which, however, reemploys the doors—still majestic in spite of extensive damage—from the 1407 facade. The central door, by Antonio Baboccio, features a *Madonna and Child* by Tino da Camaino under its arch. Inside, the splendid nave welcomes all, with a gilt wooden ceiling (1621) and golden roundels painted above the pillars by Luca Giordano and his school depicting various saints. From the nave head to the right side of the church to see the chapel devoted to the city's patron saint.

The **Cappella del Tesoro di San Gennaro,** or Chapel of the Treasure of San Gennaro, was built in 1608–37 by the Theatin architect Francesco Grimaldi to fulfill a desperate vow pronounced by city fathers during an outbreak of the plague (January 13, 1527), some 80 years earlier. The chapel honors Saint Gennaro (250–305), one of the earliest Christian martyrs; as bishop of Benevento, he was executed at Pozzuoli during the rule of Emperor Diocletian. The entrance to the chapel is marked by a heavy gilt-bronze baldequin gate (1668–86) by noted architect Cosimo Fanzago, who also designed the chapel's superb floor, and is flanked by statues of Sts. Peter and Paul by Giuliano Finelli. Inside, the elegant Greek-cross plan is decorated everywhere possible with gold, colored marble, bronze, and paint, but nothing could be too overdone for the home of St. Gennaro's most famous DNA sample and the fabulous treasure of jeweled offerings bestowed by numerous sovereigns. The 40-odd *brocatello* columns, with their musty tones of dried roses, were sent from the quarries of Tortosa in Valencia, Spain. Numerous bronze statues of saints keep permanent watch over the chapel. The high altar on the back wall (1689–90), designed by the painter Francesco Solimena, seems to swell as it tries to contain the opulence of the central relief, created in silver (circa 1692) by Giovan Domenico Vinaccia (who inserted into it a portrait of himself holding eyeglasses). Above the altar, against the wall, is a large bronze of St. Gennaro on his bishop's throne by onetime Bernini assistant Giuliano Finelli. Also behind the altar are two silvered niches donated by Charles II of Spain to house the reliquaries containing the blood of the saint (the right-hand one) and his skull. This latter reliquary consists of the famous gilded medieval bust done by three French artists (1305) set on a silver base from 1609, the actual repository of the precious vials of the saint's blood.

Most of the frescoes are by the Bolognese artist Domenichino, but his compatriot Guido Reni was originally engaged to paint the cycle, and thereby hangs a tale. The celebrated painter came to Naples only to find his life made miserable by jealous local artists indignant at such an honor being given to an outsider. Ultimately, the commission went to the great Domenichino, who came to Naples only after the viceroy himself guaranteed his protection. He started painting under armed guard in 1630 and had almost completed the ensemble in 1641 when he died suddenly. Poisoning was suspected, and the committee at this point refused to even consider a Neapolitan painter, so the Roman Giovanni Lanfranco was called in to bravely (and quickly) finish the dome, and it was he who painted the dome's frescoed vision of Paradise. Also note Il Ribera's *San Gennaro in the Furnace* (1647), on the right-hand wall—perhaps the most beautiful church painting in Naples. Dating from his early Neapolitan period, it clearly shows the influence of Velasquez in the figures on the left, and it is imbued with a Mediterranean luminosity that is rare in his work. The chapel, a veritable church-within-a-church, also has its own sacristy (sometimes closed), which contains a luxurious washbasin by Cosimo Fanzago. This room leads into a suite of rooms with frescoes by Giacomo Farelli and a splendid altarpiece by Massimo Stanzione; at the back are kept the 51 statues of the "co-patron" saints, displayed in the chapel proper in May and September and which accompany the reliquary of the blood on its annual procession to Santa Chiara.

The main altar sits in the resplendent apse redesigned in 1744 by Paolo Tosi and framed by two magnificent jasper columns found in a dig in 1705. The paintings in the apse are the work of Stefano Pozzi (ceiling and left wall) and Corrado Giaquinto (right wall). A staircase on either side of the entrance to the presbytery (high altar area) descends to the Caraffa Chapel, better known as the **Succorpo di San Gennaro,** or, more simply, the crypt (1497–1506), a Renaissance masterpiece by Tommaso Malvito in the form of a rectangular room divided into three naves by rows of columns. Malvito also carved the imposing statue of Cardinal Oliviero Caraffa, who commissioned the chapel. A simple antique terra-cotta vase underneath the main altar contains the bones of St. Gennaro.

Coming back up into the nave and continuing in a counterclockwise direction, you find the Chapel of San Lorenzo, with highly restored frescoes by Lello da Orvieto (circa 1314–20). This chapel hides an elevator that ascends through one of the corner towers to the roof, which offers an intimate yet panoramic view of the historic quarter. Nearby is the tomb of Pope Innocent, sculpted in 1315 and redone in the 16th century by Tommaso Malvito. The sarcophagus to the left belongs to Andrea of Hungary, the unfortunate consort of Queen Joan I, who allegedly had him strangled in Aversa (at least the dogs at the foot of the deceased show a little sadness). Beyond the tombs of Pope Innocent XII and the late-Renaissance chapel of the Brancaccio family, a door leads to the Chapel of Santa Restituta.

The **Cappella di Santa Restituta** is in fact the oldest church in Naples, dating from the 4th century AD and, according to tradition, built by order of the first Christian emperor, Constantine, on the site of a temple to Apollo. It was dedicated to St. Restituta in the 8th century when the martyr's relics were transferred to the church. To the left is a ticket booth for the visit to the baptistery and underground archaeological area (entrance: €2.58). This allows you to visit a fairly dry exhibit of ancient fragments; the Baptistery of San Giovanni in Fonte (off to the right), however, is in itself worth the ticket price—a square room with an octagonal dome, built by Bishop Soterus in the middle of the 5th century, it still dazzles with its rare, gorgeous, and important early Christian mosaics. ⊠ *Via Duomo 147, Spaccanapoli* ☎ *081/449097* ⊘ *Daily 9–noon and 4:30–6:30* ▭ *Santa Restituta Chapel €2.50* Ⓜ *Metro: Piazza Cavour (in construction: Duomo).*

★ ⑪   **Gesù Nuovo.** *Opulenza* and *magnificenza* are the words that come to mind when describing this floridly Baroque church, the centerpiece of the Piazza del Gesù Nuovo. Its formidable diamond-point facade is actually a remnant of the Renaissance palace of the Sanseverino princes (1470), destroyed to make way, in 1584–1601, for a generically stupendous exercise in the full-throated Jesuit style, albeit one with an unusual Greek-cross plan. The dome has been rebuilt twice (this is an earthquake zone); the present version dates from the early 19th century. The bulk of the interior decoration took more than 40 years and was completed only in the 18th century. You will find the familiar Baroque sculptors (Naccherino, Finelli) and painters. The gracious *Visitation* above the altar in the second chapel on the right is by Massimo Stanzione, who also contributed the fine frescoes in the main nave: they are in the presbytery (behind and around the main altar). In the chapel to the left of this are some interesting frescoes by the young Francesco Solimena, who became a leading Baroque painter, and to the left of that is a wonderful gallery of reliquary portraits, each placed in its own opera box, and around the corner is a small devotional room where statues are draped head to toe with silver body-part votive offerings. ⊠ *Piazza del Gesù Nuovo, Spaccanapoli* ☎ *081/5518613* ⊙ *Mon.–Sat. 6:30–12:45 and 4:15–7:30, Sun. 6:30–1:30* Ⓜ *Metro: Piazza Dante.*

㉒ I Girolamini. The Girolamini is another name for the Oratorians, followers of St. Philip Neri, to whom this splendid church is dedicated. Built in 1592–1619 by the Florentine architect Giovanni Antonio Dosio, the dome and gray-and-white facade were rebuilt after a design by Ferdinando Fuga (circa 1780) in the most elegant Neoclassic style. Hit by Allied bombs in 1943, the intricate carved-wood ceiling is still being restored, and the church is essentially closed off. Yet you can still get a good look at the grandiose fresco (1684) by Luca Giordano on the inside of the entrance wall. The Oratorians also built the Casa dei Padri dell'Oratorio, down the block at Via Duomo 142. Step through its gate to see the two improbably calm and disciplined cloisters, designed by the Florentine architects Giovanni Antonio Dosio, Dionisio di Bartolomeo, and Dionisio Lazzari sometime around 1600. Just off the larger cloister enclosing a prolific forest of lemon and loquat trees is the Girolamini Pinacoteca. With its high-quality, intimate collection of 16th- and 17th-century paintings, the gallery more than compensates for the adjacent church being closed. Here, too, is one of the most gloriously decorated 18th-century libraries in Europe, the 60,000-volume Biblioteca dei Girolamini, now used by scholars. In fact, this area was an important nucleus of intellectual life in the Renaissance and Baroque periods, thanks to the presence of the Girolamini Library. Directly across the street as you exit the Girolamini, note an inscription by Naples's profusely subtle philosopher, historian, and politician Benedetto Croce (1866–1952) to that marks the house in which his illustrious predecessor, Giambattista Vico, lived for nearly 20 years. On the left is the Palazzo Manso, where the Marchese di Villa hosted the noted 16th-century poet Torquato Tasso. ⊠ *Via Duomo 142, Spaccanapoli* ☎ *081/449139* ⊙ *Daily 9:30–12:50* Ⓜ *Metro: Piazza Cavour (in construction: Duomo).*

⓯ Monte di Pietà. Lush and lavish, this Baroque-era landmark is a must-see for anyone interested in Neapolitan decorative arts. As Spaccanapoli was home to both Naples's poorest and richest residents, the latter formed several charitable institutions, of which the Monte di Pietà was one of the most prominent. At the beginning of the 16th century, it constructed this palazzo (F. Cavagna, 1605), with a grand courtyard leading to the Cappella della Pietà, with gilt stuccoes and beautiful frescoes by Belisario Corenzio. Leading off the chapel are a number of salons, including the Sala delle Cantoniere, with inlaid marbles and precious intarsia woodwork. Since most Neapolitan residential palace interiors are private or have disappeared, this 17th-century enfilade of salons offers a rare glimpse of Naples at its most sumptuous. Concerts and theatrical performances are often held in the courtyard during the summer. Today the palazzo is an office for the Banco di Napoli. ⊠ *Via Biagio dei Librai 114, Spaccanapoli* ☎ *081/5517074* ⊙ *Sat. 9–7, Sun. 9–2* Ⓜ *Metro: Piazza Cavour (in construction: Duomo).*

FodorsChoice
★

⓰ Museo Civico Filangieri. Housed in the Florentine-style Palazzo Cuomo, this is now a unique museum—the residue of a once-important collection created by Prince Gaetano Filangieri, who donated it to the city in 1888. The palazzo was originally built in the Tuscan Renaissance style, only to be demolished when Via Duomo was laid out. It was reconstructed (1879), then World War II scattered the important canvases. Still, it preserves the private air of a connoisseur's house, with weapons, paintings, furniture, medallions, and costumes displayed in 19th-century-style salons. The vast central hall is now used to showcase temporary art exhibitions. ⊠ *Via Duomo 288, Spaccanapoli* ☎ *081/203211* ✉ *€2.58* ⊙ *Tues.–Sat. 9–2, Sun. 9–1* Ⓜ *Metro: Piazza Garibaldi (in construction: Piazza Borsa).*

㉕ Napoli Sotterranea. Outside San Paolo Maggiore (on your right as you're coming out) on Piazza San Gaetano along Via dei Tribunali is one of the entrances to *Napoli Sotterranea*—Underground Naples. This is a fascinating tour (be prepared to go up and down a lot of steps and squeeze through some tight spaces) through a portion of Naples's fabled underground city and a good initiation into the complex layering of history in the city center. Most of the tufa mound on which Naples rises is honeycombed with successive layers of tunnels, well shafts, and underground halls whose interconnections permit a passage from Porta Capuana to the Palazzo Reale without ever seeing the light of day. Used by the soldiers of Belisarius in the 6th century AD, and again by the troops of Holy Roman Emperor Otto IV of Brunswick in the Middle Ages, the complicated network remained largely forgotten until the Neapolitan architect and engineer Guglielmo Melisurgo undertook a well-documented exploration beginning in 1880. The surprisingly large caves served a vital military purpose during the popular uprising against the Nazis in 1943. The Germans, cognizant of the location of some of the principal caverns but unable to mount a credible assault given the general chaos in the streets, bombed a number of entrances in a departing act of gratuitous vengeance, trapping the crowds underground, but arriving American soldiers dug out thousands of desperate people. Tours are provided every day at 10, noon, 2, and 4. ⊠ *Piazza San Gaetano, Spaccanapoli* ☎ *081/296944* ✉ *€5* Ⓜ *Metro: Piazza Cavour (in construction: Duomo).*

⑰ Pio Monte della Misericordia. One of the defining landmarks of Spaccanapoli, this octagonal church was built around the corner from the duomo (practically in front of its constantly used side door) for a charitable institution founded in 1601 by seven noblemen. The institution's aim was to carry out acts of Christian charity: feeding the hungry, clothing the poor, nursing the sick, sheltering pilgrims, visiting prisoners, ransoming Christian slaves, and burying the indigent dead—acts immortalized in the history of art by the famous altarpiece painted by Caravaggio (1571–1610) depicting the *Sette Opere della Misericordia* (or *Seven Acts of Mercy*) and now the celebrated focus of the church. In this haunting work the artist has brought the Virgin in palpable glory, unforgettably borne atop the shoulders of two angels, right down into the street—and not a rhetorical place, but a real street of Spaccanapoli (scholars have in fact suggested a couple of plausible identifications) populated by figures in whose spontaneous and passionate movements the people could see themselves given great dignity. Along with other paintings in the church, the sculptures by Andrea Falcone on its porch refer to this commitment. The original church was considered too small and destroyed in 1655 to make way for the new church, designed by Antonio Picchiatti in 1658–78. Pride of place is given to the great Caravaggio above the altar (for a discussion of this work, see the Close-Up box, "Chiaroscuro Plus: Caravaggio's *Seven Acts of Mercy,*" *below*) but there are other important Baroque-era paintings on view here; some hang in the church while others are in the adjoining Pinacoteca, or picture gallery.

Fodor'sChoice
★

The extraordinary expressiveness and efficiency of the Caravaggio altarpiece can be judged by comparison with the church's other paintings, commissioned from Neapolitan painters after Caravaggio hit the road again (to Malta) to stay one step ahead of the law. In particular, in the painting to the left of the altar, *St. Peter Rescuing Tabitha* (1612), Fabrizio Santafede is clearly struggling to modify his Technicolor formalist style to suggest the dramatic impact of the altarpiece—but the figures here merely occupy the space of the painting, rather than animate it. Upon seeing Caravaggio's altarpiece, a number of artists changed their styles radically, although often giving a personal interpretation to one aspect of Caravaggio's style. The painting to the right of the exit door is a beautiful work by one of the best of the Neapolitan Caravaggesques, Giovan Battista Carraciolo, who was 29 years of age when the slightly older artist came to town. Depicting the *Liberation of St. Peter* (1615), the composition is almost shockingly spartan, nearly all dark brown with contained blocks of white, red, and flesh tones. For more paintings of the Neapolitan Seicento, head up the staircase in the courtyard around the left of the church to the church's small **Pinacoteca,** a museum of 17th- and 18th-century paintings. ⊠ *Via Tribunali 253, Spaccanapoli* ☎ *081/446944* ⊗ *Mon.–Sat. 9–1; Pinacoteca museum, Tues., Thurs., Sat. 8:30–2* Ⓜ *Metro: Piazza Cavour (in construction: Piazza Borsa-Università).*

> **need a break?** When leaving the Pio Monte during the summer months, note that a street vendor named **Ciro** often sets up in the small square directly across from the church and sells a silky homemade lemon slush (*limonata*) given a shy blush by a dose of strawberry juice. Smoothly tart, ice cold, and—well—*real*, it makes for a uniquely satisfying complement to Caravaggio's vision of daily grace. ⊠ *Spaccanapoli.*

㉗ San Domenico Maggiore. One of the largest churches of Spaccanapoli, this Dominican house of worship was originally constructed by Charles I of Anjou in 1238. Legend has it that a painting of the crucifixion spoke to St. Thomas Aquinas when he was at prayer here. This early structure, however, was nearly gutted by a fire three centuries later and, in 1850, a neo-Gothic edifice rose in its place, complete with a nave of awe-inspiring dimensions. In the second chapel on the right are remnants of the earlier church—14th-century frescoes by Pietro Cavallini, a Roman predecessor of Giotto. Along the side chapels are also some noted funerary monuments, including those of the Carafa family, whose chapel, to the left of Cosimo Fanzago's 17th-century altar, is one of the most beautiful Renaissance-era set-pieces in Naples. ⊠ *Piazza San Domenico Maggiore 8/a, Spaccanapoli* ☎ *081/5573204* ⊗ *Mon.–Sat. 8:30–noon and 5–8, Sun. 9–1 and 5–7:30* Ⓜ *Metro: Piazza Cavour (in construction: Piazza Borsa-Università).*

⑲ San Giuseppe dei Ruffi. Half a block from the Duomo, this late-17th-century church, built by Dionisio Lazzari, features one of the most impressively solid and dramatically Baroque facades in Naples. The order must have spent most of its money on it, since they wound up painting the nave walls in faux marble to keep up appearances. This place can be a relaxing stop in the morning, especially if the nuns are singing. ⊠ *Piazza San Giuseppe dei Ruffi 2, Spaccanapoli* ⊗ *Mon.–Sat. 7:30–1 and 4–6, Sun. 7:30–10:30.* Ⓜ *Metro: Piazza Cavour (in construction: Duomo).*

㉖ San Gregorio Armeno. Set on Via San Gregorio Armeno, the street that FodorśChoice ★ is lined with Naples' most adorable Presepe—or Nativity crèche scene—emporiums—and landmarked by a picturesque campanile, this convent is one of the oldest and most important in Naples. The nuns (often the daughters of Naples's richest families) who lived here must have been

CloseUp

CHIAROSCURO PLUS:
CARAVAGGIO'S *SEVEN ACTS OF MERCY*

The most unforgettable painting in Naples, Michelangelo Merisi da Caravaggio's Seven Acts of Mercy—in Italian, the Sette Opere della Misericordia—takes pride of place in the Church of Pio Monte della Misericordia, as well as in nearly all of southern Italy, for emotional spectacle and unflinching truthfulness.

Painted in 1607, it combines the traditional seven acts of Christian charity in sometimes abbreviated form in a tight, dynamic composition under the close, compassionate gaze of the Virgin (the original title was Our Lady of Mercy). Borne by two of the most memorable angels ever painted, she flutters down with the Christ child into a torchlit street scene.

Illuminated in the artist's landmark chiaroscuro style (featuring pronounced contrasts of light, chiaro, and deep shadow, scuro), a man is being buried, a nude beggar is being clothed, and—this artist never pulled any punches—a starving prisoner is being suckled by a woman.

Caravaggio, as with most geniuses, was a difficult artist and personality. His romantic bad-boy reputation as the original bohemian, complete with angry, nihilistic, rebel-with-a-cause sneer and roistering and hippielike lifestyle, has dominated interpretations of his revolutionary oeuvre and tend to present him as an antireligious painter.

This is perhaps understandable—most of the documents pertaining to his life relate to his problems with the law and make for a good story indeed (he came to Naples after killing a man in a bar brawl in Rome, where his cardinal patrons could no longer protect him).

But in spite of (or perhaps because of) his personal life, Caravaggio painted some of the most moving religious art ever produced in the West, whittling away all the rhetoric to reveal the emotional core of the subject. His genuine love of the popular classes and for the "real" life of the street found expression in his use of ordinary street folk as models.

If his art seems to surge directly from the gut, his famous "objectivity" of observation and reduced palette have clear antecedents in paintings from his home region in northern Italy. The simplicity and warts-and-all depictions of his characters show a deeply original response to the Counter-Reformation writings on religious art by Carlo Borromeo, a future saint, also from Lombardy.

The Seven Acts of Mercy, the first altarpiece commissioned for the new church of the charitable institution, has been called "the most important religious painting of the 17th century" by the great 20th-century Italian art critics Roberto Longhi and Giuliano Argan, and if that may not be immediately obvious, it's nevertheless easy to imagine the impact this astonishing painting had on artists and connoisseurs in Naples.

It's easy to imagine that Caravaggio was a natural Neapolitan of the heart, like the recent soccer-player-turned-hero Maradona, and that his maverick virtuosity was similarly appreciated. And like Maradona, he came, dazzled them, and left, though in the year he spent in Naples he managed to paint at least three other major works, now in Vienna, London, and the Museo di Capodimonte (The Flagellation) as well as a few lost works.

Naples affected his style, too: he began to express visual relations purely in terms of dramatic light and shadow, which further exalted the contrasts of human experience.

disappointed with heaven when they arrived—banquets here outrivaled those of the royal court, hallways were lined with paintings, and the church groaned under an orgy of gilt stucco and semiprecious stones. Described as "a room of Paradise on Earth" by Carlo Celano and designed by Niccolò Taglicozzi Canle, the church has a highly detailed wooden ceiling, unique papier-mâché choir lofts, a nuns' gallery shielded by 18th-century jalousies, a shimmering organ, candlelit shrines, and important Luca Giordano frescoes of scenes of the life of St. Gregory, whose relics were brought to Naples in the 8th century from Byzantium. Inside, the convent's cloister has a grand view of the Bay of Naples, while rooms such as the Salottino della Badessa—generally not on view, as this is still a working convent—are preserved as magnificent 18th-century interiors. ⊠ *Piazzetta San Gregorio Armeno 1, Spaccanapoli* ☎ *081/5520186* ⊙ *Daily 8:30–noon* Ⓜ *Metro: Piazza Cavour (in construction: Duomo).*

㉓ **San Lorenzo Maggiore.** One of the grandest medieval churches of the Decumano Maggiore, San Lorenzo features a very unmedieval facade of 18th-century splendor. Due to the effects and threats of earthquakes, the church was reinforced and reshaped along Baroque lines in the 17th and 18th centuries, and remaining from this phase is the facade by Ferdinando Sanfelice (1742) based on the sweeping curves of Borromini's Filomarino altar in the Church of Santi Apostoli. Begun by Robert d'Anjou in 1265 on the site of a previous 6th-century church, the church's single, barnlike nave reflects the desire of the Franciscans for simple spaces with enough room to preach to large crowds. Numerous statues and paintings from the 14th century are indicative of San Lorenzo's importance during this period. In 1334, in fact, Boccaccio met and fell in love with his fabled Lady Fiammetta here, and in 1343 another great Italian poet, Petrarch, resided in the monastery next door. During the 20th century late-Baroque accretions were stripped off to reclaim the original Gothic design. Entering the huge nave and then beginning at the right, view a number of notable tombs and chapels, including the tomb of the Admiral Ludovico Aldomorisco in the second chapel, a fine Renaissance composition by Antonio Baboccio (1421); and the Cacace Chapel, a Baroque masterpiece with a typically sumptuous marble-inlay display from the workshop of Cosimo Fanzago. The transept is announced by a grandiose triumphal arch, while the main altar (1530) is the sculptor Giovanni da Nola's masterpiece; notice the fascinating historical views of Naples in the reliefs.

The apse was built by an unknown imported French architect of great caliber, who gives here a brilliant essay in the pure French Angevin style, complete with an ambulatory of nine side chapels that is covered by a magnificent web of cross arches. The most important monument in the church is found here: the tomb of Catherine of Austria (circa 1323), by Tino da Camaino, one of the first sculptors to introduce the Gothic style into Italy. The left transept contains the 14th-century funerary monument of Carlo di Durazzo and yet another Fanzago masterpiece, the **Cappellone di Sant'Antonio**—*cappella* (or small chapel) being too diminutive a word, especially in this behemoth of a church. Outside the 17th-century cloister is the entrance to the **Greek and Roman** *scavi*, or excavations, under San Lorenzo, which are a good initiation to the ancient cities beneath the modern one. Near the area of the forum, these digs have revealed streets, markets, and workshops of another age. ⊠ *Via dei Tribunali 316, Spaccanapoli* ☎ *081/2110860* 🎫 *Excavations €2.58* ⊙ *Daily 8–noon and 5–7; excavations Mon.–Wed. 9–1 and 3–5:30, Sat. 9–5:30 and Sun. 9:30–1:30* Ⓜ *Metro: Piazza Cavour (in construction: Duomo).*

㉔ San Paolo Maggiore. Like Santi Apostoli, this church was erected for the Theatin fathers in the late 16th century (1583–1603), the period of their order's rapid expansion. This was another instance where Francesco Grimaldi, the (ordained) house architect, erected a church on the ruins of an ancient Roman temple, then transformed it into a Christian basilica. Spoils from the temple survive in the present incarnation, especially the two monumental Corinthian columns on the facade holding up a piece of their architrave to form a portal over the entrance door. The cloaked torsos of the ancient gods, which used to lie under the statues of Peter and Paul, have been moved. An earthquake knocked down the original facade in 1688, and World War II coupled with decades of neglect did further damage. ✉ *Piazza San Gaetano, Spaccanapoli* ☎ *081/454048* Ⓜ *Metro: Piazza Cavour (in construction: Duomo).*

⑭ Sant' Angelo a Nilo. Originally built by Cardinal Brancaccio in the late 1300s, this church was redesigned in the 16th century by Arcangelo Guglielminelli. Inside the graciously beautiful interior is the earliest evidence of the Renaissance in Naples: the cardinal's funerary monument, sculpted by the famous Donatello, assisted by the almost-as-famous Michelozzo, in 1426–27. The front of the sarcophagus bears a bas-relief *Assumption of the Virgin,* testament to Donatello's legendary *stiacciato* trompe-l'oeil technique. Beyond the small courtyard is the Palazzo Brancaccio, where the learned prelate opened the first public library in Naples in 1690. ✉ *Piazzetta Nilo, along Via San Biagio dei Librai, Spaccanapoli* ☎ *081/5516227* ☉ *Mon.–Sat. 8:30–noon and 5–7, Sun. 8:30–noon* Ⓜ *Metro: Piazza Cavour (in construction: Duomo).*

⑫ Santa Chiara. Across from the Gesù Nuovo and offering a stark and telling

Fodor's Choice contrast to the opulence of that church, Santa Chiara is the leading mon-

★ ument of Angevin Gothic in Naples. The fashionable church for the nobility in the 14th century, and a favorite Angevin church from the start, Santa Chiara was intended to be a great dynastic monument by Robert d'Anjou. His second wife, Sancia di Majorca, added the adjoining convent for the Poor Clares to a monastery of the Franciscan Minors so she could vicariously satisfy a lifelong desire for the cloistered seclusion of a convent; this was the first time the two sexes were combined in a single complex. Built in a Provençal Gothic style between 1310 and 1328 (probably by Guglielmo Primario) and dedicated in 1340, the church had its aspect radically altered, as did so many others, in the Baroque period, when the original wooden roof was replaced with a vault dripping in stuccos. A six-day fire started by Allied bombs on August 4, 1943 put an end to all that, as well as to what might have been left of the important cycle of frescoes by Giotto and his Neapolitan workshop: Giorgio Vasari, writing in the mid-16th century, tells us that the paintings covered the entire church. The interior, a large, luminous rectangular hall, nevertheless offers ample serenity, the 18th-century marble floor by Domenico Antonio Vaccaro has been decently restored, and the tombs, in the back, are worth a look. The most important tomb in the church towers behind the altar. Sculpted by Giovanni and Pacio Bertini of Florence (1343–45), it is, fittingly, the tomb of the founding king: the great Robert d'Anjou, known as the Wise. To the right of the altar is the tomb of Carlo, duke of Calabria, a majestic composition by Tino da Camaino and assistants (1326–33), and answering it on the side wall is Tino's last work, the tomb of Carlo's wife, Marie de Valois.

Around the left side of the church at Via Santa Chiara 49/c is a gate leading to the **Chiostro delle Clarisse,** the most famous cloister in Naples. It's clear here that we are not dealing with any normal convent; the benches and octagonal columns upholding the trellis of vine shading this privileged garden comprise a light-handed masterpiece of painted majolica designed by Domenico Antonio Vaccaro, with a delightful profusion of landscapes and light yellow and green floral motifs realized by Donato and Giuseppe Massa and their studio (1742). Where the real vines leave off and the painted ones take over was once hard to say, but much of the cloister is now being replanted, so the complete effect is missing. The elegant 14th-century porch around the garden is enlivened by fading frescoes. In the back corner you can enter the Museo dell'Opera, built on the visible remains of an old Roman bath establishment and containing some interesting sculptural fragments from the damaged church (look for Giovanni da Nola's moving wooden *Ecce Homo* of 1519 on the upper floor) and objects illustrating life in the cloister. ⊠ *Via Benedetto Croce, Spaccanapoli* ☎ *081/5526209* ⊡ *€4* ☉ *Church daily 7–12:30 and 4:30–6:30; cloister Mon.–Sat. 9:30–1 and 2:30–5:30, Sun. 9:30–1* Ⓜ *Metro: Piazza Dante (in construction: Piazza Borsa-Università).*

㉑ **Santa Maria di Donnaregina Vecchia.** The towering Gothic funeral monument of Mary of Hungary, wife of Charles II of Anjou (circa 1254–1309), who is said to have commissioned the frescoes in the church at a cost of 33 ounces of gold, is contained within this church. Don't confuse this church with another, nearby in the piazza, of the same name, but Baroque. This real gem of a church—one of the few without a Baroque-era makeover—is well worth making an appointment to see. ⊠ *Vico Donnaregina 25, Spaccanapoli* ☎ *081/299101* ☉ *By appointment mornings only* Ⓜ *Metro: Piazza Cavour.*

㉒ **Santi Apostoli.** This Baroque church in a basic Latin-cross style with a single nave shares the piazza with a contemporary art school in a typically anarchic Neapolitan mix. Built (1610–49) by the ordained architect Francesco Grimaldi for the Theatin fathers above a previous church, itself built on the remains of a temple probably dedicated to Mercury, it's worth a quick peek inside for its coherent, intact Baroque decorative scheme. There are excellent paintings on the inside of the entrance wall and on the ceiling by Giovanni Lanfranco (circa 1644), with a good number painted by his successors Francesco Solimena and Luca Giordano. The terra-cotta and marble floor is a work of the late 17th century by Francesco Viola. For lovers of Baroque architecture, there's an altar in the left transept by the great architect Francesco Borromini. Commissioned by Cardinal Ascanio Filomarino, this is the only work in Naples by this architect, whose freedom from formality so inspired the exuberance of the Baroque in southern Italy, although its massive virile flourish of monochrome gray stone comes as a bit of a shock in the midst of this polychromed city. ⊠ *Largo Santi Apostoli 9, Spaccanapoli* ☎ *081/ 299375* ☉ *Mon.–Sat. 9–noon, Sun. 9–1* Ⓜ *Metro: Piazza Cavour.*

Art & Antiquity: From the Museo Archeologico Nazionale to Porta Capuano

It's only fitting that the Museo Archeologico Nazionale—the single most important and remarkable museum of Greco-Roman antiquities in the world (in spite of itself, some observers say)—sits in the upper *decumanus,* or neighborhood, of ancient Neapolis, the district colonized by the ancient Greeks and Romans. Repository of many of the greatest surviving art treasures of antiquity—including most of the celebrated finds from Pompeii and Herculaneum—the museum has so many rooms it almost constitutes its own walking tour. As Naples's preeminent treasure trove, it deserves your undivided attention. Happily, it is open all day (its core collection, that is). But if two hours are your limit for gazing at ancient art, nearby you'll discover some of the lesser-known delights of medieval and Renaissance Naples, along with the city's lush botanical gardens (which are set in the neighborhood quarter known as Carlo III). Along the way you'll visit churches that are repositories for magnificent 15th- and 16th-century art and sculpture and the city's famed Porta Capuano, one of the historic gates to the city walls.

a good walk

Limited opening hours in some of the less-frequented churches mean you'll probably have to practice some fancy footwork here. Begin at the enormous complex of the **Museo Archeologico Nazionale** ㉘ ▶. You'll want to choose now if you want to visit any of the lesser-known collections and rooms of the museum, since some of them undoubtedly will close for the day in the afternoon hours. Happily, the fabled rooms of the core masterpiece collection are usually open until early evening, so you can always return after your walk through the neighborhood to view (or re-view) these treasures (of course this means two museum admissions, but the world's greatest collection of archaeological treasures is surely worth many more visits). If you get to the museum when its doors open at 9 AM, then spend two hours there, you can then head out to the end of Piazza Cavour and begin a walk for about six blocks along Via Forio. If you wish to pay a call on the city's botanical gardens (an appointment must be made) you can hop on one of the many buses going down Via Foria towards Piazza Carlo III, getting off some 10 blocks later when you see the towering trees of the **Orto Botanico** ㉙ on your left behind the formidable protective wall. If you are not going to the botanical gardens, simply make a right when you reach Via Carbonara and walk down it toward the important Church of **San Giovanni a Carbonara** ㉚, set back from the road 300 ft down on the left. Continue down via Carbonara to the Renaissance church of **Santa Caterina a Formiello** ㉛. On the left is the noted landmark, the **Porta Capuano** ㉜, one of the centuries-old gates to the city walls. Cross over and walk along the walls of medieval Castel Capuano (now a criminal law court, formerly a royal palace), to the main entrance of the castle. Opposite the entrance stretches via Tribunali, one of the decumani (the main Greek/Roman roads of the historic center). If your feet haven't called a sit-down strike, you can now decide to walk to the new (possible opening in 2004) metro stop near the Duomo. This, unfortunately, requires a hike back up the very steep Via Tribunalii, leading up to Pio Monte della Misericordia on your left and the Guglia di San Gennaro on your right. If this uphill hike of some 12 blocks fazes you (along with the immediate area, one of the less picturesque sectors of the Spaccanapoli), head instead to the metro stop, found some 10 blocks in the opposite direction, at the city's main Stazione Centrale on Piazza Garibaldi.

TIMING   The Museo Archeologico Nazionale now enjoys extended opening hours throughout the year. However, many of the lesser known rooms may be closed at any time, so if you are particularly keen to see, say, the exhibition on prehistory in Campania or the Egyptian section, a phone call will avoid disappointment. If you want the full feast, get an early morning start. The real problem is fitting in the churches with their limited opening hours, which means being ruthless (to your feet and flagging spirits!) if you want to fit the vast museum in on one day, along with the neighboring churches.

Sights to See

㉘ **Museo Archeologico Nazionale** (National Museum of Archaeology). Those who know and love this legendary museum have a tendency, upon hearing it mentioned, to heave a sigh: it is famous not only for its unrivaled collections but also for its off-limit rooms, missing identification labels, poor lighting, billows of dust that attack the unwary visitor, suf-

Fodor'sChoice ★

From La Sanità to Capodimonte

focating heat in summer, and indifferent personnel—a state of affairs seen by some critics as an encapsulation of everything that's wrong with southern Italy in general. Precisely because of this emblematic value, the National Ministry of Culture has decided to lavish attention and funds on the museum in a complete reorganization. This process has been ongoing for some time and looks as if it will continue for a while longer. Ticketing has been privatized, opening hours extended (for the center-core "masterpiece" collection, that is; other rooms are subject to staffing shortages and can be closed on a rotating basis), and vastly improved guide services are now on offer. New rooms covering archaeological discoveries in the Greco-Roman settlements and necropolises in and around Naples have been opened, with helpful informational panels in English. And even if some rooms may be closed, this still leaves available the core of the museum, a nucleus of world-renowned archaeological finds that puts most other museums to shame. For it includes the legendary Farnese collection of ancient sculpture, together with local sculptural finds, and almost all the good stuff—the best mosaics and paintings—from Pompeii and Herculaneum. The quality of these collections is unexcelled and, as far as the mosaic, painting, and bronze sections are concerned, unique in the world. Today, the ancient past and the modern future collide here—of all things, the basement level of the museum has been turned into a contemporary art space, with major temporary exhibitions (such as Jeff Koons's first Italian retrospective) on tap throughout the year.

History of the Museum. The museum was conceived in the mind of Charles III—Carlo III in Italian—who had inherited the various Farnese collections from his mother. The Farnese family had aggressively collected antiquities in Rome during the 16th century, when there were still quite a few important pieces to be found—their excavations of the Baths of Caracalla, in particular, produced a number of marvels, including the Farnese Bull and Farnese Hercules—and these pieces, together with the paintings, made an ideal endowment for a new museum. Charles originally intended to house the collection, together with the Farnese collection of paintings and precious objects, in a specially built palace at Capodimonte, which would be at once a dynastic monument and an avant-garde intellectual endeavor of the Enlightenment, but the antiquities collection soon outstripped the available space. In 1738, the same year the definitive project for Capodimonte got underway, excavations began at the site explored by Prince d'Elboeuf—Resina, in the Herculaneum area—which yielded a stunning sample of marble and bronze statues. Then, in 1748, a new site opened up that surpassed every archaeologist's dreams: Pompeii. By 1750 a makeshift museum had been set up in the royal palace at Portici to house the rapidly growing finds, and Naples, with its exciting excavations, had become an obligatory stop on travelers' Grand Tour itineraries.

After a time the question of a fitting museum became an international issue, and given the precarious position of Portici (it lies under Vesuvius), a solution was deemed urgent—even if it did not seem so to the king. (When Vesuvius erupted in 1767 and ministers pleaded with him to find a safe, permanent home for the collection, Charles of Bourbon replied that if the worst happened and they were buried anew, they would be the crowning joy of excavators' digs 2,000 years hence.) A decision was made in 1777 to utilize a former university, the Palazzo degli Studi, on the hill of Santa Teresa. Ferdinando Fuga was given orders to draw up a plan, but his innovations as usual stirred up controversy, and when he died in 1782, the work had not begun, and the project was passed on to the Roman architect Pompeo Schiantarelli. During this decade the Farnese collection of ancient sculpture finally arrived. This was totally illegal—Cardinal Alexander Farnese's will of 1587 specifically stipulated that the collection was to stay in Rome. But Ferdinand IV, son of and successor to Charles III, politely ignored the strident complaints of the Pope and various other personages, including Goethe, and calmly packed up the loot for transfer.

The museum, named the Royal Library of Naples, finally opened in 1801—perhaps a bit late, given that Ferdinand had just massacred nearly all of his city's intellectual elite in "appreciation" of their Republican ideas. On the whole, however, the museum, if not the Neapolitans themselves, did well from the Napoleonic wars. The French had already packed up the Farnese Hercules for transport to the new Louvre, but the new king of Naples, Joachim Murat, was able to use his considerable military clout within Napoléon's empire to keep the museum's contents in Naples (the rest of Italy was thoroughly and expertly plundered). Murat's wife, Caroline (who rather usefully happened to be Napoléon's sister), herself collected antiquities; so Ferdinand proudly added her collection to the museum in 1816, once he had reestablished himself on the throne with the help of his friends. To quell any doubts about who the owner was, or what sort of government had set it up, he renamed it the Royal Bourbon Museum. The building was finally finished in 1822, just in time to house the spectacular mosaics uncovered in the 1830s in the House of the Faun in Pompeii. With the fall of the Bourbons and unification with the emergent Italy, the collection was reorganized as a so-called National Museum. The result of course was immediate mismanagement and a number of scandals, concerning not only the ideological content underlying the display program but also the large number of pieces that simply went missing, including important items from the Boscoreale treasure, now in the Louvre. Damage inflicted on the building by the 1980–81 earthquakes was the impetus for the last two decades' campaign of modernization.

Room-by-Room Tour of the Collections. As you enter the building, the ticket booth is immediately on the left, with a sign indicating which rooms are open and which closed (read this before buying your ticket). Ahead of you is the large **Atrium of the Magistrates,** which contains a dignified but discreet introduction to the sculpture collections, including a pair of Dacians from Trajan's Forum in the middle aisle and a number of toga-wearing figures and members of the Balbi family from Herculaneum. If you want to continue with marble sculpture, wend your way back to the door near the ticket barrier, the one framed by two columns of antique Numidian yellow marble, and enter the Room of the Tyrannicides. It makes more sense, however, to start your visit on the top floor of the museum, which contains some of the more demanding works on the eye, and work your way down. Head for the stairs flanked at the base by two large reclining 2nd-century AD river deities. Placed unavoidably halfway up the stairs is a ridiculous statue of Ferdinand IV in the guise of Athena, by Canova (which shows that some people should just never wear drag, especially if they have a regal dignity to maintain). While the text below has an extensive description of the entire collection, you might wish to invest in an up-to-date printed museum guide, as exhibits are generally poorly labeled.

Go up two flights of stairs to the first floor (that's by Italian accounting; the mezzanine only counts for half a floor—except when it comes to subsidies). To the right is the important collection of bronzes. The first room (CXV) presents a delightful collection of small decorative bronzes (Silenus heads, children's portraits, leopard antefixes) from the grandiose Villa of the Papiri in Herculaneum, while the adjoining room (CXIV) has a permanent exhibition on the papyrus scrolls, from where the villa got its name, with pride of place given to the curious 19th-century device invented to unwind them. The scrolls have now almost all been read—with the aid of rather more sophisticated technology—and are now housed in the Biblioteca Nazionale. The big room (CXVI) ahead contains statues from the villa that most museums would sell their souls to get as virtually all metal objects from antiquity, especially bronze statues, were melted down. Here you have a treasury of life-size masterpieces, with a splendid set of heads along the left wall illustrating the ancient themes of illustrious men—Hellenistic princes, philosophers, poets—and generic, ideal figures referring to aspects of civilized life: theatrical figures and athletes (note the head of Thespis with the bronze curls soldered on separately). In front of these sit a pensive *Hermes* from a local workshop and the famous *Drunken Satyr,* a pair of deer, the two running athletes (copies after Lysippus) with their original encrusted eyes, and, in the corner next to the left window, a bust of Dionysus with extravagant, meticulously rendered hair. The far wall has a celebrated set of five female *Dancers* (recently reinterpreted as water carriers and identified with the Danaids, who were condemned to draw water endlessly) in the stiff but expressive Severe style. The next room (CXVII), just beyond, contains another fine series of bronze herm heads, an impressive 1st-century BC copy of a lance-throwing *Athena Promachos,* which replicates the monumental statue that once decorated the Acropolis in Athens, and the justifiably renowned portrait head known as the *Seneca,* whose world-weary expression will still move you deeply, even though you have to bend down low to receive its full impact. An equally impressive collection of small bronzes will eventually be displayed in the rooms along the courtyard.

Rooms CXVIII to CXXI shift the focus from Herculaneum to ancient Neapolis and the first Greek settlement overlooking what is now Castel dell'Ovo, Palaeopolis. Exhibits include important finds from public buildings and necropolises during the Greco-Roman period. With helpful information panels (in English), this section shows what and how much lies buried beneath the modern city center, and gives insight into religious and cultural practices during the various periods.

Back through the bronze galleries and to the right at the staircase, you come into the large **Sala della Meridiana,** designed as the reading room of the library and presently wasted space, gussied up with a series of huge 19th-century mediocrities detailing the family history of the fabulous Farnese. At the far end of the room is a famous statue of the titan *Atlas* from the Farnese collection, which bears the oldest known complete depiction of the constellations of the zodiac. Off the door to the right, a suite of rooms along the front facade of the palazzo houses newly renovated displays of findings from pre-Roman Campania, with lots of the usual pottery. On the other side of the Sala della Meridiana, a pair of Trajan-era kneeling Persians in white and purple *pavonazzetto* marble drapery provides a suitable announcement of the celebrated collection of ancient frescoes beyond.

Room 1 (or CXVI; most rooms are numbered in both Arabic and Roman styles) starts off with some excellent *Fourth-Style painted-stucco friezes from the House of Meleager* in Pompeii that refer to the cults of Dionysus and Hercules, but this is just an antechamber to the cream of the crop, spread around the rooms branching off from Room 2 (CXVIII). Handy English-language displays of information, on the left as you enter, give a good presentation of the so-called Four Styles of Roman painting as seen in Pompeii and Herculaneum, evidence of the "golden age" of Roman wall painting. The room to the right displays what's left of the Third Style *paintings from the villa at Boscoreale,* discovered in 1900; the next room (LXX) contains two versions of the *Three Graces* on the right. The third bay (LXXI) has a display case in the center with some exquisite monochrome paintings on marble, including *Fight with a Centaur,* rendered in a confident, precise line reminiscent of Ingres. The bay with the window shows off the famous paintings from the Basilica of Herculaneum, discovered in 1739, including a panel of an oddly nonchalant Hercules discovering his son Telephus being nursed by a doe in Arcadia. Room LXXII has a wonderful *Perseus Freeing Andromeda* from the House of the Dioscuri in Pompeii, plus the celebrated image of *Theseus and the Minotaur* next to the exit door. The last room (LXXIII) along the front facade houses a number of panels in the refined but cold antiquarian current of the Third Style, a reflection of Augustan classicism. Nearby are the six rooms (LXXIX–LXXXIV) that feature material recovered from the Temple of Isis.

Room LXXXV starts the **Glass Collection,** with one of the museum's showstoppers in the center: the *Blue Vase from Pompeii,* an astonishing example of antique cameo glasswork, with white swirls of vegetation and wildlife surrounding some *erotes* (cupids) against an intense cobalt blue. In an adjacent room is the spectacular 100:1 scale model of Pompeii made in 1879. The main part of the glass and jewelry collection (Room LXXXVI) has some fine mosaic glass bowls which would grace any *triclinium* (banquet room) dining table. Stairs take you back down to the mezzanine, site of the **Mosaic Collection.** And what mosaics they are! The first room, which gives just a taste of things to come, sports a striking spotted leopard and a small panel showing a drunk Silenus trying to ride a donkey. The next room on your right (LVIII) concentrates on *nymphaeum* and fountain mosaics in glass paste while Room LIX features the much-reproduced black-and-white depiction of Death. A stunningly sensitive portrait of a woman in micro-mosaic is found in Room LXIV. The finest works are saved for the last two rooms: the world-renowned *opus vermiculatum* mosaics from the House of the Faun in Pompeii. The star piece here is the gigantic *Alexander and Darius at the Battle of Issus* on the far wall. Considered to be a copy of a famous painting by Philoxenos of Eretria done for King Cassander of Macedonia (end of the 4th century BC), this mosaic copy, which dates to 125–120 BC, would be, even if clumsily rendered, of priceless documentary value for our knowledge of the lost art of Greek painting; as it happens, the mosaic itself is a masterpiece. Nearby, cat fans will appreciate the small panel with the cat attacking a bird, while the scene of the *Satyr and Nymph* next to the Alexander mosaic presents lust in an astringently frank manner.

Tucked in discreetly by the mosaic area is the **Gabinetto Segreto,** a unique collection of objects covering a gamut of sexually explicit themes, from phalluses in imaginative poses to Pan doing indescribable things to a nanny goat. After many years of closure due either to 19th-century prudery or 20th-century restoration, the Gabinetto can now be viewed (guided tours only, every 30 minutes, no children under 11) by prior request at the main ticket office. The information panels here are helpful, so you might like to browse at your own pace rather than hurry along with the hurried guided tour.

Once back on the ground floor, cross the **Atrium of the Magistrates** and go through the yellow columns on the side wall near the ticket takers to the **Room of the Tyrannicides** (Room I), named for the group in the center, a 2nd-century AD Roman copy of a famous bronze by Kritios and Nesiotes cast in 477 BC. To the right, notice the beautiful fragmentary *Head of Apollo from Baiae,* with traces of red paint still in his hair. Through the door to the left of this head, you enter the **Gallery of the Great Masters** (Rooms II–VI), which contains mostly copies of works by Greek masters, but some of these copies are among the finest, or they are the only such examples known, including the *Apollo Citharedos,* between Bays II and III, with his rich, flowing hair, and the *Doriphoros of Polycleites* in Bay II. The window-side of the leftmost bay (Room VI) shows off a pair of gorgeous, if damaged, Greek originals of the 4th or 3rd century BC: Nereids with flowing "wet" drapery carved in succulent honeycomb-color stone. Back into the Room of the Tyrannicides and to your right is the **Gallery of Flora** (or Gallery of the Carracci, Room VIII), with a beautifully intact *Artemis of Ephesus* in basalt and antique yellow marble, her fecundity underlined by her multiple breasts and the numerous animals adorning her raiment. In the middle of the gallery stands a voluptuous *Aphrodite Callipygos* ("of the beautiful buttocks"), originally found in the area of Nero's Domus Aurea in Rome.

The collections of ancient sculpture culminate in the **Gallery of the Farnese Bull** (Rooms XI–XV), whose monumentality is no less than the grandiose sculptures from the Baths of Caracalla deserve. The right end of the gallery is dominated by the awesomely powerful *Farnese Hercules,* a signed ("Glykon of Athens made this") copy of a 4th-century BC bronze by Lysippus. The left arm is a restoration, and the nearby set of legs was made by Guglielmo della Porta in the 16th century to complete the statue when it was first discovered; the originals, found afterward, were long judged inferior to these and were not reintegrated until much later. At the left end, the splendid *Farnese Bull*—the largest sculptural group to come down to us from antiquity—answers the Hercules in magnificence. Yes, it has been highly restored (this is well documented on the wall), but all in all, the restorers did a decent job. The strong composition, with its calm depiction of murder, still inspires awe, and numerous artists, from Michelangelo to Picasso, have been influenced by this sculpture.

Behind the Hercules is a discreet door leading into two small rooms housing the **Farnese Collection of Gems,** mostly ancient cameos. The centerpiece of the collection is the fabled *Farnese Cup,* a true stunner, carved to translucent thinness out of a solid layered block of agate and sardonyx; various color layers are brilliantly used to portray a group of mythological figures on the interior and a Medusa's head on the exterior. Probably a royal commission of the court of the Ptolemies in Egypt from the 2nd or 1st century BC, this masterpiece most likely became Roman imperial property before passing through the court of Frederick II Hohenstaufen in Palermo and ending up in Rome, where Lorenzo the Magnificent bought it in 1471. It takes some concentration to appreciate the rest of the collection because the pieces are small, but the ensemble as a whole is fascinating.

Once back out of the Gallery of the Farnese Bull and into the Gallery of Flora, turn right toward the rear of the building; this second half of the inner gallery contains more masterpieces, including one of the best versions of the emperor Hadrian's favorite, *Antinous,* as well as a pliant *Ganymede* with a threatening eagle farther down on the left. Below the stairs is the **Egyptian Collection.** Regrettably, there are currently few resting places and no refreshments available within the museum itself: The nearest options are in the Galleria across the road and in the pedestrianized area in front of the Accademia delle Belle Arti (Academy of Fine Arts) reachable through the Gallery. ⊠ *Piazza Museo, Decumano Maggiore* ☎ *081/440166* 🖃 *€6.50* ☉ *Wed.–Mon. 9–7:30 (center core collection; other collections may only be open 9–1:30)* Ⓜ *Metro: Piazza Cavour (in construction: Museo).*

★ ㉙ **Orto Botanico.** Founded in 1807 by Joseph Bonaparte and Prince Joachim Murat as an oasis from hectic Naples, this is one of the largest of all Italian botanical gardens, comprising some 30 acres. Nineteenth-century greenhouses and picturesque paths hold an important collection of tree, shrub, cactus, and floral specimens from all over the world. Next to the Orto Botanico, with a 354-meter (1,200 ft) facade dwarfing Piazza Carlo III, is one of the largest public buildings in Europe, the Albergo dei Poveri, built in the 18th and 19th centuries to house the city's destitute and homeless; it's now a UNESCO World Heritage Site awaiting an ambitious restoration scheme. ⊠ *Via Foria 223, Carlo III* ☎ *081/449759* 🖃 *Free* ☉ *By appointment weekdays 9–2.*

32 **Porta Capuano.** Its elegance heightened by the frantic piazza on which it stands, this great ceremonial gateway is one of Naples's finest landmarks of the Renaissance era. Ferdinand II of Aragon commissioned the Florentine sculptor and architect Giuliano da Maiano to build this white triumphal arch—perhaps in competition with the Arco di Trifono found on the facade of the city's Castel Nuovo—in the late 15th century. As at Castel Nuovo, this arch is framed by two pepperino stone towers, here nicknamed Honor and Virtue. Across Via Carbonara stands the medieval bulk of the **Castel Capuano,** once home to Angevin and Aragonese rulers until it was transformed in 1540 by the Spanish Viceroy into law courts, a function it still fulfills today. ⊠ *Piazza San Francesco, Carlo III.*

★ **30** **San Giovanni a Carbonara.** This sadly neglected church—many guides give it short shrift, if they don't omit it altogether—is a coherent complex of Renaissance architecture and sculpture that can hold its own against any church in Florence or Rome in terms of quality, if not size. Its curious name is the result of its location during medieval times near the city trash dump, where refuse was burned (carbonized); this location is just outside the Capuana Gate of the old city walls. Its history starts in 1339, when the Neapolitan nobleman Gualtiero Galeota gave a few houses and a vegetable garden to a small convent of Augustinian monks who ministered to the poor neighborhood nearby. Four years later, in admiration of the monks' simplicity and piety, he added another two contiguous gardens and built a church to his family's patron saint, John the Baptist. At this point, some monks moved out, judging the new complex too luxurious; however, King Ladislas judged it too small and 50 years later started a new church, enriching the complex enough to serve as a suitable site for his tomb (together with that of his sister and successor to the throne, Joan II). Redone in the 18th century and badly damaged in 1943, the church has been returned to its original appearance thanks to a conservation scheme.

To enter the church, go up the dramatic staircase in piperno stone with a double run of elliptical stairs—modeled after a 1707 design by Ferdinando Sanfelice (similar to other organ-curved stairways in Rome, such as the Spanish Steps). Together with the courtyard on top, this staircase formed the scene of one of the first major battles of the Neapolitan revolt against the Nazis in September–October 1943 (known as the Four Days of Naples). Upon entering the rectangular nave, the first thing you see is the Monument of the Miroballo family, which is actually a chapel on the opposite wall, finished by Tommaso Malvito and his workshop in 1519 for the Marchese Bracigliano; the magnificent statues in the semicircular arch immediately set the tone for this surprising repository of first-class Renaissance sculpture.

To the right—beyond the skeletal main altar which has been stripped of its 18th-century Baroque additions—is the suitably royal (59-ft-tall, 18 m), if not megalomaniacal, funerary monument of King Ladislas and Joan II, finished by Marco and Andrea da Firenze in 1428. Four monumental female statues of Virtues hold up the sarcophagi of Ladislas and his sister, as well as statues of the two monarchs seated on thrones, and, finally, an energetic armed Ladislas on horseback being blessed by a bishop (the king died excommunicate, but you can buy anything in Naples). A door underneath this monument leads to the **Ser Caracciolo del Sole Chapel,** with its rare and beautiful original majolica pavement—the oldest (1427) produced in Italy, from a workshop in Campania, it shows the influence of Arab motifs and glazing technique.

Coming back out into the nave and immediately turning right at the altar, you enter another circular chapel, the **Caracciolo di Vico Chapel.** This cohesive, sophisticated ensemble shows how Italian art history, first written by Tuscans with a regional agenda, tends to simplify the evolution of Renaissance art and architecture at the expense of other centers. The dating for the chapel is the object of debate; usually given as 1517, with the sculptural decor complete by 1557, the design (usually attributed to Tommaso Malvito) may go back to 1499 and thus precede the much more famous Tempietto in Rome, by Bramante, which it so resembles. In fact, the chapel's superlative quality has led some scholars to reject the traditional attribution and give it to Bramante himself or one of the Sangallos under the assumption that such a fine work should naturally be by someone quite famous. Coming once again into the nave, see if the next door on the right is open (or ask the custodian): this leads to the small rectangular room of the **Old Sacristy,** commissioned by the Caracciolo di Sant'Erasmo. The walls are decorated with 18 richly colored fresco panels depicting scenes from the Old and New testaments as well as saints and doctors of the Church, painted by Giorgio Vasari, disciple of Michelangelo and godfather of Renaissance art history. (Note that the sacristy was closed for restoration at press time.) Outside the church in the courtyard there is a chapel on the right (the Chapel of the Crucifix), with a *Crucifixion* by Giorgio Vasari, and the tomb of Antonio Seripando (1539). You can be thankful this great church is off the path of tour groups so you can absorb the ordered beauty of the decoration in peace. ⊠ *Via San Giovanni a Carbonara 5, Decumano Maggiore* ☎ *081/295873* ☉ *Mon.–Sat. 9:30–1* Ⓜ *Metro: Piazza Cavour.*

㉛ Santa Caterina a Formiello. Inspired by Brunelleschi's churches in Florence, this graceful single-nave church and convent for the Dominican Fathers, designed by Romolo Balsimelli, is a fine example of Renaissance Neapolitan architecture; luckily, later makeovers and restoration have not spoiled its harmonious lines. The ceiling was decorated by Luigi Garzi in 1695 with splendidly dramatic scenes from Saint Catherine's life. The magnificent 16th century tombs from the Caccavello–D'Auria Neapolitan workshop, set in the center of the cross and the presbytery, attest to the wealth of the Spinelli family who financed the church and used it as a sort of private Pantheon. The second chapel on the left holds the relics of those massacred during the sack of Otranto in 1480. The apse contains a particularly fine 16th-century Mannerist-style choir. ⊠ *Piazza Enrico De Nicola, Decumano Maggiore* ☎ *081/444297* ☉ *Daily 8:30–7:30* Ⓜ *Metro: Piazza Garibaldi.*

Town & Country: La Sanità to Capodimonte

The diadem to Naples, the Parco di Capodimonte is the crowning point of the vast mountainous plain that slopes down through the city to the waterfront area. Nearly three miles removed from the madding crowds in the *centro storico,* the sylvan and verdantly green mount of Capodimonte is enjoyed by locals and visitors alike as a favored escape from the overheated city center. With its picture-perfect views over the entire city and bay, the park was first founded in the 18th century as a hunting preserve by Charles of Bourbon. Before long, partly to house the famous Farnese collection which he had inherited from his mother, he commissioned a spectacular Palazzo Reale for the park. Today this palace is the Museo di Capodimonte, which contains among its other treasures the city's greatest collection of old master paintings. Here, rooms virtually wallpapered with Titians, Caravaggios, and Parmagianinos will be your reward after a tour through La Sanità, one of Naples's most densely populated neighborhoods and still studded with legendary palaces and gilded churches. In between, in the district known as I Vergini (so-called after an inscription found on a ancient Greek tomb in the area relating to the women who had dedicated their virginity to the Greek god Eunosto), you can catch your breath at the haunted Catacombs of San Gennaro.

a good walk

From the Piazza Cavour metro stop, just to the west of the complex of the Museo Archeologico Nazionale, begin by walking eastward along Piazza Cavour past the picturesque Porta San Gennaro—a relic of the old 15th-century city walls—until it becomes Via Foria. Then swing a left into Via Vergini, leading into the district known as La Sanità. Wander into the restored green and cream **Palazzo dello Spagnolo** ㉝ ▸, at No. 19 Piazza Vergini, to admire the stunning staircase built by one of the greatest Neapolitan architects of the 18th century, Ferdinando Sanfelice. Opposite lies the church he designed, Santa Maria succurrere miseris. Walk up via Arena della Sanità, where at No. 2 you'll find the sadly rundown palazzo designed by Sanfelice as his own residence. Here, the architect created his first courtyard "falcon's wing" staircase, used to such theatrical effect at the Spagnolo palazzo. Head into via della Sanità to the Baroque Church of **Santa Maria della Sanità** ㉞ with the **Catacombs of San Gaudioso** ㉟ below. Then take the elevator (only during daylight hours) from the Ponte up to corso Amedeo di Savoia and walk up to the *Tondo* (roundabout) close to the ancient **Catacombe di San Gennaro** ㊱, sited below the steps leading up to the **Museo di Capodimonte** ㊲. After extensively touring this gigantic treasure house—filled with some of Naples's finest old-master paintings and surrounded by a famous park—take Bus 24 down to the the center city, perhaps to the bus stop adjacent to the Museo Archeologico Nazionale, if you feel like paying another call on ancient Greece and Rome.

TIMING The Museo di Capodimonte enjoys the extended viewing hours of the city's biggest museums, so you'll want to tour La Sanità and I Vergini before heading up to Capodimonte.

Sights to See

㉟ **Catacombe di San Gaudioso.** One of the noted sights of the district known as the Sanità—in ancient days, this was outside the main city walls and the area was thus used as a burial site—this labyrinth was tunnelled by the Romans for use as water-cisterns. By the 5th century AD, it had become the shrine devoted to the North African hermit-bishop, St. Gaudiosus. A few early mosaics and frescoes adorn the musty caves but what will fascinate most here is the range of burial techniques on view, including a rather macabre one favored by the well-heeled of the early 17th century. The dearly departed was walled in upright in a niche with his head cemented into the rear wall. Once the body fluids had drained away, the headless body was removed and buried, the skull then placed over a frescoed skeleton portrait of the deceased with a symbol or a pose depicting their rank or profession (note the painter Giovanni Balducci, for example). Gain access to these catacombs from the church of Santa Maria della Sanità. ☒ *Via della Sanità 124, Sanità* ☏ *081/5441305* ☒ *€3* ☉ *Guided tours Sun.–Fri. 9:30, 10:15, 11, 11:45, and 12:30; Sat. 9:30, 10:15, 11, 11:45, 12:30, 5:10, 5:50, and 6:30* Ⓜ *Metro: Piazza Cavour.*

㊱ **Catacombe di San Gennaro.** These catacombs—designed for Christian burial rather than as bolt-holes—go at least as far back as the 2nd century AD. This was where St. Gennaro's body was brought from Pozzuoli in the 4th century, after which the catacombs became a key pilgrimage center. The 45-minute guided tour of the two-level site takes you down a series of vestibules with fine frescoed niche tombs. The imposing bulk of the early 20th-century church looms over the site (Madre del Buon

Consiglio), apparently inspired by St. Peter's in Rome. ⊠ *Via Capodimonte 16, next to the Madonna del Buon Consiglio church, Capodimonte* ☎ *081/7411071* 🎟 *€2.50* ⊗ *Guided tours daily every 45 mins 9:30–11:45 AM; afternoon tours for groups by appointment only.*

★ ㊲ **Museo di Capodimonte.** The grandiose 18th-century Neoclassic Bourbon royal palace, in the vast Bosco di Capodimonte (Capodimonte Park), which served as the royal hunting preserve and later as the site of the Capodimonte porcelain works, is a spectacular setting for Naples's finest collection of old master paintings and decorative arts. Perched on top of a hill overlooking all of Naples and the bay, the palace was built in 1738 by Charles III of Bourbon as a hunting retreat, then expanded by Antonio Medrano—architect of the Teatro San Carlo—to become the repository of the fabled Farnese art collection Charles inherited from his mother, Elizabeth Farnese. For this art-loving king, however, collecting was not enough; to compete with his father-in-law, Frederick Augustus, the Elector of Saxony, who had founded the celebrated Meissen porcelain factory, Charles decided to set up his own royal factory, opposite the Capodimonte Palace, and before long, the "soft-paste" porcelain figurines of Pulcinello, biscuit vendors, and pretty nymphs were the choicest collectibles for Europe's rich. Fittingly, the most unique room in the palace is entirely crafted from porcelain (3,000 pieces of it)—**Queen Maria Amalia's Porcelain Parlor** (1757–59), built for the royal palace at Portici but relocated here.

But Capodimonte's greatest treasure is the excellent collection of paintings, well displayed in the **Galleria Nazionale** on the palace's first and second stories. Before you arrive at this remarkable collection, a magnificent staircase leads to the royal apartments, where you'll find beautiful antique furniture, most of it on the splashy scale so dear to the Bourbons, and a staggering collection of porcelain and majolica from the various royal residences. The walls of the apartments are hung with numerous portraits, providing a close-up of the unmistakable Bourbon features, a challenge to any court painter. The main galleries on the first floor are devoted to work from the 13th to the 18th centuries, including many familiar masterpieces by Dutch and Spanish masters, as well as by the great Italians: Simone Martini's *St. Louis Crowning King Robert* (1317), Masaccio's *Crucifixion* (1426), Giovanni Bellini's *Transfiguration* (1480), Annibale Carracci's *Pietà* (1600), Parmigianino's *Antea* (1531), Gentileschi's *Judith and Holofernes* (1630), Caravaggio's *Flagellation* (1607–10), and a bevy of famous Titians, including the *Danaë* (1545).

On the top floor, a set of galleries features international contemporary art—including Andy Warhol's *Mount Vesuvius*, painted when the artist visited Naples in 1985—while the second floor holds extensive collections of 14th- to 19th-century Neapolitan painting and decorative arts, including plenty of dramatic renditions of Vesuvius in all its raging glory. When you've had your fill of these, take time to admire the genuine article from the shady parkland outside, designed by Ferdinando Sanfelice and then adapted into the "natural" English style, which affords a sweeping view of the bay. You can get to the museum via Bus No. 24 from Piazza Municipio or Piazza Carità. ⊠ *Via Miano 2 (Porta Piccola), Via Capodimonte, Capodimonte* ☎ *848/800288 for information and tickets for special exhibitions* 🎟 *€7.50* ⊗ *Tues.–Sun. 8:30–7:30; ticket office closes at 6:30; Closed Mon.*

㉝ **Palazzo della Spagnola.** Spectacularly dramatic, quintessentially Baroque, the architectural masterworks of Ferdinando Sanfelice (1675–1748) are among the most iconic Neapolitan buildings. Previously trained as a set designer and parade decorator for the royal court, he brought these skills to bear on a number of palazzi he designed in the borghi of I Vergini and La Sanità for a newly wealthy set of patrons. Among the largest was the Palazzo della Spagnola, built for the Marchese Moscati in 1738 (it became the property of a Spanish noble family in the 19th century, from whence came its present name). The showpiece here is the double-flight external staircase in the palace courtyard. Critics likened the form of this three-flight honeycomb of ascending bays to the wingspread of a falcon, so this setpiece became known as a stair *ad ali di falco,* a "falcon's wing" staircase. The staircase dramatically separates a smaller courtyard from a larger one and creates a scenographic effect that is typically and floridly Neapolitan. Sanfelice built this staircase ten years after he first created one for his own palazzo, which is found about three blocks to the west at Via Sanità 2. Both palazzi now contain private apartments but the courtyards are usually open to the public. ⊠ *Via Vergini 19, Sanità* ⊙ *Mon.–Fri. 7:30–2, 3:30–9, Sat, 7:30–1.*

㉞ **Santa Maria della Sanità.** This Baroque Greek-cross–shape basilica, replete with majolica-tiled dome, was commissioned by Dominican friars in the early 17th century. The church contains a small museum of 17th-century Counter-Reformation art—the most flagrantly devotional school of Catholic art—and includes no less than five Luca Giordano altarpieces. Elsewhere, the richly-decorated elevated presbytery, complete with double staircase, provides the only note of color in the grey and white decoration. This also provides access to the noted Catacombe di San Gaudioso. ⊠ *Via della Sanità 124, Sanità* ☎ *081/5441305* ⊙ *Mon.–Sat. 8:30–12:30 and 5–8, Sun. 8:30–1:30.*

> **need a break?** In teeming Via dei Vergini, give in to temptation with a pastry from **Pasticerria dei Vergini** (⊠ Via dei Vergini 66, Vergini ☎ 081/455989) to enjoy a truly calorie-bursting Neapolitan specialty. If you don't have a sweet tooth, pick up a sandwich from **da Salvatore,** a tiny snack bar next door.

Funiculì-funiculà: The Vomero to the Lungomare

When the French writer and philosopher Montesquieu visited Naples in 1728, he exclaimed: "Nothing is more beautiful than the siting of Naples in the gulf: Naples is like an amphitheater on the sea." This tour starts at the top of that theater—the Vomero Hill—then goes back down to its elegant "orchestra" level: Naples's famous waterfront area, the Lungomare, which runs from the Riviera di Chiaia to the Castel dell'Ovo, the harbor castle. Neapolitans often say their town's glories are vertical—the white *guglia* (religious obelisk) that festoon the historic quarter, the eight-story tenements of Spaccanapoli, and Vomero, the towering hill that overlooks the city center. Even longtime residents love to head up here to gaze in wonder at the entire city from the balcony belvedere of the Museo di San Martino. Before them, a rich spread of southern Italian amplitude fills the eye: hillsides dripping with wedding-cake hotels, miles of villainously ugly apartment houses, streets short and narrow—leading to an unspeakable as well as unsolvable traffic problem—countless church spires and domes, and far below, the reason it all works, the intensely blue Bay of Naples. To tie together the lower parts and upper reaches of the city, everyone uses the *funivia*—the cable-car system that runs on three separate routes up and down the Vomero. Before you know it, you can be hopping and skipping over the city with these funiculars, whistling, of course, "Funiculì-funiculà," the famous 1880 song composed by Neapolitans Peppino Turco and Luigi Danza to celebrate the opening of the first line.

Thanks to the funiculars, you can readily take in many of Naples's aristocratic pleasures and treasures: the chic Piazza dei Martiri sector; the gilded 19th-century Villa Pignatelli; three museums that crown the Vomero Hill—the Villa Floridiana, the Certosa di San Martino, and the Castel Sant'Elmo; down to the Lungomare, the grandest stretch of waterfront in Naples. In the 19th century Naples's waterfront harbored the picturesque quarter that was called Santa Lucia, a district dear to artists and musicians and known for its fishermen's cottages. The fishermen were swept away when an enormous landfill project extended the land out to what is now Via Nazario Sauro and Via Partenope, the address for some of Naples's finest hotels. Today, the waterfront promenade has lost much of its former color, but it still retains a uniquely Neapolitan charm.

a good walk

Begin at the main station of the Funicolare Centrale, on the tiny Piazza Duca d'Aosta, just opposite the Via Toledo entrance to the Galleria Umberto I. After two hillside stops, get off at the end of the line, Stazione Fuga, near the top of the Vomero Hill. To get to the Castel Sant'Elmo/ Certosa di San Martino complex, head out from the station, turning right on Via Cimarosa, then left on Via Morghen. At the next street, Via Scarlatti—the main thoroughfare of the neighborhood—turn right and walk up the steps of the hill, cut twice across the snake-like Via Morghen, then follow the path around the left side of the Montesanto funicular until you run into the Via Tito Angelini. This street, lined with some of Naples's best Belle Epoque mansions, leads to the **Castel Sant'Elmo** ㊳ ☞ and the adjoining **Certosa di San Martino** ㊴, which commands magnificent vistas over city and sea to Vesuvius. After viewing this enormous complex (its star exhibition is the collection of Presepe, or Nativity, scenes), backtrack to Via Scarlatti until you make a left on Via Bernini at Piazza Vanvitelli. This piazza, with no shortage of smart bars and trattorias, remains the center for the Vomero district, and is also the site of the city's first pedestrianism project (Via Scarlatti, between Piazza Vanvitelli and Via Luca Giordano), now a fun gathering point for talented street performers. Walk right onto Via Cimarosa for two blocks until you reach the entrance to the **Villa Floridiana** ㊵, today a museum filled with aristocratic knickknacks and surrounded by a once-regal park. After viewing the villa, make a right from the park entrance on Via Cimarosa for two blocks until you reach the Stazione Cimarosa of the Chiaia funicular, which will take you back down to the Lungomare area. From the Amedeo funicular station walk down Via del Parco Margherita, past Piazza Amedeo, making a left onto Via Colonna, and taking the first right onto the steps at the top of Via Bausan. The steps will take you down to the Riviera di Chiaia (*chiaia* means "beach" in the Neapolitan dialect), where a final right turn brings you to the **Villa Pignatelli** ㊶, whose red-velvet salons still seem warm with the spirits of the Rothschilds, Actons, and other aristos who once called this home. From here cross the Riviera to the waterfront park of the Villa Comunale and its world-famous **Aquarium** ㊷.

For a late lunch, follow the Riviera past the Piazza della Vittoria onto Via Partenope and the spectacular **Castel dell'Ovo** ㊸. In its shadow is the enchanting **Borgo Marinaro** ㊹—a dollhouse of a fishermen's village, where seafood restaurants offer good food. From here, cross back over into Via Santa Lucia opposite, and walk along until you turn left into Via Console leading to Piazza del Plebiscito. Turn left up Via Egiziaca a Pizzafalcone for a 20-minute hike to the top of the historic hill of **Pizzofalcone**, ㊺ also known as Monte Echia, site of the first Greek settlement in the area. Transformed into an elegant residential quarter in the Baroque and Rococo periods, the area is gradually shaking off its neglected, traffic-ridden reputation and undergoing a long-awaited cleanup. Explore the district's church of **Santa Maria degli Angeli** 46 (if it's after 4:30 PM when churches reopen for evening hours). View Naples's finest 18th-century palace courtyard—with a seriously spectacular double stairway—at the **Palazzo Serra di Cassano** 47, then take in **Santa Maria Egiziaca** 48. Nearby is the church of **La Nunziatella** 49. See if there's a theatrical performance you wish to attend at Pizzofalcone's theater, the Politeama. Return to the church of Santa Maria degli Angeli on Via Nicotera to find the elegant Empire-era Ponte di Chiaia, a 17th-century gateway restored in the 1880s. To view the gateway properly, take the elevator down (open during shopping hours)—*never* take the neighboring stairway, as its deserted route makes it a haunt for muggers—to the elegant shopping and dining of the Chiaia district. If you're looking for a place for a pizza dinner, not far away is Naples's most historic pizzeria, Brandi, at Salita Sant'Anna di Palazzo 1. Head back along Via Chiaia to the Piazza dei Martiri to join chic Neapolitans on their evening *passeggiata*, shopping the boutiques, bookstores, and antiques shops lining the streets that radiate off the piazza (particularly the designer-dense stretch between Via Carlo Poerio and Via dei Mille). For a particularly romantic farewell to Naples, wander over to vico Santa Maria a Cappella Vecchia, which leads out of the piazza to the Palazzo Hamilton, former home of Sir William Hamilton, the great collector of antiquities, British ambassador, and, most famously, husband to the immortal Emma, lover of Admiral Horatio Nelson. Their residence, perhaps still spirit-warm, was a former Benedictine abbey, today marked by a portal dated 1506. Nearby is that unique icon of Naples, the **Gradoni di Chiaia** 50, a wonderous staircase-cum-street. The Metropolitana Piazza Amedeo station is nearby, while the R3 bus route follows the Riviera di Chiaia, which is the main avenue of the Lungomare. Farther to the east, on the edge of the city proper lies Naples's famous park, the **Parco Virgiliano** 51 and the coastal district of Posillipo, landmarked by the haunted **Palazzo Donn'Anna** 52.

TIMING As always in Naples, it's best to start out early in the morning to fit most of your sightseeing in before the lunch break—and the midday heat. Aim to get to the San Martino complex atop the Vomero hill at opening time and allow at least three hours to take it in along with the Castel Sant'Elmo and a further half-hour for the Villa Floridiana, being careful to time your visit to coincide with the tours of the villa's ceramics museum. If you run out of steam or time at the end of the morning, there are a number of relaxed snack and dining options in the Vomero, though without the atmospheric backdrop of the Borgo Marinaro down at sea level. If you prefer a leisurely wander or wish to visit an exhibition at Castel Sant'Elmo, go straight to the Borgo from the Riviera di Chiaia following the seafront, and then swing back to Villa Pignatelli and the Aquarium.

Sights to See

42 **Aquarium.** Originally named by the Greeks after the mermaid Parthenope (who slew herself after being rejected by Odysseus, at least in the poet Virgil's version), it's only fitting that Naples should have established one of Europe's first public aquariums in 1874. At the time—when, not so incidentally, the public imagination was being stirred by Jules Verne's Captain Nemo and Hans Christian Andersen's Little Mermaid—technological innovations came into place to funnel seawater directly from the bay into the aquarium tanks, which showcase some 200 species of fish and marine plants (undoubtedly better off here than in the somewhat polluted Bay of Naples, their natural habitat). Officially named the Stazione Zoologica, founded by the German scientist Anton Dohrn,

and housed in a Stil Liberty building designed by Adolf von Hildebrandt, the aquarium quickly became the wonder of Naples for children and art-exhausted adults. Today the ground floors contain the aquarium tanks—fishy "living rooms" decorated with rocks and plants of the region and illuminated by skylights. Upstairs are research facilities and the library, which is decorated with Hans von Marées's magnificent mosaics showing the Lungomare area as it looked when the Aquarium opened, when it was directly on the water. To see the library you need to make a request when buying your ticket. ⊠ *Stazione Zoologica, Viale A. Dohrn, Chiaia* ☎ *081/5833263 for information and library visits* ⊕ *www.szn.it* ✑ *€1.50* ⊗ *Mar.–Oct., Tues.–Sat. 9–6, Sun. 9:30–7:30; Nov.–Feb., Tues.–Sat. 9–5, Sun. 9–2* Ⓜ *Metro: Piazza Amedeo.*

㊹ Borgo Marinaro. If your thoughts of Naples involve the strumming of a mandolin, fishermen singing "Santa Lucia," and idyllic seaside sunsets, the city can be a sad disappointment—that is, until you venture to the Borgo Marinaro, a toy fishermen's village nestled in the shadows of mighty Castel dell'Ovo. After the cholera epidemic of 1884, entire quarters of the city were demolished and the rubble was transported to the Santa Lucia quarter as *colmata,* or landfill. For the most part, picturesque fishermen's houses were replaced by the Lungomare's luxurious hotels, but something of old Naples remains here at this little harbor port, officially called the Porto di Santa Lucia. Adorned with kitschy seafood restaurants, lovely outdoor cafés, and thriving boat shops, it inhabits the small islet called Megaris by the ancients and now connected to the mainland by the mole-pier of the Castel dell'Ovo. From the Santa Lucia shrine (just under the mole), stroll along the Lungomare past the Hotel Excelsior to the **Fontana dell'Immacolatella** (1622), sculpted by Pietro Bernini, father of the famous Gianlorenzo, which frames a great vista of Vesuvius. ⊠ *Via Partenope, at Castel dell'Ovo, Santa Lucia.*

FodorsChoice
★

㊸ Castel dell'Ovo. The oldest castle in Naples, the Castel dell'Ovo sits on the most picturesque point of the bay, standing guard over the city it protects. Occupying the isle of Megaris, it was originally the site of the Roman villa of Lucullus—proof, if you need it, that the ancient Romans knew a premium location when they saw one (for the same reason, some of the city's top hotels share the same site today). By the 12th century, it had become a fortress under the Normans; it was once the prison of Conradin and of Beatrice, daughter of Manfred, last of the Hohenstaufen rulers. Its name refers to the legend that the poet Virgil saw a magical egg rise from the waves here. This must have been one tough egg to crack, as the fortress still looks awe-inspiring and impregnable, although it lost many of its towers and battlements centuries ago. The castle's gigantic rooms, rock tunnels, and belvederes over the bay are among Naples's most striking sights as well as a magical setting for the temporary contemporary-art exhibitions sponsored by the city council, so this is a must-do. ⊠ *Via Partenope, at the Borgo Marinaro, Santa Lucia* ☎ *081/2400055* ✑ *Free* ⊗ *Oct.–May, Mon.–Sat. 9–5; June–Sept.,Mon.–Sat. 9–7, Sun. 9–1:30.*

FodorsChoice
★

㊳ Castel Sant'Elmo. Long a powerful symbol of foreign and governmental domination, the imposing fortress of the Castel Sant'Elmo broods over the city center from its hilltop perch above the Vomero and seems to be policing you wherever you walk in Naples. Originally built by Charles I of Anjou in 1275 and enlarged by the Angevin kings in the 1330s, it was transformed in the 16th century by Pedro Scrivà under viceroy Don Pedro de Toledo into its present stoutly fortified six-point-star configuration. The castle cells housed many prisoners over the centuries, including the philosopher–monk Tommaso Campanella (1568–1639), leaders of the Masaniello rebellion, and even patriots of the short-lived 1799 Neapolitan rebellion against the Bourbons. From the ramparts, panoramic views of the city extend in all directions. Today the great rooms of the castle often host contemporary-art exhibitions and conferences. ⊠ *Largo San Martino, Vomero* ☎ *081/5784030* 🎫 *€3* 🕑 *Tues.–Sun. 9–2* Ⓜ *Funicular railway: San Martino.*

★ ㊴ **Certosa di San Martino.** Atop a rocky promontory with a fabulous view of the entire city, and with majestic salons that would please any monarch, the Certosa di San Martino is a monastery that seems more like a palace. In fact, by the 18th century Ferdinand IV was threatening to halt the order's government subsidy, so sumptuous was this *certosa*, or charter house, which had been started in 1325 under the royal patronage of Charles of Anjou. With the Carthusians' vast wealth and love of art, it was only a matter of time before dour Angevin Gothic was traded in for varicolor Neapolitan Baroque, thanks to the contributions of many 17th- and 18th-century sculptors and painters. Although the Angevin heritage can be seen in the pointed arches and cross-vaulted ceiling of the Certosa Church across the courtyard just opposite the ticket barrier, the church was overhauled from 1631 onward, partly as a response to Naples's deliverance from Vesuvius the same year. Other pre-1631 survivors are the remarkable wooden inlaid cupboards in the sacristy (1587–1600), at the back left of the church: the top row shows stories from the Scriptures while the bottom row regales us with fine (imaginary) perspectives.

The sacristy leads into the later Cappella del Tesoro, with Luca Giordano's ceiling fresco of Judith holding aloft Holofernes's head and the painting by Il Ribera (the *Pietà* over the altar is one of his masterpieces). The main Baroque style note was set by Cosimo Fanzago (1591–1678), an architect, sculptor, and decorator who was as devout as he was mad. His polychrome marble work is at its finest here in the church, while he displays a gamut of sculptural skills in the **Chiostro Grande** (Great Cloister), also adding the curious small monks' graveyard, bounded by a marble balustrade topped with marble skulls. Fanzago's ceremonial portals at each corner of the cloister are among the most spectacular of all Baroque creations—aswirl with Mannerist volutes and Michelangelo-esque ornament, they serve as mere frames for six life-size statues of Carthusian saints, who sit atop the doorways, judging all with deathless composure.

Most of the monastery, which was suppressed in 1861, now serves as a museum. For a sound introduction to monastic life and a well-signposted history of the Carthusians and San Martino, see the panoramic renovated galleries of the **Museo dell'Opera** around the Chiostro Grande. Room 24 has a helpful 18th-century scale model of the monastic complex, while Room 26 has 19th-century paintings of monastic life. Dalbono's 13 gouaches of Vesuvius in various angry poses are attractively displayed in Room 28. If you're beginning to think that the 17th century in Naples was all grand masters and opulence, Room 37 and the various paintings depicting the plague might correct that impression. Nearby is the **Sezione Presepiale**, the greatest collection of Nativity crèches in the world. Ranging in size from a nutshell to an entire room, they offer supreme evocations of 18th-century life. Many figures are garbed in exquisite costumes and have portraitlike faces. The most noted is the *Presepe Cuciniello,* with more than 160 shepherds, eight dogs, countless angels, Moors, chickens; cheese wheels, beggars, and dwarfs, all worshiping the Holy Family against a brilliant blue sky. If visiting around Christmas, expect to share the displays with hundreds of Italian schoolchildren unless you manage to arrive at opening time in the morning; note that this section is only open during the winter holiday season.

Just by the entrance to the monastery's terraced gardens and plush 19th-century carriages is the **Quarto del Priore,** the prior's apartment, which was the residence of the only monk who had any contact with the outside world. It is an extravaganza filled with frescoes, 18th-century majolica-tiled floors, and paintings, with extensive gardens where scenic *pergolati* (roofed balconies) overlook the bay—a domicile that might be called the very vestibule of heaven. ✉ *Museo Nazionale di San Martino, Largo San Martino, Vomero* ☎ *081/5781769* 💶 *€6* 🕓 *Tues.–Sun. 8:30–7. Some rooms are often closed afternoons (Quarto del Priore), while others are open seasonally (the Sezione Presepiale nativity scenes)* Ⓜ *Funicular railway: San Martino.*

★ ⑩ **Gradoni di Chiaia.** Built in the 1870s and one of the most extraordinary "streets" in the world, this amazing thoroughfare is half-chasm, half-staircase. Due to the city's hilly terrain, such *scalinatelli* were used for streets too steep to be climbed without steps. A veritable canyon lined with 19th-century six-story-high tenements, leading up to the church of S. Caterina di Siena, and backdropped by the drama of San Martino Hill, this is the most soaring and eyepopping of Naples's iconic "gradoni." Too bad most of the laundry lines hanging over the street have disappeared. ✉ *Entrances on Via Chiaia and Via San Caterina di Siena, Chiaia* Ⓜ *Metro: Piazza Amedeo.*

⑭ **La Nunziatella.** In 1736 the Jesuits asked Ferdinando Sanfelice, then at work several blocks away on the magnificent Palazzo Serra di Cassano, to transform a novitiate into a church; the result is one of the jewels of 18th-century Neapolitan architecture, with rich but not overwhelming marble-inlay work and an excellent series of contemporary frescoes by Francesco de Mura. The interior of the church can occasionally be viewed in the morning if you ask the guard or chaplain at the adjoining military college, but usually you need official permission from the Ministry of Defense. ✉ *Via Generale Parisi, Pizzofalcone* ☎ *081/7641520.*

⑫ **Palazzo Donn'Anna.** One of the great icons of romantic Naples and immortalized many times over the centuries in paintings, this bayside palace (now with privately owned apartments) adorns the shoreline of Posillipo (*see below*), the superb suburb that sits just to the west of the Mergellina harbor, the westernmost sector of the city center proper. Due to its spirit-haunted past, the palace, unfinished to begin with, has always been rather dilapidated but that is part of its centuries-old (and still powerful: Vanvitelli's 18th-century painting of *A Prospect of Posillipo with Palazzo Donn'Anna* recently sold for a record-breaking $3.5 million) charm. The palace we see was designed by Cosimo Fanzago in 1642 for Princess Donn'Anna Carafa, the beautiful local-born wife of the Duke of Medina, the Spanish Viceroy of Naples, who proceeded to abandon her when he was recalled to Spain. While the interior is closed, the porticoed terrace—with fantastic views over the Bay of Naples—may be open (ask at the gate for access to the courtyard). Fanzago's palazzo arose on a site that once housed 14th-century Queen Joan's private palace, where, according to legend, she lured young fishermen to a night of passion before throwing them into the sea. The best way to get to the palazzo is to take Bus 140 from Piazza Vittoria. Nearby is Bagni Elena, one of the most convenient city beaches, if you want a quick dip in rather murky waters or a laze in the sun. Further along the shore are the beloved beaches of Marechiaro and Gaiola, but there is no bus access to them. Just down the shoreline, closer to the city, is the fabled villa that was once home to Sir William Hamilton, the 18th-century English ambassador, great collector of antiquities, and husband to Emma. Landmarked by a semicircular portico and terrace overlooking the bay, the private house is now home to a family of the Neapolitan aristocracy. ✉ *Piazza Donn'Anna 9, Posillipo.*

★ ㊸ **Palazzo Serra di Cassano.** By the late 18th century, Via Monte di Dio had become one of Naples's poshest addresses. Lined with palazzi and villas, it was chosen by Prince Aloisio Serra di Cassano for his family palace, designed by Ferdinando Sanfelice, the most important architect of domestic architecture in Naples. In this city where spectacle and love of show have always been important, the appropriately gigantic double-flight staircase that Sanfelice built in the palace courtyard wouldn't have been out of place in a lavish 1950s MGM musical. The regal staircase was reduced to back-door status when the palazzo's main door on Via Egiziaca was closed by the prince in honor of his son Gennaro, executed as one of the participants in the 1799 revolution. Today the Istituto Italiano per gli Studi Filosofici, an institute devoted to philosophy studies, occupies much of the palazzo; it offers a full calendar of courses and lectures throughout the year. ✉ *Via Monte di Dio 14–15, Pizzofalcone* ☎ *081/2452150* ⊘ *Weekdays 7:30–1 and 3–7, Sat. 7–noon.*

㊶ **Parco Virgiliano.** At the far western end of the city lies one of Naples's most tranquil spots, the Parco Virgiliano, reached up an achingly long flight of steps and named after the great ancient Roman poet Virgil. The park is most famed for its legendary Bay of Naples vista. Immortalized in countless postcards and pizza-parlor paintings—you know, it's that one showing a lone umbrella pine tree sitting on a bluff overlooking all of the Bay of Naples and the city, with Vesuvius in the background—the vista is situated not far from "Virgil's Tomb." Unfortunately, the legendary pine tree is no longer standing. The small park is still beautiful and is, according to legend, the site of the poet's tomb, now judged to be an anonymous Roman *columbarium* (funerary monument). It's set not far from both the Crypta Neapolitana, an ancient Roman tunnel now caved in, and the tomb-memorial of Giacomo Leopardi, the noted 19th-century poet. Gain access to the park from behind the church of Santa Maria di Piedigrotta, close to Piazza Piedigrotta, just outside the Stazione di Mergellina station. The park rises to the left immediately after the railway bridge crossing Via Piedigrotta, just before the road tunnel entrance. ✉ *Parco Virgiliano, Salita della Grotta 20, Mergellina* ☎ *081/669390* ✉ *Free* ⊘ *9–1 hr before sunset.*

㊺ **Pizzofalcone.** In the 7th century BC, Pizzofalcone (Falcon's Beak) *was* Naples. The ancient Greeks had settled here because, legend says, the body of the siren Parthenope had been found washed ashore on the beach at the foot of the Pizzofalcone Hill, then known as Monte Echia. More than two millennia later, in the 18th century, the hill, mere feet from the bay and the Castel dell'Ovo, became a fashionable address as Naples's rich and titled sought to escape the congestion and heat of the city center. The rocky promontory soon became studded with Baroque palaces and Rococo churches. You can walk up to Pizzofalcone by taking Via G. Serra just to the right-hand colonnade of the Church of San Francesco di Paola, on Piazza del Plebiscito, to Pizzofalcone's main piazza, Santa Maria degli Angeli; or take the elevator during daylight hours (never the dark staircase) by the bridge on Via Chiaia. The leading sights are the palazzi along Via Monte di Dio—including Palazzo Serra di Cassano—and the churches of La Nunziatella, Santa Maria degli Angeli, and Santa Maria Egiziaca. Like other parts of Naples, Pizzofalcone harbors both palaces and slums; unlike other parts, it's off the beaten path, so don't stop to answer questions from seemingly innocuous strollers. ⊠ *Piazza Santa Maria degli Angeli, accessed via the elevator at the Ponte di Chiaia on Via Chiaia, Pizzofalcone.*

46 Santa Maria degli Angeli a Pizzofalcone. In 1590 the princess of Sulmona, Costanza Doria del Carretto, commissioned this church not far from her palace on Pizzofalcone. In the 17th century the church was given to the Theatine order and enlarged by an architect belonging to the order. The lively vault and dome frescoes are by Giovanni Beinaschi from Turin, better known as a painter of genre scenes, and there are some good paintings by Luca Giordano and Massimo Stanzione tucked away in the smaller side chapels and oratory. ⊠ *Piazza Santa Maria degli Angeli, Pizzofalcone* ☎ 081/7644974 ⏱ *Daily 7:30–11:30 and 5:30–7.*

48 Santa Maria Egiziaca a Pizzofalcone. This church is probably the masterpiece of Cosimo Fanzago, a Lombard architect and sculptor who became one of the leading innovators of Neapolitan Baroque. The octagonal form of the church was to influence the work of many of his contemporaries, although Fanzago was never to finish this church; the project died a natural death in 1665 along with that of its patron, Spanish king Philip IV. The white cupola—contrasting starkly with the rest of the skyscape in this area—was only completed in 1714 and the church first consecrated in 1717. ⊠ *Via Egiziaca 30, Pizzofalcone* ☎ 081/7645199 ⏱ *Daily 9:30–1.*

40 Villa Floridiana. Now a chiefly residential neighborhood, the Vomero Hill was once the patrician address of many of Naples's most extravagant estates. La Floridiana is the sole surviving 19th-century example, built in 1817 on order of Ferdinand I for Lucia Migliaccio, duchess of Floridia—their portraits greet you as you enter. Only nine shocking months after his first wife, the Habsburg Maria Carolina, died, when the court was still in mourning, Ferdinand secretly married Lucia, his longtime mistress. Scandal ensued, but the king and his new wife were too happy to worry, escaping high above the city and court gossip to this elegant little estate. Designed by architect Antonio Niccolini in Neoclassic style, the house is now occupied by the **Museo Nazionale della Ceramica Duca di Martina,** a museum devoted to the decorative arts of the 18th and 19th centuries. Countless display cases are filled with what Edith Wharton described as "all those fragile and elaborate trifles the irony of fate preserves when brick and marble crumble": Sèvres, Limoges, and Meissen porcelains, gold watches, ivory fans, glassware, enamels, majolica vases. Sadly, there are no period rooms left to see. Due to economic measures, escorted visits (not tours per se) are now provided through the myriad rooms. Outside is a park designed in the English style by Degenhardt, who also designed the park at Capodimonte. Nannies and their charges walk along the winding paths between spreading pines and araucarias, while joggers head for the cool of the holm-oak wood on the shady east side. Unfortunately, and despite the army of park attendants and gardeners, the park is not well tended—graffiti defaces the Grecian Tempietto and red plastic fencing prevents access to much of the panoramic viewing platform at the bottom of the park. ⊠ *Via Cimarosa 77, Vomero* ☎ *081/ 5788418* 🎫 *€2.50* ⏱ *Museum Mon.–Sat. 9:30, 11, and 12:30, escorted visits; park 9–1 hr before sunset* Ⓜ *Metro: Piazza Vanvitelli.*

----

need a break?

Walking down the fashionable Via Scarlatti in the Vomero, once a traffic-choked artery and now a bustling pedestrian precinct, you'll come upon **Bar Daniele** (⊠ Via Scarlatti 104, Vomero ☎ 081/ 5780555), a stalwart Vomero caffè producing a wide range of cakes and waist-threatening delicacies. If you need something more substantial, look at the *rosticceria* selection at the back.

④ **Villa Pignatelli.** More officially known as the Museo Diego Aragona Pignatelli Cortes, this is one of the few patrician homes of old Naples that is open to the public. When built in 1826 by architect P. Valente for the aristocratic Acton family (Sir Harold Acton, who died in the mid-1990s, was the author of many books on Neapolitan history; Princess Acton, whose family to this day hosts the best New Year's Eve parties in Naples, still occupies the family palazzo, which towers over nearby Via Chiaia), it was one was of the city's premier houses, with an imperially grand ,Grecian-temple front and a beautiful park. In 1841 the barons Rothschild took over and redid rooms in Second Empire splendor, including the leather-lined smoking salon and the Sala Rosso, a red velvet-and-gold jewel box. Prince Pignatelli Cortes's daughter donated the house to the city in 1952, and he must be spinning in his grave at the shoddy state of the house today, with its lighting dimmed, enough dust to cover Pompeii, and rooms used as warehouses. The house may be spruced up for some of the temporary exhibitions held here from time to time, but it usually looks like a set for Violetta's death scene in *La Traviata*. What makes a visit worthwhile is the Banco di Napoli art collection on the *piano nobile*, with fine works by the 19th-century sculptor Vincenzo Gemito and a delightful gallery of 18th- and 19th-century landscapes (Room 6). On the grounds is a carriage house (eternally closed for restoration) that contains the **Museo delle Carrozze** (Carriage Museum), with coaches from the late 1800s to the early 1900s. A stroll in the park here is a pleasant respite from the noisy city streets. ✉ *Riviera di Chiaia 200, Chiaia* ☎ *081/669675* ✇ *€2.00* ☉ *Tues.–Sun. 8:30–7:30.*

off the beaten path

POSILLIPO – To the west of the city's main shoreline crescent, known as the Riviera di Chiaia, is the seaside suburb of Posillipo, whose name comes from the ancient Greek *Pausilypon* ("respite from pain"). First developed as the kingdom of Poggioreale in the 15th century by Alfonso II, this coast, honeycombed with idyllic coves and beaches, became Naples's Côte d'Azur in the 19th century when many vacation villas were built here. Today, most remain private but are sadly overshadowed by modern apartment buildings. Still, the shoreline here harbors picturesque spots like the hamlet of Marechiaro ("clear sea")—home to two of Naples's best restaurants and some of the city's nicest beaches and bathing establishments— and not far from the Palazzo Donn'Anna, built by Cosimo Fanzago for the wife of the Spanish viceroy in 1637 and one of the city's most romantic, legend-haunted structures; another fabled abode, the former casino-villa of Sir William Hamilton, is nearby (both villas are still private).

Bus route No. 140 trundles along Via Posillipo and the sea, climbing steadily towards the headland at the end of the run. The headland of Posillipo at the end of Viale Virgilio, called **Parco della Rimembranza** (confusingly also known as the Parco Virgiliano) will probably become an archaeological park, but until that time, it's a semi no-go area. You can get to Posillipo's famed Marechiaro area by bus on a fairly circuitous route (Bus No. 11), although it will be quicker to be left at the main street (by Bus No. 140) and walk down to the water. (Bus No. 11 currently runs every half-hour, but only during the day and weekends—it's the only route that has a timetable posted at every bus stop and runs rather infrequently at night, so a taxi is often the best option.) ✉ *Parco Virgiliano, Salita della Grotta 20, Mergellina* ☎ *081/669390* ✇ *Free* ☉ *9–1 hr before sunset.*

WHERE TO EAT

Updated by
Francesca
Marretta and
Chris Rose

Let's be honest: you really want a traditional Neapolitan dinner with lots of tomato sauce and a great show of Neapolitan love songs to get you crying into your limoncello. There's no reason to feel guilty, because even the natives love to get into the spirit. But listening to someone warble "Santa Lucia" while feasting on a pizza *Margherita* (with basil, mozzarella, and tomatoes) from a table overlooking the bay is just one example of the pleasures awaiting diners in Naples. From *vitello alla Principe di Napoli* (veal garnished with truffles) to sea bass in *acqua pazza*—that is to say, poached in water "maddened" with anchovy, bay leaves, *peperoncino,* and olive oil, to Neapolitan pastries like the light, fluffy, exotic *babà al Rhum,* the city expresses its gastronomic self in many ways. The *haute*-hungry should look elsewhere (particularly Ristorante Don Alfonso 1890, just across the bay in Sorrento) and so should those in search of newer-than-now nouvelle flights of fantasy, designer plates, and the latest fusion dishes. While these can be found, the cuisine in Naples is by and large earthy, pungent, and *buonissima,* as attested to by those signature dishes: *mozzarella in carrozza* (mozzarella cheese fried in a "carriage" of two slices of bread); *polpo alla luciana* (octopus stewed with garlic, peppers, and tomatoes); *risotto ai frutti di mare* (seafood risotto); and *spaghetti puttanesca* (streetwalker's spaghetti with black olives and bitter capers). In Naples it is still the old reliables that apply, the recipes time-tested by centuries of mammas that still manage to put meat on your bones and smiles on your faces.

This means pizzerias aplenty. As the birthplace of pizza, Naples prides itself on its vast selection of pizzerias, the most famous of which—Da Michele, Sorbillo, or Trianon—deserve the encomium "incomparable." Many Neapolitans make lunch their big meal of the day, then have a pizza for supper or—just watch the jeweled operagoers at the Teatro San Carlo head over to Ciro a Santa Brigida—a late-night treat. Note that "pizzerias" in Naples does not simply mean the linoleum-floored, neon-lit ones you'll find back in New York City—they range here from hole-in-the-walls to full-scale restaurants.

When it comes to *i secondi* (main dishes), you can find a first-rate chicken offering, but the reason visitors to Naples want to eat seafood is a good one: geography. Naples's position, hugging a rich bay, has guaranteed that marine creatures feature prominently on local menus. Marinated seafood salad (*insalata di frutti di mare*) is a classic antipasto, as well as marinated white anchovies (*alici*). Spaghetti *con le vongole veraci* (with clams, garlic, and a baby's fistful of chopped flat-leaf Italian parsley) is of course a popular and dependable standard, as are myriad variations on linguine or fresh pasta with mixed seafood (mussels, shrimp, clams, and so forth), usually "stained" with fresh cherry tomatoes. As for seafood Neapolitan style, the best—*spigola* (sea bass), *pesce spada* (swordfish), and, if you can find it, *San Pietro* (sort of a sole for grownups)—is grilled simply and ennobled with a splash of olive oil and a squeeze of lemon. Fresh calamari, kissed lightly by a grill, can be exquisitely delicate, but the fried version, which can be uniquely satisfying, is, alas, too often done these days with frozen squid. Another good way to have fish is *all'acqua pazza* (literally, in crazy water), poached with anchovy, bay leaves, red pepper, and olive oil, a brew said to have been invented by returning fishermen using seawater to cook up a meal on the beach.

There isn't a surfeit of expensive, luxury restaurants in Naples for one simple reason—the city's rich and fashionable prefer to dine at Naples's *circoli,* or private clubs, rather than at restaurants. No matter. When it comes to Neapolitan food, veterans know that the best restaurants are the simplest. But wherever you head, you'll be delighted (or exasperated, depending on how critical you are): after all, you're in Naples, and the mise-en-scène—Vesuvius as a backdrop to your flambéed chicken Vesuvio, or a table on a charming alleyway—can't be beat. Note that many restaurants in Naples close for at least a week around August 15th to celebrate the Ferragosto holidays.

WHAT IT COSTS In Euros				
$$$$	$$$	$$	$	¢
AT DINNER	over €20	€15–€20	€9–€15	€5–€9	under €5

Prices are for a main-course entry only (known in Italian as *secondo piatto*, or second course); if only prix-fixe meals are served, price category reflects full meal.

City Center

Appropriately, the monumental city center environs feature two of Naples's most famous restaurants.

$$–$$$ ✕ **Brandi.** Forget that this historic place gave the world *pizza Margherita*—the classic combo of tomato sauce, mozzarella, and basil, named after King Umberto's queen. This is, hands down, one of the most picturesque restaurants in Italy. Set on a cobblestone alleyway just off chic Via Chiaia, it welcomes you with an enchanting wood-beamed salon festooned with 19th-century memorabilia, saint shrines, gilded mirrors, and bouquets of flowers, beyond which you can see the kitchen and the *pizzaioli* (pizza makers) at work. That's the good news. Unfortunately, most of Naples stays away, considering the pizzas are far, far better elsewhere. But there's no denying the decor is *delizioso* and if "tourists" like Luciano Pavarotti and Chelsea Clinton have dined here, why not you? ⊠ *Salita Sant'Anna di Palazzo 1, Toledo* ☎ *081/416928* ▤ *AE, DC, MC, V* ✆ *Closed Mon.*

$$ ✕ **Trattoria San Ferdinando.** The apparently brusque but actually friendly Angela and her colleagues open in the evening only on Friday and Saturday, with the fine intention of running a restaurant for the sheer pleasure of it. Their dedication shows in the traditional (but cooked with a lighter modern touch) pasta dishes (especially those with *verdura*, fresh leaf vegetables) and excellent fish. Close to the San Carlo Theater and aptly decorated with playbills and theatrical memorabilia both ancient and modern, this is an excellent place to stop after a visit to the opera. ⊠ *Via Nardones 117, Toledo* ☎ *081/421964* ▤ *AE, DC, MC, V* ✆ *No dinner Sun.–Thurs.*

$–$$ ✕ **Ciro a Santa Brigida.** Just off Via Toledo, Ciro has been an obligatory entry on any list of Neapolitan cooking (as opposed to cuisine) since 1932, when Toscanini and Pirandello used to eat here. Popular with business travelers, artists, and journalists, Ciro is famous for a wide variety of favorites, with an emphasis on rustic food, from very fine pizzas and justly famed versions of pasta *e fagioli* to the classic *sartù*—rice loaf first concocted by Baroque-era nuns—and the splendid *pignatiello e vavella*, shellfish soup. The menu looks too large for all its items to be good, but the owners must be doing something right, as the place is often packed with Neapolitan regulars. The old waiters are darling wherever you sit, but try to get a table upstairs, which has a more pleasant atmosphere. ⊠ *Via Santa Brigida 71, Toledo* ☎ *081/5524072* ⊕ *www.ciroasantabrigida.it* ▤ *AE, DC, V* ✆ *Closed Sun. and last 2 wks in Aug.*

CloseUp

HEY, IT NEVER TASTED LIKE THIS BACK HOME

There's no pizza like real Neapolitan pizza. If you don't believe it, try one at **Ciro a Santa Brigida** (✉ Via Santa Brigida 71, Toledo ☎ 081/5524072). This restaurant is a little more upscale than a typical Neapolitan pizzeria, but its pizza is the real thing, and it's proper to eat it with your napkin stuffed into your shirt to avoid tomato stains.

The restaurant's owner, Antonio Pace, president of the True Neapolitan Pizza Association, is behind an unusual initiative to upgrade the quality of pizza worldwide. Mr. Pace and Professor Carlo Mangoni di Santo Stefano, a nutritionist at the University of Naples, have written what they call a Pizza Discipline, a treatise that discusses everything from the history of pizza to the correct ingredients for the perfect Neapolitan pie.

Based on the Pizza Discipline, the city of Naples recently registered a logo that pizzerias can hang in their window if, and only if, they serve true Neapolitan pizza. That means using sinfully luscious buffalo-milk mozzarella made in certain areas near Naples, kneading the dough for a full 30 minutes, and letting it rise for four hours. (The "discipline" includes photos of dough taken through a microscope before and after it has risen.)

It may take a while before pizzerias around the globe actually hang the logo in their windows. But the city of Naples wants it to eventually be a sign of quality as distinctive as the DOC (Denominazione di Origine Controllata, or denomination of controlled origin) on wine labels. The logo will be blue, with Mt. Vesuvius in the background, a red pizza with mozzarella in the center, and PIZZA NAPOLETANA written across the foreground. Make sure you're the first to spot it!

Some pizza history, as recounted by Professor Mangoni (who scoffs at claims that pizza was invented in the United States):

Pizza marinara, which doesn't have mozzarella at all but is simply a pie with tomatoes, garlic, oregano, and olive oil, first appeared in Naples around 1760. King Ferdinand of Naples liked the pizza, but his wife, a Habsburg princess, wouldn't allow pizza in the palace. The king would often sneak out to one of the world's first pizzerias, making the places famous.

Even earlier, there's a mention of plates of flour with other food on top in Homer's Iliad, but Professor Mangoni says this was just a precursor to pizza, not the real thing. Tomato sauce, says Mangoni, dates back to 1733.

Mozzarella came later. The pizza Margherita was invented in 1889, when Naples chef Raffaele Esposito was called on to prepare a meal for the Italian queen, Margherita. He made a pizza with tomato sauce and mozzarella, and his wife had the idea of adding basil to honor Italy's red, white, and green flag.

According to the Pizza Discipline, the only true pizzas are marinara and Margherita. Anchovies, pepperoni, and so on are heresy. So don't expect to see the logo with Mt. Vesuvius at your local pizza joint anytime soon.

In Antonio Pace's family, pizza goes back a long way. He claims his grandfather's grandfather made pizza in 1856. Pizza fact or fiction aside, at Ciro a Santa Brigida, everything is delicious. Ask for a taste of plain buffalo mozzarella and just savor it in your mouth.

If you have a lactose intolerance, there's still hope—Professor Mangoni and his team of scientists are developing lactose-free mozzarella. If they manage to match the taste of real mozzarella, he says, pizzerias will be allowed to use it and still display the Pizza Napoletana logo. Go figure.

Spaccanapoli

Spaccanapoli is now one of *the* evening locations where *buona cucina* meets both low- and high-brow culture (what a change from 10 years ago, when it was a dark and dangerous part of town). The teeming alleyways and 17th-century palazzi house many inexpensive places to eat, which begin to fill up after 9 PM. Although several of the classier restaurants are closed at lunchtime, there's still plenty of choice both for lingering meals and quick streetside snacking.

$$ ✕ **'A Canzuncella.** Host Aurelio Fierro is a legend of Neapolitan light music, and people come here as much for his spread of musical entertainment as for the food. Enjoy a traditional dinner accompanied by a show of Neapolitan crooners—a performance only an entrenched curmudgeon would fail to enjoy. Saturday evenings offer a banquet and live entertainment for a combined price of €52 (reservations are essential). Standards of both *cucina* and *servizio* are high, as indeed they have to be for loyal but demanding clients, mainly drawn from *Napoli bene* (the upper crust of Naples). ⊠ *Piazza Santa Maria La Nova 17/18, Spaccanapoli* ☎ *081/5519018* ⊟ *AE, DC, MC, V* ☽ *Closed lunchtime and Sun. eves.*

$–$$ ✕ **La Taverna dell'Arte.** As its name suggests, this gracious trattoria on a small side street near Naples's main university is popular with actors in particular, but manages to remain welcomingly low-key. Warmed with touches of wood, it prides itself on its fresh interpretations of Neapolitan classics: excellent salami, mozzarella, and *frittura* (fried vegetables) among the appetizers, cabbage soup fragrant with good beef stock, and meat and fish grilled over wood. Typical Neapolitan desserts, such as babas and the familiar crunchy almond cookies called *quaresimali*, are served with homemade liqueurs. ⊠ *Rampe San Giovanni Maggiore 1/a, Spaccanapoli* ☎ *081/5527558* ⚑ *Reservations essential* ⊟ *MC, V* ☽ *Closed Sun. and last 2 wks in Aug. No lunch.*

★ **$–$$** ✕ **Lombardi à Santa Chiara.** Located right on Spaccanapoli opposite the Palazzo Croce, home to the philosopher and historian Benedetto Croce, this is one of the city's most famous pizzerias, packed night after night. The young crowd heads down into the more boisterous basement, while the atmosphere upstairs is calmer and more congenial to conversation at standard decibel levels. You can watch the owner himself, Don Luigi, working the pizza dough, manipulating each pizza as if it were a live creation. ⊠ *Via Benedetto Croce 59, Spaccanapoli* ☎ *081/5520780* ⊟ *AE, DC, MC, V* ☽ *Closed Mon. and last 2 wks in Aug.*

$–$$ ✕ **Napoli Napoli.** Young, noisy, and fashionable, decorated with a very modern take on traditional Neapolitan tiles and ceramics, this restaurant/bar/takeaway on the corner of the student-packed Piazza del Gesù is a lively mixing spot at night. Chaotic and permanently busy (but in a fun way), it's a good place for a quick lunch while discovering Spaccanapoli or a light dinner before going on to a club. The spot is known for its innovative selection of pizzas (though still no pineapple toppings) and a stimulating selection of salads for vegetarians who are tired of plain tomato and mozzarella. ⊠ *Piazza del Gesù Nuovo 26, Spaccanapoli* ☎ *081/5518427* ⊟ *AE, DC, MC, V.*

$–$$ ✕ **Ristorante Bellini.** Worth visiting just to observe the waiters, who all seem to have just stepped off the stage of a Neapolitan comedy at the nearby Teatro Bellini, this spot claims a proud perch on the corner of the chicly bohemian Piazza Bellini. But if the neighborhood remains suave, this staple Neapolitan restaurant proudly retains its Old World feel. Good bets here include a fine (if rather small) pizza, and classic fish dishes such as linguine *al cartoccio* (baked in paper) or *all'astice* (a type of small lobster). Go up the narrow stairs to get to the spacious upper rooms, or squeeze in at one of the pavement tables in summer. ⊠ *Via Santa Maria di Costantinopoli 79, Spaccanapoli* ☎ *081/459774* ▭ *MC, V* ⊘ *Closed Sun. from June to Mar.*

$–$$ ╳ **Taverna Ho La La.** A bizarre name for this former student haunt, now frequented by those who are no longer students but still feel bohemian at heart, should deter no one from this welcoming place. A mix between traditional and trendy (in terms of both food and decor), this place hosts an exhibition by a young local artist every month which you can admire while sampling the *farfalle con crema di carciofi* (pasta bows with artichoke puree), or *scaloppa di maiale al calvados* (pork chops in apple brandy). There's also a long, inviting bar if you just fancy a drink, some elegantly chilled music, or a quick surf on the Net. For such a friendly place, it's not surprising to discover that "happy hour" here lasts from 7 to 9. ⊠ *Via Santa Chiara 49, Spaccanapoli* ☎ *081/19568378* ▭ *No credit cards* ⊘ *Closed Sun. from June to May.*

$ ╳ **La Cantina di Via Sapienza.** There's a strong whiff of 1920s Paris intelligentsia in this hangout of students and young professionals, although the garb is now in Technicolor shades and every dish is spiced up with garlic. It's busy and not big enough (expect to share a table— and if your fellow diners are not shy, why should you be?), but the prices can't be beat, and the daily selection of a good dozen vegetable side plates merits a detour of its own, even if you're not a vegetarian. ⊠ *Via Sapienza 40, Spaccanapoli* ☎ *081/459078* ▭ *No credit cards* ⊘ *Closed eves. and Sun.*

$ ╳ **La Vecchia Cantina.** On a rather dark side street in the tattier side of Spaccanapoli, this place is well worth seeking out for its combination of old-style Neapolitan hospitality and hip attention to the quality of its food and wine. The place is run as a family affair, with Gianni out front while his mother Nunzia and wife Maria are busy in the kitchen, much like a typical Neapolitan household. An accumulation of kitsch decorations completes the feeling, and everyone who comes here seems to know each other. The pasta with chickpeas is a must, and *baccalà fritto* (fried salt cod) is a speciality. Backed up with a selection of wines from all over Italy, this place is a great value. ⊠ *Via S. Nicola alla Carità 13–14, Spaccanapoli* ☎ *081/5520226* ▭ *AE, DC, MC, V* ⊘ *Closed Tues.*

★ $ ╳ **Timpani e Tempura.** A tiny shrine to local culinary culture with no tables, but where you are invited to perch yourself at the bar-style counter, this place isn't comfortable but is worth the squeeze for its *timballi di maccheroni* (baked pasta cakes) and its unique *mangiamaccheroni*, spaghetti in broth with caciocavallo cheese, butter, basil, and pepper. High-quality wines by the glass make this a spot for a swift but excellent lunch. You can also buy cheese and salami to take home with you. Note that Timpani is only open for lunch. ⊠ *Vico della Quercia 17, Spaccanapoli* ☎ *081/5512280* ▭ *No credit cards* ⊘ *No dinner.*

¢–$ ╳ **Sorbillo.** Don't be put off by the queues—the locals know it's worth waiting for. Take their advice and devour a basic Neapolitan pizza cooked to perfection—after all, a third generation of pizza-makers runs this place. Try the uncommon pizza al pesto, or the sublimely simple marinara. Don't expect tablecloths: here you have the joy of eating on traditional white-marble tabletops. ⊠ *Via dei Tribunali 32, Spaccanapoli* ☎ *081/446643* ▭ *MC, V* ⊘ *Closed Sun.*

Piazza Garibaldi & Environs

Forget waterfront restaurants and outdoor candlelit terraces. This is an area noted for fine no-nonsense eating, with some of the city's most traditional restaurants offering excellent value for money. If returning to base after dark, stick to well-lighted main roads or ask one of the restaurant staff to order a taxi.

★ **$$–$$$** ✕ **Mimì alla Ferrovia.** Clients of this Neapolitan institution have included Fellini and that magnificent true-Neapolitan comic genius and aristocrat of dubious lineage, Totò. Mimì manages to live up cheerfully to its history, proudly serving fine versions of everything from pasta *e fagioli* to the sea bass *al presidente*, baked in a pastry crust and enjoyed by any number of Italian presidents on their visits to Naples. Not so much a place to see and be seen as a common ground where both the famous and the unknown can mingle, feast, and be of good cheer, Mimì's sober beige-and-green hues, accented with updated Art Deco features, pale-yellow tablecloths, and retro bentwood chairs pleasantly tone down the bustle. ✉ *Via A. D'Aragona 19/21, Piazza Garibaldi* ☎ *081/289004* ⊕ *www.mimiallaferrovia.com* ▭ *AE, DC, MC, V* ✆ *Closed Sun. and last 2 wks in Aug.*

$$ ✕ **La Fila.** To the north of the Stazione Centrale at Piazza Garibaldi, this family-run trattoria is a place to experience genuine Neapolitan food. Listen to the Signora Elvira (it's difficult not to) if she insists that you try something: the simplest dishes, so often done indifferently elsewhere, are here exquisite voyages of discovery: baked pasta with meatballs, pizza with pungent sausage kissed awake by the wood-fired oven. Even the ubiquitous potato croquette—always disappointing—is here made with respect, real mashed potatoes, and smoked provolone. The pizza, with its ricotta cheese-stuffed base, has to be tasted to be believed. ✉ *Via Nazionale 6/c, Piazza Garibaldi* ☎ *081/206717* ⚐ *Reservations essential* ▭ *No credit cards* ✆ *Closed Mon.*

$ ✕ **Triunfo.** A strikingly clean place near the Stazione Centrale, in a neighborhood that has seen better times, this restaurant sticks out for the quality of its pizza and draws a devoted clientele. The selection of cold antipasti, with lots of simply prepared vegetables, is a welcome change from the usual fried offerings, and the house pizza, with prosciutto and artichokes, makes a wonderful summer dinner. ✉ *Vicolo II Duchesca 10, Piazza Garibaldi* ☎ *081/268948* ▭ *AE, DC, MC, V* ✆ *Closed Mon.*

¢–$ ✕ **Trianon.** Across the street from its archrival Da Michele, this is a classic pizzeria with a simple yet upscale Art Nouveau ambience expressed in soothing tile and marble. More relaxed and upmarket than its rival, Trianon does the classics (Margherita, marinara) in an exemplary manner, but you can also feast on pizza with sausage and broccoli greens, while the signature pizza Trianon comes with eight different toppings. ✉ *Via P. Coletta 46, Piazza Garibaldi* ☎ *081/5539426* ▭ *No credit cards* ✆ *No lunch Sun.*

★ **¢** ✕ **Da Michele.** You have to love a place that has, for more than 130 years, offered only two types of pizza—marinara and Margherita—and a small selection of drinks, and still manages to draw in the crowds. The prices have something to do with it, but the pizza itself suffers no rivals, and even those the locals waiting in line are good humored; the boisterous, joyous atmosphere wafts out with the smell of yeast and wood smoke onto the street. Note that Neapolitans aren't always orderly queuers, so at busy times the waiter here gives you a number (collect it at the door) and has you wait outside until your number is called. ✉ *Via C. Sersale 1/3, Piazza Garibaldi* ☎ *081/5539204* ▭ *No credit cards* ✆ *Closed Sun. and last two weeks in Aug.*

Santa Lucia & Chiaia

While Santa Lucia is a classic choice for both chic and touristy fish restaurants with that just-how-you-imagined-Naples sea view, the upscale area of Chiaia is a favorite with both locals and discerning expatriates and is likely to offer better value for money.

$$$–$$$$ ✕ **Caruso.** When you get the urge to dress up, head to the panoramic rooftop restaurant of the Hotel Vesuvio—a very chic locale that is not

KEY

+——+ Rail Lines
==== Metro
——+ Funicular
1 Hotels
① Restaurant

as expensive as you might think. It's named after the great Enrico, who breathed his last up here (when this space was a suite) in 1921. The food wisely declines to compete with the view of the bay but instead accompanies it suavely. Seafood predominates, from the marinated *frutti di mare* and fish-stuffed ravioli to the classic grilled sea bass, but if you're tired of shrimp and such, try the delicate lemon risotto or the *bucatini alla Caruso* (tubular spaghetti with fresh tomatoes, sweet peppers, and sautéed zucchini). ✉ *Hotel Vesuvio, Via Partenope 45, Santa Lucia* ☎ 081/7640044 ⊕ *www.vesuvio.it* ▭ *AE, DC, MC, V.*

★ **$$$–$$$$** ✗ **La Terrazza.** Completely refurbished in 2002 in an attempt to conquer the crown of the finest restaurant in Naples, the Hotel Excelsior's Terrazza attracts A-list stars visiting the area with its Pompeian-red marble floorings and brown leather furnishings (all aimed at highlighting the gold cutlery, *capisce?*). A breathtaking buffet counts as an appetizer (but would be a banquet in itself for mere mortals), while the à la carte menu creates a fusion of Italian regional culinary styles. The owners have even risked bringing in a chef from Milan (Naples's historical rival). Dress up, and expect to be impressed. ✉ *Hotel Excelsior, Via Partenope 48, Santa Lucia* ☎ 081/7640111 ▭ *AE, DC, MC, V.*

$$$–$$$$ ✗ **Zi' Teresa** Set in the adorable center-city harbor of the Borgo Marinaro, this place is mentioned in Norman Lewis's classic account of wartime Napoli, *Naples '44*, as being a cheap dive full of local spivs and army officers. One suspects that Lewis wouldn't recognise the place now, elegantly decorated with airy Mediterranean tiles, its large terrace opening out onto the small harbor, with tables draped in linen tablecloths and silver cutlery. Book ahead to make sure you get a place as close to the seafront as possible, and enjoy the unspectacular but perfectly prepared seafood pastas and grilled fish. ✉ *Borgo Marinaro 1, Santa Lucia* ☎ 081/7642565 ▭ *AE, DC, MC, V* ☉ *Closed Mon. No dinner Sun.*

$$ ✗ **La Bersagliera.** On the picturesque Borgo Marinaro—the port at Santa Lucia—in the shadow of the looming medieval Castel dell'Ovo, this spot is touristy but fun, with an irresistible combination of spaghetti and mandolins. Dalí and De Chirico, Sophia and Marcello all came here in the grand old days to enjoy uncomplicated time-tested classics, such as spaghetti with mixed seafood and eggplant *alla parmigiana*. Recent additions to the menu include octopus and swordfish carpaccio. But as any Neapolitan will tell you, simple grilled fish always tastes better when seasoned with sea air and a view of a few yachts. ✉ *Borgo Marinaro 10, Santa Lucia* ☎ 081/7646016 ⊕ *www.labersagliera.it* ▭ *AE, DC, MC, V* ☉ *Closed Tues.*

★ **$$** ✗ **La Stanza del Gusto.** Set opposite the Teatro Sannazzaro on Via Chiaia and located on an unbelievably quiet and leafy *vicoletto* (alley) near some of the city's busiest streets, this small, refined place lives up to its name (the "room of taste"). The discreet ambience within nicely reinforces the sense of escape from the hectic world outside. This is the place to try those stalwarts of Neopolitan cuisine, *soffritto*—a sauce made from liver, kidneys, lung, and other unmentionables—and *arancini* (riceballs), here transformed almost beyond palatal recognition with prawns and local greens. ✉ *Vicoletto Sant'Arpino 21, Chiaia* ☎ 081/401578 ◿ *Reservations essential* ▭ *DC, MC, V* ☉ *Closed Sun., Mon., and Aug.*

$$ ✗ **Osteria Castello.** The walls are covered with shelves full of wine bottles, there are red-check tablecloths with candles on them, and dark wooden chairs. It looks like the quintessential Italian restaurant, and it is—simple, excellent value, and friendly service. Put as much on your plate as you can from the excellent antipasto buffet, follow it with the essential *pasta e patate con la provola* (pasta and potatoes with smoked mozzarella—it sounds like carbohydrate overload, but is actually divine) and then the grilled, flat *pleos* mushrooms. Order an extra bottle of wine (preferably the local *aglianico* red) or a liqueur and sit there for hours talking to your friends. ✉ *Via S. Teresa a Chiaia 38, Chiaia* ☎ *081/400486* ▭ *AE, DC, MC, V* ☉ *Closed lunch and Sun. and 3 wks in Aug.*

$$ ✗ **Trattoria dell'Oca.** The bright, clean, simple decor reflects this place's lighter take on occasionally heavy Neapolitan food, also echoed in the younger crowds who pack this place on weekends. The soupy pasta *e piselli* (with peas) is a wonderful surprise for anyone who has bad memories of pea soup, while the penne *alla scapariello* (pasta quills with fresh tomato, basil, and pecorino cheese) is a specialty to set the taste buds quivering. ✉ *Via S. Teresa a Chiaia 11, Chiaia* ☎ *081/414865* ▭ *AE, DC, MC, V* ☉ *Closed Sun and 3 wks in Aug.*

$$ ✗ **Umberto.** Run by the Di Porzio family since 1916, Umberto has become one of the city's classic restaurants. It is divided into a simpler pizzeria and a more elegant restaurant, but both parts offer the classy appeal of the Chiaia area and the friendliness of other parts of the city. Try the *tubettini 'do tre dita* ("three-finger maccheroni," with a mixture of fish and seafood), the nickname of the original Umberto. Owner Massimo and sister Lorella (Umberto's grandchildren) are wine experts and have a well-curated cellar. Umberto is also the only restaurant in the city that caters to those who have a gluten allergy. ✉ *Via Alabardieri 30–31 Chiaia* ☎ *081/418555* ⊕ *www.umberto.it* ▭ *AE, DC, MC, V* ☉ *Closed Mon.*

★ $$ ✗ **Vadinchenia.** Serving up all the trimmings of a first-class restaurant at surprisingly modest prices, husband-and-wife team Saverio and Silvana serve up an innovative menu against a backdrop of refreshingly minimalist decor. Adventurous palates will enjoy bold combinations like *paccheri alle alici e pecorino* (pasta with sardines and sheep's cheeses), while recidivist carnivores will delight in the *filleto al vino e sale grosso,* (steak with rock salt). ✉ *Via Pontano 21, Chiaia* ☎ *081/660265* ⌨ *Reservations essential* ▭ *AE, DC, MC, V* ☉ *Closed Sun. and Aug. No lunch.*

$–$$ ✗ **Amici Miei.** A place favored by meat eaters who can't take another bite of sea bass, this small, dark, and cozy den of comfort is well loved for specials such as tender carpaccio with fresh artichoke hearts and a rice and arugula dish featuring duck breast. Happily, there are also excellent pasta dishes, such as *orecchiette* with chickpeas or *alla barese* (with chewy green turnips) or that extravaganza, the *carnevale lasagne,* an especially rich concoction relied on to sustain the taste buds in the build-up before Lent. Everyone finishes with a slice of chocolate and hazelnut *torta caprese.* Reservations are essential Friday and Saturday evenings. ✉ *Via Monte di Dio 78, Chiaia* ☎ *081/7646063* ▭ *AE, DC, MC, V* ☉ *Closed Mon. and Aug. No dinner Sun.*

$–$$ ✗ **'A Taverna 'e Zi Carmela.** Not far from the Villa Comunale gardens, this is a reasonable, family-run alternative in the pricey Santa Lucia area. Don't pay attention to the haphazard decor; the pizza is excellent, from the ubiquitous basics to such original specialties as the brashly named *incazzata,* a calzone stuffed with spicy pasta *all'arrabbiata* (for those who can't decide if they want pizza or pasta). If you do want pasta, try the hearty gnocchi with beans, or the superb house spaghetti with fresh tomato and a perfectly cooked medley of fresh seafood. ✉ *Via Niccolò Tommaseo 11/12, Chiaia* ☎ *081/7643581* ▭ *No credit cards.*

$–$$ ✗ **Marino.** This famous pizzeria offers up its delights in a cool white-and-blue room. Try the house specialty, the Anastasia, with cherry tomatoes and lots of premium mozzarella. Recent extensions to the sidewalk and partial pedestrianization of Via Santa Lucia make this a pleasant outdoor venue in summer. ✉ *Via Santa Lucia 118/120, Santa Lucia* ☎ *081/7640280* ▭ *AE, V* ☉ *Closed Mon. and Aug.*

$ ✗ **Da Antonio.** Once you actually find this welcoming trattoria, set two minutes from Piazza dei Martiri, settle back and enjoy the informal setting of an archetypal family eatery. There *is* a menu, but—as is often the case—you're better off listening to the day's specials. The pasta dishes may be consumed as a *tris* (threesome), an attractive option if you think you might miss out on something interesting. Remember to leave room for the homemade cakes at the end of the meal. ✉ *Vico II Alabardieri 30, Chiaia* ☎ *081/407147* ▭ *MC, V* ☉ *Closed Sun.*

$ ✕ **Da Ettore.** One of Naples's classic pizzerias, and the only one in this area, Ettore is popular with locals who work in this busy neighborhood. Unpretentiously decorated, this place is great for a working lunch or dinner before going somewhere else. The selection of pizzas includes fresh tomato and rocket, or with spicy country salami. If you're really hungry, go for the *pagnottiello*, a cross between a sandwich and a pizza—the dough is folded over and stuffed with prosciutto and mozzarella or sausage and *friarielli* (a locally grown bitter, iron-rich broccoli). If you've still got space, follow this up with the deep-fried zucchini flowers. ✉ *Via S. Lucia 56, Santa Lucia* ☎ *081/7640498* ▭ *No credit cards* ☉ *Closed Sun.*

$ ✕ **La Mattonella.** A tiled trattoria ("mattonella" means "tile") set behind Piazza del Plebiscito, this tiny place offers a few classic dishes. Unchanged for years, Mattonella has a 1950s ambience—you could imagine a young Mastroianni walking in at any minute for a plate of pasta *alla genovese* (with onions and ground beef), a glass of the local red, and a read of the day's paper. As a digestive, have a limoncello lemon liqueur, served in chocolate glasses (yes, you can eat the glass afterward). ✉ *Via Nicotera 13, Chiaia* ☎ *081/416541* ▭ *No credit cards* ☉ *Closed Sun.*

$ ✕ **I Re di Napoli.** With its inviting blue-and-green custom-tile interior and tables set along the seafront drive, this chic pizzeria is an essential hangout for Naples's gilded youth and really gets going toward midnight on weekends. Thirty kinds of pizza plus a fine selection of salads and an ample buffet make the place a refreshing change from the more minimal *pizzerie*. The various stuffed pizzas named after kings are classics with a modern twist: try the *Boccone di Re Ferdinando*, filled with *speck* (lean cured pork), *provola* cheese, and artichokes. ✉ *Via Partenope 29/30, Santa Lucia* ☎ *081/7647775* ▭ *AE, MC, V.*

Mergellina & Posillipo

These ritzy bayside suburbs feature some of the most popular restaurants in Naples. Several of these spots are found at the end of bayside cul-de-sacs, so unless you have your own wheels, taxis will be the most convenient option.

$$$–$$$$ ✕ **Dora.** Though in an unflattering location up a narrow *vicolo* (alley) off the Riviera di Chiaia, this restaurant has achieved cult status for its seafood platters. It's remarkable what Giovanni, the owner-chef, can produce from his tiny *cucina*. Try to create some space for the richly garnished pasta dish *mezzanello*, with its full complement of seafood, and perhaps follow it up with a *pezzogna* (blue-spotted bream). Like most of the restaurants near the seafront, Dora has its own guitarist, Roberto, who is often robustly accompanied by the kitchen staff. ✉ *Via Ferdinando Palasciano 30, Mergellina* ☎ *081/680519* ⌕ *Reservations essential* ▭ *AE, DC, MC, V* ☉ *Closed Sun. and 2 wks mid-Aug.*

$$$–$$$$ ✕ **La Sacrestia.** Once the most famous restaurant in Naples, Sacrestia has suffered a bit from the stiff competition that has developed over the last 10 years, though Woody Allen still eats here when he's in town. Marco Ponsiglione continues his father's work in modifying traditional recipes, which can be enjoyed from the superb terrace perched above Mergellina's harbor. For starters try the risotto with baby squid or the pasta with shrimp, artichokes, and olives, or, if you're feeling regal, the *bu-*

"O SOLE MIO-O-O-O!"

If you have a hankering to hear some of the fabled Neapolitan folksongs—the canzoni napoletane—performed, you might be lucky enough to catch the city's top troupes, such as the Cantori di Posillipo and I Virtuosi di San Martino, at venues like the Teatro Trianon. But most every night at the city's more traditional restaurants, expect your meal to be interrupted by a posteggiatore. These are singers who aren't employed by the owners, but who are, nevertheless, encouraged to come in, swan around the tables with a battered old guitar, and belt out classics such as "Santa Lucia," "O' Surdat' Innamurate," "Turna a Surriento" (Come Back to Sorrento), and, inevitably "Funiculi-funiculà." Of course, these are but the most famous of a vast repertoire which found worldwide fame with the mass exodus of southern Italians to the United States in early 20th century.

"Funiculì-funiculà" was written by Peppino Turco and Luigi Danza in 1880 to herald Naples's new funicular railways. "O Sole Mio," by Giovanni Capurro and Eduardo di Capua, has often been mistakenly considered the Italian national anthem. "Torna a Surriento" was composed by Ernesto di Curtis in 1903 to help remind the Italian prime minister how wonderful he thought Sorrento was (and how many government subsidies he had promised the township). If you've got a fave, and want some baby Caruso to warble "Bella Notte" (from Walt Disney's Lady and the Tramp, remember?), the singers are more than happy to do requests, even inserting the name of your innamorato/a into the song. When they've finished they'll come and stand discreetly by your table. Give them a couple of euros and you'll have friends for life.

---

catini alla Principe di Napoli, whose pasta is ennobled by an abundance of un-Neapolitan truffles. ⊠ Via Orazio 116, Posillipo ☎ 081/664186 🗐 AE, DC, MC, V ☺ Closed Aug. No dinner Sun., no lunch Mon.

★ $$–$$$ ✕ **'A Fenestella.** One of the most beloved of Neapolitan restaurants, this is picturesquely perched over a beach in Posillipo near the end of a long winding side road. The landmark comes with its own legend: the story goes that in the 19th century any Juliet would promise herself simply by appearing at the window ("fenestella" in the local dialect) to the Romeo sailing in the boat below, thus inspiring the famous Neapolitan folk song. Today, the restaurant is blatantly traditional, with a comfortable decor and the usual suspects on the menu (for stylish food and people, head across the road to Da Cicciotto). Still, sitting at a window table overlooking the sea here remains a quintessential Neapolitan memory for many old-timers. ⊠ Calata del Ponticella a Marechiaro 23, Posillipo ☎ 081/7690020 ⊕ www.afenestella.it 🗐 AE, MC, V ☺ Closed Wed. lunch, Sun. dinner.

★ $$–$$$ ✕ **Da Cicciotto.** One of Naples's best-kept secrets, this chic and charming spot corrals more than a few members of the city's fashionable set—there's a fair chance you'll find a Neapolitan count or off-duty film star enjoying this jewel. A tiny stone terrace overlooks a pleasant anchorage, centered around an antique column, with seats and canopy exquisitely upholstered in blue-and-white matching-but-mixing fabrics. To appreciate that outdoor setting, come here for lunch, not dinner, and don't even bother with a menu—just start digging into the sublime antipasti and go with the owner's suggestions. Cicciotto is at the end of the same long winding road that leads to the famed 'A Fenestella restaurant and shoreline, so you'll need a car or taxi to get here. ⊠ Calata del Ponticella a Marechiaro 32, Posillipo ☎ 081/5751165 🗐 AE, DC, MC, V ☺ Closed Mon. in winter.

$$ ✕ **La Cantina di Triunfo.** Founded by Carmine Triunfo in 1890 and now run by great-grandson Antonio (who looks after the wines) and his mother Tina (who looks after the kitchen), this place has recently made a successful bid to move upmarket. Well-prepared *cucina povera* ("poor people's food") still dominates, from the antipasto of hot peppers, salami, and cheese to the famous *vermicelli alle vongole fujute* (pasta with "escaped" clams, flavored with a dose of seawater) and the "meatballs" made of bread, but more aristocratic specialties now take their place on the menu as well: sartù—the famous rice-based dish—or the fabulous shrimp au gratin in lemon leaves. ✉ *Riviera di Chiaia 64, Mergellina* ☎ *081/668101* ✍ *Reservations essential* ▭ *DC, V* ✆ *Closed lunch, Sun., and Aug.*

Vomero

Sitting on top of the hill, the wealthy residential Vomero doesn't look like the first place you'd pick to eat out in. However, if you've been on a shopping spree on Via Scarlatti or taking in the Castel Sant'Elmo, you could do worse than stick around for a bite. Absence of tourists means that there are still a few stalwart places frequented by locals.

$ ✕ **La Cantina di Sica.** Recently refurbished so that the quality of the interior (spacious with muted lighting and cool Pompeian-red walls) matches the quality of the food, this former no-frills trattoria has successfully upgraded itself. The food consists of variants on traditional faves: the *tubettoni al pesce spada* (small pasta tubes with succulent pieces of swordfish), *peperoni imbottiti* (peppers stuffed with breadcrumbs, olives and capers), and the *parmigiana di melanzane* (layers of tomato, eggplant, and mozzarella baked in the oven) are all excellent. The kitchen's take on the traditional Neapolitan *pastiera* is as good as, if not better than anybody's mamma ever made it. ✉ *Via Bernini 17, Vomero* ☎ *081/ 5567520* ▭ *DC, MC, V.*

$ ✕ **Osteria Donna Teresa.** Donna Teresa has managed to keep a piece of old-style Napoli alive on the otherwise modern and unspectacular Via Kerbaker. A tiny place, this restaurant is always full of clients who are treated like children (and that means being encouraged, if not actually forced, to eat everything on their plates). Patrons flock here at lunchtime, in particular for a fill of classic pasta e fagioli (with beans), pasta e ceci (with chickpeas), or solid helpings of fried anchovies or baccalà (salt cod). ✉ *Via Kerbaker 58, Vomero* ☎ *081/5567070* ▭ *No credit cards* ✆ *Closed Sun. and Aug.*

¢–$ ✕ **Acunzo.** If you see a long line of hungry-looking patrons near the top station of the Chiaia Funicular, you'll know you are close to Pizzeria Acunzo. To avoid anxious waits, many like to get here as soon as it opens for the busier evening session at 7:30. When ordering, note that few variations on the pizzas are permitted; but then owner Michele and his wife Caterina have been running the establishment since 1964 and have a tried-and-tested product. The house specialty, pizza*Acunzo*, comes replete with a daunting list of ingredients, but ends up being *fenomenale*. ✉ *Via Cimarosa 60–62, Vomero* ☎ *081/5785362* ▭ *AE, MC, V* ✆ *Closed Sun.*

Munch-on-the-Run

If you get caught up in the chaotic head-spinning atmosphere of downtown Napoli, you might not even be able to sit still for an hour to eat. If so, follow the locals and indulge in some of the delicious quick snacks that Neapolitans have dreamed up to assuage hunger in a short time and at a low price. Many of Naples's specialties can be consumed while standing up—a fantastic advantage if you've got little time or money.

¢ ✗ **Ambrosino.** Once they opened for business, the owners of this grocery store quickly realized that people were eating the produce as soon as it was handed to them so they added a counter. Now you can take your pick from the pizzas and pasta dishes, or ask the owners to make up a *panino* (sandwich) by choosing the ingredients from the huge range of excellent cheeses, vegetables, and meats on display. A uniformly excellent quality of ingredients makes up for the rather spartan surroundings. ⊠ *Via Scarlatti 49, Vomero* ☎ *081/3721170* ▭ *AE, DC, MC, V* ⊘ *Closed Sun.*

¢ ✗ **Friggitoria Pizzeria Giuliano.** A favorite place of students from the adjacent school of architecture, Giuliano has an old-style glass cabinet in which are kept *arancini* (balls of fried rice) the size of tennis balls, and deep-fried pizzas filled with mozzarella, tomato, prosciutto, or ricotta, that can fill that yawning void in your stomach—even if you have to sit down on the steps in the square afterward to recover. ⊠ *Calata Trinità Maggiore, Spaccanapoli* ☎ *081/5510109* ▭ *No credit cards.*

★ ¢ ✗ **Friggitoria Vomero.** Popular with kids heading home from school, this spot also often draws guilty-looking adults attracted by its greasy brown paper bags filled with deep fried eggplant, zucchini, zucchini flowers, *zeppole* dough balls, or potato croquets—the Neapolitan versions of Proust's madeleines. Forget all that stuff about the Mediterranean diet being so healthy and indulge in some oil-drenched bliss. ⊠ *Via Cimarosa 44, Vomero* ☎ *081/5783130* ▭ *No credit cards* ⊘ *Closed Sun. and Aug.*

¢ ✗ **La Focaccia Express.** While the flat, pan-cooked focaccia is enough to make pizza fundamentalists wince (coming as it does from Rome), this place makes mouth-watering slices of crunchy-bottomed snacks with a variety of toppings. Skip the too-obvious tomato variations and go for the delicious potato and rosemary focaccia with melted provola (smoked mozzarella). Washed down with a beer, this makes for a great speedy lunch or late night snack. ⊠ *Vico Belledonne a Chiaia 18, Chiaia* ☎ *081/ 412277* ▭ *No credit cards* ⊘ *Closed Sun.*

¢ ✗ **L.u.i.s.e.** Elbow your way through the crowds at lunchtime, point to what you want in the tempting glass counter, and pay for it at the cash desk. If you're lucky you'll get a seat, but if not you can still enjoy the usual *frittura* (fried dough balls and potato croquets stuffed with mozzarella), the tangy cheese pies (*sfoglino al formaggio*), the pizza *scarola* (an escarole pie with black olives), or slices of omelettes stuffed with spinach, peppers, or onions. The immaculately liveried waiters aren't polite, but they are quick. ⊠ *Via Toledo 7, Toledo* ☎ *081/4153367* ▭ *No credit cards.*

Caffès & Coffee

Naples is ground zero for coffee lovers, and a snappy, definitive antidote to the hysterical pretensions of Seattle. Espresso was invented here and is still considered by the Neapolitans to be an essential and priceless part of their cultural patrimony (the word *espresso,* by the way, should probably be understood here in its meaning "pressed out," rather than the more common interpretation of "quick"). For many cognoscenti, Naples has the best coffee in the world. Almost any bar you walk into, no matter how dingy or how close to the train station, is likely to serve up an espresso that would make any Malibu hotspot wilt in envy. Even Italian bars do not specialize in alcoholic beverages per se and are generally tied to, as English pubs once were with brewers, a coffee roaster–distributor. The sponsoring brand is indicated with a sign on the outside, so you can choose your bar by looking for the sign of your favorite brand. Brands tend to be highly regional; the most widely advertised Neapolitan brand is Kimbo, but Moreno and

Salimbene are considered far superior by the cognoscenti. Some small, family-run caffès still roast their own.

You won't find any double low-fat mochas with extra vanilla here; in Naples you take your coffee like a grown-up. Individuals do have a choice of certain permitted variations: *corretto,* with a shot of grappa or the local moonshine thrown in; *al vetro,* in a glass; *macchiato,* "stained" with a burst of steamed milk; and, of course, cappuccino. On the whole, coffee is a Neapolitan sacred ritual with precise rules. Cappuccino, for instance, is essentially a breakfast beverage, accepted in the afternoon with a pastry but looked strangely at after a meal (they claim it's bad for the liver). Many Italians like to order a glass of water (*bicchiere d'acqua*) with their coffee as a chaser. As for flavored coffees, Neapolitans, like all Italians, stubbornly believe that you only add flavorings to coffee to hide imperfections in the original grind. Coffee is perhaps the one feature of life in which Neapolitans don't gild the lily. Why fix what works?

Gran Caffè Aragonese (⊠ Piazza San Domenico Maggiore 5, Spaccanapoli ☎ 081/5528740) offers a fine coffee in the heart of historic Spaccanapoli: sit out on the Piazza San Domenico or inside in the elegant tearoom with its marble-topped tables. In the heart of the congested city center, the small **Caffè del Professore** (⊠ Piazza Trieste e Trento 46, Piazza Municipio ☎ 081/403041) offers a superb espresso, as well as a house specialty, the *caffè nocciolato,* which is sweetened with a coffee-and-walnut syrup.

The most famous coffeehouse in town is the **Caffè Gambrinus** (⊠ Via Chiaia 1/2, Chiaia ☎ 081/417582), catercorner to the Palazzo Reale across the Piazza Trieste e Trento. Founded in 1850, this 19th-century jewel functioned as a brilliant intellectual salon in its heyday but has unfortunately fallen into a Sunset Boulevard–type existence, relying on past glamour, at the mercy of tourists and their pitiless cameras, and with often indifferent service. However, the opening and renovation of some of its long-closed inside rooms, replete with amazing mirrored walls and gilded ceilings, still makes it an essential stop for any visitor to the city. You may find it more worthwhile to continue along the Via Chiaia shopping street with its fashionable clothes shops as far as **La Torteria** (⊠ Via Filangieri 75, Chiaia ☎ 081/405221) not only for its excellent coffee but also for its selection of beautiful-looking cakes—concoctions of cream, chocolate, and fruit that look like Abstract Expressionist paintings with their swirls of color. A fave with Via Chiaia shoppers is **Bar Guida** (⊠ Via Dei Mille 46, Chiaia ☎ 081/426570), which offers you not only the luxury of being able to sit down, but also has a decent range of savory light meals. **La Caffetteria** (⊠ Piazza dei Martiri 30, Chiaia ☎ 081/7644243 ⊠ Vomero Branch: Piazza Vanvitelli 10/B, Vomero ☎ 081/5782592) is a classic address in the chic Chiaia district, and it has a second space in Vomero. Both addresses sell their famous coffee-flavored chocolates in the shape of tiny coffeepots. The **Gran Bar Riviera** (⊠ Riviera di Chiaia 181, Chiaia ☎ 081/665026) also has good profiteroles and fresh tiramisu, and is an excellent late-night stopover for clubbers—a cappuccino and cornetto in the small hours are classic post-dancing pick-me-ups. If you're near the Borgo Marinaro waterfront, **Megaride** (⊠ Via Borgo Marinaro 1, Santa Lucia ☎ 081/7645300), on the port under the shadow of the Castel dell'Ovo, provides a romantic outdoor setting for a coffee or aperitif.

Piazza Bellini, in the Spaccanapoli area, also contains a gaggle of good and hip caffès, and almost any of the pastry shops listed in the Pastry & Gelati Shops section will have an excellent brew.

Pastry & Gelati Shops

On the whole, Neapolitan pastry tends to suffer from the excesses that mar most southern Italian desserts: Falstaffian enthusiasm rather than precision in technique, ricotta clogging up everything, embarrassingly sentimental glops of glaze, and over-effusive dousings of perfumed syrups (one local specialty, baba al rhum, often succumbs to this latter vice). But the Neapolitan tradition of pastry is an old and venerable one, and the most classic local invention in matters of *pasticceria* (pastry making), the *sfogliatella,* is a true Baroque masterpiece, with puff pastry cut on a bias and wrapped around a nugget of cinnamon-sugar ricotta to form a simple but intricate shell. These are best eaten hot, and they are easy to find in Naples this way. It's also worth noting that some cakes are strictly seasonal—if you're here at the end of October, look out for the brightly colored slabs of incredibly sweet *torrone* nougat, eaten to commemorate the Day of the Dead (Nov. 1), while Christmas brings an array of delights, including the teeth-challenging *rococo* (made from almonds) or the tiny fried pastry balls doused in honey, *struffoli.* St. Joseph has the honor of being commemorated with the *zeppola,* a baked or fried pastry base with a dollop of cream on the top, available mid-March. The classic address for sfogliatelle is **Pintauro** (⊠ Via Toledo 275, Spaccanapoli ☎ 081/417339). If you need a hot-out-of-the-oven morsel as soon as you get off the train, **Attanasio** (⊠ Vico Ferrovia 2, Piazza Garibaldi ☎ 081/285675), hidden away off Piazza Garibaldi, is justifiably famous.

Scaturchio (⊠ Piazza San Domenico Maggiore 19, Spaccanapoli ☎ 081/ 5516944) is the essential Neapolitan pastry shop. Although the coffee is top-of-the-line and the ice cream and pastries quite good—including the specialty, the *ministeriale,* a pert chocolate cake whipped with rum-cream filling—it's the atmosphere that counts here (though not the luxe, it's a rather unprepossessing sort of place). In the heart of Spaccanapoli, it's where nuns, punks, businesspeople, and housewives commune on the good things they all have in common. If all this coffee is giving you a caffeine-rush, try the city's only hot chocolate bar—**Chocolat** (⊠ Via S. Pietro a Maiella 8, Spaccanapoli ☎ 081/299840) offers 35 different types of hot chocolate as well as milk shakes and ice creams in the summer months.

The largest number of good pastry shops are in the upscale Chiaia neighborhood. **Moccia** (⊠ Via San Pasquale a Chiaia 21, Chiaia ☎ 081/ 411348) is often said to be the finest pasticceria in the city, and it has great babas (decorated, should you wish, with whipped cream and wild strawberries) and an out-of-this-world pound cake injected with just the right dose of intense lemon curd. Connoisseurs will say the most refined and tasty pastry in town can be found at **Gran Caffè Cimmino** (⊠ Via G. Filangieri 12/13, Chiaia ☎ 081/418303). Most of the city's many lawyers congregate here, to celebrate or commiserate with crisp, light cannoli; airy lemon eclairs; *choux* paste in the form of a mushroom laced with chocolate whipped cream; and delightful wild strawberry tartlets, precise and Lolita-innocent, with only a dewy spray of ruby glaze as a discreet enticement to perdition.

All these addresses will have exemplary ice cream as well, but you may prefer a more informal setting. **Scimmia** (⊠ Piazza Carità 4, Spaccanapoli), in the center of town, scoops out a luscious variety of ice cream flavors. Young Neapolitans often go down to Mergellina to have a cone at one of the outdoor chalets in the garden along the port; connoisseurs insist that **Chalet Ciro** (⊠ Via F. Caracciolo, 1 block west of

Mergellina hydrofoil pier, Mergellina ☎ 081/669928) is the best. They also whip up astonishing milk shakes and smoothies using a wide selection of fruit that looks as if it grew in fruit paradise. Just off Via Gramsci, a five-minute walk west of the Villa Comunale and the American Consulate, is the highly rated gelateria **Remy** (✉ Via F. Galiani 29/A, Mergellina ☎ 081/667304). If you're going to abandon your low-cholesterol diet, this is definitely the place to do it, preferably with a selection of their *semi-freddi* (a cross between ice cream and mousse). Some experts award the prize to Posillipo's **Gelateria Bilancione** (✉ Via Posillipo 238B Posillipo ☎ 081/7691923), where the divinely light ice cream matches the perfection of the Bay of Naples view. Keep in mind that a number of ambulant vendors around town sell absolutely first-rate lemon ice, or granita, for derisory prices; this can be a godsend in summer.

Chocolate lovers will be relieved to know that **Gay Odin** (✉ Via Toledo 214, Spaccanapoli ☎ 081/400063 ⊕ www.gay-odin.it), Naples's most famous *cioccolateria*, has seven stores distributed around town, all recognizable by their inviting dark-wood Art Nouveau decor; try the signature chocolate forest cake (*foresta*) or their unusual "naked" chocolates (*nudi*), a suave mixture of chestnuts and walnuts, some with a whole coffee bean wrapped in the center. **Cioccolateria Perzechella** (✉ Vico Pallonetto a S. Chiara 36, Spaccanapoli ☎ 081/5510025) is a new arrival to Naples but looks set to challenge Gay Odin's supremacy in the chocolate world. How can they not, since owners Pina and Giulia have rather shamelessly devised the *Tre Re* ("three kings")—three hazelnuts stuck together with chocolate in honor of King Ferdinand II, revolutionary Masaniello, and Naples's unofficial saint, the soccer player Diego Maradona. They just may tip the scales with their *Torna a Surriento*— Sorrento orange peel dipped in dark chocolate.

A small alleyway leading off the side of the Gesù Nuovo toward Via Toledo hides a little-known jewel that is worth the detour: **Gallucci** (✉ Via Cisterna dell'Olio 6, Spaccanapoli ☎ 081/5513148), founded in 1890, specializes in fruit-filled chocolates (the cherry and grape are memorable) and also produces a delightfully original local cult item, chestnuts filled with marsala. It also produces the most fantastically packaged Easter eggs, all with huge silver or gold bows, that you are ever likely to see.

Food Shopping

The makings of delicious sandwiches (panini) can be had at any neighborhood *salumerie,* which specialize in cured meats and cheese. You'll find the cheapest and freshest fruits and vegetables in the open-air markets. Cubbyhole mom-and-pop groceries offer basic foodstuffs and sometimes produce. For exotic (including American) ingredients, **Tropical Fruit** (✉ Via Montesanto 6, Spaccanapoli ☎ 081/5801006) offers a limited supply of organic products and an excellent assortment of dried fruits, and is a generally reliable source of peanut butter.

If you fancy taking home some of the region's increasingly excellent wines, head for the **Enoteca Dante** (✉ Piazza Dante 18, Spaccanapoli ☎ 081/ 5499689), which often has not-to-missed special offers. **L'Altra bottiglia** (✉ Via Martucci 103, Chiaia ☎ 081/667928) has a high-quality selection of wines, together with a range of cheeses and smoked meats. **Leopoldo** (✉ Via Colonna 46 Chiaia ☎ 081/416161) offers its legendary *taralli*—peppery biscuits—and other goodies for gourmands.

WHERE TO STAY

Updated by
Victoria
Primhak

Naples has the range of accommodations you would expect of any bustling metropolis, from the grand landmarks of luxury on the Lungomare and Posillipo to the little *alberghetti* around the Piazza Garibaldi railway station. Happily, the equivalent of the genteel *pensiones* of yesteryear are enjoying a renaissance: usually small and intimate, set in historic palazzi, they often have a quaint appeal that fortunately does not preclude modern plumbing. Since Naples is very much a businessperson's city, the better hotels can be quickly booked up by conventioneers (who are willing to pay top prices and even supplements for amenities like air-conditioning), so reserve well in advance for the finer hotels. But whether you are in a five-star hotel or a more modest establishment, you may enjoy one of the greatest pleasures of all: a room with a view. In this case it's not *any* view, but the lay-down-and-die panorama of the Bay of Naples and Vesuvius, so be sure to ask for a bayside room if your hotel can provide one.

Since Naples is not known for peace and quiet, it's good news that it features a bevy of hotels that deliver exactly that—most accommodations are cool and tranquil sanctums, with the emphasis on cool. As one of Europe's hottest and busiest cities, its hotels feature some of the strongest air-conditioning around (when making reservations, be sure to inquire if there is a supplement for air-conditioning). Bear in mind that high seasons in Naples are really the "shoulder seasons" elsewhere—April to June and September to October—so be sure to book well in advance if visiting then.

Unfortunately, rare is the hotel that fills every measure on our yardstick—character, national aura, centrality to interesting locations. Yet there are grand hotels that still conjure up the days of steamship travel and whose window views allow you to indulge in reveries of Vesuvius; several properties that set out to be ideal business hotels (with faxes, copiers, and modems at the ready); elegant 19th-century mansions renovated into homes-away-from-home that would not be too out of place in *A Room with a View;* and even a pensione that occupies the former palace of the Princes di Sangro. Assume all hotel rooms have air-conditioning, telephones, TV, and private bath, unless otherwise noted.

WHAT IT COSTS In Euros				
$$$$	**$$$**	**$$**	**$**	**¢**
over €210	€160–€210	€110–€160	€60–€110	under €60

Prices are for two people in a standard double room in high season including tax and service.

Lungomare & Santa Lucia

This prominent stretch of seacoast, with an unsurpassed view of the Bay of Naples, naturally has the greatest concentration of luxury hotels in the city, although more reasonable lodging is available on the side streets.

★ **$$$$** ✕⊡ **Excelsior.** A swarm of maharajahs, emperors, and Hollywood legends has stayed at this hotel, a grand-tradition outpost since 1909. The exterior, with the hotel's name magnificently picked out in Pompeian red, is awash in elegant detail, while the interior is a symphony of soaring columns, gilded French doors, and Venetian chandeliers. Some guest suites renovated in 2003 feature the best views of Vesuvius in Naples. Today the hotel caters to corporate chiefs, its ballrooms host company meetings, and the breakfast is delicious, but there's not a maharajah or

Hollywood legend in sight. Always a plus, discreet but attentive service gives the hotel a personal touch—if you even want to hire a yacht, the concierge can oblige. After those walks around town, repair to the quietest piano bar in Naples, where you'll find barman Francesco mixes the driest martini in town—ask for a Hemingway. La Terrazza has been renovated to within its eye teeth to become the best restaurant in town, replete with antique red accents, vermeil tableware, very ambitious dishes, and a terrace with sweeping views of the bay that make summer dining-out (and late Sunday breakfast?) a must. ⊠ *Via Partenope 48, Santa Lucia 80121* ☎ *081/7640111* 🖷 *081/7649743* ⊕ *www.excelsior. it* ➯ *109 rooms, 12 suites* ♨ *2 restaurants, minibars, health club, bar, meeting room, Internet* ⊟ *AE, DC, MC, V* ⏐○⏐ *BP.*

★ **$$$$** ✕🖪 **Hotel Santa Lucia.** There may be luxury hotels in Naples as fetching as this one, but in no other can you open your window to find the port immortalized in the song "Santa Lucia," bobbing with hundreds of boats, lined with seafood restaurants, and backed by the medieval Castel dell'Ovo. Even if your room doesn't have this bayside view of the Borgo Marinaro fishing village, the hotel's luxurious, quietly understated polish will win you over. The lobby is aglow with antiques, chandeliers, and full length portraits of Neapolitan aristocrats. The brocaded and very comfortable guest rooms are traditional (however, there are some that readers carp are too small for the price), with bathrooms paved in terra-cotta and often equipped with whirlpool bath. Just off the lobby, the restaurant Megaris makes a handy spot for luxe hotel dining. ⊠ *Via Partenope 46, Santa Lucia, 80121* ☎ *081/7640666* 🖷 *081/7648580* ⊕ *www.santalucia.it* ➯ *107 rooms* ♨ *Restaurant, minibars, bar, meeting room, Internet* ⊟ *AE, DC, MC, V* ⏐○⏐ *BP.*

$$$$ ✕🖪 **Vesuvio.** Caruso died here, Queen Sophia of Sweden stayed here (just after a cholera epidemic, as a gesture of good will), Oscar Wilde and his lover Lord Alfred Douglas escaped here—but you'd never guess that this is the oldest of Naples's great seafront hotels from its exterior, now defaced with one of the ugliest modern facades in existence. Still, if this hotel is good enough for Giorgio Armani when he stays in town, it's good enough for you, right? Happily, the interior soothes the eye and the top-class service and new beauty center and spa pamper your body. Atop the hotel is the famous Caruso restaurant, with a Cinerama vista of the bay as a garnish to some excellent dining. Guest rooms can be lullingly luxurious—traditional in style, with antique accents (framed prints, marble lamps) and vibrantly colored walls, plus cove moldings, parquet floors, gleaming bathrooms; many have grand views of the bay. Now, if they could only do something about that sickly gray-and-Miami-Beach–pink facade. ⊠ *Via Partenope 45, Santa Lucia 80121* ☎ *081/ 7640044* 🖷 *081/7644483* ⊕ *www.vesuvio.it* ➯ *146 rooms, 17 suites* ♨ *Restaurant, minibars, gym, bar, hair salon, spa, meeting room, Internet, parking (fee)* ⊟ *AE, DC, MC, V* ⏐○⏐ *BP.*

$$$–$$$$ 🖪 **Miramare.** Like a relic of a more gracious age, this turn-of-the-20th-century town house in the Stil Liberty style sits above the frantic traffic of Via Nazario Sauro like a dowager at a disco party. Once the American consulate, it still offers the air of a private home, an air much fostered by manager Enzo Rosolino, a household name in Italy thanks to his nephew, a gold-medalist Olympic swimmer. Enzo often presides over guests in the main parlor, seeing to their comfort with a courteous attention to detail, as shown by the electric teapots and the selection of videocassettes available in the rooms. Guest rooms, with an airy Deco feel to them, are handsome, quiet, and exquisitely air-conditioned. The hotel looks directly onto the bay (and that traffic, although dulled by double-pane windows; for real peace and quiet opt for a room at the back of the hotel) and you can enjoy a breakfast atop the roof garden.

A 10-minute walk takes you to Piazza del Plebiscito and the center of Naples. The hotel offers good deals on weekends, over Christmas, and during August. ⊠ *Via N. Sauro 24, Via Partenope, 80132* ☎ *081/ 7647589* 🖷 *081/7640775* ⊕ *www.hotelmiramare.com* ⇥ *31 rooms* ♻ *Minibars, meeting rooms* ☰ *AE, DC, MC, V* ❘⓪❘ *BP.*

★ **$$–$$$** ⊡**Parteno.** Undoubtedly proud of their premier address—"No. 1" on Naples's main waterfront street—welcoming owners Alex Ponzi and mother Adele have installed an exclusive and elegant bed-and-breakfast near the Villa Comunale, 5 minutes from Castel dell' Ovo and 15 from the hydrofoils to the bay islands. The spacious and serene rooms are tastefully decorated with period etchings and gouache views of Naples. One looks onto the bay; the others face a side street, happily removed from the swirling traffic on the bayside avenue. Breakfast (served in your bedroom if you wish) is the real treat here—one of a tempting range of specialty Neapolitan pastries will accompany your caffè. For those suffering from Internet addiction disorder, Alex has arranged a 24-hour connection in each room (computers can be borrowed) together with a fax and a refrigerator for downloading Neapolitan goodies. ⊠ *Via Partenope 1, Santa Lucia, 80121* ☎🖷 *081/2452095* ⊕ *www.parteno. it* ⇥ *6 rooms* ♻ *Internet* ☰ *AE, DC, MC, V* ❘⓪❘ *BP.*

★ **$$** ⊡**Chiaja Hotel de Charme.** No views, but there's plenty of atmosphere in these converted first-floor apartments that occupy a spruce 18th-century palazzo, part of which includes a converted historic brothel. Above the fireplace in the cozy entrance hall, the distinguished looking chap with the moustache in the painting is the Marchese Nicola Le Caldano Sasso III, original owner of the building (though not, one assumes, the brothel), whose granddaughter Mimi now runs the place. Antiques, many of them original to the Marquis's home, give a personal touch to the elegant, air-conditioned, period-feel bedrooms (most have whirlpool baths). A two-minute walk from Piazza Plebiscito and the Royal Palace and a stagger from the liveliest nightlife in town in the back streets around Piazza dei Martiri, this also has a top location (although its Via Chiaia locale is not quite within the purview of the Riviera di Chiaia district, covered separately below). If you're anxious to get out in the morning, vouchers for breakfast in the nearby Gambrinus caffè or the Barcadero at the Borgo Marinaro are available on request. ⊠ *Via Chiaia 216, Chiaia, 80121* ☎ *081/415555* 🖷 *081/422344* ⊕ *www.hotelchiaia.it* ⇥ *27 rooms* ♻ *Bar* ☰ *AE, DC, MC, V* ❘⓪❘ *BP.* '

Piazza Garibaldi to La Sanità

Hardly the nicest or most interesting part of town to stay in, the Piazza Garibaldi area is convenient to the train station. There's almost always a room somewhere and few neighborhoods can give you such a blast of *Napolinità.* From here the hills runs up through the quaint Sanità district.

$$$ ⊡**Suite Esedra.** Squashed into a tiny piazza off frantic Corso Umberto— one of the main traffic trunks leading away from Piazza Garibaldi—this is a hotel that's convenient to transportation as well as just a few blocks from the heart of the historic neighborhood of Spaccanapoli. The decor, based on an astrological theme, takes itself lightly enough to work. Each guest room expresses a different planet or sign of the zodiac, all in the coolest faux-Memphis style, with plenty of sleek woods and Philippe Starck–esque touches. The hotel is in a densely packed district (reach out your window and you can practically touch the building across the way), so the building has sliver dimensions with guest rooms on the petite side, except for two suites that have their own private terrace with whirlpool. Still, the lobby, library, and dining room are all suavely decorated and a nice touch at breakfast sees all the guests seated round one table, rather like a house party. ⊠ *Via A. Cantani 12, Piazza Garibaldi,*

80133 ☎ *081/5537087* 🖷 *081/287451* ⊕ *www.sea-hotels.com* ⤵ *17 rooms* ⚗ *Minibars, gym, bar* ▭ *AE, MC, V* ⦿ *BP.*

$$ ✕⊡ **Del Real Orto Botanico.** Located near Naples's noted botanical gardens, this 18th-century building has been turned into a spacious hotel, an eight-minute taxi ride from the airport and only a short bus ride from the bustling center of town. Owner Michele Catuogno's attention to detail has leapfrogged this place into one of the best hotels in town. Antiques—for sale, no less—adorn the public rooms (although the Pomodoro wall-bar in the tiny TV lounge is a modernist classic he's hanging on to), 200 guidebooks and art catalogues are available to help promote this less-frequented historic area of Naples, and service is excellent. A courtesy car will take you to the airport or train station during the day. Front rooms are noisy if you leave the balcony window open, but they face the gorgeous tropical gardens of the Orto Botanico; a better bet may be the back, particularly on summer nights, as traffic never stops in this city. All rooms are spacious, decorated in stylish, soothing greens and beiges, but the real stunner is the fabulous roof-terrace bar–restaurant—fresh grilled fish a speciality—with views over the gardens and the Sanità right up to Capodimonte. ✉ *Via Foria 192, Carlo III, 80139* ☎ *081/4421528* 🖷 *081/4421346* ⊕ *www.hotelcavournapoli.it* ⤵ *36 rooms* ⚗ *Restaurant, bar* ▭ *AE, DC, MC, V* ⦿ *BP.*

$–$$ ⊡ **Hotel Potenza.** Completely renovated, this tiny hotel up one flight of stairs is bright and cheerful, decorated in clear Mediterranean blues and greens, with pleasant bathrooms. All rooms are air-conditioned and reasonably spacious, with brand-new fittings; in addition to guest rooms, there are some quasi-student-type accommodations that fit several beds into a room. No breakfast officially, but the owners also run the bar–restaurant below so they will bring a basic breakfast to your room. ✉ *Piazza Garibaldi 120, Piazza Garibaldi, 80142* ☎ *081/286330* 🖷 *081/5633220* ⊕ *www.hotelpotenza.com* ⤵ *14 rooms* ▭ *AE, MC, V* ⦿ *EP.*

¢ ⊡ **Hotel Viola.** Here's a clean, family-run basic accommodation, just around the corner from the Stazione Centrale. All rooms have color TV and most have private bathrooms. Owner Giuseppe Viola was born in the hotel and his son and daughter help run it. Around-the-clock reception makes this a safe budget option, and some dorm-style four-bed rooms are available. Breakfast is served in the rather bleak bar or in the bedrooms. It's worth paying extra for air-conditioning in summer. ✉ *Via Palermo 22/23, Piazza Garibaldi, 80142* ☎ *081/269368* 🖷 *081/5549749* ⊕ *www.hotelviola.it* ⤵ *25 rooms* ⚗ *Bar* ▭ *AE, DC, MC, V* ⦿ *CP.*

¢ ⊡ **Pensione Mancini.** On the other side of Piazza Garibaldi from the main station, this pensione-cum-hostel is a safe and comfortable outpost in the middle of the daily carnival of Neapolitan street life. With several double rooms, but also with dormitory-type accommodation available for those on a tight budget, this is a good base if backpacking on your own and in need of company for evening forays into downtown Napoli. Human dynamo Lello in the reception area doubles as night porter, besides running a booking office for other reputable low-price hotels in the area when the Mancini is full. Book well in advance to ensure a place here. ✉ *Via Mancini 33, Piazza Garibaldi, 80142* ☎ *081/5536731* 🖷 *081/5546675* ⊕ *www.hostelpensionemancini.com* ⤵ *6 rooms, 3 with bath* ⚗ *Bar; no a/c, no room phones* ▭ *No credit cards* ⦿ *BP.*

Spaccanapoli & Piazza Municipio

Spaccanapoli is Naples's most picturesque quarter, so if you're out to spend some time *nel cuore della antica Napoli, immersei nel silenzio di settecenteschi palazzi nobilari*—"in the heart of historic Naples, immersed in the silence of 17th-century noble palaces," as the Resorts Sansevero (who run some of the quaintest hotels hereabouts) put it—this is the place to roost. The flip-side of the coin is the nearby area around Piazza Municipio—the bustling heart of the city—which sports a collection of upscale large-capacity business hotels, along with some delightful finds housed in historic buildings.

$$$$ 🏨 **Mediterraneo.** A large, modern, efficient business hotel, this place is within walking distance of both the Teatro San Carlo and Spaccanapoli. Comfortable and personable if not personal, it's a favorite for conferences. A lovely plus here is the beautiful roof garden. ⊠ *Via Nuova Ponte di Tappia 25, Toledo, 80133* ☎ *081/5512240* 🖷 *081/5525868* ⊕ *www.italyhotel.com/napoli* ⤣ *256 rooms* ⅋ *Restaurant, minibars, bar, Internet* ⊟ *DC, MC, V* ⑩ *BP.*

$$–$$$ 🏨 **Parteno Deluxe.** If you're looking for something different, the new Parteno Deluxe (mate to the cheaper Parteno along the Lungomare) comes complete with huge hi-tech, minimalist open-plan, split-level studios with kitchens and whirlpool baths. In the busy Piazza Dante area, and set in the slightly rundown 17th-century Palazzo Ruffo, it happily sits just opposite a state-of-the-art metro station and is only a five-minute stroll from the Museo Archeologico Nazionale (a nifty way to get a jump on its crowds). And how's this for a sweet idea: guests can ask for a cooking lesson in their kitchen, order a typical Neapolitan dish like *parmigiana di melazana,* shop for ingredients in the local market, assist with the cooking, and then be waiter-served in the room. ⊠ *Piazza Dante 89, Spaccanapoli, 80135* ☎ *081/2452095* ⅋ *Kitchenettes* ⊟ *AE, DC, MC, V* ⑩ *BP.*

★ **$$$–$$$$** 🏨 **Grand Hotel Oriente.** This is an excellent businessperson's hotel with all the conveniences and in a great location. Outside the hotel will be the new Toledo metro station (due to open in 2005) linking up with the Museo Archeologico Nazionale and the Vomero. A three-minute walk away is the pedestrianized Via Toledo, leading down to Piazza Plebiscito and the Royal Palace. Despite the severe marble facade, the interior is welcoming: after a long, hard day it's a boon to return here and find comfortable, soundproof guest rooms and friendly, professional staff. ⊠ *Via Diaz 44, Toledo, 80134* ☎ *081/5512133* 🖷 *081/5514915* ⊕ *www.oriente.it* ⤣ *130 rooms* ⅋ *Minibars, bar, Internet, parking (fee)* ⊟ *AE, DC, MC, V* ⑩ *BP.*

★ **$$$** 🏨 **Il Convento.** Opposite the gruesomely named Convento di Santa Maria Francesca dalle Cinque Piaghe ("of the five wounds")—women hoping to conceive trek from miles around to sit in its saint's chair, as she was famed for curing childlessness—this 17th-century building has now been winningly converted into a hotel. Fetchingly and charmingly decorated, the place comes complete with lots of wrought-iron, rose terracotta tiles, and sunny colors. The mix of antiques, rustic and repro, creates a surprising sense of harmony. The former "cells" have all been renovated delightfully. Room sizes vary but if you can afford it, book a junior suite with private flower-filled roof-garden; there's no view, but it's a haven of peace and sun in the city center. Centrally located in the *quartieri* (Spanish Quarter), you still need to keep an eye on your pocketbook, but the hotel offers 24/7 security access. ⊠ *Via Speranzella 137/A, Toledo, 80132* ☎ *081/403977* 🖷 *081/400332* ⊕ *www.hotelilconvento.com* ⤣ *12 rooms, 2 suites* ⅋ *Minibars, bar* ⊟ *AE, MC, V* ⑩ *BP.*

$$$ 🏨 **Mercure Napoli Angioino.** In the heart of town, right off Piazza Municipio in the shadows of the famed Castel Nuovo, and close to the Teatro San Carlo, this popular place has a sober yet luminous lobby and quiet, tastefully appointed guest rooms, some of which are reserved for nonsmokers. This is an especially good choice if you're taking a boat from the nearby Molo Beverello. ⊠ *Via De Pretis 123, Toledo*

80133 ☎ 081/5529500 🖷 081/5529509 🌐 www.mercure.com ⇨ 85 rooms ♁ Minibars, meeting room, no-smoking rooms ▭ AE, DC, MC, V 🍽 BP.

★ $$–$$$ **Executive.** Near Santa Maria la Nova and a 10-minute walk from both the port and Spaccanapoli, this rightly popular restored convent still grants a privileged solace from the busy world. The airy, well-insulated rooms come complete with a phone in the bathroom. The bar area is an exquisitely decorated nook. Breakfast is served on the sunny roof terrace. The hotel is on Via del Cerriglio, the first road on your right as you go up Via G. Sanfelice from Piazza Bovio (Borsa). ✉ *Via del Cerriglio 10, Toledo, 80134 ☎ 081/5520611 🖷 081/5528163 🌐 www.sea-hotels.com ⇨ 19 rooms ♁ Minibars, gym, sauna, bar, parking (fee) ▭ AE, DC, MC, V 🍽 BP.*

$–$$ **Europeo.** Right around the corner from the Spacca's Piazza San Domenico Maggiore, this is an excellent choice if you are looking for a clean, firm bed at reasonable prices in the middle of the university quarter. The international student atmosphere extends to dorm rooms available downstairs. Breakfast is served at the nearby Executive, part of the same group, and you're right around the corner from the famed pastry shrine, Scaturchio. ✉ *Via Mezzocannone 109/c, Spaccanapoli, 80131 ☎🖷 081/5517254 🌐 www.sea-hotels.com ⇨ 17 rooms, 7 with bath ▭ AE, MC, V 🍽 BP.*

$–$$ **Toledo.** A centuries-old palazzo has now been tastefully transformed into this boutique hotel, a two-minute walk up from Via Toledo, near Spaccanapoli and the Royal Palace. Rooms are furnished in a pleasing rustic style, while the leafy rooftop terrace provides a quintessentially Neapolitan backdrop for your breakfast. ✉ *Via Montecalvario 15, Toledo 80134 ☎🖷 081/406800 🌐 www.hoteltoledo.com ⇨ 18 rooms ♁ Bar ▭ AE, DC, MC, V 🍽 BP.*

★ $ **Albergo Sansevero.** This is a superbly located option, as handy to the main thoroughfare of Via Toledo as it is to the historic enchantments of Spaccanapoli. Ten blocks away from its sister establishments, the Soggiorno Sansevero and Sansevero Degas, this *albergo* (small hotel) is off caffè-set Piazza Bellini, the prettiest of the Spacca's squares, and its address is on one of the city's great 19th-century boulevards. As with many of the city's alberghi, there's no elevator (and quite a number of steps). ✉ *Via S. Maria di Constantinopoli 101, Spaccanapoli, 80131 ☎ 081/210907 🖷 081/211698 🌐 www.albergosansevero.it ⇨ 11 rooms, 9 with bath ♁ Bar ▭ AE, DC, MC, V 🍽 BP.*

★ $ **Sansevero Degas.** Just off the pulsing aorta of Spaccanapoli, the gorgeous Piazza del Gesù, this new offshoot of the Sansevero hotels is perfectly located between the historic center and all the sights of royal Naples. Rooms in this historic palace are comfortable and spacious, some with views over the piazza, and as you walk through the magnificent gateway to the hotel's courtyard you really feel part of the old Neapolitan aristocracy. A very friendly welcome is another top plus here. ✉ *Calata Trinità Maggiore 53, Spaccanapoli, 80131 ☎ 081/210907 🖷 081/211698 🌐 www.venere.it/it/napoli/sanseverodegas/ ⇨ 9 rooms, 7 with bath ♁ Bar ▭ AE, DC, MC, V 🍽 BP.*

$ **Caravaggio.** Opened in December 2002 in a 17th-century palazzo on a tiny square behind the Duomo, this place takes its name from the painter of the amazing *Sette Opere della Misericordia* altarpiece, which can be seen in the chapel opposite. Spaccanapoli's first "modernist" hotel, it's atmospherically furnished with blocks of volcanic stone in the entrance hall, while the guest rooms (some of which include a Jacuzzi) are all refreshingly light and airy. ✉ *Via Riario Sforza 157, Spaccanapoli, 80131 ☎ 081/2110066 🖷 081/4421578 🌐 www.caravaggiohotel.it ⇨ 11 rooms ♁ Bar, Internet ▭ AE, DC, MC, V 🍽 BP.*

$ ⊡ **Neapolis.** Situated on a narrow alley off the humming Via Tribunali close to Piazza Bellini, this recent addition looks out over the 13th-century Pietrasanta bell tower. A mix of modern and traditional style furnishings with a lovely warm terra-cotta floor and data ports in every room make this a good bet if you want to explore the delights of the Spacca, Naples's fascinating medieval center. ⊠ *Via Francesco Del Giudice 13, Spaccanapoli 80131* ☎ *081/4420815* 🖷 *081/4420819* ⊕ *www. hotelneapolis.com* ➳ *18 rooms* ⚲ *Bar, in-room data ports* ▤ *AE, DC, MC, V* �101 *BP.*

★ **$** ⊡ **Soggiorno Sansevero.** Replete with the atmosphere of old Naples and within the very heart of Spaccanapoli, this pensione occupies a floor in the former Baroque-era palace of the princes di Sangro di San Severo, who built the "notorious" 18th-century family chapel directly behind this building. Although the palace overlooks the opera-set-like Piazza San Domenico, the tiny Soggiorno is on the palazzo's quiet inner courtyard with simply furnished rooms—linoleum floors, modern beds, great-grandmama's boudoir bureau—and may even come with ghosts: Carlo Gesualdo, inventor of the madrigal song, murdered his wife and her lover on the palace's staircase in 1590. As with the other hotels in this local group, the staff is very friendly and helpful. ⊠ *Piazza San Domenico 9, Palazzo Sansevero, Spaccanapoli, 80131* ☎ *081/5555949* 🖷 *081/ 211698* ⊕ *www.albergosansevero.it* ➳ *6 rooms, 4 with bath* ▤ *AE, DC, MC, V* 101 *BP.*

Chiaia, Vomero & Posillipo

Chiaia is the ritziest residential neighborhood of Naples, studded with 19th-century mansions and an elegant shopping district bordering the Villa Comunale gardens by the water. Above Chiaia rises the Vomero hill, offering great vistas of the bay. The bayside atmosphere continues at Mergellina, a transportation hub set at the far western end of the Riviera di Chiaia, and beyond at the suburban coastal district of Posillipo.

★ **$$$$** ✕⊡ **Parker's.** This landmark hotel, which first opened its doors in 1870, continues to serve up a supremely elegant dose of old-style atmosphere and surprisingly personal service. The name comes from wealthy eccentric English marine biologist George Parker, a regular in the late 19th century who finally upped and bought the hotel in 1889 (legend has it that the then-owner gave up the hotel to cover his gambling debts; when the debt-collectors came to close it down one morning, they knocked at the suite where Parker was staying, waking him up, and he replied "Put the hotel on my bill!" and went back to sleep.) The hotel, officially called Grand Hotel Parker's, now welcomes visiting V.I.P.s, ranging from rock stars to Russian leaders, who probably enjoy the hotel decor, an homage to the Neoclassical style, brought to Naples by Napoléon and his general Joachim Murat. Gilt-trimmed Empire bureaus, shimmering chandeliers, fluted pilasters, and ornate ceilings all glitter. Set midway up the Vomero Hill, and a bit of a walk from its funicular stops, the hotel's perch offers fine views of the bay and distant Capri; drink it all in from the superb rooftop-garden restaurant, which proffers regional specialities. ⊠ *Corso Vittorio Emanuele 135, Vomero, 80121* ☎ *081/7612474* 🖷 *081/663527* ⊕ *www.grandhotelparkers.com* ➳ *83 rooms* ⚲ *Restaurant, minibars, bar, meeting room, parking (fee)* ▤ *AE, DC, MC, V* 101 *BP.*

★ **$$$$** ⊡ **San Francesco al Monte.** This landmark in Neapolitan history is a luxurious contender in Naples's hotel sweepstakes. Situated high up on the Vomero hill's Corso Vittorio Emanuele and famed as one of the city's most historic 16th-century monasteries, San Francesco first entered the history books when mobs charged into it during the Masaniello uprising of 1647 to aim their cannons at the Royal Palace of Castelnuovo from its terraces. After the Bourbon king Ferdinand II's visit here in 1853, a royal edict forbade building below the convent, thereby guaranteeing its panoramic views for posterity. The simple elegance of the former cells (for once a well-hidden TV and bar) enchants as much as the vistas. Their finishing touches are original frescoes above their doors—the monks never had whirlpool baths and showers, though. Parts of the ancient structure have been incorporated, such as the brick oven and the hand-painted wall tiles on the old stone staircase (note that some areas can only be accessed by steps). Best of all is the nearly 360-degree view of the city and bay from the roof terrace. Nicely set under the craggy Vigna di San Martino, the terrace also seduces with its outdoor waterfall and swimming pool. A restaurant with outdoor terrace dining, a cloister-bar, and luxurious quiet are the toppings on the cake here. A shuttle bus to the airport is available for hotel guests. ⊠ *Corso Vittorio Emanuele, 328, Vomero, 80135* ☎ *081/423911* 🖨 *081/2512485* ⊕ *www.hotelsanfrancesco.it/ing/home.html* 🛏 *30 rooms* ⚭ *2 restaurants, minibars, bar, outdoor pool, parking (fee)* ☰ *AE, DC, MC, V* ⏺ *BP.*

$$$ 🏨 **Britannique.** As one reader put it, "this is an elegant but far from pretentious place, full of history with a charm that can only be born of time." Adjacent to Grand Hotel Parker's, this reserved and traditional hotel has bright, well-appointed, spacious rooms with even better views across the bay and city, thanks to the small private garden across the street (reserved for guests), which prevents any obstruction—so if you want to immortalize the Bay of Naples in watercolor, do it here. Guest rooms are comfortably furnished and have double-glazed windows, a wise precaution on the Corso, one of Naples's busiest nighttime streets. ⊠ *Corso Vittorio Emanuele 133, Vomero, 80121* ☎ *081/7614145* 🖨 *081/660457* ⊕ *www.hotelbritannique.it* 🛏 *86 rooms* ⚭ *Restaurant, minibars, bar, meeting room* ☰ *AE, DC, MC, V* ⏺ *BP.*

$$$ 🏨 **Paradiso.** This impressive hotel on the hillside of Posillipo is famous for the views of the Bay of Naples from its rooms, its roof-garden restaurant, and its garden terrace. From your own flower-bedecked balcony you can also take in the immediate neighborhood, less enchantingly filled with apartment buildings. Although the hotel is located at the western edge of the city, the nearby funicular takes you efficiently to the harbor port and transportation hub of Mergellina, at the end of the Riviera di Chiaia. ⊠ *Via Catullo 11, Posillipo, 80122* ☎ *081/2475111* 🖨 *081/7613449* ⊕ *www.bestwestern.it/paradisohotel* 🛏 *74 rooms* ⚭ *Restaurant, minibars, bar* ☰ *AE, DC, MC, V* ⏺ *BP.*

$$ 🏨 **Delle Terme.** Want to stay in Naples while feeling like you're in the country? You might have the best of both worlds here at this hotel set in an enormous, verdant vale in the Campi Flegrei area on the western outskirts of the city. In the same complex as the Agnano Spa—its mud wallows and saunas have been on tap since the Caesars vacationed around here—this attractively priced hotel in a park is an ideal spot if you're traveling by car (it's easy to get to, with the Tangenziale highway that leads to the center city just two minutes away) and want a relaxing and convenient base to the whole area for a few days. Access is provided to Naples via municipal bus, which takes you to the Metro stop at Campi Flegrei, but late-night public transport is tricky. Modern, comfortable if impersonal rooms make this an attractive option for small conferences. The spa gives discounts to hotel guests. ⊠ *Via Agnano Astroni 24, Agnano, 80125* ☎ *081/5701733* 🖨 *081/7626441* ⊕ *www.hotelterme.it* 🛏 *62 rooms* ⚭ *Restaurant, minibars, tennis court, spa, bar* ☰ *AE, DC, MC, V* ⏺ *BP.*

★ $$ 🏨 **Pinto Storey.** A fascinating old pensione, overflowing with warmth and charm, this is on the fourth floor of an elegant late-19th-century Stil Liberty building off Piazza Amedeo in the heart of the chic Chiaia district. The main salons are lined with old engravings of bella Napoli, while the airy guest rooms have just been renovated in period style with wrought iron bedsteads; bathrooms have been completely refitted. Some rooms look out over the buildings to the bay. Pleasant and personal service make it extremely popular, so book way in advance. ⊠ *Via G. Martucci 72, Chiaia, 80125* ☎ *081/681260* 🖨 *081/667536* ⊕ *www.pintostorey.it* ⇨ *16 rooms* ☰ *AE, DC, MC, V* ⍾ *BP.*

$$ 🖾 **Ausonia.** The spic-and-span rooms of this hotel are decorated in a nautical motif, retaining a homey feel. In the courtyard of a building on the waterfront at Mergellina, this is quite handy if you're taking a boat from the Mergellina pier. On the other hand, perhaps this is why some guests have complained about suffering from cabin fever after staying here a few nights. ⊠ *Via Caracciolo 11, Mergellina, 80122* ☎ *081/682278* 🖨 *081/664536* ⇨ *20 rooms* ☰ *AE, MC, V* ⍾ *BP.*

$ 🖾 **Ruggiero.** In the same Art Nouveau building as the Pinto Storey (but on the third floor), this bright, cheerful pensione has clean rooms at reasonable prices with convenient access to the Metropolitana, the funicular to Vomero, and the Villa Comunale gardens. ⊠ *Via G. Martucci 72, Chiaia, 80121* ☎☎ *081/7612460* ⇨ *18 rooms, 17 with bath* ☰ *DC, MC, V* ⍾ *BP.*

NIGHTLIFE & THE ARTS

The Arts

Updated by
Francesca
Marretta and
Chris Rose

Lively and energetic yet also chaotic and often difficult to follow, the cultural scene in Naples reflects the city's charming yet infuriating character. Schedules of events are published in daily newspapers, particularly *Il Mattino, La Repubblica,* and *Corriere della Sera,* though they can't be relied on to cover everything that is happening, or frequent last-minute changes of program or venue. The listings magazine *Le Pagine dell'Ozio* can also give you an idea of what's going on, but publication a month beforehand means it is inevitably out-of-date by the time it hits the newsstands. The best source of information is word-of-mouth (ask the receptionists in your hotel what's going on this evening) or by keeping your eyes peeled for the theater and concert posters that wallpaper much of the city center. Information and ticket sales are provided by the following ticket agencies: **Box Office** (⊠ Galleria Umberto I 17, Piazza Municipio ☎ 081/5519188 ⊕ www.boxoffice.it); **Concerteria** (⊠ Via Schipa 23, Chiaia ☎ 081/7611221); **Botteghino** (⊠ Via Pitloo 3, Vomero ☎ 081/5564684).

Concert Halls & Theaters

In addition to the world-famous Teatro San Carlo, Naples has several other leading concert halls and theaters. Each theater generally plans its entire season—which usually runs October through May—in advance with a printed schedule. The **Augusteo** (⊠ Piazza Augusteo, Piazza Municipio ☎ 081/414243 ⊕ www.teatroaugusteo.it) is a large, centrally located theater off Via Toledo that usually presents commercial Italian theater and concerts. **Galleria Toledo** (⊠ Via Montecalvario 36, Spaccanapoli ☎ 081/425824 ⊕ www.galleriatoledo.it) attracts the hip set with high-quality fringe and avant-garde theater presentations, as does its arch-rival the **Teatro Nuovo** (⊠ Via Montecalvario 16, Spaccanapoli ☎ 081/425958 ⊕ www.nuovoteatronuovo.it). **Teatro Bellini** (⊠ Via Conte di Ruvo 14, Spaccanapoli ☎ 081/5499688) is a gilded Belle Epoque theater that presents plays and concerts of a more traditional flavor. **Teatro delle Palme** (⊠ Via Vetriera 12, Chiaia ☎ 081/418134), is a rather ugly postwar-plywood, auditorium-cum-movie theater, which regularly hosts chamber music concerts presented by the Associazione

Alessandro Scarlatti. **Teatro Mercadante** (⊠ Piazza Municipio, Piazza Municipio ☎ 081/5513396), a Belle Epoque theater with an ultra-modern foyer, hosts touring productions of invariably high quality. The **Teatro Politeama** (⊠ Via Monte di Dio 80, Chaia ☎ 081/7645001) could almost be considered an off-Broadway playhouse, considering its challenging bill of fare, which includes much contemporary dance. The Teatro San Carlo company use it for contemporary works, which they don't dare show in their hallowed temple.For a satisfying Neapolitan "soul" experience, catch a local singer like Lina Sastri or Lara Sansone warbling at the **Teatro Sannazzaro** (⊠ Via Chiaia 157, Chiaia ☎ 081/403827); traditional Neapolitan plays by Edoardo di Filippo are also often presented here. **Teatro Trianon** (⊠ Piazza Calenda, 9, Spaccanapoli ☎ 081/2440411) is a refurbished cinema opened in 2003 to provide a "home for Neapolitan song," mixing showings of classic Neapolitan movies with local comedies and frequent concerts by traditional Neapolitan musicians (not to be missed if you want to feel tearful while singing along to "Turna a Surriento").Finally, the **Palapartenope** (⊠ Via Barbagallo, Fuorigrotta ☎ 081/5706806) is an enormous hangar in the suburban Fuorigrotta area where most area pop concerts take place.

Film

Neapolitans take their cinema seriously: the city has many cinema and video stores and rental outlets, and several cinemas even run their own "cineforums" one day a week to cater to more discerning cinemagoers. From the end of June to mid-September, open-air cinemas come into their own, and provide film aficionados with a chance to catch up on movies they missed during the year. The city's love fest with the movies reaches its high point every year with the Napoli Film Festival, usually presented every June at the **Cinema Modernissimo** (⊠ Via Cisterna dell'Olio 59, Spaccanapoli ☎ 081/5511247) and the outdoor location of the Maschio Angiono in Piazza Municipio. **Astra** (⊠ Via Mezzocannone 109, Spaccanapoli ☎ 081/5520713) is a popular cinema in the historic center. **Filangieri** (⊠ Via Filangieri 43, Chiaia ☎ 081/5212408) is a favored cinema in a choicer part of town. The new **Warner Village Metropolitan** (⊠ Via Chaia, Chiaia ☎ 081/2525133) is the latest addition to the city's filmscape—an American-style seven-screen labyrinth, with gigantic buckets of popcorn at every turn.

More traditional cinemas include: **Ambasciatori** (⊠ Via Crispi 33, Chiaia ☎ 081/7613128) and **Delle Palme** (⊠ Via Vetriera 12, Chiaia ☎ 081/418134). Within a short walk of the Castel dell'Ovo and the waterfront hotels is **Santa Lucia** (⊠ Via Santa Lucia 59, Santa Lucia ☎ 081/7648837). For the most panoramic cinema foyer in town and a good selection of films, try the **America Hall** (⊠ Via Tito Angelini 21, Vomero ☎ 081/5788982) in San Martino. As elsewhere in Italy, your favorite movie star will be speaking fluent Italian on the big screen—the dubbers still have a stranglehold on the industry—unless you choose the only (usually Tuesdays) English-language cinema in town, **Abadir** (⊠ Via Paisiello 35, Vomero ☎ 081/5789447). Consult *Il Mattino, La Repubblica,* or *Corriere della Sera* for updated film programs.

Opera & Classical Music

Opera is a serious business in Naples. Not the music, that is, but the costumes, the stage design, the players, the politics. Anyone who aspires to anything absolutely has to be present at the season's major openings, where what's happening on the stage and in the pit are secondary to the news of who is there, who they're with, and what they're wearing. Given this, it's hardly surprising that the city's famous San Carlo company does not offer a particularly challenging repertoire but spends time endlessly redressing the greats. The major event of 2002, for example, was *Don Giovanni,* hardly a radical choice by anybody's agenda, but given the reaction to director Mario Martone's (interesting but relatively unadventurous) staging, you'd think they'd put on an atonal Stockhausen piece. Despite the lack of innovation, the company is usually of very high quality—and if they're not on form, the audience lets them know. Although rotten vegetables are terribly passé, catcalls and boos are perfectly acceptable. All this takes place in the historic **Teatro San Carlo** (✉ Via San Carlo 101–103, Piazza Municipio ☎ 081/7972412, box office, or 081/7972331 ⊕ www.teatrosancarlo.it), the luxury liner of opera houses in southern Italy. The concert hall still gleams with its mid-19th-century gilded furnishings and thick red-velvet drapes. For the opera and ballet season (generally December through June), many seats are presold by subscription but there are usually some seats available if you go to the box office several days before the performance (unless, Domingo, or another superstar, is performing). How far in advance can you book? This depends on the opera and time of year. For some opera performances, tickets can only be bought five days before the performance, but at other times you can buy tickets weeks in advance. You can also book ahead using a credit card by calling **Concerteria** (✉ Via Schipa 23, Chiaia ☎ 081/7611221). Unlike many leading opera companies in the United States, the San Carlo does not operate on a revolving repertory schedule: each opera or ballet is usually scheduled for a mini-run, generally over a 10-day period.

Prices vary due to both location and date. The front rows of the stalls, known as *poltronissime,* might cost as much as €200 for a performance on the first night of an opera, while up in the sixth tier, the Balconata VI, you would pay a fifth of that price, or much less if you went on a later night. Prices are always highest at first nights with the best opera *dive,* then fall off as top performers are sometimes substituted after a few nights. If you get a box seat, keep in mind that there are as many as six people sharing a box, so it's worth getting there early to get a front seat. Some people tip the *maschere* (ushers) and this is especially appreciated if they have fixed you up with a better seat than the one you were allocated originally (maybe a season ticket holder didn't show up). Ballet and concert performances are up to 50% less expensive than opera presentations. One way of getting into the San Carlo for much less would be to go on a guided tour (weekends only, 2 to 3:30). At €2.70 a shot, you soak up some of its magnificence and it might be preferable to paying 50 times as much and sitting through five hours of the Ring cycle. For complete information, contact the **box office,** which is open Tuesday to Saturday 10–1 and 4:30–6:30, and Sunday 10–1, and one hour before performances.

Naples features a reasonable calendar of classical and chamber music concerts; check the newspaper listings and street posters for information about concerts frequently held in the historic churches of the city. The **Associazione Alessandro Scarlatti** (✉ Piazza dei Martiri 58, Chiaia ☎ 081/406011 ⊕ www.napoli.com/assoscarlatti) organizes a series of chamber music concerts at the **Teatro delle Palme** (✉ Via Vetriera 12, Chiaia ☎ 081/418134), and occasionally in other locations around the city—check their Web site for details. The **Centro di Musica Antica Pietà de' Turchini** (✉ Via Santa Caterina da Siena 38, Spaccanapoli ☎ 081/402395 ⊕ www.turchini.it), based in the early Baroque church of Santa Caterina da Siena, offers an excellent season of early music that runs from October to early May. Even if madrigals aren't your thing, it's worth visiting just for the location.

A classical music festival known as **International Music Weeks** takes place throughout May in Naples. Concerts are held at the Teatro San Carlo, the Teatro Mercadante, and in the Neoclassic Villa Pignatelli. For information contact the Teatro San Carlo box office. ✉ *Mergellina.*

Nightlife

Nightlife in Naples begins well after the sun has gone down. If you're going to a club, don't even think about turning up before 11, as more than likely it'll still be empty, and don't plan on going to bed much before 3. Yet if you're willing to stay up late enough, and prepared to hang around outside places where there's sometimes more going on in the street than in the clubs themselves, Naples offers distractions for night owls of all persuasions. The designer-clad young and not-so young hang out in the area around Chiaia and Mergellina; a more artsy post-student crowd congregates around Piazza Bellini; the rawer, punkier edge prefers to hang around on Piazza del Gesù or Piazza San Domenico. Clubs tend to open and close or change name, style, or ownership with bewildering rapidity, so be sure to check locally before planning a night out. The best way to find out what's going on is to keep your eyes on the flyers that cover Spaccanapoli or check the monthly publication *Le Pagine dell'Ozio.*

Many dance clubs issue a drink card (prices vary, €10 is average) at the door that must be returned when you leave, stamped to show you've consumed at least one drink. After the first or second drink, other drinks usually run less (about €5). Long queues are common at the more popular spots as people endlessly haggle about being on the guest list or try to avoid paying in some other way. Be patient and enjoy the experience—many long-standing friendships have been formed in queues outside nightclubs in Naples. But remember that planning a night out in Napoli is rather like planning a military campaign, with many phone calls made, appointments fixed, changed, not met, and plans B, C, and D coming into action. Most of this negotiating is carried out in one of the city's growing range of good bars. Via Cisterna dell'Olio hosts the tiny but agreeably funky **Superfly** (✉ Via Cisterna Dell'Olio 12, Spaccanapoli ☎ 347/1272178), where a DJ spinning classic jazz stands next to the bartender and regularly changed photographic exhibitions line the walls. A few doors away from the Superfly club, **Kinky Bar** (✉ Via Cisterna dell'Olio 16, Spaccanapoli ☎ 081/5521571) is actually a reggae bar. The vibrant atmosphere here (and clouds of cigarette smoke) compensate for the fairly dull furnishings. This place fills up so quickly that in summer the whole scene spills out onto the pavement outside. Nearby Piazza Bellini is somewhat more relaxed than the club-studded alleyways of Spacca, and you might even be able to sit down at a proper table. **Caffè Intramoenia** (✉ Piazza Bellini 70, Spaccanapoli ☎ 081/290720) is the granddaddy of the bars here—set up as a bookshop in the late 1980s, it still has its own small publishing house and a variety of the attractive titles are on sale. Seats in the heated verandah are at a premium during winter, though many patrons sit outside year-round. Next to the Caffè Intramoenia is the **Caffè Arabo** (✉ Piazza Bellini, Spaccanapoli ☎ No phone)—as its name suggests, this is a meeting point for the city's Arabic community, and offers a variety of Middle Eastern snacks to accompany your beer. If Piazza Bellini is too packed, head down to the quieter **Kestè** (✉ Largo S. Giovanni Maggiore 26, Spaccanapoli ☎ 081/5513984) in the small square in front of the Orientale University. Cool chrome furnishings contrast with the old arched ceiling inside but try to bag one of the few tables out in the beautiful square. A DJ spins tunes and there's live jazz on the tiny stage on weekends. The nearby **Aret' 'a Palm** (✉ Piazza S. Maria La Nova 14, Spaccanapoli ☎ 339/8486949) shares the same vibe, though its dark wooden interior, marble topped bar, and red plush seats suggest Paris far more than the Mediterranean. There's often impromptu live music as owner and guitarist Alan Wuzburger picks out some of his tunes. One stalwart of the Spaccanapoli scene is **Velvet** (✉ Via Cisterna dell'Olio 11, Spaccanapoli ☎ 347/8107328 ⊕ www.velvetzone.it). It's in a dark and somewhat labyrinthine basement with arched doorways leading into ever smaller rooms, and has occasional live bands, electronic music on Fridays and Saturdays, jazz on Sundays, and even a cineforum on Wednesdays. **Musik Art Notting Hill** (✉ Piazza Dante 88/A, Spaccanapoli ☎ 081/8822687 ⊕ www.nottinghill.net) is an old favorite of the Spacca. A tunnel-like space that fills up after midnight, its techno-chrome decor contrasts with the long arched ceiling and makes the place surprisingly roomy and light—music runs the gamut from '70s revival to disco to rap and hip-hop.

If jazz is more your thing, **Bourbon Street** (✉ Via Bellini 52, Spaccanapoli ☎ 328/0687221) attracts an older crowd, possibly as much for its comforting interior as for its laid-back music. **Murat** (✉ Via Bellini 8, Spaccanapoli ☎ 081/5445919) is a small place favored by serious jazz enthusiasts.

A dressier crowd hangs out in the Chiaia zone. **S'move** (✉ Via Martucci 28/30, Chiaia ☎ 081/2461729) is somewhere between a bar and a club, with its high-tech bar leading into an oriental-style room complete with scatter cushions if you want to arrange yourself artfully on the floor to the chill-out soundtrack. It fills around midnight with a young crowd that wears its clothes so that the designer labels show.

Opened in 2003, **Miles** (✉ Via S. Pasquale 47 Chiaia ☎ 081/405000) is named after "Davis," which gives you a clue about the music—lounge jazz and chill-out leading into lots of '70s revival as the night wears on to get the slightly older crowd here moving. It's sumptuously furnished, with long leather divans and zebra-striped barstools where you can sit and watch the acrobatic barman shake and stir cocktails under the moody blue lights. Live music is on Thursdays. The bar entitled simply **66** (✉ Via Bisignano 66, Chiaia ☎ 081/415024) describes itself as a "fusion bar," presumably because it's a fusion of various things. Some prefer it as a chic place to have an aperitif (help yourself to the snacks beautifully laid out on the bar). Other patrons, who look like they've just popped out of one of the area's designer clothes shops, come here to dine and listen to the chilled-out DJ in one of the ethnic-themed rooms upstairs.

Along elegant Via dei Mille are a number of old-guard nightclubs, such as **La Mela** (✉ Via dei Mille 40, Chiaia ☎ 081/413881), popular with off-duty soccer players and older men with younger women on their arms. **Chez Moi** (✉ Parco Margherita 13, Chiaia ☎ 081/407526) is particularly simpatico for younger Neapolitan aristocrats. A cool option is the **Otto Jazz Club** (✉ Salita Cariati 23, Chiaia ☎ 081/5524373), a staple of the city's trad jazz scene. In a district just beyond Vomero, **Madison Street** (✉ Via Sgambati 47, Vomero ☎ 081/5466566) remains a vast, fun, and tacky disco that allows all persuasions to trip the night fantastic.

If you can't face any chaotic nightlife after the all-too chaotic daylife of Naples, there's the civilized option of the *enoteca,* not exactly a "wine bar," but a place where you can stop for a drink or meet up with friends without having to shout over the music or hang around on the street outside for hours, and have something more substantial to eat than peanuts and pretzels. **Berevino** (✉ Via San Sebastiano, Spaccanapoli ☎ 081/29313) looks like a shop from the outside, but go in and the long wooden tables and shelves and shelves of wines from all over Italy tell you you're in a place where you can sample as much of the produce as you fancy—peppery *taralli* biscuits, olives, and selections of cheeses and smoked meats can be used to *apoggiare* ("prop up") whatever you're drinking. Look for recommendations by the glass on the chalkboard or spend ages perusing the encyclopedic list. The **Enoteca Belledonne** (✉ Vico Belledonne a Chiaia 18, Chiaia ☎ 081/403162) is something of an institution among inhabitants of the area. Between 8 and 9 in the evening it seems like the whole neighborhood has descended into the tiny space for an *aperitivo*. Make your way through the crowd in the bar, however, and you'll find a space inside. The small tables and low stools are notably uncomfortable, but the cozy atmosphere and the pleasure of being surrounded by glass-fronted cabinets full of wine bottles with beautiful labels more than makes up for it. Excellent local wines are available by the glass at great prices. Again, look at the notices behind the bar to see what's good today—if you're lucky, the owners will have been cooking and will offer you a plate of pasta. A particularly quiet and refined option in Chiaia is **L'ebrezza di Noè** (✉ Vico Vetriera a Chaia 86/9, Chiaia ☎ 081/400104). A small bar leads into a larger dining area decorated in the style of what seems to be a very elegant farmhouse. Owner Luca has an enthusiasm for what he does that is quite moving—as you sip his recommendation you can see he's really very anxious that you like it and share his passion. The attention paid to the quality of the wine is backed up by that of the food—more than just a "prop," here you can taste delicate slices of Tuscan steak *carpaccio di chianina* or rare cheeses such as the Sicilian *ragusano di razza modicani*.

SPORTS & THE OUTDOORS

Updated by
Francesca
Marretta and
Chris Rose

For complete news and information about sporting events, check the newspapers *Il Mattino, La Repubblica,* and *Corriere della Sera,* and the free English-language monthly guide *Qui Napoli.* Many sporting facilities in Naples, such as those for golf and horseback riding, are run as private clubs, so they are not listed here. The major sports area of Naples is the Fuorigrotta area, to the west of the city center, site of the Stadio San Paolo (soccer stadium).

Participant Sports

Beaches, Spas & Water Sports

Beaches are few and far between in Naples proper, although out of desperation Neapolitans like to take to the Lungomare rocks that line the waterfront from the Castel dell'Ovo to the little port of Mergellina. The water here was recently declared officially safe to swim in, though it's still only the very young and very reckless who dive in. For true swimming pleasure, head to the Posillipo coast that lies just west of the Mergellina harbor. Here are three ancient fishing ports: **Giuseppone a Mare,** at the end of Via Ferdinando Russo; **Marechiaro,** at the end of Discesa Marechiaro; and **La Gajola** (local dialect for "The Cage"), at the end of Discesa Gajola. These are quite picturesque spots immortalized in Neapolitan songs, landscape paintings, and poetry. The more policed and costly facilities in the Posillipo zone are the **Bagno Elena** (✉ Via Posillipo 14, Posillipo ☎ 081/5755058 ⊕ www.bagnoelena.it), alongside the splendid Palazzo Donn'Anna and from where you can now rent canoes or motor boats; **Gabbiano** (✉ Via Marechiaro 115, Posillipo ☎ 081/5755650); **Le Rocce Verdi** (✉ Via Posillipo 68, Posillipo ☎ 081/5756716); **Marechiaro** (✉ Calata Ponticello a Marechiaro 33, Posillipo ☎ 081/7691215); and **Villa Imperiale** (✉ Via Marechiaro 90, Posillipo ☎ 081/

5754344). Of course, for the best paradisiacal beaches head to Ischia and the Amalfi Coast.

Fitness Facilities

The Villa Comunale along the seafront has to be one of the most spectacular jogging routes in the world, but you do have to contend with the traffic. If that's too stressful, head for the Parco Virgiliano, which has a beautiful outdoor running and gymnastics area. The Villa and the Parco are now both closed at night, the only time you'd really want to avoid them. Otherwise, most major facilities are in Neapolitan suburbs. The **Club Partenopeo** (⌗ Via Coroglio 144, Bagnoli ☎ 081/7628283) is one of the best gyms in the city, with a beautiful location on the Coroglio beach overlooking the island of Nisida, off the shore of Posillipo, with an expert, friendly staff. A central city option is the **New Athletic Club** (⌗ Via De Pretis 115, Piazza Municipio ☎ 081/5515271), an underground gym, which boasts a sauna and (albeit tiny) swimming pool.

Tennis

At the Villa Comunale near the American Consulate (Piazza della Repubblica) is the **Tennis Club Napoli** (⌗ Viale Dohrn, Mergellina ☎ 081/7614656), with six outdoor courts used from June to September. For a unique experience within the park of the Mostra D'Oltremare in Fuorigrotta, try one of the clay courts at the **Tennis Club Mostra** (⌗ Mostra D'Oltremare, Fuorigrotta ☎ 081/2390444). If you have no partner, Gino, the court manager and general dispenser of bonhomie, can arrange for both partner and racket hire once you have become a club faithful.

Spectator Sports

Soccer

Considering the position of importance and the popularity of *calcio,* or soccer, for the Neapolitan people, the San Paolo Stadium is probably a shrine only a fraction less important than the town cathedral. This shrine's last "saint" was Diego Maradona, who, in 1987 and 1989, led the town team (their name, incidentally, is just Napoli) to first place in Italy's national championships. Matches are played at the **Stadio San Paolo** (☎ 081/2395623 ⊕ www.calcionapoli.it), in a suburb to the west of Mergellina (beware: *very* raucous crowds on their way to a game can clog up public transportation throughout the city). The team has sadly fallen on hard times for the past five years and is lurking around the bottom of the Serie B second division. The positive slant on this is that the once gold-dust tickets are now easy to come by and range from about €15 for the *curva* (at the highest tier of the giant stadium) to €50 for the more comfortable *tribuna* stand. Even though the great Maradona's days are long gone, it's still worth a visit for a heady experience in which the fans are more interesting to watch than whatever's happening on the pitch. The stadium is across the piazza from the Ferrovia Cumana train station at Mostra and can also be reached via the Metropolitana stop at Piazzale Tecchio. Tickets are available through **Azzurro Service** (⌗ Via F. Galeota 17, Fuorigrotta ☎ 081/5934001) near the stadium and **Concerteria** (⌗ Via Schipa 23, Chiaia ☎ 081/7611221).

SHOPPING

Updated by
Francesca
Marretta and
Chris Rose

Naples is a fascinating and largely underrated city for shopping. From the delightful *Presepe* (Nativity scene) shops that transform Via San Gregorio Armeno into a perpetual Christmas morning to its noted leathergoods emporia, the city's rich history of skilled workmanship means it abounds in unique souvenirs and gifts, including some of the world's best ties (**Marinella**), crèche figures (**Ferrigno**), masks (**Nel Regno di Pulcinella**), shoes (**Mario Valentino**), and intarsia tabletops (**Domenico Russo**). At the other end of the price scale are world-famous, dirt-cheap bootleg CDs of Italian and Neapolitan music for you to check out. A sense of adventure is once again the key, especially in the open markets, which are worth a visit just as a social experience—bargaining here is an art (watch your wallet and leave the expensive extra camera lenses at the hotel).

Shops are generally open from around 9:30 in the morning to 1:30, when they close for lunch, reopening around 4:30 and staying open until 7:30 or 8. Most stores are closed Sunday, but certain higher-volume addresses have procured a license allowing them to open on Sunday morning. Sales run twice a year, from mid-January to mid-March for the fall–winter collections and from mid-July to early September for the spring–summer collections, with half-price discounts common.

Department Stores & Shopping Malls

La Rinascente (⊠ Via Toledo 343, Spaccanapoli ☎ 081/411511 ⊕ www. rinascente.it) is a good, basic department store with a wide variety of clothes, cosmetics, household items, and so forth. **Coin** (⊠ Via Scarlatti 100, Vomero ☎ 081/5780111 ⊕ www.coin.it), in the Vomero, is a packed department store, boasting a tasteful array of kitchenware in **Coincasa** on the top floor.

There are two shopping centers in the Vomero—**Galleria Scarlatti**, on Via Scarlatti, and **Galleria Vanvitelli**, off Piazza Vanvitelli—as well as the more famous (though increasingly lackluster) **Galleria Umberto I**, across from the Teatro San Carlo, if you want to browse indoors and under cover.

Markets

Shopping in an outdoor market is an essential Neapolitan experience; do prepare yourself against pickpockets (relax—just don't wear your tiara). Food markets are all over town, offering a Technicolor feast for the eyes as well as free street theater. The **Mercato di Porta Nolana** (⊠ Via Carmignano, Piazza Garibaldi), open Monday–Saturday 8–6 and Sunday 8–2, is just south of Piazza Garibaldi, with a great display of seafood. The **Mercatino della Pignasecca** (⊠ Spaccanapoli), several blocks west of Piazza Carità off Via Toledo, is open Monday–Saturday 8–2 and is the best place in the city for fruit and vegetables. For low price and surprisingly high-quality clothing and linen, go to the **Mercatino di Antignano** (⊠ Piazza degli Artisti, Vomero), open daily 8–1. The **Mercatino di Posillipo** (⊠ Viale Virgilio, Posillipo) takes place once a week, on Thursday mornings. Get there early to get the best bargains. In Chiaia, the **Bancarelle di San Pasquale** (⊠ Via San Pasquale, Chiaia) takes place every morning, with a smaller but higher quality selection of shoes, bags and clothing.

Specialty markets also abound. Photographers will want to explore the flower market, which opens at dawn every day in the moat of the Castel Nuovo. On the last two weekends of each month there's an **antiques market** in the Villa Comunale park, where junk from grandmother's attic nuzzles up to some surprisingly fine furniture and objects; it's open daily 8–4. ⊠ *Mergellina*.

Clothes merit a special mention. Neapolitans are the world masters of the used-clothing trade and also specialize in—well, let's call them unofficial brand-name knockoffs, sometimes of excellent quality. If you trust your eye, you can have a field day: you might find excellent shoes made by the same factories that turn out top brands, quality leather purses, or secondhand cashmere at the price of discount-store cotton. Of course, quite often you have to wade through a lot of dismal stock of no interest in order to get to the good stuff, but that's part of the fun. The best stomping ground is the **Mercato di Ponte Casanova** (✉ Porta Capuana, Piazza Garibaldi), which is open Monday–Saturday 8–sunset and which must have the world's greatest collection of jeans and a surprising number of untagged name-brand items at half price. The above-mentioned markets of **Antignano** in Vomero and **San Pasquale** in Chaia also have a good selection of clothing.

Shopping Districts

Most of the luxury shops in Naples are along a crescent that descends the Via Toledo to Piazza Trieste e Trento and then continues along Via Chiaia to Via Filangieri and on to Piazza Amedeo, as well as continuing south toward Piazza dei Martiri and the Riviera di Chiaia. Within this area, the Via Chiaia probably has the greatest concentration and variety of shops (and caffè–pastry shop Cimmino, on the corner of Via Filangieri and Via Chiaia, makes for an excellent rest stop along this route). The area around Piazza Vanvitelli, and Via Scarlatti in particular, in the Vomero also has a nice selection of shops outside the tourist zone, with the **Galleria Scarlatti** on Via Scarlatti and **Galleria Vanvitelli** in Piazza Vanvitelli; this area can be conveniently reached by funicular from Piazza Amedeo or the Cumana station. Used-book dealers tend to collect in the area between Piazza Dante, Via Port'Alba, and Via Santa Maria Constantinopoli toward Piazza Bellini. The shops specializing in Presepi (Nativity scenes) are in Spaccanapoli, on the Via San Gregorio Armeno.

Specialty Stores

ART GALLERIES   Back in the late 1970s, the late Lucio Amelio operated the finest contemporary art gallery in Naples and succeeded in luring international superstars like Andy Warhol and Joseph Beuys to the city (Warhol wound up lingering on past his summer holidays and contributed paintings of Vesuvius to the "Terrae Motus" show, held to benefit the city after the earthquake of 1980). Lia Rumma, together with her late husband Marcello Rumma and art critic Achille Bonito Oliva, helped create the Arte Povera and Transavanguardia movements, while the standard-bearers of the Neapolitan aesthetic—Francesco Clemente in painting; Philip-Lorca di Corcia in photography—maintain worldwide reputations. A depression set in following Amelio's untimely death, but recently a ferment of young artists and gallery owners have kick-started the Neapolitan visual arts scene into life again. **E-M Arts** (✉ Via Calabritto 20, Chiaia ☎ 081/7643337) provides a home for avant-garde and performance art, being an offshoot of the **Fondazione Morra** (✉ Via Vergini 19, Piazza Cavour). **Raucci Santamaria** (✉ Piazza S. Maria La Nova 19, Spaccanapoli ☎ 081/5521000) specializes in young international artists including Michael Raedecker and Mat Colishaw. **Inside Open** (✉ Via Duomo 214, Spaccanapoli ☎ 333/3442386) is an innovative "home gallery" showing work by local and international artists and fashion designers. **T293** (✉ Via Tribunali 293, Spaccanapoli ☎ 081/295882) is a tiny space hidden away in the heart of the old town and has shown a fine selection of upcoming Italian artists. **Galleria Scognamiglio** (✉ Via M. D'ayala, Chiaia ☎ 081/400871) has built up a fine reputation and shows work by international artists including Antony Gormley and local mainstay Mimmo Paladino.

Galleria Lia Rumma (✉ Via Vannella Gaetani 14, Chiaia ☎ 081/7643619) has a status-heavy array of artists, including Cindy Sherman, Anselm Kiefer, and Vanessa Beecroft, along with upcoming Neapolitan sculptors. **Galleria Trisorio** (✉ Riviera di Chiaia 215, Chiaia ☎ 081/414306) has cutting-edge exhibits by such masters as Mimmo Jodice and Luigi Ghirri.

BOOKS & PRINTS   Naples is a paradise for bibliophiles. It helps if you read Italian, of course, but you can find a reasonable selection of delightful surprises in French-

or English-language publications as well. The best area to hunt is between Piazza Bellini and Piazza Dante, along the streets of Via Santa Maria di Constantinopoli, Via San Sebastiano, and Via Port'Alba. The largest bookstore in town is **La Feltrinelli** (⌧ Piazza dei Martiri, Chiaia ☎ 081/2405411 ⊕ www.lafeltrinelli.it), with its extensive range of CDs and videos, and—unique for Naples—an inviting coffee bar on the lower ground floor and a space for daily meetings and book launches. Another branch of **Feltrinelli** (⌧ Via Tommaso D'aquino 70 Piazza Municipio ☎ 081/5521436) has a much larger selection of English-language books. **Libreria Guida** (⌧ Via Port'Alba 20/23, Spaccanapoli ☎ 081/446377) has a wide selection of local interest books in English and Italian and an expert staff.

Rare-book enthusiasts will want to check out **Casella** (⌧ Via Carlo Poerio 92, Chiaia ☎ 081/7642627 ⊕ www.abebooks.com/home/libreria casella), just above the Riviera di Chiaia, a famous source that also specializes in authors' autographs. **Colonnese** (⌧ Via San Pietro a Maiella 32/33, Spaccanapoli ☎ 081/459858), near Via Port'Alba, has a wide assortment of antique postcards and magical objets d'art. If you're an art history student and pictures are what matter, browse the booksellers near Piazza Bellini and take Via Port'Alba to Piazza Dante, where **Alpha** (⌧ Via Sant'Anna dei Lombardi 10, Spaccanapoli ☎ 081/5525013) has a great selection of cut-rate art books. For antique prints and engravings, the most famous shop in town is **Bowinkel** (⌧ Piazza dei Martiri 24, Chiaia ☎ 081/7644344), in the Chiaia area; it also has antique postcards, watercolors, photographs, and fans. **Arethusa** (⌧ Riviera di Chiaia 202/b, Chiaia ☎ 081/411551) specializes in collectible posters and has an excellent selection of both rare and inexpensive editions.

CLOTHING & ACCESSORIES Neapolitans are famous for their attention to style, and Naples abounds in clothing stores for every pocketbook. **Melinoi** (⌧ Via Benedetto Croce 34, Spaccanapoli ☎ 081/5521204) is particularly known for its originality—as well as Romeo Gigli. It also stocks clothes and accessories by a number of French designers, with an eye for uniqueness of style.

International chains are present, of course. A good selection of affordable clothes can be found at **Benetton** (⌧ Via Chiaia 203/204, Chiaia ☎ 081/405385), which continues to represent easy Italian chic to most of the world. Up the price scale, **Emporio Armani** (⌧ Piazza dei Martiri 64, Chiaia ☎ 081/425816) is in the Via dei Mille–Via Filangieri area of the Chiaia district. A landmark of the Chiaia area are the luxe outfitters **Versace** (⌧ Via Calabritto 7, Chiaia ☎ 081/7644210). Beloved by stylemeisters, **Prada** (⌧ Via Calabritto 9, Chiaia ☎ 081/7641323) is yet another Chiaia area emporium.

A number of smaller, local, or more exclusive shops are also worthy of notice. **Amina Rubinacci** (⌧ Via dei Mille 16, Chiaia ☎ 081/415486) is the queen of knitwear, featuring her famous "ostrich" pullover and a wide range of colors in sweaters. **Maxi Ho** (⌧ Via N. Nisco 23/27, Chiaia ☎ 081/427530) has the latest in men's and women's fashion trends. Italy wouldn't be Italy without shoes, and **De Liberti** (⌧ Via Chaia 10, Chiaia ☎ 081/416064) offers a wide range of cutting-edge fashion footwear (often at the edge of the wearable).

Women can find provocative clothes by the local designer and erstwhile pal-of-Andy-Warhol Ernesto Esposito at **Staffelli** (⌧ Via Carlo Poerio 12, Chiaia ☎ 081/7646922), off the Piazza dei Martiri above Riviera di Chiaia. **Barbaro** (⌧ Galleria Umberto I 3/7, Piazza Municipio ☎ 081/414940) has a stylish choice of name designers. If your credit card is crying in pain by this time, head for **Lo Stock** (⌧ Via Fiorelli 7, Chiaia

☎ 0812405253), a large basement in which designer-label end-of-lines can be found at hugely reduced prices. You have to be prepared to rummage and hope they've got your size, as all items are one-offs only.

Naples is a surprisingly good city for male fashion and tends to completely spoil its male clotheshorses (many would use the word *peacocks*). An excellent address for the hip but easygoing is **Giorgio** (✉ Via Calabritto 29, Chiaia ☎ 081/7644122). Finely tailored shirts with hand-sewn buttonholes can be found at **Luigi Borelli** (✉ Largo Sant'Orsola a Chiaia 3b, Chiaia ☎ 081/410070). If you feel like indulging in a custom-made suit, try **Blasi** (✉ Via dei Mille 29/31/35, Chiaia ☎ 081/415283), which also has some soigné ready-to-wear items. Superb ready-to-wear items are on tap at **Sartoria dal Cuore** (✉ Piazza Vittoria 6, Chiaia ☎ 081/2451056). You'll find high-class souvenirs that are more immediate and more accessible at **Marinella** (✉ Riviera di Chiaia 287, Chiaia ☎ 081/2451182), where Maurizio Marinella, grandson of the founder, Eugenio, cuts made-to-measure ties for the world's royalty and other sensitive necks—these are widely considered by globe-trotting VIPs to be the finest ties in the world, and most important, they are never considered vulgar. The selection of fabrics is so vast it's impossible *not* to find the perfect tie. **Argenio** (✉ Via Filangieri, 15, Chiaia ☎ 081/418035) is another famous and exclusive address for men's accessories, and former supplier of scarves, cuff links, buttons, tiepins, and so forth to the royal Bourbons of the House of the Two Sicilies.

Mario Valentino (✉ Via Calabritto 10, Chiaia ☎ 081/7644262) offers fine handmade footwear in his fashionable shoe store. **Spatarella** (✉ Via Roma 29, Spaccanapoli ☎ 081/401376) is a top source for shoes by local craftsmen, as well as for high-quality belts, purses, and luggage.

CRAFTS & GIFTS The classic handicraft of Naples is the Presepe—or Nativity crèche scene—with elaborate sets and terra-cotta figurines and elements of still life. The tradition goes back to the medieval period, but its acknowledged golden age arrived in the 18th century. Famous sculptors of the day churned out stunningly lifelike figurines, which were then custom-dressed by the chicest tailors to the aristocracy, providing a delightfully picturesque, if idealized, view of Neapolitan street life. The most stunning masterpieces from this period are the Presepe Cuciniello, in the Museo di San Martino; one that belongs to the Banco di Roma displayed in the Palazzo Reale; and the Royal Nativity Scene in Capodimonte. The tradition is alive and flourishing; although the sets and figurines retain their 18th-century aspect, the craftsmen keep their creativity up-to-date with famous renditions of current political figures and other celebrities: porn star and member of parliament Ilona Staller, better known as La Cicciolina, was a big hit a few years back (not as the Virgin Mary—there's a limit to everything, even in Naples), as was exiled political leader Bettino Craxi, represented, with typical Neapolitan humor, in Arab dress (he was hiding out in Tunisia at the time) as one of the wise men. More recent heroes and villains have included the inevitable bin Laden and the recently returned Savoy ex-royal family (though whether the latter were portrayed as heroes or villains isn't quite clear). The scenes are appropriately completed with a profusion of domestic animals and food of all sorts, meticulously rendered. A number of the smaller articles make great Christmas tree ornaments, if you don't feel up to adopting an entire Bethlehem-on-the-bay Nativity scene. Shops cluster along the Via San Gregorio Armeno in Spaccanapoli, and they're all worth a glance, but the undisputed master is **Giuseppe Ferrigno** (✉ Via San Gregorio Armeno 10, Spaccanapoli ☎ 081/5523148), who still faithfully uses 18th-century techniques. If you're seriously bitten by the Presepe-collecting bug, you can find rare antique Nativity figures at **Marisa Catello** (✉ Via Santa Maria Costantinopoli 124, Spaccanapoli ☎ 081/444169). **Gramendola** (✉ Via San Gregorio Armeno 51, Spaccanapoli ☎ 081/5514899) offers the noted creations of Matteo Principe.

The **Ospedale delle Bambole** (✉ Via San Biagio dei Librai 81, Spaccanapoli ☎ 081/203067)—a tiny storefront operation—is a world-famous "hospital" for dolls, a wonderful photo-op, and a great place to take kids. **Nel Regno di Pulcinella** (✉ Vico San Domenico Maggiore 9, Spaccanapoli ☎ 081/5514171) is the workshop of famous Pulcinello-maker Lello Esposito. This shop, a converted 16th-century stable, also offers some wonderful model volcanoes and the traditional good-luck symbol of the city, a red horn.

Music lovers can get a prestigious mandolin at **Liuteria Calace** (✉ Vico San Domenico Maggiore 9, Spaccanapoli ☎ 081/5515983 ⊕ www.calace.it) or a greater range of instruments along Via Costantinopoli, close to the Naples Conservatorio. You'll get a spontaneous and more accessible musical experience at any of the *bancarelle,* or ambulant sellers, specializing in bootleg CDs; you'll find them in most outdoor markets, or along Corso Umberto I, or walking around the city center with boomboxes blasting the latest songs. Bear in mind that both purchaser and vendor risk hefty fines if caught in mid-transaction, and that your bootleg product is unlikely to have any liner notes and may well be substandard, if that.

Elegant office supplies—notebooks, pens, and stationery—can be had at **P & C** (✉ Largo Vasto a Chiaia 86, Chiaia ☎ 081/418724), a treasure trove for writing enthusiasts. Many adore the gifts at **Gli Artigiani del Libro** (✉ Calata Trinità Maggiore 4, Spaccanapoli ☎ 081/5511280). **Bottega della Carta** (✉ Via Cavallerizza a Chiaia 22, Chiaia ☎ 081/421903) has a stylish array of goodies. **Bruno Acampora Profumi** (✉ Via G. Filangieri 70, Chiaia ☎ 081/414162) is a famous local perfume maker selling prized fragrances in signature minimalist aluminum flasks.

HOUSEHOLD DECORATION & ANTIQUES

For household linens, **La Cage** (✉ Largo Duca della Ferrantina 10, Chiaia ☎ 081/403811) has the most exclusive selection in Naples. The national chain **Frette** (✉ Via dei Mille 2, Chiaia ☎ 081/418728) is justifiably famous throughout Italy for the quality of its sheets, towels, and bedspreads.

Galleria Elena (✉ Viale Gramsci 15/c, Mergellina ☎ 081/667822) crafts luxury floors in wood, marble inlay, mosaic, and terra-cotta and has a splendid collection of high-quality reproductions of Renaissance majolica tiles. Another good address for hand-painted ceramic tiles is **Capri Due** (✉ Via Scarlatti 61–65, Vomero ☎ 081/5789400), in the Vomero. **Domenico Russo e Figli** (✉ Via Bisignano 51, Chiaia ☎ 081/7648387) continues the centuries-old Neapolitan tradition of marble-inlay work, creating precious tables and console tops. Mario Muscariello produces museum-quality replica furniture (they copied the ancient furniture from Herculaneum for the Getty Museum) at **Il Cirmolo** (✉ Via Santa Maria di Costantinopoli 32, Spaccanapoli ☎ 081/451140). **Salvatore Molino** (✉ Via Alabardieri 21/22, Chiaia ☎ 081/426505) painstakingly handcrafts furniture, using time-tested techniques. Fine bronze reproductions can be found in the area of Capodimonte at the foundry called **Patrizio di Pietro** (✉ Corso Amedeo di Savoia 248, Capodimonte ☎ 081/7410217).

If you're interested in original antiques, several prestigious dealers are clustered along Via Domenico Morelli south of Piazza dei Martiri. **Arte Antica** (✉ Via Domenico Morelli 45, Chiaia ☎ 081/7646897) has a fine display of porcelain objects. **Maurizio Brandi** (✉ Via Domenico Morelli 11, Chiaia ☎ 081/7643906) is known for its 17th- and 18th-century

Neapolitan antiques. **D'Amodio** (✉ Via Domenico Morelli 6/bis, Chiaia ☎ 081/7643872) is the place for historic majolica. **Florida** (✉ Via Domenico Morelli 13, Chiaia ☎ 081/7643440) is famous for its painting on glass and silver Rococo and Neoclassic style candelabra. Fine collectible 20th-century furniture and objects (basically Art Nouveau and Art Deco) can be seen in Chiaia at **Nabis** (✉ Via Cavallerizza a Chiaia 52, Chiaia ☎ 081/422493). For current designs, go by **Agorà** (✉ Via Orazio 138/a, Posillipo ☎ 081/651056) in Posillipo; **Novelli** (✉ Piazza Amedeo 21/22, Chiaia ☎ 081/413233) in Piazza Amedeo; or **San Patrignano Casa d'Arte** (✉ Via Santa Lucia 133, Santa Lucia ☎ 081/7640878), which shows high-quality, limited-edition, handcrafted furnishings and objects and is worth a visit even if you have no intention of buying.

JEWELRY The best selection of goldsmiths' and jewelers' shops is, fairly incongruously, located in what has become one of the poorest areas of town, on and around Via degli Orefici (Street of the Goldsmiths) between Corso Umberto and Via Marina. The nearest you get to a gold supermarket in Naples is **Presta** (✉ Via Scialoia 2–10, Piazza Garibaldi ☎ 081/5545282), which has unbelievably competitive prices. In the center of Spaccanapoli is **Gioielleria Caso** (✉ Piazza San Domenico Maggiore 16, Spaccanapoli ☎ 081/5516733), which has antique jewelry and silver and great coral works. **Brinkmann** (✉ Piazza Municipio 21, Piazza Municipio ☎ 081/5520555) is noted for its exquisite collection of wathches that incorporate rare coins. **Ventrella** (✉ Via Carlo Poerio 11, Chiaia ☎ 081/7643173) is a posh salon showing original designs by the most exclusive contemporary workshop.

Naples has also long been famous for its coral and cameos, and although the raw material now comes most often from the Far East, it's Neapolitan technique and inspiration that transform the shells and coral into works of art. A number of touristy shops along the Sorrento coast sell cameos of varying quality and price, but if you want to see how beautiful they can get, go to Torre del Greco and visit **B. e M. Mazza** (✉ Via E. De Nicola 45, Torre del Greco ☎ 081/8812665). **Murizio Apa** (✉ Via de Nicola 1, Torre del Greco ☎ 081/8811155) is a long-standing source for coral.

SIDE TRIPS

Updated by
Francesca
Marretta and
Chris Rose

While the modern town of Caserta is unbelievably dull, a day trip is worthwhile to see the Reggia, the Bourbon monarchs' answer to Versailles. If you go by car, make the effort to drive up to the old medieval town of Casertavecchia to see the atmospheric cathedral and tiny, winding stone streets, though avoid the overpriced touristy restaurants. Benevento is similarly unspectacular, having been bombed flat during World War II, but the almost perfectly preserved Roman arch makes it worth a brief stop.

Caserta

25 km (16 mi) northeast of Naples.

The royal palace known as the **Reggia di Caserta** is exemplary of mid-18th-century Bourbon royal living. Architect Luigi Vanvitelli devoted 20 years to its construction under Bourbon ruler Charles III, whose son, Ferdinand IV, moved in when it was completed in 1774. The story goes that Charles III was envious of Louis XIV's creation of Versailles, and decided to show that the Bourbons could do something that if not exactly better would at least be bigger. The otherwise talented Vanvitelli was thus given the unenviable task of transforming a country hunting lodge into a larger-scale replica of Versailles. The result is vast: four interconnecting courtyards and miles of draughty corridors connect 1,200 rooms, surrounded by an enormous park. It ends up being impressive largely just because of its sheer size—the palace can be seen for miles and miles around in the flat countryside. Inside, much of the palace disappoints, with room after room after room of heavy gilded furniture and overdone portraits of some incredibly ugly minor royalty. It seems that having built something awesome just because of its size, the Bourbon kings (never famed for their good taste) couldn't think of anything to put in it. However, the main staircase (which movie fans may recognize as being from Queen Amidala's palace on Naboo from George Lucas's "Phantom Menace" *Star Wars* film) is breathtaking—a kaleidoscope of marble inlay and long, wide steps on which it's impossible not to walk (or rather, glide) up looking regal and graceful. Some of the sumptuous **royal apartments** impress due to their lack of taste—the royal bathrooms with their enormous gold-plated bathtubs give you a glimpse into the Bourbon mentality, where big meant good and the more gold the better. A number of the empty rooms now fortunately provide a semi-permanent home to the Terrae Motus exhibition of contemporary art. Following the terrible earthquake in 1980, curator Lucio Amelio called a number of his important friends and commissioned works of art on the theme of earthquakes from them, resulting in some fine, if disturbing, work from Andy Warhol, Anselm Kiefer, Richard Long, and Tony Cragg, among others. It was here, in what Eisenhower called "a castle near Naples," that the Allied High Command had its headquarters in World War II, and here German forces in Italy surrendered in April 1945.

One of the main reasons to visit the palace is for its wonderful gardens. Coming out of the back of the palace, you are presented with a mile-long avenue of gently raising terraces, interrupted only by the occasional fountain. If you're tempted to try walking to the far end, be warned—it's much farther than it looks. Some enterprising carriage drivers will offer to take you up there in a horse-drawn buggy, but you'll pay highly for the privilege. Better to wait for the shuttle bus, which leaves every 15 minutes. Once arrived, admire the Grande Cascata fountain and its life-size statues showing the story of Actaeon (who was turned into a stag and torn apart by his own dogs after observing the goddess Diana bathing naked—a story, one suspects, which titillated the Bourbon kings). Alongside this is the famous Giardino Inglese, the "English Garden" landscaped for Queen Maria Carolina in the late 18th century through the auspices of Sir William Hamilton, husband to the famous Emma, and reflecting the supposed English approach to landscape gardening, much less ordered and formal than the otherwise symmetrical perspectives of the park. ⊠ *Piazza Carlo III* ☎ *0823/447147* 🖃 *Royal apartments €4.20, park €2.10, Giardino Inglese €1.10, shuttle bus €.20* ⊙ *Royal apartments Tues.–Sun. 8:30–7:30; park Tues.–Sun. 8:30–1 hr before sunset; Giardino Inglese 8:30–1 hr before park closure, guided visits (Italian only) every 30 mins.*

Benevento

35 km (22 mi) east of Caserta, 60 km (37 mi) northeast of Naples.

Benevento (which means "place of the good winds," its name reflecting its rather harsh microclimate) owes its importance to its establishment as the capital of the Lombards, a northern tribe that invaded and settled what is now Lombardy before being ousted by Charlemagne in the 8th century. Tough and resourceful, the Lombards moved south and set up a new duchy in Benevento, later moving its seat south to Salerno, where they saw the potential of the natural harbor. Under papal rule in the 13th century, Benevento built a fine cathedral and endowed it with bronze doors that were a pinnacle of Romanesque art. The cathedral, doors, and a large part of the town were blasted by World War II bombs. The **duomo** has been rebuilt; look for the remaining panels of the original bronze doors in the chapter library. Fortunately, the majestic 2nd-century AD **Arco di Traiano** survived unscathed. The arch honors Roman emperor Trajan, who sorted out Rome's finances, added parts of the Middle East to the empire, and extended the Appian Way through Benevento to the Adriatic. The friezes show the emperor himself, involved in many good deeds. The ruins of the **Teatro Romano,** which had a seating capacity of 20,000, are still in good enough shape to host a summer pop concert season. ⊠ *Take Via Carlo from the duomo* ⌑ €2.06 ⊙ *Daily 9–1 hr before sunset.*

NAPLES A TO Z

AIR TRAVEL TO & FROM NAPLES

CARRIERS Alitalia, Lufthansa, and British Airways all fly from Naples, though it may be necessary to change at a hub in Rome or Milan to reach world capitals.

🚹 Airlines and Contacts **Alitalia** ☎ 848/865641 reservations on national flights; 848/ 865642 international ⊕ www.alitalia.it. **British Airways** ☎ 199712266 reservations ⊕ www.britishairways.com. **Lufthansa** ☎ 06/65684004 ⊕ www.lufthansa.it.

AIRPORTS & TRANSFERS

Capodichino Airport, 8 km (5 mi) north of Naples, has many domestic and European connections but hosts few international flights.

🚹 Airport Information **Capodichino Airport** ☎ 081/7896259.

AIRPORT Bus 3S runs from Piazza Garibaldi to the airport (every 30 minutes, the
TRANSFER journey lasts around 30 minutes) between 5:30 AM and midnight, €.77. The quicker shuttle bus, Alibus, runs from 6:30 AM to midnight between the airport, Piazza Garibaldi (where the main railroad terminal is), the port, and the very center of town, the Piazza Municipio (every 30 minutes, the journey lasts approximately 20 minutes, €3). If you take a taxi from Piazza Garibaldi, expect to pay between €15 and €20 for the 20-minute trip.

🚹 Taxis and Shuttles **Shuttle bus** ☎ 081/5311706.

BOAT & FERRY TRAVEL

If you're heading to the Aeolian Islands, other parts of Sicily, or Sardinia, Naples may be a convenient departure point. A major long-distance carrier is Tirennia, which departs from Stazione Marittima, near Piazza Municipio. Tirennia's main competitor is Linee Lauro, which departs from Molo Belvedere below Castel Nuovo.

Boats leave once weekly for Tunis (18 hours southwest, €90–€125), and more frequently for Sardinia (14 hours west, €35–€110), Palermo (11 hours southwest, €39–€50), and the Aeolian Islands (8–14 hours, €40–€45), among other places. There are now also connections with Sete (France) and Palma de Majorca (Spain) (15 hours west, €40–€120).

For trips around the Bay of Naples, the main port is Molo Beverello, below Castel Nuovo. Many carriers send boats to the islands all day until 7 or 8, though in the off-season service is less frequent. Carriers include Medmar, Caremar, and Navigazione Libera del Golfo. Hydrofoils (but not ferries) also leave from the port at Mergellina, a short walk below the Mergellina train station; these are run by SNAV and Alilauro.

Major destinations from both ports include Capri (hydrofoils: 40 minutes south, €12; ferries: 1 hour 20 minutes, €8), Procida (hydrofoils: 30 minutes southwest, €11; ferries: 1 hour, €8), and Ischia (hydrofoils: 40 minutes southwest, €11–€12.50; ferries: 1 hour 20 minutes, €8). Several hydrofoils also ply to Sorrento (25 minutes southeast, €11).

FARES & SCHEDULES Departure times and additional info on some routes, including the local ferry and hydrofoil lines listed below, can be found in *Qui Napoli?* ("Which Naples?") or in the newspapers *Il Mattino, La Repubblica,* and *Corriere della Sera.*

🚢 Boat and Ferry Information **Alilauro** ☎ 081/7614909 ⊕ www.alilauro.it. **Caremar** ☎ 081/5513882 ⊕ www.caremar.it. **Medmarnavi** ☎ 081/5513352 ⊕ www.medmarnavi. it. **Navigazione Libera del Golfo** ☎ 081/5527209 ⊕ www.navlib.it. **SNAV** ☎ 081/ 7612348 ⊕ www.snavali.com. **Tirennia** ☎ 081/7201111 ⊕ www.tirrenia.it.

BUS TRAVEL TO & FROM NAPLES

Medium- and long-distance buses out of Naples are handled by several companies. The main operator is SITA, whose buses leave from either Piazza Garibaldi or Via G. Pisanelli near Piazza Municipio, but a host of other coach companies operate on long-haul routes southeastward into Puglia. For detailed information check the local paper *Il Mattino* with its comprehensive list of operators and destinations.

FARES & SCHEDULES 🚌 Bus Information **SITA** ☎ 081/5522176 ⊕ www.sita-on-line.it.

BUS TRAVEL WITHIN NAPLES

Bus routes in Naples change frequently, the signs posted at bus stops aren't too helpful, and there's no bus map available. That said, there's a network of frequent routes that shuttle you efficiently among a few major junctions. These are the R1, which runs between Piazza Medaglie d'Oro in Vomero and Piazza Bovio (at the end of Corso Umberto near Piazza Municipio) by way of Via Toledo and Via Diaz; the R2, which runs between Piazza Garibaldi and Piazza Municipio; the R3, which runs between Piazza Municipio and Piazza Trieste e Trento and Mergellina; and the R4, which runs from Piazza Bovio and the Ospedale Cardarelli above Vomero by way of the Museo Archeologico Nazionale. Other useful buses include the 24, which takes you from downtown (Piazza Castello by way of Via Monteoliveto) to Capodimonte; the C25, which connects Piazza Bovio, Piazza Municipio, Via Santa Lucia, and Piazza Amedeo; the 140, which takes you from Via Santa Lucia to Posillipo by way of Piazza Sannazzaro; and the 152, which runs between Fuorigrotta and Piazza Garibaldi, passing through Mergellina. The E1 is handy in the city center; it makes a loop from Piazza del Gesù Nuovo around the Museo Archeologico Nazionale and the duomo and back by way of Via Monteoliveto. Since transfers are free, a few mistakes won't deplete your bank account. For further information call ANM. Bus tickets are included on the popular Giranapoli pass. A pass costs €0.77 and is valid for 90 minutes on all public transit within the city boundaries; €2.32 buys a *biglietto giornaliero* (ticket for the whole day).

FARES & SCHEDULES 🚌 Bus Information **ANM** ✉ Via G. B. Marino 1, Fuorigrotta ☎ 081/7631111 ⊕ www.anm.it.

CAR RENTAL

Be careful if you rent a car outside Campania; there's always extra insurance for this region, and most companies refuse to let you take a Mercedes or BMW into Campania and make you sign a retainer accepting all responsibility for the car if you do take it there. Car thieves here are some of the fastest and most organized in the world; the car is usually dismantled and in Eastern Europe the next day (there's a big market with the new Eastern European mafiosi for relatively inexpensive trophy cars). Some excellent deals can sometimes be arranged through local hotels on the spot, especially for the faint-hearted who may prefer a driver. Some rental agencies in Naples are listed below; Maggiore has offices at the airport and central train station.

🚗 Major Agencies **Avis** ⊠ Stazione Centrale, Piazza Garibaldi ☎ 081/284041 ⊠ Aeroporto di Capodichino Capodichino ☎ 081/7805790 ⊕ www.avis.com. **Europcar** ⊠ Aeroporto di Capodichino, Capodichino ☎ 081/7805643; 800/014410 toll-free ⊕ www. europcar.it. **Hertz** ⊠ Aeroporto di Capodichino, Capodichino ☎ 081/7802971; 199112211 toll-free ⊕ www.hertz.it ⊠ Piazza Garibaldi 93, Piazza Garibaldi ☎ 081/206228. **Maggiore** ⊠ Via Cervantes 92, Piazza Municipio ☎ 081/5521900 or 800/867196 ⊕ www. maggiore.it.

CAR TRAVEL

Naples is located on the major north–south Autostrada del Sole, more commonly known as the A1 to Rome and Milan and the A3 to Salerno. The A30 acts as an express highway through Campania, enabling travelers to avoid the busy A3 between Naples and Salerno where traffic jams are endemic; the A16 winds southeast in the direction of Bari. As they near Naples, the autostradas meet the Tangenziale di Napoli (€.65 toll), a busy six-lane highway that borders the city's northern sector. The Tangenziale is the main access route from the airport to the city center, and continues on to Pozzuoli and the Phlegrean Fields region to the west of the city center. From Naples, the A3 for Salerno is best reached via the Tangenziale (follow the green signs for the motorways) unless you are close to Santa Lucia and the port area, in which case follow the traffic eastward along the waterfront and the port until you reach the autostrada sliproad at the end of Via Marina.

Those entering Naples and wanting to reach one of the main hotels close to the seafront should take the Tangenziale and exit at Fuorigrotta, then follow signs to Mergellina and Napoli Centro. For access to the port, stay on the autostrada until you see the signs for Napoli Centro and then follow signs for the Porto.

GASOLINE Gas and service stations can be found—somewhat surprisingly—in several monumental city-center locations: Piazza Mergellina (AGIP); Via Manzoni (Esso); Via Foria (Q8); Via Falcone (IP); and Corso Europa (AGIP) are likely to be open at night while the gas stations at the Tangenziale ringroad exits at Capodimonte and Agnano are open 24 hours.

PARKING For those who decide to tempt fate, it is advisable to leave your car only in designated parking areas. Leaving it anywhere else will almost certainly attract the attention of an illegal *parcheggiatore* who will demand a euro for keeping an eye on your car. The *parcometro*, the Italian version of metered parking in which you put coins into a machine for a stamped ticket that you leave on the dashboard, has been introduced in Naples, but the safest option is to park your car in a garage. Most of the hotels in the Santa Lucia district have (expensive) garages, but the following are some of the more centrally located and reasonably priced options. In Santa Lucia, try the Garage Chiatamone. In the historic center—Garage Santa Chiara. In the Molo Beverello zone by the harbor, try Garage Turistico, and near the Mergellina train and Metropolitana stations Garage Mergellina and Garage Sannazzaro are good bets.

🚗 Garages **Garage Chiatamone** ⊠ Via Chiatamone 26, Chaia ☎ 081/7642863. **Garage dei Fiori** ⊠ Via Colonna 21, Chaia ☎ 081/414190. **Garage Mergellina** ⊠ Via Mergellina 112, Mergellina ☎ 081/7613470. **Garage Sannazzaro** ⊠ Piazza Sannazzaro 142, Mergellina ☎ 081/681437. **Garage Santa Chiara** ⊠ Pallonetto Santa Chiara 30, Spaccanapoli ☎081/5516303. **Garage Turistico** ✉Via dei Gasperi 14, Piazza Municipio ☎081/5525442.

TRAFFIC Traveling by car through Naples calls to mind the many circles described in Dante's *Inferno*. Congestion and stunt-driving are par for the course, as is the rush-hour gridlock that sets in on weekdays. Weekends aren't much better: suburbanites like to pile into their cars, enter Naples from Via Marina, and do a traffic loop to Mergellina and the Via Caracciolo waterfront. This nightlife traffic-jam phenomenon takes hours to get through and seems to now be a favorite pastime. At peak hours, even buses (which usually have their own traffic lanes) get blocked. Clearly, walking, funicular, railway, or the metro are better alternatives.

When driving through Naples, be careful to place valuables and bags containing them out of sight, as scooter riders sometimes attempt smash-and-grabs. If traveling with a lot of baggage, never leave your car unattended. We may have mentioned these points elsewhere, but they can never be overstated.

CONSULATES

🛈 **United Kingdom** ✉Via Dei Mille 40, Chiaia ☎081/4238911 ⊕ www.britain.it
🕙 weekdays 9–12:30 and 2–4.
🛈 **United States** ✉Piazza della Repubblica 2, at west end of Villa Comunale, Mergellina ☎081/5838111 ⊕ www.usembassy.it 🕙 Weekdays 8–1.

EMERGENCIES

The main police station has an *ufficio stranieri* (foreigners' office) that usually has an English speaker on staff. For an English-speaking dentist or for a general physician, call one of the numbers listed below. You can also consult the English Yellow Pages, available in major hotels. Naples has some excellent general hospitals, which are also listed below. In case of a medical emergency after 8 PM, call the Medical Emergency number below and ask for an English-speaking nurse.

If you need a late-night pharmacy, try the one in Via Carducci above the Villa Comunale, or the one in the hallway of Stazione Centrale. If these are closed, they will post the addresses of those that are open (the others take turns staying open late); you can also call 192 or buy a copy of the newspapers *Il Mattino, La Repubblica,* or *Corriere della Sera* for a daily list of pharmacies that are open nights and weekends.

🛈 **Doctors and Dentists Dentist** ☎081/664436. **Doctor** ☎081/5567253 ⊕ www.englishyellowpages.net.
🛈 **Emergency Services Ambulance** ☎118. **Fire** ☎115. **General emergencies** ☎113. **Police** ☎112. **Police Station** ✉Via Medina 75, Piazza Municipio ☎081/7941111 ✉foreigners' office: ✉Via Ferraris 131, Piazza Garibaldi ☎081/6064307.
🛈 **Hospitals Ospedale Cardarelli** ✉Via Cardarelli 9, Vomero ☎081/7471111. **Ospedale dei Pellegrini** ✉Via Portamedina 41, Piazza Garibaldi ☎081/2543333. **Ospedale San Paolo** ✉Via Terracina 219, Fuorigrotta ☎081/7686274. **Universitaria Policlinico Federico II** ✉Via S. Pansini, Colli Aminei ☎081/7461111.
🛈 **Hot Lines Medical Emergency** in central Naples ☎081/2542424 and in Chiaia–Posillipo ☎081/7613466.
🛈 **Late-Night Pharmacies Pharmacy** ✉Via Carducci 21–23, Spaccanapoli ☎081/417283.

ENGLISH-LANGUAGE MEDIA

BOOKS For romance, philosophy, or a handy thesaurus, head to Universal Books, inside a palazzo off Corso Umberto near Piazza Bovio, open weekdays 9–1 and 4–7, and on Saturdays 9–12.
🛈 **Bookstores Universal Books** ✉Corso Umberto 22, Piazza Garibaldi ☎081/2520069.

NEWSPAPERS & *See* English-Language Media *in* Smart Travel Tips (before Chapter 1).
MAGAZINES

FUNICOLARE & TRAM TRAVEL

If you're heading up to the Vomero Hill, *funicolari* (cable cars) can make the trek for you. The Funicolare Centrale from its Via Toledo station links the city center with the Piazza Fuga station atop the Vomero Hill. The Funicolare di Chiaia links Via del Parco Margherita to the Via Domenico Cimarosa station on the Vomero Hill. The Funicolare di Montesanto travels from Piazza Montesanto to the station at Via Morghen. In addition, the Funicolare di Mergellina links the waterfront at Via Mergellina with Via Manzoni. Funicolare and tram tickets are included on the popular Giranapoli pass. A pass costs €0.77 and is valid for 90 minutes on all public transit within the city boundaries; €2.32 buys a *biglietto giornaliero* (ticket for the whole day). The Chiaia and Centrale funiculars usually run from 7 AM to 1 AM with departures every 10–15 minutes, while the others close at 10 PM. The city's tram system runs northwest–southeast; Tram 1 will take you from Piazza Garibaldi to Mergellina along the waterfront. Contact ANM for more information.

🛈 **ANM** ☎ 081/7631111 ⊕ www.anm.it and **Metronapoli** ☎ 800/568866 ⊕ www.metro.na.it

MAIL & SHIPPING

The main post office has *fermo posta* (held mail) and a *sportello filatelico* (philatelic counter) for stamp collectors. The postal code is 80100. Branch offices are usually open weekdays 8:15–1:30 and Saturday 8:15–12:10.

🛈 **Post Offices** **Post office** ⊠ Piazza Matteotti, off Via Diaz, Piazza Municipio ☎ 081/5511456 ⊙ Weekdays 8:15–6 and Sat. 8:15–1:30.

MONEY MATTERS

ATMS   With cash available virtually on tap from any number of ATMs throughout the city, the traditional exchange offices near the port area have felt the squeeze. The only charge on the ATM card will be whatever your bank charges for using a bank not your own, and the exchange rate is whatever you'd get charging something on a credit card. The only disadvantage is you won't know the exact rate until you get home and look at your bank statement to see precisely how many dollars were deducted from your account.

CURRENCY   If you want convenience and aren't changing a big wad, use the Ufficio
EXCHANGE   Cambio near the ticket office inside Stazione Centrale (*see* Train Travel); it's open daily 7:30 AM–7:30 PM. Most banks are geared to changing cash and travelers' checks, although the queuing and red tape can be frustrating. Also, banks in Naples are equipped with metal detectors, so you have to leave all your worldly goods outside in lockers before entry.

SAFETY

After a decade-long offensive against crime, Naples is now as safe as any other modern metropolis. Employment is up, poverty is down, and armies of *polizia* now patrol the city's main thoroughfares. Provided you stay clear of the remaining pockets of crime (most of these neighborhoods, like the Sanità, Forcella district, and the Spanish Quarter, are well off the beaten tourist path), you can enjoy a safe stay. That noted, some advice is in order. In the city's picturesque quarters, streets aren't just streets—they are literally "living rooms," so act as you would as a guest in someone's house: don't gawk at residents as you stroll through Spaccanapoli or the Pignasecca market. Have fun taking photographs—most Neapolitans are extremely proud of their neighborhoods—but don't make a production number out of it. In the poorer sectors, don't wave a 20-carat diamond around, or an expensive Nikon, or, for that matter, your guide book. It's best to blend in with the natives, so you might even camouflage yourself by storing your camera and pocketbook in a shopping bag from one of the city stores.

The main hazard in Naples is *lo scippo,* or bag-snatching, usually perpetrated by two youths riding a souped-up motor scooter. As a general rule, give all scooters a wide berth, and use a small daybag rather than a handbag, which can be an inviting target. For safe, undisturbed shopping, opt for the pedestrianized areas like Via Toledo and Via Scarlatti, where scooter fiends are less likely to strike. Wear a concealed money belt or remain aware of the stray pickpocket on the jammed buses and subways. As they are fond of saying in Naples, if you think something bad is going to happen to you, it will: so smile and enjoy yourself.

SUBWAY TRAVEL

Naples's main urban Metro line, Metropolitana Napoli, nicknamed the Metronapoli, runs through the city from Gianturco, east of Stazione Centrale, through the lower level of Stazione Centrale, and takes you out to the city's suburbs as far west as Bagnoli before terminating in Pozzuoli. This line is best known as "Metro Linea 2" and is the older of the two main subway routes threading through the city. It is also the one that will prove most useful to tourists, since its stops include Piazza Cavour (just up the street from the Museo Archeologico Nazionale), Montesanto (near the Cumana railway station and Montesanto funicular line), Piazza Amedeo (in the ritzy Chiaia district and near the Chiaia funicular line), Campi Flegrei (for the San Paolo stadium and occasional mainline trains), and the Stazione Mergellina (near the Mergellina funicular line and hydrofoils for the islands). The complete list of stops is the following: Piazza Garibaldi (at the end of Piazza Garibaldi, same as the main station); Piazza Cavour; Montesanto (just off Piazza Montesanto); Piazza Amedeo; Mergellina (right at the bottom of the Corso Vittorio Emanuele, just above Piazza Sannnazaro and next to Virgil's Tomb). At this point the line enters the "suburbs" and goes off the general tourist map, as it heads to Piazza Leopardi (on Viale Giulio Cesare); Campi Flegrei–Piazzale Tecchio (opposite San Paolo Stadium); Cavalleggeri Aosta; Bagnoli; and, finally, Pozzuoli.

The other subway line is popularly known as "Metro Linea 1," which is a state-of-the-art line extending north to the suburbs—giving the line its official name, the Metropolitana Collinare—but also, more importantly, this is the line that is currently being tunneled, in the opposite direction, into the very heart of the city center. Currently, the main Naples nexus for this line is Piazza Vanvitelli, way atop the Vomero Hill. The line, however, descends the hill into the popular area around the Museo Archeologico Nazionale and Piazza Dante (making this useful for anyone who's staying in Vomero—but it's still quicker to use the funicular in this case). The line running from the Vomero down to the Piazza Dante will eventually go to the two biggest squares in the city center—the Piazza Municipio and Piazza Garibaldi—and even up to the airport, but don't hold your breath. The stops on this line all feature new works by contemporary artists—Joseph Kosuth's neon rendering of a passage from Dante's *Inferno* being a blackly humorous choice for the Piazza Dante stop.

Following this line from the Vomero to the city, the stops are (or will be): Piazza Vanvitelli (atop the Vomero hill); Via Cilea/Quattro Giornate (on Piazza Quattro Giornate, next to the Stadio Collana); Via Salvator Rosa (at the junction of Salvator Rosa and Via Girolamo Santacroce); Materdei (just opened on Piazza Materdei); Museo (on Piazza Cavour, right next to the archaeological museum); Piazza Dante; Via Diaz (not open yet in 2003, at the interesection between Via Diaz and Via Toledo/Roma); Piazza Borsa–Università; and, back to the beginning, Piazza Garibaldi. Consult the helpful map on the metro web site, www.metro.na.it/metronapoli/img/map.pdf.

FARES & SCHEDULES Subway tickets cost €.80; the main line usually runs from 6:40 AM to 10:54 PM, with departures every 15 minutes. Metro tickets are also included on the popular Giranapoli pass. A pass costs €0.77 and is valid for 90 minutes on all public transit within the city boundaries; €2.32 buys a *biglietto giornaliero* (ticket for the whole day).
🚇 Subway Information **Metronapoli** ☎ 800568866.

TAXIS

Maligned and mistrusted for decades, Neapolitan taxi drivers are now beginning to shake off their somewhat tarnished image. However, tricks-of-the-trade are still used (taking you from the airport to your seafront location in Naples via the Tangenziale exit of Agnano and failing to switch on the meter are two favorites). Never take an "unofficial taxi" (the people who accost you at the airport and train station, offering you a taxi: real taxi drivers wait at a taxi stand). Do make sure that the meter has been turned on. It will start at €2.6, although the minimum fare is €4.5. Regular supplements are charged for the following services: €1.6 for Sundays and holidays, €2.1 for nighttime service (10 PM to 7 AM), €.60 for each bag, €2.6 for service to or from the airport, and €.80 for a radio call. Expect to pay €6–€15 for most trips in town during the day, and €20–€25 to or from the airport. If taking a taxi to a location outside the city boundaries, you will have to pay double the fare on the meter, in addition to any supplements like autostrada tolls.

Taxis in Naples rarely cruise, but if empty they will stop if you flag them down. Taxis wait at stands or can be paged by telephone. Radio taxi numbers are listed below. When you phone, you should wait until you're given the taxi's I.D. (always the name of a city combined with a number). Obviously it's cheaper and occasionally quicker to reach a nearby taxi stand. The principal ones are: in the center, Piazza Garibaldi and Piazza Carità; near the seafront, Via Partenope, Piazza Vittoria, Piazza Amedeo, and Piazza Mergellina; and on the hills, Piazza Medaglie d'Oro and Piazza Vanvitelli in the Vomero.
🚕 Taxi Companies **Radio taxi** ☎ 081/5707070, 081/5525252, 081/5560202, 081/5564444, or 081/5515151.

TELEPHONES

PHONE CARDS For making long-distance calls, pick up a prepaid *scheda telefonica* (telephone card), sold at most newspaper kiosks and tobacconists and usable in any pay phone.

TOURS

EXCURSION TOURS You can book tours to Pompeii, Vesuvio, and the islands with CIT and through Bopa, conveniently open on Sundays, too.
🚌 Fees and Schedules **Bopa** ✉ Stazione Centrale, Piazza Garibaldi ☎ 081/267125. **CIT** ✉ Piazza Municipio 70, Piazza Municipio ☎ 081/5525426.

SPECIAL-INTEREST TOURS If you're a spelunker at heart, call the Libera Associazione degli Escursionisti Sottosuolo for adventurous tours of Naples's underground; tours take place on the weekends, and meet at 10 AM at the Piazza Trieste e Trento in front of Bar Gambrinus. Other exciting tours of Naples's underground are offered weekends at 10 AM by Napoli Sotterranea.

For personalized tours specializing in art history contact the **Fine Arts Cultural Association.**
🚌 Fees and Schedules **Fine Arts Cultural Association** ✉ Vico San Marcellino 8, Spaccanapoli ☎ 081/291634. **Libera Associazione degli Escursionisti Sottosuolo** ✉ Via

Santa Teresa degli Spagnoli 24, Piazza Municipio ☎ 081/400256 ⊕ www.
lanapolisotterranea.it. **Napoli Sotterranea** Meeting point: ✉ Piazza San Gaetano to
the left of San Paolo Maggiore ☎ 081/449821.

GUIDES   Agencies in town offering guided tours with official guides include Carrani Tours, Milleviaggi, and Tourcar.
▪ **Carrani Tours** in Rome ☎ 06/4880510 or 06/4742501. **Milleviaggi** ✉ Riviera di Chiaia 252, Chiaia ☎ 081/7622064. **Tourcar** ✉ Piazza Matteotti 1, Piazza Municipio ☎ 081/
5520429 ⊕ www.tourcar.it.

TRAIN TRAVEL

Stazione Centrale overflows onto Piazza Garibaldi, northeast of old Naples
and the port. Services in this hectic station include a pharmacy, travel
agency, money exchange office, 24-hour luggage check (€2.7 every 12
hours), post office, and visitor information office. A Wasteels branch
office sells BIJ train tickets Monday–Saturday 9–7:30. If you're staying
in Mergellina, many trains stop first at Stazione Mergellina, also near
a hydrofoil port. If you arrive at night, consider taking a taxi to your
hotel, especially as local rail transport around the stations grinds to a
halt between 10 and 11 PM.

Other than the two center city metro lines—the Metropolitana Napoli
and the Metropolitana Collinare (*see* Subway Travel), Naples has two
sets of commuter rail lines, each with its own tickets, that link the city
with its environs. The Ferrovia Circumvesuviana leaves for points east
from the Stazione Circumvesuviana, on Corso Garibaldi; its trains also
stop on the lower level of Stazione Centrale. Destinations include Ercolano (Herculaneum), Pompei (Pompeii), and Sorrento. SEPSA manages two railway lines that leave from the Stazione Cumana, near
Montesanto Metro station. Both end at Torregaveta, at the west end of
the Gulf of Naples; the Cumana line goes along the coast and stops at
Pozzuoli and Lake Lucrino, among other places.

FARES &   Trains from the Stazione Centrale leave at least hourly for Rome (2½
SCHEDULES   hours northwest, €14–€23) and several times daily for Milan (7 hours
northwest, €35–€55) and Reggio di Calabria (4½ hours southeast,
€22–€35).
▪ **Train Information Ferrovia Circumvesuviana** ☎ 081/7722244 ⊕ www.vesuviana.
it. **SEPSA** ☎ 081/7354111 ⊕ www.sepsa.it. **Stazione Centrale** ✉ Piazza Garibaldi, Piazza Garibaldi ☎ 848/888088 ⊕ www.fs-on-line.it. **Stazione Mergellina** ✉ Corso Vittorio Emanuele 4, Mergellina ☎ 848/888088 ⊕ www.fs-on-line.it. **Wasteels branch
office** ☎ 081/201071.

TRANSPORTATION AROUND NAPLES

A major saving grace in the city's transit system is the Giranapoli (€.77),
a 90-minute ticket that works for the Metropolitana (subway), the
Cumana network, tram, funiculars, and AMN city buses, as long as you
are within the city limits. You can purchase tickets at most tobacco shops
(look for the TABACCHI sign) or newsstands. If you buy a day pass
(€2.32), remember to stamp it the first time you use it.

A novel integrated transport system called Campania Unico now allows
you to travel all over Campania. Combining several transportation
modes, the new *biglietto unico* varies in price and time validity depending
on how many zones you have to cross (for more information on this,
see Transportation Around Naples & Campania *in* the Smart Travel Tips
chapter). A Fascia 1 ticket (€1.40 for 100 minutes) covers trips between
Naples and a radius of about 10 km (6 mi), which includes Pozzuoli
and Portici; Fascia 2 (€1.70 for 120 minutes) takes in Ercolano (Herculaneum), Baia, and Cuma; Fascia 3 (€2.20 for 140 minutes) includes

Pompeii, Boscoreale, and Castellammare; Fascia 4 (€2.70 for 160 minutes) will take you as far as Vico Equense; and Fascia 5 (€3.10 for 180 minutes) covers trips to Sorrento and beyond.

TRAVEL AGENCIES

Every Tour travel agency, open weekdays 9–1:30 and 3:30–7, and Saturdays 9–1, provides the entire range of American Express services. Dedicated to helping students, Eurostudy Travel, open weekdays 9:30–1:30 and 3–6, is across from the central university building; its ticket office is also open Saturday 9:30–12:30.

⨏ Local Agents Every Tour ⊠ Piazza Municipio 5–6, Piazza Municipio ☏ 081/5518564. **Eurostudy Travel** ⊠ Via Mezzocannone 119, Spaccanapoli ☏ 081/5520947 ⊠ Ticket office: ⊠ Via Mezzocannone 87, Spaccanapoli ⊕ www.vacanzegiovani.

VISITOR INFORMATION

The numerous tourist offices in Naples aren't always open when they claim to be, but most are generally open from Monday to Saturday 8:30–8 and Sunday 8:30–2 except where noted. There's an EPT (Ente Provinciale per il Turismo) office in Stazione Centrale, where the people are quite friendly and helpful; the main administrative center (with an atmosphere of Baroque mothballs) is in Piazza dei Martiri, and is open weekdays 8:30–2. There's also a branch at Stazione Mergellina. An AACST office specializes in information on old Naples but generally just gives out brochures. A second office, which is closed on Sundays, is handily inside the Palazzo Reale.

⨏ Tourist Information AACST ⊠ Piazza Gesù Nuovo, Spaccanapoli ☏ 01/5523328 ⊠ Palazzo Reale Piazza Municipio ☏ 081/2525726. **EPT** ⊠ Stazione Centrale, Piazza Garibaldi ☏ 081/268779 ⊠ Piazza dei Martiri 58, Chiaia ☏ 081/4107211 ⊠ Stazione Mergellina Mergellina ☏ 081/7612102 ⊠ Via S. Carlo 9, Piazza Municipio ☏ 081/402394 ⊕ www.ept.napoli.it.

AROUND THE BAY: FROM POMPEII TO THE PHLEGREAN FIELDS

2

FODOR'S CHOICE

Cumae, *for the fabled Cave of the Cumaean Sibyl*

Herculaneum, *better preserved than Pompeii*

Lago d'Averno, *Virgil's "Gateway to Hell"*

Oplontis, *Nero's "Home Sweet Home"?*

Pompeii's Villa of the Mysteries, *for love among the ruins*

Portici's Palazzo Reale, *where Emma Hamilton partied*

Pozzuoli, *hallowed by both St. Paul and Sophia Loren*

The Solfatara, *to enjoy a walk through a volcano*

Vesuvius, *because it is (still?) there*

HIGHLY RECOMMENDED

ARCHAEOLOGY Baia's Museo Archeologico, *near Caesar's villa*

Cumae, *and the spectacular vistas from the Acropolis*

Pompeii's Anfiteatro

HOTELS Hotel Amleto, *Pompeii*

Azienda Agrituristica Il Casolare, *Baia*

RESTAURANTS Il Principe, *Pompeii*

La Mammola, *Torre del Greco*

Ristorante Don Antonio, *Pozzuoli*

Ristorante President, *Pompeii*

Many other great sights enliven this area. For other favorites, look for the black stars as you read this chapter.

By Mark
Walters

Updated by
Mark Walters

YOU CAN GET TO NAPLES by train, bus, or car, or you can "arrive" aboard a boat. If you're lucky enough to travel by water, a peacock's tail of splendor unfolds before you as you enter the vast Golfo di Napoli, the Bay of Naples. Enshrined in 1,001 travel posters, this pulse-tingling vista offers a turquoise-rimmed crescent of isles, hills, azure sky and sea, ancient cities, and modern villas, all arrayed around the bay to the east and west of Naples. But on each side of the city the earth fumes and grumbles, reminding us that all this beauty was born of cataclysm. Along the coast to the west are the Campi Flegrei, or the Phlegrean Fields of the ancients, where the crater of the Solfatara spews satisfyingly Dante-esque gases and where hills like Monte Nuovo have a habit of emerging overnight. Nearby are the dark, deep waters of Lago d'Averno, the lake that was allegedly the ancient doorway to Hell, or Hades, as it was then called. To the southeast slumbers Vesuvius, the mother of all mounts, looking down from its 4,000-foot height at the coastal strip stretching from modern and ancient Pompeii all the way to Naples. With potential destruction ever at hand, it is small wonder that southern Italians—and in particular the inhabitants of Campania around Naples—obey to the letter Horace's precept—*carpe diem*, "seize the day."

Even with the world's most famous volcano looming over the scene like a perpetual standby tombstone, visitors should feel relatively safe. The observatory on Vesuvius's slopes keeps its scientific finger on the subterranean pulse and will warn when signs of misbehavior become evident, so you need not worry about becoming an unwilling exhibit in some encore of Pompeii. You can simply concentrate on the memorable sights that fringe the spectacularly blue bay. The entire region is rife with legend and immortal names. Sixteen kilometers (10 mi) to the west of Naples lies an area where the emperors Claudius and Nero schemed and plotted in their villas, Virgil composed his poetry, and the Apostle Paul landed to spread the Gospel. Here, in and around what was called the Phlegrean (burning) Fields, are ancient sites, such as the Greeks' first colony in mainland Italy, the city of Cumae, home of the famed Cumaean Sybil; the luxury-loving Baiae, whose hot springs and dissolute living made it ancient Rome's most fashionable pleasure dome; and the Amphitheater of Pozzuoli, whose subterranean galleries are better preserved than even Rome's Colosseum. Here are the Campi Flegrei—inspiration for Dante's *Inferno*—and the sulfur-bound Solfatara, the "Little Vesuvius." Leapfrogging over Naples and spread out east along the bay are the glittering Bourbon palaces of Portici, the ancient palace at Oplontis, and, under the shadow of Vesuvius, Herculaneum and Pompeii—two of the largest archaeological sites in Europe. Nowhere else in Italy is there a comparable mingling of natural beauty with the remains of antiquity.

Rich archaeological and literary evidence reveals a continuous human presence in the area for millennia. Used as an outpost probably by the Minoans and Mycenaeans in the second millennium BC, the area was first colonized by Greeks from Euboea in the 8th century BC; they settled on the island of Pithekoussai (modern-day Ischia) and later on the mainland at Cumae. So much we have learned from a very valuable literary source, the Greek geographer Strabo (64 BC–after AD 21), who appears to have traveled extensively in the area. The early Greeks traded widely with the Etruscans and local Italic peoples, eventually extending their sphere of influence to Neapolis and southward and northward along the shores of the Tyrrhenian Sea.

Greek civilization flourished for hundreds of years along this seaboard, but there was nothing in the way of centralized government until centuries later, when the Romans surged southward and began to set up colonies of their own for added protection, especially after incursions led by such flamboyant figures as Pyrrhus and Hannibal in the 3rd century BC.

From the 1st century BC onward, Campania became synonymous with sybaritic wealth. It was here that wealthy Romans built palatial residences, tapping the naturally hot springs for their fabled baths and harnessing the area's rich volcanic soils to produce wines lauded by Latin poets. Here emperors indulged in vices that would have been unseemly in the capital, and there was the usual complement of public baths and theaters to keep the plebeians happy.

The merrymaking to the east of Naples was stilled in AD 79 by a jolt from Vesuvius, believed by few at the time to harbor any danger for those living at its base. We are fortunate to have Pliny the Younger's memorable description of his uncle being overwhelmed by fumes and dying of asphyxiation in Stabiae, now Castellammare di Stabia. Although written some years after the event, Pliny's letter to Tacitus is a unique and moving account of the disaster. But as so often happens in history, other people's catastrophes are an archaeologist's dream: Pompeii, Herculaneum, and outlying lesser-known settlements such as Oplontis were spared the ravages of the centuries and have been remarkably preserved for posterity.

Following the fall of the Roman Empire and the period of general decay that prevailed during Byzantine times, more than 1,000 years were to pass before the area's classical greatness was once again appreciated, this time by young, well-heeled 18th- and 19th-century travelers from northern Europe, for whom a visit to Vesuvius and the various ancient sites was the culmination of their Grand Tour.

Many would say that the region is now experiencing a second Renaissance. The *artecard* scheme—a pass experimentally introduced in 2002 combining access to Campania's major historic sites and travel by public transport—has proved immensely successful. Partly in response to a massive rise in local demand, new sites and museums have been opened and visitor facilities have been globally improved.

Exploring the Bay

When it comes to Campania's overflowing basket of treasures of the ancient world, everyone starts with Pompeii, and rightly so. After touring this massive ghost town, work your way clockwise around Mt. Vesuvius to nearby Oplontis and Herculaneum, two other spectacular excavations, and then shoot off at a tangent to the Museo Archeologico Nazionale in Naples to study the many artistic masterworks excavated from these towns. The lower slopes of Vesuvius—the most densely inhabited volcanic region in the world—are crisscrossed by major roads and several railway lines, providing easy access to most of the archaeological sites. To make a chronological departure from classical times, while in Ercolano make a short detour to take in the sumptuous Royal Palace of Portici and a Vesuvian villa, such as the attractively restored Villa Campolieto, both built during Bourbon rule in the 18th century. The best form of transportation is the Circumvesuviana light railway, its stations never more than a 10-minute walk from the major sites.

But—pause, emphasis, gesture—this is just the beginning of ancient wonders the Bay of Naples has in store for travelers. Pompeii and the towns mentioned above are set to the east of Naples, but you'll really get awash in mythical folklore if you also head to the *west* of Naples. Pompeii and Herculaneum were favored by middle and upper-middle class Romans but when the emperors wanted to party they headed to

With limited time at your disposal, priority should be given to the sites of **Herculaneum** ② and **Pompeii** ⑥–㉖ ►, although a single day will merely whet the appetite. While these are two of the most popular day trips for travelers based in Naples or Sorrento, a practical minimum for really absorbing the splendors of this area and getting a healthy balance of archaeology, history, museums, and cuisine is about three days. To take in the entire span from the Campi Flegrei to Pompeii, including some of the undeservedly less-visited sites such as **Baia** ㉚, you would be advised to make a weeklong trip with at least two base camps, one on either side of Naples.

2

Numbers in the text correspond to numbers in the margin and on the East of Naples, Pompeii, and West of Naples maps.

If you have
3 days

Begin at **Pompeii** ⑥–㉖, allowing at least half a day for the archaeological site, which will be just enough time to take in the main civic buildings, a representative sampling of villas, and the hotspots of ancient Roman entertainment, such as the Amphitheater. Given the part it played in AD 79, **Vesuvius** ③ also merits a visit, though temperatures at the peak in winter months can be pretty frigid. Then head for **Herculaneum** ②, for its less-visited but more evocative ruins. In between, you should slot in the villa of **Oplontis** ⑤, located in the town of Torre Annunziata, a stop now included in the three-day archaeological pass, the *biglietto cumulativo*. With time left over, sample the opulence of a Vesuvian villa on the so-called Miglio d'Oro, or "Golden Mile," built by the Bourbon aristocracy close to the Royal Palace of **Portici** ①.

If you have
5 days

More time in the area will enable you to head west of Naples into the Campi Flegrei, where a little exploring will pay immediate dividends. To experience the volcanic nature of this otherworldly terrain, walk across the crater of the **Solfatara** ㉘ and then soak up the archaeological sites of **Pozzuoli** ㉙ and **Baia** ㉚. Reserve half a day for the site of **Cumae** ㉛ and appreciate the sweeping views of Italy's Tyrrhenian coastline from its impressive acropolis.

this area, from Pozzuoli (where Petronius set much of his famous *Satyricon*, the unique novel that looks though some keyholes during Nero's time) to Baiae, where the Caesars built their pleasure palaces, to Cumae, home of the famed Cumean Sibyl. Every tour group since Cicero has marched through Pompeii and environs, but you'll really win the classical sweepstakes if you also tour the sites west of Naples.

About the Restaurants & Hotels
With prices substantially lower than those in the city center, the restaurants located outside of Naples, especially those in the Campi Flegrei, become popular stopovers for day-trips at weekends and evenings—so book well in advance to get the pick of your choice.

To avoid what might seem like glorified Pompeian *lupanaria*—those favored abodes of ancient ladies of the night—you should be careful when choosing a hotel in the area. Most hotels give excellent value compared with locations in the city of Naples, and will be a good deal quieter as well. However, where hotels are close to main roads—and that means motor scooters at night—ask for quiet rooms at the back, especially in the busy towns of Pompeii and Pozzuoli. As throughout the rest of Italy, high season in this region is usually at Christmas, Easter, and in summer, when temperatures, prices, and visitor numbers reach a crescendo. Avoid visiting Pompeii during religious festivities—in particular, Easter Week, May 8th, and the first Sunday in October—as hotels are likely to be booked up with pilgrims months in advance. As a general rule, to ensure you get the right room at the right time, book well ahead of your expected arrival.

WHAT IT COSTS In euros				
	$$$$	**$$$**	**$$**	**$**	**¢**
RESTAURANTS	over €20	€15–€20	€9–€15	€5–€9	under €5
HOTELS	over €210	€160–€210	€110–€160	€60–€110	under €60

Restaurant prices are for a main-course entry only (known in Italian as secondo piatto, or second course); note that if a restaurant offers only prix-fixe (set-price) meals, it has been given the price category that reflects the full prix-fixe price. Hotel prices are for a standard double room in high season, excluding tax and service charges; higher prices (inquire when booking) prevail for any board plans.

Timing

This part of the Mediterranean is at its best in spring and fall. Winter months occasionally reserve chilly surprises for visitors, with roads on the upper slopes of Vesuvius becoming dangerously icy at times. In April and May watch out for the hordes of (nonpaying) schoolchildren at archaeological sites and, as a general rule—to avoid the crowds—visit sites first thing in the morning or in the late afternoon before closing time (usually an hour before sunset). Pozzuoli rewards its overheated summer visitors with evening performances in the amphitheater, and other sites such as Cumae and Oplontis may have rival attractions. Nature lovers will be pleased to know that this part of the Mediterranean, especially the verdant Campi Flegrei, becomes a floral feast at springtime, while the north-facing slopes of Vesuvius are still awash with color as late as June and July.

UNDER THE SHADOW OF VESUVIUS: PORTICI TO HERCULANEUM

Though barely more than a third as tall as Mt. Etna, its Sicilian counterpart, Vesuvius, with its relatively modest 4,189-ft height, has achieved unparalleled status in the collective consciousness of the Italians and the world. "Vesuvius is nature committing suicide," Madame de Staël reported back to Parisians during the Age of Enlightenment. For centuries this still-active volcano had offered a spectacle to visitors who flocked to the Bay of Naples to marvel at its small-scale eruptions, ever-present plumes of smoke, and thundering fumaroles. In the mid-18th century, in fact, the entire court of Naples set up shop in Portici, at the foot of the mountain, building summer villas that served as ringside seats to the volcano's hypnotic pyrotechnics. Artists painted the mountain in eruption, streams of lava rendered in lurid hues of blood. Romantic poets climbed the peak under the full moon to create odes extolling its sublime and terrible power. Duchesses (fashionably attired with earrings and cameos exquisitely carved of lava stone) would hire chair porters to bear them up to the rim, where, down below, rainbow mounds of sulfurous ash, vents of hissing steam, lunarlike boulders—everything, it seems, but little imps dashing about with long Luciferian pitchforks—presented a hellish sight.

2

Noble Dust
Home to Pompeii, Herculaneum, Baia, and Cumae, the regions to the west and east of Naples are two of of the world's greatest treasure troves of Greek and Roman antiquity. While the best relics of ancient art have been carted off to the Museo Archeologico in Naples, many of the towns and cities where they were first created still grace the countryside. Quick to appreciate the sybaritic possibilities of such a lovely land—which they dubbed *Campania Felix,* or the "Happy Land"—the ancient Romans arrived to build palatial country residences and create resort towns like Pompeii. Cosmopolitan and eclectic, Roman art absorbed whatever its tastemakers thought modish in other cultures, but it retains a candor and insight that is positively modern—just visit the eye-opening murals at Pompeii's Villa of the Mysteries, the finest surviving paintings from classical antiquity. Today, the extraordinary archaeological wonders on view in this region—Pompeii, preserved by Vesuvius's dust; Herculaneum, founded by that famous Greek, Hercules; Baia, pleasure pot of the Roman emperors; Lake Averno, legendary entrance to Hades; Oplontis, once home to Mr. and Mrs. Nero; Pozzuoli's great amphitheater; and Cumae's Cave of the Cumean Sibyl—startlingly bridge the centuries to bring alive the world of the ancients.

As the Caesars Dined
If *Betae garo cum olivis capparibusque* and *Cassata oplontis* seem somewhat unusual menu listings, fitting perhaps for an antiquarian Vatican dinner party, further surprises will be in store when dining out in the modern town of Pompeii. At the Principe restaurant, Roman banquets are re-created with ingredients that would have been used 2,000 years ago. You might even be able to taste one of the dishes mentioned above (the first is beet with fish sauce, olives, and capers, the second a sweet made from ricotta cheese and honey). Fortunately, the ancients committed much of their culinary expertise to writing, thanks mainly to authors like Cato, Cicero, and the renowned gourmet of Augustan times, Apicius.

To the west of Naples, Cumae is thought to have been the setting for part of Petronius's *Satyricon,* a picaresque novel probably written in the 1st century AD, containing the memorable scene of a dinner hosted by the nouveau-riche Trimalchio. In the same area of the Campi Flegrei, the tradition of abundance, if not excess, continues in a host of local restaurants and trattorias. This is where many Neapolitans migrate on weekends to buy their *frutti di mare* (seafood) or dine in Lucullan style at one of the many waterside restaurants, and at half the price they would spend at restaurants nearer home.

Wines: In Vino Veritas
Two thousand years ago, wine from Campania was considered some of the best in the Roman Empire. Latin poet Horace in the first century BC extolled the merits of the wines, such as Falernian and Massic, grown around Mondragone, northwest of Naples; a century later, Pliny the Elder praised several grape varieties thought to have been cultivated in the area. The latter author was less complimentary about wines from Surrentum (Sorrento), which he claimed were little more than vintage vinegar and recommended for those recovering from illness; wines from Pompeii, he reported, could provoke a hangover lasting until noon the following day.

Today, after centuries of mediocre wine production, Campania is once again arousing the passions and palates of wine connoisseurs: traditional grape varieties like Aglianico and Piedirosso (reds), and Fiano and Falanghina (whites) have halted the southward expansion of "foreign" intruders like Sangiovese and Trebbiano. One of the few reputable producers in the 1980s, Mastroberardino, now has to compete with Campanian producers like Feudi di San Gregorio, Antonio Caggiano, and the Cantina del Taburno, which have all become major players on the national circuit. Like those in Tuscany to the north, vineyards are increasingly opening their doors to the public, while some, like Mustilli and Villa Matilde, have cashed in on the agriturismo boom and are offering first-rate meals with *degustazioni,* or tastings. There is renewed interest in preserving traditional training systems, such as the Etruscan *alberata* still used around the Aversa area north of Naples, where vines grow spectacularly up live supports—mainly poplars—to heights of 40 ft. On the research front, vines have been replanted within the site of ancient Pompeii with the same characteristics as in antiquity, though hopefully modern wine-making techniques will prevent the finished product having the same day-after effect sorely lamented by Pliny.

Vesuvius's eruptions—from the ancient era through the 18th century—had long been legendary, but the volcano's lethal handiwork only became apparent to modern minds when the Roman towns of Pompeii and Herculaneum were discovered by accident and then excavated in the late 18th century. As it turned out, having been buried since the famous AD 79 eruption, these towns promptly became the most celebrated archaeological sites in Europe, offering up untold artistic treasures (the finest of which are on display at Naples's incredible Museo Archeologico Nazionale). Today, thousands of visitors arrive every day to sites around the bay, most with one eye monitoring *Il Vesuvio,* just a few miles away. There have been around 30 eruptions of various magnitudes in the past 2,000 years, the most recent of which took place in 1944. This might be construed as good news, but many vulcanologists think it is ominous when a living volcano is so silent—only two eruptions have occurred in the 20th century—and they now maintain a constant watch.

Portici

❶ *7 km (5½ mi) southeast from Naples, 1 km (½ mi) northwest from Ercolano.*

Portici, whose Reggia, or Royal Palace, offers a peek into the gilded lives of the 18th-century rich and famous, is set rather incongruously within the urban sprawl of the *Comuni Vesuviani.* A little more than 250 years ago, the area was chosen by the first Bourbon king of the Two Sicilies, Charles III, as the site for a royal palace that would be sufficiently close to Naples for him to be able to return to the capital at a moment's notice, yet far enough away for the king and his entourage to indulge in hunting, one of the main Bourbon pursuits. No matter that courtiers were worried by the proximity of Vesuvius; Charles refused to show concern at any imminent danger, proclaiming, "God, the immaculate Virgin, and San Gennaro will protect us." The royal presence in the area triggered a boom in real estate, with more than 120 ducal villas being built in the subsequent half century on a stretch of land that came to be known as the *Miglio d'Oro* (Golden Mile). Here life became one long gala, with costume balls, picnics, concerts, and entertainment, some of which enchanted the likes of Goethe and Lord Byron. Today, progress

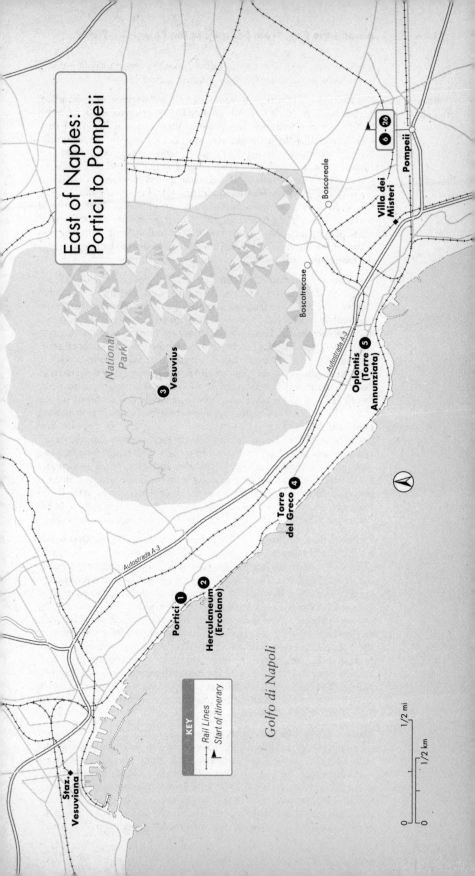

is being made by the *Ente per le Ville Vesuviane* (Vesuvian Villa Agency) to purchase and restore the villas to their former glory.

Fodor'sChoice The showpiece is Portici's Reggia (palace), or **Palazzo Reale**. Straddling
★ the Via Nazionale delle Calabrie (Statate 18), the main road that led south of Naples in past centuries, now renamed Via Università, this royal palace was designed by the architect Canevari, complete with a layout of 75 acres of woodland, but its actual construction was overseen and executed by another architect, Ferdinando Fuga, 1738–42. It stands impressively at the foothills of Vesuvius and enjoys sweeping views across the Bay of Naples from both its south-facing inner courtyard and its upper floors. Although the agriculture department of Naples University still occupies most of the palace, the cultural heritage ministry has taken over a few of the rooms on the *piano nobile* (main floor) and currently uses them for temporary exhibitions, thereby restoring to the public one of the main landmarks of Bourbon history and architecture.

The palace is conveniently located on a trolley-bus route (No. 255) between Ercolano and Portici, a 10-minute walk northwest up Corso Resina from the Herculaneum archaeological site. The bus stop is unmistakable, in the middle of the courtyard right between the northern and southern wings. Head for the university porters' lodge on the seaward side (in parking lot just beyond) and mount the monumental staircase leading up to the piano nobile. At the risk of developing a crick in your neck, admire the well-preserved 18th-century trompe l'oeil frescoes decorating the walls and the ceiling and generally enjoy these now-hallowed halls of academe. Horatio Nelson would have walked up the same staircase on his way to a royal banquet held in his honor by King Ferdinand IV and Queen Carolina in 1798, where he sat opposite and first met Sir William Hamilton and his wife, Emma. At the time the palace was used as a repository for many of the early finds from Herculaneum, now in the Museo Archeologico in Naples, and it was noted particularly for the decorative 18th-century panels from the finest salon—called the porcelain, or china, room—which were subsequently moved to the Royal Palace of Capodimonte, where they can still be admired today. ⊠ *Via Università 100* ☎ *081/7751251* ☞ *Free* ☉ *Sept.–July, weekdays 8:30–7.*

Opposite the entrance to the Royal Palace of Portici lies the **Orto Botanico** (Botanical Garden), founded in 1872. It's housed within the palace grounds and abuts the magnificent Holmoak Wood, the hunting preserve of the Bourbon kings. The garden's original specimens were severely damaged in World War II, when the botanical institute was requisitioned and the garden used as a vehicle parking area by Allied forces. Since then the collection has recovered and expanded, with a delightfully shady palmery, an impressive variety of cycads, and some unusually large specimens of the exotic Asian tree *Ginkgo biloba*. Since there are virtually no signposts in the garden, ask to see the rare southern African desert plant *Welwitschia mirabilis*, and the native but endangered primrose *Primula palinuri* if assistance or guidance is at hand. During normal opening hours, guided visits can be arranged by appointment with the curator. ⊠ *Via Università* ☎ *081/7754850* ☞ *Free* ☉ *Mon.–Sat. 8–1.*

There are other signature villas of the famed Miglio d'Oro, but many—including the Villa d'Elbeuf, Villa Signorini, and Torre del Greco's Villa delle Ginestre—are either being renovated or are only open for group visits. However, to the west of Portici (in the rather dreary suburban town of San Giorgio a Cremano) is the **Villa Bruno**, now restored to its original late 18th-century grandeur. Past its gentle yellow-and-gray outer walls and remodeled Neoclassical façade you'll find a small museum devoted to locally-born actor and film director Massimo Troisi. At the back of the villa is a pergola walkway, a small auditorium used for concerts, and extensive lawns offering a welcome respite from San Giorgio's incessant traffic. The villa is best reached from the Cavalli di Bronzo stop of the Circumvesuviana railway between Naples and Portici. Outside the station, turn right down Via Cavalli di Bronzo for about five minutes until you come to the villa on your left. ✉ *Via Cavalli di Bronzo 20, San Giorgio a Cremano* ☎ *081/5654395* 🎫 *Free* ⊙ *Daily 9–5.*

Where to Eat

¢–$ ✕ **A' Cantinella do Cunvento.** A short walk down Via Università from the Royal Palace of Portici brings you to this unpretentious ristorante-pizzeria, known to the locals as Da Peppino after its owner-manager Giuseppe. Although crowded at lunchtime with staff from the nearby college, this spot has down-to-earth service and prices which are hardly donnish. The competitive all-in-one price—an incredibly good value—includes first course (pasta or rice), main course (octopus salad is a specialty), and fruit. ✉ *Via Università 64, Portici* ☎ *081/7755301* 🚫 *No credit cards* ⊙ *Sometimes closed weekends.*

Herculaneum (Ercolano)

2 *12 km (8 mi) southeast of Naples, 40 km (25 mi) northwest of Salerno.*

Fodor'sChoice ★

A visit to the archaeological site of Herculaneum neatly counterbalances the hustle of its larger neighbor, Pompeii. And although close to the heart of the busy town of Ercolano—indeed, in places right under it—the ancient site seems worlds apart, and you have the sensation of being catapulted back into the past, for here there is ample supply of ancient allure and splendor (unlike Pompeii, whose site is much more ruined). Like Pompeii, Herculaneum was buried by Vesuvius's eruption in AD 79. Unlike Pompeii, it was submerged in a mass of volcanic mud that sealed and preserved wood and other materials (whereas at Pompeii, most organic matter rotted away over time). Much smaller than its famous neighbor, the settlement of Herculaneum was wealthier and more select, and a greater portion of what was found has been left in place. Several villas have inlaid marble floors that evoke the same admiration as the mosaics in Naples's Museo Archeologico. Elsewhere it's possible to gauge how the less privileged lived: more remains of the upper stories than in Pompeii, so you can view the original stairs to the cramped, poorly lighted rooms that gave onto the central courtyard. Here there's more of a sense of a living community than Pompeii is able to convey. Like all the other sites in the Vesuvian area, Herculaneum is served efficiently by the Circumvesuviana railway, which provides fast, frequent, and economical connections; from Naples's Stazione Centrale or Stazione Vesuviana, take the Circumvesuviana train to the Ercolano stop (five per hour, 20 minutes east, €1.70). The ruins are a five-minute walk down Via Novembre toward the Bay of Naples. Archaeology buffs will want to bring a flashlight to better see into the dark corners of the excavated houses.

Lying more than 60 ft below the town of Ercolano, the **Scavi di Ercolano** (Excavations of Herculaneum) now stand among acres of greenhouses that make this area one of Europe's chief flower-growing areas. It was named, like several other Greek colonies around the Mediterranean, after its legendary founder Heracles (Hercules), but details surrounding the date of its foundation date by its Greek settlers have yet to be revealed. Certainly the grid plan of the town's layout suggests affinities with nearby Neapolis (now Naples), so it could have been an offshoot of its neighbor on the Bay of Naples. Like many Greek sites in southern Italy, in about the 4th century BC it fell under Samnite influence. It finally became a *municipium* (municipality) under Roman dominion in 89 BC. At the time of its destruction in AD 79, it had about 5,000 inhabitants (as compared to Pompeii's 20,000), many of whom were fishermen, craftsmen, and artists, while a lucky few patricians owned villas overlooking the sea. In contrast to Pompeii, most of the damage here was done by volcanic mud. This semiliquid mass seeped into the crevices and niches of every building, covering household objects and enveloping textiles and wood—sealing all in a compact, airtight tomb.

Casual excavation—and haphazard looting—began at the beginning of the 18th century under the prince of Elbeuf, who purchased the land after a farmer had made several chance finds of marble relics. The excavation technique at the time consisted of digging vertical shafts and horizontal galleries, and whenever possible, gunpowder was used to speed up the work—techniques that make those of the much-maligned Heinrich Schliemann, discoverer of Troy, sound positively scrupulous. It was precisely through this network of underground tunnels that 18th-century visitors from northern Europe on their Grand Tour—such as Horace Walpole and Thomas Gray—were to experience the buried city. Systematic digs were not initiated until the 1920s, by which time many of the sugarplums buried within the cake had already been plucked or damaged. Today less than half of Herculaneum has been excavated; with present-day Ercolano and the unlovely Resina quarter (famous among bargain hunters as the area's largest secondhand-clothing market) perched on top of the site, progress is understandably limited.

Although Herculaneum had only one-fourth the population of Pompeii and has been only partially excavated, what has been found is generally in a better state of preservation. In some cases you can even see the original wooden beams, staircases, and furniture. Lending a touch of verdant life, some of the peristyle gardens have been replanted. Today much excitement is focused on one excavation in an inaccessible corner of the site, the **Villa dei Papiri,** built by Julius Caesar's father-in-law. The building takes its name from the 1,800 carbonized papyrus scrolls dug up here in the 18th century, leading scholars to believe it may have been a study center or library. Now Italian archaeologists and geologists have uncovered part of the villa itself and hope to unearth more of the library—given the right funds and political support. In the spring of 2003, amid much fanfare, the villa was reopened to the public for weekend viewing (make separate reservations at www.arethusa.net).

For standard visits to the site, walk through the ticket office down the slope to the southern end of the site toward the large modern structure of the Antiquarium (yet to be opened). This is a good point at which to view the grid system of roads, with the three *cardines* (avenues, from northeast to southwest) being intersected by two *decumani* (roads) from left to right. The blocks, as in Pompeii, are referred to as *insulae*, each containing four or five main villas and sometimes a row of shops. In general, and unsurprisingly, the best mosaics, wall paintings, and any organic remains such as wooden furniture are found in those parts that were excavated in the 20th century. The 19th-century open-air excavators—though systematic—took few precautions to preserve the upper stories (just note the ruinous state of Insula II, in the southwest corner) and, in addition, the artwork has been exposed to the air for an extra century.

At this stage you may want to pick up an audioguide to the site (€6 for one, €9 for a pair; I.D. required), which gives helpful house-by-house information. Entry to the site is currently gained via an underground passage, which cuts down through 60 feet of volcanic deposits and emerges by the southern (lower) end of the site. The path then crosses a marshy area, which was the original sea level and the site of a small port. This means that thanks to various eruptions (especially AD 79 and AD 1631), the topography of the land has changed beyond all recognition. It's now hard to believe that Herculaneum lay *"inter duos fluvios infra Vesuvium"* (between two rivers below Vesuvius). Visitors are ★ nowadays channeled up to the town past the **Terme Suburbane** (Suburban Baths, usually open mornings only). In the courtyard outside the building is an altar erected by the town benefactor, Marcus Nonius Balbus, and the base for his marble statue, long since removed to the Museo Archeologico in Naples. Much of the volcanic mud here has been left in situ, so you get a good idea not only of a Roman baths complex, but also of the problems the archaeologists were confronted with when excavating it. ⊠ *Il Quartiere Suburbano.*

In antiquity, the **Casa dei Cervi** was one of the first houses that visitors to the town would have passed as they entered the city from the seaward side. As in most top-notch town residences, however, the entranceway is plain and leads into a long narrow corridor called the *fauces,* or *vestibulum,* which then opens onto an atrium. The showpiece in this particular house is the garden area, surrounded by a cryptoportico and terminating in a partially reconstructed gazebo. Of course, prior to the eruption, the house would have had a fine view over the Bay of Naples. ⊠ *Insula IV.*

As you walk around Herculaneum, you'll notice the narrow entrances of the houses and the wider entrances for shops, inns, and other buildings where large numbers of people required access. A case in point is at the corner of Cardo V and the Decumanus Inferior, where you'll see two access points and counters with large amphoras for keeping dishes warm. This was one of the town's **Thermopolia**, the fast-food outlets of the ancient world. Next door, for relaxed, discreet dining where, judging from the warren of private chambers within, more than just food and drink was on offer, there was the **Taverna di Priapo** (Priapus's Tavern), complete with its waiting room at the back right. ⊠ *Insula IV.*

Of course, no town would have been complete without its sports facilities, and Herculaneum was no exception. Just opposite the *thermopolium* on Cardo V is the entrance to the large **Palaestra** where a variety of ball games and wrestling matches were staged. Here, when you look at the peristyle columns and realize that only three of a total of more than 20 have been excavated, you appreciate how much of the ancient town still lies buried under solidified volcanic mud. ⊠ *Insula Orientalis II.*

On Cardo IV parallel to Cardo V, close to the Forum Baths, is the **Casa del Nettuno ed Anfitrite** (House of Neptune and Amphitrite). It takes its name from the mosaic that still sports its bright blue coloring and adorns the wall of the small secluded *nymphaeum,* or shrine with fountains, at the back of the house. According to legend, in the time-honored fashion of the Olympians, Neptune (or Poseidon) saw Amphitrite dancing with the Nereids on the island of Naxos, carried her off, and married her. The adjacent wall, in similar mosaic style though less well preserved, has a hunting scene with a stag being pursued by a dog. Annexed to the same house is a remarkably preserved wineshop, where amphorae still rest on carbonized wooden shelves.

In addition to its fine mosaics, this house has a good example of an atrium (courtyard) with an *impluvium* in the middle which collected rainwater and channeled it to an underground cistern (just lift the metal lid to have a look). At the back of the atrium there would have been a *tablinum,* a main reception room where the *patronus* (host) would receive his *clientes* (guests). In some houses there would have been a screen to provide more privacy for the master of the house. Where there was space, a colonnaded garden (peristyle) was considered desirable, complete with fountains and a *triclinium* (open-air dining room). *Cubicula* (bedrooms) were sometimes on either side of the entrance, although this is by no means the rule in Herculaneum. Also try to spot the service area (kitchen), with the servants' quarters often immediately above. ⊠ *Insula V.*

Stories of Roman licentiousness are belied by the **Terme del Foro** (Forum Baths), where there were separate sections for men and women. Here you see most of the architectural ingredients of *thermae* (baths). But besides the mandatory trio in the men's section (a round *frigidarium,* a cool swimming pool; a *tepidarium,* a semi-heated pool; and a *calidarium,* or heated pool), there's also an *apodyterium,* or changing room, with partitioned shelves for depositing togas and a low podium to use as seating space while in line to use the facilities. For more attractive mosaics—particularly a spectacular rendition of Neptune—go around into the women's baths (with seemingly no frigidarium). The heating system in the tepidarium was also different (no hot air piped through or under, only braziers). Note the steam vents ingeniously built into the bath's benches and the small overhead cubbies in which bathers stored their togas. ⊠ *Insula VI.*

An outstanding example of carbonized remains is in the **Casa del Tramezzo di Legno** (House of the Wooden Partition), as it has been prosaically labeled by archaeologists. Following renovation work in the mid-1st century AD, the house was designed to have a frontage on three sides of Insula III and included a number of storerooms, shops, and second-floor habitations. This suggests that the owner was a wealthy *mercator,* a member of the up-and-coming merchant class that was starting to edge the patricians out of their privileged positions. The airy atrium has a lovely garden. Look closely at the impluvium, and you'll see the original flooring below, which was later replaced with marble, perhaps after a change of owners. Next to the impluvium is an elegant marble table, or *cartibulum,* while behind is the tablinum, partially screened off by a bronze-studded wooden partition (the central part of which is missing) that would also have had hooks for hanging *lucernae* (lamps). ⊠ *Insula III, 11–12.*

If you're looking for decorations, these are especially delicate in the **Casa del Atrio a Mosaico** (House of the Mosaic Atrium), with a geometrically patterned flooring in the vestibulum leading into a black-and-white checkerboard pattern in the atrium, with the tablinum in the background. The tablinum is unusually elaborate, with its three aisles separated by two rows of pillars topped by Corinthian capitals, conforming to the design described by the great Roman architect Vitruvius as *"oecus aegyptius,"* or Egyptian-style room. Like many other houses in both Herculaneum and Pompeii, this is likely to be kept locked, and you could be restricted to a peek through the entrance. This villa enjoyed a sweeping view of the sea, a vantage point utilized in the many rooms that had windows. ⊠ *Insula IV, 1–2.*

One of the more spectacular sights at Herculaneum is also a well-guarded secret: the **underground theater** dating to about the 1st century BC, in the northwest corner of the site but accessible only by prior arrangement with site guides or local travel operators. Access is gained from a small building painted in Pompeian red at Corso Resina 23, about a five-minute walk farther along the road to Portici, opposite the Church of Santa Caterina. One of the more sensational finds to be unearthed in the past decade at Herculaneum are the storehouses located in its ancient port by the sea. Here, about 300 skeletons were excavated, all "frozen" in place as they slept their troubled sleep after the first day of volcanic destruction when a thermoclastic cloud swept the town (their brain pans were stained red as their heads exploded from the heat). Using silicon technology, a cluster of about ten are now on display in Naples's Museo Archeologico Nazionale special "Tales of an Eruption" exhibition. They cannot be viewed in situ. The Garden of the Fugitives in Pompeii is, if anything, more poignant, for there you get to see the casts in situ at the bottom of the garden. ⊠ *Corso Resina 6, Ercolano* ☎ *081/ 7390963* 🖃 *€10 for Herculaneum only; €18 for the "biglietto cumulativo" ticket to 5 sites (Pompeii, Herculaneum, Boscoreale, Oplontis, and Stabiae) valid for 3 days* ☉ *Nov.–Mar., daily 8:30–5, ticket office closes at 3:30; Apr.–Oct., daily 8:30–7:30, ticket office closes at 6.*

Leave the archaeological site of Herculaneum and head southeast along Corso Resina, keeping Vesuvius on your left and the Bay of Naples on your right; after about a five-minute walk you'll pass the entrance to **Villa Campolieto,** one of the most attractive Vesuvian villas, which, like most historic buildings still standing in the area, has survived centuries of volcanic eruptions, earthquakes, and post-Bourbon neglect. Go in through the well-tended gardens past the information kiosk (leaflets are available in English) and turn left into the main building. If you're motorized, ask at the kiosk to use the parking facilities at the far end of the gardens.

The construction of Villa Campolieto was commissioned by Prince Luzio of Sangro and entrusted to no less than four architects during its troubled conception from 1755 to 1775, with the final touches added by the architect Luigi Vanvitelli, better known for his work on the Royal Palace of Caserta, and his son Carlo. After entering through the gardens—this was the original main entrance, as the large doorway on the Via Nazionale delle Calabrie (now Corso Resina) was reserved for carriages—proceed up the Vanvitellian staircase (similar to the one at the palace at Caserta) to the piano nobile, currently used for art exhibitions. Note the classical scenes in most of the frescoes on this floor, with fine illusionist work by Jacopo Cestaro, including depictions of Minerva and Mercury set in a Vanvitelli-style colonnade. Cestaro was also responsible for the beautifully restored frescoed ceilings in both of the front rooms facing Vesuvius. At ground-floor level, the main peculiarity is the elliptical rotunda, which provides a picturesque setting for outdoor concerts and theatrical performances during the Vesuvian Villas Festival in July. Note the natural gray shading of the steps and lower facade, characteristic of many buildings erected in the Bourbon era, from the local volcanic *piperno* stone. This villa is the headquarters for the Ente per le Ville Vesuviane association. ⊠ *Corso Resina 283, Ercolano* ☎ *081/7322134* ⊕ *www.villevesuviane.net* 🖃 *Free* ☉ *Tues.–Sun. 10–1.*

Where to Eat

$ ✕ **Trattoria da Calcagno.** Catering to locals and foreigners alike—always a good sign in areas with large tourist flows—this eatery is a five-minute walk up from the excavations of Herculaneum just off Via 4 Novembre. Dishes and wines vary according to season: pasta *e fagioli* (with beans) is a winter favorite, while richly garnished spaghetti with clams is a summer stalwart, all washed down by lively Vesuvian wines. ⊠ *Corso Italia 17, Ercolano* ☎ *081/7390405* 🖃 *No credit cards* ☉ *Closed Sun.*

Shopping

Donadio Manifattura Coralli (⊠ Via del Corallo, by the Ercolano exit of the Napoli-Salerno autostrada, Ercolano ☎ 081/7752900 ⊕ www. donadio.net) is first and foremost a cameo factory; it also sells directly to the public. Local artisans can be observed making the cameos, an age-old tradition in which shells—now virtually all imported—are meticulously carved to produce mythological scenes in relief, exploiting the natural layering and contrasting colors of the raw material.

Vesuvius

❸
Fodor'sChoice
★

16 km (10 mi) east of Naples, 8 km (5 mi) northeast of Herculaneum, 40 km (25 mi) northwest of Salerno.

Vesuvius may have lost its plume of smoke, but it has lost none of its fascination—especially for those who live in the towns around the cone. They've now nicknamed it the "Sterminator." In centuries gone by, their predecessors would study the volcano for signs of impending destruction. "*Napoli fa i peccati e la Torre li paga,*" the residents of nearby Torre del Greco used to mutter—"Naples sins and the Torre suffers." When reports of depraved behavior circulated about Neapolitans across the bay, chastisement was only to be expected. Today, the world continues to watch Il Vesuvio with bated breath. Although its destructive powers are undoubtedly diminished, the threat of an eruption is ever present. In bygone ages the task of protecting the local inhabitants fell to the martyred patron saint of Naples, San Gennaro, or St. Januarius, whose statue was often borne aloft through the streets of the city in an effort to placate the volcano's wrath. Today, volcanic activity is attentively monitored by the Osservatorio Vesuviano. Founded under Bourbon king Ferdinand II in the mid-19th century, it's the facility where the seismic scale was invented. The original observatory, conspicuous with its Pompeian-red facade, has survived unscathed on the volcano's upper slopes and now serves as a conference center and small museum: the **Museo dell'Osservatorio Vesuviano** houses a mineralogical display, characteristic landscape gouaches, early seismographs, and information panels. Access during the week is restricted to scientific groups, associations, and schools. ✉ *Via Osservatorio, Ercolano* ☎ *081/7777149 or 081/7777150* ⊕ *www.ov.ingv.it* ✒ *Free* ☉ *Weekends 10–2.*

Seen from the other side of the Bay of Naples, Vesuvius appears to have two peaks: on the northern side is the steep face of Monte Somma, possibly part of the original crater wall in AD 79; to the south is the present-day cone of Vesuvius, which has actually formed within the ancient crater. The AD 79 cone would have been considerably higher, perhaps peaking at more than 2,150 ft. The upper slopes bear the visible scars left by 19th- and 20th-century eruptions, the most striking being the lava flow from 1944 lying to the left (north side) of the main approach road from Ercolano on the way up. On earlier lava flows, such as that of 1872, the grayish lichen named after the volcano, *Stereocaulon vesuvianum,* has had more time to break up the volcanic rocks and prepare the way for pioneer plants like red valerian and the characteristic leggy Mt. Etna broom, which transform the upper slopes into a blaze of dark pink and yellow in late spring.

Under its status as a national park and having been designated a World Biosphere Reserve by UNESCO, Vesuvius currently enjoys substantially greater protection from urban encroachment and other land uses that have ravaged the towns lying at its base. The **park office** (☎ 081/7717549 ⊕ www.parks.it) has mapped out a series of trails open to the public; a popular one includes the Valle del Gigante (Giant's Valley) and the Valle dell'Inferno (Hell's Valley). To reach this, head downhill from the summit parking lot on the north side and look for the footpath descending on the other side of the guardrail at the first bend. Those seeking a barren lunar landscape will be disappointed: the flora here is remarkably diverse, including 23 species of orchid set amid an interesting combination of montane vegetation and Mediterranean maquis. Birders should watch out for peregrine falcons soaring over Monte Somma and for ravens at lower altitudes, in addition to various warbler species that have found their eco-niches on the upper slopes of Vesuvius.

For public transport users, the Vesuvius bus run by **Transporti Vesuviani** (☎ 081/5592582) makes about five trips a day (one-way from Pompeii, €3; from Herculaneum (Ercolano), €1.70). It starts from Piazza Anfiteatro in modern Pompei (which is spelled with one "i" in Italian), stops at Piazza Esedra near the *autostrada* (highway) toll booths, does another pickup at the Ercolano station, snakes its way up the mountain to the foot of the long-defunct *seggiovia* (chairlift) and the aborted *funicolare* (cable car) of the 1980s, and then after a brief stop heads farther uphill to Quota 1000, the car park near the top (let the driver know if you want to visit the museum located halfway up). This is the end of the road for all but service vehicles that go up to the crater, and the best place to reward yourself with a drink after the ascent; take a seat outside the caffè, weather permitting (unlike much of Italy, it's the same price whether you're sitting or standing). For those driving up, the road is sometimes confusingly marked, but as a general rule look for the brown PARCO NAZIONALE DEL VESUVIO signs from the Herculaneum (Ercolano) or Torre del Greco autostrada exits and keep heading upward for about 20 minutes. (For taxi rides up Vesuvius from Torre del Greco or Pompeii, expect to pay about €80 round-trip.)

The road is not much better than in the days of Lord and Lady Hamilton, but it's certainly more littered with garbage. When you get to the parking lot at the top, for extra security opt to pay the €2.50 parking charge. The parking lot and bus terminal at Quota 1000 lie roughly 30 minutes' walk (about a 400-ft climb) from the nearest viewing point down into the crater. You will be handed a sturdy walking stick on leaving the parking lot (a small tip is appreciated on your return). The path is kept in good repair, but wear nonskid shoes (not sandals) and come prepared for strong winds. You have to pay a fee near the crater of €6 (open from 9 to two hours before sunset), which covers the cost of a compulsory but somewhat elusive guide service. Once you've seen the fumaroles and gazed down as much as 600 ft into the wondrous depths of the crater, take in the broad sweep around the Bay of Naples—though you'll probably find the city of Naples more photogenic from lower down the slopes, near the observatory. As you walk up the volcano path, you cannot look too long or unwarily at the splendid views without worrying about your feet—there are some spots where a little chain fence is all that prevents you from taking a steep fall. Near the top is the ticket seller's booth and postcard stands. In the old days, postcards at this lofty outpost cost twice as much as the ones found at the car park at the foot of the mountain, but today that charming scheme has been abandoned.

Torre del Greco

❹ *16 km (10 mi) southeast of Naples, 11 km (7 mi) northwest of Pompeii.*

Being in an area of high volcanic risk, Torre del Greco has borne the brunt of Vesuvian eruptions over the centuries. The demolition of the historic center begun by Vesuvius was almost completed by the time of the postwar building boom; with more than 100,000 inhabitants, Torre del Greco is now close behind its neighbor Portici as one of the most densely populated towns in the world. However, some architectural jewels have survived—including the 18th-century Vesuvian villa Palazzo Vallelonga, on Via Vittorio Emanuele—and the **Museo dei Coralli** on Piazza Palomba. As it turns out, this museum is sited on the first floor of an art school and is only opened as and when the hard-pressed teaching staff gets time off between lessons. No admission is charged and the times more or less coincide with classes (usually from 8:30 to 1 PM), but there are no permanent staff attached to the museum, so it is all on a very informal, ad hoc basis. In any event, the exhibits reveal why the Torresi (the townspeople) are still considered the world's best fashioners of coral and cameos. Torre del Greco is a good base camp for exploring the Vesuvian area, with well-paved, clearly signposted roads north of the Torre del Greco autostrada exit.

Where to Stay & Eat

★ **$$–$$$** ✕ **La Mammola.** A secluded restaurant on the grounds of the Hotel Marad, La Mammola has departed imaginatively from the standard platters found around the Bay of Naples. It has succeeded in achieving a touch of stylishness without succumbing to pretension. Ask for a sample of its seafood *primi piatti* (first courses), including pasta with rockfish *paccheri con ragù di scorfano*, served with pumpkin or peppers. Wash it down with either Falanghina or Greco di Tufo, both a blend of ancient grape varieties—Biancolella and Forastera—that Tiberius and Nero might have enjoyed. Reservations are essential for Saturday evening. ⊠ *Via Benedetto Croce 20* ☎ *081/8825664* ▭ *AE, DC, MC, V* ⊘ *Closed Mon. No dinner Sun.*

$$ ▦ **Hotel Marad.** Dominated by huge spreading umbrella pines and conveniently close to the Torre del Greco exit of the Naples–Salerno A3 Autostrada, the Marad bristles with efficiency and is an obvious base for exploring the area around Vesuvius and Herculaneum. Booking in advance makes good sense, as the hotel doubles as a conference center. At the lower end of the price range, the hotel offers four-star facilities at three-star prices, and a choice of two excellent restaurants. If you are without a car, you'll appreciate the pickup service from the nearest Circumvesuviana station. ⊠ *Via Benedetto Croce 20, 80059* ☎ *081/8492168* 🖷 *081/8828794* ⊕ *www.marad.it* ⇱ *74 rooms* ⌂ *2 restaurants, minibars, pool* ▭ *AE, DC, MC, V* ⦿ *BP.*

Oplontis (Torre Annunziata)

❺ *20 km (12 mi) southeast of Naples, 5 km (3 mi) west of Pompeii.*

Fodor'sChoice
★

Surrounded by the fairly drab urban landscape of Torre Annunziata, thrown up in the 1960s, Oplontis justifies its reputation as one of the more mysterious archaeological sites to be unearthed in the 20th century. The villa complex has been imaginatively ascribed—from a mere inscription on an amphora—to Nero's second wife, Poppaea Sabina, whose family was well known among the landed gentry of neighboring Pompeii. As Roman villas go, Poppaea's Villa, or Villa A, as it's called more prosaically by archaeologists, is way off the top end of the scale. What has so far been excavated covers more than 7,000 square meters (75,000 square ft), and because the site is bound by a road to the west and a canal to the south, we are unlikely to ever gauge its full extent. Complete with porticoes, a large peristyle, *piscina* (pool), baths, and extensive gardens, besides the standard atria, triclinia, and a warren of cubicula, the villa is thought by some to have been a training school for young philosophers and orators. Certainly, for those overwhelmed by the throngs at Pompeii, a modern-day visit to the site of Oplontis offers a chance for contemplation and intellectual stimulation.

Access is easiest from the Circumvesuviana station of Torre Annunziata (about 600 ft away). Outside the station turn left and then right downhill, and the site is just after the crossroads down on the left. If coming by car, take the Torre Annunziata turnoff from the Naples–Salerno autostrada, turn right, and then look for signs on the left for Oplontis at the first major crossroads. Try to negotiate a parking space in the site car park, especially if your car is laden with luggage. The main entrance to the site is from the north—you basically go into the villa through the gardens, with the atrium on the southern side lying under about 16 ft of pumice and pyroclastic material from Vesuvius.

Oplontis offers the full gamut of Roman wall paintings, with its occupants showing a particular penchant for the illusionist motifs of the so-called Second Pompeian Style. There are some good examples in the west wing of the villa, especially in the triclinium (Room 14—look for the room numbers above the doors) giving onto the small portico (Room 13), which abuts the west end of the site and the road above. Although the stucco work in the thermae, or baths, is less impressive than in Pompeii and Herculaneum, the calidarium (Room 8) has a delightful miniature landscape scene surmounted by a peacock in a niche at its eastern end, above a more visible fresco of Hercules in the Garden of the Hesperides. Nearby, in the tepidarium (Room 18) there's an interesting glimpse into the structural design of Roman baths; here the floor is raised by *suspensurae*, small brick supporting pilasters, enabling warm air to pass beneath.

Such initial opulence sets the scene for the rest of the site. Although there are exceptions to the rule—for example, from their relatively small size and less elaborate frescoes, the cubicula, or bedrooms, are perhaps conspicuous by their simplicity—a visit to the eastern wing confirms the earlier impression. The warren of rooms gives way to much larger spaces, featuring long corridors, peristyles fit for large gaggles of stoics, and a large swimming pool, with its complement of porticoes and terraces, at the eastern end. Note that Oplontis is now back in use as a theater venue between June and September, with productions usually featuring ancient Greek and Latin playwrights (in Italian); tickets can be bought at the Proloco in Torre Annunziata (close to the Oplontis site). ✉ *Via Sepolcri 1, Torre Annunziata* ☎ *081/8621755* 💶 *€5 for Oplontis, Stabia and Boscoreale; €18 for the "biglietto cumulativo" pass to 5 sites (Pompeii, Herculaneum, Boscoreale, Oplontis, and Stabiae) valid for 3 days* ⊙ *Nov.–Mar., daily 8:30–5, ticket office closes at 3:30; Apr.–Oct., daily 8:30–7:30, ticket office closes at 6.*

POMPEII: CITY OF VESUVIUS

Mention Pompeii and most travelers will think of ancient Roman villas, prancing bronze fauns, writhing plaster casts of Vesuvius's victims, and the fabled days of the Caesars. Mention Pompeii to many southern Italians, however, and they will immediately think of Pompeii, home to the Santuario della Madonna, the 19th-century basilica in the center of the town of Pompei (to use the modern-day Italian spelling, not the ancient Latin), with the archaeological ruins taking second place. Although millions of culture seekers worldwide head for ancient Pompeii every year, the same number of Italian pilgrims converge on Pompei's basilica as a token of faith—joining processions, making *ex-voto* offerings, or just honoring a vow. Wealthy Neapolitans come to make their donations to help the Church carry out its good deeds. New-car owners come to get their vehicles blessed—and given driving standards in these parts of the world, insurance coverage from on high is probably a sensible move.

Caught between the hammer and anvil of cultural and religious tourism, the modern town of Pompei has shaken off its rather complacent approach and is now endeavoring to polish up its act. In attempts to ease congestion and improve quality at street level, parts of the town have been pedestrianized and parking restrictions tightened. Departing from the rather sleazy reputation of previous years, several hotels have filled the sizable niche in the market for quality deals at affordable prices. As for recommendable restaurants, if you deviate from the archaeological site and make for the center of town, you will be spoiled for choice. Unlike many archaeological sites in the Mediterranean region, those around Naples are almost all well served by public transport. Pompei has three railway stations, and it's a short hop from here to the impressive villa of Oplontis, in Torre Annunziata.

Pompeii

★ *24 km (15 mi) southeast of Naples, 11 km (7 mi) southeast of Herculaneum.*

▶ ★ **6–26** Tomb of a civilization, petrified memorial to Vesuvius's eruption on the morn of August 23, AD 79, the **Scavi di Pompei** is probably the most famous system of excavations anywhere. It's certainly the most accessible and one of the largest. Today Pompeii is choked with both the dust of 25 centuries *and* more than 2 million visitors every year; only by escaping the hordes and lingering along its silent streets can you truly fall under the site's spell. On a quiet backstreet, all you need is a little imagination to sense the shadows palpably filling the dark corners, to hear the ancient pipe's falsetto and the tinny clash of cymbals, to envision a rain of rose petals gently covering a Roman senator's dinner guests. Come in the late afternoon when the site is nearly deserted and you will understand that the true pleasure of Pompeii is not in the seeing but in the feeling.

Ancient Pompeii was much larger than Herculaneum; a busy commercial center with a population of 10,000–20,000, it covered about 160 acres on the seaward end of the fertile Sarno Plain. In 80 BC the general Sulla turned Pompeii into a Roman colony, a place where wealthy patricians could escape the turmoil of city life. The town was laid out in a grid pattern, with two main intersecting streets. The wealthiest took whole blocks for themselves; those less well endowed built a house and rented out the front rooms, those facing the street, to shopkeepers. The facades of these houses were relatively plain and seldom hinted at the care and attention lavished on the private rooms within. An arriving visitor entered through a narrow corridor giving onto an open atrium, in the rear of which was a reception room. Behind this was another open area, called the peristyle, with rows of columns and perhaps a garden with a fountain. Only close friends ever saw this private part of the house, which was surrounded by the family's bedrooms and a dining area.

Pompeian houses were designed around an inner garden so that families could turn their backs on the outside world. Today we install picture windows that break down visual barriers between ourselves and our neighbors; the people in these Roman towns had few windows, preferring to get their light from the central courtyard—the light within. How pleasant it must have been to come home from the Forum or from the baths to your own secluded holding, with no visual reminders of a life outside your own preserve. Not that public life was so intolerable. There were wineshops on almost every corner, and frequent shows were given at the Amphitheater. The public fountains and toilets were connected to huge cisterns by lead pipes beneath the sidewalks. Since garbage and rainwater collected in the streets of Pompeii, the sidewalks were raised, and huge stepping stones were placed at crossings so pedes-

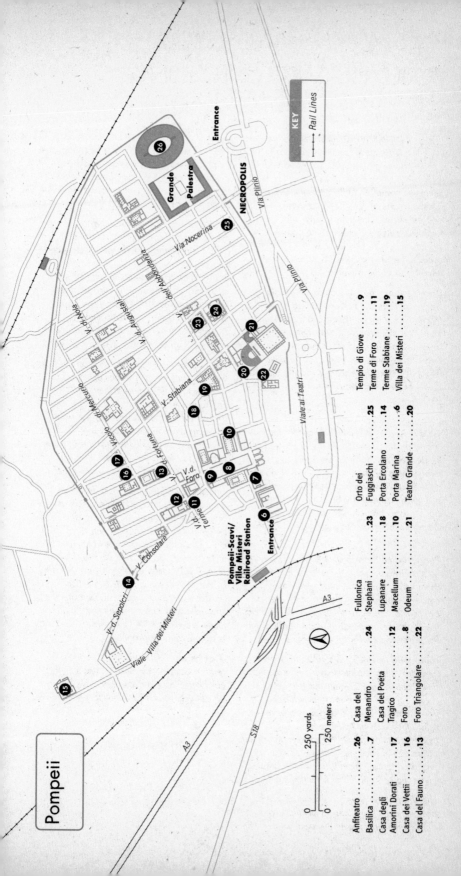

Pompeii

KEY
→ *Rail Lines*

Entrance

NECROPOLIS

Via Plinio

Grande Palestra

Via Nocerina

Via dell'Abbondanza

Via Stabiana

V. d. Nola

V. d. Augustali

di Mercurio

Vicolo di Fortuna

V. d. Foro

V. d. Terme

V. Consolare

V. d. Sepolcri

Viale Villa dei Misteri

Pompeii-Scavi/ Villa Misteri Railroad Station

Entrance

Viale ai Teatri

A3

S18

A3

250 yards
250 meters

Anfiteatro **26**
Basilica **7**
Casa degli Amorini Dorati **17**
Casa dei Vettii **16**
Casa del Fauno **13**
Casa del Menandro **24**
Casa del Poeta Tragico **12**
Foro **8**
Foro Triangolare **22**

Fullonica Stephani **23**
Lupanare **18**
Macellum **10**
Odeum **21**
Orto dei Fuggiaschi **25**
Porta Ercolano **14**
Porta Marina **6**
Teatro Grande **20**

Tempio di Giove **9**
Terme di Foro **11**
Terme Stabiane **19**
Villa dei Misteri **15**

BURIED PLEASURE: UNLOCKING THE VILLA OF THE MYSTERIES

A **FUNNY THING HAPPENS** on the way to the forum as you walk through Pompeii. Covered with dust and decay as it is, the city seems to come alive. Perhaps it's the familiar signs of life observed along the ancient streets: the beer shops with tumblers' rings still fresh in the counter, the stanchion where horses were tethered outside the taverna, the tracks of chariot wheels cut in the pavement.

Coming upon the thermopolium (drinking bar), you imagine natives calling out, "One for the road." But a glance up at Vesuvius, still brooding over the scene like an enormous headstone, reminds you that these folks—whether imagined in your head or actually wearing a mantle of lava dust—have not taken a breath for centuries.

In its day, Pompeii was celebrated as the Côte d'Azur, the seaside Brighton, the Fire Island of the ancient Roman empire. Evidence of a Sybaritic bent is everywhere. In the town's grandest villas as well as rowdiest lupanaria (brothels), murals still reveal a worship of hedonism. Satyrs, bacchantes, hermaphrodites, and acrobatic couples are pictured indulging in hanky-panky.

People came here to do the things Greeks had a word for, and there is no more astounding, magnificently memorable evidence than the world-famous frescoes on view at the Villa dei Misteri, or Villa of the Mysteries, a palatial abode built at the far northwestern fringe of Pompeii.

Unearthed in 1909, this villa had more than 60 rooms painted with frescoes; the finest are in the triclinium, or banquet room. Painted in the most glowing Pompeian reds and oranges, the panels relate the saga of Ariadne, a young bride, and her initiation into the sacred mysteries of the cult of Dionysus, who was a god imported to Italy from Greece and then given the Latin name of Bacchus.

The Villa of the Mysteries frescoes were painted circa 50 BC, most art historians believe, and represent the peak of the Second Style of Pompeian wall painting. The triclinium frescoes are thought to have been painted by a local artist, although the theme may well have been copied from an earlier cycle of paintings from the Hellenistic period.

In all there are 10 scenes, beginning with the reading of the ritual by a child (Dionysus, perhaps) assisted by a seated matron, followed by a servant pouring libations to carry out some type of sacrificial ceremony. The third picture (on the left-hand wall), depicting a silenus (troll) with his musical instrument, is somehow connected with the fourth, which shows a frightened woman.

The slightly damaged frescoes on the front wall depict Dionysus (recognized by his staff, or thyrsus) slumped over an enthroned Ariadne, flanked by a silenus and satyrs on the left and, on the right, a kneeling woman (perhaps a bacchante) unveiling a phallus with a winged figure wielding a flagellum (sacred whip) standing over her.

The south wall (on the right) depicts a woman being flogged while a naked bacchante (perhaps the same girl) does a twirl—but is the woman being flogged or does she simply want to veil her eyes from the phallus? The last two scenes show a seated woman, possibly preparing for a bridal ceremony, while the last also portrays a mantled woman, perhaps the spouse and priestess of the god, but more likely the wife of the villa owner—her face is an uncanny portrait.

After nearly 2,000 years, historians remain puzzled by many aspects of this celebrated fresco cycle. For now, it may be enough for visitors here to ponder love among the ruins.

trians could keep their feet dry. Herculaneum had even better drainage, with an underground sewer system that led to the sea.

To get the most out of Pompeii, rent an audio guide (€6 for one, €9 for two; you'll need to leave an I.D. card) and opt for one of the three itineraries (2 hours, 4 hours, or 6 hours). If hiring a guide, make sure the guide is registered for an English tour and standing inside the gate; agree beforehand on the length of the tour and the price, and prepare yourself for soundbites of substandard English mixed with dollops of hearsay. For refreshments, the only restaurant inside the site is both overpriced and busy, so it makes sense to bring along water and snacks. If you come so equipped, there are some shady, underused picnic tables outside the Porta di Nola, to the northeast of the site. The archaeological site of Pompeii has its own stop (Pompei–Villa dei Misteri) on the Circumvesuviana line to Sorrento, close to the main entrance at the Porta Marina, which is the best place from which to start a tour. If, like many potential visitors every year, you get the wrong train from Naples (stopping at the other station "Pompei"), all is not lost. There's another entrance to the excavations at the far end of the site, just a seven-minute walk to the Amphitheater. Two buildings within Pompeii—Terme Suburbane (daily, 10–2) and Casa del Menandro (weekends, 2–4)—are open for restricted viewing on a first-come, first-served basis. Ask for a free coupon when you purchase your ticket and you will be assigned a visiting time. For information on reaching the other sites nearby (Boscoreale, Oplontis, and Stabiae), ask about transport and access at the helpful information kiosk at Porta Marina. If you intend to visit both Pompeii and Herculaneum within the space of three days, then you should buy the *biglietto cumulativo* pass, which also includes the above three sites.

The first buildings to the left after you've gone through the ticket turn-stiles are the **Terme Suburbane** (Suburban Baths), built—by all accounts without planning permission—right up against the city walls. Opened to public viewing in 2002 partly to compensate for the closing of other sites for restoration, the baths have eyebrow-raising frescoes in the *apodyterium* (changing room) that strongly suggest more than just bathing and massaging were on offer. The frigidarium next door contains some of the best frescoes on either side of the nymphaeum shrine, which contains a small artificial waterfall with a pool below.

6 Enter the city through **Porta Marina**, so called because it was on the seaward side prior to the eruption in AD 79 (the sea would have been accessible from here via a narrow canal). The layout here is less gridlike than in other parts of town because you're in the oldest section of Pompeii, originally a smallish Oscan or pre-Roman settlement. In Roman times the road up to Porta Marina itself would have been steep and difficult for larger conveyances to negotiate—fortunately there were seven other gates to choose from—although this was by far the quickest way of getting to the hub of civic life, the Forum. In this case there were two passages, the one on the left for pedestrians and the one on the right for animals and light vehicles.

7 Beyond the Porta Marina and past the Temple of Venus is the **Basilica**, the law court and the stock exchange of the town. These oblong buildings ending in a semicircular projection (apse) were the model for early Christian churches, which had a nave (central aisle) and two side aisles separated by rows of columns. Standing in the Basilica, you can recognize the continuity between Roman and Christian styles of architecture, though here, instead of a sacral area being placed at the end, there was the tribunal.

❽ The Basilica opens onto the **Foro** (Forum), with which it shares some elements of its design: a large rectangular area with a colonnade surmounted by a loggia, running along three sides. This served as the political, commercial, and religious center of city life, with the main temples, law courts, and commercial and government buildings grouped around it. It was here that elections were held and speeches and official announcements made. In AD 79 the Forum would have been adorned with statues of the great and the good, many of them probably in equestrian form, as testified by some larger bases left on the south side. One of the bases is wider and more massive than the others, indicating that it may have been the *suggestum,* or orator's rostrum.

❾ At the far (northern) end of the Forum is the **Tempio di Giove** (Temple of Jupiter), sacred to the Capitoline triad of Jupiter, Juno, and Minerva, with the brewing cone of Vesuvius behind. Little more than the base of this 2nd-century BC temple has been preserved. Like many buildings in Pompeii, it was severely damaged in an earthquake in AD 62 and was still in a ruined state at the time of the eruption in AD 79.

❿ On the eastern side of the Forum, fronted by an elegant three-column portico, is the **Macellum,** the covered meat and fish market dating to Augustan times. Like the ancient Greek *agora* in Athens, the Forum was a busy shopping area, complete with public officials to apply proper standards of weights and measures.

⓫ The **Terme di Foro** (Forum Baths), on Via delle Terme, are smaller than the Terme Stabiane but have more delicate decoration. The tepidarium and calidarium in the men's section are extremely well preserved and provide a useful insight into heating systems. The tepidarium was warmed by a brazier while beneath the calidarium were brick pillars, or *suspensurae,* which together with hollow walls, ensured the passage of hot air. Note the inscription in bronze letters around the great *labrum* (fountain) recording the names of the officials who installed the labrum, as well as its cost (5,420 sesterces) in the years AD 3–4.

⓬ The **Casa del Poeta Tragico** (House of the Tragic Poet), opposite the Forum Baths, is a typical middle-class house from the last days of Pompeii. On the floor is a mosaic of a chained dog and the inscription CAVE CANEM ("Beware of the dog"). The house owes its name and fame to a mosaic found in the tablinum representing a *choregos,* or theatrical sponsor, along with, on the walls of the atrium and peristyle, a superb series of pictures, now in the Museo Archeologico in Naples, of mythological subjects like the Sacrifice of Iphigenia.

The **Thermopolium Caupona** was one of about 90 shops selling hot food and drinks. The structure of this one is fairly typical of those found in Pompeii: easy access from the street, a counter in masonry with built-in *dolia* (earthenware storage jars) sunk into it, and rudimentary back rooms so that customers could sit and consume on the premises. A famed delicacy was *garum,* made from marinated fish innards (or anchovies, if you were lucky).

⓭ The renowned **Casa del Fauno** (House of the Faun) gets its name from the small bronze statue in the middle of its spacious impluvium. The original—this is the case for many of the best works of art unearthed in Pompeii—is housed in the Museo Archeologico Nazionale in Naples. This is both one of the earliest and the most sumptuous private dwellings in Pompeii. The front part of the house is arranged around two atria, behind which is the peristyle with a portico of 28 Ionic columns. On its discovery in 1830, particular attention was focused on the fine mosaic, done in tiny tesserae depicting the Battle of Issus fought between Alexander the Great and the Persian emperor Darius III in 330 BC. This masterwork—again, on display in the Museo Archeologico Nazionale in Naples—was found in the *exedra* (discussion room) fronted by stuccoed columns immediately behind the first peristyle. The exedra was flanked by two *triclinia* (dining rooms) giving onto a megaperistyle at the back.

⓮ The beautiful **Porta Ercolano** (Herculaneum Gate) was a main gate that led to Herculaneum and Neapolis. The gate has three archways—the central one for wheeled conveyances and the two side openings for pedestrians. It is thought to have been constructed without a defensive strategy in mind. This would imply a fairly late construction date, when the colonization of southern Italy was well consolidated and the native Italic peoples were no longer restless.

One of the most evocative roads in Pompeii, the Via dei Sepolcri, leads out from the Porta Ercolano and is lined with tombs—a favorite spot for painters and photographers of the early 20th century. This road leads to the world-famous **Villa dei Misteri** (Villa of the Mysteries), lying 200 meters (660 ft) outside Pompeii's walls and therefore in theory not part of the ancient town. It contains what some consider the greatest surviving group of paintings from the ancient world, telling the story of a young bride, Ariadne, being initiated into the mysteries of the cult of Dionysus (*see* the Close Up box, "Buried Pleasure: Unlocking the Villa of the Mysteries"). Bacchus, to give Dionysus his Latin name, was the god of wine, fertility, theater, and other forms of racier entertainment. So he was naturally popular in a town so devoted to the pleasures of the flesh. But he also represented the triumph of the irrational—of all those mysterious forces that no official state religion could fully suppress. The cult of Dionysus, like the cult of the Cumaean Sibyl, gave people a sense of control over fate, and in its focus on the Other World helped pave the way for Christianity.

Fodor's Choice
★

With its background panels spectacularly painted in Pompeiian red (in fact, made from cinnabar, the most expensive pigment of the time), the great fresco cycle is found in the triclinium, the villa's banquet hall. This is the room where Dionysiac rites may have been "celebrated" before they were consummated in the adjoining bedrooms. Scholars are divided on the sequential order of the frescoed scenes: some believe it is one story unfolding from left to right, while others see the painted figures interacting across the room with the optimal vantage point being in the dead center of the salon. But all agree the scenes build to a climax on the back wall, where Dionysus and Ariadne preside over the unveiling of the phallus found within the "sacred basket." At this crucial moment, an initiate bares her back to be flagellated; the following scene reputedly shows the same girl at one with the mysteries as she blissfully executes a celebratory dance. The figure nearest the spectactor on the left wall is a stolid, luxuriantly garbed matron with a questioning face and now believed to be the *domina,* the female head of the household of the Villa of the Mysteries (which, incidentally, is only partly excavated). Unfortunately, while top scholars in classical art have come up with more than 20 theories explaining what is depicted in this fresco cycle, no consensus has been reached. The frescoes at the Misteri remain a mystery, in part due to the fact that after 3,000 years no written account has ever surfaced describing the exact nature of the Dionysiac Mysteries themselves.

⓰ The **Casa dei Vettii** (House of the Vettii) is the best example of a house owned by wealthy *mercatores* (merchants). Closed for restoration at the time of writing, it contains vivid murals—a magnificent *pinacoteca* (picture gallery) within the very heart of Pompeii. The scenes here—except for those in the two wings off the atrium—were all painted after the earthquake of AD 62. Within this visual feast, cast an admiring glance at the delicate frieze around the wall of the triclinium (on the right of the peristyle garden as you enter from the atrium), depicting cupids engaged in various activities, such as selling oils and perfumes, working as goldsmiths and metalworkers, acting as wine merchants, or performing in chariot races. This is definitely the place to refresh your memory of Greek mythology. In another *oecus* (room) facing onto the peristyle (in the right-hand corner) are other masterpieces of the Fourth Style of Pompeian painting, including one scene showing Pasiphaë, Minos's wife, as a wooden cow, a disguise that would enable her to consummate her divine-inflicted passion for a bull. Opposite this scene is the omnipresent Dionysus surprising Ariadne while asleep, and on the end wall is Ixion bound to a wheel by Hephaestus with Hera standing by disdainfully—a torture devised by Zeus to punish Ixion for having dared to seek the love of Hera, Zeus's wife. Given Zeus's amply testified philandering, Ixion could have been forgiven for thinking the coast was clear.

Another room close to the exit (such is the throng of visitors here that a one-way traffic system has been introduced) depicts the baby Hercules strangling snakes sent by Hera, while the opposite wall shows the punishment inflicted on Dirce—she was bound to the horns of a bull and dragged to death—in return for enslaving and maltreating Antiope, daughter of a Boeotian river-god. On the far wall is Pentheus, King of Thebes, prior to dismemberment by a group of Maenads for having opposed the introduction of the cult of Dionysus. Not everyone's choice of sitting-room decor perhaps: but then the Vettii brothers were unlikely to be considered arbiters of fine taste amongst the area's old-style patricians. Another of the main attractions in the Casa dei Vettii is the small cubicle beyond the kitchen area (to the right of the atrium) with its faded erotic frescoes now protected by Perspex screens.

⓱ The **Casa degli Amorini Dorati** (House of the Gilded Cupids) is an elegant, well-preserved home with original marble decorations in the garden. The house may well have belonged to the Poppaei family, better known for their family connections with Nero, who married the notorious Poppaea the second time around. Its pictorial decorations express elegant and refined theatrical tastes dating to Nero's time (AD 54–AD 69). The house is named after the cupids engraved in gold leaf that adorn one of the *cubicula* (bedrooms). Stroll around the peristyle in the garden, which would have been adorned with sculptures, marble tables, and a pool.

⓲ On the walls of the well-preserved **lupanare** (brothel) are scenes of erotic pastimes in which clients could engage. Several of the rooms were on the upper floor, served by an independent staircase, suggesting separate facilities for customers who wanted to keep a lower profile. At ground level, small painted panels above the entrances illustrated the specialty offered by each *meretrix* (courtesan).

⓳ The **Terme Stabiane** (Stabian Baths) were heated by underground furnaces whose warmth circulated among the stone pillars supporting the floor, rose through flues in the walls, and escaped through chimneys. The water temperature could be set for cold, lukewarm, or hot. Bathers took a lukewarm bath to prepare themselves for the hot room. A tepid bath came next and then a plunge into cold water to tone up the skin. A vigorous massage with oil might be followed by rest, reading, horseplay, or conversation. The Stabian Baths are the most complete in Pompeii and among the oldest baths from Roman times. This was the basic pattern used for the grand imperial baths of antiquity, such as the Baths of Caracalla in Rome, although the latter were built to a massive scale. Like the

Forum Baths, these had a palaestra, or porticoed area (note the fine stucco work on the palaestra walls), where athletes could train, play a *sphaeristerium* (ball game), and then remove dirt and oils from their bodies with a strigil before cooling off in the frigidarium. Most of the Stabian Baths complex is roped off, and access is currently limited to the men's entrance hall, *apodyterium* (changing room), and palaestra from the entrance on Via dell'Abbondanza. To compensate, there are two cases with plaster casts of bodies in their original agony throes, found nearby during excavations in the 19th century. It was Giuseppe Fiorelli, appointed Professor of Archaeology after Italy's unification in 1860, who invented the ingenious method of pumping liquid plaster into cavities left by the decayed bodies within the hardened deposits of volcanic ash and pumice.

20 Not far from the Stabian Baths was the theater area on the southern side of town. The **Teatro Grande** (large theater), originally dating from the 2nd century BC but subsequently restored, had a seating capacity of about 5,000. It was designed to fit into the natural slope of the hill, so that spectacles would be performed against a backdrop of the *Mons Lactarius* (Lattari Mountains). Little remains of the original *cavea* (seating area) except for some of the lower tiers, some of the *media cavea* halfway up, and the framework of the *summa cavea* (top gallery). Behind the theater lie the gladiators' barracks, though this porticoed area is thought to have also served as a space for the audience to unwind between plays. Of course, with the advent of racier entertainment down in the Amphitheater, this large theater lost much of its pull.

21 Adjacent to the Teatro Grande is the **Odeum,** also called Teatrum Tectum (Covered Theater). Built between 80 BC and 75 BC and with a seating capacity of 1,000, the Odeum is a gem of theatrical architecture and was far less heavily restored in antiquity than its predecessor next door. The semicircular cavea was truncated and transformed into an almost square-shape design to facilitate the building of a roof. With theatrical performances often held on hot summer days, ancient Pompeians would have welcomed the shade provided.

22 Some of the oldest structures in Pompeii are to be found in the **Foro Triangolare** (Triangular Forum), west of the theater complex. In the middle of the Forum are the remains—just a few column capitals in Doric style—of a temple dating as far back as the 6th century BC, originally dedicated to Hercules, the founder of the city. This is one of the quietest areas of the archaeological site, and the ample shade afforded by trees here makes it a good spot to pause and muse on what you've seen.

The main street running most of the way from the Forum to the Amphitheater was the bustling **Via dell'Abbondanza** (the name was made up by archaeologists). Shops were by no means restricted to the Forum area, and many were located along this thoroughfare. Shops can easily be distinguished from private houses by their much broader fronts (6–10 ft wide) with wooden shutters for nighttime security. Private houses had narrower—almost poky—entrances, thereby reducing exposure at street level to an absolute minimum. As you go along Via dell'Abbondanza away from the Forum, two blocks beyond the Stabian Baths you'll notice on the left the current digs at the Casa dei Casti Amanti (House of the Chaste Lovers), screened off behind unsightly corrugated-iron fencing. A team of plasterers and painters were at work here when Vesuvius erupted, redecorating one of the rooms and patching up the cracks in the bread oven near the entrance—caused by earth tremors a matter of days before. Thanks to modern archaeological techniques and the assistance of many scientific disciplines, the site has provided a mine of information and is expected to be opened shortly to public viewing.

㉓ Togas, the required Roman attire, were washed at **Fullonica Stephani**. The cloth was dunked into a tub full of water and chalk, then stomped upon like so many grapes. Once clean, the material was stretched across a wicker cage and exposed to sulfur fumes. The fuller (cleaner) carded it with a long brush, then placed it under a press. The harder the pressing, the whiter and brighter it became. When excavated in 1911, the entrance to the fuller's premises was still shuttered and locked. Behind was a body clutching a bagful of sesterces. Could these have been the last takings of the *fullonica*? Or had a passerby, carrying his worldly wealth, stopped inside and sought refuge behind the door from the hail of lapilli outside?

㉔ Many paintings and mosaics were executed at the **Casa del Menandro** (House of Menander), a patrician's villa. The Greek comic poet Menander is depicted in a rectangular niche on the far wall in the peristyle, although you need go no farther than the atrium to see three scenes from the Trojan War in a small exedra to the left: the death of Laocoön and his sons (right); Cassandra trying to dissuade the Trojans from making the fatal mistake of bringing the wooden horse into Troy; and (left) one of the Greek heroes with Helen. This impressive residence also had a small complex of private baths, just next to the kitchen to the right of the peristyle. The siting of the baths next to the kitchen quarters was common practice in many of the larger villas, enabling heat from cooking to be exploited for warming the calidarium. The Casa del Menandro is open only on weekends from 2 to 4.

㉕ The **Orto dei Fuggiaschi** (Garden of the Fugitives), close to the Nocera gate, contains the lifelike casts of a group of victims overwhelmed by the AD 79 eruption and left in situ. Huddled together close to the wall at the bottom of the garden, the group was overwhelmed a day after the initial eruption not by the rain of lapilli and ash but by the first surge— a dense cloud of vapor, ash, and other solids that swept down the slopes of the volcano like a boiling avalanche at 40–50 mi per hour.

★ **㉖** The **Anfiteatro** (Amphitheater) was the ultimate in entertainment for local Pompeians and offered a gamut of experiences, but essentially this was for gladiators rather than wild animals. Unlike the amphitheater at Pozzuoli, there are no underground *cellae* for the penning of animals and, besides, *venationes* (battles with wild animals) only really became popular later on. With the large palaestra close by and the gladiatorial barracks near the theater area, there were extensive facilities to train gladiators in many types of combat. Teams worked for impresarios, who hired them out to wealthy citizens, many of whom were running for office and hoping that the gory entertainment would buy them some votes. Most gladiators were slaves or prisoners, but a few were men from the far-flung reaches of the empire who enjoyed fighting. When a gladiator found himself at another's mercy, he extended a pleading hand to the president of the games. If the president turned his thumb up, the gladiator lived; if he turned his thumb down, the gladiator's throat was cut. The arena got pretty bloody after a night's entertainment and was sprinkled with red powder to camouflage the carnage. The victorious gladiator got money, or a ribbon symbolizing his exemption from further fights. If he was a slave, he was often set free. If the people of Pompeii had had trading cards, they would have collected portraits of gladiators; everyone had his favorite. Says one piece of graffiti: "Petronius Octavus fought thirty-four fights and then died, but Severus, a freedman, was victor in fifty-five fights and still lived; Nasica celebrates sixty victories."

By Roman standards, Pompeii's Amphitheater was quite small (seating capacity: 20,000). Built in about 80 BC, it was oval and divided into three seating areas, like a theater. There were two main entrances—at the north and south ends—and a narrow passage on the west, called the *Porta Libitinensis,* through which the dead were most probably dragged out. A wall painting found in a house near the theater (now in the Naples Museum) depicts the riot in the Amphitheater in AD 59 when several citizens from the nearby town of Nucera were killed. After Nucerian appeals to Nero, shows in the Amphitheater were suspended for 10 years.

Just behind the Amphitheater is the second entrance to Pompeii (at Villa dei Misteri there is only an exit), with the main town square and its 19th-century basilica a short walk to the east. By the Amphitheater is a poorly signposted **Percorso Extramurario** (Outside the Walls Promenade), a walkway that links the Amphitheater, three of the old city gates, and the Porta Ercolano Necropolis at the northern and eastern sides of the site (within the site fence); the route takes about 30–40 minutes in all. ⊠ *Pompei Scavi, Via Villa dei Misteri 2* ☎ *081/5365154* 🖾 *€10 Pompeii only or the 3-day "biglietto cumulativo" pass for €18 covering 5 sites (Pompeii, Herculaneum, Boscoreale, Oplontis, and Stabiae)* ⊙ *Nov.–Mar., daily 8:30–5, ticket office closes at 3:30; Apr.–Oct., daily 8:30–7:30, ticket office closes at 6.*

Where to Stay & Eat

★ **$$$$** ✕**Il Principe.** This is the closest you'll get to experiencing the tastes of ancient Pompeii, though the wines (fortunately) will be quantum leaps better. At times the food is so artistically presented that it seems boorish to pick up a knife and fork. Try the *pasta vermiculata garo,* otherwise known as spaghetti with *garum pompeianum,* a fish-based sauce consumed widely in Roman times. Round off the meal with the *cassata Oplontis* (a sweet made with ricotta cheese and honey), inspired by a famous still-life fresco found in a triclinium at the site of Oplontis. On rare evenings between September and March, the restaurant offers theme menus devoted to ancient Roman cooking. The decor is luxe, with echoes of Stil Liberty (Italian Art Nouveau) in its style. ⊠ *Piazza B. Longo 8* ☎ *081/8505566* 🖨 *081/8633342* ⊕ *www.ilprincipe.com* 🖃 *AE, DC, V* ⊙ *Closed Sun. dinner, Mon. (except lunch in summer), and 3 wks in Aug.*

★ **$$-$$$** ✕**Ristorante President.** The Gramaglia father-and-son team is well versed in top-level catering and makes sure that customers sigh with satisfaction after every course. For something different, try the *astice ubriacata* (drunken lobster) accompanied by some imaginative side dishes, like *sfoglie di zucca in agrodolce* (sweet-and-sour pumpkin strips). Beautiful presentation, impeccable service, and excellent value for money all add up to a stellar meal. ⊠ *Piazza Schettini 12* ☎ *081/8507245* 🖨 *081/8638147* 🖃 *AE, DC, MC, V* ⊙ *Closed Mon.*

$-$$ ✕**Ristorante Pizzeria Carlo Alberto.** This is a small, efficiently run restaurant with an impressive culinary repertory, comfortably out of the reach of large tour groups. If you're a vegetarian, try pizza *con mozzarella, rucola, e mais* (with mozzarella, arugula, and corn) or just have a plain *focaccetta* instead of bread to accompany your meal. Those who make it through to the *dolce* (desserts) should sample the delicate *grappa del Vesuvio,* made from Lacrima Christi grape varieties. Reservations are essential on weekends. ⊠ *Via Carlo Alberto 15* ☎ *081/8633231* 🖃 *DC, MC, V.*

★ **$** 🏨**Hotel Amleto.** *Appassionati* and connoisseurs of historical styles of furnishings will find this hotel a real treat. Enjoy the Pompeian-type mosaic in the reception room and the mesmerizing House-of-the-Vettii–type scene in the breakfast room before retiring to your quarters, either 19th-century Neapolitan in style or Venetian in taste. Convenient to say the least, this spot is near the archaeological site and close to Pompeii's cathedral. ⊠ *Via B. Longo 10, 80045,* ☎ *081/8631004* 🖨 *081/8635585*

⊕ *www.hotelamleto.it* ⇄ *26 rooms* ⚮ *Internet, meeting room* ☱ *AE, D, MC, V* ⍟❙ *BP.*

¢   ▦ **Casa del Pellegrino.** A safe, convenient base for cash-strapped travelers, this former convent was pleasingly converted into a hostel in 2001. It's a 10-minute walk from the Amphitheater entrance and close to the action in Pompei's main square—yet seemingly miles away from the tourist throngs. Fairly spartan accommodation consists of dormitories (each bed €13) and family rooms (each bed €16). ⊠ *Via Duca D'Aosta 4, 80045* ☎ *081/8508644* ⊕ *www.hostels-aig.org* ⇄ *12 rooms with shared bath* ⚮ *No a/c, no room phones, no room TVs* ☱ *No credit cards* ⍟❙ *EP.*

Nightlife & the Arts

A *son-et-lumière*, sound-and-light-show extravaganza, **"Pompeii by Night"** was introduced in 2002 as a way to tour the ancient city at night. Groups of up to 80 are taken through a multimedia reconstruction of life in ancient Pompeii, culminating in something like a Sensurround experience in the Basilica (recordings of galloping horses, clanging swords, etc.). Though no substitute for a thorough visit—you only see a small fraction of the site—the show gives you privileged nighttime access and an atmospheric immersion, replete with extravagantly colored spotlights, into the sights and sounds of the ancient city (€24; daily at 9:30 in English, 10:20 and 11:10 in Italian). You can advance book tickets on the web site. Note that the nearby site of Oplontis (in Torre Annunziata) is now the venue for summer plays. (☎ 081/8575347; 081/5365154 ⊕ www.arethusa.net)

WEST OF NAPLES: THE PHLEGREAN FIELDS

Extinct volcanoes, steaming fumaroles, natural spasms, and immortal names, all steeped in millennia of history, are the basic ingredients of the Campi Flegrei, or Phlegrean Fields (from the ancient Greek word *phlegraios,* or burning). Pompeii and Herculaneum, to the east of Naples, may be the most celebrated archaeological sites in Campania, but back in the days of the Caesars they were simple middle-class towns compared to the patrician settlements to the west of Naples. Here, at Baiae, famed figures like Cicero, Julius Caesar, Nero, and Hadrian built sumptuous leisure villas (*villae otiorum*) and ports for their gigantic pleasure barges; here St. Paul arrived at Pozzuoli on board an Alexandrian ship; here the powerful came to consult the oracles of the Cumaean Sibyl; and here Virgil visited Lago d'Averno—the legendary entrance to the underworld—to immortalize it in his *Aeneid.* Although several villas have now sunk beneath the sea, there are many archaeological sights still extant: the Flavian Amphitheater, which, if not as imposing above ground as the Colosseum at Rome, is far better preserved in the galleries and cages below the arena in which wild beasts, gladiators, and stage props were kept in readiness; the ancient commercial area of Pozzuoli now known as Rione Terra, which was opened to the public in 2002; the ruins of the Sibyl's cave in Cumae; and the ancient baths of Baia. To such archaeological riches, add a pinch of local hospitality and an essence of gastronomy, and you'll soon see why the area holds so much fascination for the present-day traveler.

The Solfatara

㉗   *8 km (5 mi) west of Naples, 2 km (1 mi) east of Pozzuoli.*

★   Here at the sunken volcanic crater Solfatara you can experience firsthand the otherworldly terrain of the Campi Flegrei. The only eruption of this semiextinct volcano was in 1198, though according to one legend, every crater in the area is one of the mouths of a 100-headed dragon named Typhon that Zeus hurled into the crater of Epomeo on the island of Ischia. According to another, the sulfurous springs of the Solfatara are poisonous discharges from wounds the Titans received in their war with Zeus. Both legends, of course, are attempts to dramatize man's struggle to overcome the mysterious and dangerous forces of nature. Appropriately, the crater was given the name of *Forum Vulcani* by the ancient Romans, who thought it the residence of the god Vulcan. The Solfatara has been a powerful magnet for travelers over the past 300 years. No self-respecting 18th-century aristocrat taking the Grand Tour would have returned to northern Europe without visiting the site, which has always been much more accessible from the center of Naples than the better-known Vesuvius on the other side of the city.

The Solfatara lies on two bus routes out of Naples (152, M1), with stops just outside the main entrance, and is a 15-minute walk uphill (1 km [½ mi]) from the Metropolitana station of Pozzuoli. By car take the Tangenziale (bypass) from Naples toward Pozzuoli, getting off at the Agnano, Exit 11, about 4 km (2½ mi) away from the crater. Then follow signs to Pozzuoli and look for the VULCANO SOLFATARA sign when beginning the descent into Pozzuoli. Enter the Solfatara through the arch of the turn-of-the-20th-century, long-defunct baths complex (parking facilities and ticket office inside). You approach the volcanically active area down an avenue of holm oak trees, with the attractive Solfatara campsite making full use of all available shade on either side. Complete with year-round bar and **seasonal restaurant** (☎ 081/5268144 or 081/5262341), open April–October, providing honest fare to campers and other visitors, this must be one of the best-appointed volcanic craters in the world. After you have cleared the refreshment area, emerge from the vegetation into a light clay expanse that in bright sunlight makes you reach instinctively for your sunglasses. Helpful information panels about the surrounding vegetation and the volcanic action at the core of the crater will steer you past the century-old brick *stufe* (ovens) resembling a Roman *sudatorium* (sauna), where you can be parboiled in a matter of seconds. The sulfur fumes were supposed to cure those afflicted with diseases of the respiratory tract, the skin, and the joints. While musing on advances in modern medicine, move on to the fenced-off area of the fumaroles, known as the *Bocca Grande*, where steam whooshes out at about 160°C. Continuing the circuit, note the *fangaia*, or mud baths, whose mineral-rich mud is highly prized for medicinal purposes. The dark veining on the mud surface consists of bacteria that are super-resistant to high acidity and temperature. The walk continues past a 19th-century well that was sunk to tap mineral water from an underlying aquifer 30 ft below and which was in active use until the 1920s. ⊠ *Via Solfatara 161, Pozzuoli* ☎ *081/5262341* ⊕ *www.solfatara.it* ☜ *€5* ☉ *Daily 8:30–1 hr before sunset.*

Where to Stay & Eat

$–$$ ✕**Taverna Viola.** A three-minute walk down the road from the Solfatara, this rustic-style restaurant–pizzeria has a pleasing view over the Bay of Pozzuoli and the added attraction of serving pizzas at lunchtime. This is the place to deviate from a pizza Margherita and have one *con prosciutto e rughetta* (with ham and arugula) or even branch out into a fish-based dish, depending on the season. ⊠ *Via Solfatara 76, Pozzuoli* ☎ *081/5269953* ▬ *MC, V.*

$$ ▦ **Hotel Solfatara.** A clean, functional hotel built in 1983 and constantly refurbished, this is handily located just outside the Solfatara entrance. For extra peace and quiet, ask for a room at the back (no view). ⊠ *Via*

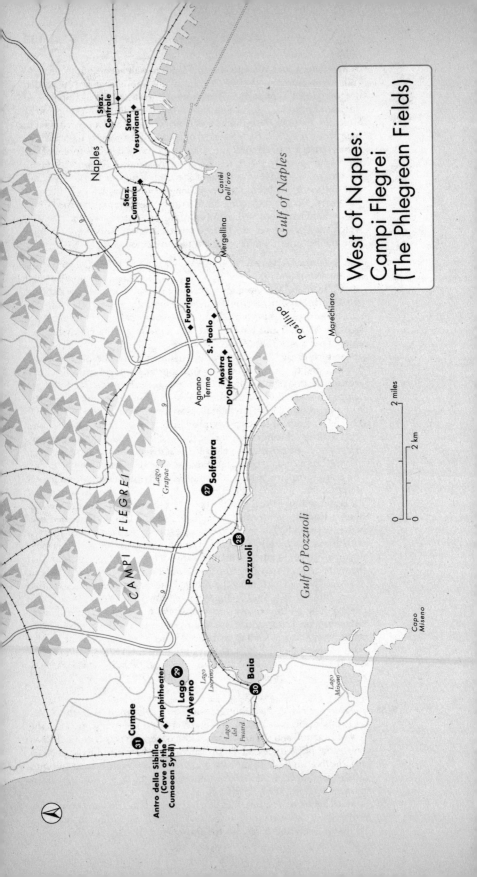

West of Naples:
Campi Flegrei
(The Phlegrean Fields)

Gulf of Naples

Naples

Staz. Centrale

Staz. Vesuviana

Staz. Cumana

Castel Dell'ovo

Mergellina

Posillipo

Marechiaro

Fuorigrotta

S. Paolo

Agnano Terme

Mostra D'Oltremari

27 Solfatara

Lago Grapae

CAMPI FLEGREI

28 Pozzuoli

Gulf of Pozzuoli

Cumae

Amphitheater

29 Lago d'Averno

Antro della Sibilla (Cave of the Cumaean Sybil)

31

Lago Lucrino

Baia

30

Lago del Fusard

Lago Miseno

Capo Miseno

2 miles

2 km

0

0

Solfatara 163, 80078 ☎ *081/5267017* 🖷 *081/5263365* ⊕ *www.hotelsolfatara.it* ⤳ *34 rooms* ⚭ *Restaurant* ☰ *AE, DC, MC, V* �𝌆 *BP.*

¢ ⊡ **Camping Vulcano Solfatara.** With its gamut of bungalows, caravans, and tents for hire, this campsite set in Mediterranean woodland within the Solfatara Crater offers tranquillity, unique ambience, and good facilities at very reasonable prices. Reservations are essential for bungalows. ⊠ *Via Solfatara 161, 80078* ☎ *081/5267413* 🖷 *081/5263482* ⊕ *www.solfatara. it* ⚭ *Restaurant, pool, shop* ☰ *AE, DC, MC, V* ☉ *Closed late Oct.–late Mar.* 𝌆 *EP.*

Pozzuoli

28
Fodor'sChoice
★

8 km (5 mi) west of Naples.

Legendary spirits populate Pozzuoli. St. Paul stepped ashore at the harbor here in AD 61 en route to Rome: his own ship had been wrecked off Malta, and he was brought here on the *Castor and Pollux,* a grain ship from Alexandria that was carrying corn from Egypt to Italy. Not far from the harbor esplanade, San Gennaro, patron saint of Naples, earned his holy martyrdom by being thrown to the lions at an imperial gala staged in the town's enormous amphitheater, constructed by the Flavian emperors (the wild beasts were said to have torn the rags from Gennaro's body but to have left him unharmed—at which point he was taken to the public square and finished off). More recently, that latter-day goddess Sophia Loren was born in a house still standing on a backstreet; later she set off to Naples and celluloid fame. Today Pozzuoli is a well-connected, busy town with about 70,000 inhabitants who are mainly employed by its fisheries, ship yards, and archaeological sites. Built on geologically unstable land, the area near the port was partially evacuated in the early 1980s due to a phenomenon known locally as *bradyseism,* or the rise and fall of the land surface. Since then it has been gradually recolonized and partially gentrified: many of the buildings in the Centro Storico have been given a face-lift, the main park (Villa Avellino) has become a mecca for open-air summer festivals, and the town's reputation as a center for gastronomy has been firmly established. Pozzuoli has also capitalized on its strategic position close to two of the islands in the Bay of Naples, Procida and Ischia. One of its main selling points is its main arena—apart from Rome, Puteoli (to use the ancient Latin name of the town) was the only place in the empire to boast two amphitheaters—offering glimpses into the life of *panem et circenses* (bread and circuses) in classical times, when Puteoli was one of the busiest ports in the Mediterranean and easily eclipsed Neapolis (today's Naples).

★ The **Anfiteatro Flavio** (seating capacity, 40,000) is a short walk from the Pozzuoli Metropolitana railway station and about 15 minutes' walk down from the Solfatara. Despite the wear and tear of the millennia and the loss of some of the masonry to lime-making in the Middle Ages, the site is one of the marvels of Roman architecture in the Campi Flegrei area. The foundation date is open to question. Like many sites in antiquity, the period from conception to completion could stretch over decades. It was probably built under Vespasian (AD 70–AD 79), given various inscriptions reading COLONIA FLAVIA AUGUSTA PUTEOLANA PECUNIA SUA ([built] by the Flavian colony of Puteoli with its own money), although some maintain that work may have started under Nero (AD 54–AD 69) and merely completed later. As you approach the site, note the external part in *opus reticulatum* (masonry arranged in a net-shape pattern) and brick, which is typical of the Flavian emperors, while the pillars of the external portico are all in brick, which would suggest a 2nd-century addition. Although we now get a fairly good idea of the horizontal ground plan in ancient times, comparison with the Colosseum in Rome shows that much of the superstructure has been lost: the outside part consisted of three stories surmounted by an *atticus* (decorative attic), while the *cavea,* or sitting area, would have had a portico above the top row of seats, decorated with a number of statues and supported by columns. At ground level there was an *ambulacrum* (walkway) along which spectators would have passed to reach the *vomitoria* (exits).

Judging from the complex underground network of *carceres,* or cells, which definitely merit a visit, entertainment consisted mainly of *venationes,* or fights, often involving exotic animals like lions and tigers brought from far-flung corners of the Roman Empire through the port of Puteoli. The *fossa,* or large ditch in the middle of the arena, may well have contained the permanent stage setting, which could be raised when necessary to provide a scenic backdrop. According to tradition, several early Christians—including the Naples protector St. Januarius, or San Gennaro—were condemned to be savaged by wild beasts in Puteoli under the Fourth Edict, passed in AD 305, but the sentence was later commuted to a less spectacular *decapitatio* carried out farther up the hill on Via Solfatara at a site now commemorated by the Church of St. Januarius.

Down near the port, a three-minute walk from the Cumana railway stop of Pozzuoli in Piazza Serapide, are the evocative remains of the ancient **macellum,** or food market, a porticoed courtyard with a *sacellum* (shrine) at its northern end. Known commonly—but erroneously—as the Temple of Serapis and proven to have been below sea level (see the perforations in the columns made by mollusks) for much of its history, this is almost all that remains of the ancient harbor district of Puteoli. The macellum is closed to the public but easily visible and photographed from Via Roma on the waterfront. ⊠ *Anfiteatro Grande, Via Terraciano 75* ☎ *081/5266007* ✍ *€4, including admission to Cumae and the museum and site of Baiae* ☉ *Daily 9–1 hr before sunset.*

Rione Terra is the name given to the natural acropolis overlooking the port of Pozzuoli. Probably the site of a Greek settlement in the 6th century BC, it acquired importance when the area was parcelled out in 194 BC to Scipio's veterans from the Second Punic War fought against Hannibal. After decades of neglect and underground pillaging Rione Terra was partially excavated, and opened to the public in 2002. The site, which occupies the basement of a historic palazzo, is a seeming warren of roads and it will take you time to find your bearings. As the area adjoined the ancient forum, many of the buildings were commercial: lengthy information panels—at press time, only in Italian—guide you through a labyrinth of *tabernae* (taverns), *horrea* (storerooms) designed as a cryptoporticus, and a *pistrinum* (bakery). At the end of the passageway you turn left and come out near the Duomo built around the ancient Roman temple. When the Duomo caught fire in 1964, much of the original Roman structure was suddenly revealed. Given the complexity of the site and the fairly impenetrable information displayed, call and try to arrange a free guided tour. ⊠ *Rione Terra, Strada Duomo* ☎ *848/800288* ✍ *€3, or €5.50, including admission to other sites in the Campi Flegrei* ☉ *Weekends 9–6:15. Call for a free guided tour in Italian (11, noon, 3, 4, or in English by request (minimum 5 people).*

Where to Eat

$$–$$$ ✕ **La Taverna di Angelo.** A three-minute walk from the ferry terminal, this welcoming restaurant run by husband-and-wife team Angelo and Teresa fills a quality niche in the Pozzuoli dining scene. Try the *antipasti* with their unusual combinations such as prawns and oranges, and for a pasta dish sample the *paccheri con coccio* (pasta with rockfish). Round

off your meal with an *ottimo* sweet. ⊠ *Via Maria Puteolana 12* ☎ *081/3031002* ⊟ *DC, MC, V* ⊘ *Closed Mon. No dinner Sun.*

★ **$-$$** ✕ **Ristorante Don Antonio.** Despite its unflattering location up a *vicolo* (alley) one block from the Pozzuoli waterfront, this restaurant has achieved cult status in Neapolitan circles for its fresh seafood and unbeatable prices. Unlike other eateries, which will happily serve well into the afternoon siesta or late at night, this spot rolls down the shutters as soon as the day's catch has been consumed. ⊠ *Via Magazzini 20, off Piazza San Paolo* ☎ *081/5267941* ⚘ *Reservations not accepted* ⊟ *No credit cards* ⊘ *Closed Mon.*

Lago d'Averno

㉙ *11 km (7 mi) west of Naples, 3 km (2 mi) north of Baia.*

Fodor'sChoice
★

When the great poet Virgil wrote *"Facilis descensus Averno"*—"The way to hell is easy"—it was because he knew what he was talking about. Regarded by the ancients as the doorway to Hades, the fabled Lago d'Averno (Lake Avernus) was well known by the time the great poet settled here to write *The Aeneid.* Today the scene has changed a fair amount: in summer, the whole area pulsates to the sound of down-market disco music booming from lakeside clubs, and you would be more likely to come across members of the 21st-century underworld than meet the shades of the dead that Virgil so evocatively describes. As with Lago Lucrino (Lake Lucrino) less than 1 km (½ mi) to the south, a tarmac road skirts much of the lake, opening out at times into litter-strewn lay-bys. However, some of the spell is restored by the backdrop: forested hills rise on three sides and the menacing cone of Monte Nuovo looms on the fourth. Landscaping in 2002 restored the path skirting the lake, and bilingual information panels are found at various stages around the perimeter. The water is indeed "black," the smell of sulfur sometimes hangs over the landscape, and blocked-off passages lead into long-abandoned caves into which Virgil might well have ventured. On the approach road from Lago Lucrino, look for remnants of the Roman channel dug in the 1st century BC, which transformed Avernus into a protected inner harbor and linked it to the Lucrine lake and the sea beyond. An even greater feat of engineering was the tunnel (now blocked off) dug from the northwestern side of Avernus leading to the center of Cumae. Also not far away is the Mare Morto of ancient Romans, who identified it as the Stygian Lake of the Dead, where Charon plied his trade, ferrying souls into the underworld. Nearby is the spring that was thought to flow directly from the River Styx, and it was there that Aeneas descended into Hades with the guidance of the Cumaean Sibyl, as famously recounted in *The Aeneid* of Virgil. To reach Lake Avernus, take the Cumana railway to Lucrino (a 10-minute walk away); by car, drive westward from Pozzuoli, hugging the coast where possible, and turn right (inland) at Lucrino, about 4 km (2½ mi) away.

Where to Eat

$$$-$$$$ ✕ **La Ninfea.** In antiquity the site of some of the most celebrated oyster beds and fish farms, Lake Lucrino is now the setting for this stylish restaurant, which treats cooking as one of the fine arts. On your way in, admire the aquarium brimming with crustaceans of all shapes and sizes, and if overwhelmed by the choice of seafood consult the waiter or even Antonio, the experienced sommelier. For a *primo piatto* with a difference, pamper yourself with the *tagliolini alla Sofia,* with its garnish of lobster, cream, and cheese. ⊠ *Piazza Italia, Lucrino* ☎ *081/8661326* ⊟ *AE, DC, MC, V.*

$-$$ ✕ **La Cucina di Ruggiero.** Starting with a bizarre but simpatico welcome announced through a booming megaphone, your visit to this restaurant is likely to be very different from anything you've previously experienced. Besides running this homely restaurant on the western shore of Lake Lucrino, Ruggiero is also a writer and poet—though his clients would insist that the real artist is his wife, Maria, whose culinary repertory and imagination are boundless. There are no written menus here and no choice—for a fixed price of €20–€30, you eat what has been prepared that day. ⊠ *Via Intorno al Lago Lucrino, Lucrino* ☎ *081/8687473* ⚓ *Reservations essential* ▭ *No credit cards* ⊘ *Closed Mon. and Tues. No lunch Wed. and Thurs., no dinner Sun.*

Baia

㉚ *12 km (7 mi) west of Naples, 4 km (2½ mi) west of Pozzuoli.*

Now largely under the sea, ancient Baiae was once the most opulent and fashionable resort area of the Roman Empire, the place where Sulla, Pompey, Cicero, Julius Caesar, Tiberius, and Nero built their holiday villas. Petronius's *Satyricon* is a satire on the corruption, intrigue, and wonderful licentiousness of Roman life at Baiae. (Petronius was hired to arrange parties and entertainment for Nero, so he was in a position to know.) It was here that Cleopatra was staying when Julius Caesar was murdered on the Ides of March (March 15) in 44 BC; here that Emperor Claudius built a great villa for his third wife, Messalina (who is reputed to have spent her nights indulging herself at local brothels); and near here that Agrippina (Claudius's fourth wife and murderer) is believed to have been killed by henchmen sent by her son Nero in AD 59. Unfortunately, the Romans did not pursue the custom of writing official grafitti—"Here lived Crassus" would help—so it's difficult to assign these historical events to specific locations. Consequently, conjecture is the order of the day: Julius Caesar's villa is now thought to be at the top of the hill behind the archaeological site and not near the foot of the Aragonese castle, though we cannot be absolutely certain. We do know, however, that the Romans found this area staggeringly beautiful. A visit to the site can only confirm what Horace wrote in one of his Epistles: *Nullus in orbe sinus Baiis praelucet amoenis* ("No bay on Earth outshines pleasing Baiae").

★ Access to the **Parco Archeologico e Monumentale di Baia** (Archaeological Park) is relatively straightforward on the Cumana railway (trains leave every 15–20 minutes from Montesanto in Naples, travel time 30 minutes, nearest stop Lucrino) followed by a shuttle bus for the last 3 km (2 mi). On Fridays, weekends, and public holidays, take the Archeobus Flegreo from Piazza della Repubblica in Pozzuoli (or from other sites in the area). Where the bus stops in the square outside the Baia station, cross the disused railway line on a footbridge, noting the impressive dome of the so-called Temple of Diana, part of the ancient baths complex sundered from the rest of the archaeological site by the railway, obviously built well before the days of impact assessment. Continue upward for about five minutes until you reach the entrance to the site (limited parking is available). Unlike Pompeii, Oplontis, and Herculaneum, where visitors are left stranded with very little site information—it's good for sales of guidebooks and guiding services—at the Baia ticket office you should receive a small map to the site while information panels in readable English are at strategic intervals. In antiquity this whole area was the Palatium Baianum (the Palace of Baiae), dedicated to *otium*—the ancient form of dolce far niente—and the residence of emperors from Augustus to as late as Septimius Severus in the 3rd century AD. The first terrace, the aptly named Villa dell'Ambulatio, is one of the best levels from which to appreciate the topography of the site: the whole hillside down to the level of the modern road near the waterfront has been modeled into flat terraces, each sporting different architectural features. While up on this terrace look for the exquisite stuccoed artistry, with its depictions of dolphins, swans, and cupids in the *balneum* (bathroom) (Room 13), and admire the elaborate theatrical motifs in the floor mosaic in Room 14. Below the balneum and inviting further exploration is a nymphaeum shrine, which can be reached from the western side. The suggested itinerary around the site is somewhat confusing, especially as part of the site is roped off. This regrettably includes the Temple of Mercury, on the lowest level, which has held so much fascination for travelers from the 18th century onward. It has been variously interpreted as a frigidarium and as a natatio and is the oldest example of a large dome (50 BC–27 BC), predating the cupola of the Pantheon in Rome. If possible, have a peek inside the temple and test the impressive echo within.

If visiting during weekends and you have some surplus energy after touring the main archaeological site, continue up Via Fusaro away from Baia and branch left at the next roundabout. After walking about 450 ft along Via Bellavista look for a large gate on the left with a panda symbol. This marks the entrance to the newly created archaeological heritage park run by dedicated WWF volunteers. A short walk through small vegetable plots and vineyards will take you up to the summit and what is now believed to be Julius Caesar's villa, complete with the remains of a World War II gun emplacement and a commanding view both east and west. The park now hosts traditional concerts and poetry readings throughout much of the year (entrance is free but donations are welcome) and provides a focal point for local *contadini* (farmers) to sell their produce. For the schedule of events, ask at the archaeological site ticket office or at the Museo Archeologico dei Campi Flegrei (081/5233797). ⊠ *Parco Archeologico e Monumentale di Baia, Via Fusaro 75, Baia* ☎ *081/ 8687592* ◪ *€2* ☉ *Tues.–Sun. 9–1 hr before sunset.*

Housed in the Castle of Baia, which commands a fine 360° view—eastward across the Bay of Pozzuoli and westward across the open Tyrrhenian—is the exquisite **Museo Archeologico dei Campi Flegrei.** A regular bus service leaves the old Baia station (in the direction of Bacoli; buy a ticket for the return journey, too, at the kiosk outside the old railway station) and stops about a minute's walk away, just opposite the ramp ascending to this impressively located castle. On Fridays, weekends, and public holidays, take the Archeobus Flegreo from Piazza della Repubblica, Pozzuoli or from other sites. Though its foundation dates to the late 15th century, when Naples was ruled by the House of Aragon and an invasion by Charles VIII of France looked imminent, the castle was radically transformed under the Spanish viceroy Don Pedro de Toledo after the nearby eruption of Monte Nuovo in 1538. Indeed, its bastions bear a striking resemblance to the imposing Castel Sant'Elmo in Naples, built in the same period. This is an ideal spot for museumphobes: spacious, uncluttered rooms display tastefully contextualized finds; there's a virtual absence of large tour groups; there's access to bastion terraces; and it only takes about an hour to see. The south side of the castle is also the venue for outdoor classical music recitals and other performances (on summer evenings; ask at the ticket office about coming events).

Of the various exhibitions, the first on the suggested itinerary consists of plaster casts from the Roman period found at the Baia archaeological site. This gives valuable insights into the techniques used by the Romans to make copies from Greek originals in bronze from the Classical and Hellenistic periods. Displayed in the cases are plaster molds and casts from a local sculptor's workshop active around the 1st century BC, which were then used to produce marble copies of well-known works, such as that of the Athenian Tyrannicides, which probably once stood in the Agora of Athens. Thanks to the Romans' love of Greek art and their fondness for marble copies of the bronze originals, we have been able to reconstruct much of the history of ancient Greek sculpture.

Pride of place in the museum goes to the sacellum, or small sanctuary, transported from nearby Misenum and tastefully displayed inside the Aragonese tower, the Torre Tenaglia. Standing about 20 feet high, the sacellum has been reconstructed, with two of its original six columns (the rest in steel) and a marble architrave with its dedicatory inscription to the husband-and-wife team of *Augustales* (imperial cult devotees), who commissioned restoration of the sanctuary in the 2nd century AD, this surmounted by a pediment depicting the beneficent couple. Behind the facade are the naked marble figures of Vespasian (left) and Titus (right) in a flattering heroic pose, at least from the neck downward. To the right outside the sanctuary is a bronze equestrian statue (1st century AD) originally depicting Domitian. After his death and the subsequent *damnatio memoriae* (the imperial decree issued by emperors who wanted to disgrace predecessors by destroying all sculpted likenesses of them) the statue was extensively—but all too visibly—remodeled to represent his successor, Nerva. Such changes in favor and falls from grace were common in the 1st century AD, and there are cases where faces were resculpted so many times that the statues ultimately became unrecognizable.

Moving on to the upper floor of the tower, you come to the other *capolavoro*, or showpiece, of the museum, the reconstruction of Emperor Claudius's nymphaeum. Discovered in 1959 but only systematically excavated in the early 1980s, the original nymphaeum now lies together with much of the ancient site of Baiae under 20 feet of water in the Bay of Pozzuoli. The sculptural elements salvaged from the seabed include a recognizable scene of a headless Odysseus plying Polyphemus (statue never found) with wine, aided by a companion with a wineskin. The other statues filling the niches along the two longer walls of the nymphaeum include one depicting Claudius's mother, Antonia, and a rather poignant sculpture of perhaps one of his daughters who died young. She is depicted holding a butterfly about to take wing, thought to be symbolic of the spirit of life departing. In contrast, there are two statues of the youthful Dionysus (one crowned, the other with panther), making any thematic connections between the statues rather hard to draw. The function of the nymphaeum is suggested by the marble supports for *klinai* (couches) set on the floor near the entrance: this must have been a showy triclinium, with its full complement of statues and fountains designed to ease the weight of imperial cares and provide due source for reflection and inspiration. ⊠ *Via Castello 39, Bacoli* ☎ *081/5233797* ▣ *€4, including Cumae, the site at Baiae, and the Flavian amphitheater in Pozzuoli* ☉ *Tues.–Sat. 9–1 hr before sunset, Sun. 9–2.*

Boat Excursions

From the small modern-day port of Baia you can board a boat with glass panels on its lower deck and view part of the *città sommersa*, the underwater city of ancient Baiae. The guided tour—usually in Italian, but given in English by prior appointment—takes about 1¼ hours and is best undertaken in calm conditions, when you can get good glimpses of Roman columns, roads, villa walls, and mosaics. The fare (€8) also includes a brief talk about significant changes in the coastline over the last two millennia and the main underwater sights. There are sailings from mid-March to mid-November, Saturday at noon and 4, Sunday at 10:30, noon, and 4. Night sailings are offered mid-June–mid-September, Saturday and Sunday at 9 and 10:30. For further information and bookings, contact **Associazione Aliseo** (⊠ Piazza della Repubblica 42, Baia ☎ 081/5265780).

Where to Stay & Eat

¢–$ ✕▦ **Azienda Agrituristica Il Casolare.** Il Casolare offers the rare chance of dining and lodging within a 10,000-year-old volcanic crater (thankfully extinct). This place is particularly known for its restaurant, perched on the inner slopes of the volcano, offering a view of the patchwork of farmed plots on the crater floor. Specializing in *cucina contadina napoletana* (Neapolitan rustic cuisine) the owner Tobia serves whatever is in season. No agonizing over menus here (the all-inclusive set price is about €26): expect a cornucopia of antipasti (possibly including goat-milk ricotta, and *poppacelle,* peppers done in vinegar) and some novel vegetarian dishes like pasta *e cicerchia* (vetchling). The inn's four guest rooms, or *mini-appartmenti,* are small but tastefully furnished, a perfect base for exploring the surrounding area. Transfers can be arranged from the nearby railway station of Lucrino. ⊠ *Via Selvatico, Contrada Coste dei Fondi di Baia, 80070* ▦*081/5235193* ⏴*Reservations essential* ⬲*4 rooms* ⏶ *Restaurant* ▭ *No credit cards* ⏱ *Closed Mon. No dinner Sun.* ⏅*EP.*

Cumae

③① *16 km (10 mi) west of Naples, 5 km (3 mi) north of Baia.*

Fodor's Choice
★

Being perhaps the oldest Greek colony on mainland Italy, Cumae overshadowed the Phlegrean Fields and Neapolis in the 7th and 6th centuries BC, since it was home to the **Antro della Sibilla,** the fabled Cave of the Cumaean Sibyl—one of the three greatest oracles of antiquity—who is said to have presided over the destinies of men. In about the 6th century BC the Greeks hollowed the cave from the rock beneath the ridge leading up to the present ruins of Cumae's acropolis. Today you can walk—just as Virgil's Aeneas did—through a dark, massive 350-foot-long stone tunnel that opens into the vaulted Chamber of the Prophetic Voice, where the Sibyl delivered her oracles. Standing here in one of the most venerated sites of ancient times, the sense of the *numen*—of communication with invisible powers—is overwhelming. "This is the most romantic classical site in Italy," wrote famed travelogue H. V. Morton. "I would rather come here than to Pompeii."

Cumae was founded in the third quarter of the 8th century BC by Greek colonists. The name has legendary origins: myth has it that Euboean mariners found a woman who had miscarried a baby on the beach here, and the fetus was washed out to sea by great breakers on the shore. Thinking this an omen from the gods of fertility, the mariners built an altar here and called their new settlement *kuema* (or "fetus" in Greek). Centuries later Virgil wrote his epic of *The Aeneid,* the story of the Trojan prince Aeneas's wanderings, partly to give Rome the historical legitimacy that Homer had given the Greeks. On his journey, Aeneas had to descend to the underworld to speak to his father, and to find his way in, he needed the guidance of the Cumaean Sibyl. Virgil did not dream up the Sibyl's Cave or the entrance to Hades—he must have actually stood both in her chamber and along the rim of Lake Avernus, as you yourself will stand. When he described the Sibyl's Cave in Book VI of *The Aeneid* as having *"centum ostia"*—a hundred mouths—and depicted the entrance to the underworld on Lake Avernus so vividly, *"spelunca alta . . . tuta lacu nigro nemorum tenebris"*—"a deep cave . . . protected by a lake of black water and the glooming forest"—it was because he was familiar with this awesome landscape. In Book VI of *The Aeneid,* Virgil describes how Aeneas, arriving at Cumae, sought Apollo's throne (remains of the Temple of Apollo can still be seen) and "the deep hidden abode of the dread Sibyl/An enormous cave . . ."

In general, Sibyl was the title given to inspired prophetesses, usually of Apollo. As the god of light who pierced through all darkness, Apollo was also the god of divination, and there were oracles throughout the ancient world interpreting his will. Although Cumae never achieved the status of Delphi, it was the most important oracular center in Magna Graecia, and the Sibyl would have been consulted on a whole range of matters. Governments consulted the Sibyl before mounting campaigns. Wealthy aristocrats came to channel their deceased relatives. Businessmen came to get their dreams interpreted or to seek favorable omens before entering into financial agreements or setting off on journeys. Love potions were a profitable source of revenue; women from Baiae lined up for potions to slip into the wine of handsome charioteers who drove up and down the street in their gold-plated four-horsepower chariots. Still, it was the Sibyl's prophecies that ensured the crowds here, prophecies written on palm leaves and later collected into the corpus of the Sibyline books. However, with the coming of the Olympian gods, the earlier gods of the soil were discredited or given new roles and names. Ancient rites, such as those surrounding the Cumaean Sibyl, were now carried out in secret and known as the Mysteries. The Romans—like the later Soviets—tried in vain to replace these Mysteries by deifying the state in the person of its rulers. Yet even the Caesars appealed to forces of the Other World. And until the 4th century AD, the Sibyl was consulted by the Christian bishop of Rome, one reason why Michelangelo portrayed the Cumaean Sibyl—one of his most magisterial creations—on the Sistine Chapel ceiling.

However little of ancient Cumae now stands above ground—and the Temple of Apollo has suffered woefully over the millennia—the underground passages are virtually intact, though not entirely visitable. There are detailed information panels to guide you through the site. As you walk through, you'll soon appreciate what a good choice it was to colonize this site: it was surrounded by fertile land, offered opportunities for development on various levels, had relatively easy access to the sea (though no natural harbor), and an acropolis at the top providing an excellent view in all directions. Allow at least two hours for this visit to soak up the ambience and study the ruins. Unlike in Greek and Roman times, when access to Cumae was through a network of underground passages, an overground bus service leaves the old Baia station at regular intervals. On Fridays, weekends, and public holidays, take the Archeobus Flegreo from Piazza della Repubblica, Pozzuoli or from other sites in the area. If driving, leave the Naples Tangenziale at the Cuma exit and then continue to follow signs for about 3 km (2 mi). There's a free parking lot. ⊠ *Via Acropoli 39, Cumae* ☎ *081/8543060* ✍ *€4, including the museum and site at Baiae and the Flavian amphitheater in Pozzuoli* ☉ *Daily 9–1 hr before sunset.*

Where to Stay

$–$$ ⌂ **Villa Giulia.** Built with characteristic yellow tuff walls and restored in immaculate taste, this historic farmhouse is a welcome addition to the Cumae area. The decor and atmosphere are those of a top-notch hotel, while the price is refreshingly accessible. As the villa is hard to find, owner-manager Giulia will prearrange a meeting-point closer to Naples and escort you to her home. For an extra €20, try Giulia's inventive cuisine (evenings only) served under her leafy pergola. ⊠ *Via Cuma–Licola 178, 80078* ☎ *081/8540163* FAX *081/8044356* WEB *www. villagiulia.info* ⇥ *6 rooms* ⚇ *Pool* ▭ *MC, V.* ⦿ *BP*

AROUND THE BAY A TO Z

BUS TRAVEL

In general, in this area it's best to travel on rails rather than on wheels, as local roads can be frustratingly slow. However, for the trip up Vesuvius the bus operated by Transporti Vesuviani (€3 from Piazza Anfiteatro in Pompei, €1.70 from Ercolano Circumvesuviana station) will take you up to the car park and the starting point of the path up to the top of the cone.

Since Easter 2003 the major archaeological sites both east and west of Naples have been linked by a special Archeobus which runs from Friday to Sunday. In the Campi Flegrei, the bus leaves Piazza della Repubblica, near Rione Terra in Pozzuoli, on the hour between 9 AM and 4 PM and takes an 80-minute circular route via Pozzuoli's amphitheater, Lago Lucrino, the port in Baia, Baia castle, Capo Miseno, Lago Fusaro, and Cumae, then returning via the Temple of Serapis to Pozzuoli. This means you can site-hop throughout the Phlegrean Fields. A similar, though less frequent, service has been arranged for the Pompeii area, linking the archaeological sites, the main train stations, and the nearby port of Torre Annunziata.

🚌 Bus Information **Circumvesuviana Archeobus Vesuviano** ☎ 081/7722444 ⊕ www. vesuviana.it.**SEPSA Archeobus Flegreo** ☎ 081/5513328 ⊕ www.sepsa.it. **Transporti Vesuviani** ☎ 081/5592582.

CAR TRAVEL

Pompeii is a very short distance off the A3 Autostrada (toll from Naples or Nocera: €1.20), though this major highway with only two lanes in each direction can get very congested with ill-disciplined drivers.

A car could be useful for exploring the Campi Flegrei region on the west side of Naples, especially for sites like Cumae and Lake Avernus where public transport is either infrequent or nonexistent. From Naples, travel toward Pozzuoli on the Tangenziale—the Naples bypass (toll: €.65)—exiting at the appropriate junction.

PARKING Most archaeological sites are fairly accessible by car and usually have reasonably safe parking facilities. Take customary precautions when parking and leaving your vehicle: use a *parcheggio custodito* (attended parking lot) and avoid on-street unattended parking when possible.

ROAD CONDITIONS Off the main highways, signposting is sometimes poor, with road signs suffering intense competition from advertising placards, so navigating becomes an invaluable skill. The westbound Tangenziale (Napoli–Pozzuoli) should be avoided Saturday evenings and Sundays in summer (crowds heading out of Naples for nightlife or beaches). Road surfaces are usually fair, though conditions near the top of Vesuvius can become icy in winter.

EMERGENCIES

🚑 Pompeii **Ambulance** ☎ 081/8637816. **First Aid** ✉ Via Colle San Bartolomeo 50, Pompeii ☎ 081/5359111. **Police** ☎ 081/8506172.

🚑 Ercolano (Herculaneum) **Ambulance** ☎ 081/7775600. **Hospital** ✉ Ospedale Maresca, Via Montedoro, Torre del Greco ☎ 081/8824033. **Police** ✉ Ercolano [Herculaneum] ☎ 081/7321858.

🚑 Pozzuoli **Ambulance** ☎ 081/5266954. **Hospital** ✉ Ospedale S. Maria delle Grazie, Via Domiziana, Pozzuoli ☎ 081/8552111. **Police** ☎ 081/8041100.

CURRENCY EXCHANGE In Pompeii, besides the Banco di Napoli, there are several exchange bureaus around and off the main square, Piazza Longo, near Porta

Marina, and an ATM located by the main ticket office at Porta Marina. Exchange services in Pozzuoli and Ercolano are listed below.

🚩 Exchange Services **Banco di Napoli** ✉ Piazza B. Longo 37, Pompeii 📞 081/8631001 ✉ Via N. Terracciano 18, Pozzuoli 📞 081/5256111. **Exchange Bureau, A.T.I. Viaggi** ✉ 1 Traversa IV Novembre 12, Ercolano 📞 081/7397587.

TAXIS

🚩 Taxi Companies **Ercolano** ✉ Stazione Circumvesuviana 📞 081/7393666. **Pompeii** ✉ Piazza Santuario 📞 081/8632686 ✉ Piazza Esedra 📞 081/5367852. **Pozzuoli** ✉ Piazza della Repubblica 📞 081/5265800.

TRAIN TRAVEL

The main station in Naples (Stazione Centrale, at Piazza Garibaldi) is also the main interchange node for public transport both east and west of Naples. A branch of the aptly named Circumvesuviana railway serves the main archaeological sites at the foot of Vesuvius. Trains leave from the Corso Garibaldi station in Naples, stop at the main terminal at Piazza Garibaldi 10 blocks away to link up with the Naples *metropolitana*, and then head southeast for Sorrento (about two trains per hour; €1.70 to Ercolano and Torre Annunziata, and €2.20 to Pompei Scavi–Villa Dei Misteri). Confusingly, the station called "Pompei," which is the stop for the modern city, lies on a different line, which will leave you not at the main entrance to the archaeological site but just behind the cathedral, close to the amphitheater.

For the Phlegrean Fields to the west of Naples, take the Cumana line run by SEPSA, with trains every 15–20 minutes, from the terminus at Piazza Montesanto near Montesanto Metropolitana station. Alternatively, take the Metropolitana all the way to Pozzuoli from one of the railway stations in Naples, either Piazza Garibaldi or the more welcoming station of Mergellina, with one departure every 10–15 minutes. This will drop you near the amphitheater and the Solfatara crater.

When not affected by wildcat strikes or landslides, the railway network on either side of Naples is cheap and reliable, though with the many stops along the way you're unlikely to experience nerve-tingling velocity. As in any mass transit system through a fairly depressed area, not all your fellow-passengers will be well versed in train etiquette so brace yourself for clandestine smoking, etc., especially on the Circumvesuviana.

🚩 Train Information **Circumvesuviana railway** 📞 081/7722444 ⊕ www.vesuviana. it. **Mergellina** 📞 081/5543188. **SEPSA** 📞 081/5513328.

TRAVEL AGENCIES

🚩 Local Agents **A.T.I. Viaggi** ✉ 1 Traversa IV Novembre 12, Ercolano [Herculaneum] 📞 081/7397587 🖷 081/7772872 ⊕ www.ativiaggi.com. **Amorini Viaggi** ✉ Via Lepanto 235, Pompeii 📞 081/8502614 🖷 081/8561689. **Campi Elisi Viaggi e Turismo** ✉ Via Solfatara 13, Pozzuoli 📞 081/5266466 🖷 081/5266845.

VISITOR INFORMATION

Azienda Autonoma di Cura Soggiorno e Turismo offices in Pompeii and Pozzuoli are open 8–2, closed Sunday. Ufficio Informazione in Ercolano (Herculaneum) is open 9–5 daily. Ufficio Turistico in Ercolano is open 9–2, closed Sunday.

🚩 Tourist Information **Azienda Autonoma di Cura Soggiorno e Turismo** ✉ Via Sacra 1, Pompeii 📞 081/8508451; 800/013350 toll-free 🖷 081/8632401 ⊕ www.uniplan. it/pompei/azienda ✉ Piazza Matteotti 1/a, Pozzuoli 📞 081/5266639 🖷 081/5265068 ⊕ www.campnet.it/aziendaturismo/pozzuoli. **Ufficio Informazione** ✉ Piazza Porta Marina 12, Ercolano [Herculaneum] 📞 081/8575347 ⊕ www.pompeiisites.org. **Ufficio Turistico** ✉ Via IV Novembre 82, Ercolano [Herculaneum] 📞 081/7881243.

CAPRI, ISCHIA & PROCIDA

3

FODOR'S CHOICE

Castello Aragonese, Ischia, *a spectacular seaside castle*
Certosa di San Giacomo, Capri, *the island's "palace"*
Grotta Azzura, Capri, *the legendary Blue Grotto*
Hotel Caesar Augustus, Capri, *a clifftop Xanadu*
Hotel Punta Tragara, Capri, *buonissima! bellissima!*
I Faraglioni, Capri, *three rocky colossi that are Capri's icons*
La Mortella, Ischia, *a garden of cactus and orchids*
Marina di Corricella, Procida, *a horizontal Positano*
Marina Piccola, Capri, *lined with fashionable lidos*
Santa Maria a Cetrella, Capri, *relentlessly picturesque*
Villa Jovis, Capri, *where Emperor Tiberius ruled the world*
Villa San Michele, Capri, *a sky-kissing villa "all'antica"*

HIGHLY RECOMMENDED

RESTAURANTS
La Canzone del Mare, Capri
La Conchiglia, Procida
Le Grotelle, Capri
Ristorante Pizzeria Aurora, Capri

HOTELS
Grande Albergo Mezzatorre, Ischia
La Scalinatella, Capri
Pensione Il Monastero, Ischia
Villa Krupp, Capri

Many other great sights, restaurants, and hotels enliven this area. For other favorites, look for the black stars as you read this chapter.

By Mark
Walters

Updated by
Victoria
Primhak

THE ISLANDS OFF NAPLES ARE SO DIFFERENT FROM EACH OTHER that you wonder how they can possibly be in the same bay—indeed, some would say they are not true water mates, as they lie just beyond the bay's outer fringes. The contrast goes beyond mere geology and vegetation. They all occupy different niches in the traveler's mind, with Capri pandering to the whims of the international great-and-good, Ischia servicing the needs of a predominantly German and Italian clientele, and Procida—the closest to the mainland—being more dependent on the weekend and summer influx of Neapolitans. Chosen by the Greeks, the supreme connoisseurs and aesthetes of antiquity, as their first base in Italy, the islands of Capri, Ischia, and Procida combine a broad gamut of experiences.

Islandophiles, of course, have always had a special love for Capri (the first syllable is accented—"CA-pri"). Pleasure dome to Roman emperors, and still Italy's most glamorous seaside getaway, this craggy, whale-shape island tips one of the two points of the crescent formed by the Bay of Naples (Ischia tips the other). The island's beauty is an epic one: cliffs that are the very embodiment of time, bougainvillea-shaded pathways overlooking the sea, trees seemingly hewn out of rock by the Greeks. It's little wonder that tales tell of tourists snapping up villas while their unsuspecting wives were, so they thought, doing last-minute souvenir shopping, or of American industrialists who, determined to stay on, sent a wire home with a brisk "sell everything" order. Capri has always been a stage that lesser mortals could share with the Beautiful People, often an eclectic potpourri of duchesses who have left their dukes home, fading French film actresses, pretenders to obscure thrones, waspish couturiers, and sleek supermodels. Today Capri's siren song continues to seduce thousands of visitors. The summer scene calls to mind the annual bull stampede of Pamplona: meaning, if you can visit in spring or fall, do so. Yet even the crowds are not enough to destroy Capri's very special charm. The town itself is a Moorish stage-set of sparkling white houses, tiny squares, and narrow medieval alleyways hung with flowers, while its hillsides are spectacular settings for luxurious seaside villas. The mood is modish but somehow unspoiled. The upper crust does its sunbaking in private villas, hinting that you, also, should retreat when the day-trippers take over—offering yourself to the sun at your hotel pool or exploring the hidden corners of the island. Even in the height of summer, you can enjoy a degree of privacy on one of the many paved paths that wind around the island hundreds of feet above the sea.

In terms of settlements, conquests, and dominion, the history of the islands echoes that of the mainland. For eastern Mediterranean traders in the second and first millennia BC, Capri and Ischia were both close enough to the mainland to provide easy access to trade routes and impervious enough to afford natural protection against invaders. Ischia, or Pithekoussai, as it used to be called—a word probably derived from the Greek term for a large earthenware jar (*pithos*) rather than the less plausible word, *pithekos*, meaning monkey—is renowned in classical circles as the first colony founded by the Greeks on Italian soil, as early as the 8th century BC. Capri, probably colonized a century or so later, is amply described in the early years of the Roman Empire by authors such as Suetonius and Tacitus, as this was the island where Tiberius spent the last 10 years of his life.

After the breakup of the Roman Empire, the islands, like many other parts of the Mediterranean, suffered a succession of incursions. Saracens, Normans, and Turks all laid siege to the islands at some stage, be-

3

Emperors, kings, and artists have made the Bay of Naples's sea-wreathed isles their abodes for more than 2,000 years. And well they might, for the islands of Capri, Ischia, and Procida are compact realms of undiluted beauty. Bathed in 24-karat sunshine, Capri has been a chic resort ever since the Caesars made it their private playpen; Ischia is famous for its volcanic spas, where there's nothing between you and the rest of the world except for a layer of fango mud; and the magical waterfront of Procida has been immortalized in the Oscar-winning film *Il Postino*. If archaeology and history are at the top of your list of priorities, choosing between Ischia and Capri can be difficult. Moving around Capri to the main sites is generally easier—and can be done in a day if pushed—while Ischia calls for more chilling out at your destination, especially in summer months. If time is limited, Procida can be tacked on to your stay as a day trip from Ischia or from the mainland.

Numbers in the text correspond to numbers in the margin and on the Capri and Ischia maps.

If you have
1 day

With no chance of overnighting, take an early ferry from the mainland to Capri so that you get to the main sites before the human tsunami hits the island. Take a quick tour of glamorous Capri—**La Piazzetta ❷**, the idyllic Via Tragara, and the famed **I Faraglioni ❾** and **Punta Tragara ❿**. Return by route of the romantic **Certosa di San Giacomo ⓫**, then, if you're up for an hour's hike, head up to the **Villa Jovis ❺** to gaze in wonder at Tiberius's Leap and the sea views. After lunch, take a breathless bus ride up to Anacapri to visit the mountaintop gardens of Axel Munthe's **Villa San Michele ⓮**. From Anacapri catch the bus to the **Grotta Azzurra ⓴**—the matrix-blue light at this grotto scintillates even in late afternoon, and by then the crowds are gone.

If you have
4 days

After the day outlined above, overnight on Capri—even more magical when the day-trippers have departed—and enjoy more of its sights on your second day. Begin with a morning jaunt around the Giro dell'Arco Naturale to view the **Grotta di Matermania ❼** and the **Villa Malaparte ❽**. For more scenic splendor, head back up to Anacapri and the chairlift up **Monte Solaro ⓯**, then explore the churches of **Santa Maria a Cetrella ⓰** and **San Michele ⓳**. If you just want to be busy doing nothing, opt instead to laze the afternoon away at the bathing lido at **Marina Piccola ⓭**. On Day 3 head to Ischia on the afternoon direct hydrofoil (limited service). Visit **Ischia Ponte ㉒** and the "doorman" to the island—the magnificent Castello Aragonese—then visit the museum of Greek and Roman antiquities at **Lacco Ameno ㉕** and **Forio ㉖**, where you'll find the island's most picturesque church, the Santuario del Soccorso, and the famous gardens of La Mortella. On your final day you'll want to save time for a welcome dip into Ischia's soothing waters, either at Citara Beach or at one of the noted spas: if you want the gamut of natural saunas and access to a dreamy beach, head to Poseidon in Forio; for more stylish surrounds and landscaped Mediterranean gardens, check out Negombo in Lacco Ameno. Or take the ferry and explore nearby Procida on your way back to the mainland.

If you have
7 days A week should be enough to sample a gamut of pleasures ranging from natural saunas to trails winding through thick Mediterranean maquis, with plenty of time left over for experiencing the local brands of dolce vita in the evenings. On Capri, go for a round-the-island boat trip. Spend a lazy day on Procida combining a walk on Vivara with a lingering lunch at a quayside restaurant in the enchanting fishing village of Corricella. Then trek up to the walled village of Terra Murata for the best view of the bay of Naples and a visit to the fascinating abbey and its underground chapels.

---

tween periods of relative stability under the Swabians, the Angevins, the Aragonese, and the Spanish. After a short interregnum under the French at the beginning of the 19th century, a period of relative peace and prosperity ensued.

From the opening of its first hotel in 1826 and especially in the early decades of the 20th century, Capri saw an influx of visitors that reads like a Who's Who of literature and politics. Ischia and Procida established themselves as holiday resorts much later, with their development quickening from the 1950s onward. Recent years have seen a diversification of the experiences offered on the three islands. Once entirely dependent on its thermal springs, Ischia is now the archaeological front-runner in the bay, thanks to its noted museum in Lacco Ameno. Procida has opened up to tourism, with some newer, smaller hotels remaining open throughout the year. As always, you need to book a room well in advance to fully discover Procida's fascinating Easter procession, replete with handcrafted wooden sculptures representing religious scenes. On Capri, for those seeking peace and quiet away from its main thoroughfares, walks introducing some of the island's major geological landmarks have been mapped out through species-rich Mediterranean maquis.

EXPLORING CAPRI, ISCHIA & PROCIDA

Lying equidistant from Naples (about 25 km [16 mi]), Ischia and Capri stand like guards at the main entrance to the Bay of Naples, with Ischia to the west and Capri to the south, while Procida is like a small stepping-stone halfway between Ischia and Capo Miseno (Cape Misenum), on the mainland. The islands can be reached easily from various points in and near Naples, with the port of Pozzuoli offering the closest access to Procida and Ischia, and the port of Sorrento lying almost opposite Capri.

All the islands are well served by road networks, with buses plying the main roads and a funicular on Capri reaching the main town from the Marina Grande, as well as a chairlift ascending &to the top of Monte Solaro (1,932 feet) from Anacapri. Note that on a few of Capri's major roads only cars, taxis, and buses are permitted—elsewhere on the island, foot power is the preferred mode of transportation. Life on Capri gravitates around the two centers of Capri Town (on the saddle between Monte Tiberio and Monte Solaro) and Anacapri, higher up (984 feet). Ischia's larger population is distributed among six main urban areas and countless smaller villages and farmsteads dotted around the slopes of Monte Epomeo, the highest point on the island (2,582 feet). Much of Procida is built-up, apart from the less developed southwestern end and the island of Vivara (linked by a pedestrian causeway to Chiaiolella). Small buses ferry locals around Procida, but for real exploring you need to walk down the less-explored paths.

About the Restaurants & Hotels

Unfortunately, international tourism and the euro have pushed prices sky-high on Capri. Happily, the wider choice on Ischia means meals are still reasonably priced. While Caprese cuisine is touted the world over, standards are sadly wavering as international trends make incursions—choose dishes with fresh vegetables or local fish rather than overpriced lobster flown in from Africa. Don't be dismayed to find menus in German in Ischia—thanks to the flocks of Germanic tourists, virtually a second language there—although the food may well be a pleasant surprise. Procida restaurants focus on local produce and traditional cuisine but are overcrowded in summer and on weekends, so be prepared to reserve or wait in line. In general, reservations are a must in summer and on weekends at all good restaurants, especially those on beaches.

Although island prices are generally higher than those on the mainland, it is definitely worth paying the difference for an overnight stay. On Capri, once the day-trippers have left center stage and headed down to the Marina Grande for the ferry home, the streets regain some of their charm and tranquillity. Again, although Ischia can be sampled piecemeal on day excursions from Naples, given the size of the island, you'd be well advised to arrange a stopover. Bear in mind that there is considerable competition for hotel rooms, especially at moderate prices. Procida can be easily seen on a day trip but try for a mid-week visit, as all three islands are popular with Neapolitans on weekends (especially during July and August). On Capri hotels seem to fill almost as quickly as your wallet empties, so book well in advance to be assured of getting first-pick accommodations. While they are included in one section, hotel and restaurant listings indicate whether the place is located in either Capri Town and its environs or Anacapri. Assume all hotel rooms have air-conditioning, telephones, TV, and private bath, unless otherwise noted.

WHAT IT COSTS In euros				
	$$$$	**$$$**	**$$**	**$**	**¢**
RESTAURANTS	over €20	€15–€20	€9–€15	€5–€9	under €5
HOTELS	over €210	€160–€210	€110–€160	€60–€110	under €60

Restaurant prices are for a main-course entry only (known in Italian as secondo piatto, or second course); note that if a restaurant offers only prix-fixe (set-price) meals, it has been given the price category that reflects the full prix-fixe price. Hotel prices are for a standard double room in high season, excluding tax and service charges; higher prices (inquire when booking) prevail for any board plans.

Timing

The islands in the Bay of Naples, at a latitude of just more than 40° north, enjoy a typical Mediterranean climate, with hot dry summers, which means the area can be pretty torrid in July and August. Spring is excellent for wildflowers and birds, although it also attracts large numbers of vacationers, especially from northern Europe. If you're looking for a quiet break, the holiday season calms down considerably at the end of September, while sea temperatures are still pleasantly warm by Mediterranean standards even to the end of October. At any time of year except summer, conditions can be stomach-churning in the Bay of Naples, and on exceptionally rough days ferry services to the mainland may be canceled. In winter *la caccia* (hunting) is a common pursuit, especially on Ischia, so it's best to schedule country walks for nonhunting days (usually Tuesday and Friday, check locally). Watch out for Pasquetta (Easter Monday), when ferries to the islands are crammed with Neapolitans hell-bent on their annual country picnic. This is definitely a no-go day for travel or country walks.

CAPRI: A SIREN LANDSCAPE

D. H. Lawrence once called Capri "a gossipy, villa-stricken, two-humped chunk of limestone, a microcosm that does heaven much credit, but mankind none at all." He was referring to its once rather farouche reputation as well as its unique natural beauty. Fantastic grottoes, soaring conical peaks, caverns great and small, plus villas of the emperors and thousands of legends combine with Suetonius's ancient Roman tales of "exquisite tortures" to brush the isle with an air of whispered mystery and an intoxicating quality as heady as its rare and delicious wines. Emperor Augustus was the first to tout the island's pleasures by nicknaming it Apragopolis—the city of sweet idleness—and Capri has drawn escapists of every ilk since. Ancient Greek and Roman goddesses were moved aside by the likes of Jacqueline Onassis, Elizabeth Taylor, and Brigitte Bardot, who made the island into a papparazzo's paradise in the 1960s. Today, new generations of glitterati continue to answer the island's call, among them Harrison Ford, Julia Roberts, and Whitney Houston.

Of all the peoples who have left their mark on the island during its millennia of history, the Romans with their sybaritic wealth had the greatest effect in forming the island's psyche. Capri became the center of power in the Roman Empire when Tiberius scattered 12 villas around the island and decided to spend the rest of his life here, refusing to return to Rome even when, 10 years on, he was near death. Far from being a dirty old man only interested in orgies, this misunderstood gentleman used Capri as a base to run the ancient Roman Empire. All Tiberius's hard work and happy play—he indulged in his secret passion for astronomy here—were overlooked by ancient scandalmongers, prime among them Suetonius, who wrote: "In Capri they still show the place at the cliff top where Tiberius used to watch his victims being thrown into the sea after prolonged and exquisite tortures. A party of mariners were stationed below, and when the bodies came hurtling down, they whacked at them with oars and boat-hooks, to make sure they were completely dead." Thankfully, present-day Capri is less fraught with danger for travelers, or even to dignitaries from afar. The main risks now are overexposure to the Mediterranean sun and overindulgence in pleasures of the palate.

Capri Town & Environs

From the main harbor, Marina Grande, you can take a bus or funicular to reach the island's hub, Capri Town. This fantasy of white-on-white Capriote architecture, flower-filled windowboxes, and stylish boutiques rests on a saddle between rugged limestone cliffs to the east and west, where huge herds of *capre* (goats) once roamed, hence the name of the island. Beyond Capri Town lies some of the island's most spectacular sights, including I Faraglioni and the Villa Jovis. As you disembark at the marina quay, note that unlike the other islands in the Bay of Naples, Capri is not of volcanic origin but was formed by marine deposits laid more than 100 million years ago and then uplifted during plate tectonic activity in the Pleistocene era (as recently as 1–2 million years ago); Monte Tiberio, to the south of the Marina Grande, and Monte Solaro, to the west, powerfully attest to these upheavals.

3

Scenic Wonders

While Capri may first conjure up chichi caffès and Gucci stores, it's also a wonderland of idyllic pathways running beside cactus-covered cliffs and whitewashed Arabian houses overlooking some of the bluest water on earth. So when Capri Town swarms with summer crowds and begins to feel like an ant farm, take to the hills—in a few minutes, you can find yourself atop a cliff without a trace of humanity in sight. The island is a novice hiker's paradise, with plenty of moderate hikes that lead to stunning vistas. One of the simplest routes is to take Anacapri's Via Caposcuro and Via Migliera south to the Belvedere di Migliera, a lookout point above a cliff on the island's south side. For another great hike, from Capri Town follow Via Camerelle–Via Tragara past the ritzy hotels and villas to the terrific southside vista, within spitting distance of the Faraglioni rocks. From here there's a path leading down to the secluded beaches under the Faraglioni. From the area around the the island's famous Arco Naturale, descend hundreds of steps past the Grotto di Matermania to find the stunning southern hillside path called the Via Pizzo Lungo, passing several famous villas. At Via Arco Naturale, you can climb the hill to see this famous natural rock bridge that overlooks the sea. To return to town, exit the Via Pizzo Lungo onto enchanting Via Tragara and head back to Capri Town. A short but dizzying hike descends the cliff beneath the Giardini di Augusto. Via Matteotti has been closed just beneath the gardens because of the risk of falling rocks, but some people climb around the gate and walk down the cliff's series of switchbacks. After the path straightens out, there's a path on your left; veer left where it divides, and you'll come to the Grotta dell'Arsenale, a large cave in the base of the cliff and one of Capri's most secluded beaches. Once you're back on the main path, you can go downhill to Marina Piccola. Capri is considered by many to be one of the most beautiful places on Earth, and the good news is that its trailways allow you to discover its every nook and cranny.

On the Menu

Although relatively close together, the three islands enjoy different culinary traditions. Capri has lent its name to two dishes that are also widely consumed on the mainland: *insalata caprese*, a dish with a color scheme like the Italian flag—made with alternating slices of mozzarella and tomato and served with a sprig of basil; and *torta caprese*, a plain cake combining chocolate and finely chopped almonds and topped with a sprinkling of powdered sugar. Unlike Capri and Procida, where seafood tends to predominate, the Ischitani exploit their naturally fertile volcanic soils to good effect: wine flows—notably from Biancolella and Forestera grape varieties—and is a pleasing accompaniment to the renowned dish from Ischia, *coniglio all'ischitana*, rabbit in a rich tomato-base sauce together with aromatic herbs like basil, rosemary, thyme, and marjoram. The sauce is also used as an accompaniment to *bucatini*, spaghetti-shape pasta with a hole running from one end to the other. Procida's claim to fame is its lemon groves— a special variety used for salads and the local pastry, a lemon cream in puff pastry known as *lingua al limone*.

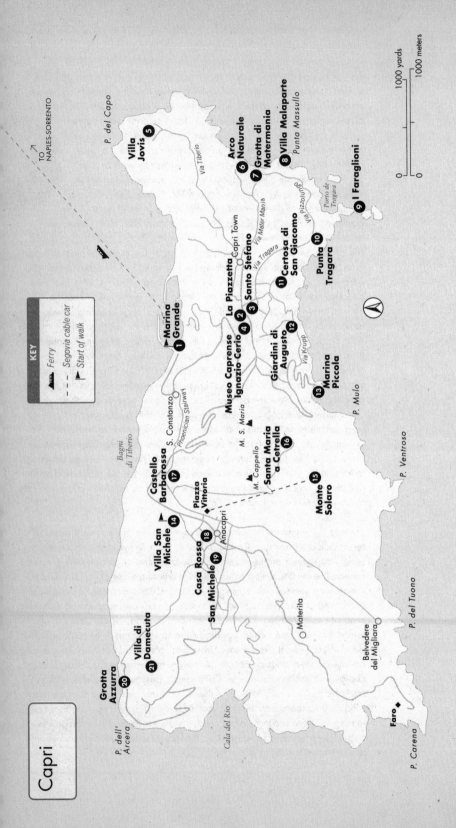

Capri

KEY

- Ferry
- --- Segovia cable car
- ▶ Start of walk

TO NAPLES-SORRENTO

P. del Capo

P. dell' Arcera

Bagni di Tiberio

S. Constanzo

Phoenician Stairway

Via Tiberio

Capri Town

Via Mater Mania

Via Tragara

Via Pizzolungo

Porto de Tragara

Via Krupp

P. Mulo

Cala del Rio

Materita

P. Ventroso

P. del Tuono

P. Carena

Belvedere del Migliara

Faro

M. S. Maria

M. Cappello

Punta Massullo

1 Marina Grande
2 La Piazzetta
3 Santo Stefano
4 Museo Caprense Ignazio Cerio
5 Villa Jovis
6 Arco Naturale
7 Grotta di Matermania
8 Villa Malaparte
9 I Faraglioni
10 Punta Tragara
11 Certosa di San Giacomo
12 Giardini di Augusto
13 Marina Piccola
14 Villa San Michele
15 Monte Solaro
16 Santa Maria a Cetrella
17 Castello Barbarossa
18 Piazza Vittoria
19 Casa Rossa / San Michele
20 Grotta Azzurra
21 Villa di Damecuta

Anacapri

1000 yards

1000 meters

a good
walk

Once you get off the ferry and have picked up a decent map of Capri (€.80 at the information office on the main jetty), take a funicular ride up from the harbor area of **Marina Grande** ❶ ▶ to Capri Town (only one stop, €1.3 one-way; if for any reason it's not working, there's a bus and taxi service). For energetic foot soldiers, there's a former mule track starting from a small square on the quayside called Largo Fontana that will place you at the top in about 15 minutes, emerging just below the clock tower in Capri Town. The top funicular station brings you out onto Piazza Umberto I, better known locally as **La Piazzetta** ❷. On peak days in summer this area gets so crowded it's rumored the local police only give you 20 minutes to sip your Campari before encouraging you to move on. Admire the majolica decoration of the clock tower dial and inspect the 17th-century church of **Santo Stefano** ❸, just off the upper side of the square in Piazzetta Cerio. On the same tiny square is the **Museo Caprense Ignazio Cerio** ❹, a small four-room exhibition of archaeological and fossil finds, and useful as a backup site on a rainy day. Then forge your way across the main Piazzetta to Via Le Botteghe; if you're thinking about a picnic lunch, you can stock up on provisions here (try Sfizi di Pane, a baker at Via Le Botteghe 4 for a slice of frittata *di maccaroni* or a more orthodox *panino,* or roll, and fixings). Look to the right for the small supermarket to complete the meal or just to stock up on liquid refreshments at reasonable prices.

The farther away you get from La Piazzetta, the quieter this pedestrianized road becomes. Via Le Botteghe becomes Via Fuorlovado and then Via Croce, developing gradually into an avenue fringed by bougainvillea and spreading oleander trees. This is an area where real estate now changes hands for at least €7,000 a square meter (more than $650 per square foot). After about 10 minutes the road to the Arco Naturale branches off to the right. Archaeology buffs will instead want to continue straight on up Monte Tiberio for about 45 minutes to reach Tiberius's famous mountaintop **Villa Jovis** ❺—on the way you'll pass the entrance to the Villa Lysis, one of Capri's most legendary private homes, built by the poet Baron Fersen and now the property of a very lucky Chilean millionaire. The caffè at the crossroads is one of the last watering holes before heading out to the Arco Naturale. Follow the ceramic signs for Arco Naturale along Via Matermania for about 15 minutes until the path forks (Arco Naturale, to the left; Grotta di Matermania, to the right). Peer at the **Arco Naturale** ❻ (Natural Arch), keeping in mind that the path is a cul-de-sac, so every step you go down has to be retraced. Then, knee joints permitting, take the hundreds of steps—and we mean hundreds (don't worry, you won't have to backtrack)—down to the **Grotta di Matermania** ❼, an impressive natural cave where ancient Romans worshiped the goddess Cybéle every dawn.

Where the path levels out begins one of the most beautiful seaside walks in the world—the Via Pizzo Lungo. This path continues southward through fine Mediterranean maquis vegetation (most of the evergreen trees are holm oak) high above the shoreline, affording fine views of Punta Massullo where **Villa Malaparte** ❽—possibly the most important creation of 20th-century Italian architecture—perches over the sea. Two hundred yards farther on is a panoramic point from which you can gaze at the famous **I Faraglioni** ❾, Capri's three, striking offshore rocks, which now loom magnificently into view. As you continue westward, look first for the most romantic house on Capri, the Villa Solitaria—once home to novelist Compton MacKenzie, it's set on a bluff high over the sapphire sea and was built in the early 1900s by architect Edwin Cerio—then look for the towering rock pinnacle Pizzo Lungo (High Point), which the ancients thought was the petrified form of Polyphemus, the giant blinded by Odysseus's men. The end of the Giro dell'Arco Naturale (Natural Arch Circuit) is reached at another panoramic point, the **Punta Tragara** ⑩, which marks your arrival back in Capri Town. From here take Via Tragara—lined with elegant hotels and villas, it's the most beautiful street on Capri (some say in the world)—until it joins with Via Camerelle. Look for a left turn down Via Cerio to the **Certosa di San Giacomo** ⑪ (Charterhouse of St. James), a former monastery that is Capri's grandest architectural set-piece. About five minutes' walk away up Via Matteotti are the **Giardini di Augusto** ⑫ (Gardens of Augustus), which give an excellent view over the southern side of the island toward the Faraglioni. Here the road stops. The impressive Via Krupp has been blocked off for years, making access to Marina Piccola impossible from this point. So retrace your steps until you get to Via Serena—you'll recognize it from the vast oleander bushes on either side of the walkway, which form a picturesque arch; it's a mere five-minute walk from the Piazzetta. Once back at base, reward yourself with a granita or a fruit-based cocktail (perhaps fresh peaches or strawberries with spumante) at the Gran Caffè, the very first bar to grace the square 40 years ago. You might as well splurge on something really memorable; even standard drinks like caffè espresso and cappuccino are outrageously expensive.

TIMING   Allowing time for a refreshment stop, a little shopping, and a fair amount of camera-lens focusing, the walk will take between three and five hours, plus an extra half hour if you visit the Certosa museum. Those who aren't up for a lot of hiking should choose either the trek to the Villa Jovis or the Giro dell'Arco Naturale; the latter is a cliffside path that includes hundreds of steps (going downhill mostly), so be prepared. Most of the sites and shops are open throughout the day, but as there's more than a fair amount of up-and-down, you'd be well advised to avoid the stickiest hours—weather-wise—from noon to 3 during summer.

What to See

⑪ **Certosa di San Giacomo** (Charterhouse of St. James). Nestled between
FodorśChoice   the Castiglione and Tuoro hills, this grand, palatial complex was for cen-
★   turies a Carthusian monastery dedicated to St. James. It was founded between 1371 and 1374 by Count Giacomo Arcucci, who was given the lands and the means to create the monastery by Queen Giovanna I of Naples; the count and the queen both died during the upheaval of the Angevin monarchy. After the monastery was sacked by the pirate Dragut in the 16th century, it was heavily restored and rebuilt—thanks in part to heavy taxes exacted from the populace. The friars within were often detested by the *Capresi* because they refused to open their gates to minister to them when plague broke out.

You enter the complex via a grandly imposing entryway, which leads to the **Biblioteca Comunale Popolare Luigi Bladier** (public library) and the spacious church of **San Giacomo** (built in 1690). After admiring the church's Baroque frescoes, follow the signpost down toward the *Parco*, which leads down an avenue flanked by pittosporum and magnolia toward the monastery gardens and some welcome benches. Beyond a covered road lies the **Chiostro Grande** (Large Cloister)—originally the site of the monks' cells and now the temporary home of a high school. Nearby is the much prettier 15th-century **Chiostro Piccolo** (Small Cloister), now the venue for summertime open-air concerts. Before leaving be sure to visit the **Museo Diefenbach**, a collection of large canvases by the German painter K. W. Diefenbach, who visited Capri in 1900 and stayed until his death in 1913. Not even a protracted stay on such an uplifting island was able to cure Diefenbach of his chronic depression, and his tormented soul emerges clearly in his stunningly powerful paintings, filled with apocalyptic storms and saintly apparitions. For years, Diefenbach rivaled the Blue Grotto for sheer picturesqueness—he was given to greeting visitors replete with flowing white beard, monk's cowl, and primitive sandals. For a peek at Diefenbach's paintings, log on to www.capriweb.com/Capri/Diefenbach. From La Piazzetta take Via Vittorio Emanuele and then Via F. Serena to reach this beautiful monastic complex. ✉ *Via Certosa, Capri Town* ☎ *081/8376218* ✉ *Free* ⊙ *Tues.–Sun. 9–2, park 9–1 hr before sunset.*

⓬ **Giardini di Augusto** (Gardens of Augustus). You'll see some spectacular views of the southern side of Capri from the southernmost terrace of this well-kept park lying on both sides of Via Matteotti. The gardens are merely pretty (a tacky fountain doesn't help). In one corner of the gardens is a monument to Lenin, who visited Gorky and his Capri-based school for revolutionaries between 1907 and 1913. Above the gardens is the Villa Krupp, now a hotel of the same name. This was the home of the German industrialist Friedrich Alfred Krupp, who commissioned the zigzagging Via Krupp, temporarily closed to the public, designed by Emilio Mayer and built in 1902. An amateur marine biologist, Krupp fell in love with Capri after coming to Naples to visit its aquarium. Although heir to a munitions fortune, Krupp was the most peaceful of men and bestowed monies on many island charities. Despite his good works, he was hounded by malicious gossip that he held orgies at his villa and in the island grottoes, and he committed suicide in 1902. More than one critic has observed that Via Krupp shows that roads can be works of art as well as functional structures. Currently undergoing a massive renovation, it usually connects Giardini di Augusto and the Punta del Cannone with the Marina Piccola. ✉ *Via Matteotti, Capri Town.*

❼ **Grotta di Matermania.** Set in the bowels of Monte Tuoro, this legend-haunted cave was dedicated to Cybele, the Magna Mater, or Great Mother of the gods—hence the somewhat corrupted name of the cave. A goddess with definite eastern origins, Cybele did not form part of the Greek or Roman pantheon: worship of her was introduced to Italy in 204 BC at the command of the Sibylline oracle, supposedly for the purpose of driving Hannibal out of Italy. At dawn the cave is touched by the rays of the sun, leading scholars to believe it may also have been a shrine where the Mithraic mysteries were celebrated. Hypnotic rituals, ritual sacrifice of bulls, and other orgiastic practices made this cave a place of myth, so it is not surprising that later authors reported (erroneously) that Emperor Tiberius used it for orgies. Nevertheless, the cave was adapted by the Romans into a luxurious nymphaeum (small shrine), but little remains of the original structure, which would have been covered by tesserae, polychrome stucco, and marine shells. If you want to see the few ancient remains, you have to step inside the now-unprepossessing cavern. ✉ *Giro del'Arco Naturale.*

❾ **I Faraglioni.** Few landscapes set more artists dreaming than that of the famous Faraglioni—three enigmatic, pale-ochre limestone colossi that loom out of the sea just off the Punta Tragara on the southern coast of Capri. Soaring almost 350 feet above the water, the Faraglioni have become for most Italians a beloved symbol of Capri and have been poetically compared to Gothic cathedrals or modern skyscrapers. The first rock is called Faraglione di Terra, since it is attached to the land; at its base is the famous restaurant and bathing lido Da Luigi, where a beach mattress may accompany the luncheon menu. The second is called di Mezzo or Stella, and little boats can often be seen going through its picturesque tunnel, which was caused by sea erosion. The rock farthest out to sea is Scopolo and is inhabited by a wall lizard species with a strik-

FodorśChoice
★

ing blue belly, considered a local variant by biologists although legend has it that they were originally brought as pets from Greece to delight ancient Roman courtiers. ⊠ *End of Via Tragara, Capri Town.*

⑩ The "three sons of Capri" can be best seen from the famous lookout point at **Punta Tragara** at the end of gorgeous Via Tragara. At this point, a path—marked by a plaque honoring the poet Pablo Neruda, who loved this particular walk—leads down hundreds of steps to the water and the feet of I Faraglioni, and perhaps to a delightful lunch at one of the two lidos at the rock base: Da Luigi, a household name in the Bay of Naples, or La Fontelina, an exclusive sun-drenched retreat nearby. After lunch, habitués then hire a little boat to ferry them back to nearby Marina Piccola and the bus back to town. Near the start of the Neruda path turn left to find the most gorgeous seaside walk in Capri—the Via Pizzo Lungo. Another place to drink in the view of I Faraglioni, which is most romantic at sunset, is the Punta Del Cannone, a hilltop belvedere reached beyond the Certosa di San Giacomo and the Giardini di Augusto. ⊠ *End of Via Tragara, Capri Town.*

❷ **La Piazzetta.** The English writer and Capriophile Norman Douglas called this square, officially known as Piazza Umberto I, "the small theater of the world." The rendezvous point for international crowds, this *"salone"* became famous as the late-night place to spot heavenly bodies—of the Hollywood variety, that is: Frank Sinatra, Rita Hayworth, Julie Christie, and Julia Roberts are just a few of the celebs who made La Piazzetta the place where the rich and famous came to watch other rich and famous folk. If, in fact, *le tout Capri* bothers to make an appearance any longer, they show up at 8 in the evening to enjoy an aperitif and some peppery *tarallucchi* breadsticks, only to return for a late-night limoncello.

In any event, the square is never less than picturesque and has been a natural crossroads and meeting point since Roman times. The religious complex of Santo Stefano was built around the square in the 17th century, but the clock tower and Municipio, or town hall (once the archbishop's palace) are the only remnants of its cathedral. Capri's version of Big Ben—the charming bell tower, or Torre de'Orologio—is perched over the ancient gateway. Just above the gateway on the lower side is a Latin inscription erected by an American man of letters, Thomas Spencer Jerome, at the beginning of the 20th century; Jerome wished to restore "honor and dignity" to the much-maligned Emperor Tiberius. ⊠ *At intersection of vias Botteghe, Longano, and Vittorio Emanuele, Capri Town.*

❶ **Marina Grande.** Besides being the main gateway to Capri and the main disembarkation point for the mainland, Marina Grande is usually the starting point for round-island tours and trips to the Blue Grotto. Originally a conglomeration of fishermen's houses built on ancient Roman foundations, it's now an extended hodgepodge of various architectural styles, with buildings that almost exclusively service the tourist industry. Warehouses and storerooms in which fishermen once kept their boats and tackle are now shops, restaurants, and bars, most either tacky or overpriced. The marina has faded in the glare of neon since the days when it was Sophia Loren's home in the 1958 film *It Started in Naples.* To the west lies the historic church of San Costanzo, Palazzo a Mare (the former palace of emperor Augustus), and the chic Baths of Tiberius beach. ⊠ *Marina Grande.*

⑬ **Marina Piccola.** A 10-minute ride from the main bus terminus in Capri (Piazzetta d'Ungheria), Marina Piccola is a delightfully picturesque inlet that provides the Capresi and other sun worshipers with their best access to reasonable beaches and safe swimming. The entire cove is ro-

FodorśChoice ★

mantically lined with *stabilimenti*—elegant bathing lidos where the cabanas are often air-conditioned and the bodies can be Modigliani-sleek. The most famous of these lidos (there's a fee to use the facilities), found closest to I Faraglioni, is La Canzone del Mare, once presided over by the noted British music-hall singer Gracie Fields and for decades favored by the smart set, including Noël Coward and Emilio Pucci (who set up his first boutique here). La Canzone del Mare's seaside restaurant offers a dreamy view of I Faraglioni and a luncheon here, although pricey, can serve as an iconic Capri moment. Jutting out into the bay is the **Scoglio delle Sirene**, or Sirens' Rock—a small natural promontory—which the ancients believed to be the haunt of the Sirens, the mythical temptress whose song seduced Odysseus in Homer's *Odyssey*. This rock separates the two small beaches: Pennaulo, to the east, and Marina di Mulo, site of the original Roman harbor, to the west. ✉ *Via Marina Piccola,.*

❹ Museo Caprense Ignazio Cerio. The small but interesting museum conserves interesting Pleistocene fossil finds of pygmy elephant, rhino, and hippopotamus (Room 1), which all grazed here 200,000–300,000 years ago, when the climate and terrain were very different. Although most of the important archaeological finds—such as the statues found in the Blue Grotto—have been shipped off to Naples, Room 4 displays the leftovers, a scantily labeled collection of vases, mosaics, and stucco work from the Greek and Roman periods. ✉ *Piazzetta Cerio 8a, Cerio Capri Town* ☎ *081/8376681* 🖷 *081/8370858* 💷 *€2.6, guided tours by appointment €16* 🕐 *Tues.–Wed. and Fri.–Sat. 10–1, Thurs. 3–7* 🕐 *Closed Sun. and Mon.*

❸ Santo Stefano. Towering over La Piazzetta, with a dome that is more sculpted than constructed and with *cupolettas* that seem molded from frozen zabaglione, Capri's mother church is a prime example of *l'architettura baroccheggiante*—the term historians use to describe Capri's fanciful form of Baroque architecture. Often using vaulting and molded buttresses (since there was little wood to be found on such a scrubby island to support the ceilings), Capri's architects became sculptors when they adapted Moorish and Grecian styles into their own "homemade" architecture. Sometimes known unglamorously as the ex-cathedral, the church was built in 1685 by Marziale Desiderio of Amalfi on the site of a Benedictine convent (founded in the 6th century), whose sole relic is the clock tower campanile across the Piazzetta. As in so many churches in southern Italy, there has been a good deal of recycling of ancient building materials: the flooring of the high altar was laid with polychrome marble from Villa Jovis, while the marble in the Cappella del Sacramento was removed from the Roman villa of Tragara. Inside the sacristy are some of the church treasures, including a silver statue of San Costanzo, the patron saint of Capri, whose holy day is celebrated every May 14. Opposite the church on the tiny Piazzetta I. Cerio are the Palazzo Cerio, with its Museo Caprense Ignazio Cerio; the Palazzo Farace, which houses the Biblioteca Caprense I. Cerio (I. Cerio Library); and the Palazzo Vanalesti, the executive offices of the Capri tourist board. Ignazio Cerio's son, Edwin, is the author of many eloquent books about Capri and was also the architect of some of the island's most celebrated early-20th-century villas. ✉ *Piazza Umberto I, Capri Town.*

❺ Villa Jovis. Named in honor of the ancient Roman god Jupiter, or Jove, the villa of the emperor Tiberius is riveted to the towering Rocca di Capri like an eagle's nest overlooking the strait separating Capri from Punta Campanella, the tip of the Sorrentine peninsula. Lying near the easternmost point of the island, the villa is reached by a well-signposted 50-minute walk that climbs gradually from the Piazzetta in Capri Town and offers

Fodor's Choice
★

several opportunities along the way to slake your thirst and catch your breath (if possible, resist temptation until you get to the welcoming Bar Jovis, on Via Tiberio, about five minutes' walk from the site). Although criticized by locals for the visible conditions of neglect, Villa Jovis is nonetheless a powerful reminder of the importance of the island in Roman times. What makes the site even more compelling are the accounts of the latter years of Tiberius's reign from Capri, between AD 27 and AD 37, written by authors and near-contemporaries Suetonius and Tacitus. They had it that this villa was famous for its sybaritic living, thus sounding a leitmotif whose echo can be heard at the luxurious hotels of today.

There are remarkably few discrepancies between the accounts of the two historiographers. Both point to Tiberius's mounting paranoia in Rome, while Tacitus outlines his reason for choosing Capreae (*Annals*, Book IV). "Presumably what attracted him was the isolation of Capreae. Harborless, it has few roadsteads even for small vessels; sentries can control all landings. In winter the climate is mild, since hills on the mainland keep off gales. In summer the island is delightful, since it faces west and has open sea all round. The bay it overlooks was exceptionally lovely, until Vesuvius's eruption transformed the landscape." Capri in Roman times was the site of 12 spacious villas, but Villa Jovis is both the best preserved and must have been the largest, occupying nearly 23,000 square ft. It was believed by ancient tattletales that Tiberius, fearful of assassination, slept in different villas every night, even putting wax effigies of himself in all of them to confuse those bent on doing him harm. Although Tacitus spits with characteristic venom in his account, Suetonius leaves little to the imagination: Tiberius's character is systematically vilified and pilloried, while the atrocities committed at Villa Jovis are described in gory detail in *The Twelve Caesars*.

The entrance to the site lies just beyond the *pharos* (lighthouse) built under Tiberius and used until the 17th century to warn ships away from the narrows between Capri and the mainland. Pick up a site map at the ticket office, which gives a useful breakdown of the various areas of the villa to be visited. Nearby, you'll find the **Salto di Tiberio** (Tiberius's Leap), the place where ancient gossips believed Tiberius had enemies, among them his discarded lovers and even unfortunate cooks, hurled over the precipice into the sea some 1,000 ft below. After taking stock of this now-harmless viewing platform and its information panels, take the upper path past the baths complex around the palace residential quarters to view the heavily restored Chapel of Santa Maria del Soccorso and its large bronze statue of the Madonna. The walk around the perimeter of the site gives an idea of the overall layout of the palatial residence, which in places rose to five stories in height. From here descend some steps and then a ramp to the *ambulatio* (walkway), which offers additional spectacular views and plenty of shade, as well as a *triclinium* (dining room) halfway along. The center of the site is a complex devoted to cisterns. Unlike in Pompeii, there was no aqueduct up here to provide fresh running water, so the cisterns next to the bath complex were of prime importance. ⊠ *Via A. Maiuri* ☎ *081/8370381* ✆ *€2* ☉ *Daily 9–1 hr before sunset.*

❽ **Villa Malaparte.** Nicknamed the *Casa Come Me* (House Like Myself) and perched out on the rocky Punta Massullo, this villa is considered by some historians to be a great monument of 20th-century architecture. Built low to be part of the ageless landscape, the red-hued villa was designed in Rationalist style by the Roman architect Adalberto Libera in the late 1930s for its owner Curzio Malaparte (author of the novel *La Pelle*, which recounts various World War II experiences in Naples). Unfortunately, the aesthetic concerns of the villa are inextricably entailed with political ones: Curzio Malaparte was a full-blown Fascist and the only reason why this house was allowed to be built along this otherwise unsullied stretch of coast was by special fiat from none other than Mussolini. Malaparte was unhappy with the design and made a number of alterations during the construction phase, including the famous trapezoidal staircase that seems to grow out of the roof. The villa is private, but if you want to see it up close, it was featured as a suitably striking backdrop for Brigitte Bardot in Jean-Luc Godard's underrated film *Contempt* (1963). ⊠ *Giro dell'Arco Naturale*.

From Anacapri to the Blue Grotto

One of the most breathtaking bus rides anywhere follows the tortuous road from Capri Town 3 km (2 mi) up a dramatic escarpment to skyswimming Anacapri. Set 930 feet high over the bay, Anacapri is the island's only other town and leading settlement on the island's peaks, poetically referred to as the Monte Sirene (Siren Heights). Crowds are thickest around the square that is the starting point of the chairlift to the top of Monte Solaro and close to Villa San Michele, the main magnet up here for tour groups. To get here, take the bus from the terminus in Via Roma (Capri Town) or go directly from the port of Marina Grande (€1.30). Allow plenty of time for getting back down again, as space on the local buses is usually at a premium. The athletically inclined could try the 900 steps of the Scala Fenicia, or Phoenician Stairway (more likely to have been built by the Greeks than the Phoenicians), leading all the way down to Marina Grande (about 20 minutes' walk away; for access to this elusive path, continue walking past Villa San Michele away from Piazza Vittoria). Long in a state of disrepair, this ancient pathway has been restored and reopened. As a fitting finale, take the convenient bus down the hill from Anacapri to the water's edge and the fabled Blue Grotto.

a good walk

From Anacapri's main square of Piazza Vittoria, take Via Capodimonte to **Villa San Michele** ⑭ ▶, about a 10-minute walk on the right, past a formidable array of garish boutiques, bars, and liqueur factories, all vying to ensnare unwitting passersby. As with many sites on the island, it's best to get to the villa shortly after it opens, or in the early evening when the day-trippers have moved through. After browsing through its rooms and strolling through the gardens and the ecomuseum, retrace your steps to Piazza Vittoria and make for the lower station of the *Seggiovia* (chairlift) to **Monte Solaro** ⑮. You will soon be whisked out of town over whitewashed houses and carpets of spring-flowering broom and rockrose to the viewing platform at the top of Solaro. From here a path leads northward downhill toward the sublimely picturesque church of **Santa Maria a Cetrella** ⑯ through some of the most beautiful wooded countryside on Capri. During spring and autumn, watch for migrating birds. A splash of yellow combined with an undulating flight could be the golden oriole; the multicolor bee-eater also migrates via Capri in May and September. On the way back down from Cetrella, follow the signs to Anacapri along Via Monte Solaro (downhill), passing close to the ruins of the **Castello Barbarossa** ⑰ and then emerging close to the Villa San Michele. If you have time and energy left over, make for Via Orlandi, a useful street for stocking up on provisions. Pass the impressive **Casa Rossa** (Red House) ⑱, on your right, and then take the next right turn (Via San Nicola) to Piazza San Nicola and the church of **San Michele** ⑲. If possible, climb to the organ loft to savor its magnificent majolica tile floor depicting the Garden of Eden, then head back to the Piazza Vittoria. By mid- to late afternoon, the crowds will have vanished from the

Grotta Azzurra ⑳ (Blue Grotto), at the sea below Anacapri. Catch the convenient bus that links the town with the grotto and enjoy this fabled sight around 4 PM or 5 PM, when connoisseurs swear that the light is best. History buffs and vista lovers will want to top out their day with a trek to the nearby **Villa di Damecuta** ㉑, thought to have been one of Emperor Tiberius's secret retreats.

TIMING The walk takes approximately three hours, allowing at least one hour for the visit to Villa San Michele and its gardens, and a further two hours' leisurely ambling on the round-trip. If armed with a packed lunch, you're most likely to find a picnic site near Cetrella—in attempts to discourage low-spending day-trippers from the mainland, consumption of picnics is made fairly difficult on Capri.

Sights to See

⑱ **Casa Rossa** (Red House). Capri is famous for its villas built by artists, millionaires, and poets who became willing prisoners of Capri during the Gilded Age. Elihu Vedder, Charles Coleman, Lord Algernon, and the Misses Wolcott-Perry were some of the people who constructed lavish Aesthetic Movement houses. Built by the American colonel J. C. MacKowen, this particular villa, near the center of Anacapri, was erected between 1876 and 1898. With walls hued in distinctive Pompeian red, the villa incorporates a noted 14th-century Aragonese tower. A historian and archaeologist, MacKowen wrote a guide to Capri and brought to light marble fragments and statues inside the Blue Grotto, thus revealing and validating its importance as a nymphaeum in Roman times. ✉ *Via G. Orlandi, Anacapri* 🎫 *€2* ⊙ *Tues.–Sun. 11–1 and 6–8:30.*

⑰ **Castello Barbarossa.** The foundation of this ruined castle, almost clinging to the side of the cliff above Villa San Michele, dates to the late 10th century, when Capri was ruled by the ancient maritime republic of Amalfi. Named after the admiral of the Turkish fleet, Khair-Eddin, or Barbarossa (Redbeard), who stormed and took the castle in 1535, much of the original layout has been changed over the centuries. The castle is part of the Swedish-run Axel Munthe Foundation, which organizes weekly guided visits on Thursday afternoons from May to October (call the foundation to reserve a place) besides carrying out ornithological research in the surrounding area. ✉ *Axel Munthe Foundation, Anacapri* ☎ *081/8371401.*

⑳ **Grotta Azzurra** (Blue Grotto). Only when the spectacular Grotta Azzurra was "discovered" in 1826 by the Polish poet August Kopisch and his Swiss friend, the artist Ernest Fries, did Capri become a tourist heaven. The watery cave's breathlessly blue beauty quickly became a symbol of the era of Romanticism—a monument to man's return to Nature and revolt from Reason. The pair's discovery triggered widespread interest and began the flow of Grand Tour visitors to the island. In fact, however, the grotto had been an island landmark since time immemorial. In the Roman era, as testified by the extensive remains primarily below sea level and several large statues, it had been the elegant, mosaic-decorated nymphaeum of the adjoining Roman villa of Gradola. Historians can't quite agree if it was simply a lovely little pavilion where rich patricians would cool themselves for midday picnics or if it was truly a religious site where sacred rituals were practiced.

FodorśChoice
★

The Grotta Azzurra can be reached from Marina Grande or from the small embarkation point below Anacapri on the northwest side of the island, reached by bus from Anacapri. If you're pressed for time, skip this sometimes frustrating and disappointing excursion. You board one boat to get to the grotto, and you have to transfer to another smaller

MY BLUE HEAVEN:
THE LURE OF THE GROTTA AZZURRA

CERTAINLY ONLY A completely soulless being could fail in his mind's eye to people Capri with nymphs, dryads, and centaurs, its grottoes and caverns with mermaids and dancing fauns, while in the imagined palatial villas strewn about the island Greeks and Romans mingle with pirates, Saracens, Norman princes, and Renaissance courtiers in a vast and gay time-forgetting revel. But nowhere is Capri's hold on the imagination greater than at its Blue Grotto, or Grotta Azzurra.

Famously, it was once thought to be the haunt of Emperor Tiberius. Legend had it that the old gent stayed incognito at the nearby Villa di Dame Occulte (the modern Capri landmark Damecuta is said to derive from the name) and gained access to the wondrous grotto by a secret passage, which many thought to be the cloaca maxima (sewer) of Anacapri.

After the mists of legend swept in, the Grotta Azzurra was only "rediscovered" on August 18, 1826 by the two painters August Kopisch and Ernst Fries, with their Capri host Don Giuseppe Pagano. Then, believe it or not, it was forgotten again. Only when, two years later, the young German poet Wilhelm Waiblinger came to Capri and wrote an ode about the blue cave, which became an overnight sensation back in Germany and which inspired Hans Christian Andersen to use the Grotta Azzurra as a setting in his 1835 novel, The Improvisor, was the Blue Grotto's modern fame assured.

As one of the most famous tourist attractions in the world, it can be overrun with tour boats during peak midday hours. Perhaps this is why, after hours, Capri's prowling young and daring often steal into the watery cavern, its midnight-blue waters and opaline walls—once so dear to Emperor Tiberius's heart—the irresistible lure.

Legend claims a ship with a cargo of Tyrian purple dye (a color the exclusive province of Roman emperors) sank below the grotto and has forever colored its waters a wine-dark blue. Of course, making Emperor Tiberius's reputed retreat your own is frowned upon and officially banned by the authorities. Since local convention (and Fodor's) never considers such unofficial dunking, hail instead a magic carpet over to your hotel pool to indulge your craving for lavish soaking.

If thrill-seekers cannot avoid the grotto's lure, they attempt to swim into the cave early in the morning or after 5:30 in the evening, when the boats have left. Needless to say, they do this only if the sea is perfectly calm—fatalities have occurred in rougher weather—and always with companions at hand.

Swimming in the Blue Grotto can be an ethereal experience, and is now enjoyed by many who arrive and leave their clothes at the bar just above the entrance (no doubt it would be politic to have an aperitivo there after the swim).

Swimmers enter the cave by holding onto the chain that threads the entrance, but all swimmers attempting entry should keep in mind that the only resting place inside is on a ledge on the back wall and the distance to it a good 100 feet. This area was once the site of an ancient Roman nymphaeum, and marble statues that were found here are now on view at Capri's Certosa di San Giacomo museum.

With a face mask, snorkel, and flippers, experienced snorkelers like to swim into the cave in the usual way, then about-face and dive under for 10 or so feet, then swimming toward and under the huge undersea arch to finally pop up in the sea outside. The distance is about 65 feet, so this should only be attempted by seasoned snorkelers with companions. Old-timers tell you to watch out for the small purple jellyfish that deliver a rather annoying sting. If you decide to be venturesome here, always take extra precautions and be ever alert for your own safety.

one in order to get inside (the opening is only just over 3 feet high). If there's a backup of boats waiting to get in, you'll be given precious little time to enjoy the gorgeous color of the water and its silvery reflections. Instead, tour Anacapri first, then head to the Piazza Vittoria for the bus that connects the town with the seaside grotto. Be prepared to dicker with the boatmen at the grotto entrance. Swimmers enter "free." Yes, adventuresome types (who know that this type of activity is officially banned) can enjoy the intoxicating experience of a grotto swim, but only after-hours. Note that the Blue Grotto is just one of Capri's many seaside caves: there's also a Grotta Bianca (White Cave), Grotta Verde (Green Cave), Grotta Rossa (Red Cave), and numerous other caves, many of which can be explored if you hire a boat for a classic *giro,* or tour, of the island. And what about the best time to see the fabled blue color? It's often been said that the optimum time is from 10 AM to 1 PM; however, those hours were said to be prime by native Capresi, who, in truth, actually preferred to siesta their early afternoons away. The best time to come—especially as unknowing crowds have long since departed—is around 4 PM or 5 PM (note that at this hour, many—but not all—of the boatmen have departed with the tour buses). If you are lucky, you'll have the Blue Grotto all to yourself. ⊠ *Grotta Azzurra* 🖃€15 *from Marina Grande, €8.10 by rowboat from Grotta Azzurra near Anacapri* ☉ *9–1 hr before sunset, closed if sea is even minimally rough.*

⑮ Monte Solaro. An impressive limestone formation and the highest point on Capri (1,932 feet), Monte Solaro affords gasp-inducing views toward the bays of Naples and Salerno. A 12-minute chairlift ride will take you right to the top (refreshments available at bar), which is a starting point for a number of scenic trails on the western side of the island. Picnickers should note that even in summer it can get windy at this height, and there are few trees to provide shade or refuge. ⊠ *Piazza Vittoria, Anacapri* 🕾 *081/8371428* 🖃 *€4 one-way, €5.5 round-trip* ☉ *Daily: Mar.–Oct. 9:30–sunset, Nov.–Feb. 10:30–3.*

⑲ San Michele. The octagonal Baroque church of San Michele on Piazza San Nicola, finished in 1719, is best known for its exquisite majolica pavement (1761), designed by Solimena and executed by the Abruzzese *mastro-riggiolaro* (master tiler) Leonardo Chiaiese. A walkway skirts the rich ceramic carpet depicting Adam and a duly contrite Eve being expelled from the Garden of Eden, but you can get a breathtaking overview from the organ loft, reached by a winding staircase near the ticket booth. Outside the church is the Via Finestrale, which leads to Anacapri's noted **Le Boffe quarter.** This section of town, slightly lower on the hillside, is centered around the Piazza Ficacciate and the church of Santa Sofia and owes its name to the distinctive domestic architecture prevalent here, which uses vaults and sculpted groins instead of cross beams. The word *boffe,* as it turns out, comes from the Neapolitan dialect for "swollen." ⊠ *Piazza Nicola, Anacapri* 🕾 *081/8372396* 🖃 *€1* ☉ *Nov.–Mar., daily 9:30–4; Apr.–June, daily 9:30–5; July–Oct. daily 9:30–7.*

⑯ Santa Maria a Cetrella. Scenically perched on the slopes of Monte Solaro, this small sanctuary in late-Gothic style—with its older parts dating to the late 14th century—offers a truly picturesque frame for a panorama that takes in much of the island. It also marks the top of the second access route (Il Passetiello) used in ancient times, which linked Capri Town with Anacapri. This is the pathway that the Carthusian monks of San Giacomo would have used to reach their properties in the upper part of the island. Congregants were mainly fisherfolk whose boats were moored in the Marina Piccola directly below; they also used this clifftop aerie as a lookout against Saracen pirates. The church was substantially

FodorsChoice
★

rebuilt by Franciscan monks in the early 17th century, when a sacristy was added. To reach Santa Maria, you can climb a path leading off Viale Axel Munthe (an hour-long walk); an alternative is to descend a path leading from the Monte Solaro chairlift. The church itself is open Saturday afternoon until sunset, May to September, but the site remains unforgettable year round. ⊠ *Monte Solaro*.

㉑ Villa di Damecuta. Sited strategically on a ridge with views sweeping across the Bay of Naples toward Procida and Ischia, the main access to this Roman villa would have been from the landing stage right by the Blue Grotto at Gradola. This was probably one of the villas mentioned by Tacitus in his *Annals* as having been built by Tiberius: "Here on Capreae, in twelve spacious, separately named villas, Tiberius settled." Like Villa Jovis to the east, Villa di Damecuta was extensively plundered over the centuries prior to its proper excavation in 1937. Below the medieval tower (Torre Damecuta) there are two rooms (*domus* and *cubiculum*) that are thought to have been Tiberius's secret summer refuge. Affinities with Villa Jovis may be seen in the *ambulatio* (walkway), complete with seats and stunning backdrop. To reach Villa Damecuta, get the bus from Anacapri to Grotto Azzurra and ask the driver to let you off at the right stop. Alternatively, you can walk from the center of Anacapri down the bus route (about 30 minutes, but no sidewalks) or try your luck in the network of virtually traffic-free little alleyways running parallel to the main road. ⊠ *Via A. Maiuri* 🎟 *Free* ☉ *Daily 9–1 hr before sunset*.

► **⑭ Villa San Michele.** Henry James called this villa and garden "the most
Fodor'sChoice fantastic beauty, poetry, and inutility that one had ever seen clustered
★ together," and this encomium can't be topped. At the ancient entranceway to Anacapri just at the top of the Scala Fenicia and occupying the site of an ancient Roman villa, Villa San Michele was built (beginning in 1896) in accordance with the instructions of its owner, Axel Munthe (1857–1949). Physician to the Swedish royal family, Munthe practiced both in Paris and in Rome, thereby building up a substantial fortune, much of which he plowed into real estate in Anacapri. He was also known as a philanthropist because of his lifelong dedication to the sick and destitute. Munthe's *The Story of San Michele* is an evocative—if not entirely reliable—autobiography.

Those 19th-century artists Alma-Tadema and Lord Leighton—specialists in painting scenes *all'antica* ("of antiquity")—would have set up their easels in a minute at the villa, thanks to its Roman-style courtyards, marble walkways, and atriums. Rooms display the doctor's varied collections, which range from bric-a-brac to classical antiquities (once thought so important J. Pierpont Morgan arrived to spend millions on them, but the good doctor knew that most were fakes so refused all offers). Medieval choir stalls, Renaissance lecterns, and gilded statues of saints adorn various rooms, while the doctor's personal memorabilia enables the visiting public to find out more about this enigmatic patron of the arts and humanist. The villa is connected by a spectacular pergola path overlooking the entire Bay of Naples. This leads to the famous **Sphinx Parapet,** where an ancient Egyptian sphinx sits and looks out over to Sorrento (you cannot see its face—on purpose). It's said that if you touch the sphinx's hindquarters with your left hand while making a wish, it will come true. The parapet is connected to the little Chapel of San Michele, which once stood on the grounds of one of Tiberius's villas. When Munthe bought the property, its missing bells were said to ring as a sign that Tiberius was seeking forgiveness for having sentenced a certain carpenter from Galilee to death. Oddly enough, the only person Munthe allowed to live at the Villa San Michele (the doctor's real home was the

Torre di Materita, up the mountainside) was the Marchesa Casati, the notorious fin de siècle fashion plate who was fond of walking diamond-collared leopards down the Champs-Élyseès.

Besides hosting summer concerts, the Axel Munthe Foundation has an ecomuseum that fittingly reflects Munthe's fondness for animals, where you can learn about various bird species—accompanied by their songs—found on Capri. Not only did Munthe aid people, he bought up the hillside as a sanctuary for birds, which prevented the Caprese from capturing quail by terrible means (lured by songbirds that had been blinded to make them sing better). Today, thanks to the good Dr. Munthe, this little realm is still an Eden. ⊠ *Viale Axel Munthe, Anacapri* ☎ *081/8371401* ⊕ *www. caprionline.com/axelmunthe* ⊠ *€5* ☉ *Daily: Nov.–Feb., 10:30–3:30; Mar., 9:30–4:30; Apr., 9:30–5; May–Sept., 9–6; Oct., 9:30–5.*

Where to Stay & Eat

Most restaurants and hotels are either in Capri Town—on the lower haunch of the island—or in Anacapri, atop its dizzying Siren Heights. Each review lists whether the restaurant or hotel is in lower or upper Capri. As you can imagine, even basic accommodations come at a premium on Capri and all the zeros on the hotel bills are likely to make you feel dizzy. Many hotels charge extra for breakfast, so you might just wish to enjoy a coffee and *cornetto* pastry at a town caffè. Some hotels even add a hefty surcharge for air-conditioning. Note that although many hotels close for the winter months, some that do so are open during the Christmas and New Year holidays.

Since cars are generally not permitted on Capri, most hotels will arrange porterage from the Marina Grande port if you tell them when you're arriving (on what boat/hydrofoil, etc.). Sometimes this is a complimentary service. **Porterage services** (☎ 081/8370896) can be obtained for a fee down at the port.

★ $$$$ ✕ **La Canzone del Mare.** This is the legendary bathing lido of the Marina Piccola, erstwhile haunt of Gracie Fields, Emilio Pucci, Noël Coward, and any number of 1950s and '60s glitterati. The VIPs may have departed for the Bagni di Tiberio beach, but this setting is as magical as ever: enjoy luncheon (no dinner served) in the thatched-roof pavilion looking out over the sea and I Faraglioni in the distance—this is Capri as picture-perfect as it comes. You need to pay a fee (€16) to actually use this bathing *stabilimento* (club) but why not make a day of it? ⊠ *Via Marina Piccola 93, Capri Town* ☎ *081/8370104* ▭ *AE, DC, MC, V* ☉ *Closed Nov.–Mar. No dinner.*

★ $$$–$$$$ ✕ **La Capannina.** Isn't that Whitney Houston at the table by the door? Known as one of Capri's most celebrity-haunted restaurants, La Capannina is only a few steps from the busy social hub of the Piazzetta. It has a discreet covered veranda—opened up in the summer—for dining by candlelight in a garden setting, with most of the regulars avoiding the stuffy indoor rooms. The specialties, aside from an authentic Capri wine with the house label, are homemade *ravioli capresi* and *linguine con lo scorfano* (flat spaghetti with scorpion fish). ⊠ *Via Le Botteghe 14, Capri Town* ☎ *081/8370732* ♣ *Reservations essential* ▭ *AE, DC, MC, V* ☉ *Closed mid-Jan.–mid-Mar. and Wed. in Mar. and Nov.*

★ $$$–$$$$ ✕ **Le Grottelle.** Enjoying one of Capri's most unique settings, this extremely informal trattoria is built up against the limestone rocks not far from the Arco Naturale—a cave at the back doubles as the kitchen and wine cellar. Whether you stumble over this place, or make it your pointed destination after an island hike, Le Grottelle will prove memorable, thanks to that ambience and sea view. The food? Oh, that . . . the menu is chiefly seafood, with *linguine con gamberetti e rucola* (pasta with shrimp and arugula) one of the more interesting specialties. ⊠ *Via Arco Naturale 13* ☎ *081/8375719* ⚲ *Reservations essential* ⊟ *AE* ⊘ *Closed mid-Nov.–Mar.*

★ **$$$–$$$$** ✕ **La Fontelina.** Lying just below Punta Tragara at the base of Capri's impressive offshore rocks (the Faraglioni), this is the place to enjoy a delightfully comatose day on the island. Given its position right on the water's edge, seafood is almost de rigueur. For a slightly different starter, try the *polpette di melanzane* (eggplant fritters), and then dip into the vegetable buffet. Highly recommendable is the house sangria, a blissful mix of white wine and fresh fruit. If you're overwhelmed by large portions of pasta, order half portions (and pay half). La Fontelina also functions as a lido, with steps and ladders affording access to fathoms-deep blue water. Access is by boat from Marina Piccola or on foot from Punta Tragara (10 minutes). Only lunch is served. Across the way is the archrival lido-restaurant, Da Luigi, with a more evocative setting but now a bit too famous for its own good. ⊠ *I Faraglioni, at end of Via Tragara, Capri Town* ☎ *081/8370845* ⊟ *AE* ⊘ *Closed mid-Oct.–Easter. No dinner.*

$$–$$$$ ✕ **I Faraglioni.** With natural shade provided by a 100-year-old wisteria plant, this is a popular, fairly stylish restaurant, which is both centrally located and yet almost immersed in Mediterranean greenery. Meals here usually kick off with *uovo alla Monachina,* an egg-shape dish stuffed with mystery ingredients. For a first course, try the *straccetti con gamberi e pomodorini* (fresh green pasta with shrimp and small tomatoes). Reservations are essential for dinner. ⊠ *Via Camerelle 75, Capri Town* ☎ *081/8370320* ⊟ *AE, DC, MC, V* ⊘ *Closed Nov.–Mar.*

$$$ ✕ **Da Tonino.** It's well worth making the short detour off the beaten track to the Arco Naturale to be pampered by creative chef Tonino. With the emphasis more on land-based dishes, try pasta with fresh anchovies, tomatoes, and wild fennel, followed by local rabbit stuffed with cheese and olives, or ask for the pigeon dish with pesto, rosemary, and pine nuts, accompanied by wine from an unbelievably well-stocked cellar. ⊠ *Via Dentecala 12–14, Arco Naturale, Capri Town* ☎ *081/8376718* ⊟ *AE, DC, MC, V* ⊘ *Closed Jan. 10–Mar. 15.*

$$$ ✕ **Il Cucciolo.** Nestling in thick maquis high above the Blue Grotto and a five-minute walk from the Roman site of Villa Damecuta, this must be one of the most romantic locations in the Mediterranean. The cucina is refreshingly inventive: ask for the specialty, *fagottini all'ortica,* pasta stuffed with cheese and stinging nettles. There's evening chauffeur service to and from Anacapri. Reservations are essential in the evening. ⊠ *Via La Fabbrica 52, Anacapri* ☎ *081/8371917* ⊟ *AE, DC, MC, V* ⊘ *Closed Nov.–mid-Mar. No lunch July and Aug.*

$$–$$$ ✕ **Al Grottino.** This small and friendly family-run restaurant, which is handy to the Piazzetta, has arched ceilings and lots of atmosphere; autographed photos of celebrity customers cover the walls. House specialties are gnocchi with tomato sauce and mozzarella and linguine *ai gamberetti* (with shrimp and tomato sauce). ⊠ *Via Longano 27, Capri Town* ☎ *081/8370584* ⚲ *Reservations essential* ⊟ *AE, MC, V* ⊘ *Closed Nov. 3–Mar. 20.*

$$–$$$ ✕ **La Rondinella.** This is an airy ristorante-pizzeria looking onto the main pedestrianized street of Anacapri. In summer make sure you reserve a table out on the popular terrace. If you have difficulty choosing from the extensive menu, ask for advice or opt for one of their best pasta dishes, linguine *macchiavelle,* with capers, olives, and cherry tomatoes. ⊠ *Via Orlandi 295, Anacapri* ☎ *081/8371223* ⊟ *AE, DC, MC, V* ⊘ *Closed Jan. 10–Feb. and Thurs. Oct.–May.*

★ **$$–$$$** ✕ **Ristorante Pizzeria Aurora.** Though often frequented by celebrities—photographs of famous guests adorn the walls inside—this restaurant offers courtesy and *simpatia* irrespective of your persona. If you want to eat out and be seen, reserve one of the tables outside on one of Capri's most chic thoroughfares; otherwise go for extra privacy and ambience within. The cognoscenti start by sharing a pizza all'Acqua, a thin pizza with mozzarella and a sprinkling of *peperoncino* (chili). If tiring of pasta, try the *sformatino alla Franco* (rice pie in prawn sauce) but leave room for the homemade sweets. ✉ *Via Fuorlovado 18–20, Capri Town* ☎ *081/8370181* ⚏ *Reservations essential* ▭ *AE, DC, MC, V* ⊘ *Closed Jan. and Feb.*

$–$$ ✕ **Da Gelsomina.** Set amid its own terraced vineyards with inspiring views to the island of Ischia and beyond, this is much more than just a well-reputed restaurant. It has an immaculately kept swimming pool and is located close to the island's finer walks—an excellent base for a whole day or longer. There's also a five-room pensione, with free transfer service by request from Anacapri center. ✉ *Via Migliera 72, Anacapri* ☎ *081/8371499* ▭ *AE, DC, MC, V* ⊘ *Closed Jan.–mid-Feb. and Tues. in winter.*

$–$$ ✕ **Mamma Giovanna.** This ristorante-pizzeria sits below Piazza Diaz in the heart of the old town of Anacapri, facing the 16th-century church of Santa Sofia. The no-frills ambience belies the quality of the cucina: besides *pizze* (served midday and evenings), Mamma Giovanna specializes in *primi piatti*, (first courses) such as *maccheroncelle al cartoccio* (baked pasta with seafood). ✉ *Via Boffe 3/5, Anacapri* ☎ *081/8372057* ⚏ *Reservations essential* ▭ *No credit cards* ⊘ *Closed Jan.and Feb. and Wed. Oct.–Apr.*

★ $$$$ ▦ **La Scalinatella.** If you're bronzed and beautiful, or just bronzed, or even just beautiful, this is your kind of hotel. A white Moorish mansion out of the Arabian Nights, it conjures up Capri in finest Hollywood fashion. The name means "little stairway," and that's how this charmingly small hotel is built, on terraces following the slope of the hills, with winding paths and bougainvillea arbors. Inside, the decor is *Architectural Digest*—opulent, with Venetian blackamoor statues, Empire-era consoles, and Valentino fabrics. Guest rooms have overstuffed sofas, bright colors, large terraces, and his-and-her bathrooms (with whirlpool baths). Outside, one of Capri's bluest pools is the fetching setting for delicious luncheons. ✉ *Via Tragara 8, Capri Town 80073* ☎ *081/8370633* 🖷 *081/8378291* ⊕ *www.scalinatella.com* ⬿ *52 rooms* △ *Restaurant, minibars, tennis court, pool, bar* ▭ *No credit cards* ⊘ *Closed Nov.–mid-Mar.* ⊮ *BP.*

$$$$ ▦ **Punta Tragara.** Soigné, adorable, and drop-dead gorgeous, this is eas-
Fodor'sChoice ily the finest hotel on Capri. Clinging to the Punta Tragara, it has a hold-
★ your-breath perch directly over the famed rocks of I Faraglioni. Originally a villa enjoyed by Churchill and Eisenhower, its exterior was renovated by Le Corbusier in traditional Capri style, then opened as a hotel in the 1970s by Countess Manfredi. Baronial fireplaces, gilded antiques, and travertine marble set the style in the main salons, while guest rooms—no two are alike—are sumptuously cozy-casual. The dreamy garden area is the showstopper here and it comes studded with two saltwater pools. One is adorned with exotic trees and cacti, and bordered with flag-poles flying yachting colors. The other is a jet-powered, aquamarine jewel set a foot away from La Bussola, an idyllic, arbor-covered restaurant that just might be the prettiest spot on the island. To top it off, the entire staff seems to have been sent to the finest finishing schools. If you really want to taste the good life, stay here. ✉ *Via Tragara 57, Capri Town 80073* ☎ *081/8370844* 🖷 *081/8377790* ⊕ *www.hoteltragara.com* ⬿ *48 rooms* △ *Restaurant, minibars, 2 pools, bar* ▭ *AE, DC, MC, V* ⊮ *BP.*

$$$$ ▦ **Quisisana.** This was one of Capri's first and most celebrated hotels, and it still packs them in. This seems to be the operative phrase, for this place seems nearly as elephantine as a Las Vegas hotel (rather a sacrilege on tiny Capri, don't you think?). The mile-long lobby leads to the pool area—gorgeous, yes, but the size of a set for an Esther Williams MGM movie. The Quisisana remains a favorite with some because of its shiny and luxe restaurants, see-and-be-seen bars, professional service, array of facilities, and location (just down the street from the crowded Piazzetta, this is *too* convenient). Spacious guest rooms have arcaded balconies—the only problem is that there are floors and floors of them. Still, the Quisisana's legend is strong: the hotel's Krug Bar is Capri's latest hangout for the rich and famous. ⊠ *Via Camerelle 2, Capri Town 80073* ☎ *081/8370788* 🖷 *081/8376080* ⊕ *www.quisi.com* ⇆ *150 rooms* ♿ *Restaurant, minibars, tennis court, pool, sauna, bar* 🖃 *AE, DC, MC, V* ⊙ *Closed Nov.–mid-Mar.* ⅋⊙⅋ *BP.*

$$$$ 🏨 **Villa Brunella.** This quiet family-run gem is set in a garden just below the lane leading to the Faraglioni. Comfortable and tastefully furnished, the hotel also has spectacular views, a swimming pool, and a terrace restaurant known for good food. ⊠ *Via Tragara 24, Capri Town 80073* ☎ *081/8370122* 🖷 *081/8370430* ✉ *villabrunella@capri.it* ⇆ *18 rooms* ♿ *Restaurant, minibars, pool, bar* 🖃 *AE, DC, MC, V* ⊙ *Closed Nov.–Mar.* ⅋⊙⅋ *EP.*

$$$–$$$$ 🏨 **Caesar Augustus.** A favorite of the Hollywood set, this landmark
Fodor'sChoice hotel has long been considered a Caprese paradise thanks to its breath-
★ taking perch atop an Anacapri cliff and the grandeur of its villa and gardens. As for accommodations, think chic, charming, and casual: the chairs are plump, the beds enormous, the bouquets fragrant. You won't give a second's thought to décor, however, once you catch sight of the fabled stone terrace and its Cinerama view of the Bay of Naples or the pool—a jaw-dropping extravaganza nearly levitating 1,000 ft over the sea and easily one of the most glamorous spots on Earth. Blissfully distant from Capri Town's crowds, the hotel has a private van to shuttle pampered guests back and forth, but chances are they'll rarely want to leave this dreamy domain. ⊠ *Via G. Orlandi 4, Anacapri 80071* ☎ *081/8373395; 081/8371421 reservations* 🖷 *081/8371444* ⊕ *www.caesar-augustus.com* ⇆ *56 rooms* ♿ *Coffee shop, minibars, pool, bar, lounge* 🖃 *AE, DC, MC, V* ⊙ *Closed Nov.–mid-Apr.* ⅋⊙⅋ *BP.*

$$$$ 🏨 **La Palma.** Though the oldest on Capri (1822), this attentively run hotel has certainly not rested on its laurels. When you arrive at its front door you're immediately given a blast of island glamour, with gleaming lobby, palm trees, and majolica-tiled rooms providing a delightful contrast to the hustle at street level outside (this is just down the street from La Piazzetta). Room prices dip substantially outside peak season, making it more affordable to enjoy this oasis of style and tranquillity in the town center. ⊠ *Via V. Emanuele 39, Capri Town 80073* ☎ *081/8370133* 🖷 *081/8376966* ✉ *palma@mbox.caprinet.it* ⇆ *72 rooms* ♿ *Restaurant, minibars, bar, meeting room* 🖃 *AE, DC, MC, V* ⊙ *Closed Jan.–Easter* ⅋⊙⅋ *MAP.*

$$$ 🏨 **San Michele.** You'll find this large white villa-hotel next to Axel Munthe's home. Surrounded by luxuriant gardens, the San Michele offers solid comfort and good value, along with spectacular views. It's modern, with some Neapolitan period pieces adding atmosphere. Most rooms have a terrace or balcony overlooking either sea or island. ⊠ *Via G. Orlandi 5, Anacapri 80071* ☎ *081/8371427* 🖷 *081/8371420* ⊕ *www.sanmichele-capri.com* ⇆ *59 rooms* ♿ *Restaurant, minibars, pool* 🖃 *AE, DC, MC, V* ⊙ *Closed Nov.–Mar.* ⅋⊙⅋ *MAP.*

$$–$$$ 🏨 **Gatto Bianco.** A literary atmosphere pervades this spacious but discreet hotel located only two minutes' walk from the Piazzetta. Jacqueline Kennedy sought refuge here when hounded by paparazzi. It now provides old-world charm and character with a distinct local flavor. ⊠ *Via*

Vittorio Emanuele 32, Capri Town 80073 ☎ *081/8370203* 🖷 *081/ 8378060.* 📧 *h.gattobianco@capri.it* 🛏 *44 rooms* 🖃 *AE, DC, MC, V* ☉ *Closed Nov.–mid-Mar.* 🍽 *BP.*

$$ 🏨 **Biancamaria.** This tastefully refurbished hotel with its pleasing facade and whitewashed spreading arches lies in a traffic-free zone close to the heart of Anacapri. The front rooms have large terraces looking toward Monte Solaro; those at the back are quieter and more private. ⊠ *Via G. Orlandi 54, Anacapri 80073* ☎ *081/8371000* 🖷 *081/8372060* ⊕ *www. villasarah.it* 🛏 *25 rooms* 🖃 *AE, MC, V* ☉ *Closed Nov.–Mar.* 🍽 *BP.*

★ $$ 🏨 **Villa Krupp.** Occupying a beautiful house overlooking the idyllic Gardens of Augustus, this historic hostelry was built by the tortured German munitions millionaire Friedrich Krupp and was once the home of Maxim Gorky, whose guests included Lenin. Rooms are plain but spacious, with comfy beds (" . . . crisp white sheets accentuate the blueness outside," waxed poetic one Fodor's reader), and some have south-facing terraces with awesome views. The Punta Cantone viewpoint, Certosa di San Giacomo, and I Faraglioni are all just a few minutes away. ⊠ *Viale Matteotti 12, Capri Town 80073* ☎ *081/8370362* 🖷 *081/ 8376489* 🛏 *12 rooms* 🖃 *MC, V* ☉ *Closed Nov.–Feb.* 🍽 *BP.*

$$ 🏨 **Villa Sarah.** This whitewashed Mediterranean building has a homey look and bright, simply furnished rooms. It's close enough to the Piazzetta (a 10-minute walk) to give easy access to the goings-on there, yet far enough away to ensure restful nights. There are a garden and a small bar. ⊠ *Via Tiberio 3/a, Capri Town 80073* ☎ *081/8377817* 🖷 *081/8377215* 🛏 *20 rooms* ♿ *Bar* 🖃 *AE, DC, MC, V* ☉ *Closed Nov.–Mar.* 🍽 *BP.*

$–$$ 🏨 **Villa Helios.** The charming Villa Helios is set in a 19th-century, lilachued, Moorish-inspired villa, surrounded by extensive orchards and located on a quiet Capri lane. Don't come here for luxe—floors are linoleum-covered and some rooms share baths. Do come here for peace— a lovely chapel occupies part of the first floor. For a small fee (€2.1) all guests become members of the Centro Italiano Turismo Sociale, a Christian organization operating Italy-wide. Profits from the operation are thoughtfully channeled by the villa's owners (Franciscan nuns) into a local hospice. ⊠ *Via Croce 4, Capri Town 80073* ☎ *081/8370240* 🖷 *06/2332–01945* ⊕ *www.villahelios.it* 🛏 *25 rooms, 20 with bath* 🖃 *MC, V* ☉ *Closed mid-Oct.–Apr.* 🍽 *BP.*

$ 🏨 **Aida.** A 10-minute walk from the town center in a tiny lane that borders the Gardens of Augustus, the Aida offers a tranquil haven from Capri's bustle and hard sell. The staff is sociable, and the rooms, which look onto a small garden, are spacious, comfortably furnished, and immaculate. ⊠ *Via Birago 18, Capri Town, 80073* ☎ *081/8370366* 🛏 *7 rooms* 🖃 *MC, V* ☉ *Closed Nov.–Mar.* 🍽 *BP.*

$ 🏨 **Villa Eva.** Named after its dynamic owner-manageress, this is a popular international stopover for young *Wandervögel* (travelers) who have a laid-back approach to traveling. Accommodation is in small, low-impact villas set in luxuriant gardens. When not tending the grounds, Vincenzo, Eva's husband, will take you down to the nearby Blue Grotto for a late-afternoon swimming expedition. ⊠ *Via La Fabbrica 8, Anacapri 80073* ☎ *081/8371549* 🖷 *081/8372040* ⊕ *www.caprionline. com/villaeva* 🛏 *24 rooms* 🖃 *AE, DC, MC, V* ☉ *Closed mid-Nov.–mid-Feb.* 🍽 *BP.*

Nightlife & the Arts

As would be expected, Capri offers a fair spread of evening entertainment, especially on weekends and during the busier months of July and August, when many upper-crust Italians from the mainland occupy their holiday homes on the island. For music that is fairly gentle on the ears, try one of the traditional *taverne,* which are peculiar to Capri Town. There are also a number of discos and piano bars from which to choose but the nightlife is more laid-back than Naples or even Ischia. On summer nights the place to be seen showing off your tan and sipping your extra-dry martini is the Piazzetta. Christmas on Capri is a special time, when most of the island visitors are Italians. On New Years' Eve, the Piazzetta is definitely the place to be seen, with dancing and music culminating in a magnificent fireworks display. On New Year's Day there are marching bands, pageants, and all the revelry you would expect on this exuberant island.

Discos

For 360° music almost any night of the year, **Underground** (✉ Via Orlandi 259, Anacapri ☎ 081/8372523) is the clubbing spot for cognoscenti of various ages. Unlike most other discos in Italy, no admission fee is charged, though you are expected to knock back the odd drink (about €10 each). A new "wine corner" is pulling in the thirtysomethings. This is the only club open all year. On Tuesdays in July and August, make a point of going down to Antonio Beach near the Faro, where Underground arranges open-air discos by the water's edge beginning at 10:30 PM. **Zeus** (✉ Via Orlandi 103, ☎ 081/8371169) pulls in a much younger crowd that dances the night away at the beach parties held at the Faro di Punto Carena in summer.

Bars

Bar Tiberio (✉ Piazza Umberto 8 ☎ 081/8370268) is where the locals go to people-watch in the Piazzetta. Great cakes and a good selection of nibbles with your pricey cocktail make this a classic choice in the square. Under the shadow of the Piazzetta's clock tower is **Pulalli** (✉ Piazza Umberto 4 ☎ 081/8374108) where you can enjoy tapas-style snacks while sipping wine on the open terrace.

Taverne

Anema e Core (✉ Via Sella Orta 39/e, Capri Town ☎ 081/8376461) means "soul and heart" in Caprese dialect. This popular place is tucked down a quiet side street two minutes' walk from the Piazzetta. Admission (€25) includes an eclectic range of lightish live music (after 11 PM) and a drink from the bar. No food is served, so come well-sated. There's no dancing here officially, though some patrons—including celebrities—occasionally take to the tables. The spot is closed Mondays and is usually open 9 PM to 3 AM. Reservations are essential on weekends. Tucked well away from the hub of the Piazzetta is **Guarracino** (✉ Via Castello 7, Capri Town ☎ 081/8370514), the place for traditional Neapolitan guitar music with a hint of Latin-American rhythm.

The Arts

Culturally speaking, Capri has a fairly long hibernation. Recitals and other low-key cultural events are held in winter in the Centro Caprense Ignazio Cerio, though from June through September the island comes alive with various events, including an outdoor concert season. It's a magical experience to see works performed at the Villa San Michele or in the Certosa di San Giacomo. In general, for information about cultural events and art exhibitions, ask at the local tourist information office or scan the posters in shop windows.

Music & Concerts

Concerts are held regularly at the Certosa di San Giacomo in the attractive Chiostro Piccolo from June through September (usually Wednesday and weekends), while the Axel Munthe Foundation co-sponsors free concerts on the grounds of Villa San Michele on weekends. This means that if you're interested in either, you'll also have to arrange an overnight stay on the island.

Sports & the Outdoors

Although there are several tennis courts on the island, most are restricted access, so the vast majority of people looking to burn up excess energy do so at sea level or below. For naturalists, bird-watching is particularly good in spring and autumn as Capri lies on a migration pathway, and botany lovers will be thrilled by the island's various nature trails, especially from April to June.

Scuba Diving

For those who want something more adventurous than a little snorkeling off Marina Piccola, scuba diving can be arranged from Marina Grande, and you can rent your own Zodiac (no license required) to take you round the coast to one of the island's many lesser-known grottoes. As a general rule, avoid weekends, as island sea traffic makes navigation trying. When scuba diving, always use safety buoys to signal your presence underwater. The main outfitter is **Whales** (⊠ Via Colombo 17, Marina Grande, Capri ☎ 081/8375833), which charges about €40 per hr(2 hrs minimum) to hire a six-seat *gommone* (Zodiac). For the inexperienced, **Sercomar** (⊠ Via C. Colombo 64, Marina Grande ☎ 081/8378781 ⊕ www.caprisub.com) organizes diving courses leading to certification, mainly around the Marina Piccola area.

Swimming & Stabilimenti

Capri is not noted for fine beaches. "Strand-ed" habitués cram onto **Marina Piccola,** generally considered to have the best beach on the island. It's certainly the most historic: Homer believed this to be the legendary spot where the Sirens nearly snared Odysseus. ⊠ *Marina Piccola.* Social go-getters seem to prefer the less picturesque Bagni di Tiberio beach near Marina Grande. At Marina Piccola, expect to pay about €12 per person for the use of showers, lockers, and a sun chair/sun bed. It's definitely worth investing in snorkeling gear, as the sea is rich in marine life, and visibility is often excellent.

Rather than visiting public beaches, many sunworshippers opt to enjoy the fabled *stabilimenti balenari* (private bathing lidos) scattered around the island, some of which offer real relaxation and unbelievable views. One of the most famous is **La Fontelina** (⊠ Località Faraglioni, Capri Town ☎ 081/8370845 ☎ €12 admission includes locker and sun chair; €6 for beach umbrella), open from April to October. Situated at the foot of the Faraglioni rocks, the lido's magical setting will enchant you. There is no beach here, so the lido isn't suitable for children. You can get to La Fontelina by using a rocky path that begins at the end of Via Tragara; others prefer to take a ferry (€2.50) from the more accessible Marina Piccola during the afternoon. The excellent but pricey restaurant is only open for lunch. The **Lido del Faro** (⊠ Località Punta Carena, Anacapri ☎ 081/8371798 ⊕ www.lidofaro.com ☎ €8 admission includes locker and sunchair; €12 sunbed, €5 beach umbrella), on the Anacapri side of the island, is set amid rocks with a natural basin as a sea-water swimming pool and is open from April to October during daylight hours (special evening hours during August). The sun usually beats down on this westerly headland all day while on summer nights the restaurant provides a unique setting for enjoying the freshest fish. The lido is easily accessible by bus from Anacapri Town. Note that many other stabilimenti are set on the enchanting Marina Piccola, particularly the famous Canzone del Mare (*see* Where to Stay & Eat, *above*).

Tennis

Almost right in the town center but pleasingly secluded are the three clay courts of **Tennis Capri** (✉ Via Camerelle 41, Capri Town ☎ 081/8388245 ⊠ €25 per hr per court, €31 per lesson, racquets for hire). Access is off Via Sella Orta.

Shopping

Although Capri is unlikely to be a bargain hunter's paradise, shopping here is almost an experience in its own right. In the main town near the Piazzetta, the shop windows are usually immaculately dressed, although the shops themselves are generally designed to be low impact and pleasing on the eye. Large neon signs are definitely out. Frustratingly though, goods are often displayed without price tags, which means you have to shop Italian-style: decide whether you like an article first and then inquire about its price, rather than vice versa.

Bookstores

An antiquarian's delight and one of the most elegant bookstores in Italy, **La Conchiglia** (✉ Via Camerelle 18, Capri Town ☎ 081/8378199 ⊕ www.laconchigliacapri.com ✉ Via Le Botteghe 12, Capri Town ☎ 081/8376577 ✉ Via Orlandi 205, Anacapri ☎ 081/8372646) not only offers the largest selection of books on Capri and the Bay of Naples islands but publishes many sumptuous tomes through its own imprint. In addition to their own books, an attractive array of 19th-century prints, gouaches, and vintage editions of English books on Capri and the south of Italy is offered at their art gallery–cum–store, although a greater variety of titles is offered at their Via Le Botteghe location. There's also a branch in Anacapri.

Jewelry

The extra security of being on a virtually crime-free island means that you can actually wear the expensive items you might want to buy. Some tax-free "bargains" might be possible from **Cartier** (✉ Via Vittorio Emanuele 47, Capri Town ☎ 081/8370618), though their range of goods is unlikely to vary worldwide. Alternatively, try **Alberto and Lina** (✉ Via Vittorio Emanuele 18, Capri Town ☎ 081/8370643 ⊕ www.capridream.com/linacapri) for a distinctive locally crafted brooch or some cuff links displaying ancient Roman coins.

Perfume

If you're looking for something that's easily portable to take back from Capri, then eau de toilette, a potpourri, or perfumed soap might be just the thing. **Carthusia** has been making perfumes since 1948, but—as they will proudly tell you—the tradition of perfumery on the island stretches back hundreds of years to the days of Queen Giovanna of Anjou. The factory, close to the Certosa di San Giacomo, is open for visits and a limited range of purchases, although there are no official guided tours of the premises. (✉ *Factory: Via Matteotti, Capri Town* ☎ *081/8370368 Showrooms:* ✉ *Via Camerelle 10, Capri Town* ☎ *081/8370529* ✉ *Via Capodimonte 26, Anacapri* ☎ *081/8373668* ⊕ *www.carthusia.com.*

Resortwear

Capri's main shopping streets—the Via Vittorio Emanuele and Via Camerelle, down the road from the island's main square, La Piazzetta—are crammed with world-famous names (Fendi, Gucci, Benetton, Ferragamo, Hermès). But if you're overwhelmed by the choice and are looking for something stylish but Capri-distinctive—in an astonishing range of colors—then check out the bright hand-block prints on clothes, bags, and shoes by Capri-local Livio De Simone at **La Parisienne** (✉ Piazza Um-

berto 7 Capri Town ☎ 081/8370283 ⊕ www.laparisiennecapri.it);
here, too, you can purchase copies of the original capri pants worn by
such gilded folk as Audrey Hepburn. The boutiques of Roberto Russo
are favored by fashion folk. **Capri Uomo** (✉ Piazzetta Quisisana, Capri
Town ☎ 081/8388200 ⊕ www.russocapri.com) has one of the largest
selections. **Capri Donna** (✉ Via Vittorio Emanuele 5, Capri Town ☎ 081/
8388200) has many fans. Browse around **Rubinacci** (✉ Via Camerelle
9, Capri Town ☎ 081/8377295) for something smart yet casual in cotton, linen, or cashmere. Sandals are a Capri speciality. With a family
business stretching back 82 years, **Giuseppe Faiella** (✉ Via Vittorio
Emanuele 49, Capri Town) is justifiably proud of his made-to-measure
footwear. Expect to pay €35–€50 for a carefully handcrafted pair.

ISCHIA: THE SEASIDE CURE

Although Capri leaves you breathless with its charm and beauty, Ischia
takes time to cast its spell. In fact, an overnight stay is definitely not long
enough for the island to get into your blood. Here you have to look harder
for the signs of antiquity, the traffic is reminiscent of Naples—albeit on
a good day—and the island displays all the hallmarks of rapid, uncon-
trolled urbanization. Ischia does have its jewels, though. There are the
wine-growing villages beneath the lush volcanic slopes of Monte Epomeo,
and unlike Capri, the island enjoys a life of its own that survives when
the tourists head home. Ischia has some lovely hotel-resorts high in the
mountains, offering therapeutic programs and rooms with dramatic views.
Should you want to plunk down in the sun for a few days and tune out
the world, then go down to sea level: against the towering backdrop of
Monte Epomeo and with one of the island's inviting beaches—or natural hot baths—close at hand, you might wonder what Emperor Augustus could have been thinking when he surrendered Ischia to the
Neapolitans in return for Capri. Still, many find Ischia's physical charms
pale in comparison to Capri's splendor.

Unlike Capri, Ischia is volcanic in origin. From its hidden reservoir of
seething molten matter come the thermal springs said to cure whatever
ails you. Today the island's main industry, tourism, revolves around the
100 or so thermal baths; some of them are attached to hotels. In the
height of summer, the island's population of 60,000 swells more than
sixfold, with considerable strain placed on local water resources and public transport facilities and with decibel counts rising notably. However,
most of the *confusione* is concentrated within the island's six towns and
along its main roads, and it's relatively easy to find quiet spots even close
to the beaten path.

With easy access to the coastline, the area from Ischia Ponte to Forio is
almost a continuum of *stabilimenti balneari* (private bathing establishments) in summer, set against the scenic backdrop of Monte Epomeo and
its verdant slopes. Most port traffic to the island—mainly ferries and hydrofoils from the mainland—is channeled into Ischia Porto and Casamicciola, both towns also being burgeoning resorts and busy spa centers.
The Castello Aragonese in Ischia Ponte, which is a vast medieval complex rather than just a castle, is probably the island's main historic sight;
Lacco Ameno, with its immense archaeological heritage and more up-
market ambience, is a good base for exploring the north of the island;
Forio is famous for the grand gardens of La Mortella. Buses between the
main towns are frequent and cheap, though somewhat overcrowded.

Ischia Ponte

22 *2 km (1 mi) southeast of Ischia Porto.*

★ Marked by the spectacular **Castello Aragonese**, the harbor at Ischia Ponte is Ischia's main gateway. From afar you can make out the brooding, towering castle, which sits atop an islet just off the main shore at Ischia Ponte (or Ischia Bridge), so-called because of the causeway built in the mid-15th century to connect it with the rest of Ischia. The little island was settled as early as the 5th century BC, when the tyrant Hiero of Syracuse came to the aid of Cumae in its power struggle against the Etruscans. This was his reward: an almost unassailable natural islet more than 300 ft high, on which he erected high watchtowers to monitor movements across the Bay of Naples. The island changed hands in the succession of centuries, with Greeks from Neapolis, Romans, Visigoths, Vandals, Ostrogoths, Saracens, Normans, Swabians, and Angevins successively staking successful claims to the island and modifying the fortifications and settlements. Ischia Ponte was where the population of Ischia sought refuge in 1301, when Epomeo's last eruption buried the town of Geronda on the other side of the causeway. The new influx of inhabitants led to a flurry of building activity, most notably the construction of the **Cattedrale dell'Assunta,** built above a pre-existing chapel that then became its crypt. In the following century the Angevin castle was rebuilt by Alfonso of Aragon (1438), who gave it much of its present form. However, its turbulent history continued well into the 19th century, when it was seriously damaged by the English in their attempts to dislodge the French during the Napoleonic Wars (1809). Parts of the citadel were then used to house political (anti-Bourbon) prisoners until the Risorgimento and Italy's unification in 1861.

Two hours should be enough to give you a feel of the citadel, stroll along its ramparts, and visit its key religious sites. Don't miss the frescoed 14th-century crypt beneath the cathedral (Giotto school), although the ruined cathedral itself, with its noticeable 18th-century additions—such as the Baroque stucco work—is quite atmospheric. Access to the citadel is via an elevator from the base, and the various walks at the top are clearly signposted. While taking in the whole site, enjoy the stunning views from the various vantage points. ⊠ *Castello Aragonese, Ischia Ponte* ☎ *081/ 992834* ⊠ *€8* ☉ *June–Sept., daily 9–7; Mar.–Apr., Oct.–mid-Nov., daily 9–5; closed mid-Nov.–Dec. 26 and Jan. 7–Mar. 1.*

Where to Stay & Eat

With signs like BIER VOM FASS and SPAGHETTI-EIS HIER, you could be forgiven if you thought you were actually in northern Europe rather than on the Mediterranean. Fortunately, the Germans who flock to Ischia tend to be fairly discerning customers when it comes to dining and lodging, and standards in both departments tend to be high when measured against respective prices. In general, when choosing a hotel on Ischia, make sure it does not look onto the busy Strada Nazionale, the main road linking the six towns on the island. When choosing wines, the draught house wines—especially whites—are usually quite palatable and significantly cheaper than the bottled variety. Note that restaurant and hotel reviews for Ischia are listed under each town.

$–$$ ✕ **Ristorante Cocò Gelo.** This inviting restaurant sits on the causeway linking the Aragonese castle to the rest of Ischia and is renowned for its fresh fish, which is highly prized by the Ischitani. Try the linguine *ai calamaretti* (with squid); a good starter in winter months is the vegetable-based *zuppa di fagioli e scarola* (bean and escarole soup). ⊠ *Via Aragonese 1* ☎ *081/ 981823* ⊟ *AE, DC, MC, V* ☉ *Closed Jan.–Feb. and Wed. Oct.–Mar.*

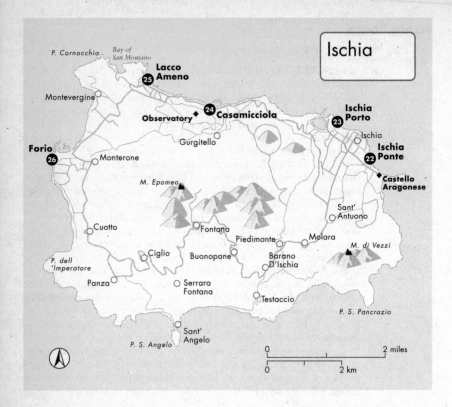

★ $$ 🏨 **Pensione Il Monastero.** Uniquely located within the Castello Aragonese at Ischia Ponte and with rustic rooms that peer down into the Mediterranean hundreds of feet below, this is the ultimate in ambience combined with the peace and quiet of a traffic-free area. Rooms are on the simple side, but the new (2003) management is friendly and tries to warm things up. This is a highly popular hotel, so book way in advance. ⊠ *Castello Aragonese 3, 80077* 🕾 *081/992435* ⊕ *www. castelloaragonese.it* 🖙 *21 rooms, 20 with bath* ⊟ *MC, V* ☉ *Closed Oct. 20–late Mar.* ⊺◎⊺ *BP.*

★ $ 🏨 **Villa Antonio.** Blessed with a stunning perch over the Bay of Cartaromana, with the Castello Aragonese posing front and center in a panoramic vista, the Antonio offers a quiet haven just five minutes from the crowds. Direct access to the sea is a few private steps away from the lovely whitewashed and casual villa, but sun-beds abound at several garden levels so most guests tend not to stray too far. Owner Antonio's brother Giovanni is a scupltor—his granite and marble works are scattered around the flower-decked terraces. Rooms are basic, but all have sea views. ⊠ *Via S. Giuseppe della Croce, 80077* 🕾 *081/ 982660* 🖷 *081/983941* ⊕ *www.villantonio.com* 🖙 *14 rooms* ♨ *Bar* ⊟ *No credit cards* ☉ *Closed Nov.–Mar.* ⊺◎⊺ *BP.*

Nightlife & the Arts

There's a rich tradition in Ischian local festivals, with the feast of Sant'Anna (July 26) holding pride of place with its skillful choreography and floating procession in the marina at Ischia Ponte below the Aragonese Castle. For year-round frolicking, Ischia Ponte has a well-known discotheque, actually within the Aragonese Castle, which in its heyday (1960s and 1970s) attracted world celebrities (now it's a magnet for the teenage scooter brigade): **Castillo D'Aragona** (⊠ Castello Aragonese 39/e, Ischia Ponte ☎ 338/1829107).

Ischia Porto

② *4 km (3 mi) east of Casamicciola.*

Ischia Porto is the largest town on the island and the usual point of debarkation. It's no workaday port, however, but a pretty resort with plenty of hotels and low, flat-roofed houses on terraced hillsides above the water. Its narrow streets often become flights of steps that scale the hill, and its villas and gardens are framed by umbrella pines. The port area was originally a landlocked volcanic crater: the Bourbon king Ferdinand II had a channel cut to create an opening seaward, and then created a sheltered port (1854). As you walk into the town along the waterfront, note the grandiose facade of the municipal baths (where Ferdinand II used to take the waters), now used for town council offices and occasional art exhibitions. While exploring Ischia Porto, be sure to stop by **Ciccio** (⊠ Via Jasolino), near the ferry piers, for the best gelati on Ischia.

Where to Stay & Eat

$$–$$$ ✕ **Da Gennaro.** This small family restaurant on the seafront at Ischia Porto serves excellent fish in a convivial atmosphere. Specialties include spaghetti with clams and linguine *all'aragosta* (with lobster). ⊠ *Via Porto 66* ☎ *081/992917* ⊟ *AE, DC, MC, V* ☉ *Closed Nov.–mid-Mar.*

$$$ 🏨 **La Villa Rosa.** A highlight at this gracious family-run hotel, in a villa with bright and airy rooms, is the thermally heated pool in the garden. In high season half-board is required, and you must reserve well in advance. Prices fall into the lower end of this category. It's in the heart of Ischia Porto and only a short walk from the beach. ⊠ *Via Giacinto Gigante 3, 80077* ☎*081/991316* 🖷*081/992425* ⊕*www.lavillarosa.it* ⟲*37 rooms* ♢ *Restaurant, minibars, pool* ⊟ *AE, DC, MC, V* ☉ *Closed Nov.–Mar.* ⍥ *MAP.*

$$ 🏨 **Del Postiglione.** This attractive pink Mediterranean-style edifice is smaller than it appears, with only 15 guest rooms. A couple of minutes' walk from the seafront, its aura of understated luxury is created by marble floors, tropical plants adorning the exterior, and generous balconies overlooking one of Ischia Porto's quiet back streets. Half board is required in August. ⊠ *Via Giacinto Gigante 19, 80077* ☎ *081/991579* 🖷 *081/985956* ⊕*www.hotelpostiglione.it* ⟲*15 rooms* ♢ *Restaurant, bar, babysitting* ⊟ *V* ⍥ *MAP.*

Nightlife & the Arts

In Ischia Porto, nightlife is concentrated around what the locals know as the Rive Droite, the eastern side of the port. In some private gardens, occasional concerts and cultural events are offered during the summer months. Nightlife on Ischia starts late in the evening, and you should be prepared to stay the course until the early hours. **Valentino Club** (⊠ Corso Vittorio Colonna 97, Ischia Porto ☎ 081/982569), in the center of Ischia Porto, is the focal point for all but the gel-and-scooter set, with clientele in its early twenties and above. Admission varies between €16 and €25, depending on what's on offer.

In season (from April to the end of October) the town hall of Ischia Porto (and sometimes that of Lacco Ameno) may be used to display paintings and sculptures, primarily by local artists. For information on forthcoming cultural events throughout the island, check at the Azienda Autonoma di Cura, Soggiorno e Turismo (information office) in Ischia Porto, or inquire at a local *agenzia di viaggi* (travel agency).

Sports

Tennis has the most facilities of any sport on Ischia, with an average of three to four clubs in each town, in addition to those attached to hotels. Playing at a well-established club with good clay courts is likely to set you back about €12 per hour. The **Tennis Club Pineta** (⊠ Corso Vittorio Colonna 84/G, Ischia Porto Ischia Porto ☎ 081/993300) is a centrally located club that welcomes temporary members.

Shopping

For leather goods and clothing boutiques, most islanders head straight for Via Roma in Ischia Porto, a two-minute walk from the harbor. A number of shops sell competitively priced leather articles such as bags and belts, and there's also a fair array of clothing boutiques. But don't expect any of the big names found on Capri. The best shops in Ischia are to be found along the pedestrianized streets of Ischia Porto and Forio (along with Ischia Ponte and, to a lesser extent, Sant'Angelo)—although the island as a whole is not renowned as a shoppers' paradise.

Casamicciola

24 *2 km (1 mi) east of Lacco Ameno.*

Known properly as the spa town of Casamicciola Terme, the town revolves around the busy Piazza Marina with its statue of the Italian king Vittorio Emanuele II and its marble plaque honoring Henry Ibsen, who was inspired by the beauty of the area to write *Peer Gynt* here. The town has retained some charming examples of 19th-century architecture. About 2 km (1 mi) from the center is a small **geophysical observatory** from the 19th century, set up to monitor the seismic activity on the island. The *osservatorio* has various antique monitoring devices and a cranky seismic tank designed by the scientist Giulio Grablovitz. ⊠ *Osservatorio Geofisico, Località Sentinella* ☎ *081/996163* ☉ *By appointment only.*

> **need a break?** While out and about, make for **Gelateria Calise** (⊠ Piazza Marina, Casamicciola), opposite the landing stage, for some divine gelati and ices.

Where to Stay

$–$$ 🏨 **Albergo l'Approdo.** Located directly on the sea near Casamicciola's port, spas, and town center, this is a small hotel with a fine array of facilities. Guest rooms have private terraces, but tear yourself away to pamper yourself with the beauty treatments on offer, including ayurveda massage and reflexology. ⊠ *Via Eddomade 29, 80074* ☎ *081/994077* 🖨 *081/980185* ⊕ *www.albergoapprodo.it* 🛏 *33 rooms* 🍴 *Restaurant, indoor pool, outdoor pool, spa, bar* ⊟ *AE, DC, MC, V* ❑ *MAP.*

$ 🏨 **Hotel Villa D'Orta.** Set outside the center of town but adjacent to the Gurgitiello spa springs, this comfortable hotel is situated on the hillside, with great views down to the sea. Guest rooms are simple and bright. You can laze all day on the large terrace-solarium. ⊠ *Via Piccola Sentinella 1, 80074* ☎ *081/994700* 🖨 *081/995921* ⊕ *www.hotelvilladorta.it* 🛏 *14 rooms* 🍴 *Restaurant, outdoor pool, spa; no a/c* ⊟ *MC, V* ☉ *Closed Nov.–Easter* ❑ *FAP.*

Lacco Ameno

25 *6 km (4 mi) west of Ischia Porto, 3 km (2 mi) north of Forio.*

The smallest of the six *comuni* (municipalities) on the island, Lacco Ameno is a mecca for some of Italy's rich and famous. Magnate Gianni Agnelli used to anchor his yacht every summer close to the Fungo, a most distinctive mushroom-shape rock in volcanic tufa sculpted by wave action in the small marina, now one of the most notable natural landmarks in the Bay of Naples. Luchino Visconti, the noted realist film director and opera designer, had his Villa La Colombaria nearby in Baia San Montano, now used by the local council to promote the film industry on the island. The Bay of San Montano, a brilliant blue-sapphire buckle along the coast, is now the setting for the Giardini Negombo, the most stylish of the thermal complexes on the island. Lacco Ameno was colonized by the Greeks as early as the 8th century BC, and the landscape here has remained epic: it was used as the backdrop for the barge scene in Elizabeth Taylor's *Cleopatra*. The main road along the seafront (Corso Rizzoli) has thankfully been pedestrianized and is now virtually a large promenade flanked by low-key shops, caffès, and restaurants.

Lacco Ameno's archaeological importance—it rests below the first Greek settlement on the island, at Monte Vico to the west—is amply reflected by the finds displayed in Ischia's top museum, the **Museo Archeologico di Pithecusae,** and the ancient site beneath the church of Santa Restituta. The museum occupies much of the Villa Arbusto, built by Carlo d'Aquaviva in 1785 on top of a Bronze Age settlement. Its eight rooms house a wide range of Greek pottery unearthed at the ancient necropolis site near the Baia di San Montano, much of it dating to the earliest years of the Greek colony (late 8th century BC), including Nestor's Cup, a kotyle vase in geometric style. Villa Arbusto combines musical *serate,* or evening soirées, in summer months with visits to the antiquities museum. ⊠ *Villa Arbusto* ☎ *081/900356* ⊕ *www.pithecusae.it* ▣ *€5.2* ⊘ *Tues.–Sun. 9:30–1 and 3–7.*

From the nearby church of Santa Restituta, almost completely rebuilt following a catastrophic earthquake in 1883, you can gain access to the underground excavations at the **Museo e Scavi Santa Restituta,** which are a memorable lesson in stratigraphy. Discovered in 1950 when the old majolica pavement above was removed, the underground site shows the building activities of several different periods (archaic Greek, Hellenistic, Roman, and early Christian), faithful reconstructions of an ancient loom and a miller's workshop, and the various finds discovered in situ. Although the structures are poorly labeled and it takes an expert eye to discern which buildings belong to which periods, this gives you a good idea of historical continuity on the island. ⊠ *Piazza Santa Restituta* ☎ *081/ 980538* ▣ *€2.58* ⊘ *Mar.–May and Sept. and Oct., Mon.–Sat. 9–noon and 3–6, Sun. 9–noon; June–Aug., Mon.–Sat. 9:30–12:30 and 5–7, Sun. 9:30–noon.*

Where to Stay

★ **$$$$** ⊡ **Grande Albergo Mezzatorre.** Far from the madding, sunburnt crowds that swamp Ischia, this luxurious forgetaway perches in splendid isolation on the extreme promontory of Punta Cornacchia. Standing on the terraces of this renovated castello, set over the blue Bay of San Montano, with yachts parading below you, it's not hard to understand why film director Luchino Visconti chose to live just up the hill. This hotel has nearly everything to tempt its privileged guests to stay put and *relax*: storybook cove, glamorous pool area, a cossetting restaurant, full health and beauty treatments—although the vast Negombo spa is just down the road—serious chef, and hundreds of pine trees for true peace and quiet. The ancient fortress has been sleekly renovated, perhaps too much so from the look of its umber-red exterior. Inside, all is white-on-white with antiques and ancestral portraits as accents. The official address is Forio but this is much closer to Lacco Ameno, where you should get off if you're using the bus. ⊠ *Via Mezzatorre 13, Località San Montano, Forio d'Ischia, 80075* ☎ *081/986111* 🖶 *081/986015* ⊕ *www.mezzatorre.it* ➲ *58 rooms* ⚲ *Restaurant, minibars, tennis court, pool, hair salon, sauna, spa* 🖃 *AE, DC, V* ⊙ *Closed Nov.–mid-Apr.* ⍾⃝ *BP.*

$$$$ ⊡ **Regina Isabella.** Built in the early 1960s (not the most elegant of eras) and tucked away in an exclusive corner of the beach in Lacco Ameno, Ischia's largest luxury hotel has full resort facilities and also pampers guests (some of whom are here to attend conventions) with spa treatments. The 90 rooms—with this number, be sure to pick the one you'll be most happy with—are ample and decorated in warm Mediterranean colors, and most have terraces or balconies, some overlooking the sea, others the "piazzetta" of the town. Don't miss the fun of socializing with chic vacationers in the elegant bar or restaurant—a meal here is worth it just for the fabulous views over the harbor. When filming *Cleopatra* on Ischia, Elizabeth Taylor and Richard Burton camped out here. ⊠ *Piazza Santa Restituta, 80076* ☎ *081/994322* 🖶 *081/990190* ⊕ *www.reginaisabella.it* ➲ *90 rooms, 20 suites* ⚲ *Restaurant, minibars, tennis court, 2 pools (1 indoor), spa, beach, bar* 🖃 *AE, DC, MC, V* ⊙ *Closed mid-Oct.–mid-Apr.* ⍾⃝ *BP.*

$$–$$$ ⊡ **Hotel Della Baia.** A small, tastefully furnished hotel on a pedestrianized road, this is near the magical bay of San Montano and opposite the elegant Negombo Gardens, with their luxuriant thermal pools. Half-board terms include free entry to Negombo, except in August. ⊠ *Baia di San Montano, 80076* ☎ *081/995453* 🖶 *081/986342* ✑ *negombo@mclink.it* ➲ *20 rooms* ⚲ *Minibars, bar* 🖃 *AE, DC, MC, V* ⊙ *Closed mid-Oct.–mid-Apr.* ⍾⃝ *MAP.*

Nightlife & the Arts

The main theatrical venue on Ischia is the **Teatro-Arena** (⊠ Baia di San Montano ☎ 081/986152 ⊕ www.negombo.it) in the Giardini Negombo spa complex. This outdoor theater has hosted some pretty big music and rock stars, including Tina Turner and Mireille Mathieu. To find out the schedule of upcoming summer performances—usually on tap from June through September—log onto the Web site. For reservations, call or go to the arena box office (tickets not available elsewhere).

The Outdoors

If you visit one of Ischia's many *terme,* or spa baths, you will not only be following a well-established tradition stretching back more than 2,000 years but also sampling one of the major contemporary delights of the island. You should allow at least half a day for this experience, but better value is to get there early and indulge until sunset. If you do decide to restrict yourself to half a day, then go in the afternoon, when the hefty entrance fee is lowered. The larger establishments have a plethora of pools offering natural hydromassage at different temperatures and in different settings, with a complement of bars and restaurants to enable customers to stay on the premises right through the day. Most terme are equipped with beauty centers, offering an unbelievably broad range of services, from mud-pack treatments and manicures to tattoo removal and bioenergetic massage.

For the ultimate Ischian spa escape, try the stylishly landscaped park of **Giardini Negombo.** Designed around a beach of the finest sand, by the scenic bay of San Montano, it was created decades ago by Duke Luigi Camerini, a passionate botanist (who named his resort in honor of its resemblance to a bay in Sri Lanka). There are 12 saltwater or thermal pools here, plus facilities for hydromassage, a beauty center with sauna and Turkish bath, sports facilities for diving, windsurfing, volleyball, yoga, a bar, restaurant, and, according to the brochure, "a boutique for irresponsible purchases." All this is set in gardens with 500 species of Mediterranean plants and several panoramic views. Everything here—modern stone waterfalls, elegant poolside tables with thatched-leaf umbrellas, sensitive landscaping—is in the finest taste. At night, the outdoor arena hosts big-name concerts. ✉ *Baia di San Montano, Lacco Ameno* ☎ *081/986152* ⊕ *www.negombo.it* 🎟 *€24 all day, €17.50 after 12:30* PM*, €12.50 after 4:30* PM ☉ *Apr.–Oct., daily 8:30–7.*

There are facilities for windsurfing, waterskiing, and sailing at virtually every beach around Lacco Ameno.

Forio

26 *9 km (6 mi) west of Ischia Porto.*

Lying close to the main wine-producing area of the island, Forio is a busy seaside resort with beaches barely a minute's walk from its town center. At first glance, it seems to provide sad evidence of suburban sprawl, and its natural setting of flat coastline is not the most alluring. However, the island's most picturesque church is here: the 14th-century whitewashed church of Santa Maria della Neve, down at the harbor,

★ better known as the **Santuario del Soccorso.** This is a good spot for a sunset stroll and for getting an overview of the town from the Torrione, one of 12 towers built under Aragonese rule in the 15th century to protect Forio's inhabitants from the ever-present threat of pirate raids.

Fodor'sChoice   Two kilometers (1 mi) north of Forio is one of the most famous gardens in Mediterranean Italy, **La Mortella.** The garden was a labor of love
★ designed in 1956 by the landscape architect Russell Page for Sir William Walton and his Argentine-born wife, Susana. The garden was created within a wide, bowl-shape, rocky valley, originally not much more than a quarry, overlooking the Bay of San Francesco and with spreading views toward Monte Epomeo and Forio. Lady Walton, now a talented gardener in her own right, first planted the trees of her childhood here: jacaranda and the rare bromeliad. Native wild plants were encouraged in the upper reaches of the gardens, with dainty vetches and orchids as well as myrtle, from which the garden got its name, La Mortella. Besides some soothing strolls among the well-labeled flower beds and landscaped rock gardens, try to spend some time in the museum dedicated to the life and works of the late English composer, William Walton. The gardens have excellent facilities, including a shop selling Sir William's music and Lady Walton's lively biography of her husband, *Behind the Facade,* as well as light, homemade refreshments. There's also a concert series scheduled in the gardens on weekends in summertime. Book well in advance for these tickets. ✉ *Via Calise 35* ☎ *081/ 986220* ⊕ *www.ischia.it/mortella* 🎟 *€8* ☉ *Tues., Thurs., and weekends 9–7.*

Where to Stay & Eat

$$$–$$$$ ✕ **Il Melograno.** Ischia's only award-winning restaurant is tucked away on the road leading to Citara Beach. Japanese chefs train here, so try the sushi to start and then just indulge in food that tastes as good as it looks. New dishes with a twist are introduced every year—the fried anchovies stuffed with provola cheese and homemade tomato bread was one year's winner. Those on a higher budget and with a healthy appetite should treat themselves to the featured special menu, replete with local fish and vegetables given a nouvelle twist. There's an excellent if pricey wine-cellar. Popular as this place is, be sure to reserve for summer dinners. ✉ *Via G. Mazzella 110* ☎ *081/998450* ▭ *AE, DC, MC, V* ☉ *Closed Jan.–mid-Mar., Mon.–Tues. Nov.–Dec.*

$$ ✕ **Bar-Ristorante Bagno Teresa.** This is an unpretentious restaurant on Citara Beach (no dress code) that offers a range of fresh seafood at reasonable prices served with lively local wine. If you want to stay light for the afternoon swim, this is the place to come—there's no need to order a full Mediterranean splurge. ✉ *Baia di Citara* ☎ *081/907647* 🚫 *No credit cards* ◷ *Closed Nov.–Mar.*

★ **$$–$$$** 🏨 **La Bagattella.** *The* place to stay in Forio, this high-style oasis has a white wedding-cake, Arabesque ambience, with flower-covered balconies, sleek illuminated pool, exotic plants, and palm trees. The lobby is handsomely accented with antique wood furniture, and guest rooms are as modern and spacious as apartments. Most are warmed up with charming Stil Liberty antiques or Baroque-style mirrors. The restaurant menu has all the usual suspects, with an ambitious array of Mediterranean specialties. A newer wing has less desirable accommodations, but everyone staying here can enjoy the truly orchidaceous atmosphere. ✉ *Via Tommaso Cigliano 8, 80075* ☎ *081/986072* 🖨 *081/989637* ⊕ *www. labagattella.it* 🛏 *56 rooms* ♦ *Minibars, pool, bar* 🖃 *AE, MC, V* ◷ *Closed Nov.–Mar.* ⦿ *MAP.*

$ 🏨 **La Pergola.** This is one of the very few opportunities to stay on a working farm on Ischia. La Pergola is a whitewashed villa perched attractively on the slopes of Monte Epomeo and surrounded by vineyards and olive and fruit trees, with sweeping views westward over Citara Beach. Its dynamic young owners also operate a thriving restaurant serving local specialties, including the fabled rabbit dish *coniglio all'ischitana.* The delicious meals of country produce make half board a real bargain here. The owners offer cooking courses on occasion and have a small farm shop with homemade jams, liqueurs, and olive oil. ✉ *Via San Giuseppe 8, 80075* ☎ *081/909483* 🖨 *081/909483* ⊕ *www.terranostra.campania. it/cciaana/lapergol.html* 🛏 *7 rooms* 🚫 *No credit cards* ⦿ *BP.*

$ 🏨 **Hotel Semiramis.** A quiet family-run hotel, this is within a minute's walk of Citara Beach and the crowded Giardini Poseidon spa. The rooms are decorated tastefully in thematic styles, with the best and most expensive in the panoramic wing on the upper terrace. To cap it all, there's a child-friendly, secluded swimming pool tapping water from geothermal aquifers 30 feet down. ✉ *Spiaggia di Citara, 80075* ☎ *081/ 907511* 🖨 *081/907511* ⊕ *www.hotel-semisischia.com* 🛏 *33 rooms* ♦ *Pool, bar* 🚫 *No credit cards* ◷ *Closed Nov.–Mar.* ⦿ *BP.*

The Arts

The William Walton Foundation arranges a busy schedule of summer late-afternoon concerts that take place within the magical gardens of La Mortella, admission to which is included in the price of the ticket. For schedules and tickets, call La Mortella or visit its Web site (☎ 081/ 986220 ⊕ www.ischia.it/mortella).

Sports & the Outdoors

The largest spa on the island, with the added boon of a natural sauna hollowed out of the rocks, is the **Giardini Poseidon Terme.** Here you can sit like a Roman senator on two stone chairs recessed in the rock and let the hot water cascade over you. With countless thermally regulated pools, promenades, and steam pools, plus lots of toga-clad kitschy statues of the Caesars, Poseidon exerts a special pull on Germans, many of them grandparents shepherding grandchildren. On certain days, the place is overrun with people, so be prepared for crowds and wailing babies. ✉ *Citara Beach, Forio* ☎ *081/907122* ⊕ *www.giardiniposeidon. it* 🎟 *€25 all day, €20 after 1 PM, €5.20 for visitors (no bathing) between 6 PM and 7 PM* ◷ *Apr.–Oct., daily 8:30–7.*

Unlike on Capri, aficionados of water sports are unlikely to leave Ischia dissatisfied. On a calm day a canoe will carry you into that secluded bay you've spotted from afar, perhaps with its sea cave that's worth exploring. A good place to start—considered by locals to be one of the best beaches on the island—is Citara, near the Giardini Poseidon, on the edge of the township of Forio. Canoe and boat rental from many beaches on Ischia is run by **Dario Mazzara Marine Service** (✉ Via F. Di Lustro 10, Forio ☎ 081/5071328).

Shopping

With all the beauty farms on Ischia, ladies may enjoy visiting the main cosmetics factory on the island, **Ischia Thermae** (✉ Via Schioppa 17, Forio ☎ 081/997745 ⊕ www.omnitel.it/shopcenter/ischiathermae), which occupies an 18th-century palazzo in the town center of Forio. Besides poring over some of the formidably named articles in their retail outlet (such as Thermal Mud Purifying Mask Exfoliator), you may enjoy guided tours of the factory, offered twice a week (Wednesday and Friday at 5) with the bonus of a free sample of their products.

PROCIDA: ISLAND OF CONTRASTS

Lying barely 3 km (2 mi) from the mainland and 10 km (6 mi) from the nearest port (Pozzuoli), Procida is an island of enormous contrasts. It's the most densely populated island in Europe—almost 11,000 people crammed into less than 3½ square km (2 square mi)—and yet there are oases like Marina Corricella and Vivara, which seem to have been bypassed by modern civilization. The inhabitants of the island—the Procidani—have an almost symbiotic relationship with the Mediterranean: many join the merchant navy, others either fish or ferry vacationers around local waters. And yet land traffic here is more intense than on any other island in the Bay of Naples.

In scenic terms this is the place to admire what the Italians call "Spontaneous," or folkloric Mediterranean, architecture: look for the tall archways on the ground floor, which signal places where boats could be stowed in winter, the outside staircases providing access to upper floors without cramping interior living space, and the delicate pastel colors of the facades contrasting with the deeper, bolder blues of the sea. Picturesquely scenic, it's no surprise that Procida has strong artistic traditions and is widely considered the painters' island par excellence. If you're here at Easter, make sure you see the striking Good Friday procession through the island's major streets.

Terra Murata & Abbazia di San Michele

Boats pull into the main port, **Marina Grande Sancio Cattolico**, which is fetchingly adorned with pastel-hue houses and the church of Santa Maria della Pietà (1760). Hike up to the Piazza di Martiri on your way up to the **Castello** (now a prison). Magnificent views can be seen from the piazza in front of the castle, including the enchanting fishing village of the Marina della Corricella. For a fascinating glimpse of the traditional architecture, once you reach the Piazza turn left and walk about 600 ft until you come to a tiny passageway that leads to the **Vascello,** originally a gated area of tumbling-down fishermen's cottages. Continue along Via San Michele to the highest point on the island, the town of Terra Murata—a fascinating cluster of ancient buildings, including churches, palazzi, fortifications, ancient walls, and gateways, mostly in yellow-gray tufa stone. A Benedictine abbey was founded here in the 7th century, safely tucked away from mainland marauders, and the area became the focal point for the inhabitants of the island. Perched precariously at the top of a cliff facing the small bay of Corricella is the 16th-century **ex-convent of Santa Margherita Nuova,** now undergoing restoration. The easily distinguishable and now abandoned **Palazzo Reale,** built at the same time—confusingly, sometimes called Il Castello—was used as a prison until 1986. Rumor has it that its inmates were a little miffed at having to abandon the sun-drenched island of Procida.

Within Terra Murata is the **Abbazia di San Michele.** San Michele (St. Michael) is the island's patron saint and a key figure in its history and traditions. Legend has it that in 1535, when the sultan of Algeria's admiral laid siege to the island, San Michele appeared above the pirate force and put them to flight (the 17th-century painting depicting the scene is in the choir of the abbey's 17th-century church; one of the invaders' anchors can also be viewed). On the wall close to the richly coffered ceiling of the church is another depiction of San Michele, this time by the grandmaster Luca Giordano (1699). As you walk around the church, note the holes in marble flagstones on the floor, which were in effect trapdoors through which bodies could be lowered to the underground crypt below. There are also a remarkable number of statues, several of which are still borne through the streets of Procida during its Easter processions. Children will be fascinated by the skulls still lurking in the maze of catacombs leading to a secret chapel. ⊠ *Terra Murata* 🕾 *081/8967612* ⊕ *www.abbaziasanmichele.it* ⊠ *Free* ☞ *Guided tours (€2 per person) to the museum and catacombs available on request at the bookstore at entrance to abbey* ♥ *Apr.–Oct., Mon.–Sat. 9:45–12:45 and 3–6; Nov.–Mar., Mon.–Sat. 3–5.*

Corricella

Fodor'sChoice ★ Perched under the citadel of the Terra Murata, the **Marina di Corricella** is Procida's most iconic sight. Singled out for the waterfront scenes in *Il Postino (The Postman,* the 1995 Oscar-winner for Best Foreign Film), this fishermen's cove is one of the most eye-popping villages in Campania—a rainbow-hue, horizontal version of Positano, comprising hundreds of traditional Mediterranean-style stone houses threaded by numerous *scalatinelli* (staircase streets). The inhabitants of Corricella have been relatively immune to life in the limelight, and apart from the opening of an occasional restaurant and bar, there have been few changes in this sleepy fishermen's village. This is the type of place where even those of us with failing grades in art classes feel like reaching for a paintbrush to record the delicate pinks and yellows of the waterfront buildings.

Where to Stay & Eat

With such a strong seafaring tradition on Procida, you'd be wise to stick primarily to seafood, especially in summer. And if you have space left over at the end of the meal, try the local variety of *torta di limone,* made from the island's wondrously large lemons.

★ $$$ ✕ **La Conchiglia.** A dinner at this beachfront spot really lets you appreciate the magic of Procida. Beyond the lapping of the waves, Capri twinkles in the distance. The seafood is divinely fresh, the pasta dishes usually soul-warming. Access here is either by foot down the steps from Via Pizzaco or by boat from the Corricella harborfront—phone owner Gianni if you want the boat to pick you up. ⊠ *Via Pizzaco 10* 🕾 *081/8967602* ⊟ *AE, DC, MC, V* ♥ *Closed mid-Nov.–Mar.*

$–$$$ ✕ **La Gorgonia.** This atmospheric restaurant sits right on the waterfront down at Corricella. The specialty here is a combination of seafood and locally grown vegetables, such as pasta *con fagioli e cozze* (with beans and mussels). ⊠ *Marina Corricella* 🕾 *081/8101060* ⊟ *AE, DC, MC, V* ♥ *Closed Nov.–Feb. and weekdays Mar.–May and Oct.*

$$ ✕ **La Medusa.** Owner Biagio is in front of the stove in this smallest of the harbor restaurants, just where the ferries dock. The locals bring him their catch direct, so don't be surprised if he closes early because he's run out of fish. On tap are traditional Procida dishes such as spaghetti with sea urchin and lemon, fish soups, and delicious antipasto, all washed down with locally produced wine. ⊠ *Via Roma 116* ☎ *081/8967481* ⊟ *MC, V* ☉ *Closed Jan. and Feb. and Tues. Oct.–May.*

$–$$ ⌂ **La Casa sul Mare.** One of Procida's best boutique hotels, this charmer overlooks the fishing village of the Corricella and the bay. The south-facing private terraces of the jewel-like, individually designed bedrooms have stunning views and are the perfect place to lap up winter sunshine. Antiques and traditional ceramics complete the decor. Breakfast is served in the garden, and a boat service is provided to the nearby sand beach La Chiaia. ⊠ *Salita Castello 13,* ☎ *081/8968799* 🖷 *081/8967255* ⊕ *www.lacasasulmare.it* ⇨ *10 rooms* △ *Bar* ⊟ *AE, DC, MC, V* �101 *BP.*

Vivara

On the western coast of Procida, beyond the quiet beach of Pozzo Vecchio and the busy Lido is the small port of the **Marina di Chiaiolella,** studded with a few hotels and bars and basically known as a port-of-call for all sorts of water activities, ranging from boating to scuba diving. The shortest way to get to Chiaiolella is from the main port of Marina Grande Sancio Cattolico. Opposite Chiaiolella is Vivara, a crescent-shape island and terminal segment of a volcanic cone, today a living museum of natural history with unsullied Mediterranean maquis vegetation. It has miraculously survived the designs of property speculators over the past 30 years and is now awaiting a proper management plan from the Regione Campania. Survived, indeed. Unfortunately, Vivara is currently "closed" to the public, since its access bridge was greatly damaged in a major storm. However, this doesn't seem to stop the locals scrambling across the ruined waterfront mole.

Apart from a few historic buildings on the island, including a Napoleonic fort near the entrance gateway, the main cultural interest lies in its rich archaeological finds dating to prehistoric times, especially the Bronze Age, as testified to by a wealth of Mycenaean pottery fragments. The island is at its best in springtime, with most of its plants in flower and lots of birds on the move. The main path winds up from the causeway to a cluster of abandoned settlements at the highest point of the island (357 ft above sea level). On the way, admire the dense maquis on either side, with characteristic plant species like tree heather, strawberry tree, and rockrose, the latter of which sports delicate pink flowers in spring. Although you'll hear birds—especially the blackcap—don't expect to see any of these skulking warblers except perhaps around the clearing at the center of the island. At migration times, watch for two of the Mediterranean's more exotic-looking summer visitors; the hoopoe, a bird that looks more in keeping with the African savanna, and the bee-eater, a splash of unusually vivid colors.

Where to Stay & Eat

$ ✕⌂ **Crescenzo Hotel-Ristorante.** A short walk from Vivara, this is a three-story whitewashed hotel overlooking the small yachting marina of Chiaiolella. Half board is required here in August, although with specialties like spaghetti *ai ricci di mare* (with sea urchins) you should consider half board at other times of the year as well. Even if you're not a hotel guest, enjoy a seafood delight or two here. The small hotel has recently been refurbished. Rooms facing the tiny port are charming but noisy in summer. ✉ *Marina di Chiaiolella* ☎ *081/8967255* 📠 *081/8101260* 🛏 *10 rooms* ⚭ *Restaurant, bar, free parking* ≡ *AE, DC, MC, V* ⟐ *MAP.*

$ 🏨 **Sol Calante.** A haven of peace well away from the crowds even in high summer, this bright, traditional Procida country house has recently opened as a small, friendly hotel. All rooms have balconies or patios onto a garden that overlooks the bay facing Ischia. Guest rooms are simple, with Mediterranean-style accents. Guests can enjoy breakfast under the shady pergola in the garden in pleasant weather (note this hotel is open year round). ✉ *Via Serra 1 bis, 80079* ☎ *081/8101856* 📠 *081/ 8101856* 🛏 *12 rooms* ⚭ *Cable TV, bar* ≡ *MC, V* ⟐ *BP.*

Nightlife & the Arts

Procida's nightlife revolves around Via Roma in the port town of Marina Grande Sancio Cattolico, although there are also a number of late-closing bars and restaurants around the Marina di Chiaiolella. The one disco on the island tends to be populated almost exclusively by high school students. The rest of the islanders while away their summer evenings strolling the bayside strip along the Marina Grande and the new tourist harbor. The **Birreria Pub Sotto Sopra** (✉ Via Roma 11, Procida ☎ 081/ 8101013) serves good draft lager for a young crowd almost around the clock in a congenial quasi-nautical setting. **Bar del Cavaliere** (✉ Via Roma 42 ☎ 081/8101047) is where yachting types, wealthy Neapolitans, and thirtysomethings gather to drink cocktails until the wee hours in a relaxing but crowded atmosphere—get here early for the people-watching tables outside. And after a really heavy night, grab your breakfast here.

Procida was the setting for Elsa Morante's novel *L'Isola di Arturo,* which has lent its name to the literary competition held here every September. There are occasional art exhibitions down at the port, in several of the palazzi along Via Roma; the Abbazia di San Michele in Terra Murata lays on special exhibitions connected with religious and literary themes.

The Outdoors

With its famous nautical school and centuries-old seafaring traditions, Procida is an ideal base for chartering yachts of various sizes or just exploring the seabed with one of the diving schools on the island.

SAILING One of the market leaders in Italy is **Sail Italia** (✉ Via Roma 10, Sancio Cattolico Marina Grande ☎ 081/8960336 ⊕ www.sailitalia.it). Except for the even-pricier month of August, chartering a 10-berth 40-foot yacht for a week—enough time to visit the other islands in the bay as well as the gorgeous island of Ponza, farther afield—will set you back about €4,000 inclusive of skipper and final clean. If reckoned on a daily per-person basis, this is an interesting alternative to hotel stays on the various islands. Hire a typical Procida wooden fishing boat for the day to chug around the island and escape the crowds from **Ippocampo** (✉ West side, Marina Chiaiolella ☎ 081/8101437). Prices run from €62 per day for up to 10 people excluding fuel; no prior boating experience is said to be required. For those of you who prefer the easy life, **Protours** (✉ Marina Chiaiolella ☎ 360/6644634 ⊕ www.protours.it) provides a boat-taxi service and island tours from €30 depending on the number of passengers. And if you fancy a night out clubbing in Ischia, the taxi service can prove costly (€21 is one proffered rate).

SCUBA DIVING The **Procida Diving Center** (✉ Lido di Procida, Marina Chiaiolella ☎ 081/ 8968385) organizes courses and provides equipment for divers of all levels. You may be taken into shallower waters, like Secca delle Formiche, near Vivara, or shown the coral formation off one of the headlands on the island. The cost for a session averages about €30 per person, and the season runs roughly from May to October.

CAPRI, ISCHIA & PROCIDA A TO Z

Capri

BOAT & FERRY TRAVEL

Capri is well connected with the mainland in all seasons, though there tend to be more sailings between April and October. However, you can't return to Naples after about 9.30 PM, so if you want to see an evening concert, you'll have to arrange for hotel accommodations. Ferries, hydrofoils, Seacats, and similar vessels leave from Molo Beverello (below Piazza Municipio) in Naples and from Sorrento's Marina Piccola, while *aliscafi* (hydrofoils) also sail from the small marina of Mergellina, a short distance west of the Villa Comunale in Naples. For locals in Naples there are restrictions on taking cars onto the island, while non-Italians can move relatively freely. Bear in mind that much of Capri Town is pedestrianized, and a car on the island may well be more of a hindrance than a help.

Caremar offers five hydrofoil departures from Molo Beverello (€10.7, with a travel time of 40 minutes) and six ferry departures per day (€5.8 high season, with a travel time of 1 hour, 15 minutes). Four ferries leave daily from Sorrento (€6, travel time 30 minutes).

Linee Marittme Partenopee offers one to three hydrofoil departures every hour from Sorrento (€8, travel time 20 minutes), seven ferries per day from Sorrento (€6.5, 50 minutes), and one hydrofoil per day from Ischia (in the morning, €12, one hour).

From Naples, Navigazione Libera Del Golfo has roughly one hydrofoil departure per hour (€12, travel time 40 minutes). From Easter to October, the company also offers one jetfoil from Positano and Amalfi (approximately €12.5, travel time 50 minutes), and one ferry from Positano and Amalfi (€10, travel time 1 hour, 20 minutes).

SNAV offers one hydrofoil every hour from Mergellina or Molo Beverello (€12, travel time 40 minutes).

FARES & SCHEDULES — Departure schedules are listed every day in several daily papers (*Corriere della Sera, Il Mattino, La Repubblica*). If you're planning to move on from Capri to Ischia or the Amalfi Coast, there's regular service from May to October. As for ferry costs, there's little to be gained—sometimes nothing—from buying a round-trip ticket, which will just tie you down to the return schedule of one line. Book in advance in spring and summer for a Sunday return to the mainland.

🚤 Boat & Ferry Information **Caremar** ☎ 081/5513882 or 081/8370700 ⊕ www.caremar. it. **Linee Marittme Partenopee** ☎ 081/8781430 or 081/8071812. **Navigazione Libera Del Golfo** ☎ 081/5527209 hydrofoils from Naples; 089/875092 ferry and hydrofoils from Positano. **SNAV** ☎ 081/7612348.

EMERGENCIES

🚹 Capri **Police** ☎ 081/8370000. **First Aid** ☎ 081/8381205. **Hospital** ✉ Ospedale Capilupi ☎ 081/8381111.
🚹 Anacapri **Police** ☎ 081/8371011. **First Aid** ☎ 081/8381205. **Hospital** ✉ Ospedale Capilupi ☎ 081/8381111.

CURRENCY EXCHANGE — 🚹 Exchange Services **Banca di Roma** ✉ Piazza Umberto I, Capri Town ☎ 081/8375942. **Banco di Napoli** ✉ Via Orlandi 150, Anacapri ☎ 081/8371202. **Cambio** ✉ Via Roma 33, Capri Town ☎ 081/8370785. **La Piazzetta 2** ✉ Piazza Vittoria 2b, Anacapri ☎ 081/8373146.

TAXIS

⏩ Taxi Companies **Taxis** ☎ 081/8371175 in Anacapri; 081/8370543 in Capri Town.

TOURS

Gruppo Motoscafisti offers excursions to Blue Grotto from Marina Grande (€ 15, with Sunday supplement) and round-island tour, or *giro* (€11), taking in other grottoes and getting good close-ups of the Faraglioni. For just the Faraglioni expect to pay €9 with Sunday supplement. Laser Capri leads excursions to Blue Grotto from Marina Grande (€13, with Sunday supplement) and a round-island tour (€9). For a more personal giro around the island on a wooden boat, Giancarlo Guarracino will skipper you around the hidden bays of Capri (fees vary). Cooperativa Battellieri Capresi manages the rowboats covering the short distance to the Blue Grotto.

⏩ Fees and Schedules **Cooperativa Battellieri Capresi** ✉ Via C. Colombo 23, Marina Grande, Capri ☎ 081/8370973. **Gruppo Motoscafisti** ✉ Molo del Porto, Marina Grande, Capri ☎ 081/8375646. **Giancarlo Guarracino** ✉ Capri ☎ 081/8376520. **Laser Capri** ✉ Via Ruocco 45, Marina Grande, Capri ☎ 081/8375208 ⊕ www.lasercapri.com.

TRANSPORTATION AROUND CAPRI

Most of Capri's sights are reasonably accessible by either boat or bus, except for Villa Jovis and Cetrella, which involve some walking (about 40 minutes). The bus service is relatively cheap and frequent, while taxis are likely to cost 10–20 times as much as public transport. Don't be tempted into buying a *biglietto giornaliero* (day pass) for the bus and funicular (€7) unless you're thinking of covering almost every corner of the island—you would need to make six separate trips to make it pay, and locals deem it a bit of a rip-off.

Access to the Blue Grotto is usually from Marina Grande in a 20-seat boat, decanting into smaller rowboats near the grotto. Some prefer to take the bus to Anacapri and then change onto another line that passes close to the grotto on the northwest side of the island. This operation involves taking just one boat and will reduce your overall cost by about €5. However, don't set your heart on an excursion to the Blue Grotto, as visits cannot be made when the sea is even minimally choppy. An alternative is the Giro dell'Isola (round-island tour), which is a better value than the Blue Grotto excursion. However, some giros do not include a stop at the Blue Grotto, which is fiercely and territorially the private province of its own boat operators; you can be sure that giro tours that do pay a call on the Blue Grotto will require extra payment for this stop.

Off the major bus routes, many roads are pedestrianized. The trails close to Villa Jovis and the Arco Naturale are all well paved and well maintained; those on the steeper parts of Monte Solaro are the only ones where walking shoes are advisable. If you go down the Scala Fenicia footpath from Anacapri, take your time. Although not dangerous, some stretches are quite steep and should be undertaken with caution.

TRAVEL AGENCIES

Grotta Azzurra can arrange ticketing for flights, trains, etc. on the mainland and provide services such as hotel reservations, customized tours of the island, and mainland tours to Herculaneum, Pompeii, and the Amalfi Coast, as well as scooter rentals.

⏩ Local Agents **Grotta Azzurra** ✉ Via C. Colombo 64, Capri ☎ 081/8370410 🖷 081/8377528.

VISITOR INFORMATION

Azienda Autonoma di Cura, Soggiorno e Turismo offices in Capri, Capri Town, and Anacapri are open 8:30–8:30 in high season, and 9–1 and 3–7 (approximately) in winter. Their excellent Web site has an English-language version.

fl Tourist Information **Azienda Autonoma di Cura, Soggiorno e Turismo** ⊠ Banchina del Porto, Marina Grande, Capri ☎ 081/8370634 ⊠ Piazza Umberto I, Capri Town ☎ 081/8370686 ⊠ Via G. Orlandi, 19/A, Anacapri ☎ 081/8371524 ⊕ www.capritourism.com.

Ischia

BIKE TRAVEL

About 100 yards from Ischia Porto's ferry terminal, Del Franco, opposite Hotel Jolly, has a fair range of sturdy bicycles costing €10 per day.

fl Bike Rentals **Del Franco** ⊠ Via Alfredo De Luca 121 Ischia Porto ☎ 081/991334.

BOAT & FERRY TRAVEL

Like the other islands in the Bay of Naples, Ischia is well connected with the mainland in all seasons. However, the last sailings leave for Naples and Pozzuoli at about 8 PM, and you should allow plenty of time for getting to the port and locating the relevant ticket office. Unlike Capri and Procida, Ischia has three ports—Ischia Porto, Casamicciola, and Forio (hydrofoils only)—so you should choose your ferry or hydrofoil according to your destination. The closest mainland port to Ischia is that of Pozzuoli, where you have the added bonus—besides paying lower fares—of walking through the colorful fish market on your way to the jetty. Many of the sailings go via Procida, giving you an attractive glimpse of its waterfront but also extending travel time by 10–15 minutes. As on Capri, residents are subject to restrictions on taking cars over to the island, while non-Italians can move relatively freely.

Alilauro has roughly one hydrofoil per hour traveling from Mergellina, Naples to Ischia Porto (€12 high season, €11 low season, travel time 40 minutes). From May through September, five hydrofoils per day depart for Forio (€13 high season, €12 low season, travel time, 50 minutes).

Caremar offers six hydrofoil departures from Molo Beverello, Naples to Ischia Porto (€10.70, travel time 50 minutes), and six ferry departures per day (€5.8, travel time 1 hour, 10 minutes). Ferry departures are also available from Pozzuoli (€6, travel time 1 hour).

Linee Lauro sends roughly one hydrofoil every two hours from Molo Beverello, Naples to Ischia Porto (€12.5, travel time 40 minutes), and eight ferry departures per day to Ischia Porto (€7, travel time 1¼ hours).

SNAV offers a hydrofoil every hour from Mergellina or Molo Beverello, Naples, to the marina of Casamicciola (€11, travel time 50 minutes).

Traghetti Pozzuoli has a ferry departing every hour from Pozzuoli, sometimes docking at Casamicciola (€6, travel time 1 hour).

FARES & SCHEDULES Departure schedules are listed every day in several daily papers (*Corriere della Sera, Il Mattino, La Repubblica*). Buy a single ticket rather than a round-trip, which would tie you to the same line on your return journey.

fl Boat & Ferry Information **Alilauro** ☎ 081/7611004 ⊕ www.alilauro.it. **Caremar** ☎ 081/5513882 ⊕ www.caremar.it. **Linee Lauro** ☎ 081/5522838. **SNAV** ☎ 081/7612348. **Traghetti Pozzuoli** ☎ 081/527736 ⊕ www.traghettipozzuoli.it.

BUS TRAVEL

The main bus terminus is in Ischia Porto at the start of Via Cosca, where buses run by the company SEPSA radiate out around the island. There are also convenient *fermate* (stops) at the two main beaches—Citara and

Maronti—with timetables displayed at the terminus. At €1 per ticket the service may be considered good value, though conditions can get very hot and crowded at peak beach-visiting times.

🚹 Bus Information **SEPSA** ☎ 081/991808.

CAR RENTAL

🚹 Local Agencies **Del Franco** ⊠ Via Alfredo De Luca 121, opposite Hotel Jolly, Ischia Porto ☎ 081/991334.

CAR TRAVEL

Given the much larger size of Ischia compared to the islands Capri and Procida (where cars are virtually redundant), having your own transport on Ischia could be handy, especially if you have to schlep large quantities of diving equipment, say, around the island. However, in most towns there are now strict parking restrictions, and *vigili urbani* (traffic police) are constantly on the lookout for aberrant motorists. The police are also clamping down on seat belt violations, so if you do drive, be sure to wear your seat belt even on the shortest journey.

CURRENCY
EXCHANGE
In general, look for exchange bureaus or signs saying WECHSEL (German for "exchange"). Commission rates may be marginally higher than in the local banks, but red tape is virtually nonexistent, and service is likely to be considerably faster.

🚹 Exchange Services **Alilauro Biglietteria** ⊠ Hydrofoil ticket office, Ischia Porto ☎ 081/7611004. **Viaggi e Turismo Di Leva** ⊠ Piazza Medaglia d'Oro 11, Forio ☎ 081/997711.

EMERGENCIES

🚹 Police ⊠ Ischia Porto ☎ 081/991336. **First Aid** ⊠ Ischia Porto ☎ 081/994044. **Hospital** ⊠ Ospedale Rizzoli, Lacco Ameno ☎ 081/994044.

TAXIS

Taxis—and microtaxis—are to be found near the major ferry and hydrofoil terminals, and there are taxi ranks close to all the town centers on the island. The fleet of microtaxis is gradually being upgraded from roaring two-stroke *api*, little more than scooters with a cabin attached but regrettably no earplugs provided, into gently purring state-of-the-art minibuses (carrying six passengers), where intelligible conversation can now be attempted. By law all taxis and microtaxis have to use their meters, so make sure the meter is activated as soon as your journey begins. If the taxi doesn't have a meter, beware: some drivers seem to be pirates in disguise, so work out a flat fee before you set out. If you just go along for the ride, you could wind up being very unpleasantly surprised when you're charged $15 for a two-minute trip.

TRANSPORTATION AROUND ISCHIA

Ischia has an excellent, competitively priced bus network, with all the major sites and beaches within easy reach of one of its 10 lines. Runs continue on some routes until well after 10 PM, making evening sorties feasible even if you haven't got your own transport. A number of car and scooter rental facilities are available, although Ischia already has more than its fair share of motorized two-wheelers on the roads and many have undergone engine tampering to improve performance (and boost noise levels). If you use a bicycle on the island, be prepared for lots of ups and downs, and where possible take to the minor roads. Boat and Zodiac rentals are available at most major beaches, and ferrying service is sometimes arranged to reach out-of-the-way beaches.

TRAVEL AGENCIES

Most travel agencies supply the following services: hotel booking, car rentals, guided tours, flight and ferry bookings, and day excursions to the mainland and other islands.

🛈 Local Agent Referrals **Isolaverde Viaggi** ✉ Piazzetta Pontile 1, Lacco Ameno, ☎ 081/980455 🖨 081/995329 🌐 www.isolaverdeviaggi.it. **Viaggi Romano** ✉ Via Porto 5–9, Ischia Porto ☎ 081/991215 🖨 081/991167 🌐 www.ischiadirecttours.it.

VISITOR INFORMATION

Azienda Autonoma di Cura, Soggiorno e Turismo in Ischia Porto is open 9 AM–1:30 PM; April through October it's also open 3–7:30 PM.

🛈 Tourist Information **Azienda Autonoma di Cura, Soggiorno e Turismo** ✉ Ufficio Informazioni, Banchina Porto Salvo, Ischia Porto ☎ 081/5074231 🖨 081/5074230 🌐 www.ischiaonline.it/tourism.

Procida

BIKE TRAVEL

Signor Basilea Luoni of Associazione Azione Verde has a cycle shop opposite the Scuola Media, which is about a 30-minute walk from the ferry terminal. The shop can arrange for bike delivery to the port. The travel agency at the port, Graziella Travel, also has a small selection of bikes for hire.

🛈 Bike Rentals **Associazione Azione Verde** ✉ Piazza Sant'Antonio da Padova, Marina Grande Sancio Cattolico ☎ 081/8967395. **Graziella Travel** ✉ Via Roma 117 ☎ 081/8969594 🌐 www.isoladiprocida.it.

BOAT & FERRY TRAVEL

Procida's ferry timetable caters to the many daily commuters who live on the island and work in Naples or Pozzuoli. The most frequent—and cheapest—connections are from the Port of Pozzuoli. After stopping at Procida's main port, Marina Grande Sancio Cattolico, many ferries and hydrofoils continue on to Ischia, for which Procida is considered a halfway house.

Caremar has six hydrofoils departing from Molo Beverello, Naples (€7.80, travel time 35 minutes), and seven ferry departures per day from Molo Beverello, Naples (€4.70, travel time 1 hour, 10 minutes). There are three ferry departures per day from Pozzuoli (€2.7, travel time 40 minutes).

SNAV hydrofoils leave every two hours from Mergellina or Molo Beverello, Naples (€8, travel time 35 minutes).

The Procida Lines 2000 ferry leaves six times a day from Pozzuoli (€2.3 Monday–Saturday, €2.8 Sunday, travel time 40 minutes).

FARES & SCHEDULES As with the other islands, buy a single ticket rather than a round-trip (there's virtually no saving on a round-trip ticket, which is usually twice the single fare, and it ties you down to one operator on your return).

🛈 Boat and Ferry Information **Caremar** ☎ 081/5513882 🌐 www.caremar.it. **Procida Lines 2000** ☎ 081/8960328. **SNAV** ☎ 081/7612348.

BUS TRAVEL

The bus terminus in Procida is at the disembarkation point in Via Roma. Provided there is no traffic gridlock along the island's narrow streets, the buses run by the company SEPSA will get you to most destinations within about 10 minutes for €.80. Chiaiolella is the most frequently served destination (about every 15 minutes) and timetables are displayed—and tickets bought—at a newsstand next to the hydrofoil ticket office. In summer the bus service runs until about 4 in the morning. Tickets can be bought for a supplement from the bus driver. Keep in mind that on-the-spot checks and hefty fines are frequently imposed on riders without a ticket.

🛈 Bus Information **SEPSA** ☎ 081/8101241.

EMERGENCIES

🛈 Police ☎ 081/8967160. **First Aid** ☎ 081/8969058. **Hospital** ☎ 081/8101213.

🛈 Exchange Services **Credem** ✉ Via Roma 102, Procida.

TAXIS

For about €14, microtaxis with a capacity of about five passengers will take you from the port to Chiaiolella. This can be a welcome service in summer, when buses get overcrowded and steamy. For a round-island tour, expect to pay upward of €30. This includes frequent stops along the way plus a shotgun-quick visit to the Abbazia. Although by law all microtaxis have to use their meters, it may be worth your while to agree on a fixed price beforehand. Taxis can be hired at Marina Grande. On the southern coast, taxis can be hired at Marina Chiaiolella.

🛈 Marina Chiaiolella ☎ 081/8968785. **Marina Grande** ☎ 081/8968785.

TRANSPORTATION AROUND PROCIDA

There are four main bus lines that will take you to practically every corner of the island as well as a fleet of microtaxis operating round island tours and plying the route between the port and the Marina di Chiaiolella, on the southwest of the island. To get to Vivara, a road climbs westward out of Chiaiolella, and motorized access is barred shortly before reaching the causeway linking the two islands. Although Procida has fewer hills than either Ischia or Capri, cycling is really only feasible when the roads are closed to motorized traffic (evenings in summer). Most islanders get around on mopeds and scooters, which means the streets between the port and the center of the island are both noisy and loaded with pollutants, making casual strolling and window-shopping stressful. Beaches can be reached by sea or land, with fishermen improvising as water-taxi drivers.

TRAVEL AGENCIES

Graziella Travel provides listings of guided tours in the area.

🛈 Local Agent Referrals **Graziella Travel** ✉ Via Roma 117, Procida ☎ 081/8969594 🖷 081/8969190 ⊕ www.isoladiprocida.it.

VISITOR INFORMATION

Tourist information, left luggage, and guided tours (be sure to book in advance) are now provided by the Pro Loco Procida, a voluntary organization, open weekends April–September 9–1 and 3–7, October–March 9–1.

🛈 Tourist Information **Pro Loco Procida** ✉ Stazione Marittima Ferry ticket office, Via Roma, Procida ☎ 081/8101968 ⊕ www.procida.net.

SORRENTO & THE AMALFI COAST

FODOR'S CHOICE

Amalfi's Cappuccini Convento, *you'll gasp (everyone does)*

Atrani, *a village of corkscrew alleys and staircases*

Conca dei Marini, *truly paradiso sur terra*

Don Alfonso, Sant'Agata, *Prince Rainer loves this place, too*

Hotel Bellevue Syrene, Sorrento, *fave of kings and queens*

Hotel Excelsior-Vittoria, Sorrento, *half palace, half resort*

La Fenice, Positano, *the prettiest little hotel in the world*

Lorelei et Londres, Sorrento, *a music-box of a hotel*

Marina di Furore, *a pastel-hued fishermen's hamlet*

Paestum, *for its great Greek temples*

Positano's Via Positanesi, *the best seaside promenade*

Ravello's Villa Rufolo, *whose seaside gardens inspired Wagner*

Ravello's Villa Cimbrone, *and its Belvedere of Infinity*

HIGHLY RECOMMENDED

RESTAURANTS Eolo, *Amalfi*

La Sponda, Hotel Le Sirenuse, *Positano*

O' Capurale, *Positano*

Ristorante il Ritrovo, *Montepertuso*

HOTELS Cocumella, *Sant' Agnello*

Caruso Belvedere, *Ravello*

Il Saraceno, *Conca dei Marini*

Le Sirenuse, *Positano*

Palazzo Murat, *Positano*

San Pietro, *Positano*

Santa Caterina, *Amalfi*

Many other great sights, restaurants, and hotels enliven this area. For other favorites, look for the black stars as you read this chapter.

By Lea Lane
Stern

Updated by
Chris Rose and
Francesca
Marretta

THANK ODYSSEUS FOR LETTING THE SIRENS LURE HIM to their lair near Sorrento's coastal waters. Here, the *Odyssey* relates, the first traveler of record first heard the seductive song of the *Sirene*—actually two formidable monsters with the heads of women and the bodies of birds. The wily navigator managed to outwit them by having himself tied to the ship's mast and sealing his crew's ears with wax. The myth was further elaborated by later mariners' tales: The number of the Sirens increased to three, the monsters morphed into physically attractive beings, and the search was on to identify the ancient location. The current consensus is that the three Sirens spitefully chose to live out eternity as rocky outcrops, right here on the islands called Li Galli, in the waters off Positano on the Amalfi Coast. Even today, it is difficult to resist the allure of this part of southern Italy, a palmy and balmy land stretching south from the Bay of Naples and the Sorrento Peninsula to the Amalfi Coast and the Bay of Salerno, rimmed by the true-bluest waters of the Mediterranean. Like Homer, you'll be able to spin your own tale around lemon-scented breezes, emerald grottoes, sun-kissed vistas, sea-fresh food, and an embracing, generous people. Like a 21st-century Odysseus, to leave these blessed shores willingly you may have to secure yourself to the ferry rail, close your eyes, and turn your Discman up to full blast.

The Sorrento Peninsula was first put on the map by the ancient Romans. The emperors—who knew a good thing when they saw it—claimed the region for their own, crowning the golden, waterside cliffs of what was then called "Surrentum" (or Land of Sirens) with palatial villas. Modern resorts now stand where emperors once staked out vacation spots. Reminders of the Caesars' reigns—broken columns, capitals, marble busts—lie scattered among the region's orange trees and terraces. Sorrento goes as far back as the Etruscans, the bon viveurs of the early ancient world, and for much of Sorrento's existence it has remained focused, in fact, on pleasure. The Sorrento Peninsula became a major stop on the elites' Grand Tour itineraries beginning in the late 18th century, thanks to glowing reports from Goethe, Lord Byron, Shelley, and Richard Wagner. By the mid-19th century, grand hotels and wedding-cake villas had sprung up to welcome the flow of princes, khans, and tycoons.

Gently faded, in the manner of a stereopticon image, and set with sherbet-hued villas, Sorrento still exudes a robust pull—from its bustling piazza named for the famous 16th-century poet Tasso, a native son, to the belvederes framing the slowly setting sun. For anyone suffering *"nostalgia di Napoli"*—a longing for tarantellas, strumming mandolins, and dolce far niente—this is the ideal place, since Naples itself is now so urbanized. As a hub for a banquet of must-see sites—Pompeii, Naples, Capri, and the Amalfi Coast to the south—Sorrento is unequaled. Because of its convenient location the city can become overrun with visitors in summer, so it's fortunate that the rest of the Sorrento Peninsula, with plains and limestone outcroppings, watchtowers and Roman ruins, groves and beaches, monasteries and villages, winding paths leading to isolated coves and panoramic views of the bays of both Naples and Salerno, remains relatively undiscovered. Eons ago, when sea levels dropped during the glaciations, the peninsula's tip and Capri were joined by an overland connection, and today it still seems you can almost make it in a single jump. Separating grande dame Sorrento from the relatively arriviste Amalfi Coast, this hilly, forested peninsula provides the famed rivals breathing space, along with inviting restaurants and an uncrowded charm all its own.

South of the Sorrento Peninsula, the Amalfi Coast—the Costiera Amalfitana—stretches from Positano to Vietri sul Mare. This area is ar-

4

One of the gigglingly gorgeous places on Earth, this corner of Campania tantalizes, almost beyond bearing, the visitor who can stay but a day or two. Poets and millionaires have long journeyed here to see and sense its legendary sights: Sorrento—Italy at its Belle Epoque best; perfect Positano—a claim that is more than alliteration; Amalfi—a shimmering medieval city; and romantic mountain-high Ravello. Connecting these towns is the Amalfi Drive, a cliff-hugging stretch of road that tests one's faith in civil engineering. This roller-coastal route offers views that are drop-dead breathtaking (literally, it sometimes seems).

The coastal sections—steep, winding, and ultrascenic—can only be traversed by boat or by two-lane roads. When driving round-trip, many choose to go only in one direction on the coastal roads, going the other way via the highway or by train from Salerno, or by boat from Amalfi or Positano. If a once-over of the region's most fascinating sights is enough, three days will allow you to see Sorrento, Positano, Amalfi, and Ravello—the absolute musts. A practical minimum for an overview of the splendors to be found on the Sorrento Peninsula, and in Positano, Paestum, and smaller villages along the coast, is five days. To take in the entire span from Sorrento to Paestum, you can put together a glorious 10-day trip.

Numbers in the text correspond with numbers in the margin and on the Sorrento, Sorrento Peninsula, Amalfi Coast, and Amalfi maps.

If you have
3 days

If staying in one place is a priority, and you will not be going exploring, start by picking a favorite base. If you plan to comb the coasts, it's best to arrange for at least two overnight destinations. **Sorrento** ❶–❾ could be one hub, especially if you're interested in covering the tip of the peninsula. If you stay in Sorrento, you can easily get to the Amalfi Coast by a short hop on the bus; boat, ferry, and hydrofoil services also connect you with Naples and environs, plus the islands of Capri or Ischia. And the train from Sorrento will deposit you right in front of Pompeii. You'll need a day to enjoy the Sorrento area, plus another leisurely day to explore the Sorrento Peninsula, enjoying the best beaches in the area or taking a rural hike. For the third day, whizzing past the Sorrento Peninsula, it's a rise-early, full-day excursion along the Amalfi Drive with a cruise through **Positano** ❶❺, a stop at the Emerald Grotto in **Conca dei Marini** ❷⓿, and brief stops in **Amalfi** ㉑–㉛, at least for the Duomo, and in **Ravello** ㉝ for the villas and a panoramic view; if you want to linger, you can return from Salerno to Sorrento at night via the highway and Sorrento Coast. If you prefer to spend more time along the coast, or if you want to visit **Paestum** ㊲, spend one of your nights in Amalfi; in so doing, you'll also be able to enjoy nearby adorable **Atrani** ㉜. If you don't mind staying overnight in three different places, a day each in Sorrento and Amalfi and a third day in Ravello or Positano would maximize this brief regional experience. If you're traveling by water, keep in mind that Sorrento, Positano, Amalfi, and Salerno have the most frequent connections. And although these itineraries start in Sorrento, you could travel east to west on the coastal roads just as easily—but remember, if you want to stay late before returning to Sorrento, you don't want to take rural, scenic roads at night.

If you have
5 days

With the three-day itinerary as a base, add the extra two days wherever you feel you want to spend more time relaxing or sightseeing. You might opt to stay two days each in **Sorrento** ❶–❾ or **Amalfi** ㉑–㉛, and spend the fifth either in **Positano** ⓯, taking in its shops and resort atmosphere, or calmer **Ravello** ㉝, with its gardens, villas, and panoramic views. After reading this chapter through, you'll have a better idea.

If you have
10 days

With a 10-day tour, you'll have the luxury of staying on at your favorite places, and still being able to see just about everything of note in the region. After enjoying **Sorrento** ❶–❾ and environs, work your way slowly south across the Sorrento Peninsula, then along the Amalfi Coast, and include a separate day trip to **Paestum** ㊲ for a rousing finale. You can take the highway or train back from Salerno to Naples, Rome, or wherever, on the 10th day. A possible itinerary would be three days in Sorrento and environs; one day at a small rural town by a beach, such as Marina della Lobra below **Massa Lubrense** ⓭ or **Marina del Cantone** ⓮ or, by the sea, sublimely exquisite **Conca dei Marini** ⓴; one day in **Positano** ⓯; two in **Amalfi** ㉑–㉛; and two in **Ravello** ㉝. If visiting from May to October, some travelers will want to fit in a long day exploring coves, islets, and grottoes—either by land or through a blissful sea cruise.

---

guably the most divinely sensual 48-km (30-mi) stretch of water, land, and habitation on Earth. Legends abound, but the Greeks were early colonizers at Paestum to the south, and Romans fled their own sacked empire in the 4th century to settle the steep coastal ridge now called the Lattari Mountains (because of the milk, or *latte,* produced there). Despite frequent incursions by covetous Lombards, Saracens, and other hopefuls, the medieval Maritime Republic of Amalfi maintained its domination of the seas and coast until the Normans began their conquest of southern Italy in the 11th century. By 1300, Naples, the capital of the Angevin Kingdom, had become the dominant ruler of the region and remained so until Italy unified in the mid-19th century.

By the late 19th century tourism had blossomed, giving rise to the creation of the two-lane Amalfi Drive, the ultimate in "road" shows. One of the most exciting drives in the world, the road appears to be merely pasted onto the facades of dizzying precipices and far-flung headlands. Wind and water erosion have carved limestone mountains into spires and crags that seem to defy gravity, cliffs plummet headlong into the sea, and crushed rock washes up along turquoise inlets. Ravines and valleys, formed by torrential flows from the highlands, are folded into the limestone coast, softening the scene with meadows and stands of chestnut trees. Thanks to the engineering marvel that is the Amalfi Drive, the world soon discovered what has come to be called the "Divina Costiera." The justly famed jewels along this coastal necklace are Positano, Amalfi, and Ravello, but today's traveler will find the satellite baguettes—including Conca dei Marini, Atrani, Scala, and Cetara—just as sparkling. The top towns along the Amalfi Drive may fill up in high season with tour buses, but in the countryside not much seems to have changed since the Middle Ages: mountains are still terraced and farmed for citrus, olives, wine, and dairy; and the sea is dotted with the gentle reds, whites, and blues of fishermen's boats. Vertiginously high villages, dominated by the spires of *chiese* (churches), are crammed with houses on, into, above, and below hillsides to the bay; crossed by mule paths; and navigated by flights of steps called *scalinatelle* often leading to outlooks and belvederes that take your breath away—in more ways than one. Songs have been composed about these serpentine stone steps, and they may come to haunt your dreams as well; some *costieri* (natives of the coast) count them one by one to get to sleep.

Semi-tough realities lurk behind the scenic splendor of the Divina Costiera, most notably the extremes of driving (potentially dangerous, although accidents are reassuringly rare), the endless steps, and nonexistent parking. Furthermore, it rains in the spring, the hills burn dry in summer, museums are few, and until you adjust, people seem to talk at maximum decibels. So what? For a precious little time, you are in a land of unmarred beauty.

EXPLORING SORRENTO, THE SORRENTO PENINSULA & THE AMALFI COAST

From Sorrento on the north coast of the Sorrento Peninsula to Vietri at the eastern edge of the Amalfi Coast, from the Bay of Naples to the Bay of Salerno, this small ledge of land is a poem of compressed beauty, with two main "verses" and a bridge. Sorrento, on the Bay of Naples, is set solidly on a steep cliff, and neighboring towns slope over the gulf, with deep valleys breaking the terraced watershed behind. The rural, sometimes mountainous peninsula is rimmed by the two bays and Statale (or state highways) 145 and 163, the two narrow, winding roads that feed into the Amalfi Drive at the peninsula's southern edge, which faces the Bay of Salerno, near Positano. If you think a road is just for getting from here to there, the twisty Amalfi Drive is not for you. The natives joke that to journey it from end to end by car in the English manner takes three hours; in the Italian style, a half hour. The going is tense until Minori—as John Steinbeck once observed, the Amalfi Drive "is carefully designed to be a little narrower than two cars side by side"—then tapers off; so expect the ride of your life. In fact, via bus or car, don't dare miss this seaside road, one of the most beautiful drives in the world.

About the Restaurants & Hotels

Having much higher levels of tourism than Naples, the area around Sorrento and Amalfi has fewer cheap and cheerful restaurants for locals, but you are more likely to find waiters who speak some English, *trattorie* which stay open right through August, and generally higher levels of cuisine and service. Betraying their rural origins, however, eating hours are earlier and you may have trouble finding a place open after 11 PM in the smaller towns. As a rule of thumb, avoid set menus (often called *menu turistico*) and go for whatever looks freshest to you. Remember that fish and steak prices on menus are often indicated by a price per 100 grams—look carefully if it seems suspiciously cheap!

The ghosts of a trysting Garbo in Ravello or ailing Caruso in Sorrento haunt the hotel corridors here. Because of logistics, major chains are absent for the most part and, consequently, the lodging scene offers a true sense of place. Sorrento's 18th- and 19th-century cliffside villas and palazzos, with their big gardens and grand staircases, huge baths and tile floors, have been transformed into spacious hotels, as have Amalfi's former convents with their peaceful cloisters. *Agriturismo* (country living) sets up farmhouse stays in rural and upland areas; check with local tourist boards. For "cheaper" rates, head to an *albergo* (small hotel or inn); the quote marks are used because many of these places cost more than 100 euros a night, due to their prime real estate overlooking the sea. As for the beloved hotel landmarks, many of them—Amalfi's Cappuccini Convento, Ravello's Villa Cimbrone, and Caruso Belvedere, to name three—are undergoing renovation, with scheduled reopening dates from 2004 to 2005. Aficionados are terrified that the special flavor of these hotel legends may be tampered with. Time will tell.

Great vistas, and balconies from which to ponder them, are available at most lodgings along these coasts. Assume all hotel rooms have air-conditioning, TV, telephones, and private bath, unless otherwise noted. If a breakfast is included in the room rate, the review lists BP, or Breakfast Plan, under the Meal Plan category. Otherwise, hotels operate on the European Plan (EP, with no meals), the Modified American Plan (MAP, with breakfast and dinner daily), called *"mezza pensione"* in Italy, or the Full American Plan (FAP, with all meals), called *"pensione completa."* When booking, note that a few hotels *require* half or even full board, usually hand-in-hand with a minimum stay of two or three nights. Some hotels have minimum stays for the peak periods of July and August and around holidays. Few business or fitness centers are available—who needs them here?—even at luxury establishments. Reserve ahead, as rooms are scarce in high season and hotels may be closed altogether in low.

If you're traveling by car and reserving rooms in advance, ask about parking fees. Many guests staying in Positano and Amalfi suffer a nasty shock when they find they have to shell out up to €20 per day for parking a car that they're unlikely to use during their stay. Porterage is run by co-operatives, not by hotels, in central Positano and Amalfi, and is another extra charge to be factored in.

Most lodgings in this part of Campania have been owned by the same families for generations, and whether the owner is plain mamma-and-papà or an heir to a ducal line, personality is evident. Along with local management may come quirks, even in the fanciest establishments—floors that dip a bit, faucets off-center, wake-up calls when you're already brushing your teeth. But you just may get your hand kissed or an invitation to chat, or get to know a glossy family dog named Lorenzo, or a cat named Luca, and isn't that sort of thing more memorable in the long run?

WHAT IT COSTS In euros					
	$$$$	**$$$**	**$$**	**$**	**¢**
RESTAURANTS	over €20	€15–€20	€9–€15	€5–€9	under €5
HOTELS	over €210	€160–€210	€110–€160	€60–€110	under €60

Restaurant prices are for a main-course entry only (known in Italian as secondo piatto, or second course); note that if a restaurant offers only prix-fixe (set-price) meals, it has been given the price category that reflects the full prix-fixe price. Hotel prices are for a standard double room in high season, excluding tax and service charges; higher prices (inquire when booking) prevail for any board plans.

Timing

Sheltered by the Lattari Mountains arcing east to west across the peninsula and inland from the Amalfi Coast, and exposed to cool breezes from two bays, the region of the Sorrento Peninsula and the Amalfi Coast enjoys a climate that is among the mildest in Italy; the temperature rarely falls below 50°F (10°C) in winter, or climbs above 90°F (31°C) in summer. Winter is least crowded but is sometimes overcast, and many hotels close from November to March. Easter time can be rainy and wet—locals call it *passione de Pasqua* ("tears of passion"), and it's safe to assume it will rain on Good Friday. On Italian public holidays (in particular, Easter Monday, April 25th, and May 1st) and Sundays, the

4

Beaches

Except for the showpieces at Positano, Atrani, Maiori, and Minori, the area's beaches are generally disappointing, as they usually consist of small patches of coarse gray sand, or just a few rocks below the precipices. In these parts, it's the water that compels: infinite shades of aquamarine, lapis, and amethyst—shimmering in sunshine, glowing silver in moonlight, and becoming transparent in coves. Sometimes the best regional beaches are the most unheralded, such as those hidden along the Sorrento Peninsula, to the west and south, many of them reachable only by footpath or boat. The longest and widest beaches on the Amalfi Coast are in Maiori and Minori. As space is at a premium, few organized beachside activities are available, the best being at Positano, where you should opt for beautiful Fornillo, the more secluded (but very popular) beach to the west of Spiaggia Grande. For exercise, folks descend (and later ascend) the scalinatelle to rocky coves, where the adults dip and sunbathe and the children play hide-and-seek. The terrain below sea level is as craggy and steep as the land above—a boon for good swimmers—but as most of the beaches shelve quite steeply, caution needs to be taken, especially with kids.

Boating

People take to boats here with the ease others use around buses and subways. Ferries and hydrofoils run on regular schedules during high season. The waters are calm and beckoning, and boating for pleasure frees you from the tension of coastal driving, so try to arrange to spend at least one day on the water. Bright red-and-blue fishing boats are for hire by the day or for a few hours at the major harbors of Sorrento, Positano, and Amalfi, and by almost any beach wherever you see fishermen. Boats can take you around the Sorrento area, to the Emerald Grotto, to Capri and offshore islets, to major towns, and otherwise inaccessible cove beaches. They will drop you off and pick you up, or stay with you, depending on your budget. Look for established sites on major beaches and come a day or so ahead to reserve and bargain, especially if you're with a group. Pricing could be around €20 an hour, more or less, depending on the market, the season, and your talent at haggling. If in doubt, ask for recommendations about local boatmen at your hotel or at the town tourist board. And don't expect fishermen to speak much English; you'll have to learn to speak with your hands, as many Italians do.

Dining: La Cucina Costiera

Locals say they have "one foot in the fishing boat, one in the vineyard"—and a fortunate stance it is, as you can count on eating simple, fresh, seasonal food, and lots of it, with *tutti i sapori della campagna verace* (all the true flavors of the countryside). From the gulfs come *pesce alla griglia* (grilled fish), *calamari* (squid), *aragosta* (lobster), and *gamberone* (shrimp). Wood oven–baked thin-crust pizzas start with the classic *Margherita*—tomato sauce, basil, and cheese—and *marinara*—"marinated" with tomato, garlic, and oregano—and go from there to infinity.

Food seems more sensuous amid all this beauty. Sun-dried tomatoes and chili peppers hang in bright red cascades on balconies and shopfronts ("VI-AGRA NATURALE" boasts a hand-lettered sign in Amalfi). After spring and autumn rains, peasants still scour the ravines for snails, to serve up with hot sauce. Oranges are as big as grapefruits, and lemons as big as oranges are cultivated on seemingly endless net-covered pergolas. From linguine with lemon at trattorias to lemon soufflés at fancy restaurants, the yellow citrus is everywhere, and all parts are used, as can be seen from the delicious habit of baking raisins, figs or pieces of cheese wrapped in lemon leaves, bound up with thin red thread. Not only are lemons a main component of meals and drinks, but they are used as a remedy for everything from flu to bunions.

Ingredients grown in terraced plots include plump olives pressed into oil or eaten whole, tiny spring *carciofi* (artichokes), and sweet figs. *Sponzini*, or *pomodori del pendolo*, the tomatoes carried from Egypt long ago by fishermen, grow in the mountains and muddy fields of Furore and Conca dei Marini. Eggplant, asparagus, and mushrooms thrive in the Tramonte uplands, while tomatoes come from Campora. Soft *fior di latte* (cow's-milk cheeses)—try *treccia*, the braided variety sold in Sorrento—are from the high hill pastures of Agerola, while the world's best buffalo mozzarella comes from Paestum. Unusual fruits worth seeking out are carobs, and *ponceri*—citrus the size of a melon, often used in pastries or extremely aromatic liqueurs.

Pasta is often served with seafood, but regional dishes include *crespelle al formaggio*—layers of crepes with béchamel cheese sauce, and fettuccinelike *scialatielli*, sometimes a house specialty, served with varied sauces. Clams and pasta baked in a paper bag—*"al cartoccio"*—is popular in Amalfi. In Positano, try traditional squid with potatoes, stuffed peppers, and slow-simmering ragù (tomato sauce with meat, garlic, and parsley). Around Cetara, salted anchovies, eggplant, and peppers in oil are the base of the famed sauce called *"garum,"* handed down from the Romans. A lighter version is *colatura di alici*, an anchovy sauce developed by Cistercian monks near Amalfi, served on spaghetti as a traditional Christmas Eve treat. Holidays and celebrations especially inspire the sweet tooth, with *zeppole, mustacciuoli*, and *struffoli* pastries at Christmas and New Year's, and eggy fruit tarts and almond cakes at Easter time. On their saint day, different villages serve different specialties. Residents in Conca dei Marini devour *"Santarosa sfogliatella"*—cakes in the shape of a nun's hood, made from milk, sugar, dried cherries, and dough mixed with San Nicola wine.

Wine here is light, drinkable, and inexpensive, and often consumed mere months after crushing; don't be surprised if it's the color of beer, and served from a jug (*"sfuso"*–loose wine). Practically all of it comes from Campania, often from the town or village in which it's poured, perhaps even from the restaurant's own centuries-old vines. Little of it transports well. Furore, Gragnano, and Ravello produce good bottled wines, both rosso and bianco, with Furore's Cuomo perhaps the finest white. In Sorrento look for rosolio, a liqueur traditionally served to Neapolitan nobles, created by the court of France's king Louis XIV. But the most renowned local digestif is limoncello, capturing in a bottle the color, fragrance, and taste of those tart-sweet lemons. Drink it cold in a tiny, frosty glass or after a shot of hot espresso—a golden memory quenched with each sip.

Although a few restaurants are world renowned, most are family affairs ... *papà* out front, the kids serving, and mamma, aunts, and even old *nonna* in the kitchen. Smile a bit, compliment the cuisine, and you're apt to meet them all.

Shopping

In the 19th century, travelers to Sorrento loved shopping for regional trifles—local crafts, embroideries, ceramics, inlaid wooden furniture (intarsia), music boxes, dolls in tarantella costumes—and, today, these rather kitschy gifts still enchant the hordes of shoppers along Sorrento's Via San Cesareo. The most esteemed products in the Amalfi Coast area are ceramics from Vietri sul Mare, but some towns also produce local pottery. Amalfi still produces some fine handmade paper, a local industry since the Middle Ages. Ravello offers coral jewelry and wines; and Positano is world famous for its handmade, blazingly colorful resortwear. Lemon-based goods of all sorts are available, and other travel-friendly foodstuffs include honey, citrus and olive products, and pasta. Bargaining is acceptable sometimes, and as everywhere, prices are best where the locals trade. Shops stay open late, 'til 9 or so, but close from about 3 to 5.

Vistas

Dolce far niente—literally "the sweetness of doing nothing"—seems the major leisure activity around here, and balustrade bend, belvedere gaze, and bench butt are by-products of doing nothing. The Sorrento area and the Amalfi Coast are studded with belvederes ("beautiful sights") and rest stops built off the roadside for you to pull into safely, especially important if you're the driver and miss what your passengers are oohing and ahhing about. Sorrento's cliffside bay vistas are wider and more serene than the Amalfi Coast's mountain-meets-sea drama. Positano and Ravello have the most dramatic in-town vistas, although great ones also peek out and pop up just about everywhere else. The Lattari Mountains behind the coast are exceptional for wider panoramas. When booking hotels, ask to be on the water side, throw open the shutters and, at least once, worship the sun: rising on the Amalfi Coast, setting in Sorrento, or doing both on the peninsula.

Walking & Hiking

Throughout this entire region, walking *is* hiking, so be prepared. Positano, where streets usually take the form of staircases, is a resort where you may leave more fit than you were when you arrived. These towns are picturesque for a reason, and you've probably never seen so many flights of steps—those bothersome scalinatelle: thousands of them, leading down to beaches, up to churches, across the hills. Getting around will take a healthy set of lungs, strong calves, comfortable footwear, time-outs for rest, and a big bottle of Ferrarelle water—slow and steady is the way to go. As for intentional hiking, mule paths and footpaths were the only land-means to get around before the car, and most remain in place for hikers' delight. The Sorrento Peninsula has several downhill paths from hubs such as Sant'Agata sui due Golfi, and you can even hike the highlands from Positano to Agerola and thence to Amalfi and Ravello. Check out Julian Tippett's excellent walking book, *Landscapes of Sorrento and the Amalfi Coast* (Sunflower Press), often found at bookstores and newsstands in the area. Even if you're not in shape, you can still participate: take transportation uphill, and let gravity guide you down.

roads heave, lemming-like, with Neapolitan motorists, so if you plan on taking a long walk in the country, schedule it for one of these busier days. Although April and May are sublime, Italian students are then on break and can overrun major sites. Summer is filled with festivities and offers the best weather for sunning and swimming, bringing dense crowds and higher prices, especially during the middle two weeks of August, when Italians vacation en masse.

SORRENTO

Like the familiar song "Come Back to Sorrento," with its long, mournful closing notes (listen to the Pavarotti version and you may shed a few tears), Sorrento's beauty is tinged with melancholy. Its streets seem like 19th-century sepia photographs, vestiges of the Roman Empire's ruins are strewn about, and tiers of votive offerings of hopeful Sorrentines flicker in the crypt of the basilica of Sant'Antonino. Vesuvius, as always, looms in the distance. And with the sun's heart-stopping descent into the Bay of Naples, the isle of Capri fades into the purple twilight, as if to disappear forever. But touched with sadness or not, Sorrento is a temptress above all. Around the 6th century BC, Greeks appear to have settled in the area, and the town was given the name Surrentum—"city of the Sirens." A brief period of Etruscan occupation followed, then Oscans and Romans came; later rulers included Goths and Byzantines, followed by sacking Lombards, Saracens, and Amalfitans. Next were the Normans, in the early part of the 12th century, and the beneficent Aragonese. Decimated in 1558 by the Turks, the city later rebuilt its walls, and in the early 1700s began a comeback that peaked in the following century when Sorrento became a prescribed stop for "Grand Tour" travelers, who savored its mild winters while sopping up its culture and history. Among the literati who played and wrote here were Byron, Keats, Scott, Dickens, Goethe, and Ibsen. According to a letter from his traveling companion in 1876, the philosopher Nietzsche, not generally known for effervescence, "laughed with joy" at the thought of going to Sorrento, and French novelist Stendhal called it "the most beautiful place on earth."

The tourist industry that began centuries ago is still dominant, although the lords and ladies of bygone days have been replaced with (mainly English) tour groups. Sorrento has become a jumping-off point for visitors to Pompeii, Capri, and Amalfi, but you will find countless reasons to love it for itself. The Sorrentine people are fair-minded and hardworking, bubbling with life and warmth. The tufa cliff on which the town rests is like a great golden pedestal spread over the bay, absorbing the sunlight in deepening shades through the mild days, and orange and lemon trees waft a luscious perfume in spring. In the evening, people fill caffès to nibble, sip, and talk nonstop; then, arms linked, they stroll and browse through the maze of shop-lined lanes. The central piazza is named after the poet Torquato Tasso, born here in 1544. What greater delight than a cozy, burnished town that commemorates a poetic native son—and serves great pasta, too? Chances are, you will *turna a Surriento* ("come back to Sorrento"), as the famous song's lyrics predict. Or, at least, hope to.

Sorrento

48 km (30 mi) south of Naples, 50 km (31 mi) west of Salerno.

Sorrento's population (less than 20,000) swells with tourists in season, all of whom are here to luxuriate in Italy's prettiest Belle Epoque resort. Winding along a cliff above a small beach and two harbors, the

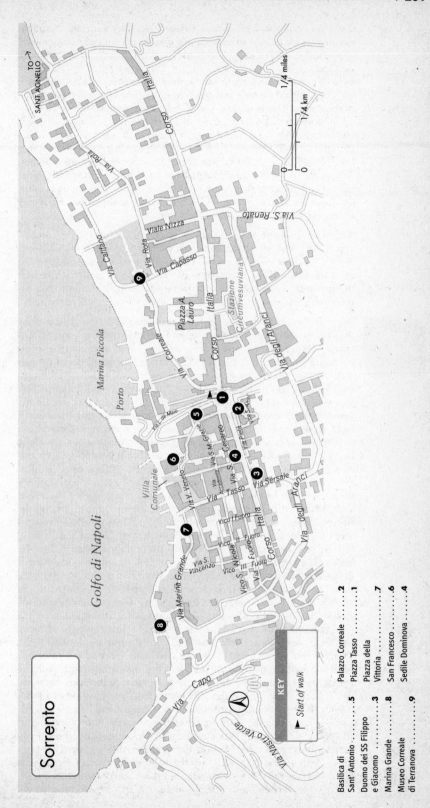

Sorrento

Golfo di Napoli

Marina Piccola

Porto

Villa Comunale

TO →
SANT' AGNELLO

1/4 miles
1/4 km

Italia
Corso Italia
Via Rota
Via Califano
Viale Nizza
Via Rota
Via Capasso
Piazza A. Lauro
Via Correale
Via Correale
Corso Italia
Via S. Renato
Stazione Circumvesuviana
Via degli Aranci
Via de Maio
Via M. Grazie
Via S. Cesareo
Via Pietà
Via Sedil
Via V. Veneto
Via Accademia
Via Tasso
Via Sersale
Vico I Fuoro
Vico II Fuoro
Vico III Fuoro
Via S. Nicola
Via Fuoro
Corso Italia
Via degli Aranci
Via S. Vincenzo
Via Marinà Grande
Via Capo
Via Nastro Verde

KEY
▲ *Start of walk*

Basilica di
Sant' Antonio 5
Duomo dei SS Filippo
e Giacomo 3
Marina Grande 8
Museo Correale
di Terranova 9

Palazzo Correale 2
Piazza Tasso 1
Piazza della
Vittoria 7
San Francesco 6
Sedile Dominova 4

town is split in two by a narrow ravine formed by a former mountain stream. To the east, dozens of hotels line busy Via Correale along the cliff—many are "grand" (an enconium sometimes included in the hotel's very name), and some, indeed, still are. Farther east (and usually out of sight of most tourist itineraries) is modern Sorrento, engulfed in a wave of "concretitis." Fodor's has received more than one letter despairing of this "ugly" Sorrento, and if you make the wrong turn, you can easily think the city is only made up of apartment blocks and other modern detritus, so beware. To the west, however, is the historic sector, which still enchants—it's a relatively flat area, with winding, stone-paved lanes bordered by balconied buildings, some joined by medieval stone arches. This part of town is a delightful place to walk through, especially in the mild evenings, when people are out and about, and everything is open. Craftspeople are often at work in their stalls and shops and are happy to let you watch; in fact, that's the point.

Most visitors arrive at the Stazione, the end of the line for the Circumvesuviana Railway; a 10-minute walk to the left along Corso Italia will bring you to the Piazza Tasso and the center of the historic quarter. At the station (which also functions as the main bus terminal), note the bust of Ernesto De Curtis, composer of *Turna a Surriento*, that music-box anthem you'll find yourself humming or whistling long after you return home.

a good
walk

Begin at Sorrento's historic center, **Piazza Tasso** ❶ ☞, watched over by the statues of the eponymous poet and the city's patron saint, St. Anthony Abbot. Avoid congested Corso Italia and head instead to the southeast corner of the piazza to Via Pietà to take a look at the noted Palazzo Veniero (No. 14) and the **Palazzo Correale** ❷ (No. 24), whose 18th-century majolica courtyard, now a flower shop, overflows with charm. Follow this street until you reach the Largo Arcivescovado, site of the **Duomo dei SS Filippo e Giacomo** ❸. After viewing this grand cathedral, head for its wedding-cake campanile, then make a right off Corso Italia down Via Giuliani to enter Sorrento's most picturesque quarter. Here, on Via S. Cesareo, is the beautifully frescoed **Sedile Dominova** ❹, the ancient, open-air site of civic discourse. At night, its little square, called the Largo Dominova, is illuminated and makes a fetching backdrop for diners at Caffè 2000. Return to Piazza Tasso along Via S. Cesareo, lit with 19th-century lanterns and one of Sorrento's most picturesque streets. When you arrive at the edge of Piazza Tasso, turn left toward the bay, a block or so along Via De Maio, to pretty Piazza S. Antonino, the site of stately palm trees and the 11th-century **Basilica di Sant'Antonino** ❺. Across the piazza is the Municipio (town hall), the former monastery of Santa Maria delle Grazie, with cloister and church. From there, take Via Santa Maria delle Grazie and Via Donnorso to the church of **San Francesco** ❻, and its legendary 14th-century "Paradise" cloister. Relax in the adjoining Villa Comunale gardens and enjoy the Cinemascope-wide view of the Bay of Naples. Keep going west along Via Veneto to the **Piazza della Vittoria** ❼. Here the rear facade of the Hotel Tramontano bears a faded "Casa di Tasso" sign, marking the birthplace of the revered poet. Cross the piazza to the aristocratic Hotel Bellevue Syrene, perhaps to enjoy a drink on the hotel's garden belvedere out front. At the back of the hotel is the Villa Pompeiana, a re-creation of a Pompeian villa built for Lord Astor (whose own magisterial house—still private—is just along the cliff), functioning now as the hotel's restaurant. Its spectacular terrace offers a caffè for luncheon snacks, although you may wish to opt instead to chow down at the Albergo Lorelei et Londres. Continue past the hotel to exit the walls near the Porta Greca (Greek Gate) and take the stairway down to the fishing port of **Marina Grande** ❽, where seafood restaurants offer good deals. Catch a bus on the Via del

Mare (they run frequently) back up to the old town, or just hike back along Via Marina Grande and the Strettoia San Vincenzo. Once back at Piazza Tasso, walk east along the Via Correale, lined by villas-turned-hotels, to the **Museo Correale di Terranova** ❾, where its collection of ancient artifacts is set within a pretty garden. End the walk by heading toward the bay to Via Califano and its Albergo Lorelei et Londres, a relentlessly picturesque 19th-century pensione; its magical terrace caffè, which seems to levitate over the Bay of Naples, is the perfect spot for an idyllic luncheon, sundowner drink, or dinner.

TIMING This complete walk is most enjoyable if you leave sufficient time for discovery and rests; if you wish to include everything, allow at least half a day. If you're not planning to tour the Museo Correale (open only until 2), you may want to throw a sweater over your shoulders the way the Italians do and start your walk—but call it a promenade—in late afternoon; even if you don't visit the Museo Correale, we suggest a walk in that direction, as a visit to the terrace caffè of the Albergo Lorelei et Londres should be part of your Sorrento sojourn.

What to See

❺ **Basilica di Sant'Antonino.** Gracing Piazza Sant'Antonino and one of the largest churches in Sorrento, the Basilica di Sant'Antonino honors the city's patron saint, St. Anthony Abbot. The church and the portal on the right side date from the 10th century. Its nave and side aisles are divided by recycled ancient columns, and the interior is Baroque style, with fine paintings, including one on the nave ceiling painted by Giovan Battista Lama in 1734. Directly opposite across the piazza is the turn-of-the-20th-century *Municipio* (town hall). ⊠ *Piazza Sant'Antonino.*

❸ **Duomo dei SS Filippo e Giacomo.** Ancient, but rebuilt from the 15th-century right up to 1924, the town's cathedral follows a Latin-cross design; its nave and two side aisles are divided by thick piers with round arches. A Renaissance-style door and artworks, including the archbishop's 16th-century marble throne and ceiling paintings attributed to the 18th-century Neapolitan school, are easily viewable. Outstanding 19th- and 20th-century marquetry ornaments a magnificent choir loft, entrance panels, and representations of the stations of the cross. Look for the unusual 10th-century marble slab used as a gravestone, with a lioness on the front and a depiction of the deceased on the back. The delightfully florid three-story campanile, topped by a clock and a belfry, has an open, arcaded base and recycled Roman columns. ⊠ *Largo Arcivescovado, at the corner of Corso Italia and Via. R.R. Giuliani.*

❽ **Marina Grande.** Close to the historic quarter (but not that close—many locals prefer to use the town bus to shuttle up and down the steep hill), the port, or "borgo," of the Marina Grande is Sorrento's fishing harbor. There's a small beach area with its *stabilimento* (beach concession), complete with colorful changing cabins and bright umbrellas, and a few good seafood restaurants within easy reach. It's especially picturesque in early morning, when water-weary fishermen head in, their primary-color boats brimming with the day's catch. Don't confuse this harbor with Marina Piccola, at the base of the cliff, below Piazza Tasso and the Hotel Excelsior Vittoria; that is the area where ferries and hydrofoils dock. ⊠ *Via del Mare.*

❾ **Museo Correale di Terranova.** Set in an 18th-century villa and lovely garden on land given to the patrician Correale family by Queen Joan of Aragon in 1428, this museum has an excellent private collection amassed by the count of Terranova and his brother. The building is fairly charmless, with few period rooms, but the garden offers an allée of palm trees, citrus groves, floral nurseries, and an esplanade with a panoramic view of the Sorrento coast. The collection is one of the finest devoted to Neapolitan paintings, decorative arts, and porcelains, so for connoisseurs of the Seicento (Italian 17th century), this museum is a must. Magnificent 18th-century inlaid tables by Giuseppe Gargiulo, Capodimente porcelains, and Rococo portrait miniatures remind us of the age when pleasure and delight was all. Also on view are regional Greek and Roman archeological finds, medieval marble work, glasswork, Old Master paintings, 17th-century majolicas—even Tasso's death mask. ⊠ *Via Correale 50* ☎ *081/8781846* 🎫 *€5.16* ☾ *Wed.–Mon. 9–2.*

★ ❷ **Palazzo Correale.** Just off the southeast corner of Piazza Tasso, this palazzo was built in the 14th century in Catalan style but transformed into a Rococo-era showstopper, thanks to its exquisite **Esedra Maiolicata** (Majolica Courtyard, 1772). This was one of the many examples of majolica and faienceware created in this region, a highlight of Campanian craftsmen (other notable examples are the Chiostro delle Clarisse in Naples's Santa Chiara and the grand terrace of Positano's Hotel San Pietro). In 1610 the palazzo became the Ritiro di Santa Maria della Pietà and today remains private, but you can view the courtyard beyond the vestryway. Its back wall—a trompe l'oeil architectural fantasia, entirely rendered in majolica tile—is now a suitably romantic setting for the Ruoppo florist shop. Buy a rose here and bear it through the streets of old Sorrento, an emblem of your pleasure in the moment. As you leave the palazzo, note the unusual arched windows on the palace facade, a grace note also seen a few doors away at **Palazzo Veniero** (No. 14), a 13th-century structure with a Byzantine-Arab influence. ⊠ *Via Pietà 24.*

⚑ ❶ **Piazza Tasso.** This was the site of Porta Catello, the summit of the old walls that once surrounded the city. Today it remains a symbolic portal to the old town, overflowing with apricot-awninged caffès, Stil Liberty (Italian Art Nouveau) buildings, people who are attracted here day and night, and horse-drawn carriages clip-clopping by. In the center of it all is Torquato Tasso himself, standing atop a high base and rendered in marble by sculptor Giovanni Carli in 1870. The great poet was born in Sorrento in 1544 and died in Rome in 1595, just before he was to be crowned poet laureate. Tasso wrote during a period when Italy was still recovering from devastating Ottoman incursions along its coasts—Sorrento itself was sacked and pillaged in 1558. He is best known for his epic poem *Jerusalem Delivered,* which deals with the conquest of Jerusalem during the First Crusade. At the northern edge of the piazza, where it merges into Corso Italia, is the church of Maria del Carmine, with a Rococo wedding-cake facade of gleaming white and yellow stucco. Step inside to note its wall of 18th-century tabernacles, all set, like a jeweler's display, in gilded cases, and the fine ceiling painting of the Virgin Mary. ⊠ *Center of town, along Corso Italia and above the Marina Piccola, at the western edge of the historic district.*

❼ **Piazza della Vittoria.** Tree-shaded Piazza Vittoria is book-ended by two fabled hotels, the Bellevue Syrene and the Imperial Tramontano, one wing of which was home to famed 16th-century writer Torquato Tasso. Set by the bayside balcony, the facade of the **Casa di Tasso** is all the more exquisite for its simplicity and seems little changed since his day. The poet's house originally belonged to the Rossi family, into which Tasso's mother married, and was adorned with beautiful gardens (not surprisingly, Tasso's most famous set piece—the meeting of Rinaldo and the Saracen girl Armida—takes place within a sylvan setting). The piazza itself is supposedly the site where a temple to Venus once stood, and the scattered Roman ruins make it a real possibility. ⊠ *Via Veneto and Via Marina Grande.*

★ **❻** **San Francesco.** Near the Villa Comunale gardens and sharing its vista over the Bay of Naples, this church is celebrated for its 14th-century cloister. Filled with greenery and flowers, the Arab-inspired cloister has interlaced pointed arches of tufa rock, alternating with octagonal columns topped by elegant capitals, supporting smaller arches, and makes a suitably evocative setting for summer concerts and theatrical presentations—make this a must if you can catch one event. The church portal is particularly impressive, with the original 16th-century door featuring intarsiated (inlaid) work. Note the exterior bronze work by Nena. The interior's 17th-century decoration includes an altarpiece depicting St. Francis receiving the Stigmata, by a student of Francesco Solimena. The convent is now an art school, where students' works are often exhibited. ⊠ *Piazza Gargiulo off Via S. Maria delle Grazie.*

★ **❹** **Sedile Dominova.** Enchanting showpiece of the Largo Dominova—the little square that is the heart of Sorrento's historic quarter—this is a picturesque open loggia with expansive arches, balustrades, and a green-and-yellow-tile cupola, originally constructed in the 15th century. The open-air structure is frescoed with Baroque-era trompe l'oeil columns and the family coats of arms, which once belonged to the *sedile* (seat), the town council where nobles met to discuss civic problems as early as the Angevin period in the 15th century. The sediles resolved regional differences and members were granted privileges by powerful Naples during the days of the Spanish occupation. Today, Sorrentines still like to congregate around the umbrella-topped tables near the tiny square; in the evening, under the still vibrant and now softly illuminated frescoes, men sitting in the forecourt may still be discussing civic problems while playing cards. Note that the festive Caffè 2000 is opposite the Sedile and a table here makes for a great front-row seat to the passing parade. ⊠ *Largo Dominova, at the corner of Via S. Cesareo and Via R. R. Giuliani.*

★ **Villa Comunale.** The largest public park in Sorrento, the Villa Comunale sits on a clifftop overlooking the entire Bay of Naples and offers benches, flowers, palms, and people-watching, plus a seamless vista that stretches from Capri to Vesuvius. From here steps lead down to Sorrento's quieter and more picturesque harbor, the Marina Grande. ⊠ *Adjoining the church of San Francesco.*

need a break? The unassuming **Bar Villa Comunale** (⊠ Villa Comunale ☎ 081/8074090), closed November to April, is the perfect spot to sit with Sorrento's cardplayers and slip perfectly into the perfect scenery. For an afternoon delight, why not head over to **Piemme** (⊠ Corso Italia 161 ☎ 081/8072927) to partake of espresso and sweet, raisin-stuffed lemon leaves?

Where to Stay & Eat

$$$–$$$$ ✕ **Ristorante Caruso.** A classic international and operatic theme is carried out from *"preludio"* appetizers, such as Malossol caviar, to the "rapsodia delicatesse" desserts, including crêpes suzette. Sorrentine favorites are tweaked creatively as well, including ravioli with broccoli sauce and squid with almonds. The staff is warm and helpful, the singer on the sound system is the long-departed "fourth tenor" himself, and the operatic memorabilia with posters and old photos of Caruso is viewed in a flattering blush-pink light. This elegant restaurant deserves its long-time reputation and popularity. ⊠ *Via S. Antonino 12* ☎ *081/8073156* 🖃 *AE, DC, MC, V.*

$$–$$$ ✕ **Aurora-'O Canonico.** This 100-year-old institution in the heart of Sorrento is the place for wood-oven pizza with a choice of 50 toppings, home-

made gnocchi, and fresh seafood. The outdoor caffè, informal trattoria, and more formal ristorante sit side by side, and all are appealing. Try the *scarzette del Cardinale* (Cardinal's hat)—a special pastry here—and choose from a list of more than 600 wines. ⊠ *Piazza Tasso 7/10* ☎ *081/8783277* ⊕ *www.ristorantecanonico.com* ⊟ *AE, DC, MC, V* ⊘ *Closed Mon.*

\$\$–\$\$\$ ✕ **Da Emilia.** Near the Marina Grande and not the most visually prepossessing place in Sorrento, this spot has a happy plus with Signora Emilia herself in the kitchen (and often out front as well). The rickety wooden tables and red-checked tablecloths are a refreshing change from the town's (occasionally pretentious) elegance. Go for a plate of honest spaghetti with clams, wash it down with a carafe of the slightly acidic white wine, and watch the fishermen mending their nets. ⊠ *Via Marina Grande 62* ☎ *081/8072720* ⊟ *No credit cards* ⊘ *Closed Nov.–Mar. No lunch Tues.*

★ **\$\$–\$\$\$** ✕ **La Favorita—"O' Parrucchiano."** This restaurant is set in a sprawling, multilevel, high-ceilinged greenhouse and orchard, with tables and chairs amid enough tropical greenery to fill a Victorian conservatory—the effect is enchantingly 19th century. Opened in 1890 by an ex-priest (O' Parrucchiano means "the priest's place" in the local dialect), La Favorita continues to serve classic Sorrentine cuisine. Although the white-bean soup, cheese baked in lemon leaves, ravioli caprese, lemon tart, and profiteroles are all excellent, they can't compete with the unique decor. ⊠ *Corso Italia 71–73* ☎ *081/8781321* ⊕ *www.parrucchiano.it* ⊟ *DC, MC, V* ⊘ *Closed Wed. from mid-Nov. to mid-Mar.*

\$\$–\$\$\$ ✕ **Zi 'Ntonio.** The sixth generation of Uncle Tony's family now runs this rustic restaurant, which offers huge portions of sensational food. Try specialties including St. Peter's fish with artichokes, lobster and lemon risotto (which—exclamation point—comes on a plate featuring a picture of Sorrento that you can take home with you afterward), and savory San Daniele ham served with mozzarella (from the same distributor since the 1950s), or the Zi 'Ntonio pizza with the aforementioned ham, mozzarella, and arugula. Local wines are well priced. Up a chestnut-wood staircase, it's fun to eat aloft in the balcony, but all of the three floors and several rooms are evocative and filled with tiles, flags, murals, and plates, along with hearty diners. ⊠ *Via Luigi de Maio 11* ☎ *081/ 8781623* ⊟ *AE, DC, MC, V* ⊘ *Closed Tues.*

\$–\$\$ ✕ **Delfino.** Right on the sea, you can eat in the sunshine or in a glassed-in nautical-motif dining area. Cod, anchovies, and octopus are fresh and flavorful, and this informal, economical venue also has a snack bar for light meals. You can even swim off the pier—but please: wait for half an hour after eating! ⊠ *Via Marina Grande 216* ☎ *081/8782038* ⊟ *No credit cards.*

\$–\$\$ ✕ **La Lanterna.** On the site of ancient Roman thermal baths (you can still see ruins under a glass section in the floor), this is a historic venue as well as a beloved eatery. Whether dining outdoors under the lanterns, or indoors under the beamed ceiling and stucco arcades, you'll enjoy *cucina tipica, locale e nazionale,* traditional local and national dishes, including old favorites such as *scaloppina a marsala* (veal scallops in marsala wine) ⊠ *Via S. Cesareo 23/25* ☎ *081/8781355* ⊟ *AE, DC, MC, V* ⊘ *Closed Wed.*

\$ ✕ **Giardiniello.** The garden is the seating of choice at this big, inexpensive, simply decorated enterprise with a congenial owner out front and mamma in the kitchen, typical of Sorrento trattorias catering to tourists as well as locals. Pizza is best for lunch; otherwise go for the *gnocchi alla Sorrentina,* small potato dumplings with tomato and mozzarella sauce. ⊠ *Via Accademia 7* ☎ *081/8784616* ⊟ *AE, DC, MC, V.*

$$$$
Fodor'sChoice
★
🏨 **Bellevue Syrene.** In the late 19th century, Empress Eugénie of France came here for a week and wound up staying three months. You'll understand why if you stay at this soigné retreat, magisterially placed on a bluff high over the Bay of Naples (wait until you see the view of Sorrento from the glass-enclosed lobby). One of Italy's most legendary hotels, this connoisseur's favorite is a gentle fantasia of Venetian chandeliers, Louis-Phillipe rugs, and Belle Epoque murals (recently retouched) painted to make the King of Bavaria feel more at home back in the 1860s. All this luxe makes for quite a contrast when you step outside and see bathers, a beach, and all of the Bay of Naples at your feet. Guest rooms are sanctums of cozy calm, and if your room doesn't have a bayside balcony, drink in the views from the grand terrace of the hotel's Villa Pompeiana restaurant (built in 1905 as part of Lord Astor's villa). No less an authority than Heinrich Schliemann, discoverer of Troy, declared the hotel's vistas of distant Vesuvius the grandest in the land. Other hotels enjoy the same Cinerama vista but at this hotel Il Vesuvio is right in the center of the panorama. ⊠ *Piazza della Vittoria 5, 80067* ☎ *081/ 8781024* 🖷 *081/8783963* ⊕ *www.bellevue.it* ↪ *73 rooms* 🍴 *2 restaurants, minibars, gym, beach, dock, bar, meeting room, some pets allowed* 🖃 *AE, DC, MC, V* ⦿⦿ *MAP.*

$$$$
Fodor'sChoice
★
🏨 **Excelsior Vittoria.** Overlooking the Bay of Naples, this Belle Epoque dream offers gilded salons worthy of a Proust heroine; gardens and orange groves; and an impossibly romantic terrace where musicians sometimes lull guests with equal doses of Cole Porter and Puccini. This complex of two mansions and two 19th-century chalets has been run by the same family for centuries; they have traded witticisms with Alexandre Dumas and Oscar Wilde, welcomed crowned heads, and comforted Caruso in his final days. The public salons are virtual museums, with potted palms, Victorian love seats, and Stil Liberty ornamentation; like the Hotel Bellevue Syrene, this hotel offers the truly magical experience of staying in a veritable "palace" in a casual resort town. Guest rooms are usually spacious and airy, with tile floors, minimal furnishings, and balconies and terraces overlooking bay or gardens. If you—like Princess Margaret, Luciano Pavarotti, and Sophia Loren—want the full treatment, opt for one of the historic suites. Dine in the open-air seaside restaurant or in the magnificently grand dining hall, where waiters in starched white jackets don't look a bit foolish (unhappily, critics have been waiting for years for the culinary standards of the kitchen to improve). Outside is a lulling, better-than-Edenic park, lined with arbored promenades, shaded by orange trees, studded with statues, and home to a giant pool. Step outside the protected gates and you are in the heart of Sorrento. ⊠ *Piazza Tasso 34, 80067* ☎ *081/8071044 or 800/325–8451* 🖷 *081/ 8771206* ⊕ *www.exvitt.it* ↪ *105 rooms* 🍴 *2 restaurants, minibars, in-room safes, pool, hairdresser, bar, meeting rooms, parking, some pets allowed* 🖃 *AE, DC, MC, V* ⦿⦿ *MAP, FAP.*

$$$$
🏨 **Imperial Hotel Tramontano.** What a past! Emperor Augustus's son had a villa here millennia before this hotel was built in the 18th century. Italian poet Torquato Tasso was born on the site, which still has a 15th-century chapel from that era. In its glory days it hosted Shelley, Byron, and Goethe, and royalty of many lands; today it sees mostly tour groups. The dining room overlooks the water, the pool nestles in a lush garden, and the view of Vesuvius remains as it was in ancient times. Rooms are large, with antiques and small balconies. The high-tech elevator gives audio instructions like the ones in department stores, and the lobby, with atrium ceiling, is a bit tacky and too pink. But how can you not fall for a place upon whose terrace *Turna a Surriento* was both written and sung for the first time? ⊠ *Via V. Veneto 1, 80067* ☎ *081/8782588 or 081/*

8781940 🖷 081/8072344 ⊕ *www.tramontano.com* 🛏 *116 rooms*
♨ *2 restaurants, café, pool, beach, bar, some pets allowed* ▤ *AE, MC,*
V ⊗ *Closed Jan. and Feb.* ⧫◎⧫ *MAP, FAP.*

$$$–$$$$ ▦ **Ambasciatori.** This salmon-color stucco hotel on a cliff over the sea
is gracious inside, with marble floors, antiques, period wall sconces, Ori-
ental rugs, large windows—and a black cat. Rooms have bold mosaic
tile floors and standard furnishings, but many open onto balconies or
terraces with sea views. Gardens surround the pool and a spacious ter-
race-on-the-sea beckons guests to lounge or enjoy the occasional dances
and buffet dinners organized by the Manniello family, longtime hotel
owners. ⊠ *Via A. Califano 18, 80067* ☎ *081/8782025* 🖷 *081/8071021*
⊕ *www.manniellohotels.it* 🛏 *103 rooms* ♨ *Restaurant, minibars, pool,*
beach, dock, bar, some pets allowed ▤ *AE, DC, MC, V* ⊗ *Closed*
Nov.–Easter ⧫◎⧫ *MAP, FAP.*

$$$–$$$$ ▦ **Royal.** Lush, landscaped gardens surround this hotel, which features
a pool with sun lounges practically leaning over the bay. An elevator
descends to sea level and a private beach. The hotel is an oasis of quiet
and cool, with a spacious lobby, lounge, and indoor or alfresco dining.
Ask for a room with a balcony and superb view of the pool, gardens,
and bay. ⊠ *Via Correale 42, 80067* ☎ *081/8073434* 🖷 *081/8772905*
⊕ *www.manniellohotels.it* 🛏 *96 rooms* ♨ *2 restaurants, minibars,*
pool, beach, 3 bars, some pets allowed ▤ *AE, DC, MC, V* ⊗ *Closed*
Nov.–Easter ⧫◎⧫ *MAP, FAP.*

$$ ▦ **Del Corso.** This centrally located, colorful pensione is clean and basic,
with quirky touches such as psychedelic-pattern tablecloths and bed-
spreads. Fresh flowers, an occasional antique, a solarium, the wooden
bar in the lounge, courtyard entrances for some rooms, and rooftop breakfast room nudge up the comfort zone. Lodgings are on the second floor
(an elevator is provided from the street). Front-facing rooms are noisy
and only some rooms have air-conditioning. ⊠ *Corso Italia 134, 80067*
☎ *081/8071016* 🖷 *081/8073157* ⊕ *www.hoteldelcorso.com* 🛏 *26*
rooms ♨ *Bar* ▤ *AE, DC, MC, V* ⊗ *Closed Nov.–Feb.* ⧫◎⧫ *BP.*

$–$$ ▦ **Villa di Sorrento.** The best and the worst thing about this self-pro-
claimed "homely environment," built in 1854, is its central location—
an easy walk to most attractions, but right off a noisy street, so request
a room overlooking the quiet rear garden. Tile-floored rooms are
meticulously clean, with Danish-modern furnishings. The lobby has
wood trim, vintage photos, and old-fashioned touches such as embroidered antimacassars on its many, many chairs. Most rooms have
either balconies or terraces, with views of the azure sea and red-clay
rooftops. ⊠ *Viale Caruso 6, 80067* ☎ *081/8781068 or 081/8785767*
🖷 *081/8072679* ⊕ *www.belmare-travel.com* 🛏 *21 rooms* ♨ *Dining*
room, some pets allowed ▤ *AE, DC, MC, V* ⧫◎⧫ *BP.*

$ ▦ **Lorelei et Londres.** Dream: sunlight on lemon trees, blazing bougainvil-
lea, a tiny, inexpensive inn with all the warm charm of the 19th century, suspended over the Bay of Naples. Reality: the Lorelei et Londres.
This amazing relic was once favored by Room-with-a-View ladies from
England and still looks like E. M. Forster's Lucy Honeychurch might
pull up at any moment. Out front is a magnificently beautiful terrace
caffè, aflutter with red awnings and tablecloths. The welcoming lobby
always seems to be filled with laughter, so it seems that few guests mind
that the rooms upstairs are tatterdemalion, furnished with simple beds,
linoleum flooring, and creaking cupboards. Ask for sea-view rooms away
from the noisy road. For luxe and modernity, go elsewhere; come here
to take a trip back to the *bella* 19th century. ⊠ *Via Califano 2, 80067*
☎ *081/8073187* 🖷 *081/5329001* 🛏 *27 rooms* ▤ *AE, DC, MC, V*
⊗ *Closed mid-Nov.–mid-Mar.* ⧫◎⧫ *BP.*

FodorśChoice
★

Nightlife & the Arts

At night, most weary sightseers will content themselves with dinner, then an evening passeggiata through the old quarter, topped off by coffee and dessert at a caffè. For a particularly festive *notte,* head to the Largo Dominova on Via S. Cesareo—floodlit with the 17th-century Sedile Dominova—and an inexpensive meal or nightcap at **Caffè 2000,** with serenading musicians crooning Neapolitan favorites. Music spots and bars cluster in the side streets near Piazza Tasso, among them Fauno, Artis Domus, and the Chantecler. Ask at your hotel about clubs that might interest you and to get the latest news. The main watering hole for Sorrento visitors is the **Circolo dei Forestieri** (✉ Via Luigi de Maio 35 ☎ 081/8074033 ✆ Closed early Dec.–late Feb.), traditionally packed with Americans, Brits, and Australians. Crowds begin to descend on this large villa (also home to the Sorrento tourist office) for an aperitif or beer at sunset; others arrive for casual dinner, while merrymakers hold out for the late-night band and karaoke.

The Tarantella Show (✉ Fauno Notte Club and La Mela Club ☎ 081/8781021 or 081/8784463) presents tarantella dances with masks, costumes, and tambourines, plus 17th-century mandolin serenades and 16th-century Neapolitan *pulcinella* (pantomime); a *pazzariello* (jester) is on hand.

Feste (religious festivals) include an atmospheric procession in the thick of Thursday night before Easter, with locals donning white hoods—eerily evocative of the Ku Klux Klan—followed by a less awesome "black" procession on Good Friday evening. Christmas has its usual accompaniment of crèches, while further celebrations are held on February 14th—not St. Valentine's Day, but St. Anthony's Day; he's the patron saint of Sorrento.

Estate Musicale Sorrentina (✉ Cloister of the Chiesa di San Francesco ⊕ www.estatemusicalesorrentina.it/) is the main cultural event of the year, offering a bevy of concerts and theatrical entertainments from the first week of July to the first week of September, many held in the famous Moorish-style cloister of the church of San Francesco. Tickets usually run around €10; check with your hotel or the Sorrento tourist office for schedules and information. Throughout the year, free municipal concerts—usually jazz or classical music—are held in several other venues. A three-minute bus ride away in the adjacent township of Sant'Agnello, the **Concerti di Cocumella** hosts weekend chamber music concerts between May and September at the gorgeous 17th-century church of Santa Maria, now part of the luxurious **Hotel Cocumella** (✉ Via Cocumella 7, Sant'Agnello ☎ 081/8782933 ⊕ www.cocumella.com).

Shopping

The main shopping street is Via San Cesareo—along this pedestrian thoroughfare, lined with dozens of shops selling local and Italian crafts, the air is pungent with the perfume of fruit and vegetable stands. Corso Italia has more modern boutique offerings. Wood inlay (intarsia) is the most sought-after item, but you'll be surprised by the high quality of embroidery and metalwork. Keep your eye out for stalls that feature tiny crèche figures—miniature Punchinellos, hunchback dwarfs, and Magi figures.

Apreda (✉ Via Tasso 6 ☎ 081/8782351) produces delicious *treccia* cheese, the local equivalent of mozzarella made from cow's milk. **Fattoria Terranova** (✉ Piazza Tasso 161 ☎ 081/8781263) sells all kinds of produce—from cheeses to preserves to liqueurs—made on the eponymous family-run farm in nearby Massa. **Bottega d'Arte** (✉ Via Luigi de Maio 18/20 ☎ 081/8781162) offers a top selection of old glass, tiles,

and jewelry—antique and new. **Rosbenia** (⊠ Piazza Lauro 34 ☎ 081/
8772341) is renowned for traditional hand-embroidered linen and lace.
La Bottega del Gioiello (⊠ Corso Italia 179 ☎ 081/8785419) employs
master goldsmiths producing jewelry, including cameos and coral. **Libreria
Tasso** (⊠ Via San Cesareo ☎ 081/8071639) has a browseworthy stock
of English books and maps. **Limonoro** (⊠ Via S. Cesareo 51 ☎ 081/
8072782) produces the lovely local lemon liqueur, limoncello. You can
observe the production process in the back of this tiny white shop, and
watch the owners paint designs on the pretty bottles. **Olga** (⊠ Via Cesareo 18 on the Decumano Maggiore) sells handmade embroidered articles for children. **Stinga Tarsia** (⊠ Via L. De Maio 16 ☎ 081/8781165)
has been crafting and selling fine quality marquetry and inlaid wood,
coral, and cameos since 1890.

It's worth making the trek out to the **Wine Corner** (⊠ Via Capo 12, the
start of the main road leading westward out of town ☎ 081/8074731),
which has an excellent range of competitively priced local wines and a
well-versed shop manager for advice.

THE SORRENTO PENINSULA: SANT'AGNELLO TO MARINA DEL CANTONE

Grand monasteries, the finest beach along the Gulf of Positano, an
Edenic botanical park, and southern Italy's finest restaurant are just a
few of the discoveries that await the traveler willing to leave Sorrento's
Belle Epoque splendor behind and take to the scenic hills and coasts of
the Sorrento Peninsula. As it turns out, many people do just that—the
towns here get crowded with weekenders from Naples and Rome, and
the two-lane state roads 145 and 163 are often congested. The sights
here, however, are worth the bother. If you don't have a car, blue-color
SITA lines and municipal orange-color buses run regularly throughout
the peninsula, with most routes stopping in Sorrento. Bus stops are frequent along the peninsula roads, but it's always best to be armed with
a local timetable to avoid long waits at stops. The destinations here are
mapped out in two directions: Northeast of Sorrento, the route leads
to Sant'Agnello di Sorrento and Meta; south of Sorrento, the road heads
through Sant'Agata sui Due Golfi, Massa Lubrense, Punta Campanella,
and Marina di Cantone.

Sant'Agnello

🔟 *2 km (1 mi) south of Meta, 2 km (1 mi) north of Sorrento.*

Back in the 18th and 19th centuries, the tiny hamlet of Sant'Agnello was
an address of choice. To escape Sorrento's crowds, Bourbon princes and
exiled Russian millionaires vacationed here, some building sumptuous
villas, others staying at the Hotel Cocumella, the oldest hotel on the Sorrento Peninsula. Today, some modern motels sadly blemish its main street,
but Sant'Agnello still possesses a faintly ducal air. The 15th- to 16th-
century parish church, Chiesa Parrocchiale di Sant'Agnello, is as lyrical as its name: swirls of lemon-yellow and white, decorated with
marble-gloss plasterwork. Nearby is a spectacular belvedere, the Terrazza Punta San Francesco, complete with caffè, which offers a hold-
your-breath view of the Bay of Naples. Sant'Agnello's two most famous
estates sit side by side nearby. In the early 19th century, the **Cocumella
monastery** was transformed into a hotel, welcoming the rich and famous.
Today, only lucky guests can enjoy its gardens, but everyone can attend

The Sorrento Peninsula

Golfo di Napoli

Sc. Rovigliano

Castellammare di Stabia

Terme d. Scário

Vico Equense

M. Faito 1131

Marina di Equa

Alimùri

Moiano

Piano di Sorrento

11 **Meta**

Marina di Puolo

Sorrento

10 **Sant'Agnello**

Positano

Il Deserto

Massa Lubrense

Marina d. Lobra 13

12 **Sant'Agata sui Due Golfi**

Golfo di Salerno

Annunziata

Metrano

Términi

Li Galli

14 **Marina del Cantone**

Bocca Piccola

TO CAPRI

Punta Campanella

0   4 miles

0   4 km

the chamber music concerts presented by the hotel in its 16th-century church of Santa Maria. Next door is the **Parco dei Principi**, a botanical park laid out in 1792 by the Count of Siracusa, a cousin to the Bourbons. Traversed by a diminutive Bridge of Love, this was a favorite spot for Désireé, Napoleon's first amour, who came here often. Shaded by horticultural rarities, this park leads to the count's Villa di Poggio Siracusa, a Rococo-style iced birthday cake of a house perched over the bay. Green-thumbers and other circumspect visitors can stroll through the romantic park, now part of the Hotel Parco dei Principi.

Where to Stay & Eat

★ $$$$ ✕▥ **Cocumella.** Cognoscenti adore this hotel, one of the most aristocratic in Italy. With a guest list littered with names like Goethe and the Duke of Wellington, set in a cliff-top garden overlooking the Bay of Naples, the Cocumella occupies a Baroque monastery, complete with frescoed ceilings, antique reliquaries, and a marble cloister. The lobby is Italian-Victorian, and 19th-century grace notes continue in grand suites that offer stone fireplaces, Empire-style bureaus, and marble-clad bathrooms; even smaller rooms have great charm. The del Papa family has gilded this lily with a vast pool, a beauty-spa and exercise room, one of the most cornucopic breakfasts around, the superb Scintilla restaurant, a 90-foot-long 19th-century yacht for daily excursions on the bay, and even summer-night chamber-music recitals in the monastery's former church. Ah, the sweet life! ⊠ *Via Cocumella 7, 84067* ☎ *081/8782933* 🖷 *081/8783712* ⊕ *www.cocumella.com* ➦ *56 rooms* ⚄ *Restaurant, minibars, tennis court, pool, gym, hair salon, sauna, beach, boating, some pets allowed* ▤ *AE, DC, MC, V* ☯ *Closed Nov.–Mar.* ⊙❙ *BP.*

★ $$$–$$$$ ▥ **Parco dei Principi.** This hotel offers the best of both worlds—a stunningly romantic park, complete with gilded 19th-century villa, plus a hotel that's 1960s-modern. Up to a decade ago, the latter might have been considered a debit, but now that Sixties Moderne has entered the history books, this building is newly chic. In fact, when opened, this striking white-on-white structure raised the bar for Sixties design, thanks to Gio Ponti, Italy's coolest designer of the era. Inside, all is white walls and blue-glass accents; outside blooms the fabled Parco dei Principi, the lush giardino laid out by the Duke of Siracusa, cousin to the Neapolitan Bourbons, in the early 19th century. Paths lined with rare Washingtonia palm trees and African marigolds still lead to a romantic Rococo villa, set on a terrace over the bay—today, a splendiferous setting for the hotel's pool area. Long a tour-group favorite, this hotel is usually jammed and is joyously festive as a result. ⊠ *Via Rota 1, 80067* ☎ *081/8784644* 🖷 *081/8783786* 📞 *96 rooms* ⟡ *Restaurant, minibars, pool, beach, meeting rooms, some pets allowed* ▤ *AE, DC, MC, V* ⊗ *Closed Nov.–Mar.* ⦿ *MAP.*

Meta

⓫ *4 km (2½ mi) northeast of Sorrento, 3 km (2 mi) northeast of Sant'Agnello.*

Set on a steep slope, hovering above the gulf on Statale 145, this charming town is lined with orange trees and its ancient buildings spill right down to the sea. Off the coastal road is the church of the Madonna del Lauro, thought to be the site of an ancient temple built to worship the goddess Minerva. Outstanding are its 16th-century wooden door and its chapel, with frescoes and wood carvings from the 18th century.

Where to Stay & Eat

$ ✕▣ **Giosue' a Mare.** Locals crowd this modern albergo and ristorante on the bay, and for good reason: it's the best food around these parts. Seafood is pristine (try the cold combo), but you can have popular standbys such as veal marsala, too. If you care to stay on, compact rooms have balconies overlooking the water, tile floors, showers, and crisp blue-and-white decor. ⊠ *Via Caruso 2, 80062* ☎ *081/8786685* 🖷 *081/5323450* 📞 *27 rooms* ⟡ *Restaurant* ▤ *AE, DC, MC, V* ⦿ *BP.*

Sant'Agata sui Due Golfi

⓬ *7 km (4½ mi) south of Sorrento, 10 km (6 mi) east of Positano.*

Because of its panoramic vistas, Sant'Agata was an end-of-the-line pilgrimage site for beauty-lovers through the centuries, especially before the Amalfi Drive opened up the coast to the southeast. As its name suggests, this village 1,300 ft above sea level looks out over the bays of Naples and Salerno (Sant'Agata refers to a Sicilian saint, honored here with a 16th-century chapel) and it found its first fame during the Roman Empire as the nexus of merchant routes uniting the two gulfs. Now that the town has become slightly built up, you have to head to its outskirts to actually take in the vistas. The most famous vantage point, however, has always been on the far north side of the hill, where an ancient Greek sanctuary was dedicated to the Sirens of fable and legend. That choice
★ location became **Il Deserto,** the Convento dei Padri Bigi built by the Carmelite fathers in the Middle Ages. Now crumbling, the monastery's famed belvedere—with panoramic views of the blue waters all around, and of Vesuvius, Capri, and the peninsula—was a top sight for Grand Tour–era travelers. To gain entry, ring the buzzer at the gate for the attendant, who will supply you with a key to the belvedere tower (the monastery often closes for religious retreats, so you or your hotel concierge must call ahead to check that it's open). To get to the Deserto from the center of Sant'Agata, with your back to the hotel, take the road

to the left of the Hotel delle Palme (Corso Sant'Agata 32), pass the church of Santa Maria delle Grazie, and keep walking uphill on Via Deserto for a little more than half a mile. ⊠ *Via Deserto* ☎ *081/8780199* 🎟 *Free; donation requested* ☉ *When not closed for retreats, daily 3–6.*

Today's travelers head to Sant'Agata less for the sublime beauties of Il Deserto than for its lodging options and to dine at Don Alfonso 1890, the finest restaurant in Campania. Across the way from Don Alfonso on the town square is the beautiful 16th-century Renaissance church of **Santa Maria delle Grazie.** The shadowy, evocative interior features an exceptional 17th-century altar brought from the Girolamini church in Naples in the 19th century. Attributed to Florentine artists, it's inlaid with lapis, malachite, mother-of-pearl, and colored marble.

Where to Stay & Eat

$$$$
Fodor'sChoice
★

✕🏨 **Don Alfonso 1890.** The greatest restaurant in Campania, this is the domain of Alfonso Iaccarino, who counts Prince Rainier of Monaco as one of his many fans. *Haute*-hungry pilgrims head here to feast on culinary rarities, often centuries-old recipes given a unique Iaccarinian spin. Lobster, for instance, is breaded with traditional Sorrentine "porri" flour, then drizzled with sweet-and-sour sauce influenced by the Arabian traders who came to Naples. The braciola of lamb with pine nuts and raisins is a recipe that dates back to the Renaissance, while the cannoli stuffed with foie gras pays homage to the Neapolitan Bourbon court. Nearly everything is home-grown, with olive oils *de nostra produzione* created on the family farm, vegetables so lovingly grown they have bodyguards, not gardeners (jokes the staff). Hand-churned butter finds its way into sublime desserts such as the *pizzo di cioccolato* (white sugar "mozzarella" on a chocolate "pizza") or the *soufflé di Nirvana.* The restaurant decor is pastel and staidly traditional—the fireworks are reserved for the food (and the occasional Vesuvio flaméd cocktail). Don Alfonso has one of the finest wine cellars in Europe, set deep in an Oscan cave—don't be surprised if the sommelier tells you his earliest bottle is a Roman amphora dating from 30 BC. If you want to make a late night of it, Alfonso and his enchanting wife, Livia, also run an inn above the restaurant, with five apartments furnished in traditional style. Light sleepers should note that the nearby church bells ring on the half-hour (!) throughout the entire night. ⊠ *Corso Sant'Agata 13, 80064* ☎🖨 *081/ 8780026* ⊕ *www.donalfonso.com* ⇲ *5 apartments* ♻ *Restaurant* ⊟ *AE, DC, MC, V* ☉ *Closed Mon. and Tues. Oct. 1–May 31; Mon. June 1–Sept. 31; and Jan. 10–Feb. 25* ⏢ *BP.*

$

🏨 **Sant'Agata.** If you wish to stay in hilltop Sant'Agata sui Due Golfi, this comfortable hotel provides clean and pleasant lodging and a good bed to fall into after a meal at Don Alfonso 1890 or a walk to the Il Deserto belvedere. ⊠ *Via dei Campi 8/A, 80064* ☎ *081/8080363* 🖨 *081/ 5330749* ⊕ *www.hotelsantagata.com* ⇲ *33 rooms* ⊟ *AE, DC, MC, V* ☉ *Closed Dec.–Feb.* ⏢ *BP.*

Massa Lubrense

⑬ *6 km (4 mi) southwest of Sorrento, 7 km (4½ mi) northeast of Punta Campanella.*

Near the far western tip of the peninsula, off Statale 145, the township of Massa Lubrense—settled in the 10th century and now with a population of about 12,000—sprawls its way through farming and fishing hamlets. Its name derives from the early–Middle Ages *massa* (rural dwellings) and the Latin *delubrum* (a temple, probably dedicated to Minerva). Faithful to the Angevins, it was made a duchy, and later destroyed in 1451 by Ferrante of Aragon. When the Jesuits founded a college here in the 17th century, the town grew into a cultural center. Today, Massa Lubrense is a relaxation destination, close to, but so far from, Sorrento's bustle.

Landmarking the central village, the cathedral of **Santa Maria delle Grazie,** on the central square, Largo del Vescovado, was renovated in the late 18th century, and features a majolica pavement; in the apse is a painting of the Madonna by Andrea da Salerno. The 16th-century **Sanctuary of Santa Maria della Lobra,** on Via Marina in the fishing village of Marina della Lobra, is on a site where pagans once worshiped. The church organ is supported by two ancient columns, perhaps from the original temple. Note also the majolica floor, the coffered ceiling, and the 18th-century wooden crucifix. The adjacent cloister was constructed in the 17th century when the complex was a Franciscan convent.

Where to Stay & Eat

$$$–$$$$ ✕ **Antico Francischiello da Peppino.** Overlooking olive groves seeming to run into the sea, this fourth-generation establishment has been welcoming hungry travelers for more than 100 years. Two huge, beamed rooms with sprays of fernery, antique mirrored sideboards, hundreds of mounted plates, brick archways, old chandeliers, fresh flowers, and tangerine-hued tablecloths is quite a sight. *Tagliolini con zafferano, zucchine e gamberi* (pasta with saffron, zucchini, and prawns), ravioli with clams and arugula, and other bountiful country cuisine is *tutto buono.* Reservations are essential for Saturday dinner and Sunday brunch. ⌂ *Via Partenope 27, halfway between Sorrento and Massa Lubrense* ☎ *081/ 5339780* ⊟ *AE, DC, MC, V* ☉ *Closed Wed. from Nov. to Mar.*

$ ⊡ **Villa Pina.** A comfortable country inn across the road from the restaurant is managed by the same family which presides over the Antico Francischiello restaurant. Stick to the newer rooms with long decks and tile floors perched over the restaurant, and content yourself with serene views of the bay of Naples and Capri from the balconies. ⌂ *Via Partenope 40, Massa Lubrense, 80061* ☎ *081/5339780* ⊟ *081/8071813* ⊕ *www. francischiello.com* ⇝ *25 rooms* ⊟ *AE, DC, MC, V* �ｦ *BP.*

Marina del Cantone

⑭ *5 km (3 mi) southwest of S. Agata sui due Golfi, 5 km (3 mi) southeast of Massa Lubrense.*

The largest (pebble) beach on the Sorrento Peninsula attracts weekend sunworshipers and foodies determined on great country dining at the seaside restaurants here. To get to the beach, usually dotted with dozens of festive umbrellas, a slender road winds down to the sea through rolling vineyards and the small town of Nerano, ending at the Gulf of Positano near the Montalto watchtower. To escape the jam, hire a boat to visit the islets of Li Galli—Gallo Lungo, Castelluccia, and La Rotonda—which sit on the horizon to the east of the beach. They are also called Isole Sirenuse (Isles of the Sirens), after the mythical girl-group that lured unwitting sailors onto the rocks. What goes around comes around: legend says the sirens' feet became flippers, because the Three Graces were envious of how they danced the tarantella; and, as the folkloric tale concludes, the mermaids' dancing days were really finito when they petrified into the isles themselves. With all this dancing going on, it's not surprising that the great Russian ballet choreographer Leonide Massine purchased the Li Galli islands as his home in the 1950s; in the 1980s, they were sold to Rudolf Nureyev, who made them his last abode. The beach at Marina del Cantone was reputedly the superstar dancer's favorite coastal hangout.

Where to Stay & Eat

\$\$–\$\$\$ ✕ **Lo Scoglio.** Dramatically set on a pier by the beach, you can hear, smell—even *taste*—the waves from here on a rough day. For those wanting to indulge in raw mollusks, this is a no-risk restaurant thanks to owner Peppino, who selects his seafood with an expert eye—all accompanied by home-grown vegetables. Even if you only stop by for a gelato, you're likely to enjoy yourself immensely in such informal surroundings (especially if you're a water baby, or are accompanied by one). ☒ *Marina del Cantone, on the pier* ☎ *081/8981026* ▤ *AE, V.*

\$\$–\$\$\$ ✕ **Maria Grazia.** A great story lies behind this area favorite. Signora Maria was running this little waterfront trattoria between the world wars when an aristocrat came round unexpectedly to eat with the marina fishermen; Maria cooked up the best she had on hand—spaghetti with stuffed zucchini blossoms. Through an aristocrat, the dish and the restaurant became famous. You can still enjoy it, even without a noble title, in season. ☒ *Spiaggia di Marina del Cantone* ☎ *081/8081011* ▤ *AE, DC, MC, V* ☉ *Closed Wed., except in summer; closed weekdays Nov.–Feb.*

\$\$–\$\$\$\$ ✕🏨 **Quattro Passi.** "A hop, skip, and a jump" is how the name of this hotel and Italian-nouvelle restaurant translates colloquially—appropriately so, in that it's in Nerano, a five-minute drive from Marina del Cantone, in the groves of the peninsula hillsides. Here, the focus is on relaxation and fine food but the comfortable environs also make it a pleasure to fall into bed. Some of the young chefs are Japanese, and their delicate touches are evident in the dollop of ham and cheese Napoléon, or a petit shrimp potpie. Dine indoors in modern white decor, on the big terrace in a lemon grove, or have a homemade limoncello in the brick-arched cantina stocked from fine vineyards north of Salerno. Guest rooms are simple, and casually elegant, with tile floors, quilts, antiques, and some two-person whirlpool tubs. This is one of the few places with absolutely no sea view, but to make up for it, you can help harvest olives in October. ☒ *Via A. Vespucci 13, Nerano, 80061* ☎ *081/8082800* 🖷 *081/8081271* ⊕ *www.ristorantequattropassi.com* ➽ *7 rooms* ☧ *Restaurant, minibars, bar, parking (fee)* ▤ *AE, DC, MC, V* ☉ *Closed Nov.–mid-Dec.* ⬦❍⬦ *BP, MAP.*

\$\$ ✕🏨 **Taverna del Capitano.** The fascinating cuisine here is based on old recipes from the various cultures—Norman and Moorish among them—that loom large in the history of the region. The captain's son, Chef Alfonso Caputo, is a wizard at conjuring up not-available-anywhere-else combinations: for example, chicory and prawn soup, and tagliatelle with anchovies, sardines, and fennel. You can rely on the knowledgeable maitre d' for an absorbing commentary on the various dishes and advice on the right wine from a siege-ready cellar. For dessert, opt for candied eggplant filled with ricotta and topped with chocolate sauce. Above the restaurant area is a select 10-room hotel—called La Locanda del Capitano—run by the same family, with the best rooms overlooking the waterfront. Lodging prices include full beach facilities. ☒ *Piazza delle Sirene 10/11* ☎ *081/8081028* 🖷🖷 *081/8981892* ⊕ *www.tavernadelcapitano.it* ▤ *AE, DC, MC, V* ☉ *Closed Jan. and Feb. and Mon., except in summer* ❍⬦ *MAP.*

POSITANO & THE AMALFI COAST

Europe's unsurpassingly beautiful coastline is ". . . the only delectable part of Italy, which the inhabitants there dwelling do call the coast of Malfie, full of towns, gardens, springs and wealthy men." Thus raves Boccaccio in his 14th-century *Decameron,* writing about the Costiera Amalfitana—the Amalfi Coast. Rugged, craggy, and extending around the Bay of Salerno from Positano on the west to Vietri sul Mare on the east, this is where the Amalfi Republic held sway in the Middle Ages, when Amalfi was one of the richest towns in Italy. Today, the coast's scenic sorcery makes this a top destination, drawing visitors who gaze longingly at the surroundings almost as much as they do at each other—after all, this is a prime honeymoon location.

Statale 163—the Amalfi Drive, as we call it—was hewn from the lip of the Lattari Mountains and completed in 1852, varying from 50 ft to 400 ft above the bay. You can thank Ferdinand, the Bourbon king of the Two Sicilies, for commissioning it, and Luigi Giordano for designing this seemingly improbable engineering feat. A thousand or so gorgeous vistas appear along these almost 40 km (29 mi), stretching from just outside Sorrento to Vietri, coursing over deep ravines and bays of turquoise-to-sapphire water, spreading past tunnels and timeless villages. This is the only coastal road in the region, and the slender two lanes hovering over the sheer drops sometimes seem impossible to maneuver by auto, let alone by buses and trucks.

Many arrive from Sorrento, just to the north, connecting to the coast through Sant'Agata sui Due Golfi on the Statale 145—the Strada del Nastro Azzurro (Blue Ribbon Road), whose nickname aptly describes its width, and the color at your alternating right and left. This inland region presents rolling hills of olive, lemon, and orange groves and is dotted with rural hamlets. The white-knuckle part, or, as some call it, the Via Smeraldo (Emerald Road), begins as the road connects back to Statale 163, threading through coastal ridges at Colli di S. Pietro, and continuing to wend its way around the Vallone di Positano. From ravine to ravine, Positano beckons, appearing and disappearing like a flirtatious coquette. Just east of Positano, at Punta San Pietro, Statale 163 again winds sharply around valleys, deep ravines, and precipices, affording more stunning ridge views. Past Praiano, the Furore gorge is crossed by viaduct. From here on to Amalfi, the ridges soften just a bit.

Positano

15 *56 km (35 mi) southeast of Naples, 16 km (10 mi) east of Sorrento.*

The most photographed fishing village in the world, this fabled locale is home to some 4,000 Positanesi, who are joined daily by hordes arriving from Capri, Sorrento, and Amalfi, eager to celebrate the fact that Positano is, impossibly, there. The town clings to the Monti Comune and Sant'Angelo and has been called by artist Paul Klee "the only place in the world conceived on a vertical rather than a horizontal axis." Its arcaded, cubist buildings, set in tiers up the mountainside, reflect the sky in dawn-color walls: rose, peach, purple, some tinted the ivory of sunrise's drifting clouds. In fact, the colors on these Saracen-inspired dwellings may have originally served to help returning fishermen spot their own digs in an instant. When John Steinbeck lived here in 1953, he wrote that it was difficult to consider tourism an industry because "there are not enough [tourists]." Alas, there are more than enough now. What Steinbeck wrote, however, still applies: "Positano bites deep. It is a dream place that isn't quite real when you are there and becomes beckoningly real after you have gone."

It may have started with bread. Roman Emperor Tiberius, son of poison-happy Livia, sent his three-oar boat to a mill in Positano, understandably afraid that his neighbors on Capri would poison him. The (now modernized) mill still grinds healthful flour, but Positano is now more than just a grocery stop. Its name could be a corruption of the Greek "Poseidon," or derived from a man named Posides, who owned villas

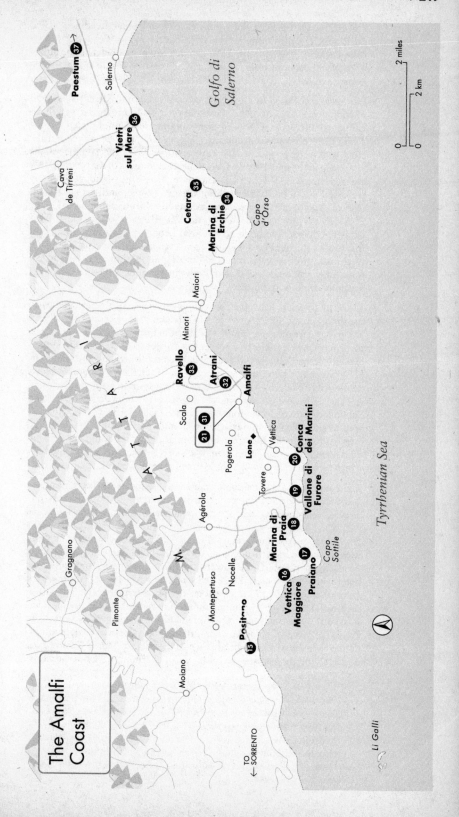

The Amalfi Coast

Paestum **37** →

Salerno

Golfo di Salerno

Cava de Tirreni

Vietri sul Mare **36**

Cetara **35**

Marina di Erchie **34**

Capo d'Orso

Maiori

Minori

Ravello **33**

Atrani **32**

Amalfi

Scala

21 · 31

Pogerola

Lone

Vettica

Conca dei Marini **20**

Tovere

Vallone di Furore **19**

Agérola

Marina di Praia **18**

Praiano **17**

Capo Sottile

Montepertuso

Nocelle

Vettica Maggiore **16**

Gragnano

Pimonte

Positano **15**

Moiano

TO SORRENTO ←

Tyrrhenian Sea

Li Galli

2 miles

2 km

here during the time of Claudius; or even from Roman freedmen, called the Posdii. The most popular theory is that the name "Positano" comes from Pestano (or Pesitano), a 9th-century town by a Benedictine abbey near Montepertuso, built by refugees of Paestum to the south, whose homes had been ransacked by the Saracens.

Pisa sacked the area in 1268, but when an elaborate defensive system of watchtowers was in place, Positano once again prospered, briefly rivaling Amalfi. As a fiefdom of Neapolitan families until the end of the 17th century, Positano produced silk and, later, canvas goods, but decline began again in the late 18th century. With the coming of the steamship in the mid-19th century, some three-fourths of the town's 8,000 citizens emigrated to America—mostly to New York—and it eventually regressed into a backwater fishing village. That is, until artists and intellectuals, and then travelers, rediscovered its prodigious charms in the 20th century, especially after World War II; Picasso, Stravinsky, Diaghilev, Olivier, Steinbeck, Klee—even Lenin—were just an inkling of this town's talented fans. Lemons, grapes, olives, fish, resort gear, and, of course, tourism keep it going, but despite its shimmery sophistication and overwrought popularity, Positano's chief export remains its most precious commodity: beauty.

Most car travelers leave their wheels either in one of the few free parking spaces on the upper Sorrento-Amalfi main road or in one of the scarce and pricey garages a few minutes' walk from the beach if their hotel doesn't provide parking. The best bet for day-trippers is to get to Positano early enough so that space is still available. Even those arriving in Positano by SITA bus should get a morning start, as traffic on the Via Smeraldo grows combustible by noon. The bus has two main stops in Positano: Transita, or Upper Town—near the large church of Santa Maria delle Grazie—and Sponda, or Lower Town, to the east of the main beach. Those who can't wait to start the Positano triathalon should get out at the first stop and start walking down. Most, however, opt to begin their walking tour from the Sponda bus stop. From here, it's a step to Via Cristoforo Colombo, which winds down through the heart of town toward the main beach.

Make sure you have some comfortable walking shoes—no heels, please!—and that your back and legs are strong enough to negotiate those picturesque, but daunting and ladderlike scalinatelle. If not, ride the municipal bus, which frequently plies the one-and-only-one-way Via Pasitea, hairpinning from Positano's central Piazza dei Mulini to the mountains and back, making a loop through the town every half hour. Continuing down from the Sponda bus stop toward the beach, you pass Le Sirenuse, the hotel where John Steinbeck stayed while he wrote his famous essay for *Harper's Bazaar* in 1953. The hotel's stepped terraces offer vistas over the town, so you might splurge on lunch or a drink on the pool terrace, a favorite gathering place for Modigliani-sleek jet-setters. Continue to Piazza dei Mulini, and make a left turn onto the pedestrianized, boutique-flanked Via dei Mulini to head down to the Palazzo Murat, Santa Maria Assunta, and the beach—one of the most charming walks of the coast.

need a break? If you want to catch your breath after a bus ride to Positano, take a quick time-out for an espresso, a slice of Positanese (a chocolate cake as delectable as its namesake), or a fresh-fruit iced "granita," check out **Bar-Pasticceria La Zagara** (⊠ Via dei Mulini 8 ☎ 089/875964). Deservedly famous for its lemon profiteroles as much as for its tree-lined terrace, suspended on a wooden platform above the lower town, Zagara is ideal for morning coffee, pre-dinner aperitivo, or post-dinner digestivo.

★ Past a bevy of resort boutiques, amble down Via dei Mulini to find the prettiest garden in Positano—the 18th-century courtyard of the **Palazzo Murat,** named for Joachim Murat, who sensibly chose the palazzo as his summer residence. This was where Murat, designated by his brother-in-law Napoleon as King of Naples in 1808, came to forget the demands of power and lead the simple life. Simple may not be the right word—this "palace" looks like it was airlifted in from the heart of Naples and seems all the grander next to the adjacent low-lying houses and harbor beach. Built in the early 18th century, the palazzo is replete with soaring limestone walls, shell sconces, and wrought-iron balconies (in summer, adorned with waterfalls of incredible bougainvillea flowers). Since Murat was one of Europe's leading stylesetters, Neapolitan Baroque suited him perfectly, and he is unlikely to have filed complaints about the views from the palazzo (now a hotel). ✉ *Via dei Mulini 23* ☏ *089/875177* ⊕ *www.palazzomurat.it.*

Beyond the Palazzo Murat is the Chiesa Madre, or parish church of **Santa Maria Assunta,** its green-and-yellow majolica dome, topped by a perky cupola, visible from just about anywhere in town. Built on the site of the former Benedictine abbey of St. Vito, the 13th-century Romanesque structure was almost completely rebuilt in the 18th century. The last piece of the ancient mosaic floor can be seen under glass near the apse. Note the carved wooden Christ, a masterpiece of devotional religious art, with its bathetic face and bloodied knees, on view to the left of the choir stalls. At the altar is a Byzantine 13th-century wooden painting of Madonna with Child, known as The Black Virgin, carried to the main beach every August 15 to celebrate the Feast of the Assumption. Legend claims that the painting was once stolen by Saracen pirates, who, fleeing in a raging storm, heard a voice from on high, *Posa, Posa*—"Put it down, put it down." When they placed the statue on the beach near the church, the storm calmed down, as did the Saracens. Positano was saved, and the town's name was established (yet again). Embedded over the doorway of the church's bell tower, set across the tiny piazza, is a medieval bas-relief of fishes, a fox, and a Pistrice—the mythical half-fox, half-fish sea monster, which supposedly characterizes the town's mixture of mountainous and marine activities. This is one of the sole relics of the medieval abbey of St. Vito. ✉ *Piazza Flavio Gioia, above the Spaggia Grande beach.*

The walkway from the Piazza Flavio Gioia leads down to the **Spaggia Grande,** or main beach, bordered by an esplanade and some of Positano's best restaurants. Take in the seaside beauty, then be sure to head over to the stone pier to the far right of the beach as you face the water. **Fodor's**Choice Here, a staircase leads to the **Via Positanesi d'America,** the loveliest seaside walkway on the coast. Halfway up the path you'll find the Torre ★ Trasìta, the most distinctive of Positano's three coastline defense towers, which define the edges of Positano in various states of repair. The Trasìta—now a residence occasionally available for summer rental—was one of the defense towers used to warn of pirate raids. Beyond the tower is O'Guarracino, a stunningly idyllic, arbor-covered restaurant. As you continue along the Via Positanesi d'America, you'll pass tiny inlets and emerald coves until the large Spaggia di Fornillo beach comes into view. Once you've explored Positano top to bottom (or vice versa), you may want to head heavenwards and visit two villages perched directly over Positano high in the crags of the Lattari Mountains. For this excursion, *see* the Close Up Box, "Above It All: Montepertuso and Nocelle."

ABOVE IT ALL: MONTEPERTUSO AND NOCELLE

The Dream: an Eden oasis with just thee and me and the cook. The Reality: tour buses, Nikons, and elbows. Thousands of travelers head to Positano every summer for some escapist entertainment, but how do you escape them?

The answer lies way up in the Lattari Mountains, directly above Positano's coastline, where two adorable villages perch on a rocky spur 1,700 ft above the sea. It's hard to believe that two such different settlements share the same ozone belt as their jet-set neighbor and, for the most part, have still escaped the glare of discovery.

Take Positano's village bus 3 km (2 mi) and climb the mountain to the village of **Montepertuso** (Pierced Mountain). This sky-high village is where Emperor Frederick II of Sicily bred and trained hawks; some feathery descendants—mainly kestrels and peregrine falcons—still nest on seemingly precarious ledges around the area.

The dramatic hole in the arched rock (arco naturale) below Monte Sant'Angelo a Tre Pizzi is one of only three in the world which both the sun's and the moon's rays can penetrate (April–July); the other two are in India. Try to see it in the morning, when the sun shines through.

Legend says the hole was created when the devil challenged the Madonna that whoever pierced the rock would own the village. In 10 attempts, the devil could only scratch the limestone, but when the Madonna touched the rock, it crumbled, the sky appeared, and she walked right through, sinking the devil into the hole.

On July 2, a holy performance, games, and fireworks commemorate the Virgin's success. Another popular village festival is the Sagra del Fagiolo, held on the last Saturday in August, which celebrates the humble bean. The town is lined with numerous stalls full of beans and other fare, with waiters in traditional folkloric garb (but no beanies). Storm the Montepertuso heights by taking the municipal Positano bus, which leaves from Piazza dei Mulini (one-way €1).

From Montepertuso you can hike up to the "lost village" of **Nocelle,** pasted to the mountainside some 1,400 feet above Positano. A trinket of a town, cloud-riding Nocelle is a car-less universe: only two stone pathways and myriad scalinatelle thread the hamlet, which looks out on a panoramantic vista.

To the east of the village, the *Sentiero degli Dei,* or Pathway of the Gods hiking trail begins, climbing 600 ft up the mountain range, crossing the Lattari Mountains east to Agerola.

This well-trod, steep, and scattered path was once the mountaintop route connecting settlements until the Amalfi Drive was built through the rock below; it's a true challenge (only experienced hikers should attempt it), but rewards with uninterrupted views the gods seem to have personally blessed.

As it turns out, just getting to Nocelle from Montepertuso—the end of the line for the Positano bus—can test your mettle. Along a well-paved road, then a curving, tree-shaded pathway, you skirt bottomless crevasses, hike under towering cliffs that appear to embody flight and gravity simultaneously, and skip up stairways that are easily tackled, if not befriended.

Finally, Nocelle appears and, in two minutes, the hamlet fully reveals itself: a stone alley, a scattering of houses and stairways, a doll-issue piazza, a church.

Oh, yes, and a view. This hold-your-breath one resets your inner clock. Sheep bleat, children giggle, birds call melodiously, and the rustling wind congratulates you on being far from the maddening crowd.

need a break? Up at the top of the town, **Bar Internazionale** (✉ Via G. Marconi 306 ☎ 089/875434) is more than just a place to wait for the bus (being opposite the main SITA bus stop). As a meeting place for locals and visitors alike, it's a happy spot where you can read newspapers from several countries while mulling over a fine creamy cappuccino.

Beaches

The Marina is the main boating area, with taupe-color, semi-sandy Spiaggia Grande the largest and widest beach of the 10 or so in the area. Fishermen—once the dominant workforce—now function as a cooperative group, supplying local kitchens; they can be seen cleaning their colorful, flipped-over boats and mending their torn nets throughout the day, seemingly oblivious to the surrounding throngs. To the west of town is the less crowded Spiaggia di Fornillo, which you can get to by walking the impossibly beautiful Via Positanesi d'America (leading off from Spiaggia Grande). Fornillo is worth the walk, as it is vast and hemmed in by impressive cliffs. To the east of Positano is a string of small, pretty beaches, separated by coves—La Porta, Fiumicello, Arienzo, San Pietro, and Laurito—most of which are accessible only by boat.

Boat Excursions

From Marina Grande you can board a scheduled day boat or hire a private one, including yachts that sleep six or more—with or without a captain—for as long as you'd like, to visit Capri, the Emerald Grotto in Conca dei Marini, or coves and inlets with small beaches. Close by, in the large cave at La Porta (650 ft east of the town center), tools, utensils, and hunting weapons from the Paleolithic and Mesolithic ages have been discovered, the oldest known remains on the coast. The favorite boating destinations, however, are the rocky Li Galli islets (6 km [4 mi] southwest), seen from any point in Positano (as they are from the beaches of the peninsula), whose name derives from their resemblance to pecking birds. Originally the site of an ancient Roman anchorage, the islands then became medieval fiefdoms of Emperor Frederick II and King Robert of Anjou. The isles remain tempting enough to lure purchasers in search of an exclusive paradise: Russian choreographer Leonide Massine in 1925, and, in 1988, dancer Rudolf Nureyev, who discovered the islands in 1984 when he came to accept the Positano Prize for the Art of Dancing, given each year in honor of Massine. The islands are still private. **L'Uomo e il Mare** (✉ Spiaggia Grande pier ☎ 089/811613 or 089/875211 📠 089/875475 ⊕ www.gennaroesalvatore.it) is an outfit run by Gennaro Capraro and his friendly English wife, Valeria, offering boating excursions to Li Galli and many other coastal destinations. Offering both short transfers (especially to beaches and night spots) and all-day affairs, including luncheon stopovers, he usually fills up an excursion party with nine people (€77 per person, including lunch), so it's best to reserve in advance. The boat is a bit on the bare-bones side, but no one knows more about the coast than Gennaro. Boating excursions can also be arranged through **Noleggio Barche Lucibello** (✉ Spiaggia Grande pier ☎ 089/875032 📠 089/875326 ⊕ www.lucibello.it), which also rents motorboats and rowboats by the hour.

Where to Stay & Eat

$$–$$$$ ✕ **La Cambusa.** Two stone lions guard this "pantry" right off the Marina Grande, a safe haven for tasty local cuisine for 25-plus years. Linguine with mussels and fresh fish with new potatoes and tomato sauce are among the favorites. Owners Luigi and Baldo are well known around town for maintaining high standards even during the hectic summer season. The outdoor dining terrace holds pride of place directly above

the entrance to the Spiaggia Grande. ✉ *Piazza Amerigo Vespucci 4* ☎ *089/ 875432* ▭ *AE, DC, MC, V* ✷ *Closed Wed. from Nov. to Mar.*

$$–$$$ ✗ **Chez Black.** A local institution, allegedly nicknamed after owner Salvatore Russo's eternal tan, this nautically themed place is probably no longer the restaurant it once was, having given in to the temptation of serving up mediocre food for the day-tripping coachloads. However, it can't be beaten for location (right on the Spiaggia Grande) or as a great spot for people-watching. Avoid the fish, stick with the decent pizzas, and follow up with a *grotta dello smeraldo*—gin, lemon, and crème de menthe. ✉ *Via del Brigantino* ☎ *089/875036* ▭ *AE, DC, MC, V* ✷ *Closed Nov.–Mar.*

★ **$$–$$$** ✗ **O' Capurale.** Even though *o' capurale* ("the corporal") himself no longer runs the place, his eponymous restaurant is still a great find in the crowded center of Positano. Positano is about easy-come elegance, and this dining spot sums it all up. Graced with a coved ceiling awash with colorful Fauvist-style frescoes, the dining room is filled with happy, stylish diners, literally unwinding before your eyes, thanks to the delicious, serious food (veal cutlet in white wine, fresh pasta with mussels and pumpkin, or rockfish *all'acqua pazza* with a few tomatoes and garlic are favorites) and lovely setting. Walk downstairs to wind up on a back street that has a charmingly framed view of the beach at tables set for alfresco dining. One luncheon here and you'll forget about all those ugly headlines back home. ✉ *Via Regina Giovanna 12* ☎ *089/875374* ▭ *AE, DC, MC, V* ✷ *Closed Nov.–mid-Feb.*

★ **$$–$$$** ✗ **Ristorante il Ritrovo.** Stretching alongside the tiny town square of Montepertuso, set 1,500 ft up the mountainside from Positano, the Ritrovo is one of the finest restaurants in the area. Take a table in the outside part of the restaurant (heated during the winter months) and admire the dizzying view down over the coast while seated in a wood-paneled room that almost has the feeling of a ship's cabin. A mixture of sea and mountain food is on the menu—try the *scialatielli ai frutti di mare* heaped up with all manner of things from the sea, accompanied by some excellent grilled vegetables or followed by the scamorza cheese baked in lemon leaves. Leave space for the hazelnut *semifreddi* mousses and a homemade liqueur (with carob or even camomile). Ask for advice on the excellent wine list from Teresa or Salvatore (if he's not too busy in the kitchen). ✉ *Via Montepertuso 77, Montepertuso* ☎ *089/812005* ⌂ *Reservations essential* ▭ *AE, DC, MC, V.*

★ **$–$$$** ✗ **O' Guarracino.** Enjoy a setting to make you fall in love, or rekindle it (be careful who you sit with)—this arbor-covered, perched-on-a-cleft aerie is about the most idyllic place to enjoy your lemon pasta and glass of vino as you watch the yachts come and go. Set a few steps above Positano's prettiest seaside path, the terrace vista takes in the cliffs, the sea, and Torre Trasìta. Thick, twining vines, little tables covered in cloths that match the tint of the bay, and fine fish specialties are among the big pluses. The super-charming arbor section of the restaurant is home to a pizzeria oven (adorned with an icon of Saint Pizza). ✉ *Via Positanesi d'America, between Spiaggia Grande and Spiaggia Fornillo* ☎ *089/875794* ▭ *AE, DC, MC, V* ✷ *Closed Nov.–Mar., except for Dec. 24–Jan. 7.*

$–$$$ ✗ **Saraceno D'Oro.** Although open also at lunchtime, this is most definitely an evening venue (the outside tables are on the other side of the busy Via Pasitea). Living up to its name, the restaurant's ambience inside is distinctly Moorish without being kitschy. This is one of the few restaurants patronized by the *Positanesi*: *antipasti misti* is a favorite starter, while bass with leeks, veal with provolone, and local wines are all delicious. ✉ *Via Pasitea 254* ☎ *089/812050* ⌂ *Reservations essential* ▭ *MC, V* ✷ *Closed Nov.–Feb.; open Dec. 24–Jan. 7.*

$–$$ ✕ **Da Adolfo.** Several coves away from the Spiaggia Grande, on a little beach where pirates used to build and launch their boats, this laid-back trattoria is a favorite Positano landmark. The pirates are long gone, but their descendants now ferry you free to the private cove, round-trip from Positano (look for the boat named for the restaurant; you can also make a steep descent from the main coastal road off the hamlet of Laurito). Sit under a straw canopy on a wooden terrace to enjoy *totani con patate* (squid and potatoes with garlic and oil), then sip white wine with peaches until sundown. Some diners even swim here—so bathing suits are just fine. ✉ *Spiaggia di Laurito* ☎ *089/875022* ▤ *No credit cards* ☉ *Closed Oct.–Apr.*

$ ✕ **Il Grottino Azzurro.** High on a hill above Positano, by a church on a pretty piazza, this family-run trattoria serves delicious fresh pasta and fish to locals as well as savvy tourists. Mamma will be happy to help you choose. The bus stops near here, and if you want to burn off the meal, walk; it's downhill, all the way back to town. ✉ *Via Chiesa Nuova* ☎ *089/875466* ▤ *No credit cards* ☉ *Closed Wed.*

★ **$$$$** ✕▥ **Le Sirenuse.** As legendary as its namesake sirens, this exquisite, in-town 18th-century palazzo vies with the Hotel San Pietro for best in show, but less flamboyantly. Venetian and Neapolitan museum-quality antiques and artwork, spacious vine-entwined terraces, a private yacht for free boating excursions, refined service, and the coast's most beautiful pool terrace—*the* place to have lunch in Positano—are only parts of the whole. A world-class operation results from the noble Sersale family's constant attentions, Swiss training, and lots and lots of cash. Rooms, each one special and many with whirlpool tubs, are accented with great art and artifacts, such as antique bedsteads or refectory tables. At night the La Sponda restaurant offers some of the best (and perhaps the priciest) food in Italy. Later, repair to the aristocratic reading room or serpentine bar, where contented patrons swap experiences and toast their good luck at being here—and *here.* ✉ *Via Cristoforo Colombo 30, 84017* ☎ *089/875066* ▤ *089/811798* ⊕ *www.sirenuse.it* ⇌ *61 rooms* ⌂ *Restaurant, minibars, in-room safes, pool, spa, 2 bars, parking (fee)* ▤ *AE, DC, MC, V* ▥ *BP.*

★ **$$$$** ✕▥ **Palazzo Murat.** With a perfect location in the heart of town between the beachside promenade and Santa Maria Assunta, and an even more perfect entrance through a bougainvillea-draped patio and garden, the Murat is one of Positano's winners. The courtyard—part-orchard, part-terrace—is one of the most drop-dead-gorgeous settings in all Campania, the lower section of which offers a sublime area for dining alfresco (the restaurant, Il Palazzo, has a superb and ambitious chef) and the occasional summer concert. The old wing is Positano's very grandest palazzo, with massive limestone walls, carved Rococo delicacies, and wrought-iron balconies swimming in pink flowers; it was built in the early 18th century and used as a summer residence by Joachim Murat, King of Naples. The new wing, also overlooking the garden, is a modern, Mediterranean-style building with arches and terraces—it's cool, lovely, with scattered nautical motifs and tile accents, and very, very pleasant in ambience. Rooms 5, 24, and 32 have the best views of the Bay of Positano. ✉ *Via dei Mulini 23, 84017* ☎ *089/875177* ▤ *089/811419* ⊕ *www.palazzomurat.it* ⇌ *30 rooms* ⌂ *Restaurant, minibars, in-room safe, bar; air-conditioning in new wing only* ▤ *AE, DC, MC, V* ☉ *Closed Nov.–Mar.* ▥ *BP.*

★ **$$$$** ✕▥ **San Pietro.** Extraordinary is the word for this luxurious oasis, favored by the likes of Julia Roberts and Princess Caroline of Monaco, both of whom prefer this place because it's several leagues out of town (a shuttle bus whisks you back and forth), far from the crowds and the paparazzi. The place itself is more than camera-ready: set on a cliff high over the sea, with seven levels of gardened terraces, the San Pietro has a frilly, pretty decor that mixes modern (the hotel was built in the early 1970s) with magnificent (great antiques, elegant Vietri tilework). Who can resist idling away hours on the famous majolica benches of the grand terrace? Before you spread a god's view of Positano and its bay, magnificently framed by gigantic urns of flowers. Most of the elegantly furnished rooms come with terraces (most look out to the sea, not toward Positano) and plate-glass views; room decors mix chic and charming in best country-style manner. The pool on an upper level is not large, so most guests opt to take an elevator fit for James Bond through hundreds of feet of mountainside to the private beach and beach bar, where Mozzarella and Pomodoro, the bilingual macaws, greet you. The proprietors organize boating excursions and parties, while the restaurant's menu is both super-ambitious and stylish. Don't you dare leave without trying the hotel's incredibly delicious signature drink, called Elephant's Milk. ✉ *Via Laurito 2, 84017* ☎ *089/875455* 🖨 *089/811449* ⊕ *www. ilsanpietro.it* 💤 *60 rooms* ⌂ *Restaurant, minibars, in-room safe, gym, tennis court, pool, beach, dock, 2 bars* ☰ *AE, DC, MC, V* ⊗ *Closed Nov.–Mar.* ¶⊙ *BP.*

$$$–$$$$ ✕⊡ **Buca di Bacco.** The *Buca* in this hotel and restaurant's name is for tavern and the *Bacco* for the Greek god of wine. Originally an early 19th-century mansion that became a nightspot, its cellar continues to attract artists and intellectuals. Upstairs, white-on-white guest rooms have balconies and tile floors, while suites feature glass walls with sliding doors to terraces or gardens. Specialties include the Buca's signature *arancini* (rice croquettes), along with *zuppa di cozze* (mussel soup), fresh *spigola* (bass), and figs and oranges in caramel, which can be enjoyed in the loggia dining room, with its fetching geranium-bordered view of the beach. (The street-level bar-rosticceria confusingly has the same name but is under different management.) ✉ *Via Rampa Teglia 4, 84017* ☎ *089/ 875699* 🖨 *089/875731* ⊕ *www.bucadibacco.it* 💤 *47 rooms* ⌂ *Restaurant, minibars, in-room safe* ☰ *AE, DC, MC; V* ⊗ *Closed Nov.–Mar.* ¶⊙ *BP.*

$$ ✕⊡ **Pupetto.** A simple place perched on the Fornillo beach, the Pupetto's main feature is its long terrace, set under heavily perfumed lemon trees and facing the sea. Opt for the excellent grilled fish, best followed by the (inevitable) homemade limoncello. ✉ *Via Fornillo 27, 84017* ☎ *089/875087* 🖨 *089/811517* ⊕ *www.hotelpupetto.it* 💤 *32 rooms* ⌂ *Restaurant* ☰ *AE, DC, MC, V* ⊗ *Closed Jan.–Mar.* ¶⊙ *MAP, FAP.*

$$$$ ⊡ **Casa Albertina.** Clinging to the cliff, this little house is well loved for its Italianate charm, its homey restaurant, and its owners, the Cinque family, with Mamma Annamaria ruling in the kitchen (the hotel requires half board and the lodging price includes the evening meal). Rooms have high ceilings, bright fabrics, tile flooring, and sunny terraces or balconies overlooking the sea and coastline. Car or motorboat excursions to surrounding towns and attractions can be arranged. You can't drive your car to the doorway, but porters will ferry your luggage. Note: it's 300 steps down to the main beach. ✉ *Via della Tavolozza 3, 84017* ☎ *089/ 875143* 🖨 *089/811540* ⊕ *www.casalbertina.it* 💤 *21 rooms* ⌂ *Restaurant, minibars, parking (fee)* ☰ *AE, DC, MC, V* ¶⊙ *MAP only from Apr. to Oct. 31.*

$$$$ ⊡ **L'Ancora.** Close to everything—set back a little from the main road and just a few minutes up from the main beach—this sunny Mediterranean-style hillside hostelry commands expansive views of the deep blue, and of local color, too. The lobby has a sprinkle of antiques, while the guest rooms are bright with local artwork and boldly patterned mosaic tiling. All rooms have balconies or terraces and sea views. ✉ *Via Cristo-*

foro Colombo 36, 84017 ☎ 089/875318 🖾 089/811784 ➛ *14 rooms* ⚓ *Free parking* ▤ *AE, DC, MC, V* ⊘ *Closed Nov.–Mar.* ⏀ *BP.*

$$$$ 🏨 **Le Agavi.** Most Positano hotels sit at the base of the town but this one perches spectacularly just steps from the sky-high Belvedere di Positano, offering views of the entire town from on high. And we do mean on high—guest-room balconies jut out over truly dizzying heights, so people with vertigo beware. The hotel's communal terraces are breathtaking, built right into the mountainside from local stone and connected by a tiny funicular that waterfalls down the levels (note that rooms close to the rails can be disturbed by mechanical noises). Spacious lobbies and public rooms are eclectic: modern design, wooden floors, Empire and Italianate furnishings with Oriental rugs and accessories. For swimming you can choose between the lavish pool area, which seems to float over all Positano, or take an elevator to the private beach—a treat in a town where most share the sand body-to-body. ⊠ *Via G. Marconi 127, 84017* ☎ *089/875733* 🖾 *089/875965* ⊕ *www.agavi.it* ➛ *70 rooms* ⚓ *2 restaurants, minibars, pool, beach, bar, business services* ▤ *AE, DC, MC, V* ⊘ *Closed Nov.–Mar.* ⏀ *MAP, FAP.*

$$$$ 🏨 **Poseidon.** More than yet another place with an amazing view and terrace restaurant, the Poseidon now aims at those who wish to holiday and keep themselves trim at the same time. The Laura Elos Beauty Centre offers gym, sauna, and hydromassage if you need a break from the stress of lying on the beach. Last time we met the hotel's "social director," she promised a party time for all—and delivered—with a full range of events, from boat rides to group excursions. If she's still in residence, say hello for us. ⊠ *Viale Pasitea 148, 84017* ☎ *089/811111* 🖾 *089/875833* ⊕ *www.hotelposeidonpositano.it* ➛ *49 rooms* ⚓ *Restaurant, pool, gym, health club* ▤ *AE, DC, MC, V* ⊘ *Closed Jan.–Mar.* ⏀ *MAP.*

$$$–$$$$ 🏨 **Covo dei Saraceni.** In Positano sea and town interact, and you see this best from the Covo dei Saraceni, perched on the main beach at the foot of Monte Comune, just steps from the main pier. Modern, charming, and increasingly luxe, this large hotel has a rooftop pool and bar set over the sea. Crisp and cool, the lobby is built around a curved staircase (with a bit too much glitzy marble for some tastes). The Bougainvillea restaurant features a pizza oven, and its glass-walled dining area is overhung with namesake vines. Guest rooms are simple but stylized, with wrought-iron balconies; newer rooms and suites are ultra-deluxe and spacious, with whirlpools, larger terraces, and fanciful furnishings. The major plus here is the absolutely blissful location—you'd need to stay on a yacht to get any nearer the bay. ⊠ *Via Regina Giovanna 5, 84017* ☎ *089/875400* 🖾 *089/875878* ⊕ *www.covodeisaraceni.it* ➛ *61 rooms* ⚓ *2 restaurants, snack bar, minibars, pool, health club, bar* ▤ *AE, DC, MC, V* ⊘ *Closed Nov.–mid-Mar.* ⏀ *MAP, FAP.*

$$$–$$$$ 🏨 **Villa Franca.** Bay blue, lemon yellow, and cool white are the palette here, making for a stress-dissolving retreat, set halfway up the town from the beach. Tile-and-mosaic floors, decorative urns, and graceful archways open to sea air and views, and conversation-seating done in bold fabrics marks the public rooms and piano bar. Similarly furnished, guest rooms all have terraces over the town, while the smallish pool enjoys a delightful view. ⊠ *Viale Pasitea 318, 84017* ☎ *089/875655* 🖾 *089/875735* ⊕ *www.villafrancahotel.it* ➛ *28 rooms* ⚓ *Restaurant, minibars, pool, health club, Turkish bath, bar* ▤ *AE, DC, MC, V* ⊘ *Closed Nov.–Mar.* ⏀ *MAP* ⏀ *BP.*

$$–$$$$ 🏨 **Conca d'Oro.** The name says gold, and the look sure shines at this bright, white-stucco hillside lodging. Chintz and hand-painted antique furnishings compete with boldly patterned tile flooring on the terrace. Guest rooms have ceiling fans and balconies, and there's a broad, casual dining verandah and a private stretch of beach. All, of course, over-

look the sea and coastline, though some are away from the hub of the main town center. One of few hotels in Positano to stay open year-round, prices dip considerably from November to March (the lodging price includes the evening meal). ⊠ *Via Boscariello 16, 84017* ☎ *089/811494* 🖷 *089/812009* 🌐 *www.albergoconcadoro.it* 🖈 *38 rooms* △ *Restaurant* ☷ *MC, V* ✸ *MAP.*

$$-$$$ ⊡ **Miramare.** Prime views, central location, and comfortable elegance are pleasing elements of this albergo converted from a 100-year-old mansion. Outdoor and indoor terraces are draped with bougainvillea, and antiques and comfy seating abound. Charming rooms, some with fireplace, are upgraded constantly and offer glazed tiles, balconies or terraces, and windows overlooking the sea. Room 201 is a large suite, and Room 210 has a huge window wall opening to the terrace. ⊠ *Via Trara Genoino 27, 84017* ☎ *089/875002* 🖷 *089/875219* 🌐 *www.starnet.it/miramare* 🖈 *15 rooms* △ *Bar, parking (fee)* ☷ *AE, DC, MC, V* ✸ *Closed Nov.–Mar.* ✸ *BP.*

$$ ⊡ **Casa Cosenza.** This 200-year-old lemon-yellow upscale pensione is a distant cousin to the more luxe accommodations in town. Still, it's set halfway up the hills, meaning you get a great view and can still easily walk to the beach. Breakfast is on a terrace overlooking town and sea, and rooms are clean and comfortable, many with coved ceilings. ⊠ *Via Trara Genoino 18, 84017* ☎ *089/875063* 🖈 *7 rooms, 2 apartments* ☷ *No credit cards* ✸ *BP.*

$$ ⊡ **La Fenice.** Paradise found. This tiny and unpretentious hotel on the
Fodor'sChoice outskirts of town beckons with bougainvillea-laden vistas, castaway cot-
★ tages, and a turquoise pool, all perched over a private beach, just across a cove from Franco Zefferelli's famous villa. Once past the gate, you climb a steep stairway to the main house—but tread slowly: the paths and stairways here enchantingly frame (sometimes literally with vines) vistas over land and sea. Thanks to the wonderful family of the owner, Constantino Mandara, you'll feel right at home in just a few minutes—that's because this *is* his home. Guest rooms, accented with coved ceilings, whitewashed walls, and native folk art, are simple havens of tranquility. Several accommodations are in a house perched above the road (a bit noisy if trucks rumble by, but this rarely happens at night), although the best are the adorable little cottages set close to the sea. All are linked by *very* steep walkways—covered with arbors and zigzagging across the hill, they tie together these little acres of heaven. ⊠ *Via G. Marconi 4, 84017* ☎ *089/875513* 🖷 *089/811309* 🖈 *10 rooms* △ *Pool; no a/c, no room TVs, no minibars* ☷ *No credit cards* ✸ *BP.*

¢ ⊡ **La Ginestra.** About 2,000 ft over Positano in the dizzy heights of the Lattari Mountains, the farming cooperative La Ginestra dominates the coastline from its converted 18th-century manor house. The peasants' quarters have been upgraded into a thriving restaurant, while the guest rooms above are decorated in simple country style. A popular retreat for ecologically sensitive townies, rooms here need booking well in advance. Positano is accessed via a network of footpaths—remember it's a good hour's slog up from the bottom. This is a perfect base if you want to combine the simplicity and organic cuisine of the Italian countryside with a good measure of hiking across the Amalfi Coast. Usually only half-board terms are offered. If arriving by train, get off the Circumvesuviana train at Vico Equense and take the local orange bus uphill to Santa Maria del Castello. ⊠ *Via Tessa, Santa Maria Del Castello, Vico Equense 80069* ☎ *081/8023211* 🖈 *8 rooms* ☷ *AE, MC, V* ✸ *MAP.*

¢ ⊡ **Pensione Maria Luisa.** With four resident cats and eight other felines who are "regular visitors," this place should unfortunately be avoided by anyone suffering from allergies, but is a real find for cat-lovers. Very small but very friendly, and wonderfully located in a quiet winding street just above the Fornillo beach, this is as close to staying in a friendly family home as you'll get in Positano. Even dog-lovers could become converts. ✉ *Via Fornillo 42, 84017* ☎☎ *089/875023* ⊕ *www.pensionemarialuisa. com* ➷ *10 rooms* ▤ *No credit cards* ⫯⧆*BP.*

Nightlife & the Arts

No longer the haven for wealthy, artsy, alternative types that it was in the 1960s and 1970s, Positano is remarkably quiet in the evenings. For entertainment, head down to the waterfront, where the restaurants lined up along the border of the Spiaggia Grande turn into an open-air party on summer nights. For the latest and most complete information on all the nightspots, concerts, and special events along the Amalfi Coast, from Positano to Salerno, be sure to consult the monthly periodical *Memo,* available at most regional newsstands. It's a day-by-day, event-filled cornucopia of information.

CHAMBER MUSIC   The **International Chamber Music Courses and Festival** (✉ Via G. Marconi 45 ☎☎ 089/812045 ⊕ www.Positanonline.it/music_Courses) offers two-week master classes, lectures, and concerts open to the public throughout July. Summer concerts are staged in the atmospheric setting of the Hotel Sirenuse in Positano and the Hotel Cocumella in Sorrento.

CULINARY   On a centrally located roof-garden with sweeping views of the coast-
LESSONS   line, **Diana Folonari** (of the famous wine family) holds weeklong seminars on Italian country cooking, offered in English from May through June and September through October, with wine tastings. Bring a notebook, pencils, and your own apron. ✉ *Viale Pasitea 246, 84017* ☎☎ *089/875784* ⊕ *www.cookingschoolpositano.it.*

DANCE CLUBS   **Music on the Rocks** (☎ 089/875874) is a popular bar with occasional live music set in a seaside cave off the Spaggia Grande beach, favored by the likes of Sharon Stone and Luciano Pavarotti.

FESTIVALS   Yearlong, the Positano calendar is filled with festivities and religious *feste.* Early spring brings the Cartoons on the Bay festival of short animated films, while early June plays host to the Moda Mare fashion show, when concerts are set up on the beach and in Nocelle, the sky-high village that looks down on Positano. The first week in September sees the Premio Leonide Massine dance awards—officially known as the Positano Prize for the Art of Dancing—and the Vittorio de Sica Film Festival, while the last week brings the Sagra del Pesce (Fish Festival); acrobats and musicians take to the streets of Montepertuso for Artisti in Strada. The star event of the year and the town's main religious festa is the **Feast of the Assumption,** held every August 15, commemorated by mock battles with the Saracens and evening fireworks on the main beach.

During Christmastime, Natale wreaths are fashioned from bougainvillea, and orchestra and choir concerts pop up all over town; the *Nuovo Anno* (New Year) is greeted with a big town dance and fireworks on the main beach, with other folklore and caffè-concerti musical events. In neighboring Montepertuso a living crèche is enacted. Outside Positano, heading east, is the tiny chapel of San Pietro, named in honor of St. Peter's landing here in AD 40 (and now marking the entrance to the luxurious Hotel San Pietro). Each year on New Year's Eve, the 120 villagers of San Pietro—give or take a few—greet the dawn telling stories, singing, and eating around a bonfire in the piazza in front of the town church. Visitors are always welcome; bring a blanket.

Sports & the Outdoors

High-flying aficionados can join an organized group of hang gliders soaring on the thermals along with the hillside swifts and gulls; check for information at the tourist board by the Chiesa Madre. Hikers often pass through Positano on their way to the region's most famed mountainside trail, the **Sentiero degli Dei** (Pathway of the Gods), which can be picked up outside nearby Nocelle. For less professional hikers, Ponte dei Libri (a bridge several miles west) spans a pretty valley with soaring rock pinnacles and is a moderate walk. More serious climbers can hike up to Santa Maria del Castello (just over 2,000 ft) from where paths radiate out eastward and westward along the Lattari Mountains. Plant-lovers will find hillside walks particularly rewarding in May, when the mountains turn into a flowering rock-garden with fine displays of orchids. As a general rule, allow plenty of time for what look like short distances on paper, take lots of water, and stick to the paths mapped out in red and white stripes by the CAI (Italian Alpine Club). Julian Tippet's hiking guide, *Landscapes of Sorrento and the Amalfi Coast* (available at stores on the coast), is a wonderful book—invest in it.

Sooner or later, everyone takes to the water in Positano. Divers can check out **Centro Sub Costiera Amalfitana** (⊠ Via Fornillo, on the beach beneath the Pupetto and Vittoria hotels ☎ 089/812148 🖷 089/812884) for dive classes and guided excursions, including night and archeological dives—there's also a branch in Praiano, at Via Capriglione 21. Day or night trips can be organized with local fishermen, who can even cook your catch and serve it on board. Ask at your hotel or check at the beach. Waterskiing facilities are offered on the main beach, where boats and skis can be rented.

Shopping

Although the traditional gaudily colored and lace-trimmed Positano-style clothes have started to look rather too frou-frou and dated, some contemporary designers are keeping the fashion alive with a more 21st-century spin. Goods still range from haute to kitsch, often tight tops and loose pareus in vibrant hues, with prices generally higher than in other coast towns. The fabric industry here began long ago with silk, canvas, and hand embroidery, then made headlines in 1959 when Positano introduced Italy to the bikini (following the reasoning that less is more, boutiques now sell even more highly abbreviated ones). The most concentrated shopping area, and the least difficult to maneuver, is the souk-like area near the cathedral by the beach, where the crowded pedestrian pathway literally runs through boutiques. Lining steep alleyways covered with bougainvillea, small shops display items such as local foodstuffs, wood, lace, pottery, wines and limoncello, and ceramics; you'll even find artisans who can hand-stitch a pair of stylish sandals while you wait.

Sfizio (⊠ Via Pasitea 54 ☎ 089/812014) has a fine selection of bags, shoes, and accessories (there's another branch at (⊠ Via del Saracino 55 ☎ 081/811818). It's worth splurging at **Marilù** (⊠ Via del Saracino ☎ 089/811709) if you want to take something unique home in Positano wear. **Amanda Tabber** (⊠ Via Cristoforo Colombo 167 ☎ 089/811855) offer an economical selection of T-shirts, beachwear, and similar portable souvenirs. **Delikatessen Positano** (⊠ Via dei Mulini 5, 13, 15 ☎ 089/875489) is the place to pick up your limoncello or biscuits and also offers candles and soaps made from lemons. At **I sapori di Positano** (⊠ Via dei Mulini 6 ☎ 089/812055) you can find anything that it's conceivably possible to make from citrus fruits.

Vettica Maggiore

⑯ *3 km (2 mi) southeast of Punta San Pietro, 2 km (1 mi) northwest of Praiano.*

From afar, Vettica Maggiore looks as alluring as a landscape painting. Up close, it turns out to be just your standard-issue village-along-a-road, but what makes it worth stopping for is its vast piazza, almost levitating over the water. This is a fine place to stretch your legs and view distant Positano, the coast, and the sea. Paved with an intricate, colorful pattern in majolica, the piazza is a fitting setting for the church of San Gennaro, rebuilt in the 16th century, with its notably ornate facade and a gleaming majolica-tiled dome (at night, often spectacularly trimmed with festive lights). Paintings from the 16th and 17th centuries include *Martyrdom of S. Bartholomew,* by Giovanni Bernardo Lama, decorating the side chapel. Elsewhere, in this most westerly village in the township of Praiano, you'll find a pretty but hard-to-reach cliffside beach if you follow the "Spiaggia" signs from the church; it's at the end of an olive grove, hidden at the bottom of the hillside, next to a tiny anchorage.

Where to Stay & Eat

$–$$$ ✕ **La Brace.** On the second floor of a simple storefront, on the inland side of the drive, the little restaurant you enter looks disappointingly simple. Its fine reputation, however, is validated as soon as you see the fresh, homemade antipasti and when you dig into the hearty Amalfitan cuisine. The friendly owner recommends the seafood (at remarkably accessible prices), and if you sit next to the big windows, you can see the jagged coastline and serene sea from whence it comes. ⊠ *Via G. Capriglione 146, Vettica Maggiore* ☎ *089/874226* ▭ *AE, DC, MC, V* ☉ *Closed Nov. and Wed. Oct.–Mar.*

$–$$ ✕ **La Taverna del Leone.** A crowd ranging from Ferrari owners to local fishermen is drawn to this rustic, convivial trattoria because of the pizza—reputedly the best around (evenings only). You can choose from a variety of antipasti and creative pizza toppings, or go for a big meal topped off with a cold beer or glass of local wine, in a lusty roadhouse setting where folks mingle happily and noisily. And if you want to stay over rather than face the drive, a few simple rooms with private baths are here as well. ⊠ *Via Laurito 43, Positano, Amalfi Drive, between Positano and Vettica Maggiore* ☎ *089/875474* ▭ *AE, DC, MC, V* ☉ *Closed Tues. and Jan. 7–Feb.*

★ **$$$$** ▦ **Tritone.** From afar on the Amalfi Drive, this looks like a shimmering white palace perched on the cliffs. Upon arriving, you'll see no other hotel has such a dizzying roost above the sea. Flagstone terraces and gardens set amid soaring rock pinnacles take full advantage of the location, while the seaside bathing area, accessed by an elevator excavated through 1,000 ft of rock, is jaw-dropping and complete with private beach, rocky tunnels, buffet, and bar. Not jaw-dropping, however, are the public and guest rooms, all very standard-issue and staidly traditional in style. Still, they are cossettingly restful and come with grand views of the sea and nearby Vettica Maggiore. All in all, this is a delightfully low-key and relaxing place. A small rock chapel in a grotto is on the property, if you care to give thanks for the region's natural wonders. ⊠ *Via Campo 5, Vettica Maggiore, 84010, about 1 mi outside Vettica Maggiore on the road to Positano* ☎ *089/874333* ▭ *089/813024* ⊕ *www. tritone.it* ➪ *59 rooms* ♿ *Restaurant, minibars, 2 pools, beach, 2 bars* ▭ *AE, DC, MC, V* ☉ *Closed Nov.–Mar.* ⦿*l MAP, FAP.*

$$$ ▦ **Tramonto d'Oro.** In the middle of Vettica Maggiore and picturesquely sited close to the town's glorious church of San Gennaro, this hotel is a much-loved option on the coast. Modern, clean, and sleek, the guest rooms are casual-traditional in style. The real plus here is the Esposito family—they also run Conca dei Marini's Terrazze Hotel—which has presided over the Tramonto d'Oro for more than 50 years with true warmth and charm. The restaurant has a vast glass wall that frames a picture-perfect view over the church and piazza, while the roof has a pleasant pool. A free shuttle bus will take you to the nearby beaches.

✉ *Via G. Capriglione 119, Vettica Maggiore 84010* ☎ *089/874955* 🖶 *089/874670* 🌐 *www.tramontodoro.it* ➦ *40 rooms* ⚐ *Restaurant, minibars, pool, gym, Turkish bath, sauna, free parking, some pets allowed* ▱ *AE, DC, MC, V* ⃝ *MAP, FAP.*

$ ▦ **Le Fioriere.** Blue-tile rooms are casually furnished, and low-key ambience is in keeping with the slow pace of the village. If you request it, breakfast can be served on your awning-covered balcony over the blue sea. This basic hotel offers easy access to the beach and to public transportation for trips along the coast. ✉ *Via G. Capriglione 138, Vettica Maggiore 84010* ☎ *089/874203* 🖶 *089/874343* 🌐 *www.lefioriere.it* ➦ *14 rooms* ⚐ *Bar, free parking* ▱ *AE, DC, MC, V* ⃝ *BP.*

Praiano

❶⑦ *2 km (1 mi) southeast of Vettica Maggiore, 1 km (½ mi) northwest of Marina di Praia.*

Just past Capo Sottile, the fishing village of Praiano juts to the sea at the base of the Lattari Mountains. Praiano has less wealth and sophistication than its neighbors and more olive and lemon trees than tourists. The town's name comes from Plagianum, as the people who first inhabited the site were called. Back in the 13th century, King Charles I of Anjou founded a university here, the doges of Amalfi established a summer residence, and, for a while, Praiano was renowned for its silk industry. But the decline of Amalfi's 12th-century maritime republic hit hard; the charming parish church of San Luca, at the top of the village, is a reminder of those headier times. A medieval lookout tower on the rocks still keeps guard over the coast, and hidden coves are for boating, bathing, and sunning off the rocks. In summer, boats leave the beach here for Capri each morning, and you can glimpse the Faraglioni rocks from here. If you look closely, you may be the first person in years to spot the giant *a mama de cernie* (mother of wreckfishes), the local equivalent of the Loch Ness monster.

Where to Stay

$ ▦ **Margherita.** Basic rooms have crucifixes over the beds, French doors to terraces over a side road lined with olive groves, and partial sea views. Tile flooring, velour seating, '70s-type lighting fixtures, and potted rubber trees make up the modest surroundings. Breakfasts are minimal, as is heat. But the price is right, and Margherita and her daughter are helpful. ✉ *Via Umberto I, 70, 84010* ☎ *089/874628* 🖶 *089/874628* 🌐 *www.wel.it/Hmargherita* ➦ *28 rooms* ⚐ *Restaurant, bar* ▱ *AE, DC, MC, V* ⃝ *MAP, FAP.*

$ ▦ **Open Gate.** This is a real deal, with much the same view as million-dollar-plus villas nearby. True, you're right on the main road, but the tile-floor guest rooms are white and clean, the private balconies are spacious, and the informal, vine-covered restaurant serves up tasty fare. The obliging staff will drive you to the nearest beach, at Marina di Praia, and the Grotto dello Smeraldo is only 2 km (1½ mi) away. ✉ *Via Roma 38, 84010* ☎ *089/874148* 🌐 *www.hotelopengate.it* ➦ *12 rooms* ⚐ *Restaurant, bar* ▱ *AE, DC, MC, V* ⃝ *MAP, FAP.*

Marina di Praia

★ ❶⑧ *1 km (½ mi) southeast of Praiano, 2 km (1 mi) west of Vallone di Furore.*

"Whoever wants to live a healthy life spends the morning in Vettica and the evening in Praiano," goes a local adage. The larger township of Praiano may not fulfill that advice, but its scenic satellite, Marina di Praia, indeed does; it's home to a landmark eatery and famous disco. Nestling by the sea at the bottom of a dramatic chasm, this is the only anchorage along this rocky stretch where you can hire a boat and dock it and where ferries depart for points and islands along the coast. The superpicturesque hamlet comprises some parking spaces, a small sand beach tucked within cliffs, a few excellent seafood restaurants, a hotel, and a tiny church. Reached along a pretty path through the cliff rocks edging the sea is the L'Africana disco.

Where to Stay & Eat

$$–$$$$ ✕**Alfonso a Mare.** A few steps from the Marina di Praia cove, this landmark restaurant is set in a rustic flagstone structure, once a dry haul for boats, partly open to the sea breezes on one side with an open kitchen on the other. Inside are country-style wooden tables, netting, and ceiling baskets, while outside, colorful boats, peasant dwellings, and the chasm's sheer rock walls catch the eye. In nearby Praiano, Alfonso also runs a hotel, where small rooms have tile floors, windows opening to terraces overlooking the gulf, and a few antique touches. ⊠ *Via Marina di Praia, 84010* ☎ *089/874091* 🖷 *089/874161* 🖃 *AE, V.*

$$$ 🏨**Onda Verde.** Built on a rock dramatically jutting over the tiny cove of Marina dei Praia, this fine hotel overlooks a Saracen tower and coastal ridges. Terraces overhang the sea, and common rooms and dining room feature panoramic glass walls and marble flooring. You can climb down a winding path to the beach, where daily boat excursions leave for Positano, Capri, and Ischia. Both a plus and a minus is the minutes-away walk to L'Africana disco. If you like to party, you can climb right into bed without having to drive; if you don't, be sure to ask for a quiet room. ⊠ *Via Terra Mare 3, 84010* ☎ *089/874143* 🖷 *089/8131049* ⊕ *www.ondaverde.it* ⤵ *20 rooms* ⚓ *Dock, bar* 🖃 *AE, DC, MC, V* ⊙ *Closed Nov. 5–mid-Mar., except for Dec. 27–Jan. 7* ⲓⲟⳑ *MAP.*

Nightlife

Off a mile-long footpath from the Marina del Praia—or accessed via an elevator from Statale 163—**L'Africana** (⊠ Via Torre a Mare ☎ 089/874042) is a classic from the 1960s, a golden-oldie on the coast. Even Jackie O danced on the glass-aquarium floor. With open-to-the-sea atmosphere, an indoor boat that's a buffet of antipasti, animal prints, and wildish shows with partial nudity, you can eat lightly, drink heavily, and dance 'til the Gulf of Salerno sunrise. Longtime owner Luca Milano has been around the block quite a few times, lives on a cliff beneath the premises, and may even show you his parrot. If coming from Positano, you can also get here on one of the boats down at the Spiaggia Grande.

Vallone di Furore

⑲ *8 km (5 mi) southeast of Positano, 2 km (1 mi) west of Conca dei Marini.*

Fodor'sChoice ★ The enchanting hamlet of **Marina di Furore**—perhaps 10 houses?—beckons as you pass over it on a towering viaduct. This tchotchke of a fishermen's village (once a favored hideout of bandits and smugglers, including the notorious Fra' Diavolo) seems sculpted out of rock walls; once mills, these houses (known as *monazzeni,* "places to live in solitude") and the adjoining paper mill were abandoned when the tiny harbor here closed. After the hamlet was discovered by vacationers, the municipality moved in, restoring and gloriously painting it in pastels. The hamlet now calls itself an "eco-museum" and short botanical trails have been laid out (down the steps, upstream from the viaduct). It's apparently possible to see Peregrine falcons here, as well as some rare species of ancient plants found nowhere else in the region. The Lilliputian settlement is at the base of a high-walled fissure in the limestone mountains—sometimes hyped as a fjord. The name is from the "furor" of stormy water that once rushed down the Torrente Schiato here, now a mere trickle—with a substantial effluent load from Agerola upstream and uncleared rock slides creating a less-than-gorgeous gorge, though a recent cleanup operation has made a significant change. From the beach, the *sentiero della Volpe Pescatrice* ("the fox-fish's path") and the *sentiero dei Pipistrelli Impazziti* ("the mad bats' path") climb up some 3,000 steps (but who's counting?) and were built to portage goods from the harbor to the town of Furore above it. The hard walk up takes a couple of hours, as you climb from sea to sky. To see any of this by car, you have to pay to park in the layby on the Amalfi side of the gorge, just before the gas station. Unless you're in fantastic shape, it's better to boat to the beach and just rubberneck. (Call 089/8304711 for information on guided tours offered by the local council information service.

Furore, the town high above the Vallone di Furore gorge, can be reached by car via a sharp turn uphill off Statale 163 about five km (3 mi) east of the gorge in Vettica Minore; look for the sign to Agerola. Beyond Furore, the landscape differs from that of the rock-ribbed coast below, containing meadows, terraced fields, dry stone walls (*macere*), chestnut forests, and wild dolomitic mountains dotted with pine and cypress trees. The local pitched-roof houses seem almost Alpine. The region is noted for dairy products, especially cheeses. You can hike all the way here from Positano, and among the villages you will pass is San Lazzaro; check out its belvedere, whose view stretches from Capri to the Monti del Cilento.

Furore is best known for its delicate, lightly tinted wine, Gran Furore Divina Costiera. Furore used to trade wine and foodstuffs for fish and foreign goods and still makes a profit being a larder for regional restaurants, as the garlands of bright red peppers and tomatoes hanging from many roof beams attest. Today Furore is becoming unexpectedly artsy; murals of agricultural scenes, modern sculptures, and house gates patterned in fuchsia and lime enliven the scene. More ancient art can be seen at the church of Sant'Elia Profeta, which has what some consider the most important Renaissance painting on the coast, a 15th-century triptych by Angelo Antonello.

Where to Stay

$ 🏨 **Le Rocce.** Set in the agricultural zone high above the coast, this odd, stone-and-stucco edifice commands the crest of a sheer rock face overlooking the Bay of Salerno and the coastal towns. The lobby looks like an old Italian airport (and the view below seems appropriate), but some redeeming features are the wraparound windows in the restaurant, pleasant rooms with balconies, a rock grotto honoring the Virgin Mary, a nightclub in a cave, and the gentle price tag. ⊠ *Via Belvedere 73, Agerola, 80051* 🕿*081/8791182* 🕿🕿*081/8740738* ⊕*www.hotelristorantelerocce. com* ⇆ *33 rooms* ⌂ *Restaurant, bar, nightclub, free parking, some pets allowed* ⊟ *AE, DC, MC, V* ⦿⧼ *MAP, FAP.*

Conca dei Marini

❷⓿ *2 km (1 mi) east of Vallone di Furore, 4 km (2½ mi) southwest of*
Fodor'sChoice *Amalfi.*
★

In her 2001 book of memories, *Happy Times,* Lee Radziwill declares that when she thinks of paradise, it is Conca dei Marini that first comes to mind. If you stay overnight here, we're sure you'll agree. Long a favorite of the off-duty famous and rich, the town hides many of its charms, as any sublime forgetaway should. Set on the most dramatic promontory of the coast, Conca dei Marini (the name means "seafarers' basin") was originally a province of ancient Rome called Cossa and later became an important naval base of the Amalfi Republic. Much later, it became a retreat for high-profile types, including John Steinbeck, Gianni Agnelli, and Carlo Ponti, who erected a white villa here by the sea (built for his first wife, not Sophia). You can see why: The green of terraced gardens competes with (and loses to) the blue sea, while the town's distinctive houses flanking the ridges have thick, white walls, with cupolas, balconies, and external staircases, testimony to former Arabic, Moorish, and Greek settlements. Below, on Capo di Conca, a promontory once used as a cemetery, a 16th-century coastal tower dramatically overlooks the sea. On a curve in the road sits the village's most famous attraction, the Emerald Grotto. Coral is still harvested in the waters off the coast here, while boats fish for sardines and squid through the night, their prow lanterns twinkling as if stars had slipped into the sea.

The main Conca dei Marini SITA bus stop is directly in front of the Hotel Belvedere. From here head west along the highway to the Saracen Tower (a private bathing beach sits within its shadow, but you might ask to dine at its caffè) and farther on for the Emerald Grotto. To the east, you can walk along the highway for views of Conca's harbor and lagoon. But the must-do is a jaunt down the staircase to the left of the Hotel Belvedere. This leads past some gorgeous houses to the dollhouse-size

★ **harbor of Santa Maria della Neve,** one of the most idyllic sights along the entire coast. Closed because of a major landside several years ago, its beach and marina have now reopened, but its darling little Chapel of Santa Maria della Neve is still under renovation.

For Conca in excelsis, however, head up the mountainside to the northern reaches of the town (the road leads upward opposite the Hotel Belvedere, and then you can opt to take the gently climbing roads or the steeper staircase ever upward). Your reward as you climb up the hillside roads and steep scalinatelle is three stunningly sited churches. The first is neo-Byzantine **San Pancrazio,** set in a lovely palm-tree garden. Opposite this church, in the direction of Positano, is a road leading to a sky-high lookout over the coast. Back at San Pancrazio, head up the Scalinatella San Pancrazio to the tiny town piazza.

To the east along the cliff-side road is the sky-swimming church and

★ **Convento di Santa Rosa,** which perches, "closer to heaven than to earth," on a bluff 1,000 ft over the sea, looking like some sort of Amalfitan Xanadu. Built as a university in the 15th century, and transformed into a Dominican monastery in the 16th century, the convent was abandoned in the 1920s and subsequently renovated into an albergo-inn. Alas, the owners closed up shop. Today, this wondrous structure is reputedly someone's private home, but its **Chiesa di Santa Rosa,** a 14th-century church, is the site for numerous recitals hosted by the Ravello Concert Society, so attending a performance is the only way you can get past the gates these days. For information, contact the Ravello Concert Society (☎ 089/858149 ⊕ www.rcs.amalficoast.it/). In the 18th century the nuns of the convent created one of the great local dishes, *sfogliata Santa Rosa* (sweet cheese and ricotta pastry shaped like a nun's hood). The mother superior distributed this delicacy free back then. Today, on every Saint's Day in August, the pastries are baked, and savored, by locals and visiting revelers. You can head up to the Santa Rosa bluff by following the road leading up into Conca from the coastline, but if you want to take in the view of the convent from adjacent hills, use the mountaintop highway connecting Amalfi to Sorrento, which (unfortunately) runs right by the convent gates.

★ Heading back to the town piazza from the Convento di Santa Rosa, take Via Due Maggio and Via Roma to **Sant' Antonio di Padova**—an elegant Neoclassical white church spectacularly cantilevered hundreds of feet over the coastline on a stone parapet. The church is only open for Sunday-morning services, but you might ask locals if someone can open the church with a key for a quick visit ("Dov'è la persona che ci può far visitare la chiesa?"). For those who want to see churches in coastal villages, this may be the only way to gain entry.

On the outskirts of Conca dei Marini, the **Grotta dello Smeraldo** (Emerald Grotto) is a much-touted stop for day-trippers. The rather tacky sign on the road and the squadron of tour buses may put you off, but it's definitely worth a stop. Steps and an elevator bring you almost to sea level, but more delightful is to arrive by boat, which you can hire at just about any port up and down the coast. The karstic cave was originally part of the shore, but the lowest end sank into the sea when the peninsula subsided (the coast remains active, so it may eventually sink even lower—or rise). Intense greenish light filters into the water from an arch below sea level and is reflected off the walls of the cave, quite living up to emerald expectations. You wait to board a large rowboat with about 20 fellow passengers, and then you set off with a guide, gondolier fashion, through the smallish cavern filled with huge stalactites and stalagmites. Don't let the boatman's constant spiel detract from the half-hour experience—this is one of those tours that points out stalactites that look like Lincoln (for Americans), Napoléon (for the French), and Garibaldi (for the Italians); just tune out and enjoy the sparkles, shapes, and Harry Winston–esque color. A tourist from Amalfi raved in a hotel log in 1858 that the cave "... can compete with Vesuvius," but it was forgotten about for years afterward until the grotto was rediscovered by a local fisherman in the 1930s. The light is best from noon to 3 PM, which is fortunately when hordes of potential visitors will be tucking into their pasta elsewhere. At Christmas there's a special celebration conducted around the underwater crèche. ⊠ *Beyond Punta Acquafetente by boat, or off Amalfi Drive* ☎ *089/871107 Amalfi tourist board* ☞ *€5.5* ☉ *Apr.–Oct., daily 9–4; Nov.–Mar., daily 10–3.*

Where to Stay

★ **$$$$** ⌂**Il Saraceno.** Gothic, Arabic, Oriental—and Las Vegas—influences combine to form this gorgeous extravaganza set on a chunk of cliff 3 km (2 mi) from Amalfi (note that this is its official address, but the hotel is really just a few steps away from Conca dei Marini). The evocatively exotic decor, which refers to Saracen pirates who roamed this coast centuries ago, begins in the lobby adorned with museum-quality 19th-century Orientalist oil paintings and antiques. Below, night-illuminated garden terraces descend the entire hillside to the enormous private beach, which features a saltwater pool. Dining options include a Romanesque cellar with candelabra and fireplace, and a formal restaurant called Castello, an alfresco terrace under a vine-covered lattice. Mosaic floors, elaborate antique lighting fixtures, a medieval warrior in full armor, and gilded murals are accents, and guest rooms have crown-molded ceilings, rich colors, antiques, and terraces with floor-to-ceiling window panoramas. The hotel also maintains a private Romanesque stone chapel. Whew. ⊠ *Via Augustariccio 33, Conca dei Marini/Amalfi, 84011* ☎ *089/831148* 🖷 *089/831595* ⊕ *www.saraceno.it* ⇆ *56 rooms* ⌂ *2 restaurants, minibars, pool, beach, 2 bars, meeting rooms, free parking* ⊟ *AE, DC, MC, V* ☉ *Closed Nov.–Mar.* ⫶◯⫶ *MAP, FAP.*

★ **$$–$$$** ⌂**Belvedere.** One of the coast's most beloved hotels, the Belvedere is really not a hotel but a "home." This is the sort of place where guests ask for the room their great-grandparents favored. Happily, everyone, not just regulars, is treated like family here, and you'll find it difficult to say goodbye to the remarkably friendly and helpful staff. Set in one of the grande dame villas of Conca dei Marini, featuring salons top-heavy with overstuffed sofas and a ravishing pool area resting by water's edge, the Belvedere is handily located for exploring Conca dei Marini, as it is equidistant from the town's lagoon and Saracen tower. ⊠ *Via Smeraldo 19, Conca dei Marini, 84010* ☎ *089/831282* ⎙ *089/831439* ⊕ *www.belvederehotel.it* ⌨ *36 rooms* ⚲ *Restaurant, minibars, pool, bar, some pets allowed* ☰ *AE, DC, MC, V* ☉ *Closed Nov.–Mar.* ⎟⊙⎟ *MAP, FAP.*

$$ ⊡ **Le Terrazze.** As opposed to the yesteryear glow of the Hotel Belvedere, this place, a few feet down the road, is a spankingly modern alternative. The *Wallpaper* crowd might love this place for its sleek, retro-chic '60s style; you half expect to see Monica Vitti and Alain Delon haunting the shadowy corridors, waiting for their cue from director Michelangelo Antonioni. Most rooms have their own balconies, which allow you to look down across the bay at the grand villa built by Carlo Ponti, and—best of all—you are just a few staircases away from Conca's adorable harbor. Guest rooms, delightfully clean and airy, are accented with local Vietri majolica tiles. For those seeking *tranquillità*, this is a fine option. A restaurant is set to open here in 2004. ⊠ *Via Smeraldo 11, 84010* ☎ *089/831290* ⎙ *089/831296* ⊕ *www.hotelleterrazze.it* ⌨ *27 rooms* ⚲ *Restaurant, bar; no room phones* ☰ *AE, DC, MC, V* ☉ *Closed Nov.–Mar.* ⎟⊙⎟ *BP.*

AMALFI: FIRST OF THE SEA REPUBLICS

★ *18 km (11 mi) southeast of Positano, 32 km (20 mi) west of Salerno.*

On Amalfi's main waterfront, a commemorative statue bears this inscription: "The judgment day, when Amalfitans go to Heaven, will be a day like any other." Visitors to this charming city, set in a verdant valley of the Lattari Mountains, will soon understand what it means. At first glance, it's hard to imagine that this resort destination, with its cream-color and pastel-hue buildings tightly packing a gorge on the Bay of Salerno, was in the 11th and 12th centuries the seat of the Amalfi Maritime Republic, one of the world's great naval powers, and a sturdy rival of Genoa and Pisa for control of the Mediterranean. The harbor, which once launched the greatest fleet in Italy, now bobs with ferries and blue-and-white fishing boats. The main street, lined with leather shops and *pasticcerie,* has replaced a raging mountain torrent, and terraced hills where *banditti* (bandits) once roamed now flaunt the green and gold of lemon groves. Bearing testimony to its great trade with Tunis, Tripoli, and Algiers, Amalfi remains honeycombed with Arab-Sicilian cloisters and covered passages that suggest Asian caravansaries. In a way Amalfi has become great again, showing off its medieval glory days with sea pageants, convents-turned-hotels, ancient paper mills, covered streets, and its mosquelike cathedral. "The sun—the moon—the stars and—Amalfi," Amalfitans used to say. Standing on the terrace of the town's Cappuccini Convento (Capuchin Convent), you'll have to agree.

Amalfi's origin is clouded. One legend says that a general of Constantine's army, named Amalfo, settled here in 320; another tale has it that Roman noblemen from the village of Melphi (in Latin, "a Melphi"), fleeing after the fall of the empire, were first in these parts, shipwrecked in the 4th century on their way to Constantinople. Myth becomes fact by the 6th century, when Amalfi is inscribed in the archives as a Byzantine diocese, and the historical pageant really begins. Its geographic position was good defense, and the distance from Constantinople made its increasing autonomy possible. Continuously hammered by the Lombards and others, in 839 it rose against and finally sacked nearby Salerno, to which its inhabitants had been deported. In the 10th century, Amalfi constructed many churches and monasteries and was ruled by judges, later called doges—self-appointed dukes who amassed vast wealth and power.

From the 9th century until 1101, Amalfi remained linked to Byzantium but also was increasingly independent and prosperous, perhaps the major trading port in southern Italy. Its influence loomed large, thanks to its creation of the Tavola Amalfitana, a code of maritime laws taken up by most medieval-era kingdoms. Amalfi created its own gold and silver coins—or *tari,* engraved with the cross of Amalfi—and ruled a vast territory. With trade extending as far as Alexandria and Constantinople—where a large colony of Amalfitan merchants resided—it became Italy's first maritime republic, ahead of rivals Pisa, Venice, and Genoa; the population swelled to about 100,000, many of them seafarers and traders. As William of Apulia wrote in the 11th century, ". . . No other is richer in silver, cloth and gold. A great many navigators live in this city . . . famous almost throughout the world as those who travel to where there is something worth buying."

But the days of wine and doges were about to end. In the 11th century Robert Guisgard of Normandy—in the duplicitous spirit of politicos to this day—first aided, then sacked the town, and the Normans from Sicily returned, after a short Amalfitan revolt, in the 12th century. Then, when the Republic of Pisa twice conquered it, Amalfi fell into decline, hastened by a horrific storm in 1343, then by an indirect blow from Christopher Columbus's discoveries, which opened the world beyond to competing trade routes. By the 18th century, the town had sunk into gloom, looking to its lemons and handmade paper for survival. After the state road was built by Ferdinand, the Bourbon king of Naples, in the 19th century, Amalfi evolved into a tourist destination, drawing Grand Tour–era travelers like Richard Wagner, Henry Wadsworth Longfellow, and Henrik Ibsen, all of whom helped spread Amalfi's fame.

Exploring Amalfi

Amalfi's compact tourist center is split between the bustling *lungomare* (waterfront), with its public and private transportation hubs, and the piazza in front of the Duomo. Parking is a big problem, as the small lot in the center of town fills up fast. Traveling here via ferry and bus or staying in a hotel with a parking garage are good ideas. Once you explore the main sights near the waterfront, take off and explore the souk-like center, then escape to the outskirts and the terraced hills of the Valle dei Mulini, site of Amalfi's ancient paper mills. At a little waterfall a block or so north of the Museo della Carta, look to the left for a set of scalinatelle and climb the 20-plus steps; follow a footpath to the right, where there's a bench at the edge of a lemon grove. If you buy a fresh lemon along the way—its leaves will be intact and its taste sweeter than you're accustomed to—and down it with a pinch of salt, you'll be passing time as the locals have since the age of its republic.

a good walk

Start on the festive waterfront, near the **Porta della Marina** ㉑ ⌐, where a ceramic panel honors Amalfi's merchant seamen. Past the traffic-filled harborside **Piazza Flavio Gioia** ㉒, which is centered around the Flavio Gioia Monument—named for the Amalfitan inventor of the maritime compass—head east up the waterfront esplanade, lined with palm trees and Victorian streetlights, to the Palazzo dei Municipio (town hall) and its **Museo Civico** ㉓, devoted to civic history (a sculpted overview is on the museum's southern wall). You may wish to continue along the wa-

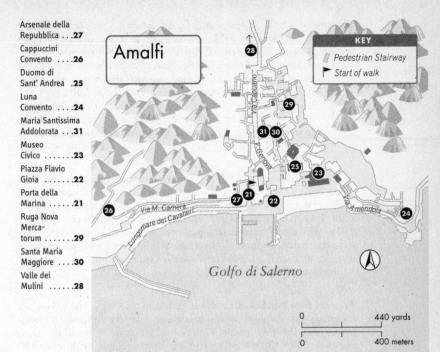

Amalfi

KEY

Pedestrian Stairway

▶ Start of walk

Golfo di Salerno

0   440 yards

0   400 meters

terfront up the gentle hill to the Torre di Amalfi, one of the 16th-century defensive towers along the coast, now part of the **Luna Convento** 24, a former Franciscan monastery-turned-hotel, where you can relax in its famous 13th-century cloister. From the museum (three minutes) or from the Luna Convento (10 minutes), look for the campanile of the Duomo di Sant'Andrea and head for the piazza in front. This is the very heart of the city, adorned with caffès and the Fontana del Popolo, graced (only in Italy, folks) by both a statue of St. Andrew and a marble female nymph whose breasts spout water. Take a deep breath and head up the monumental staircase to the **Duomo di Sant' Andrea** 25, with its museum, crypt, and noted Paradise Cloister. Unfortunately, for the next year or so, you will not be able to head up to the hilltop **Cappuccini Convento** 26, reached from the small Piazza dei Dogi off Piazza Duomo by climbing Via Annunziatella—one of Amalfi's most evocative, covered passageways (or by heading out along the waterfront on busy Via M. Camera to the hotel's cliffside elevator). This enchanting landmark is being extensively renovated and the property will be closed until the hotel reopens. The view from this 13th-century monastery, with all Amalfi at your feet, is definitely worth the blisters.

Instead, from Piazza Duomo go through the medieval arch facing the piazza to the Piazza dei Dogi, also called the blacksmith area, where the doges' palazzo stood. The **Arsenale della Repubblica** 27 is just south. North, you'll cross covered passageways and little lanes such as Vico dei Pastai and Via Herculano Marini as you head up to the Contrada Campo. From here you can descend to the Via Capuano, which cuts through the center of Amalfi along the riverbed of the mountain torrent. With the sound of water gurgling below the road, head up Via Lorenzo di Amalfi toward Via delle Cartiere (Paper Street), a 15- or 20-minute, slightly uphill stroll. Here's the beginning of the **Valle dei Mulini** 28, where the mostly converted mills and waterfalls and the Museo della Carta are evidence of Amalfi's paper industry, still hanging on from the Middle Ages. You can picnic here if you've shopped for take-out *panini* (sandwiches) along the Via Lorenzo d'Amalfi on the way. Back down the same road, and close to the Porta dell'Ospedale, is the marble entrance to the well-known and nearly straight **Ruga Nova Mercatorum** ㉙, also known as Via dei Mercanti, an old covered street. From here, Salita dei Curiali wends among houses with gardens, and ends at a charming square with the churches of the **Santa Maria Maggiore** ㉚ and the **Maria Santissima Addolorata** ㉛. Look for the nearby campanile of the duomo, and it's back to the piazza there, with a cathedral visit if you haven't seen its splendors yet.

TIMING   You'll need at least a half day, perhaps more, depending on how long you spend in the Duomo and museums, whether or not you take the optional meanderings—leading to hidden piazzas, the Valle dei Mulini, or the hike to the Cappuccini Convento. Most properties close up by 1 PM, so it's best to start early. Small churches are often open only during mass; ask at your hotel. If you leave right after breakfast and keep a blistering pace, you could finish in time for a late lunch, followed by a long beach siesta.

What to See

㉗ **Arsenale della Repubblica.** From the middle of the 11th century, Amalfi's center of shipbuilding, custom houses, and warehouses was the Arsenale, today the only (partially) preserved medieval shipyard in southern Italy. Ships and galleys up to 80 ft long, equipped with up to 120 oars, were built at this largest arsenal of any medieval maritime republic. The boat now used for the historical regatta (held every four years, next in Amalfi in June 2005) and other ship models are kept in the arsenal's two large Gothic halls. Ten of the original 22 stone piers remain; the others were destroyed by storms and changes in the sea level on this ever-active coast. ⊠ *South of Piazza dei Dogi, on corner of Via Camera, by the waterfront* ☾ *Mon.–Sat. 10–1.*

㉖ **Cappuccini Convento.** Currently closed and undergoing restoration work
Fodor'sChoice   by new owners, this fabled medieval monastery enjoys a magnificent hill-
★   top perch and was a noted stop for Grand Tour–era travelers. Long famous for its gardens, its ½-km-long (¼-mi-long) terrace over Amalfi's harbor, and its Arab-Sicilian cloister, the monastery was founded by Cistercian monks in the 13th century as the Convento di S. Pietro della Canonica. Then abandoned, the complex was taken over by the Capuchins in 1583, only to be transformed into a hotel in the mid-19th century when the king of Naples suppressed the religious orders. Immortalized in postcards and paintings, the view of Amalfi's waterfront from the hotel terrace became one of the first travel icons of the 19th century. Henry Wadsworth Longfellow composed a poem to celebrate its beauty and Richard Wagner forsook his guest room to camp out under the stars. In the recent past, visitors could stroll through the monastery and let the centuries unwind: the 13th-century cloister has the intertwined Arabic columns of the Amalfi cathedral's great Paradise Cloister, the little church is a Rococo confection, and the spirit-warm hallways and salons were barely changed from the 19th century. Let us hope they survive the ongoing renovation to bring them all into the 21st century. ⊠ *Hotel Cappuccini Convento, Via Annunziatella 46* ☎ *089/871877* ⊕ *www.hotelcappuccini.it/principale.*

★ ㉕ **Duomo di Sant' Andrea.** Complicated, grand, delicate, and dominating, the 9th-century Amalfi cathedral has been remodeled over the years with Romanesque, Byzantine, Gothic, and Baroque elements, but retains a predominantly Arab-Norman style. Cross and crescent seem to be wed here: the campanile looks like a minaret wearing a Scheherazadian turban, the facade conjures up a striped burnoose, and its Paradise Cloister is an Arab-Sicilian spectacular.

The power of Amalfi is evident in the approach to the cathedral, set atop 62 broad steps that lead to a mosaic facade, redone in the 19th century, and framed by bands, arches, and patterned squares. The imposing bronze doors, the first in Italy, were cast in Constantinople before 1066 and signed by Simeon of Syria; they were commissioned by the leader of the large Amalfitan colony there. Silver incrustations on the doors, now difficult to see, are images of Christ, Mary, and saints.

Visitors are now channeled first into the adjoining **Chiostro del Paradiso** (Paradise Cloister): built around 1266 for Bishop Augustariccio as a burial ground for Amalfi's elite, it's one of the architectural treasures of southern Italy. Its flower-and-palm-filled quadrangle has a series of exceptionally delicate, intertwining arches on slender double columns in a combination of Byzantine and Arabian styles. Note the geometric patterns of colored mosaics in the walls, comprising parts of former pillars and pulpits of the earlier church. The striking 12th-century bell tower in front of the complex has a Romanesque base and an elaborate yellow-and-green-tile top with arches in the local style, a round center surrounded by four smaller cupolas. Spiced with Saracen colors and the intricate tile work of High Barbary, Amalfi's jaunty duomo seems to bring a touch of old Istanbul to town.

The chapel at the back of the cloister leads into the earlier (9th century) basilica. The structure, called the Basilica of the Crucifix, is in Romanesque style, with a nave, two aisles, and a high, deep apse. Of special note is a 14th-century crucifixion scene by a student of Giotto. This section has now been transformed into a museum, housing sarcophagi, sculpture, Neapolitan goldsmiths' artwork, and other treasures from the cathedral complex.

Steps from the basilica lead down into the crypt of St. Andrew. The cathedral above was built in the 13th century to house the saint's bones, which came from Constantinople and supposedly exuded a miraculous liquid believers call the "manna of St. Andrew." Amalfi's cathedral had always lured pious devotees—from Francis of Assisi to Pope Urban IV—but after the 14th-century manna manifestation the pilgrim trade really picked up. The saint's remains (sans head, which is in the Vatican) are kept under the 13th-century high altar in this exceptionally beautiful crypt adorned with marble statues sculpted by Pietro Bernini, father of the famed Gianlorenzo Bernini.

Following the one-way traffic up to the cathedral itself, you finally get to admire the elaborate polychrome marbles, and painted, coffered ceilings from its 18th-century restoration; art historians shake their head over this renovation, as the original decoration of the apse must have been one of the wonders of the Middle Ages. However, the original basilica plan has been preserved. The first chapel on the left of the entrance has a red porphyry baptismal font, supposedly crafted from the ruins of ancient Paestum. Other treasures include a mother-of-pearl cross given by the people of Jerusalem in 1930, in gratitude for Amalfi's help in establishing a 2,000-bed hospital there in 1112, which later became the first military and religious order, the Knights of St. John. ⊠ *Piazza Duomo* ☎ *089/871324* ✎ *€2.50* ☾ *Daily: Mar.–June and Oct., 9–7; July–Sept., 9–9; Nov.–Feb., 10–1 and 2:30–5:30.*

❷❹ Luna Convento. Legendarily founded by none other than St. Francis of Assisi, the Luna Convento was built in the 13th century and retains its famous cloister, with distinctive Arab-Sicilian arcaded columns and a crypt with frescoes. Transformed into the earliest hotel on the Amalfi Coast in the early 19th century, the hotel was where Henrik Ibsen wrote a large chunk of *A Doll's House*. The hotel also owns the famous Torre Saracena (now home to a bar and disco) that sits across the highway and stands guard over Amalfi's seaside promontory. ✉ *Via Pantaleone Comite 19* ☎ *089/871002* ⊕ *www.lunahotel.it.*

㉛ Maria Santissima Addolorata. This church is adjacent to the confraternity founded in 1777 to organize Amalfi's Good Friday celebrations. The entrance gate bears a late-Gothic bas-relief of the Crucifixion, once belonging to nobility from the nearby village of Scala and identified by its coat of arms at the foot of the cross. The interior is Neoclassical, with a harmonious scale and coffered ceiling; note the 16th-century marble Madonna and Child in the sacristy. ✉ *Largo Santa Maria Maggiore.*

㉓ Museo Civico. The Municipal Museum of Amalfi contains artifacts from Amalfi's medieval period, including paintings, ancient coins, banners, and jeweled costumes. The highlight is the original 66-chapter draft of the code of the *Tavole Amalfitana,* the sea laws and customs of the ancient republic, used throughout the Italian Mediterranean from the 13th to the 16th centuries. The Tavole established everything from prices for boat hires to procedures to be followed in case of shipwreck. Long one of the treasures of the Imperial Library of Vienna, the draft was returned to Amalfi after more than 500 years. Note the ceramic panel on the south outside wall of the museum, between Corso delle Repubbliche Marinare and Piazza del Municipio, created by Diodoro Cossa in the 1970s. The scenes provide an overview of local history: Roman refugees establishing themselves in nearby Scala in the 4th century; the founding of Amalfi by these same Romans; Amalfi's commercial and diplomatic role in the Mediterranean; the arrival of St. Andrew's body; the invention of the maritime compass; and other historic events. ✉ *Piazza Municipio, entrance off Corso Roma* ☎ *089/871066* ✉ *Free* ☉ *Mon.–Sat. 8:30–1.*

㉒ Piazza Flavio Gioia. A statue, set in an ironically disorientating traffic roundabout in front of the harbor, honors the Amalfitan credited with inventing the maritime compass in 1302. Many say it was the Chinese who invented the compass, passing the idea along to the Arabs, who traded with Amalfi; Gioia may have adapted it for sea use (some even believe there was no such person as Gioia). ✉ *On the waterfront.*

▶ **㉑ Porta della Marina.** This gateway "door" to the harbor bears a ceramic panel, created by Renato Rossi in the 1950s, commemorating the trade routes of the republic during the Middle Ages. For one example, ships loaded up with timber from Italy, traded it in North Africa, then used the gold obtained from those sales to buy gems, spices, and silks in Asia to trade in Italy. ✉ *Across from Piazza Flavio Gioia, next to arsenal.*

㉙ Ruga Nova Mercatorum. Also known as Via dei Mercanti, evocative Ruga Nova was the main thoroughfare of medieval Amalfi, and it remains the most fascinating "street" in town. Claustrophobes, beware: it's completely covered, like a tunnel, but is especially wonderful when the light from alleys and windows plays on its white walls. Stretching from the Porta dell'Ospedale to the Salita dei Curiali, it ends at a medieval-era *contrada,* or neighborhood, filled with gardens and churches. ✉ *Contrada S. Simone, just north of Maria Santissima Addolorata.*

㉚ Santa Maria Maggiore. Constructed by Duke Mansone I in 986, as inscribed on a capital at the entrance, the church has a Byzantine layout, although a 16th-century overhaul inverted the entrance and high altar, and the decoration is now mostly Baroque. The remains of San Felice and an 18th-century crèche scene are worth noting. The campanile dates from the 12th century. ✉ *Largo Santa Maria Maggiore, near cathedral.*

28 **Valle dei Mulini.** The Valley of the Mills, uphill from town, was for centuries Amalfi's center for papermaking, an ancient trade learned from the Arabs (who learned it from the Chinese). Beginning in the 12th century, former macaroni mills were converted to the production of paper made from cotton and linen, among the first in Europe to do so. In 1211 Frederick II of Sicily prohibited this lighter, more readable paper from being used in the preparation of official documents, favoring traditional sheepskin parchment; but by 1811 more than a dozen mills here, with more along the coast, were humming. Natural waterpower ensured that the handmade paper was cost-effective, but catastrophic flooding in 1954 closed most of the mills for good, and many of them have now been converted into private housing. The **Museo della Carta** (Museum of Paper) opened in 1971 in a 15th-century mill; paper samples, tools of the trade, old machinery, and the audiovisual presentation are all enlightening. The admission price gets you a guided tour in English. A 20-minute stroll from the Piazza Duomo will take you to the valley via the main thoroughfare of Via Genoa, turning onto Via Capuano, at the edge of town. ✉ *Palazzo Pagliara, Via delle Cartiere* ☎ *089/8304561* 🎟 *€3.40* ⊕ *www.museodellacarta.it* ⊙ *Mar.–Oct., daily 10–7; Nov.–Feb., Tues.–Sun. 10–3:30.*

off the beaten path

VIA MAESTRA DEI VILLAGGI - - West to Pogerola, with its two small churches and tower overlooking an expanse of the coast, you will have to climb about 1,000 steps through a valley—more or less; you can also take a bus or car along the upland road. A trek by foot along a path called Via Maestra dei Villaggi, which cuts inland just past the west end of the Amalfi road tunnel, will bring you to Vettica, Lone, Pastena, and Tovere, a series of villages William Wadsworth Longfellow—who didn't just stay in New England writing about Hiawatha—described as "heaven beyond the sea."

Where to Stay & Eat

$$$–$$$$ ✗ **Da Gemma.** Cognoscenti have sung the praises of this understated landmark since 1872. Tile floors, green tablecloths, and a terrace set above the main street are soothing elements. The kitchen glistens, the menu is printed on local handmade paper, and Italian foodies appreciate dishes such as fish baked with lemon peel, and *tubettoni alla masaniello*, tiny pieces of pasta with capers, mussels and prawns. Traces of Amalfi's Arabic roots can be found in the sweets made with almonds and citrus fruits. ✉ *Via Fra Gerardo Sasso 9* ☎ *089/871345* ⚓ *Reservations essential* 🖃 *AE, DC, MC, V* ⊙ *Closed Jan. 15–Feb. 15 and Wed. Sept.–June.*

★ $$$–$$$$ ✗ **Eolo.** This is both one of the newest restaurants on the Amalfi Coast and one of the most sophisticated. The decor is suavely tranquil—white coved ceilings, Romanesque columns, mounted starfish—although the kitchen is anything but: masterminded by a member of the Gargano family (who also own the Hotel Santa Caterina), it tosses out gastronomic delights like lobster risotto, sea bass with lemon salt and fennel leaves, zucchini flan, and a fine dessert of eggplant and chocolate. Many dishes are fetchingly adorned with blossoms and other visual allures, but nothing compares to the view of Amalfi's harbor from one of the tables in Eolo's picture-window alcove. If you don't land one of these, don't fret—the entire room is pretty enough as it is. ✉ *Via Pantaleone Comite 3* ☎ *089/871241* ⚓ *Reservations essential* 🖃 *AE, MC, V* ⊙ *Closed Jan.–Feb. and Wed.*

$$$–$$$$ ✕ **La Caravella.** Cobalt-blue napery, antiques, tall candles, lace tablecloths, floral curtains, marble floors, and Andrea Bocelli's golden voice on the sound system make this the most romantic restaurant in Amalfi. A tasting menu is available, but don't miss out on the antipasti—especially the slices of fish grilled in lemon leaves—and the *panzerottini neri,* ravioli stuffed with ricotta cheese and squid, or the *vellutata di limone* lemon sauce with which the fish are dressed. ☒ *Via Matteo Camera 12, near Arsenale* ☎ *089/871029* ☰ *AE, MC, V* ☉ *Closed Nov. and Dec. and Tues.*

$$–$$$$ ✕ **Lo Smeraldino.** Open since 1949, this airy, popular fish restaurant on Amalfi's almost-emerald waterfront dishes out reasonably priced seafood and *cucina tipica Amalfitana,* such as the tasty penne with tomatoes, cream, eggplant, peppers, basil, and cheese, or excellent simply grilled fish (*grigliata di pesce*). You can see the boats bringing in the day's catch and at night there's pizza on the terrace amid the twinkling lights of hills, sea, and sky. ☒ *Piazzale dei Protontini 1* ☎ *089/871070* ☰ *AE, DC, MC, V.*

$$–$$$ ✕ **Al Pesce d'Oro.** The big-hearted brothers who oversee the place, their kids who serve you, and mamma and the other family-folk who keep the kitchen hopping at this comfortable roadside restaurant west of town will win your heart. None of them speak much English—it's a local fave, so they don't have to—but you'll have fun getting by, and you'll have a terrific meal, featuring—what else?—*pesce,* fresh as the sea. Try the spaghetti *al cartoccio,* served up in what look like pieces of ancient parchment, with squid, olives, capers, and shellfish. ☒ *Via Giovanni Agustariccio* ☎ *089/831231* ☰ *AE, MC, V.*

$$–$$$ ✕ **Il Tari.** Locals highly recommend this cozy little ristorante named after the ancient coin of the Amalfi Republic and located a few minutes' walk north of the Duomo. Appealing touches include local art, red tablecloths, old photos, and tile floors—not to mention wood-oven-baked thin-crust pizza with fresh sauces, and pasta specialties including *scialatielli alla Saracena,* long spaghetti-style pasta seemingly laden with everything you can imagine from the sea. ☒ *Via P. Capuano* ☎ *089/ 871832* ☰ *AE, DC, MC, V* ☉ *Closed Nov. and Tues.*

$$–$$$ ✕ **Trattoria da Ciccia-Cielo-Mare-Terra.** Big windows overlook the sky, sea, and land, and there's ample free parking, so this modern seafood restaurant is a good place to stop if you're driving. Young owner Francesco Cavaliere will give you a warm welcome. After some perfect pasta, finish up with the ricotta and pear cake, designed to accompany a tiny glass of well-chilled limoncello. ☒ *Via Giovanni Agustariccio, across from Al Pesce d'Oro* ☎ *089/831265* ☰ *AE, DC, MC, V* ☉ *Closed Nov. and Tues.*

$–$$$ ✕ **Il Teatro.** Once a children's theater, this informal, high-ceiling, white-stucco restaurant in the medieval quarter is 50 steps above the main drag and most charming. A house specialty is grilled squid and calamari with mint sauce, reflecting the position of the place—suspended between sea and mountains. The pizzas are terrific. ☒ *Via E. Marini 19* ☎ *089/872473* ☰ *AE, MC, V* ☉ *Closed Wed. and Jan.–mid-Feb.*

$$$$ ▥ **Luna Convento.** Founded as a convent in 1222, allegedly by no less a personage than St. Francis of Assisi, the hotel has been owned by the Barbaro family since 1822 and visited by Otto van Bismarck, Mussolini, Ingrid Bergman, and Tennessee Williams, among other noted figures. The restaurant and bar are in the 15th-century Saracen tower, perched on a rock over the sea, providing a view that spans from Capo dei Conca to Capo d'Orso. Coved ceilings, graceful arches, and marble columns mark the architecture, along with Flemish religious artwork, church and convent artifacts, antique furnishings, and mosaic flooring, all of which mix with modern comforts. The heart of the hotel is the famed southern Romanesque cloisters and the beautiful Baroque chapel. Below the tower is a rocky beach and waterside pool. Ask for a room in the renovated wing, and try to get one with a balcony over Amalfi's bay. The food, alas, does not measure up. Half-board is sometimes required here; inquire when booking. ⊠ *Via P. Comite 33, 84011* ☎ *089/871002* 🖷 *089/871333* ⊕ *www.lunahotel.it* 🖘 *45 rooms* 🖧 *Restaurant, pool, bar* ⊟ *AE, DC, MC, V* 🍽 *BP, MAP.*

★ **$$$$** 🏨 **Santa Caterina.** When Elizabeth Taylor and Richard Burton wanted to escape, they headed here, and little wonder. Owned by the Gargano family for generations, this quietly elegant, supremely comfortable, and very cherished hotel has long been one of the treasures of the coast. Indeed, many guests have been coming here since grandmother's grandmother's day. Just outside Amalfi proper (giving it a grand vista of the town), the Santa Caterina takes full advantage of its hillside location. There are vast, terraced gardens and orchards overlooking the sea, and down by the water is a luscious seawater-pool area, complete with an idyllic thatched-roof, open-air caffè. The lobby is charmingly coved, while decor is unobtrusively traditional, with Belle Epoque accents. The luckiest guests are allowed to book the hotel's extraordinary, 19th-century hunting-box châlet, set at water's edge at the far end of the hotel's romantic orchards. ⊠ *Strada Amalfitana 9, 84011* ☎ *089/871012* 🖷 *089/ 871351* ⊕ *www.hotelsantacaterina.it* 🖘 *62 rooms* 🖧 *Restaurant, minibars, bar, pool, gym, free parking* ⊟ *AE, DC, MC, V* 🍽 *MAP, FAP.*

$$$–$$$$ 🏨 **Miramalfi.** High above the main coastal drive, this white-stucco hotel overlooks deep blue water and coastal ridges. The hotel's elevators, or a steep hike, deposit you at the pool, with a rock ledge for sunbathing carved from the cliff. Lobbies are sleekly decorated, and the dining room serves up wraparound panoramas along with a nightly buffet; guests may also dine on the sea-air terrace. Rooms have vibrant tile flooring, brightly painted furnishings, floral fabrics, wicker, and lots of windows. All have private sea-view balconies, and some have whirlpools. ⊠ *Via Quasimodo 3, 84011* ☎ *089/871588* 🖷 *089/871287* ⊕ *www.miramalfi. it* 🖘 *49 rooms* 🖧 *Restaurant, minibars, pool, beach, bar, parking (fee), some pets allowed* ⊟ *AE, DC, MC, V* ☉ *Closed Nov.* 🍽 *BP.*

$$$ 🏨 **Aurora.** Regarded for its location near the beach of Spiaggia delle Sirene and the fishing harbor, this well-run little hotel is a good deal for sand potatoes who prefer absorbing rays to hiking the highlands. Amid a greenery-filled setting with three levels of arched windows, guest rooms are clean, with water views, and although just a flat and easy 10-minute walk from the Duomo, crowds rarely venture to this nook. ⊠ *Piazzale dei Protontini 7, between Scalo d'Oriente and Lungomare dei Cavalieri, 84001* ☎ *089/871209* 🖷 *089/872980* 🖘 *29 rooms* 🖧 *Minibars* ⊟ *AE, MC, V* ☉ *Closed Nov.–Mar.* 🍽 *BP.*

★ **$$$** 🏨 **Cappuccini Convento.** Currently undergoing restoration work at the hands of new owners and due to reopen in 2005, this place was (and will hopefully continue to be) the most richly atmospheric hotel on the Amalfi Coast—if not in all of Italy. The convent was founded in the 14th century and transformed into a hostelry in the early 19th; its ambience was little changed from the days when it welcomed Longfellow, Wagner, kings, queens, dukes, and duchesses. Set on a sky-touching cliff above the sea, its bougainvillea-draped terrace frames a view of Amalfi's harbor so perfect it became the iconic image of the region in the 19th century—Wagner decamped from his room to sleep under the stars on the fabled loggia, just the perch for food-with-a-view meals. With its umbilical cord to the past, this hotel sublimely forgot about the present and future—so people never came here looking for what any other hotel could give them: enormous buffets of four-star food, high-tech facilities, pools.

Guest "activities?" People wrote novels, painted watercolors, and escaped to the sepia-toned past, creaking beds, dusty corridors, and all. The public areas are threaded with intriguing passages lined with Victorian lecterns and Savonarola chairs; other decor treasures include a famous Arab-Sicilian cloister (now a reception center) and a Rococo-era chapel. Most guest rooms were converted friar's cells and suites—some as bare as two beds, a bureau, and a chandelier—but they also came with unforgettable views overlooking the blue, blue sea and, more important, six centuries of peace and quiet. The Cappuccini's many fans will be holding their breath until the doors reopen here. Let's hope this hotel's unique frozen-in-time spell will not be broken. ⊠ *Via Annunziatella 46, 84011* ☎ *089/871877* 🖷 *089/871886* ⊕ *www.hotelcappuccini.it/principale.*

$-$$ 🏨 **Amalfi.** Located up a tiny side street not far from the Piazza Duomo, the Amalfi is unassumingly decorated with small, somewhat characterless modern-style rooms (get one with a geranium-filled balcony if you can) without a great view. However, the place's central location, the friendly welcome of the Lucibello family (who also run a boat-hire business), and the roof terrace where you can breakfast in the warm morning sun make this a great deal for those who want to be in the center of the action while keeping an eye on the budget. ⊠ *Via dei Pastai, 3, 84011* ☎*089/872440* 🖷*089/872250* ⊕*www.hamalfi.it* 🗪*40 rooms* ⚫ *Restaurant, parking (fee), some pets allowed* ▭ *AE, MC, V* ⫸ *MAP, FAP.*

$-$$ 🏨 **Piccolo Paradiso.** A location in the Amalfi harbor area across from the Arsenale already makes this upscale B&B a special choice. The atmosphere is more pleasing and elegant than that of a typical pensione. A common area has tile flooring, and rooms are smallish but comfortable, with wicker seating and wrought-iron headboards; some have private terraces. Open only a few years, everything sparkles, and you'll get to know your fellow international guests in this little paradise. ⊠ *Via M. Camera 5, 84011* ☎ *089/873001* 🗪 *6 rooms* ▭ *AE, MC, V* ⫸ *BP.*

★ $ 🏨 **Hotel S. Andrea.** With everyone gazing at the magnificent steps leading to Amalfi's cathedral, few turn around to notice that this tiny pensione occupies one of the top spots in town. The cute "Room-with-a-View" lobby is as big as a Victorian closet and as crowded with dried flowers and swagged fabrics. Guest rooms are small and cozy; a few overlook the Duomo, with quieter ones on a side alley. ⊠ *Piazza Duomo, 84011* ☎ *089/871145* 🗪 *9 rooms* ▭ *No credit cards* ⫸ *EP.*

$ 🏨 **Sole.** This three-story, white-stucco pensione near the municipal museum and an easy stroll from the harbor has a caffè and flower boxes on the balconies. The lobby is clean and airy, with a graceful staircase, archways, and wrought-iron lighting fixtures, and there's an old mahogany bar. Some simply furnished rooms have balconies or terraces. Though the place is pretty basic, choose a double room and you will have adequate accommodations; with half- or full-board, you get extra-special value. ⊠ *Largo della Zecca 2, 84011* ☎ *089/871147 or 089/871559* 🖷 *089/871926* ⊕ *www.starnet.it/hsole* 🗪 *13 rooms* ⚫ *Bar* ▭ *MC, V* ⫸ *BP.*

Festivals

Amalfi's festivals best reflect the splendor of its past. The **St. Andrew Race** every June 27, dedicated to Amalfi's protector of seamen, is a joyous religious celebration commemorating the defeat of Barbarossa and the Moslem fleet in 1544. A procession of white-robed men carry a silver-gilt replica of the saint to the harbor, and fishermen at the beach run it back to the cathedral and—in one dramatic dash—straight up its 62 steps. Later, the statue gleams silver in the sunshine of the piazza, as fishermen hang tiny wooden and gilt fish amulets from the saint's left wrist as tokens of gratitude. In the evening, guitar music drifts from many boats, and candlelight flickers.

Even more of a pageant is the **Regatta Storica delle Antiche Repubbliche Marinare** (Historical Regatta; ☎ 089/871107), the mock battles in which four boats, each with eight oarsmen, represent the medieval maritime republics of Amalfi, Pisa, Genoa, and Venice. The prize, held by the winner for a year, is a scale-model gold-and-silver replica of an antique sailing ship. Each of the former republics is represented by 80 participants; Amalfi's musical contingent is adorned in jewel-encrusted costumes on loan from the town museum—doges, dogaressas, merchants, and commoners from the prosperous past come colorfully to life, with the day's festivities culminating in a show of fireworks. Held yearly on the first Sunday in June every four years, with the four cities alternating as the urban stage sets, the pageant is scheduled to be in Amalfi in 2005.

Amalfitans love to celebrate holidays. The Good Friday candlelight procession, Easter Sunday, and Christmas pageants with crèche competitions (with cribs mounted in the city fountains) are all excuses for lavish family occasions, with special foods and church ceremonies.

Nightlife

Amalfi doesn't have many clubs for music or dancing. However, flyers and posters often go up announcing concerts and theatricals during the peak summer months. Check out **Torre Saracena** (✉ across from Luna Convento Hotel, on the water ☎ 089/871064)—a historic watchtower recycled to offer music and dancing.

Shopping

A must-must-must for lovers of art, vintage prints, and fine books is the exquisite store of **Andrea de Luca** (✉ Largo Cesareo Console 8 ☎ 089/872976), a publisher of fine books and postcards, whose shop, located down on the waterfront near the Arsenale, sells desk accessories, objets d'art, and beautiful art tomes about Amalfi. The **Cartiera Amatruda** (✉ Via Fiume 100, beyond the museum ☎ 089/871315), in the Amatruda Mill, is run by descendants of an Amalfi papermaking dynasty dating from at least 1500; it's probably the oldest crafts paper shop in Italy and still produces and sells fine parchment-color handmade paper. The shop is a short uphill walk north of Largo Marini on Via delle Cartiere. If you're pining for English-language newspapers, wanting a book on Amalfi's history, or just looking for a suitable poolside novel, try the **Libreria-Edicola Internazionale** (✉ Via Repubbliche Marinare 17 ☎ 089/871180) near the tourist office. Leather goods are popular items in small shops along the main streets; one good option is **Bazar Florio** (✉ Via P. Capuano 5/7 ☎ 089/871980), with a fair and friendly owner. It features handbags, wallets, and backpacks. **D'Antuono** (✉ Piazza Duomo 10 ☎ 089/872368 ⊕ www.cartadiamalfi.it) sells art books, old prints, and fine paper goods. **Mostacciuto** (✉ Piazza Duomo 22 ☎ 089/871552) is run by a well-known and respected coral craftsman.

Atrani

32 *1 km (½ mi) east of Amalfi, 5 km (3 mi) southwest of Ravello.*

Fodor'sChoice
★

Ask hotel owners and longtime residents of the Costiera Amalfitana where their favorite spot is along the coast, and they often respond "Atrani." Most actually whisper, as if it were some secret treasure—and in some respects, it is: set atop a crag between cliffs overlooking the sea, and just a 10-minute walk from the western outskirts of Amalfi—take the seaside stairs off the drive, past the Luna Convento—this stage-set of a medieval town is centered around a small piazza. When closely linked to the republic, the town was the residential choice of Amalfi aristocracy. Now home to 1,000 or so residents, Atrani is largely overlooked by tourists, who drive right by it over the riverbed of the Torrente Dragone. But its special charms are most evident from the sea, as it looks like an amphitheater ready for a royal pageant.

Adorable Piazza Umberto I, entirely enclosed by four-story houses, is the setting for the basics of Italian life: general store, stationery store, coffee shop, bar, fruit stand, restaurant, barber, and, of course, police station (the constable struts about as though in command of the pigeons strutting alongside him). The uncrowded square is filled with simple scenes: children giggle at hide-and-seek, *duenas* gossip, and men debate and take sips from the venerable fountain as if the world had little changed from the days of the doges. An arcade to one side offers a glimpse of beach, fishing boats, a mule or two, and the sea beyond. At Christmas the whole town congregates here at dawn to drink cappuccino and share traditional cakes.

Atrani's closely packed, dollhouse-scaled backstreets are filled with pastel-and-white houses and shops, fragrant gardens, arcaded lanes, and spiraling scalinatelle. But the hamlet's stellar attractions are the Baroque-style churches, which dominate the skyline, and around which parish houses cluster in true medieval style.

The bell of the 10th-century church of **San Salvatore de Bireto** tolled to announce the crowning of a new doge. The coronation ceremony was restricted to those wearing a *bireto*, the cloth caps that would be ceremoniously placed on the new doge's head, and someday worn attending his burial in the same church. The church was remodeled in 1810; the dome is beautifully tiled, and the paneled bronze doors cast in the 11th century came from Constantinople, as did the doors in the Amalfi Duomo. Within is a 12th-century marble plaque showing two peacocks, one standing over a human head between two sirens, the other on a hare being attacked by two birds; peacocks were considered immortal, but the symbolism of the two in this setting is open to interpretation.

The church of **Santa Maria Maddalena,** set on a piazza, was built in 1274 and given a neo-Baroque facade in 1852. The dome is covered in majolica tile, and the bell tower has an octagonal belfry similar to the campanile of the Carmine church in Naples. Among the treasures here are an altar in richly colored marbles and 16th-century paintings attributed to Amalfi Coast artists: *St. Magdalen between St. Sebastian and St. Andrew* by Giovannangelo D'Amato of Maiori, and *The Incredulity of St. Thomas* by Andrea da Salerno.

Feisty little Atrani, which produces colorful ceramics along with its charm, gained its independence from Amalfi in 1578, with which it maintains a friendly rivalry; locals say the town holds its processions on its narrow inner streets to discourage Amalfitans from participating.

Where to Stay & Eat

$$–$$$ ✕ **A' Paranza.** At the back of the piazza on the main walkway is the best dining option in Atrani. White coved ceilings reflect immaculate linen tablecloths in a place that is at once homely and quite formal. Entirely seafood-based, each day's menu depends on the catch, though a taster menu (antipasti ranging from marinated tuna to fried rice balls, with a helping of pasta and risotto, followed by a choice of dessert) is recommended. If that sounds like too much, go for the *scialatielli ai frutti di*

mare, but be sure to leave room for the divine cakes (provided by Salvatore de Riso of Maiori). ⊠ *Via Dragone 1/2* ☏ *089/871840* ▤ *AE, DC, MC, V* ☉ *Closed Dec. 8–26 and Tues. Oct.–May.*

$$–$$$ ✕ **Le Arcate.** A cave is not where you'd normally expect to find good food, but this one changes the rules. The simple, dark, old restaurant tucked under the road also has a large terrace overlooking the beach. Folks dig its *Scialatielli Masaniello*—fresh pasta named after the local boy who became a revolutionary in Naples—as well as its pizza and grilled fish. It's been here for 50 years, a drop in the gulf around these parts. Get a table out on the seafront where you can lean over and see exactly where your meal has come from. ⊠ *Via G. Di Benedetto 4, under arcades of roadway connecting Amalfi and Atrani* ☏ *089/871367* ▤ *AE, DC, MC, V* ☉ *Closed Jan. and Mon. Nov. to Easter.*

¢–$ ✕ **Wayout Winebar.** Tucked snugly into the corner of Atrani's delightful little town square, this new place offers a superb range of wines from all over Italy as well as cheeses, smoked meats, and grilled vegetables to be enjoyed "tapas style." ⊠ *Piazza Umberto I, 84010* ☏ *089/873516* ▤ *No credit cards* ☉ *Closed Wed., Jan.–Apr. and Oct.–Dec.*

¢–$ ▦ **A Scalinatella.** Filippo, the Donald Trump of Atrani, runs just about the only game in the village, with hostel beds, private rooms, and apartments (some with kitchens and washing machines) spread all over the place. These are only modest digs, but if you want to wake up in Atrani, you'll have to deal with it. Breakfast is served up in the small restaurant on the square (also owned by Filippo), and you can enjoy inexpensive meals (from €4) there too. ⊠ *Piazza Umberto I 5, 84010* ☏ *089/ 871492* ▨ *089/871930* ⊕ *www.amalficoast.it/hotel/scalinatella* ⥱ *12 rooms, 10 with bath* ▤ *No credit cards.*

RAVELLO TO PAESTUM

Just a few minutes west of Amalfi, perched atop a ridge of Monte Cerreto, and "closer to the sky than the sea"—according to French writer André Gide—the achingly lovely town of Ravello gazes down on the Bay of Salerno and the humbler villages surrounding it. This cloud-riding perch is just one reason why some travelers give Ravello the laurel as the Amalfi Coast's—some say Italy's—most beautiful town (in fact, the town has long been nicknamed *La Bellissima*). Languor becomes Ravello's mood, a bit out of sync with the world below, and it makes this town a lovely place to catch your breath. The slightly aloof star high above the coast, it remains there for the reaching and is worth the stretch. Hearty souls trek between Atrani and Ravello by a path that climbs through the Valle del Dragone, or Dragon's Valley, a name inspired by the morning mists here. Most Ravello-bound travelers, however, take the municipal bus from Amalfi's Piazza Flavio Gioia, which corkscrews its way up 1,000 ft along a road in the southern Monti Lattari. Cars follow the same route and really come in handy when driving farther south along Statale 163 to the towns rimming the Bay of Salerno, which have their off-the-beaten-track appeal. If you're based in Naples and have singled out Ravello for a day's sampling of the Amalfi Coast, by far the quickest route is via the mountain pass called the Valico di Chiunzi, easily reached via the A3 Naples–Salerno Autostrada from the exit at Angri.

Many visitors end their southward journey along the Amalfi Coast in Ravello. They might have a point (what can top that mountaintop paradise?), but other savvy travelers keep heading southward, for ahead lie less crowded seaport villages, the bustling city of Salerno, and fabled Paestum, site of three of the greatest ancient Greek temples in the world.

After dropping down to sea level from Ravello or going eastward from Amalfi, the coast road, Statale 163, descends into Minori, known for its good beach and ancient Roman heritage. The road climbs up the cape by Torre Mezzacapo, then drops back down to sea level near the 15th-century church of San Francesco. Statale 163 then goes though the town of Maiori, with its much broader river valley producing another good beach, and passes Capo di Baia Verde, near the misleadingly named 17th-century Torre Normanna. The coast here becomes dramatic again, giving grand views of the sea as you climb past the promontory topped by Torre di Badia. Capo Tummolo and then Vallone di San Nicola, with the little village of Marina di Erchie, are ahead of you. The drive then descends to the fishing village of Cetara, set along a narrow inlet, continues along the coast, passing Torre de Fuenti and Vallone di Albori, and then faces the sea near Torre della Marina di Albori. At the junction of Raito, a lush little village, you cross the bridge over the Vallone Bonea to the town of Vietri, at which point traffic-light reality returns. Follow Statale 163 to the city of Salerno. Autostrada A3 south connects to E45, which leads to Battipaglia and the exit for the ancient temples of Paestum. Alternatively, hug the coast, driving along Salerno's *lungomare,* and continue along the fairly degraded coastline until you reach Paestum, 40 km (25 mi) from Salerno.

Ravello

★ 33 *6½ km (4 mi) northeast of Amalfi, 29 km (18 mi) west of Salerno.*

Positano may focus on pleasure, and Amalfi on history, but cool, serene Ravello revels in refinement. Thrust over Statale 163 and the Bay of Salerno on a mountain buttress, below forests of chestnut and ash, above terraced lemon groves and vineyards, it early on beckoned the affluent with its island-in-the-sky views and secluded defensive positioning. Gardens out of the *Arabian Nights,* pastel palazzos, tucked-away piazzas with medieval fountains, architecture ranging from Romano-Byzantine to Norman-Saracen, and those sweeping blue-water, blue-sky vistas have inspired a panoply of large personalities, including Wagner and Boccaccio, princes and popes, aesthetes and hedonists, and a stream of famous authors from Virginia Woolf to Tennessee Williams. Author and part-time resident Gore Vidal, not an easy critic, has called the town's Villa Cimbrone panorama "the most beautiful view in the world."

Though its origins are lost in obscurity, Ravello may have been settled by Romans fleeing the sack of their dying empire. The town itself was founded in the 9th century, under Amalfi's rule, until residents prosperous from cotton tussled with the superpower republic and elected their own doge in the 11th century; Amalfitans dubbed them *rebelli* (rebels). In the 12th century, with the aid of the Norman King Roger, Ravello even succeeded in resisting Pisa's army for a couple of years, though the powerful Pisans returned to wreak destruction along the coast. Even so, Ravello's skilled seafaring trade with merchants and Moors from Sicily and points east led to a burgeoning wealth, which peaked in the 13th century, when there were 13 churches, four cloisters, and dozens of sumptuous villas. Neapolitan princes built palaces; life was privileged.

But as is inevitable with all supernovas, Ravello's bright light diminished, first through Pisa's maritime rise in the 14th century, then through rivalry between its warring families in the 15th century. When the plague cast its shadow in the 17th century, the population plummeted from upward of 30,000 to perhaps a couple of thousand souls, where it remains today. When Ravello was incorporated into the diocese of Amalfi in 1804, a kind of stillness settled in. Despite the decline of its power and populace, Ravello's cultural heritage and special loveliness continued to blossom. Gardens flowered and music flowed in the ruined villas, and artists, sophisticates, and their lovers filled the crumbling palazzos. Grieg, Wagner, D. H. Lawrence, Chanel, Garbo and her companion, conductor Leopold Stokowski, and then, slowly, tourists, followed in their footsteps. Today, at the Villa Rufolo, the noted Fèstival Musicale di Ravello is held in its shaded gardens. Here, special Wagnerian concerts are often held to pay homage to the great composer, who was inspired by these gardens to compose scenes of *Parsifal.*

With the exception of the Villa Rufolo concerts, however, the hush lingers, especially in off-season, when there seem to be more cats than cars. Empty, narrow streets morph into whitewashed staircases rising into a haze of azure, which could be from the sea, the sky, or a union of both. About the only places that don't seem to be in pianissimo slow motion are Piazza Duomo, in front of the cathedral, during the evening passeggiata, or caffès at *pranzo* (luncheon) or *cena* (dinner). Note that the town likes to celebrate religious festas throughout the year—one of the nicest celebrations is the blossom-strewn celebration of Pentecost (usually the first week of June), when Piazza Duomo is ornamented with sidewalk pictures created with flower petals.

Although cars must park in the municipal lot, most arriving buses deposit their passengers near the hillside tunnel that leads to Piazza Duomo. On the square you'll find the tourist office, just to the left of the 11th-century duomo stairs, and the Bric-a-Brac Shop, a great resource for books on Ravello. Pride of place on the town piazza is taken by the **Duomo,** the town cathedral, dedicated to patron San Pantaleone and founded in 1086 by Orso Papiro, the first bishop of Ravello. Rebuilt in the 12th and 17th centuries, the Duomo retains traces of medieval frescoes in the transept, an original mullioned window, a marble portal, and a three-story 13th-century bell tower playfully interwoven with mullioned windows and arches. The 12th-century bronze door features 54 embossed panels depicting Christ's life, and saints, prophets, plants, and animals, all narrating biblical lore. It was crafted by Barisano da Trani, who also fashioned the doors of the cathedrals of Trani and Monreale. (The door is currently under restoration, and won't be visible until 2004, at the earliest.) The nave's three aisles are divided by ancient columns, and treasures include sarcophagi from Roman times and paintings by southern Renaissance artist Andrea da Salerno. Most impressive are the two medieval *ambos,* or pulpits: The earlier one, used for reading the Epistles, is inset with a mosaic scene of Jonah and the Whale, symbolizing death and redemption. The more famous one, used for reading the Gospels, was commissioned by Nicola Rufolo in 1272 and created by Niccolò di Bartolomeo da Foggia. It seems almost Tuscan in style, with exquisite Cosmatesque mosaic work and bas reliefs and six twisting columns sitting on lion pedestals. An eagle grandly tops the colonnette fronting the inlaid marble lectern.

A chapel left of the apse is dedicated to San Pantaleone, a physician, who was beheaded in the 3rd century in Nicomedia. Every July 27 devout believers gather in hope of witnessing a miracle (similar to that of San Gennaro in Naples), in which the saint's blood, collected in a vial and set out on an inlaid marble altar, appears to liquefy and become clearer. Use one of the side doors to go behind the altar in the small chapel to get a closer look at the pint of the saint's blood. In the crypt is the **Museo del Duomo,** which displays treasures from around the 13th century, during the reign of Frederick II of Sicily, in an elegant setting. You'll find gold and silver work, sculpture, and a classic Campanian marble bust of a half-smiling woman from the Rufolo dynasty, whose name was Sichelgaita (try saying that one with a mouthful of scialatielli). ⊠ *Museo del Duomo, Piazza del Duomo* ☎ *089/858311* 🎫 *€2.00* 🕙 *Church daily, 9–1 and 3–7. Museum Apr.–Oct., daily 9:30–1 and 3–7; Nov.–Mar., weekends only.*

Hard by the Duomo on the main piazza is the three-aisle 13th-century **Santa Maria a Gradillo** with its lovely dome. This was the place where the town noblemen gathered to discuss civic issues; its atrium collapsed in the 18th century. The small Sicilian-Saracenic bell tower has two light mullion windows. Next door is the private **Museo del Corallo** (Coral Museum), which shows the venerable tradition of Italian workmanship in coral, harvested in bygone centuries from the gulfs of Salerno and Naples and crafted into jewelry, cameos, and figurines. Look in particular for a carved Christ from the 17th century and a tobacco box covered in cameos. ⊠ *Piazza Duomo* 🕙 *Mon.–Sat. 10–noon and 3–5.*

Fodor's Choice ★ Opposite the duomo is the **Villa Rufolo**, which—if the master storyteller Boccaccio is to be believed—was built in the 13th century by Landolfo Rufolo, whose immense fortune stemmed from trade with the Moors and the Saracens. Now the setting for the Fèstival Musicale di Ravello, its Romanesque walls contain a scene that seems from the earliest days of the Crusades. Norman and Arab architecture mingle in a welter of color-filled gardens so lush that composer Richard Wagner used them as inspiration for Klingsor's Garden, the home of the Flower Maidens, in his opera *Parsifal.* Beyond the Arab-Sicilian cloister and the Norman tower are two flower-bedded terraces that offer the prime vista of the Bay of Salerno, set off by the cupolas of the 13th-century church of Santissima Annunziata and a dramatic umbrella pine tree. In 1851 the villa was acquired by Sir Francis Nevile Reid, a Scotsman, who hired Michele Ruggiero, head of the excavations at Pompeii, to restore the villa to its full splendor and replant the gardens with rare cycads, cordylines, and palms. Highlights of the villa are its Moorish cloister—an Arabic-Sicilian delight with interlacing lancet arcs and polychromatic palmette decoration—and the 14th-century Torre Maggiore, the so-called Klingsor's Tower, renamed in honor of Richard Wagner's landmark 1880 visit and today a dramatic spot for chamber music recitals (note that when weather is rainy, concerts are moved into a charmless room). Beyond lie two spectacular terrace gardens, with the lower one, the "Wagner Terrace," often the site for concerts, with the orchestra perched on a precarious-looking platform constructed over the precipice. ⊠ *Piazza Duomo, 84010* ☎ *089/857866* 🎫 *€4, concerts extra charge* 🕙 *Daily 9–sunset; closes earlier on concert days.*

For a closer look at the **Santissima Annunziata** (now a center hosting conferences of the Center for Research for Villas and their Urban Environments, based at the Villa Rufolo), exit the villa and take a sharp right to reach the Via dell'Annunziata stair path, which plummets you down the hillside past the church to the scenic Via della Repubblica. Head back up the road—which offers a panoramic vista of the blue bay—to the town square and take Via Richard Wagner, behind the tourist office, to Via San Giovanni a Toro, the address of Ravello's grandest palazzi (now hotels). **Villa Episcopio**, a 12th-century bishop's residence, was formerly called Villa di Sangro. Amid the gardens and ruins, Italy's King Vittorio Emanuele III abdicated in favor of his son, and Jackie Kennedy enjoyed breaks from her public obligations. Wine merchants here have been cultivating grapes since 1860, and varieties of Ravello rosso and bianco, as refined as their namesake, can be purchased in town.

★ Set along the bayview Via San Giovanni del Toro, the **Hotel Caruso Belvedere**, set in a historic palazzo, has the most ravishing room on the entire Amalfi Coast: an Empire-era *grande salone,* with frescoed ceiling, walls adorned with dozens of 19th-century Neapolitan paintings, and grand antiques. Don't miss the legendary belvedere whose bifore Gothic window offers one of the most picturesque vantage points on the entire coast. This terrace area leads out to the achingly beautiful hotel gardens and arbors. If the hotel is still undergoing renovation (it was shuttered in 2001), picnickers can opt instead to enjoy the wonderful view of the adjacent Belvedere Principessa di Piemonte. Across the tiny piazza from the Caruso Belvedere is the 11th-century church of **San Giovanni del Toro.** Its evocative interior has three high apses and a crypt with 14th-century frescoes of Christ and the apostles. A 12th-century ambo (pulpit) by Alfano da Termoli startles the eye with its blue Persian majolica and four columns topped with elaborate capitals. The chapel of the Coppola family in the left aisle has an exceptional 14th-century relief of St. Catherine of Alexandria. The small church's three porticos adorned with lunettes show an Arabian influence, and the tripartite back facade is exquisite. ✉ *Piazza San Giovanni del Toro.*

Fodor'sChoice
★

To the west of the main square, a somewhat hilly 10-minute walk along Via San Francesco brings you to Ravello's showstopper, the **Villa Cimbrone,** whose dazzling gardens perch 1,500 ft above the sea. The ultimate aerie, this medieval-style fantasy was created in 1905 by England's Lord Grimthorpe and made world-famous when Greta Garbo found sanctuary from the press when she vacationed here with Leopold Stokowski in 1937. The Gothic *castello-palazzo* is set in idyllic gardens, which are divided by the grand Alleé of Immensity, leading in turn to the literal highpoint of any trip to the Amalfi Coast—the legendary **Belvedere of Infinity.** This grand stone parapet, adorned with amusing stone busts, overlooks the entire Bay of Salerno and is one of the most magical spots in all Europe. The name Cimbrone derives from the rocky ridge on which the villa stands, first colonized by the ancient Romans and hailed as ìCimbroniumî back then. In the Middle Ages, the noble Accongiogioco clan built a house here. Centuries later, Ernest William Beckett, Lord Grimthorpe, fell in love with Cimbrone on a grand tour of Italy and, with the help of Nicolo Mansi, transformed the gardens into the extravaganza we see today. Since the lord hosted many of England's Bloomsbury set, it is now thought that Vita Sackville-West (just one of the many famous writers and artists who visited here), had some help in the garden design. Be sure to explore all the pathways to find the mock-Gothic crypt (now being renovated to hold a restaurant), the Temple of Bacchus *tempietto* (under which Lord Grimthorpe is buried), the tea pavilion done in the style of Florence's Pazzi Chapel, and the Grotto of Venus. Many feel the Cimbrone is the most beautiful garden in Italy; be sure to visit here and decide for yourself. Better yet, overnight at this magical domain, as the villa itself is now a hotel. Begin by logging onto the villa Web site to see its wondrous photos. ✉ *Via S. Chiara 26* ☎ *089/857459* ⊕ *www. villacimbrone.it* 🎫 *€5* ◷ *Daily 9–half hr before sunset.*

Nearly every street in Ravello has a historic church or villa. Two notable religious sites are the church and convent of **San Francesco,** founded in 1222 by St. Francis of Assisi, with a small Gothic cloister; the church was rebuilt in the 18th century (on Via S. Francesco). Majolica flooring in the 13th-century **Monastero di Santa Chiara** (on Via S. Chiara) is one special element; another is the *matronaeum,* or women's gallery, the only one left on the Amalfi Coast (not known for segregating the sexes, or anything else). Buy some gelati on the piazza by the duomo and walk east to the **Piazza Fontana Moresco,** below the Hotel Parsifal and above the gates of the walled perimeter, to check out the two stone lions on the fanciful 1,000-year-old fountain, still spewing water.

For the "best strollo in swello Ravello," begin at the cathedral in the main square of the Piazza Duomo, head up the stepped Via Wagner, to the left of the church, then turn left on Via San Giovanni del Toro and take in the magnificent view of the Belvedere di Principessa di Piemonte and the famed salons and gardens of the Hotel Caruso Belvedere. Proceed past San Giovanni del Toro, past the 13th-century convent of St. Augustine (now the Hotel Parsifal) to the Fontana Moresca fountain (near here is a good starting point for trails leading up to the chestnut forests above Ravello). Head back toward the main square via Viale Parco della Rimembranza to the church of Santa Maria a Gradillo, opposite the famous step path which leads down to Atrani. Continue along Via Roma to the Piazza Duomo. Explore the great Villa Rufolo, then return to its entrance and make a sharp left turn onto Via dei Rufolo and left again down Via Nevile Reid to the exquisitely picturesque Santissima Annunziata church. Backtrack 300 ft to pick up Via San Francesco, found off the northwest corner of the main square, to head past the underwhelming Convento di San Francesco, continuing upward until you hit Via Santa Chiara to reach the breathtaking Villa Cimbrone, thereby leaving the best until last. Tour the famous gardens, then return to the town center.

Where to Stay & Eat

$$$ ✕ **Palazzo della Marra.** The young chef-owners of this restaurant attempt to turn Campania classics into something more—and they usually succeed. Past a fireplace that flickers in season and museum-size paintings, you descend into a white, modernized 13th-century setting. The daily *menu turistica* may offer such dishes as *scarola ripiena* (stuffed endive), *risotto con zucca rossa e capesante dorate alla salvia* (red-pumpkin risotto with seafood in sage), and *lombo di agnello al rosmarino con spinaci all'uvetta* (lamb cutlets with spinach and raisins). Tasting menus—to suit various appetites and wallet sizes—are even more creative, with unexpected combinations. To match the food, the owners provide a wine list featuring the best of the region. ⊠ *Via della Marra 7* ☎ *089/858302* ⊟ *AE, DC, MC, V* ⊘ *Closed 3 wks in Nov., 6 wks Jan.–Feb., Tues. in winter.*

★ $$–$$$ ✕ **Cumpa' Cosimo.** Lustier-looking than most Ravello spots, Cumpa' Cosimo is run devotedly by Netta Bottone, whose family has owned this *cantina* for 70 of its 300-plus years. She has been cooking under the arched ceiling for more than 30 of them. You can't miss here with any of the dishes featuring classic Ravellian cuisine. A favorite (share it—it's huge) is a *misto* of fettuccine, fusilli, tortellini, and whatever other homemade pasta inspires her, served with a fresh, fragrant pesto. Meats are generally excellent—after all, they are supplied by the butcher shop next door, run by Netta's father. Local wines ease it all down gently, and homemade gelato is a luscious ending. ⊠ *Via Roma 46* ☎ *089/857156* ⌕ *Reservations essential* ⊟ *AE, DC, MC, V* ⊘ *Sometimes closed Mon. in winter.*

$$ ✕ **Vittoria.** Between the Duomo and the church of San Francesco, this is a good place for a return to reality and an informal bite. Vittoria's thin-crust pizza with loads of fresh toppings is the star attraction, and locals praise it *molto*. But also try the pasta, maybe fusilli with tomatoes, zucchini, and mozzarella. Vittoria is pretty, too, with arches and tile floors. ⊠ *Via dei Rufolo 3* ☎ *089/857947* ⊟ *AE, DC, MC, V* ⊘ *Closed Tues. Nov.–Mar.*

$$$$ ✕⌑ **Palazzo Sasso.** In this 12th-century home of the aristocratic Sasso family, Wagner penned part of his opera *Parsifal* in the 1880s, and in the fashionable 1950s, the palazzo hosted Ingrid Bergman and Roberto Rossellini. On reopening in 1997, after a 20-year hiatus, the hotel is still luring the glitterati—its first guests were Placido Domingo and his en-

tourage. Ordinary mortals, too, can come to sightsee and peek at the gleaming marble atrium, glass elevators, two rooftop hot tubs, roaring waterfall, and bar (now one of Ravello's prime watering holes). Traditionalists might look askance (if not be totally horrified) at all this glitz in quaint old Ravello, but no one will complain about immaculately furnished guest rooms, with the latest computer-operated lighting and air-cooling systems. The gilded, Empire-style Rossellini restaurant is also not to be sniffed at. ⊠ *Via San Giovanni del Toro 28, 84010* ☎ *089/ 818181* 🖷 *089/858900* ⊕ *www.palazzosasso.com* 🖙 *38 rooms, 5 suites ♢ Restaurant, café, minibars, pool, outdoor hot tub, bar, library, meeting room, parking (fee), some pets allowed* ⊟ *AE, DC, MC, V* ☉ *Closed Nov.–Feb.*

★ **$$$$** ✕🖷 **Palumbo.** Built in the 12th century as a palazzo, this famous hotel has long been a stop for visiting Someones: Wagner, who composed here; Bogart, filming *Beat the Devil*; a young Jack and Jackie. Ancient marble columns, mosaic-tile floors, and museum-quality antiques combine to provide an elegant ambience throughout the hotel, while incredible views of the Bay of Salerno can be enjoyed from your terrace or the lush gardens that sit below the hotel on the hillside. In summer, guests have the option of being whisked down to a villa at sea level and pampered in the hotel's coastal retreat. The classic yet innovative Continental cuisine—finish off your feast with lemon soufflé and Episcopio estate wine—is grandly served in the hushed 17th-century dining hall, or you can enjoy a view as delicious as the food atop the restaurant terrace (note the restaurant is closed from November to March). Most guest rooms have antiques and modern marble baths, except for those in the annex, where at just over half the cost you still have access to all the facilities of the main palazzo. The lodging prices include both a sumptuous breakfast and a choice of either a gourmet lunch or dinner. ⊠ *Via S. Giovanni del Toro 16, 84010* ☎ *089/857244* 🖷 *089/858133* ⊕ *www. hotelpalumbo.it* 🖙 *21 rooms ♢ Restaurant, minibars, bar, meeting room, parking (fee)* ⊟ *AE, DC, MC, V* ⎟◯⎟ *MAP.*

$–$$ ✕🖷 **Salvatore.** Adjacent to the Hotel Graal and sharing the same glorious view, Salvatore has a small garden you enter by walking down into it and then choosing between a large terrace or an indoor area for dining. The family creates classic Campanian cuisine, the service is friendly, and the overlook offers the best view of any inexpensive restaurant in the vicinity. Upstairs guest rooms are surprisingly upscale, with baths, TVs, air-conditioning, and balconies and with a price that makes them a great deal. ⊠ *Via della Repubbliche 2* 🖷🖷 *089/857227* 🖙 *6 rooms* ⊟ *AE, MC, V* ☉ *Restaurant closed Mon. in winter; hotel closed Nov.–mid-Mar.* ⎟◯⎟ *BP.*

★ **$$$$** 🖷 **Villa Cimbrone.** Suspended over the azure sea and set amid rose-laden gardens, this magical place was once the home of Lord Grimthorpe and the holiday hideaway of Greta Garbo. A decade ago it was exquisitely transformed into a hotel by the Vuillemeier family. Now, news comes that more renovation is underway, and the newly spruced up hotel-villa is due to reopen in spring 2004, complete with new restaurant in the Cripta, or porticoed crypt, which was built by Lord Grimthorpe to resemble the one at Fountains Abbey, near his birthplace in Malton, England. Hopefully, the Gothic-style castle will remain intact, replete with guest rooms ranging from palatial to cozy. One is covered with frescoes, but we love the small Peony Room since it is the only one with its own terrace overlooking the bay (Garbo's former room only has an enclosed balcony). Tapestried armchairs, framed prints, vintage art books, and other antiques which belonged to Viscountess Frost, the lord's daughter, still grace the enchantingly elegant sitting room. Best of all, guests have the villa's famous gardens all to themselves once their gates are closed at sunset. The villa is a bit of a hike along lanes and alleys from the town center, but porters will carry your luggage and the distance helps keep this the most peaceful place on the Amalfi Coast. You can get an advance view of the hotel at its splendid Web site. ⊠ *Via Santa Chiara 26, 84010* ☎ *089/857459* 🖷 *089/857777* ⊕ *www.villacimbrone. it* ↻ *19 rooms* ⚭ *Library* ▤ *AE, MC, V* ⊙ *Closed Nov.–Mar.* ⎮⊙⎮ *BP, MAP.*

★ **$$$–$$$$** ⊡ **Caruso Belvedere.** Now closed for an ongoing restoration (*possible* opening: March–April 2004), this is one of the most beloved hotels in the world. In decades past it has been a favored home-away-from-home for the likes of Virginia Woolf, Tennessee Williams, Graham Greene, the Khedive of Egypt, Margot Fonteyn, and Peter O'Toole (who came for a week and stayed a month). Legendarily old-fashioned, set in an 11th-century palazzo, overlooking an incomparable panorama of the Bay of Salerno, with lush gardens and a grand salon that would have made even Napoléon feel comfortable, the Caruso Belvedere is now in limbo and "sotto sequestro," which basically means all work has stopped: rumor has it that the new owners thought they could make some radical changes to this historically listed building and were caught red-handed! Let us hope that the unique aura of this place will be retained and that the wonderful Caruso family will remain as presiding spirits. ⊠ *Via Toro 52, 84010* ☎ *089/857111.*

$$$–$$$$ ⊡ **Rufolo.** D. H. Lawrence worked on *Lady Chatterley's Lover* during his 1926 visit, so it might be fun to revisit the novel's groundbreaking love scenes while you're here. Rooms have mosaic or terra-cotta floors, and some have balconies to liven up the snug quarters with gorgeous sea and sky vistas framed by the palm trees of the Villa Rufolo, just below the hotel. ⊠ *Via San Francesco 1, 84010* ☎ *089/857133* 🖷 *089/857935* ⊕ *www.hotelrufolo.it* ↻ *34 rooms* ⚭ *Restaurant, minibars, pool, bar, meeting room, free parking, some pets allowed* ▤ *AE, DC, MC, V* ⊙ *Closed Feb.* ⎮⊙⎮ *MAP, FAP.*

$$$ ⊡ **Graal.** The name comes from the Holy Grail, as in Wagner's opera *Parsifal,* but this inn is more an operetta. It's much less grand than Ravello's famous hotels, with a modern decor that's a bit of a downer. Nevertheless, it reaches high-Cs for comfort, cleanliness, and contentment. Hovering over the water on the Via della Repubblica, with a nearly unobstructed view of the breathtaking bay, this hotel possesses one of the friendliest staffs around, a pretty pool area, and whirlpools and fancy baths. In the dining room, meals from a family kitchen are delivered to tables dressed in linen and set near large, arched windows. Most rooms are smallish, some are deluxe (especially No. 342, with a double whirlpool and a bed from which you can see the great view), but all have tiled floors and balconies. ⊠ *Via della Repubblica 8, 84010* ☎ *089/857222* 🖷 *089/857551* ⊕ *www.graal.it* ↻ *35 rooms* ⚭ *Restaurant, pool, bar, meeting room* ▤ *AE, DC, MC, V* ⊙ *Restaurant closed Mon. Oct.–Mar.* ⎮⊙⎮ *BP, MAP.*

$$$ ⊡ **Villa Maria.** Fronted by a vast garden terrace, terra-cotta–color Villa Maria has more sunny warmth than most formal hotels in Ravello. Public areas have tiled floors, high ceilings, lace, and antiques. All but two rooms are standard, and there's an airy suite that has a large balcony overlooking the coast. If the hotel becomes too quiet, your hosts promote fun with dancing and music out on the terrace. Note that views here look out over the Vallone del Dragone, not the bay, but are memorable all the same. Also check out Maria's next-door sibling, the Hotel Giordano, a former 18th-century manor house, which shares facilities with the villa. The rooms are less desirable here, but the pool is closer. ⊠ *Via Santa Chiara 2, 84010* ☎ *089/858400* 🖷 *089/857071* ⊕ *www. villamaria.it* ↻ *23 rooms* ⚭ *Restaurant, minibars, pool, bar, free parking* ▤ *AE, DC, MC, V* ⎮⊙⎮ *MAP, FAP.*

$–$$ ⌧ **Parsifal.** In 1288 this diminutive property was a convent housing an order of Augustinian friars. Today the intact cloister hosts travelers simply intent on enjoying themselves mightily. Ancient, ivy-covered stone arches and a tiled walkway looking out over the coastline lead to a cozy interior that still feels a bit like a retreat. Sun lounges, a garden, a fountain with reflecting pool, and alfresco dining all overlook the sea. Rooms are small (monk's cells, after all), so ask for one with a balcony; numbers 20, 22, 23, 24, and 26 are best. The charming young manager just dotes on Americans. Half board is often required at peak season. ⌧ *Viale Gioacchino d'Anna 5, Ravello 84010* ☎ *089/857144* 🖷 *089/857972* 🌐 *www.hotelparsifal.com* ⇶ *19 rooms* ♨ *Restaurant, bar, parking (fee), some pets allowed* ▭ *AE, DC, MC, V* ⅰ⊙ǀ *MAP, FAP.*

$ ⌧ **Toro.** Right off the ladder of steps, which some consider akin to a main street, this little hotel with a big garden and lots of antiques has been in the Schiavo family for three generations. Even this modest inn once boasted visiting VIPs: composer Edvard Grieg wrote in the guest book that he was *"molto contento"* and artist M. C. Escher also stayed here (his celebrated prints of spiraling staircases were inspired by those he discovered in Ravello and Atrani). If you don't mind spare rooms and enjoy simple, good food, you, too, will be content. ⌧ *Viale Wagner 3, 84010* 🖷🖷 *089/857211* ✉ *htoro@tiscalinet.it* ⇶ *12 rooms* ♨ *Dining room, some pets allowed* ▭ *AE, DC, MC, V* ◴ *Closed Nov.–Mar.* ⅰ⊙ǀ *BP.*

$ ⌧ **Villa Amore.** A 10-minute walk from the Piazza Duomo, this charmingly secluded hotel, with a garden, is family-run and shares the same exhilarating view of the Bay of Salerno as Ravello's most expensive hotels. Rooms are small, with modest and modern furnishings. From July to September half board is required (which may not be the way to go—our meal here left a lot to be desired, but perhaps the kitchen has now improved). Reserve ahead, and specify time of arrival if you need help with luggage from the parking lot or bus stop (you pay about €5 per bag). ⌧ *Via del Fusco 5, 84010* 🖷🖷 *089/857135* ⇶ *12 rooms* ♨ *Restaurant, bar, some pets allowed* ▭ *DC, MC, V* ⅰ⊙ǀ *MAP, FAP.*

Nightlife & the Arts

Other than the concerts offered by the Fèstival Musicale di Ravello, there is little nightlife activity, unless you count moongazing. A few caffès and bars are scattered about, but the general peacefulness extends to evening hours. Hotels and restaurants may offer live music and can advise you about nightclubs, but around these parts the sound is either soft and classical—or silence.

CONCERTS Sublime music and views makes a nifty combo in Ravello, long host to the celebrated **Fèstival Musicale di Ravello** (Ravello Music Festival; ⌧ Via Trinità 3 ☎ 089/858149 🖷 089/858249 🌐 www.ravelloarts.org), held on the garden escarpments of the Villa Rufolo. Due to popular demand, this is no longer just a summer-only affair, nor is it restricted to Ravello—a few concerts are now also held in the Chiesa di Santa Rosa in Conca dei Marini and at La Gabella in Praiano. The season runs from March to November, with most concerts in May and June. The most unusual event is the *Concerto all'Alba* (dawn concert), when the entire town wakes up at 4:30 to watch the sun rise over the bay to the accompaniment of music from a full symphony orchestra; this event is usually scheduled for the second week of August. The programming is fairly traditional, and it's rare to find something outside of the Bach/Mozart/Beethoven/Brahms/Chopin repertory, although slightly less well-known Italian composers such as Scarlatti and Cimarosa also get a fair shake. Most evening concerts are held at 9:30, with occasional performances starting at 6:30. Note that the 9:30 concerts begin well after sunset, so come earlier if you want to catch the evening glow. Annual concert schedules—listed on the Ravello Concert Society web site—are posted outside Villa Rufolo and may also be picked up at tourist information offices on the Amalfi Coast.

CULINARY
LESSONS
If you fancy learning how to make some of the things you've been eating, **Mamma Agata** (⊠ Via San Cosma 9, 84010 ☎☎ 089/857019), who has cooked for Elizabeth Taylor, Federico Fellini, Jackie Kennedy, and Marcello Mastroianni, will take you into her kitchen—with the almost obligatory stunning view—and take you through the preparation of the area's pasta dishes and sweets. A four-hour morning session is followed by lunch—that you yourself will have made!

Shopping

Bric-a-Brac (⊠ Piazza Duomo 16 ☎ 089/857153) has some 19th-century antiques, including historic crèche scenes; in the front of the store is a must for history and art lovers—a great selection of books and antique prints about Ravello. **Gerardo Sacco** (⊠ Piazza Duomo 8 ☎ 089/858125) is jeweler to several divas; pictures in the shop show Glenn Close, Elizabeth Taylor, and Caroline of Monaco (among others) flashing his creations. Theatrical to say the least, his earrings, necklaces, and bracelets are large and showy and not to everyone's taste, but certainly worth a look. **Ceramiche d'Arte** (⊠ Via dei Rufolo 16 ☎ 089/857303) ships its good stock of Vietri-made and other hand-painted ceramics all over the world. Bargaining may reward you with a 10% discount, maybe more if you have a talent for it. There are also opportunities for gaining hands-on experience at their showroom and workshop a three-minute walk away in a courtyard at Via Roma 20. **Episcopio Winery** (⊠ Via Giovanni a Toro, across from Hotel Palumbo) offers selections of fine Ravello vintages. **Gruppo Petit Prince** (⊠ Via San Francesco ☎ 089/858033) has a nice selection of stationery, prints, and artworks. **Ravello Gusti & Delizie** (⊠ Via Roma 28 ☎ 089/857716) is stocked to the ceiling with *prodotti tipici e naturali della costiera Amalfitana*; this is the place for foodstuffs, as well as delicacies and wines from all over Italy. Sun-dried-tomato pasta, olive oil, and other treats are available, but most intriguing are the lemon products—candles and soaps, and even lemon honey, gathered and bottled by a town police officer.

Marina di Erchie

㉞ *13 km (7 mi) southeast of Minori, 3 km (2 mi) south of Cetara.*

With a looming Norman tower on the cliff above, the curving beach-front hamlet of Erchie is as romantic as can be, especially when there's no one around but you and the fishermen who haul in their catch in the pink sun of early morning. The little village of Erchie is built around a 10th-century Benedictine abbey destroyed and abandoned in the 12th century; Salerno took over the town in the 15th century. By the 1960s the abbey was restored in neo-Renaissance style, with a portal constructed in dark tufa and stone, and the little village was discovered by city dwellers from Salerno, who now flock here to windsurf along the cove and laze the day away.

Cetara

㉟ *3 km (2 mi) northeast of Erchie, 4 km (2½ mi) southwest of Vietri.*

Tourists tend to take a pass on the village of Cetara because of the hairpin turns off the main road. A quaint and quiet fishing village set below orange groves on Monte Falerzo, it was held in subjugation to greater powers, like most of these coastal sites, throughout much of its history. From being a Saracen stronghold in the 9th century, it became the final holding of Amalfi at the eastern edge of the republic, which all through the 11th and 12th centuries tithed part of Cetara's fishing catch, *ius piscariae*—the town's claim to fame. It's rumored that the village's Latin name comes from this big catch—*cetaria* (tuna net), but the town haul is most famous for its anchovies—thousands of years ago, salted and strained, they became a spicy liquid called *garum,* a delicacy to the rich of ancient Rome (it can be purchased at local grocery stores). After the Middle Ages, the village came under the dominion of the Benedictine abbey of neighboring Santa Maria di Erchie and then became the port of the abbey of Cava, above the coast, which traded with Africa and extracted anchorage dues. In 1534 the Turks, led by the tyrant Sinan Pasha—on the invitation, no less, of Prince Ferdinando Sanseverino of Salerno—enslaved 300 Cetaran villagers, spiriting them away in 22 galleys and executing those who would not cooperate. A few survivors fled to Naples, which immediately ordered a watchtower to be raised in Cetara to ward off future raids. This is one of the many landmarks that remind tourists that there were coastal perils previous to the one of driving on Statale 163. Beneath the tower is a rocky little beach, and a small park overlooks the harbor, where fishermen mend their nets and paint their boats. They often are away from home for months, fishing in deep waters. Other than the scenic charm of the waterfront, there are no main sights here, other than the church of San Pietro, near the harbor.

Where to Stay & Eat

¢–$ ✕ **Acqua Pazza.** Locals along this part of the coast rave about this tiny restaurant. Set on the main street, it has a modest environment—a spare interior with a few tables—but its raison d'être is remarkably fresh seafood. Everyone tries the spaghetti with *colatura di alici,* a modern, lighter version of the Roman *garum.* This is just a three-minute stroll from the harbor. ⊠ *Across from church of San Pietro* 🚫 *No credit cards* ⊗ *Closed Mon.*

$$$$ 🏨 **Cetus.** Cetara's leading hotel is set in a white-stucco building that seems to have grown right out of the living rock. The natural theme is continued within. A summer-light restaurant has floors of marble tile, a window-wall, and terraces. A steep walk leads to the hotel's private beach and "American" bar. Shutter doors open onto broad, stone-flagged spaces, with umbrella tables, casual seating, overflowing flower boxes, and close-up sea views. ⊠ *Right off Amalfi Drive, just outside Cetara, 84010* ☎ *089/261388* 🖷 *089/261388* 🌐 *www.hotelcetus.it* 📲 *40 rooms* 🍽 *Restaurant, beach, 2 bars, meeting room, free parking* 🚻 *AE, DC, MC, V* ¶❍¶ *BP.*

Vietri sul Mare

36 *5 km (3 mi) northeast of Cetara, 3 km (2 mi) west of Salerno.*

Vietri sul Mare is rich in history. Founded in a river valley by the Etruscans, who called it Marcina, it was ransacked by the Samnites, became a prosperous Roman fishing outpost, and was then destroyed by the Vandals, all before 455. Then the Lombards made it a stronghold, the Saracens attacked regularly, and, in 1648, a French fleet pillaged the town. Perhaps to brighten their troubles, Vietrians have created renowned handcrafted and fired faience work and majolica ceramics since the beginning of the Middle Ages, when the craft was sponsored by the abbey at Cava de' Tirreni. In 1086 there were already 50 kilns blasting away, and the output decorates buildings and churches all along the coast, including the town's own 18th-century San Giovanni Battista and Confraternità del Rosario. Dozens of shops in town, and hundreds throughout the region, feature Vietri's colorful designs. For a complete rundown on

Vietri's celebrated majolica and faience work, visit the **Museo della Ceramica Vietrese** (Ceramic Museum), housed in an eye-popping tile-covered edifice built in 1922, the home of King Victor Emmanuel during the Salerno government of World War II. Exhibits range from medieval and Renaissance urns to the German-influenced ceramics of the 1950s, along with today's modern style, all painted with the traditionally colorful and fanciful designs based on the folklore, flora, and fauna of the Amalfi Coast. ✉ *Torretta di Villa Guariglia (Raito)* ☎ *089/211835* 🎫 *Free* ⏲ *Tues.–Sun. 9–1 and 4–7* ⏲ *Closed Mon.*

Vietri is the end, or the beginning, of the Amalfi Coast and Drive, depending on how you look at it—a busy, bustling town, with an older section by the sea and an upper area filled with factories, shops, and that mundane sign of the encroachment of civilization: traffic lights. It may be a manufacturing center, but the residents are keenly aware of aesthetics. Recently, the town imploded a modern building, which they felt blighted the beauty of the region. "It was like a nose job," said an official.

Where to Stay

$$$ 🏨 **Best Western Lloyd's Baia Hotel.** Slightly lacking in the character that other places in the area offer, Lloyd's Baia nevertheless provides a comfortable base from which to explore the whole Cilento area. An elevator delivers you to the bottom of a cliff, where you will find one of the most beachlike swimming areas of any hotel on the coast. There are two pools, practically in the gulf, a nice strip of sandy shore, cabanas, lounge chairs, umbrellas, and a restaurant. Sea sports and boating can be arranged from the beach. Guest rooms have sea views, small writing tables, TVs, and sitting areas, and some have balconies. Reconstruction will be completed by summer 2004. ✉ *Via De Marinis 2, 84019* ☎ *089/7633111* 📠 *089/7633633* 🌐 *www.lloydsbaiahotel.it* *124 rooms* *Restaurant, minibars, pool, shops, convention center, free parking, some pets allowed* 💳 *AE, MC, V* 🍽 *MAP, FAP.*

Shopping

Dozens of shops purvey the exuberance, light, and color of the region captured in Vietri vases, dishes, statues, wall and floor tiles, and artworks. The most famous manufacturer is **Solimene Ceramica** (✉ Via Case Sparse at Fontana Vecchia ☎ 089/210188), with a huge selection and established shipping facility. Make sure you visit the astonishing **factory,** which looks like something Willy Wonka would have built if he made plates and not chocolate. (✉ Via XXV Luglio 17).

Paestum

★ 37 *45 km (27 mi) southeast of Cetara, 42 km (25 mi) southeast of Salerno, 99 km (62 mi) southeast of Naples.*

One of Italy's most majestic sights lies on the edge of a flat coastal plain: the remarkably well-preserved **Greek temples** of Paestum. The S18 from the north has now been rerouted via the train station (Stazione di Paestum), which is about 800 yards from the ruins. Access can be gained through the perfectly preserved archway **Porta Sirena,** or—if motorized—through the northern gate of **Porta Aurea.** The ruins are part of the ancient city of Poseidonia, founded by Greek colonists in the 7th century BC. When the Romans took over the colony in 273 BC and its name was latinized to Paestum, they changed the layout of the settlement, adding an amphitheater and a forum. Much of the archeological material found on the site is displayed in the helpfully labeled **Museo Nazionale.** Several rooms are devoted to the unique tomb paintings discovered in the area, rare examples of Greek and pre-Roman pictorial art. About 600 ft from the museum (in front of the main site offices), framed by banks of roses and oleanders, is the **Tempio di Nettuno** (Temple of Poseidon), a magnificent Doric edifice with 36 fluted columns and an extraordinarily well-preserved entablature (area above the capitals), which rivals the finest temples in Greece. On the left of the temple is the so-called **Basilica,** the earliest of Paestum's standing edifices; it dates from early in the 6th century BC. The name is an 18th-century misnomer, for the structure was in fact a temple sacred to Hera, the wife of Zeus. Behind it an ancient road leads to the **Foro Romano** (Roman Forum) and the single column of the **Tempio della Pace** (Temple of Peace). Beyond—on the north side of the site—is the **Tempio di Cerere** (Temple of Ceres), thought to have originally been dedicated to the goddess Athena. From the thankfully pedestrianized road which runs past the site—actually it cuts the site in half—you can view the temples in the late afternoon or early evening, when the light enhances the deep gold of the limestone. Many people touring the Amalfi Coast take a day trip down to Paestum. The easiest way to get there is to train it to Salerno and then take a 30-minute connecting train ride from there. ⊠ *Via Magna Grecia* ☎ *0828/811023* 🏛 *Site €4.25, museum €4.25, combination ticket €6.35* 🕙 *Excavations daily 9–1 hr before sunset; museum daily 9–6:30* 🕙 *Museum closed 1st and 3rd Mon. of each month.*

Where to Stay

$–$$ 🏨 **Azienda Agricola Seliano.** This working farm-with-a-difference is about 2 mi from the temples and consists of a cluster of 19th-century baronial buildings. The Baronessa Cecilia herself presides over all, with sons Ettore and Massimino handling visitor logistics. Top priority once you have settled in to your refurbished rooms is to make friends with all the farm dogs, who will then be your faithful companions on country walks past apricot orchards and fields of artichokes. Opt for half-board terms as most of the food is home-produced, including the rich buffalo stew, fresher-than-ever mozzarella, and more elaborate dishes brought with relentless regularity from the kitchens; you'll be seated, as is the tradition, with other guests around a banquet table. For those without transport, transfers can be arranged from Paestum main-line station; bicycles may be borrowed on a first-come, first-served basis. ⊠ *Via Seliano, Paestum, 84063, about ½ mi down a dirt track west off the main road from Capaccio Scalo to Paestum* ☎ *0828/723634* 🖷 *0828/724544* ⊕ *www.agriturismoseliano.it* 🛏 *9 rooms* ⬧ *Restaurant, pool, bicycles, horseback riding, some pets allowed* ⊟ *DC, MC, V* 🕙 *Closed Nov.–Feb., except Dec. 27–Jan. 7* ⅠⓄⅠ *MAP, FAP.*

$ 🏨 **Helios.** Directly across the road from the Porta della Giustizia and only a few steps from the temples, the Helios has cottage-type rooms, each with a minibar, in a garden setting. A pleasant restaurant serves local specialties and seafood. The home-produced ricotta and mozzarella are especially recommended. ⊠ *Via Principe di Piemonte 1, Zona Archeologica, 84063* ☎ *0828/811020* 🖷 *0828/811600* ⊘ *hotel-helios@one.online.it* 🛏 *30 rooms* ⬧ *2 restaurants, minibars, pool* ⊟ *AE, DC, MC, V* ⅠⓄⅠ *BP, MAP.*

SORRENTO & THE AMALFI COAST A TO Z

AIR TRAVEL

CARRIERS You can fly non-stop to Capodichino A&irport in Naples from Rome on Alitalia.

🛫 Airlines and Contacts **Alitalia** ☎ 848/865641 ⊕ www.alitalia.it.

AIRPORTS

The nearest major airport is Capodichino in Naples. Autolinee Curreri Service runs the bus from the Naples airport to Sorrento, leaving and arriving in Sorrento four times daily. Most hotels in the area will arrange airport transfers for an extra fee.

🛈 Airport Information **Autolinee Curreri Service** ✉ Piazza Tasso ☎ 081/8015420 ⊕ www.curreriviaggi.it. **Capodichino Airport** ☎ 081/7896111.

BOAT & FERRY TRAVEL

Headquartered in Naples, the Metro del Mare is an extension of urban public transport—by sea. Operating since 2002, it connects the northern ports of Bacoli and Pozzuoli to Naples and from there goes to Sorrento, Positano, and Amalfi. The service runs from May through October, with three boats a day between Naples and Positano. Check the local papers (*Il Mattino* or *La Repubblica*) for timetables or go to www.metrodelmare.com. A one-way ticket costs €10, making it the cheapest way to get around by sea. In addition to this public transport service, many commercial ferries and hydrofoils run year-round, but offer the most trips in high season. To get to smaller towns or to take private boats, you can make arrangements with private boat companies or independent fishermen. Seek out people who are recommended by the tourist office or your hotel.

Headquartered in Amalfi, ferries operated by Linee Maritime Salernitane (a consorzio which includes lines run by Alicost and Metro del Mare) cover the region. Ferries sail from Salerno to Positano (about €6); Salerno to Amalfi (€5); and Salerno to Capri (€11.50). A hydrofoil connects Amalfi to Salerno (€5.50); Salerno to Positano (€8.50; and Salerno to Capri (€13.50). Hydrofoils usually run only in summer, less frequently than ferries. Tickets can be purchased at booths usually located on piers and docks.

In Positano, the ferry and hydrofoil ticket office is on the Spiaggia Grande; ferries to Amalfi, Sorrento, Salerno, and Capri are available at a dock on Via Positanesi d'America, near the public beach in the center of town. Services are provided by Linee Maritime Partenopee and F.lli Grassi, which is located at the pier—look for the logo depicting a blue-and-white whale.

In Salerno, ferries to Amalfi and Positano leave from the main port at Piazza della Concordia; ferries continuing to Capri and Ischia leave from the west end of the waterfront at Molo Manfredi. A typical schedule is an early-morning departure and a late-afternoon return; the EPT (Ente Provinciale di Turismo, or local tourist board) office has current information, as does the Cooperative Sant'Andrea. Hydrofoil service is available in summer to Amalfi, Positano, Capri, and Sorrento.

In Sorrento, ferries and hydrofoils are operated by Alilauro, Caremar, Linee Lauro, Linee Marittime Partenopee; services—and fares—have been stepped up to Capri and there are frequent sailings of a variety of fast and slow craft (hydrofoil €8.50, ferry €6.50). Sorrento to Naples costs €10 and to Ischia Porto €12, with Salerno, Amalfi, and Positano served in the summer.

FARES & SCHEDULES 🛈 Boat and Ferry Information **Alicost** ☎ 089/871483. **Alilauro** ☎ 081/8073024. **Alilauro-Gruson** ☎ 081/8071430. **Caremar** ☎ 081/8073077. **Linee Maritime Salernitane** ☎ 089/873301 in Amalfi; 089/811164 in Positano; 081/8073024 in Sorrento. **Positano ferry and hydrofoil ticket office** ✉ Via del Brigantino ☎ 089/811986. **Travelmar** ☎ 089/872950.

BUS TRAVEL

Although some travelers opt for cars when touring the Amalfi Drive, most use the convenient and inexpensive SITA Blue Line buses. For best views on board, sit on the sea side of the bus (on your left as you board the bus if you're starting in Sorrento, on your right if you begin in Amalfi). The trip between Sorrento and Amalfi generally takes 80 minutes. The major bus stops, in order after departing from Sorrento's bus depot, are: Sant'Agnello, Piano di Sorrento, Meta, Positano (the bus stops at the Chiesa Nuova, outside the Bar Internazionale in the upper town, then at a second—and the main—stop at Sponda, in the lower town), Praiano (in the township of Vettica Maggiore), Conca dei Marini, and then Amalfi, ending at the bus hub on Piazza Flavio Gioia. The bus driver will stop anywhere on the main route as long as you inform him of your destination, be it hotel or fork in the road, when boarding.

You can best enjoy the scenery if you leave the helm to drivers and bus power. Besides, the mighty elevation of bus seats high atop the road offers an even better perch to take in the passing show. Note that buses fill up in the summer months, and Italians aren't usually orderly queuers!

AMALFI   You can purchase SITA Blue Line bus and coach tickets prior to boarding at Bar Sita or any port-side bar, travel agency, or tobacco shop displaying a SITA sticker; all SITA buses leave Amalfi from Piazza Flavio Gioia. The special express bus to Naples departs many mornings at 8 AM (€3.10); catching this bus makes for an easy and scenic ride back to the city, allowing you to bypass a transfer from bus to the Circumvesuviana railway in Sorrento.

POSITANO   Purchase SITA Blue Line bus and coach tickets prior to boarding at Tabaccheria. The Blue Line bus stops here are at Chiesa Nuova and Sponda. SITA buses pass through Positano almost hourly on the run from Amalfi to Sorrento, 7 AM–7:30 PM (later on weekdays); from Sorrento to Amalfi, 9 (earlier on weekdays)–9:30 PM (later on weekdays). In addition to the tobacconist listed below, check around for caffès and additional tobacconists selling SITA tickets.

In Positano, local Orange Line buses regularly ply even the smallest roads and make more stops than the SITA buses. Look for the orange sign and wait there. Taxis and boats are usually by the harbor, or ask at the tourist office, travel agency, or your hotel. Service on most Orange Line routes begins at 6:20 from Monday through Saturday, at 7:50 on Sunday, and ends at midnight; departures are usually every half hour on the main lines.

RAVELLO   ATACS (Orange Line) municipal buses make the run up and down the mountain between Ravello and Piazza Flavio Gioia in Amalfi, where you can catch the main Amalfi Drive bus to Sorrento. You can purchase SITA Blue Line bus and coach tickets prior to boarding at Bar San Domingo, Bar Calce, and Tabaccheria. Buses run almost hourly.

SALERNO   SITA buses run hourly to Sorrento, three times per hour to Naples, and once or twice an hour to Amalfi. Purchase tickets for preboarding at the SITA office or at tobacco shops displaying the SITA sticker; ATACS (Orange Line) buses traverse the city, while ATACS and SCAT buses, departing from the Salerno train station, run frequently to Paestum.

SORRENTO   SITA Blue Line buses and coaches depart hourly from Sorrento to Amalfi. Before boarding, purchase SITA tickets at the newspaper stand in the train station, or at Bar Tonino in the Piazza Lauro. For trips leaving from Sorrento and heading southward into the coastal towns of the Sorrentine Peninsula, the main run stops at Massa Lubrense, Sant'Agata, and Torca. Service usually begins at 5 AM and lasts until 10:30 PM, with varying schedules for weekends and holidays. The Sorrento–Nerano line at Piazza Tasso and Piazza Lauro (main destination: Termini and Marina del Cantone) either goes through Sant'Agata or through Massa Lubrense. Contact Azienda Turismo for complete information. Circumvesuviana buses are used for local Sorrento runs (€1–€2.25). In Sorrento, the main local Orange Line bus stops are in Piazza Lauro, Piazza Tasso, and down at Marina Piccola. You can also use Circumvesuviana buses (€1–€2.20) for local Sorrento runs.

🚌 Bus Information **Azienda Turismo** ☎ 081/8074033 🖷 081/8773397. **Circumvesuviana** ☎ 081/7722444 ⊕ www.vesuviana.it. **Flavio Gioia** ☎ 089/811895 🖷 089/811896. **SITA** ⊕ www.uniplan.it/sita. **SITA Blue Line tickets** ✉ Bar Sita, Piazza Flavio Gioia, Amalfi ☎ 089/871016 ⊕ www.uniplan.it/sita ✉ Tabaccheria, Piazza dei Mulini, Positano ✉ Circumvesuviana train station, Sorrento ☎ 081/7722444 ✉ Bar Calce 2 Via Boccaccio11, Ravello ☎ 089/857130 ✉ Tabaccheria, Via dei Rufolo 4, Ravello ⊕ www.uniplan.it/sita. **Sorrento bus depot** ✉ Circumvesuviana railway station near Corso Italia.

FARES & SCHEDULES SITA buses make the trip along the coast 22 times daily between 6:30 AM and 10 PM (festival, Sunday, and bank holiday schedules vary from weekday schedule). Wallet-size SITA bus schedules are available at ticket vendors, regional tourist offices, and from hotel concierges, or contact SITA in Salerno. If you're traveling along the coast by SITA bus, be sure to get a schedule, as it proves invaluable to planning your day. Schedules are also posted at the Sorrento train station and at the SITA bus office at Bar Sita, Piazza Flavio Gioia. One-way ticket prices range from €2 to €3.35. An express Amalfi–Naples line includes stops in Sorrento, Colli San Pietro, Positano, and Praiano, with the return in reverse. This bus runs daily, except Sunday and national holidays, usually leaves at 8 AM, and takes 2½ hours.

PAYING Tickets must be purchased in advance (remember to time-stamp your ticket in the machine at the front of the bus as you board because conductors often make spot checks). You'll find ticket vendors in many caffès, bars, and newsstands area-wide; heading south, the Sorrento train station newsstand is where most people stock up, but between noon and 4, when it's closed, head for the caffès on the square two blocks to the south; heading north from Amalfi, Bar Sita, at Piazza Flavio Gioia in Amalfi, is the place to buy tickets.

CAR RENTAL

If flying into Naples, you'll find that the major car rental firms have offices there. Avis also has branches in major towns, and allows one-way rentals, including drop-offs in other countries.

🚗 Major Agencies **Avis** ✉ Aeroporto di Capodichino ☎ 081/7805790 ⊕ www.avis.com. **Hertz** ✉ Via degli Aranci 9A, Sorrento ☎ 081/8071646 ⊕ www.hertz.it

CAR TRAVEL

Running between the Sorrentine peninsula and Salerno, Statale 163 (or State Highway 163) is better known to Americans and Brits as the Amalfi Drive and to Italians as the Via Smeraldo (Emerald Road). It can be reached from Naples via the A3 Autostrada to Castellammare di Stabia, then linked to Sorrento via Statale 145. Most people travel from Naples, heading southeast, but others prefer to drive directly to Salerno via the A3, then return northwest using the Amalfi Drive, a concrete ribbon that rewards visitors with mountain-meets-sea views and panoramas unfolding at every turn. If bound for Ravello and traveling by car, exit the A3 Autostrada at Angri, and approach Ravello from the north via the pass called Valico di Chiunzi.

EMERGENCY SERVICES 🚗 **Road Assistance** (Italian Auto Club) ☎ 803116.

PARKING Parking is a major problem, with spaces in Positano and Amalfi costing per day almost as much as a three-course meal, so you should factor in this additional cost.

ROAD CONDITIONS Driving the scenic and often hairpin roads of the Sorrentine Peninsula and the Amalfi Drive is both a joy and a challenge. Medium-size cars are a good compromise, and turns will be easier with automatic transmission. The round reflecting mirrors set along major curves in the road intend to show if others are coming around a bend; they may help, but remain ever alert. Honk before narrow curves to let oncoming traffic know about you, and listen for honks from oncoming curves. Buses and trucks will sometimes require you to back up; if there's a standoff, take it in stride, as it goes on all the time.

Driving will be on winding two-lane roads except for the A3 Autostrada to and from Salerno. Although (and perhaps because) driving here requires total concentration, accidents occur surprisingly infrequently.

EMERGENCIES

⚑ Countrywide Emergency Numbers **Police** ☎ 112. **Emergency Police Help** ☎ 113. **Fire Department** ☎ 115. **Emergencies at Sea** (Coastguard) ☎ 1530. **International Inquiries** ☎ 4176. **Medical Emergencies** ☎ 118. **Phone Directory Assistance** ☎ 412.
⚑ Amalfi **Police** ☎ 089/871633. **Ambulance** ⊠ Piazza Municipio ☎ 118.
⚑ Positano **Police** ⊠ Loc. Chiesa Nuova ☎ 089/875011. **Ambulance** ⊠ Via G. Marconi ☎ 118.
⚑ Ravello **Police** ⊠ Via della Marra 4 ☎ 089/857498. **Ambulance** ⊠ Piazza Fontana 9 ☎ 118.
⚑ Sorrento **Police** ☎ 081/8073111 or 081/8781010. **Ambulance** ☎ 118.
⚑ Hospitals **Ospedale Civico** ⊠ Corso Italia, Sorrento ☎ 081/5331111. **Ospedale San Giovanni di Dio** ⊠ Via San Leonardo, Salerno ☎ 089/671111.
⚑ Pharmacies **Amalfi** ⊠ Piazza Duomo 42 ☎ 089/871045. **Positano** ⊠ Viale Pasitea 22 ☎ 089/875863. **Ravello** ⊠ Piazza Duomo 14 ☎ 089/857189. **Salerno** ⊠ Via Mercanti 62 ☎ 089/253965. **Sorrento** ⊠ Via L. De Maio 19 ☎ 081/8781349 ⊠ Corso Italia 66 ☎ 081/8781174.

MONEY MATTERS

ATMS Almost all banks now have ATM machines, which provide the quickest currency exchange, of course with bank commission. Hotels have the worst exchange rate but are convenient for small change and last-minute needs.

CURRENCY EXCHANGE In Salerno, banks line Corso Vittorio Emanuele; the Salerno train station information window is open 9–7. In Sorrento, the Ufficio Cambi is open daily 9 AM–10:30 PM. The Sorrento Post Office has better rates than town banks.
⚑ Exchange Services **Bank Ufficio Cambi Spot** ⊠ Via Roma 38, Ravello ☎ 089/858086. **Banca Popolare di Salerno** ⊠ Via Roma 15, Ravello ☎ 089/857872. **Banco di Napoli** ⊠ Piazza Duomo, Amalfi ☎ 089/871005. **Deutsche Bank** ⊠ Via dei Ferrari 1, Amalfi ☎ 089/873050 ⊠ Via Cristoforo Colombo, Positano ☎ 089/811066 ☎ 089/811045. **Sorrento Post Office** ⊠ C. Italia 210, Sorrento ☎ 081/8781495. **Ufficio Cambi** ⊠ Piazza dei Mulini, Positano ☎ 089/875864 ⊠ Via Luigi de Maio 21, Sorrento.

TAXIS

Taxis are at stands by the main piazzas and harbors and can also be hired through hotels and restaurants. The following are the major taxi services in the area. Positano Car & Limo Service offers car and driver rentals, tours, and excursions.
⚑ Taxi Companies **Amalfi** ⊠ Piazza Flavio Gioia, at pier ☎ 089/872239. **Autoservizi Flavio Gioia** ⊠ Via Cristoforo Colombo 91, Positano ☎ 089/811895. **Positano Car & Limo Service** ⊠ Via Cristoforo Colombo 2, Positano ☎ 089/875541. **Ravello** ⊠ Piazza

Duomo ☎ 089/857917. **Rent-A-Car** ✉ Viale Pasitea, Positano ☎ 089/811777. **Salerno** ✉ Piazza XXIV, Maggio ☎ 089/229171. **Sorrento** ✉ Piazza Lauro ☎ 081/8782204 ✉ S. Agnello ☎ 081/8781428. **Sorrento Rent a Scooter** ✉ C. Italia 210-A ☎ 081/8781386 ⊕ www.sorrento.it.

TOURS

Private boat tours are available to the Emerald Grotto, Capri, and isolated beaches through F.lli Grassi in Positano. GoldenTours International in Sorrento offers excursions to Capri, Ischia, Positano, Amalfi, Ravello, Pompeii, Herculaneum, Paestum, and Naples; car rentals; limo services; package tours; and train, boat, and air tickets.

⑦ Fees and Schedules Divina Costiera ✉ Piazza Flavio Gioia 3, Amalfi ☎ 089/872467. **F.lli Grassi** ✉ Spiaggia Fornillo, Positano ☎ 089/811888. **GoldenTours International** ✉ Corso Italia, 38-E ☎ 081/8781042 🖶 081/8071745 ⊕ www.goldentours.it. **Wagner Tours** ✉ Via Trinità 4, Ravello ☎ 089/858416 🖶 089/858914.

TRAIN TRAVEL

The two main train stations serving the Amalfi Coast are Salerno and Sorrento. Conveniently, the stations are also hubs for cheap, efficient bus services radiating toward the major tourist destinations along the coast and inland.

State Railways trains stop in Salerno on the Milan–Reggio Calabria line. Trains leave from Salerno for Pompei town (the archeological site of Pompeii is 15 minutes' walk away) once or twice each hour; Naples twice an hour, €3.60. The station here is also an excellent starting point for buses to the Amalfi Coast.

The Circumvesuviana departs from the Circumvesuviana train station and runs approximately every half hour from Sorrento to Naples; some trains are express, only stopping at major stations, returning in the reverse order. Round-trip fares are €6 for Sorrento to Naples and €3.20 to Pompeii. In Sorrento the train station is opposite Piazza Lauro and a five-minute walk from Piazza Tasso.

⑦ Train Information Circumvesuviana ☎ 081/7722444 ⊕ www.vesuviana.it. **State Railways** ✉ Piazza V. Veneto ☎ 848/888088 ⊕ www.fs-on-line.it.

TRAVEL AGENCIES

Divina Costiera in Amalfi also rents scooters (€70 per day). Golden Tours offers boat tours to Grotta dello Smeraldo (Emerald Cave) from Amalfi docks. The American Express representative in Sorrento is Acampora Travel.

⑦ Local Agents Acampora Travel ✉ Via Correale 20, Sorrento ☎ 081/5329711 ⊕ www.acampora.it. **Arechi Viaggi** ✉ Via Sichelmanno 17, Salerno ☎ 089/759353 🖶 089/759341. **Divina Costiera** ✉ Piazza Flavio Gioia 3, Amalfi ☎ 089/872467 🖶 089/871254. **Faito Travel** ✉ Via G. Marconi 344, Positano ☎ 089/811802. **Golden Tours** ✉ Corso Repubbliche Marinare 23, Amalfi 🖶 089/871301. **Positour** ✉ Via Cristoforo Colombo 69, Positano ☎ 089/875012 🖶 089/811045 ⊕ www.positour.com. **Ravello International** ✉ Via Roma 38, Ravello 🖶 089/858086.

VISITOR INFORMATION

Azienda Autonoma di Cura, Soggiorno e Turismo in Amalfi is open weekdays 8:30–1:30 and 3–5; Saturday 8:30–1; in Sorrento the office is open Monday to Saturday, summer 8–8, winter 8:30–2:30 and 3:20–6:30.

In Positano, the Azienda Autonoma Soggiorno e Turismo is open Monday–Saturday 8:30–2, and June to September, it's also open 3:30–8. In Ravello, the office is open Monday to Saturday 8–8 in summer and 8–7 in winter.

In Salerno, the EPT office is open Monday–Saturday, 9–1 and 3–8.

The Centro di Cultura e Storia Amalfitana is open Tuesday, Thursday, and Saturday 9–1; Monday, Wednesday, and Friday 4–8.

🔢 Tourist Information **Azienda Autonoma di Cura, Soggiorno e Turismo** ✉ Corso Reppubliche Marinare 27, Amalfi ☎🔒 089/871107 ✉ Via Luigi di Maio 35, Sorrento ☎ 081/8074033 🔒 081/8773397 ⊕ www.sorrentourism.it. **Azienda Autonoma Soggiorno e Turismo** ✉ Via del Saracino 4, Positano ☎ 089/875067 🔒 089/875760 ✉ Piazza Duomo 10, Ravello ☎ 089/857096 🔒 089/877977 ⊕ www.ravello.it/aziendaturismo. **Centro di Cultura e Storia Amalfitana** ✉ Via Annunziatella, Amalfi ☎ 089/873143. **EPT Office** ✉ P. Vittorio Veneto 1, Salerno ☎🔒 089/231432 ⊕ www.salernocity.com.

UNDERSTANDING NAPLES, CAPRI & THE AMALFI COAST

NAPOLI EVER AFTER

BOOKS & VIDEOS

NAPOLI EVER AFTER

By Gregory W. Bailey

THE ACUTE STAGES ARE NOT EASY TO DI-AGNOSE: the symptoms cry out. Utter the words *Bay of Naples, Positano,* or *Capri,* and patients will close their eyes and sigh—or roll their eyeballs and moan. If it's an advanced case, they will embark on a monologue in which you will be able to discern such phrases and fragments as ". . . the lure of the Mediterranean," ". . . the magic of the Southern sun," ". . . water that out-sapphires the jewels at Tiffany's," ". . . the song of the sirens." Every ailment—physical, mental, or social—reflects a need. Acute and widespread "Campaniamania"—the hopeless infatuation with Campania and its myriad sun-wreathed resorts and starlighted isles—simply proves (with or without spots) that there is something in the organism, blood, and mental makeup of every modern-day escapist that requires a good dose of this relentlessly romantic corner of the world.

It has been this way ever since the Roman emperors escaped overheated Rome by building pleasure palaces around the Bay of Naples—and, in the process, inventing the very idea of the vacation. Back then, some Roman travel agent urged his countrymen to "See Naples and Die." Ever since, this pithy phrase has been interpreted in contrasting, equally viable ways. Lovers of Naples, asking what there is on Earth that you can't find here, get the slogan's true meaning. The hard-liners, noting the murderous traffic, Mafia doings, ever-present threat of Vesuvius erupting, and the region's earthquakey history, say, "See Naples and die." As it turns out, the saying originally advised travelers to visit the city on the bay, then check out the nearby town of Mori (Latin for "to die"). And it is in this sense that this guidebook proceeds. It's simply a given that you must first explore this relentlessly fascinating city, then move on to the rest of Campania, a province that stacks snazzy resorts, grandly Baroque palaces, Edenic gardens, the most satisfying hundred miles of coastline to be found in tourist Europe, and some of the oldest ruins this side of Constantinople into one mammoth must-see sandwich.

However, if you limit your tour to Sorrento, Ravello, Capri, Ischia, Positano, Pompeii, and Amalfi, you will "see" Campania, but you won't understand it. To do that, you must get to know Naples itself. Most guidebooks approach the capital of Campania with a degree of circumspection, treating her as the cousin who would be presentable if only she toned down her makeup, watched her mouth, and didn't try to palm her date's wallet. Of course, guidesters focus on the array of things to see in Naples: the supreme, sun-drunk, natural setting, with Dame Vesuvius tapping her feet across the Bay of Naples; the richest museum of Greco-Roman antiquities in the world; one of the finest collections of Renaissance paintings; outstanding examples of architecture, from medieval to modern; and a kaleidoscope of colorful vignettes. But you don't come to Naples to see things, as such; you come to Naples to *be.* Naples is a kinetic gust of 3-D garlic-and-basil aromatherapy for the soul, a vital and revitalizing splash of reality; Naples is rediscovering the "simple things" and finding them exalted into ecstasies of complication; Naples is fluidity among stasis, fertility spawning misery, infinite intelligence circumventing colossal stupidity. Naples is intense, and intensely poetic. Naples doesn't need defending—it does that quite well by itself, thank you. And it is not rational, despite the many grids that various rulers vainly laid down to tame it. Naples is about falling in love, not blindly—that wouldn't last long, in any case—but instead by having your senses and sensibilities shamelessly charmed into full bloom.

It's not only the scenery that will incessantly engage your senses, it's also the Neapolitans themselves. More so than in any Italian city, the engine driving Naples is its people. Sophia Ponti, *née* Loren, the most famous living Neapolitan (okay, so she's from the suburb of Pozzuoli) recently confided that her *concittadini,* or fellow citizens, "had many virtues: fantasy, sincerity, generosity, boastfulness, a sense of humor . . . Neapolitans do not have defects . . . or at least I've never noticed any." Not everyone has been so complimentary: throughout history, foreigners of all stripes have sustained a positively unseemly indignation and disdain for the Neapolitans and their anarchic and passionate approach to morality. Already in ancient times, the entire Neapolitan area (and Baia in particular) was notorious as a fleshpot. The goings-on in the court of Joan I in the 14th century make the 1980s soap opera *Dynasty* look like an unimaginative Romper Room model of treachery and lust. Naples's reputation for sexual permissiveness was sealed when the French troops of Charles VIII, chased out of Naples, took back with them an epidemic they later termed "the Neapolitan disease": syphilis. Epidemiological historians still argue over the origins of the disease in Europe, but the damage was done. The very Victorian philosopher Walter Benjamin simply dismissed Naples as "a lost city."

Yes, contrary to native daughter Sophia, others have looked upon the Neapolitans with a less generous eye, put off by their robust earthiness, their physicality, their volatility. The truth is, on deeper acquaintance, the mannerisms of the Neapolitans are found to be merely the prickly nettles that must be navigated before reaching the ripe center. Their mode of life is simply an inextinguishable belief that the art of living lies in enjoying what surrounds you, not passively, but with enthusiasm—be it the sunshine, a glass of wine, romance, a scam, a prayer, a song, an argument, a traffic jam. Sublime artists of existence, Neapolitans are skilled players in the larger, more serious world. And yet, far from being bitterly cynical, they take the same delight in the ingeniousness, the virtuosity as it were, of a crook as they do of an artist. They are free of cynicism and loaded with courage (Naples was the only city in World War II to rout its Nazi occupiers in a spontaneous revolt).

Naples is almost as old as Rome, and the main components of the historically constructed mentality are Greek and Spanish—testimony to the city's ancient Greek founders and its 16th-century Spanish rulers—rather than Italian as such. Greek was commonly spoken in Naples, even under the Roman Empire, and Naples was considered an outpost and living remnant of Greek culture in Italy, much as New Orleans retained its Frenchness in 19th-century America; the Neapolitans' brilliant, argumentative, and impossibly charming nature is ancient Greek. To this have been added Spanish pride and an intransigent sense of honor.

***

ONCE EXPERIENCED DEEPLY AND OPENLY, Naples remains a reference point while exploring the rest of Campania—at once a grounding in reality and a glimpse into the stratosphere of fantasy. There are a fair number of sights to see in this region, but many visitors find such pursuits beside the point, for they look upon Campania as a playground, a school, a way of life that insists on having its way with you. Who but the Neapolitans could have invented *dolce far niente*—the sweetness of doing nothing? But fulfillment under the Campanian sun comes in various guises. The legions of honeymooners, Main Streeters, and deadline slaves could be lounging in the very sand once trod by Nero, Tiberius, and Hadrian. Virgil's *Georgics* and Wagner's *Parsifal* came to life in view of these waters. Passion—pairs on the scene have included Admiral Nelson and Lady Hamilton and Elizabeth Taylor and Richard Burton—has a way of percolating under these skies. Numerous great and once-great names spent time here, writing, painting, philosophizing, or just drinking in the grand scenery.

Like them, you will want to depart Campania with that final sense of beauty unparalleled, with the echoes of Capri's grottoes still resounding in your ears and the perfume of the flowers of Ravello still in your nostrils, with the austere classicism of Paestum oddly blending in your mind with the Cave of the Cumaean Sibyl, and with the panorama from your window in Naples, with its splendid bay and ever-threatening volcano, all comprising one vast picture in your mind. If you're lucky, that celebrated Neapolitan vista will be yours to enjoy from your hotel room on a spring morning when the sun is just warm enough to be comfortable. Step out onto your balcony for the first time, and drink in the panorama. Down below your balcony will be the Bay of Naples, with its gently curving shoreline, docks, and palm-lined avenues. Farther along will be the Castel Nuovo of Charles I of Anjou, its eternal and primitive shape contrasting sharply with far more modern buildings near it. Follow the bay with your eyes to the horizon and Vesuvius itself. Look to your right to see a little islet that seems to spring directly out of the bay. This is Capri. Ischia is probably a little out of your vision's range, as are Pozzuoli and Cumae, but no matter. Far below you the bay is shimmering blue. In the distance gentle little waves fleck it with white. The air is fragrant with flowering vines and trees. A violently purple bougainvillea cluster clings to the hotel trellis within a few feet of your head. It would be pleasant just to sit there in the warmly comfortable sun and relax for the rest of the day—maybe for a week or so. That's what a Neapolitan would do. But we haven't time.

BOOKS & FILMS

Books

As one of the great centers of civilization in the Western World, Campania and its splendid history have been exhaustively covered by authors great and small. What follows is just a Whitman's Sampler of books that will enhance anyone's trip to the region. Back in the early 19th century, Goethe wrote his *Italian Journey* and Stendhal his *Rome, Naples, and Florence*, both setting the style for the flood of travel literature to come. The Grand Tour unleashed a stream of travelers, two of whom left written accounts that deserve special mention: Lady Blessington's *Lady Blessington in Naples* and Sir William Gell's *Letters to the Society of Dilettanti, 1831–1835*. Among the most poetic and moving of modern travel essays on southern Italy and Campania are Aubrey Menen's *Four Days in Naples*, Herbert Kubly's *An American in Italy,* and Sean O'Faolain's sublime *An Autumn in Italy*. Perhaps the most magisterially poetic (and definitely overlooked) opus is Edward Hutton's 1958 *Naples and Campania Revisited*, an enthralling read filled with provocative thoughts (". . . there is nothing like Naples in its sordid and yet tremendous vitality, a vitality that is sterile, that wastes itself upon itself . . .") and gorgeous language.

For art, architecture, and splendor, consult the array of books on Neapolitan art history. *Palaces of Naples* by Donatella Mazzoleni and Mark E. Smith, offers a tour, replete with sumptuous photos, of the city's grandest houses. The 18th-century golden age of Neapolitan painting is best captured in *Painting in Naples 1606–1705 from Caravaggio to Giordano* by Clovis Whitfield, the catalogue for a show mounted by the National Gallery of Art; *The Golden Age of Naples* is another impressive catalogue, this one for a show mounted by the Detroit Institute of Arts. In addition, consult *Neapolitan Painting of the Seicento* by Aldo De Rinaldis. That Neapolitan superstar, Caravaggio, has been the subject of several recent biographies, including *M: The Man Who Became Caravaggio* by Peter Robb, while the latest coffee-table art books devoted to this master of chiaroscuro are written by John Spike and Catherine Puglisi. For architectural trends of the 17th and 18th century, see Sir Anthony Blunt's *Neapolitan Baroque and Rococo Architecture*. George L. Hersey, the eminent Yale art historian, has written several books on the art of the region, including *The Aragonese Arch at Naples, 1443–1485,* and *Alfonso II and the Artistic Renewal of Naples*—both dealing with the Renaissance period—and *Architecture, Poetry, and Number in the Royal Palace at Caserta*, on the vast 18th-century palace outside the city. For the early 19th-century Romantic era, read C. Powell's *Turner in the South: Rome, Naples, Florence*, while *Vases and Volcanoes: Sir William Hamilton and His Collection*, written by Ian Jenkins and Kim Sloan, studies the legendary antiquities collection formed by "Mr." Emma Hamilton through the optic of Grand Tour–era esthetics.

On Naples's complicated history, start with the famous Neapolitan author and philosopher, Benedetto Croce: two of his many works are *Between Naples and Europe,* and *History of the Kingdom of Naples*. On medieval history, consult B. Kreutz's *Before the Normans: Southern Italy in the Ninth and Tenth Centuries*. On the Renaissance era, check out A. Ryder's *The Kingdom of Naples and Alfonso the Magnanimous: The Making of a Modern State,* Jerry H. Bentley's *Politics and Culture in Renaissance Naples,* and Antonio Calabria's *The Cost of Empire: The Finances of the Kingdom of Naples in the Time of Spanish Rule*. For the Baroque and Empire eras, consult Sir Harold Acton's *The Bourbons of Naples (1734–1825)* and *The Last Bourbons of Naples (1825–1861)*. On the notorious Lady Hamilton, read K. McKay's *A Remarkable Relationship: The Story of Emma Hamilton and Sir Charles Greville, Sir William Hamilton, and Horatio Nelson,* Flora Fraser's magisterial *Emma Hamilton,* and Norah Lofts' *Emma Hamilton*.

That Hamilton woman was also dealt with in Susan Sontag's award-winning novel, *The Volcano Lover*. Much of the region was put on the map of the public imagination thanks to the Victorian pot-boiler *The Last Days of Pompeii*, by Sir Edwin Bulwer-Lytton. More recent fiction efforts have been Shirley Hazzard's *The Bay of Noon* and Patricia Highsmith's devilishly clever mystery, *The Talented Mr. Ripley*, made into a film in 1999 starring Gwyneth Paltrow and Matt Damon. Other fictional forays include *The Flame of Life* by Gabriele d'Annunzio and Gregory Dowling's murder mystery, *See Naples and Kill*.

Capri has been the subject of many books, the best of which have been written by Norman Douglas, including *Siren Land* and the exceedingly witty *South Wind*; Edwin Cerio also dealt with the isle in numerous titles, including *That Capri Air* and *The Masque of Capri*. Dr. Axel Munthe's famous *Story of San Michele* was first published in 1929 and is still in print. Exquisitely written is a new entry to the field, dealing with the famous English author, Graham Greene: Shirley Hazzard's *Greene on Capri*.

For Pompeii, start with the fine exhibition catalog, *Pompeii AD 79*, edited by J. B. Ward-Perkins, to accompany a major 1978 show at the Museum of Fine Arts, Boston. An accompanying luxurious art-book volume, with the same title, has an enthralling text by the eminent professor of archeology, Richard Brilliant. A noted title is *Cities of Vesuvius: Pompeii and Herculaneum*, by Michael Grant, while more recent entries are *Pompeii: The Day A City Died*, by Robert Etienne; *Rediscovering Antiquity: Karl Weber and the Excavation of Herculaneum, Pompeii, and Stabiae*, by C. Parslow; *Pompeii: An Architectural History*, by L. Richardson, Jr.; Paul Zanker's excellent *Pompeii: Public and Private Life*; and *Roman Pompeii: Space and Society*, by Ray Laurence. A new and eye-opening look at many of Pompeii's finest artworks is provided in *Roman Sex*, written by the classical scholar John R. Clarke.

To get you to Positano before you arrive and to leave you in Ravello after you've left, there's nothing like a glossy photography book. The most recent entry is *Hidden Naples and the Amalfi Coast* by Cesare M. Cunaccia and Massimo Listri. Two other entries to the field cover many of the most beautiful spots in the region, and can come in handy for planning your trip: *Gardens of Naples*, by Elisabeth B. Mac-Dougall, and M. T. Train, with exquisite photographs by Prince Nicholas Sapieha; and *Escape to the Amalfi Coast* by Robert I. C. Fisher, which includes photographs of many of the celebrated hotels and sights covered in this guidebook (for a Web preview of some of the photos, log on to www.fodors.com/features/esc/020708/listings.cfm?display=author). For pictures of Ravello, consult the Franco Maria Ricci *edition de luxe, Ravello*, which includes an essay by part-time Ravello resident Gore Vidal. Finally, to whip up some of the great Neapolitan specialities you enjoyed on your trip, read Arthur Schwartz's delicious *Naples at Table: Cooking in Campania*.

Films

As for movies and videos, look for the wonderful series of comedic films directed by Vittoria di Sica and starring Sophia Loren, starting with the 1950s classic *The Gold of Naples* and ending in the 1960s with *Marriage, Italian Style* and *Yesterday, Today, and Tomorrow*. Two early films are difficult to find but reward efforts: Robert Hussein's bleak look at postwar Naples, *Paisan* (1951), and Roberto Rossellini's *The Miracle* (1948), in which Anna Magnani memorably plays a waif seduced by a blonde man she thinks is Christ (played by Federico Fellini, no less), filmed in glorious black-and-white around Atrani and Il Furore along the Amalfi Coast. For a more recent take on Campania, see the 1994 film, *Only You*, for scenes filmed in Positano (notably at Le Sirenuse hotel) featuring Marisa Tomei and Robert Downey Jr. Naples and Ischia star along with Gwyneth Paltrow, Matt Damon, Cate Blanchett, and Jude Law in the 1999 film version of Patricia Highsmith's novel, *The Talented Mr. Ripley*—the scenery is alluring, the sordid story is not. Now if only some great filmmaker would tackle the saga of Caravaggio, the 17th-century painter and murderer whose dramatic life has all the makings of a cinematic classic. There was a potboiler filmed in Italy back in the 1950s and Derek Jarman tried to do the great artist justice with his 1986 film but both came up a cropper.

INDEX